# Interpersonal
# Communication

# Interpersonal Communication

SIXTH EDITION

SARAH TRENHOLM
*Ithaca College*

ARTHUR JENSEN
*Syracuse University*

New York    Oxford
OXFORD UNIVERSITY PRESS
2008

Oxford University Press, Inc., publishes works that further Oxford University's objective of excellence in research, scholarship, and education.

Oxford  New York
Auckland  Cape Town  Dar es Salaam  Hong Kong  Karachi
Kuala Lumpur  Madrid  Melbourne  Mexico City  Nairobi
New Delhi  Shanghai  Taipei  Toronto

With offices in
Argentina  Austria  Brazil  Chile  Czech Republic  France  Greece
Guatemala  Hungary  Italy  Japan Poland  Portugal  Singapore
South Korea  Switzerland  Thailand  Turkey  Ukraine  Vietnam

Published by Oxford University Press, Inc.
198 Madison Avenue, New York, New York 10016
http://www.oup.com

Oxford is a registered  trademark of Oxford University Press

**Library of Congress Cataloging-in-Publication Data**

Trenholm, Sarah, 1944–
    Interpersonal communication/Sarah Trenholm, Arthur Jensen.—6th ed.
        p. cm.
    Includes bibliographical references and index.
    ISBN-13: 978-0-19-531290-4 (pbk.)
    1. Interpersonal communication.  I. Jensen, Arthur, 1954– II. Title.

BF637.C45T72 2007
153.6—dc22                                                    2006051537

Printing number: 9 8 7 6 5 4 3 2

Printed in the United States of America
on acid-free paper

# Contents in Brief

# Contents

## PART 2   SENDING AND RECEIVING MESSAGES   49

# PART 3   INTERPERSONAL PROCESSES   141

# Preface

## To the Student

Living in the 21st century means that you can do amazing things. It means that you can pick up a phone or sit down at a computer and be in instant contact with someone on the other side of the globe. It means that space and time don't mean what they used to, that you can be as close to someone in Beijing or Beirut as to someone in Bethesda or Bangor. It also means that your social world is more complex than that of any generation before yours, and that the technologies that link you to strangers can also serve to isolate you from friends and neighbors. In a world where communication technology seems to offer the solution to every problem, it's important to remember that ease of access does not mean ease of understanding. Building rewarding and lasting relationships today is more challenging than ever before. The goal of this book is to help you become a more competent communicator in a world where communication is not always easy.

One of the reasons that communicating well is not easy is that it is so hard to *see*. For most of us, most of the time, communication is an invisible process. Although you've communicated all your life, you've probably done so automatically. You've rarely stopped to analyze the choices that you make. In fact, you may not have realized that you are making choices at all, and you may have completely overlooked the fact that your communication behavior has real effects on the people around you as well as on you yourself.

We believe that, after reading this book, you'll be more aware of the power and potential of interpersonal choices. You'll have the tools to observe communication as it unfolds and you'll have the knowledge to make better communication choices. So, we invite you to take control of your world by thinking seriously about interpersonal communication: an activity that is both commonplace and uncommonly important.

## To the Instructor

Our goal in this edition, as it has been in the previous editions, is to make students aware of the impact of communication on their lives. We want them to see that interpersonal communication has real significance, that the way people talk and what they talk about make a difference in the quality of their lives and the lives of those around them. We also want them to recognize that communication is complex and that there are no easy formulas that will guide them through every situation. Although we realize that students may want their instructors to offer them simple rules for becoming better communicators, we believe students should be encouraged to find their own solutions to communication problems rather than following one-size-fits-all prescriptions. For this reason we focus on providing basic theories and principles that can be used to analyze and understand human interaction, and we provide examples to show students how these principles play out in actual interaction. Throughout, we have resisted the temptation to "dumb down" the material. We have faith that our students can handle basic social-scientific theory, if their instructors help them see its applications. We also believe that oversimplifying our field by offering simple prescriptions doesn't do justice to its complexity and integrity.

As in previous editions, we build our discussion around a model of communicative competence. We do so because we believe the model provides a theoretical structure to our discussion, because it responds to student desires to become more competent communicators, and because it encourages students to think about the abilities and understandings they must master in order to take control of their social worlds. Throughout the text we also have included boxes that focus on unusual applications of communication principles. Drawn from anthropology, neuroscience, history, psychology, popular culture, and the like, the boxes show the connections between our field and other academic disciplines, demonstrating how material students learn in one class is enriched by what they learn in others, and emphasizing how culture and context affect what it means to be a competent communicator.

At the end of each chapter, after students have thought about communication principles, they will encounter a section devoted to improving skills. This section offers suggestions about how to put the content of the chapter to work. Topics for discussion, formerly included at the end of each chapter, as well as observation guides and classroom exercises can now be found on the companion website and in the *Instructor's Manual,* which also provides test items, additional classroom activities, and handouts. We hope you will find this material helpful in the classroom.

## Changes to This Edition

As we have in the past, we have focused most of our revisions on a few chapters, with smaller changes in others. This time around, we looked closely at Chapter 3 (nonverbal communication), Chapter 6 (perception), and Chapter 9 (goal competence.) In Chapter 3 we have updated research and have reorganized our discussion of nonverbal codes into three categories: visual, auditory, and invisible. We believe that this change will make this chapter easier to teach and will help students see connections they may not have seen before. The most extensive revisions have

been made to Chapter 6. Exciting new research has begun to show connections between brain and mind, between the physical and the social. Perhaps nowhere is this more apparent than in the area of perception. In addition to reviewing this research, we have added a discussion of emotion and motivation, reorganized our discussion of social cognitive schemata, and expanded our discussion of listening to include a section on emotional intelligence. Finally, in Chapter 9, we have simplified our explanation of general theories of influence and have refocused attention on how individuals use everyday conversation to influence one another. In this chapter, we demonstrate that there is a close relationship between influence and relationship formation and maintenance.

The structure of other chapters remains the same as in the last edition and should not require any major adaptations from those who have used this text before. Additions include:

- Four new boxes. In Chapter 5, the old box on netiquette has been updated to include a discussion of how to use instant messaging in personal and business contexts, and a new box on cell-phone communication has been added. In Chapter 6, we discuss how past, present, and future become intertwined in memory, perception, and imagination. Finally, in Chapter 9, a new box discusses some of the weapons of influence that compliance professionals use to short circuit critical thinking.

- More emphasis on computer-mediated communication (CMC) and new media. Starting in Chapter 1 and continuing throughout the text, we have made an effort to integrate material on the ways that mediated communication affects interpersonal relationships.

- Recognition of the part culture plays in determining the shape of interpersonal relationships. Although we leave an in-depth exploration of cultural variables to Chapter 13, we have worked to prepare students for that discussion by offering, both in the text and in boxes, examples of how culture affects interpersonal interaction.

We are also pleased to offer two new features that have not appeared in previous editions but that we feel will give you greater flexibility in teaching the course.

- *Research in Review* sections. In this section, we abstract recent research studies in the field of speech communication. We think it important that students gain an appreciation of how research is done in our field. In choosing research to abstract, we have looked for studies that are relevant to each chapter, address an interesting research question, and are not too methodologically difficult for undergraduates (with some guidance) to grapple with. Of course, we realize that students taking the beginning interpersonal course vary widely: Some are not yet prepared to read original journal articles, while others have the sophistication to do so. Whether you decide to assign the original articles or whether you prefer to have students simply read the abstracts, we believe that this feature will give students a better sense of the range of research in our field.

- *Screening Room* sections. Everyone loves to discuss movies. Just bring up a film title in class, and even the most reticent student has an opinion. Luckily many popular feature films are more than just good stories—they are also good illustrations of interpersonal concepts. In choosing the films described in our Screening Room sections, we asked our own students for their favorites and, after visiting the local video rental store, settled down to look for movies that are both entertaining and likely to stimulate conversation. We think the films we have chosen will be useful springboards for discussion and will help students understand the concepts they read about in the text. The extent to which you want to use this feature is entirely up to you. You may decide to discuss some of the films in class, make them the basis of an assignment, show clips, or simply let students think about them as they read the chapters.

Our primary goal is to give you as much flexibility as possible in designing a course that will interest and inspire your students. We hope the changes to this edition achieve that goal.

# Acknowledgments

We are indebted to all of the fine reviewers who have offered comments and criticisms over the years. Although we may not have been able to follow all of their suggestions, we have always taken them seriously and found them to be stimulating and insightful. Any improvements over the years are due in large part to their careful work; any errors are, unfortunately, our own. Thanks to Dianne Bloomberg, Greg Boiarsky, Brant R. Burleson, Scott E. Caplan, Mindy Chang, Kenneth Cissna, Richard K. Curtis, Fred Garbowitz, Lawrence W. Hugenberg, Randall J. Koper, Sandra Metts, Martha W. Moore, Sally K. Murphy, Charles Petrie, Sally Planalp, Jeanne Posner, Marilyn Root, Karyn Rybacki, Kristina Sheeler, Gregory J. Shepherd, Ralph Smith, Robbyn J. Turner-Matthews, Michael Waltman, Lynne Webb, and Jerry L. Winsor.

We would also like to acknowledge the efforts of everyone at Oxford University Press. We give special thanks to Peter Labella, our editor, and Chelsea Gilmore, his editorial assistant, for their efficiency and patience. They made putting this edition together a pleasure. We are also grateful to the fine work of our production editor, Barbara Mathieu, and designer, Annika Sarin. Finally, we would like to thank our colleagues and students at Ithaca College and Syracuse University for their encouragement and support.

Sarah Trenholm
Arthur Jensen

# Interpersonal Communication

# PART 1

# Introductory Perspectives

The communication process is complex. It requires sensitivity, coordination, cooperation, and the desire to establish common ground with others. But communication competence enhances every aspect of our lives—from our family relationships to our friendships to our careers.

Margaret Loxton, *Celebration*, late 20th century

## CHAPTER 1

# Introduction
# Communication and Competence

Now, I do not deny, nor do I doubt, that should communication be opened, the reaction among mankind would be very strong—not because of the content of the message but simply from the fact that a message could in fact be received. Such an experience would say to us human beings "We are not alone in the universe." And this, I think . . . might by itself quite justify any expenditures made in the search for extraterrestrial intelligence.[1]

*W. H. McNeill*

Only a few years ago the idea that humans might one day communicate with extraterrestrials seemed ridiculous. Those who believed it possible were considered to be, at best, misguided and, at worst, lunatics. Nowadays, however, some very high-powered astrophysicists are taking the idea seriously. They are convinced that communication with alien intelligence may one day be possible.[2]

Think about it for a minute. Try to put yourself in the place of these scientists. Imagine that you are trying to make contact with alien beings. Remember that the beings you are trying to reach—if they exist at all—have given you no address. All you know is that they live somewhere in the vast stretches of the universe, hundreds or thousands of light years away. And even if you succeed in making contact, you still have to design an intelligible message. Movies like *E.T.* and *Close Encounters of the Third Kind* notwithstanding, extraterrestrials are unlikely to respond (or even look) like any organism you have ever seen. The chances of their being able to understand human language, let alone English, are infinitesimally small. How can you be sure that aliens will recognize your communications? How will you be able to recognize theirs? What if you have already come in contact with their messages without realizing it?

In the face of all these problems, your only choice would be to do exactly what all of us do when we communicate: rely on guesswork and faith. You would begin by assuming a desire for cooperative communication. You would then try to guess what extraterrestrials are like and how they see the world, searching for a point of similarity upon which to make connection. After that, you would simply wait and hope. Of course, the subject of this book is not interstellar communication but a much more mundane one: the way normal human beings communicate as they go about their everyday lives. We believe, though, that unusual examples help us see the commonplace in new ways.[3]

If you think about it, there are some interesting similarities between earthbound and intergalactic communication. First of all, in both cases we must resist "communicative chauvinism," the belief that everyone else thinks and acts as we do. Communication depends on sensitivity to differences and on a real desire to establish common ground. Second, people who wish to communicate must learn to "speak the same language"; they must take the time and trouble to adjust to one another. Cooperation and coordination are necessary for any kind of communication, whether it's with neighbors in the next street or with beings in the next galaxy.

We often take interpersonal communication for granted, overlooking what an amazing process it really is. The purpose of this book is to help you see interpersonal communication in a new light. While it may not be as exotic as interstellar communication, it is still a complex and fascinating process. We hope that by the time you finish this book, you will have a better understanding of how it works.

# What Is Communication?

Although communication has been written about for over 25 centuries,[4] there is still disagreement about how to define it. In this section we'll look at a number of definitions of human communication, offer our own, and then explore its implications.

## Definitions of Human Communication
In 1972 Frank Dance and Carl Larson surveyed the field for definitions of communication. They found 126.[5] Even more have been formulated since then. Obviously, a process as complex as communication is hard to summarize or define. Each person who thinks seriously about it brings a different perspective to the task. There are many valid ways to view a process, each providing a different insight.

We will give you a number of definitions to consider, but before we do, stop and jot down your own ideas about communication. Then, compare your definition with those that follow. Ask yourself which comes closest to your understanding of what communication is. More importantly, ask yourself why.

*Communication is the discriminatory response of an organism to a stimulus.*[6]

*Communication . . . is an "effort after meaning," a creative act initiated by man in which he seeks to discriminate and organize cues so as to orient himself in his environment and satisfy his changing needs.*[7]

*Speech communication is a human process through which we make sense out of the world and share that sense with others.*[8]

*Communication: the transmission of information, ideas, emotions, skills, etc. by the use of symbols . . .*[9]

*Communication is a process by which a source transmits a message to a receiver through some channel.*

The purpose of a definition is to set boundaries and to focus attention. Definitions ask people to look at certain parts of a process while ignoring others. The question to ask in evaluating a definition is not, "Is it right or wrong?" Rather, the question should be, "Is it a useful guide for inquiry?" Each focuses on a different part of the phenomenon we call communication.

The first definition is very broad. According to this view any response by any living organism counts as communication. A plant seeking out the sun, prey sensing the presence of a predator, a human being reading a book—all would be examples of communication. Furthermore, this definition concentrates on the part the receiver plays in communication and gives almost no attention to the part played by the sender. In comparison, the next definition is narrower, focusing our attention on human communication and emphasizing the reasons we communicate. The third definition adds another concept, that of sharing. According to this definition communication is more than the processing of information; it is also the transmission of that information to others. The fourth definition also takes up the idea of transmission but adds a further limitation: Messages created by humans are made up of symbols. The final definition focuses on the means by which this transmission of messages takes place and introduces the idea of the sender as the initiator of communication.

Each definition tells us something about the process of communication, yet each leaves something out. Each asks us to examine a different aspect of the process. While you may prefer one definition over another, one is not necessarily right and the others wrong. Rather, each may be useful for a different purpose. In the next section we offer yet another definition, not because our definition is necessarily closer to what communication *really* is, but because it allows us to take a more social perspective on communication and because it emphasizes the creativity of interaction. We believe that this definition will be particularly useful in helping us understand communication in the interpersonal context.

## Characteristics of Communication

For us, **communication** is *the process whereby humans collectively create and regulate social reality*. Let's try to understand what this definition has to say about communication by looking at each of its parts.

### Communication as Process

Any object or activity can be viewed as either a thing or a process. Things are static, bound in time, and unchanging. **Processes** are moving,

have no beginning and no end, and constantly change. Our first point, then, is that communication is a process, not a thing.

The communication process is like a river: active, continuous, and flowing, never the same from one minute to the next. If we try to understand a river by analyzing a bucket of water drawn from it, we are not studying the river as a whole. The same is true of communication. Individual sentences, words, or gestures make sense only when we see them as part of an ongoing stream of events. To understand communication, we have to look at how what we do and say is connected to what others do and say. We have to view communication as an ongoing process.

### Communication as Uniquely Human

The term *communication* has been used to describe the behavior of many organisms. Geneticists, for example, describe the instructions for development and growth in the DNA of cells as a kind of communication. Physiologists use the term to describe how the human body maintains and regulates itself. Biologists see all kinds of animal behaviors as communication, including the distress signals of birds, the courtship ritual of jumping spiders, the use of threat displays by Siamese fighting fish, and the play behavior of gorillas and baboons.[10]

The kind of communication we are interested in, however, is *human* communication. We believe that humans communicate in unique and powerful ways that differ markedly from those used by other animals. Although there have been several recent attempts to teach higher primates to use human communication codes, results of these studies are inconclusive. Box 1.1 summarizes some of the research on this subject.

Most everyone will agree that only people use language naturally and spontaneously, giving us a flexibility and creativity denied to all other creatures. Of course, as Aldous Huxley pointed out, this power is not always to our advantage:

*For evil, then, as well as for good, words make us the human beings we actually are.*

BOX 1.1

## Bonzo Goes to College

# Attempts to Teach Language to Primates

Part of what we are, part of how we communicate and behave, has been inherited from our animal ancestors. But how much? What is the difference between animal and human behavior, and what difference does it make? Studies of animal behavior can help answer these questions.

A number of studies have focused on whether primates other than human beings can be taught to use "language." Since the 1950s, when an infant chimpanzee named Vicki was adopted by a human family and taught four human words, a number of chimps have been given language lessons. Four of the most famous of these "students" were Washoe and Nim Chimsky (who were instructed in the use of American sign lan-

guage); Sarah (who was taught to manipulate magnetized plastic tokens); and Lana (a computer-trained chimp). The results of these experiments have led most people to revise their ideas about the nature of the boundaries between human and animal thought.

All of the chimps learned to associate arbitrary signs with physical referents. They could recognize symbols for such objects as bananas, monkey chow, and cola. They could also use symbols to ask for rewards from their keepers. Washoe, for example, could ask her trainer to tickle her, and Lana could type on her console, "Start pour coke stop" to activate a soft-drink dispenser.

The chimps were also capable of more abstract tasks. Sarah, for example, learned to use the tokens symbolizing *same* and *different* in very sophisticated ways. She was able to solve simple visual analogies. For example, if asked whether an apple and a knife were the same as a piece of paper and a pair of scissors, she would indicate that they were. When the scissors was replaced with a bowl of water, she would indicate that the sets were now different. She also

*Deprived of language, we should be as dogs or monkeys. Possessing language, we are men and women able to persevere in crime no less than in heroic virtue, capable of intellectual achievements beyond the scope of any animal, but at the same time capable of systematic silliness and stupidity such as no dumb beast could ever dream of.[11]*

### Communication as Collective Activity

All languages depend on social agreement for their meaning. This brings us to the next part of our definition: Communication is collective. The relationship between human society and human communication is circular; one could not exist without the other. On the one hand, what holds a

society together is the ability of its members to act as a coordinated whole, which would be impossible without communication. On the other hand, communication presupposes social cooperation; interpersonal communication cannot occur unless at least two people mutually engage in creating meaning.

Joost Meerloo tells us that the word *communication* comes from *munia*, meaning service and connoting "mutual help, exchange, and interaction of those belonging to the same community."[12] In ancient times, members of the community who were exempt from public service were referred to as having *immunity*. If an individual committed an offense so terrible that he or she was no longer deemed fit to experience things in common with the rest of society, the seemed able to recognize the class to which tokens belonged. Thus, when given the token "banana" and asked whether it was a name or a color, she would correctly identify it as a name. Similarly she would label the "yellow" token as a color.

Just what can we make of these achievements? The chimps were able to recognize the communicative function of symbols and make simple associations between these symbols and objects in much the same way young human children do when they begin to learn language. However, the chimps never learned to link symbols together into complex "sentences." Although they used language to gain immediate goals, they showed no interest in using it to comment on the world. The ability to make up stories, which develops very early in human children, was absent.

Chimps also did not exhibit linguistic creativity, nor did they use language to direct their activities, as human children do when they guide themselves through a task by talking out loud.

Finally, they never spontaneously developed a language of their own. As Stephen Walker points out, "In a state of nature, we expect humans to talk, and, by comparison, the most unrelenting efforts to induce our closest living relatives to reveal hidden linguistic potential have left the discontinuities [between human speech and animal communication] bloodied but unbowed."

**SOURCE** Stephen Walker, *Animal Thought* (London: Routledge & Kegan Paul, 1983).

**ADDITIONAL READINGS**

Gardner, Beatrice T., and R. Allen Gardner. "Two-Way Communication with an Infant Chimpanzee." *In Behavior of Nonhuman Primates*, vol. 4. Allan Martin Scheier and Fred Stollnitz, eds. New York: Academic Press, 1971, pp. 117–83. (Washoe.)

Hayes, Keith J., and Catharine Hayes. "The Intellectual Development of a Home-Raised Chimpanzee." *Proceedings of the American Philosophical Society* 95 (1951): 105–9. (Vicki.)

Premack, David. *Intelligence in Ape and Man.* Hillsdale, N.J.: Lawrence Erlbaum, 1976. (Sarah.)

Rumbaugh, Duane M., ed. *Language Learning by a Chimpanzee*: The LANA Project. New York: Academic Press, 1977. (Lana.)

offender was *excommunicated*. Meerloo explains, "Wherever the concept of communication comes into play, the emphasis is on the common sharing of material and ideological wealth, on social intercourse, mutual exchange, and the bestowing of feelings and thoughts onto each other."[13]

## Communication as Creative Endeavor

A direct result of human communication is human *creativity*. When we agree with others that something can be talked about, we create that thing: We cause it to exist. While some things we agree to talk about (such as books or telephones) already exist in the physical world, others (like truth or justice) exist only in the shared symbolic world created by language. This doesn't mean, however, that symbolic things do not have powerful effects upon us.

Let's take the word *demon*. For most of us, this word has little reality. For many people in many parts of the world, however, demons have a real and objective existence. In Bali, for example, demons can cause human illness; they can make crops fail, pigs die, and volcanoes erupt. In order to survive, the Balinese must pacify and cajole them. On the Day of Silence, for example, everyone must sit "silent and immobile all day long in order to avoid contact with a sudden influx of demons chased momentarily out of hell."[14] The Balinese live in a symbolic world inhabited by—among other things—demons.

Are we superior to the Balinese? Is our world any less symbolic and more real than theirs? Think for a minute about how much of what you know and believe comes to you from direct

*Through communication we learn who we are and reflect that understanding to others.*

Pablo Picasso, *Girl Before a Mirror*, 1932

experience and how much is a product of talk. You may be surprised to find that most of your reality is created and sustained through communication.

### Communication as Regulatory

Communication allows us not only to create the world around us but to take possession of it as well. Through communication we can act on our world. In this sense communication is *regulatory*. If you have ever come down with a bad case of laryngitis, you know how helpless you feel when you can't speak. Such a loss illustrates the connection between communication and power.

This connection is as old as civilization. Even today words are associated with magic. By reciting incantations or writing an enemy's name on a piece of paper and then burning it, primitive people try to control others.[15] Even sophisticated moderns retain some superstitions about communication. One of the most common is reluctance to speak about good or bad fortune. If two friends are studying for an exam and the first asks, "What if we fail?" the other is likely to respond, "Don't even talk about something like that." We still retain vestiges of the belief that talking about something can either make it come true or jinx it.

Superstitions aside, communication is a powerful regulator of action. Through communication we can persuade, dissuade, anger, hurt, comfort, soothe, entertain, or bore one another. We can even use communication to control our own actions, talking ourselves into taking risks or comforting ourselves when we are afraid. Communication is a powerful way of regulating and controlling our world.

## Summary and Implications

All definitions have implications. What are the implications of our definition of communication? Although we see at least four, perhaps you will be able to think of more.

1. Much of what we think of as real is actually the product of communication. This implies that there is no single reality. Instead, *through communication we each create our own reality.* People with different communication experiences will see the world in different ways. We can never be totally sure that others see the world as we do. If we stop from time to time to check our perceptions, if we try to view things from others' perspectives, we may be surprised to see how different the world looks.

2. The fact that reality is a product of communication also has another implication: *Too often we allow what we have created through communication to control us.* When the Balinese created demons as an explanation for natural events, they put themselves in the position of spending the rest of their lives placating a concept. We too create our own kinds of demons. The expectations we have for ourselves—about things like success, perfection, and reputation—are examples of concepts that can control our lives and relationships.

3. Of course, individuals are not totally free to create any reality they want. Most of us are strongly influenced by the cultures in which we live. *Communication always takes place in a cultural context.* To forget this fact is to become a prisoner of culture. Erving Goffman has analyzed the powerful but unstated social rules that govern

*We are bound by social rules when we communicate, but we should not deny the creative impulse.*

interaction.[16] Although we will have more to say about Goffman throughout this book, it might be useful to introduce one of his concepts now, the concept of face.

Goffman defines **face** as an approved social identity, what we present to others for their approval. He believes that we spend a great deal of our time trying to fit face both to situation and to self-image. Communication that is incongruent with face will be judged as socially unacceptable. For Goffman, although face may be an individual's most cherished possession, "it is only on loan to him from society; it will be withdrawn unless he conducts himself in a way that is worthy of it. Approved attributes and their relation to face make of each man his own jailer; this is a fundamental social constraint even though each man may like his cell."[17]

Clearly, many of our most personal behaviors are culturally derived. One tension we all experience is that between independence and conformity. To communicate successfully, we must conform to social rules; to act creatively we must often oppose them. This tension will be discussed in more detail in Chapter 2.

4. Finally, communication requires cooperation. We are influenced not only by our cultures but by every individual with whom we communicate. This means that *what is important in interpersonal communication is what people do when they are together, not what each does separately*. Throughout this text we will stress the idea that interpersonal communication is mutual. In order to understand relationships we must look at the relationship itself, not at each individual participant. Most of the time we don't do this. For example, when a relationship fails, most of us try to figure out who to blame. We may blame the other person, feeling he or she is insensitive or egocentric; or we may blame ourselves, wishing we had been more open or less selfish. The truth is that communication is never the product of only one person's efforts. In order for relationships to work, *both* parties have to strive to be competent communicators.

# A Model of Communicative Competence

Communication doesn't always run smoothly. This may be one of the main reasons you've decided to study interpersonal communication. If you're like most people, at some time in your life you've run into communication problems. You've probably been in situations where you couldn't think of what to say next. Or you may have been unable to express yourself clearly. Perhaps you insulted someone unintentionally or blurted out something thoughtlessly. If you've experienced any of these situations, you know how important it is to be able to communicate competently.

What, exactly, does it mean to communicate competently? **Communicative competence** is the *ability to communicate in a personally effective and socially appropriate manner*. Although

this definition appears very simple, competence is a complex subject that has generated a lot of research and discussion. One reason is that competent communication involves two separate levels: (1) a surface level, consisting of the part of competence that can be seen—the actual performance of day-to-day behaviors—and (2) a deeper level, consisting of everything we have to know in order to perform. Although the surface level has many different names, we will call it **performative competence**. It is demonstrated every time someone actually produces effective and appropriate communication behaviors. The second, underlying level we will call **process competence**. It consists of all the cognitive activity and knowledge necessary to generate adequate performance.

For example, when you hear someone give a particularly gracious compliment, what you observe is only the surface level. What you cannot see is the mental activity that led up to it. Giving a compliment involves a lot of thought. It entails knowing when a compliment is appropriate and when it isn't, predicting whether the recipient will be pleased or embarrassed, choosing content that sounds sincere but not ingratiating, and knowing how to phrase the compliment in a graceful and pleasing style. All of this is part of process competence.

## Individual Knowledge and Communicative Competence

There are many different models of communicative competence. Some focus on performative aspects,[18] some on process,[19] and some do a little of both.[20] The model presented in Figure 1.1 is primarily a process model. It is our way of answering the question, "*What does a person have to know or be able to do in order to communicate in a personally effective and socially appropriate manner?*" Figure 1.1 is a representation of the processes we think are involved.

We believe that people who wish to be competent communicators must know how to do five things well: (1) assign meanings to the world around them; (2) set goals strategically; (3) take

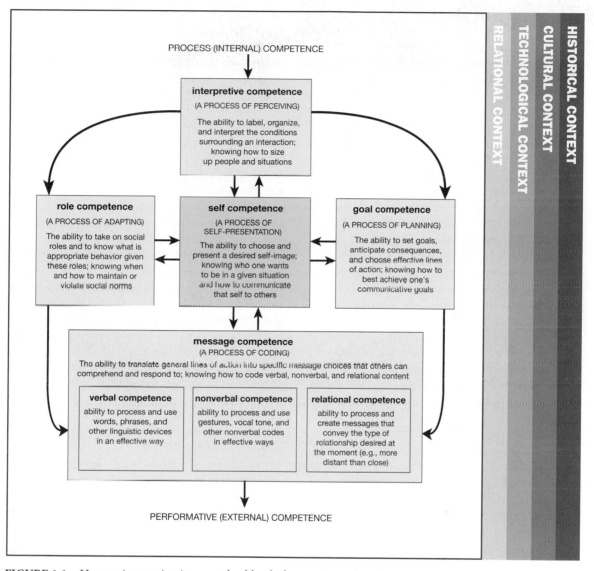

**FIGURE 1.1**  *Human interaction is a complex blend of many interrelated processes.*

on social roles appropriately; (4) present a valued image of themselves to the world; and (5) generate intelligible messages. These abilities correspond to the types of process competence outlined in our model: interpretive competence, goal competence, role competence, self competence, and message competence.

When we say that people who wish to be competent must "know" how to do the things listed previously, we are talking about implicit rather than explicit knowledge. Implicit knowledge is knowledge we don't stop to think about, that we use unconsciously to guide our behavior. Grammatical knowledge is a good example.

From the time we are quite young we can say things in well-structured and meaningful ways. We can even recognize and correct errors when we make them. However, most children (and indeed most adults) would be hard-pressed to recite the rules of grammar. The formal grammatical rules we learn in English class are attempts to express explicitly the implicit rules we follow when speaking.

The first kind of **implicit knowledge** we need about the world is perceptual. In order to communicate, we must be able to assign meaning to the world; we must know how to "see" it. This kind of competence we call interpretive competence. We must also be able to set communicative goals, to foresee the results of communication and make adequate plans. This we refer to as goal competence. Next, we must adapt to the needs and expectations of others. We must know what behaviors are appropriate and expected and what are prohibited. Doing this involves us in role competence. At the same time we are learning to adapt to others, we must also learn to be true to self. We must develop our own individual styles based on our sense of self. This is called self competence. Finally, we must be able to use all of this knowledge in actual speech situations. To do this we need message competence, the competence that allows us to express verbal, nonverbal, and relational messages. If we lack any of these kinds of process competence, communication becomes impossible: Messages are unclear and relationships flawed.

In the remainder of this chapter, we will give a brief overview of each of the elements in our model. Later in this book, we will revisit each kind of competence in more detail. As you read the brief descriptions that follow, remember that all five types of competence are interconnected. Because interpretive competence is at the top of our model and message competence is at the bottom, it may appear that interpretation comes before message-making. This isn't necessarily the case. There are times when we make language choices based on prior perceptions, but there are also times when the way we talk about something affects the way we perceive it. To emphasize the fact that the relationship between types of competence is complex and nonlinear, we will start our discussion with message competence and then move on to the other types of competence.

## Message Competence

Probably the first kind of competence most people think of when they think of communication is **message competence,** *the ability to make message choices that others can comprehend as well as to respond to the message choices of others*. Without the ability to code and decode messages, communication would be impossible. Schizophrenics, for example, use language in a bizarre and individualistic way. Their lack of message competence means that they must live apart from others in an impenetrable private world. Luckily, this kind of disruption in basic competence is rare. Most of us have an innate ability to understand and create messages.

The most obvious part of message competence is **verbal competence,** *the ability to process and use linguistic devices to convey content in effective ways*. Language is the basic currency through which meanings are exchanged. Without the ability to understand the rules of language, we would be unable to communicate in a fully human way. But language isn't everything. To communicate effectively we also need **nonverbal competence,** *the ability to process and use nonverbal codes to convey content in effective ways*. Body movement, facial expression, use of time and space, physical appearance, and vocal characteristics all convey meaning. To communicate competently, we must understand verbal codes as well as the nonverbal codes that accompany and often modify their meaning.

Verbal and nonverbal codes combine to create two kinds of meaning, content and relational meaning. Content meaning conveys the explicit topic of a message; it consists of the ideas or feelings the speaker is trying to share. Relational meaning is more implicit and contextual; it defines our relationship with the speaker. Whereas content meaning is contained in *what* is said, relational meaning lies in *how* something is said. Communicators often concentrate only on content and disregard relational meaning. To emphasize how important this second kind of message is, we have added relational competence to our model. For us, **relational competence** consists of *the ability to process and create messages that convey the type of relationship assumed or desired by a communicator at a given moment.*

The ability to make effective linguistic and nonverbal choices lies at the heart of communication. But message competence does not exist in a vacuum. It is connected to each of the other kinds of competence shown in our model.

## Interpretive Competence

In order to make effective message choices, we need to gather basic data about the context in which communication will occur. This involves **interpretive competence:** *the ability to label, organize, and interpret the conditions surrounding an interaction.* We live and communicate in a world full of diverse stimuli. Because we cannot pay attention to everything, we must learn to pick out information that is important and disregard information that is irrelevant.

If you have ever been in a completely unfamiliar situation, you know how difficult it can be to sort out sensory impressions. First-time campers lying alone in a tent in the dead of night hear all kinds of unfamiliar and inexplicable sounds, sounds that an experienced camper could easily dismiss as unimportant. Novices in any situation lack interpretive experience: They pay attention to meaningless details while overlooking important information and often don't know how to organize what they do see. If they have basic interpretive competence, however, they quickly learn what is important and what is not.

The need to interpret the world correctly is especially important in interpersonal interactions. In order to communicate effectively, we must understand the situations in which we find ourselves as well as the kind of people with whom we are dealing. We must also be able to

Communication allows us to build relationships that can endure throughout the years.

Francks Deceus, *Old Love*, 1995

identify our own feelings and needs. If we misinterpret our surroundings or misjudge our partners or overlook our own feelings, we may find ourselves in serious trouble. Without basic data about people and situations, we are likely to say the wrong thing at the wrong time. The kind of people who blurt out whatever they think, with no regard for where they are or who they are with, lack interpretive competence.

Interpretive competence helps us size up situations and people, name them, identify their outstanding characteristics, and, inevitably, decide upon an attitude toward them. If we succeed at this, we will make appropriate message choices; if not, we will do or say the wrong thing and will appear to be personally insensitive and impervious to our surroundings.

### Role Competence

Communication is a cooperative activity, a transaction in which people adapt to one another. Because of this, effective message choices must be culturally approved and socially shared. This brings us to a kind of competence we call **role competence,** *the ability to take on social roles and to know what is appropriate behavior given these roles.*

In order to communicate effectively, we must know who we may safely be in any situation; we must recognize what behaviors are appropriate and what are off limits. When conflicting social demands arise, we must be able to choose between them. We must also be able to maintain our own social identities while protecting the identities of others. If we fail to recognize the subtle rules that govern interaction, our message choices will seem odd or out of place. This often happens when we leave the safety of our own cultures. While most of us manage to learn the norms of our own groups, we're often at a loss when we have to interact with people not brought up as we were. The individual who is snatched from his or her own environment and placed in a very different one often lacks role competence. Plays and movies are full of such characters. The working-class heroine who suddenly finds herself in high society (*My Fair Lady*) or the time traveler who ends up in a different era (*Back to the Future*) are examples of characters who must somehow learn new ways of behaving. While their ineptness is a source of comedy in the movies, in real life the consequences of role-inappropriate behavior are more serious. Although a certain amount of individuality is charming, too much is socially costly. People who lack role competence often make message choices that lead others to perceive them as rude or willful or crazy.

### Self Competence

Of course communicating competently is not just a matter of following social rules. People who follow every rule of etiquette precisely, who let society define them completely, are merely social robots. We label such people as phony or fake, for they lack an essential characteristic that most of us value highly: individuality. Because all of us are individuals with our own unique thoughts and feelings, we must express them in our own ways. Thus, another important part of communicative competence is **self competence,** *the ability to choose and present a desired self-image.* Individuals with self competence know who they are and who they want to be and can convey that self to others.

One of the most important aspects of growing up is developing a sense of individuality and a personal communication style. Central to this process is the development of a healthy **self-concept,** for who we think we are is closely tied to how we present ourselves to others. If our self-concept contains negative elements (if our **self-esteem** is low) we are likely to avoid certain communication situations and to communicate tentatively and self-consciously. If, on the other hand, our self-concept is positive and our self-esteem high, we will communicate with confidence in a variety of situations. People who lack self competence lack a consistent communication style. Because they are not sure of who they are, they have trouble expressing thoughts and feelings. Others may perceive them as inconsistent or cold.

### Goal Competence

A final process necessary for communicative competence is planning. This process involves **goal competence,** *the ability to set goals, anticipate probable consequences, and choose effective lines of action.* Although not all communication is intentional, a great deal involves "strategic verbal choice-making." In order to make adequate message choices, a communicator must know what he or she is trying to achieve, determine the obstacles that lie in the path of goal attainment, and find a line of action that will overcome those obstacles.[21] This sequence is well known to salespeople who often carefully plan their approaches and use "canned" sales pitches to make sure their goals are achieved. Everyday planning takes a great deal more creativity and imagination. Seldom are our objectives completely clear and our lines of argument explicitly laid out; we must be able to think "on our feet."

Goal competence doesn't come easily. If we lack goal competence, we have few behavioral alternatives. We don't know how to approach others or what to do once we gain their attention. People without goal competence can't imagine the world as others see it, and their range of behaviors is limited. They don't know how to frame an argument or make an effective appeal. They may realize that their way of communicating is not working, but they don't know what to do about it. People who lack this form of competence make poor strategic choices. People are impervious to their messages and may well perceive them as awkward or offensive.

## Social Context and Communicative Competence

So far our discussion of the competence model has focused on individual abilities. We've looked at what a single individual has to know in order to communicate effectively. We've based our discussion on the assumption that people bring individual strengths and weaknesses with them when they communicate, and these strengths and weaknesses affect how successful they will be as communicators. For example, if Ted has trouble expressing his ideas directly, openly, and forcefully, he will lack verbal message competence, and he may have communication problems. To overcome these problems, he can work on becoming more fluent, forceful, and verbally expressive. In this sense, Ted's individual abilities make a significant difference in communication. However, this is not the whole story, for communication occurs in a social context. If we ig-

nore this context, we're oversimplifying the nature of communication. To avoid this problem, we've added context variables to the model. We've "framed" our view of what makes individuals competent with four kinds of context: cultural, historical, technological, and relational.

### Historical and Cultural Contexts

People communicate as they do not only because of individual abilities, experiences, and personalities, but also because they live in a certain place and in a certain time. In modern-day America, for example, we value direct, open, and honest communication. We believe that problems should be brought into the open and discussed. But this view is highly culture specific. Let's return to Ted, the young man who lacked message competence because he communicated indirectly. If Ted had been born in America 150 years ago, he would not be judged incompetent. At that time, a more guarded style was considered appropriate. In fact, being too open or too glib was considered a character defect. The "sell yourself" mentality we accept today is actually a product of mid-20th-century thinking. Similarly, if Ted had been reared in a country where social harmony is prized, he would be evaluated in an entirely different way. Knowing when to remain silent and, indeed, how to interpret the silence of others would be a central competence. Culture, like history, is a powerful factor in defining communication competence. In fact, the very meaning of talk changes from country to country and from group to group. Throughout this book we will offer illustrations of cultural differences in communication, and in Chapter 13 we'll examine this topic in depth. We urge you, as you read and think about the communication practices discussed in the rest of this book, to keep in mind that the way you and your acquaintances communicate—and in fact the values you hold about communication—are products of your culture. There are many other ways to approach communication that you may not yet have considered. For a first example of how the values associated

BOX 1.2

## Insulting the Meat

# An Interpersonal Communication Ritual

Cultural understandings guide virtually every aspect of our lives. They show us how to dress and move and speak. They tell us how to make friends, how to make enemies, and how to make love. They indicate what objects to hoard, what people to value, and what gods to worship. But precisely because they tell us so much, we often fail to realize their influence. Studying the customs of different cultures can remind us that the way we do things is not the only natural and proper way.

One example of how another culture communicates is described by Richard Lee, who studied the Dobe !Kung, the so-called Bushmen of the Kalahari. The !Kung are nomadic foragers who survive in a harsh environment by hunting and gathering. They have developed a number of rituals that have helped them adapt to this way of life. One of the most interesting is known as "insulting the meat."

In !Kung society the wild game and edible plants gathered by members of the group are normally shared with the entire tribe. A lot of time and attention are devoted to the fair distribution of goods, particularly of meat. One way of ensuring fair distribution is demonstrated by the following communication pattern.

Strict norms govern the way a hunter announces his results when he returns from a successful hunt. He must sit in silence until someone asks him how the hunt went. He must then say that he found nothing of any worth. On the following day, when his companions go out with him to collect the kill, they are expected to do so with a minimum of enthusiasm, complaining loudly about the distance and wretchedness

with communication are culturally constrained, see Box 1.2.

## Technological Context

One reason competence is affected by history is that, over time, new technologies are discovered, technologies that make it possible to communicate in new ways. Each time that happens, people must adapt to the technology and find ways to use it competently. Ted may be reticent in face-to-face contexts, but his confidence may change dramatically when he communicates online, while his roommate Fred may be completely ineffective when communication is mediated. New technologies present new opportunities and new challenges, although at the beginning, emerging communication technologies are often viewed with suspicion.

John Bargh and Katelyn McKenna tell us, for example, that, when the telegraph came into use, governments feared it would lead to revolution.[22] And it was generally feared that the telephone could harm social interaction by undermining the practice of visiting friends. Radio and television were also met with concern as critics warned that people would no longer engage in civic activities and children would abandon wholesome activities once these new forms of entertainment entered the home. Although a study by sociologist Robert Putnam gives some support to the fear that television can undermine social group membership, none of the other fears have been realized.[23] In fact, in all of the other cases, interpersonal communication has been enhanced. Early on, for example, telegraph operators formed social networks and used code to exchange news and of the game. Instead of being offended, the hunter agrees, apologizing for his lack of skill.

What can we make of this behavior? Wouldn't it be more "natural" for a hunter to boast of a good kill? Lee tells us that the "heavy joking and derision are directed toward one goal: the leveling of potentially arrogant behavior in a successful hunter." Lee believes that "insulting the meat" is a way of maintaining a sense of equality. Because the !Kung depend on sharing for survival, generosity is something that should not be praised but simply expected. Praise might lead to pride and arrogance, potential threats to the !Kung way of life. As Tomazho, one of the !Kung, expressed it:

> When a young man kills much meat, he comes to think of himself as a chief or a big man, and he thinks of us as his servants or inferiors. We can't accept this. We refuse one who boasts, for someday his pride will make him kill somebody. So we always speak of his meat as worthless. In this way we cool his heart and make him gentle.

For most of us, this is a peculiar way of doing things. We believe that people should take pride in their accomplishments and show gratitude for generosity. But stop for a moment and think about the social results of concepts such as "gratitude" and "accomplishment" and "generosity." How do they affect our relationships with others? The answer to this question may make you see more clearly how seemingly innocent and trivial patterns of communication are tied to larger social issues.

**SOURCE** Richard B. Lee, *The Dobe !Kung* (New York: Holt, Rinehart & Winston, 1984).

**ADDITIONAL READINGS**
Geertz, Clifford. *The Interpretation of Cultures.* New York: Basic Books, 1973.
Spradley, James P., and David W. McCurdy, eds. *Conformity and Conflict: Readings in Cultural Anthropology,* 5th ed. Boston: Little, Brown, 1984.

gossip. In fact, Thomas Edison, who started out as a telegraph operator, proposed to his wife over the telegraph.[24] The effect of the telephone was also positive: It increased contact between distant friends and relatives and strengthened local ties.[25] And radio and television both allowed the rapid dissemination of news.

Now, in the 21st century, advances in information and communication technologies are giving rise to the same old fears of social isolation and the uncontrolled spread of dangerous information. The Internet, for example, has been accused of turning people into mindless zombies who spend hours surfing the Web looking for pornography— and neglecting family and friends. In an amusing aside, Bargh and McKenna report that the Internet has even been denounced by the head of the Miss France committee as "an uncontrolled medium where rumormongers, pedophiles, prostitutes, and criminals could go about their business with impunity." This tirade occurred when rumors that the reigning Miss France was, in fact a man, spread across the world.[26] Yet, despite the hysteria, most researchers now agree that the overall effect of the new media has been to strengthen interpersonal communication, not to weaken it. In fact, national surveys have found that Internet users actually have larger offline social networks than nonusers do.[27] That the Internet is used to enhance interpersonal relationships is shown by the fact that the most frequent use of the Internet, its "killer app," is e-mail, a medium for interpersonal interaction. Most e-mail communication occurs with people the sender already knows offline, although, for those who wish to, the Internet allows individuals to meet online and

## Communication Incompetence

# Meet the Parents

Jay Roach, 2000

Meeting prospective in-laws for the first time is a situation that can challenge even the most accomplished communicator. Unfortunately, Greg Focker (Ben Stiller) is far from accomplished. His desperate attempts to make a good impression on his girlfriend Pam's (Terri Polo) parents backfire at every turn, especially when he meets Pam's father Jack (Robert DeNiro), a potential groom's worst nightmare. All Greg wants to do is make himself agreeable, but his small social lies soon escalate, especially after he claims to have milked a cat.

Anyone who's ever been in a stressful communication situation can identify with Greg, although, admittedly, most of us don't set other people's houses on fire, flood their septic tanks, or substitute counterfeit cats for beloved pets. This very funny movie explores what happens when the need to win people over triumphs over common sense, and it provides an over-the-top example of communication incompetence. It's a relief to know that no matter what social faux pas we may make from time to time or what negative impressions we inadvertently create, it will never get as bad for us as it was for Greg Focker.

form meaningful cyber relationships. Certainly, for stigmatized people, the Internet has been a boon, offering support and identity affirmation.

Despite all of these positive effects, the new media, including mobile telephones as well as networked computers, present challenges. Being able to communicate more quickly does not mean that one will communicate more competently. Because people almost never use new technologies as their inventors imagine, there is no instruction manual to tell users how to be effective communicators in a new medium. At the beginning, people have to work out ways to interact competently. For example, one of the effects of the omnipresent cell phone is an effect known as **aproximeeting.** Because we can contact one another so easily, we no longer make specific appointments. This can lead to entire evenings spent trying to figure out where everyone is and where to meet up, with the eventual outcome that nothing ever gets decided. Another challenge lies in negotiating space. Cell-phone users exist in physical space, yet they communicate in virtual space, an effect that can be confusing when trying to walk along a busy street while fighting with a friend or trying to comfort a distraught roommate. And how should attention be divided between copresent friends and a ringing cell phone?[28] Although these problems may seem trivial, they can cause disruptions to communication and, if not handled with tact and sensitivity, can harm relationships. In Box 5.1 in Chapter 5, we will offer some suggestions about ways to handle new media. For the present, just keep in mind that all five of the competences we have discussed are affected by technology. For this reason, we add it as a contextual constraint in Figure 1.1.

### Relational Context

Another kind of context that affects the way we communicate is relational context. A person like Ted, who is reticent and indirect in many situations, may open up when he is with someone about whom he cares. A close, comfortable relationship may transform Ted. Conversely, sometimes relationships cause people who are normally outgoing and expressive to turn inward. We need to remember that people change and are changed by their relationships. Communication is relational: It is a reciprocal interaction between two people. It is something two people do together, not something that they do to each other. In the next chapter, we'll focus more on this important aspect of communication.

## The Link Between Process and Performance

The five processes we have discussed are all necessary for good performance. Unfortunately, knowing how to communicate does not guarantee we will say or do the right thing. A person can know perfectly well what is required in a given situation and still not perform adequately. A number of factors can cause communication to fail: individual physical states such as fatigue or anxiety; contradictory attitudes, beliefs, and values; poor motivation; and sheer stubbornness. Finally, lack of practice can cause a performance to come off as stilted and artificial.

In this book we'll provide you with some of the theoretical knowledge you'll need to understand and analyze communication. After defining interpersonal communication in the next chapter, we revisit the five kinds of competence outlined in our model. We begin with message competence because the sending and receiving of messages is the heart of all interpersonal communication. In Chapter 3 we look at nonverbal communication codes and note the kinds of meanings they convey. In Chapter 4 we note the importance of language on thought and action, while in Chapter 5 we explore ways both codes are used to send relational messages. Chapter 6 looks at interpretive competence, examining the relationship between communication and perception. Chapter 7 investigates role competence, while Chapter 8 focuses on self competence and issues of identity formation. Chapter 9 centers on goal competence and strategic communication. Chapters 10 through 12 focus on competence in important communication contexts. These chapters discuss how we can improve our interactions with family, intimates, and colleagues. Finally, we end with a chapter dedicated to understanding how culture and history affect interpersonal patterns in all contexts.

While we believe that the first step to becoming a better communicator is understanding the basic processes of competence, we believe theory is not the whole picture. To be fully competent you must be able to translate theory into practice. To help you do that, at the end of each chapter we include a section on skill building. These sections offer guidelines to help you improve your interpersonal skills. Through classroom activities and by working through some of the assignments in the "Process to Performance" sections at the end of each chapter, we hope you will find a way to take these general guidelines and make them work for you.

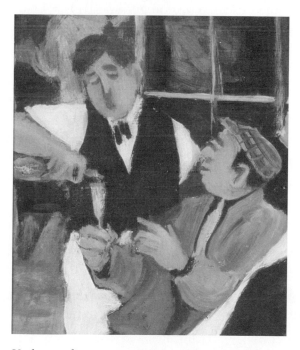

*Understanding communication processes helps us see how different types of communication are appropriate in various contexts.*

*Getting the Most out of College*

# Communication Competence in the Classroom

What does it mean to be an effective student? Is it just a matter of knowing how to study? Or is there something more? Ann Bainbridge Frymier suggests that being a good student also means being a competent classroom communicator. In her article "Students' Classroom Communication Effectiveness" she looks at some of the communication skills that increase students' abilities to communicate effectively with their teachers.

Frymier hypothesized that four communication skills are related to positive classroom outcomes. These skills, the study's independent variables, are interaction involvement (the ability to attend to, understand, and react to ongoing interaction), assertiveness (the capacity to stand up for oneself without attacking another), responsiveness (the ability to understand others' needs and to listen actively), and frequency of out-of-classroom communication (how often one meets with the instructor after class to seek advice or to get to know him or her better). The positive classroom outcomes measured in this study, the dependent variables, were student reports of learning, motivation to study, satisfaction with instructors, and grades.

Two hundred ninety-seven students enrolled in introductory communication courses were asked to think of the instructor they had immediately preceding the course in which data were collected and then to fill out scales measuring all of the independent and dependent variables.

Results showed that out of all the independent variables, interaction involvement was the best predictor of positive classroom outcomes. There were positive correlations between involvement and all of the dependent measures, which means that students who scored high in involvement also felt they learned more, were more motivated and satisfied, and reported higher grades. Responsiveness was associated with learning, motivation, and satisfaction but not with grades. Assertiveness did not appear to be of particular importance, and frequency of out-of-class communication was related most strongly to satisfaction, but not to the other dependent variables.

What can you learn from this study? The results suggest that if you want to be a more effective student, you should focus on increasing your interaction involvement. This means becoming more aware of how your teacher responds to you, listening rather than letting your attention wander, and finding ways to meet your teacher's expectations. It is easy to sit back passively in class, but the more involved you are the better you will like your instructor, the more motivated you will be to study, and the more satisfied you will be with classroom communication. Of course, communication style cannot make up for poor study skills, but combining the two may just make you happier with school and give you better grades.

Frymier, Ann Bainbridge. "Students' Classroom Communication Effectiveness." *Communication Quarterly* 53, no. 2 (2005): 197–212.

# Skill Building: On Taking a Process Perspective

As we progress through the text, we will be looking at ways to improve specific skills like listening, giving and receiving feedback, becoming more assertive, and so on. For now, we want to say a few general words about how to build skills. An important step in improving your communication is learning to take what we call a **process perspective.** This means becoming aware of what's going on when you communicate, beginning to recognize how the underlying processes involved in communication manifest themselves in everyday performance. Too often people communicate in a mindless kind of way. They are so busy thinking about *what* they are saying or doing (the content of communication) that they fail to consider *how* they are going about it (the form of communication). Taking a process perspective means concentrating on form in addition to content. It means sitting back and watching yourself as you communicate.

At first this is not an easy thing to do, for it involves a kind of "double consciousness." The competent communicator must be able to act naturally and spontaneously and at the same time observe and analyze communication patterns. This is somewhat like being a good actor. On the one hand, actors exist within the imaginary world of the play, reacting as their characters would. On the other hand, they remain aloof and in control, watching for the cues that signal exits and entrances, remembering their positions and lines, and adjusting to audience reaction. Beginning actors often have a hard time finding just the right mixture of involvement and distance.

The beginning speech communication student must also find the right balance point between performing and analyzing. At first students have problems removing themselves from the content level; they have not yet learned to see process. Later on, as they learn more about communica-

tion, they may become too analytical, annoying their friends by giving instant analyses of every interaction. But with practice it is possible to learn when to act and when to analyze. The transitions become easy and automatic.

We cannot stress strongly enough how important it is to begin to start analyzing interactions. For one thing, it will make learning theory more interesting and enjoyable. You will begin to see connections between what you read about in this text and what you and those around you actually do. Even more important, developing the ability to observe behavior will allow you to diagnose and improve your own performance.

As a beginning, look at the study described in the Research in Review box and think about your own level of interaction involvement. If it is low, think about ways you might be able to increase it.

# *Process to Performance*

## Review Terms
The following is a list of major concepts introduced in this chapter. The page where the concept is first mentioned is listed in parentheses.

communication   (5)
process   (5)
face   (9)
communicative competence   (10)
performative competence   (10)
process competence   (10)
implicit knowledge   (12)
message competence   (12)
verbal competence   (12)
nonverbal competence   (12)
relational competence   (13)
interpretive competence   (13)
role competence   (14)
self competence   (14)
self-concept   (14)

self-esteem (14)
goal competence (14)
aproximeeting (18)
process perspective (21)

## Suggested Readings

Galvin, Kathleen M., and Pamela J. Cooper. *Making Connections: Readings in Relational Communication, 4th ed.* Los Angeles, Calif.: Roxbury, 2006. The essays in this collection give an overview of the field of interpersonal communication and provide a feel for the ways in which communication affects the building of relationships.

Segerdahl, Par, William Fields, and Sue Savage-Rumbaugh. *Kanzi's Primal Language: The Cultural Initiation of Primates into Language.* New York: Palgrave Macmillan, 2005. For 18 years, Sue Savage-Rumbaugh maintained a relationship with a chimpanzee named Kanzi. In this book, she and her colleagues give a behind-the-scenes look at how Kanzi acquired the ability to use a form of language.

## Topics for Discussion

www.oup.com/us/trenholm

## Observation Guide

1. Analyze a recent conversation by applying the model of communication competence presented in this chapter. Identify the level of interpretive, goal, role, and message competence you and your partner achieved. For instance, how successful were you in sizing up the situation? Did you accurately perceive your partner's intentions? How many message strategies did you consider? Did you have a clear understanding of the social roles called for? Were there any verbal or nonverbal misunderstandings? Judge your performance. How well did you do what you wanted to?

2. Take a look at the other courses you're enrolled in this semester. How can these courses give you an understanding of communication? Make a list of at least 15 topics from other courses that are related to interpersonal communication. Take one and describe what it taught you about the communication process. For example, you may have read a short story in a literature class that described interpersonal relationships. You may have come across a theory in psychology that explains some aspect of communication. Describe in detail what you learned.

## Exercises

1. Work in pairs. Begin by individually thinking of the best and worst communicators you ever knew. Describe them to your partner. Working together, come up with a list of at least 10 attributes that differentiate your good and bad communicators. Now ask your partner to describe his or her best and worst communicators and repeat the process. How did your ideas differ? How do you stack up on both your own and your partner's list? What is your strongest point? What areas need more work? Discuss.

2. Taking a process perspective means becoming aware of how people communicate with one another. It means looking for cues that signal what's going on between people. Choose a partner and go to a public area on campus. Find a group of people who look interesting and observe them for 10 or 15 minutes. As you observe, make notes on what's going on in their interaction. Share your notes with your partner. From your combined observations, make a list of all of the things you were able to tell about interpersonal relationships just by observing. At the next class, share your list with others. Together come up with an observation guide—a list of things to look for in interaction. Use this observation guide to observe another group. You should begin to see more and more happening as you gain experience in observing others.

3. A model is a simplified explanation of a process. Models can help us understand the charac-

teristics of a process, the factors that affect it, the way it operates, and so on. There are many ways of describing any process; consequently there are many models of it.

a. To get some practice in model making, think of a fairly complex process or object that you're familiar with (a football game, eating at a restaurant, graduating from high school, a first date). Working in groups, construct a model of that process. Pretend that you are preparing materials for people from a vastly different culture who will be visiting your college. Your model will help these people learn how things are done in your culture. You can create a verbal description, a flowchart, a diagram, a rule book. Share your model with the class.

b. Now try constructing your own model of communication.

*Interpersonal communication always changes us. When it works, we touch each other's lives; when it fails, we feel disconnected and alone.*

Edward Hopper, *Nighthawks*, 1942

## CHAPTER 2

# Interpersonal Communication Building Relationships

Communication takes many forms. It can be as simple and direct as a smile or as complex and eloquent as a novel. It can occur between two people or among thousands, with a small group of friends or in an impersonal bureaucracy. Because communication takes so many different forms, it is easy to forget that all are part of the same process: the act of creating and sharing meaning. No matter how technologically sophisticated the channels or how vast the audience, communicators must share meaning with one another. It is for this reason that communication is, at heart, an interpersonal process.

One of the authors of this text was once asked at a party what he taught. When he answered, "Interpersonal communication," he was asked, "But isn't all communication interpersonal? Doesn't it always occur between people?" The question is not a bad one. Although it is common to reserve the label interpersonal for intimate communication between two people in face-to-face interaction, clearly all communication is, in a sense, interpersonal.

In this chapter we explore the relationship between interpersonal and other forms of communication. We begin by discussing some of the unique characteristics of two-person communication. We then describe how interpersonal communication enables us to form close personal relationships, and we examine some of the issues couples confront as they create relational profiles. Finally, we consider what it takes to build a healthy relationship.

## What Is Interpersonal Communication? The Nature of Dyads

What is interpersonal communication? The answer depends on the approach you take. If you take a **situational approach** you define interpersonal communication in terms of its external characteristics; you look at factors like the number of people involved and their physical proximity. If you take what has been called the **developmental approach**, you define interpersonal

**25**

communication in terms of its content; you look at the kind of information people exchange and how well they know one another. As the situational approach is the most common way to distinguish interpersonal communication from other forms of communication, we will begin with that approach. But, because the developmental approach is an interesting and intriguing way of thinking about interpersonal communication, we will also discuss it briefly.

## The Situational Approach to Interpersonal Communication

Although communication always involves the cooperative act of creating meaning, it can take on quite different forms depending on the situation. A presidential address to the nation, for example, and a heated argument between friends may both address the same political issue, but, both in purpose and structure, they are poles apart. For this reason, it is common to distinguish between different forms of communication, including intrapersonal, interpersonal or dyadic, small-group, organizational, face-to-face public, and mass media, both traditional and new.

When we're alone, our communication is often quite different from our communication when we are with others. First of all, it is silent, taking place inside our heads. Most people believe that this kind of communication, called **intrapersonal communication,** is also more disconnected and repetitive and less logical than other forms of communication.[1] Whenever you daydream or fantasize, consider a difficult personal problem, or try to make sense of the world around you, you are engaging in intrapersonal communication. You are both sender and receiver of your own message.

Intrapersonal communication can be distinguished from **interpersonal communication,** communication between two people, generally in face-to-face interaction. Another name for this form of communication is *dyadic.* Dyadic communication is generally spontaneous and informal; the participants receive maximum feedback

from each other. Roles are relatively flexible, as partners alternately act as senders and receivers. When you sit down with a friend to recall old times, when you ask a professor what will be on the test, or when you have a serious discussion with someone you love, you are engaging in interpersonal communication.

As soon as a third person joins an interaction, it ceases to be interpersonal and becomes **small-group communication.** While the size of a small group may vary, it must be small enough that everyone can interact freely. In a dyad the participants are connected directly; if the link between them is severed, the relationship no longer exists. In a small group, communication is not destroyed when the link between two of the members is cut. Members can communicate with one another in a variety of ways.

Coordinating group interaction is relatively complex. For most of us, groups are psychologically more difficult to handle than dyads. One of the reasons formalized roles like that of leader emerge is to allow groups to handle the difficult problem of coordinating activity.[2] Students working on a class project together, cabinet members setting government policy, sports teams, and social clubs all engage in small-group communication.

The next level involves **organizational communication.** This form of communication occurs in complex organizations such as large businesses and industries and government institutions. Here communication takes place within a strongly defined hierarchy. Organizational members also experience, in addition to interpersonal and group relationships with coworkers, a relationship to the organization itself and to the bureaucracy that organizes and runs it. Roles tend to be more specialized and differentiated than at other levels, and rules for behavior are more formalized. Successful communication requires knowledge of these roles and rules, often referred to as "organizational culture."[3]

When a single speaker addresses a large group of individuals simultaneously, he or she engages in **face-to-face public communication.** The speaker doesn't know audience members personally and

| Characteristics of Interaction | | |
|---|---|---|
| number of persons | few | many |
| proximity of interactants | close | far |
| nature of feedback | immediate | delayed |
| communication roles | informal | formal |
| adaptation of message | specific | general |
| goals and purpose | unstructured | structured |
| **Situational Levels:** | Intrapersonal    Small Group    Public<br>Interpersonal    Organizational    Mass | |

FIGURE 2.1 *Situational characteristics and levels of communication.*

must therefore compose the message for a hypothetical receiver. Because of the size of the audience, mutual interaction is also impossible. The speaker therefore acts as sender while the audience takes on a more passive receiver role. Clear organization, careful planning, and a fairly formal, nonconversational style are hallmarks of public communication. A political candidate on a whistle-stop tour, an evangelist exhorting a congregation, even a lecturer in a mass-enrollment course are examples of people communicating on the public level.

Finally, when speaker and audience become separated in both space and time, indirect ways of sending and receiving messages must be used. Messages must be stored until they can be received by their intended audience. When the audience is large but the transmission is indirect, we call it **mediated public** (or **mass**) communication. Whenever "a medium replicates, duplicates, and disseminates identical content to a geographically widespread population," mass communication is taking place.[4] Radio and TV broadcasts, newspaper and magazine articles, and recorded music are examples.

As we move from intrapersonal to mass communication, the following elements change: (1) the number of interactants, (2) their physical proximity, (3) their ability to deliver and receive feedback immediately, (4) the level of formality of communication roles, (5) the ability of interactants to adapt messages to others' specific needs, and (6) the degree to which communicative goals and purposes are planned and structured.[5] Of all these variables, size probably has the biggest effect, since a change in size leads to all other changes.[6] Figure 2.1 shows how these factors affect communication.

As we've seen, communication can take many forms. This doesn't mean, however, that it is always easy to figure out what kind of communication is going on. Communication contexts often blend into one another or rapidly change back and forth. For example, while sitting in class listening to a lecture (public communication), you may at the same time daydream (intrapersonal) or make eye contact with a friend (interpersonal). And when new technologies are involved, for example, e-mail or computer chat rooms, it's difficult to know whether the communication you're engaging in is interpersonal, group, or mass communication.

Instead of thinking of interpersonal communication as separate from other forms of communication, we prefer to think of all communication as having an interpersonal element. While the clearest instance of interpersonal communication takes place when two people interact directly and personally, many other interactions are partially interpersonal.

Situations overlap, and when they do communication may take on the characteristics of both situations. The Research in Review section in Chapter 8 on interpersonal blogs provides a good example of a hybrid form of interpersonal communication called mediated interpersonal communication, as does the Research in Review section in Chapter 9 on reality TV gossip. While the clearest instance of interpersonal communication takes place when two people interact directly and personally, many other interactions are partially interpersonal in nature. It may be useful to think of interpersonal communication as what philosophers and psychologists refer to as a "fuzzy set," a class that does not have completely clear boundaries.

## The Developmental Approach to Interpersonal Communication

The situational approach focuses our attention on external factors. Under the situational approach a customer directing a cab driver where to go would be just as interpersonal as a friend pouring out his heart to a buddy: Both involve two people in face-to-face interaction. But does that make sense? According to the *developmental approach*, it does not. The customer and the cabbie may be a dyad, but their communication is not truly interpersonal because they lack intimate knowledge of one another. The friends, on the other hand, are communicating interpersonally because they know each other so well. Many years ago, Gerald Miller and Mark Steinberg argued that there is a quality dimension to interpersonal communication. Initial interactions start out as *impersonal*; only over time do they develop into interpersonal interactions. In fact,

Miller and Steinberg believe that most dyadic communication is not interpersonal at all.

What does it take to communicate interpersonally? To answer that question from the standpoint of the developmental approach, we have to distinguish three levels of information available to communicators. Very general information that applies to all members of a given culture is called **cultural level data**. When communicators identify one another as middle-class Americans, for example, they are working at the cultural level. The knowledge they share makes communication possible, but it remains at a surface level. When people identify one another based on the reference or membership groups to which they belong, they use **sociological level data**. When two people find out they are both college students, for example, they have progressed to this second level; as a result their ability to predict one another's interests and attitudes has increased. **Psychological level data** provide the most information of all; they are data based on unique, personal attributes. When two people share their hopes and fears with one another, they know one another in an entirely different way. According to Miller and Steinberg, when individuals operate at the cultural or sociological levels they are engaged in "noninterpersonal communication." Only "when predictions are based primarily on a psychological level of analysis" are the communicators actually engaged in interpersonal communication.[7] Miller and Steinberg argue that people vary in their ability to communicate interpersonally. Because moving to an interpersonal level requires the ability to see others as unique individuals and to appreciate differences, rigid or dogmatic people have great difficulty communicating interpersonally. In their view, true interpersonal communication is rare, perhaps because it takes a great deal of skill and commitment to communicate interpersonally.

Whether or not you agree with their analysis, Miller and Steinberg draw our attention to the fact that some forms of dyadic communication are deeper and more profound than others. Most relationships will never progress to the level

Miller and Steinberg call interpersonal, nor should they. It would be impossible to be close and personal with everyone with whom we come in contact. Yet interactions in which both parties have a unique appreciation of one another are qualitatively different from the more fleeting and less intimate interactions that are characteristic of most dyadic relationships.

In the rest of this book, we will take the situational approach, using the term *interpersonal communication* to refer to *dyadic communication in which two individuals, sharing the roles of sender and receiver, become connected through the mutual activity of creating meaning.* Although most of the time the bonds we create by communicating with one another are short-lived and practical, they can sometimes be the first step in the creation of deeply personal, long-term relationships.

# The Role of Interpersonal Communication in Relationships

Before we begin our discussion of how interpersonal communication functions in the creation of relationships, stop for a moment and imagine what your life would be like without friends, family, or loved ones. It's easy to see that your quality of life would be threatened, but you may not realize that your health and, perhaps, your very ability to survive are also tied to interpersonal bonds. Box 2.1 offers some scientific evidence for the importance of interpersonal relationships in every aspect of our lives.

## What Is a Relationship?

Given the fact that relationships are so important in our lives, you'd think it would be easy to define the concept of relationship. In fact, it's sur-

prisingly difficult to find a single answer to the question, "What is a relationship?" Relationships have been defined in several different ways: as constellations of behaviors,[8] as cognitive constructs,[9] as mini-cultures,[10] and as collections of contradictory forces.[11] In this section, we'll review these different views of what a relationship is, and in the next we'll combine them into a discussion of six important characteristics of relationships.

Some scholars see **relationships as constellations of behaviors;** for them, a relationship is equivalent to the interdependent actions of two people. In other words, relationships are all the things two people do when they are together. For example, Tony and Tina have been seeing each other for half a year, and they have fallen into routines. Certain behaviors inevitably lead to arguments, while other behaviors smooth things out. In the process of doing things together, Tony and Tina have developed **interdependence:** What Tony does affects Tina and what she does affects him. For many people the answer to the question of what is a relationship is clear. The way two people behave toward each other *is* their relationship.

But is behavior enough, or does something else happen to create a relationship? Some theorists believe that relationships are more than behaviors: They see **relationships as cognitive constructs** that exist in our minds when we think about one another. For these theorists, a relationship is the way we *think* about our behaviors. People who see relationships in this way argue that when we interact with another person, we form a mental image of the interaction and compare it to a **relational prototype,** an idealized image of how things should be. Tina, for example, carries around in her head a version of what she thinks a romantic relationship should be like. As she thinks about Tony and how he treats her, she compares their behaviors to her version of the "romantic couple" prototype. Because the fit is a close one, she decides that they are a couple. Meanwhile, Tony is doing the same thing. Because Tony agrees with Tina, there is no conflict about what they mean to each other. Unfortunately, this does

BOX 2.1

## The Neuroscience of Love

# Why We Need Relationships

In the late 1950s Harry Harlow conducted a now-famous study on primate bonding. Harlow offered baby monkeys a choice of two surrogate mothers: one, made of wire mesh, dispensed milk through a feeding bottle; the other gave no food, but was made of soft terrycloth. Although the young monkeys went to the wire mother to drink, they formed no bonds with her. As soon as they were finished dining, they scurried to the terrycloth mother. "They clasped her, squealed at her, embraced her, hid behind her when alarmed. . . . In trial after trial, the more a doll could be made to resemble a mother monkey, the more infatuated the little monkeys became."

Why did the baby monkeys seek out the doll that looked most like their mothers? Why do human infants bond with their caregivers? And why, even in adulthood, does it hurt so much when a close relationship ends? In *A General Theory of Love,* Thomas Lewis and his colleagues examine the neurochemistry of human attachment. They argue that all mammals, including humans, are born with an instinctive need to form interpersonal bonds. Our need to attach to and love others is not just a luxury; it is an absolute necessity. Without interpersonal relationships humans and other mammals cannot lead normal, healthy lives.

Lewis shows us that humans need one another to regulate their physiology. This process was discovered by accident. Psychobiologist Myron Hofer walked into his lab one day to find that one of his rats had gnawed through her cage, abandoning her litter. Hofer noticed that the abandoned pups' hearts beat at less than half the normal rate. Further studies showed that when separated from their attachment figures, many animals show deficits in body temperature, sleep rhythms, immune function, hormone activity level, sleep, and a variety of other neurochemical levels. Behavior is affected as well. Studies by neurobiologist Gary Kraemer showed that if raised alone from infancy, monkeys cannot engage in reciprocal interactions with normal monkeys, are unable to mate, may

not always happen. Sometimes two people have very different ideas about their relationship, and because of this they experience dissatisfaction and confusion. These kinds of situations demonstrate why thoughts and expectations are just as important in defining relationships as actual behaviors are.

Whereas some theorists locate relationships in the minds of individual communicators, others feel that relationships are not individual views but shared understandings. These people view **relationships as mini-cultures.** People who come from a given national culture (say, the United States or Japan) share common percep-

tions about the world and agree to abide by common codes of conduct in order to live together in harmony. Some scholars who study close relationships suggest that, when two people form an interpersonal bond, they create their own small-scale culture, developing shared perceptions and creating roles that allow them to coexist. If we view Tina and Tony's relationship in this way, their relationship consists of more than their behaviors or their individual images of each other. In addition, it consists of the rules and obligations that govern their interactions and of their shared understandings of each other and their social worlds.

self-mutilate, and, if artificially impregnated, are indifferent or even dangerous mothers.

Lewis believes that the mammalian brain cannot develop in isolation. Mammals that lack relationships are "jagged and incomplete. Their brains produce fractured behaviors that emerge at the wrong times, in the wrong places, in the wrong ways. . . . A monkey cannot even grow up knowing how to eat or drink in a balanced way unless his mother was at his side during childhood. Love, and the lack of it, change the young brain forever." And what is true of baby monkeys is also true for human infants. Infants who are neglected or deprived of touch show greatly elevated mortality rates.

Research like this has stimulated a new understanding of human relatedness. It is becoming increasingly clear that individuals are not self-sufficient. We need others to transmit information that regulates our physical and emotional well-being. According to Lewis, when two people attach, a reciprocal process occurs simultaneously: "the first person regulates the physiology of the second, even as he himself is regulated. Neither is a functioning whole on his own. . . . Together they create a stable, properly balanced pair of organisms." This process of mutual regulation is called *limbic regulation*. Although the need for the presence of another regulating being is strongest in infancy, adults "continue to require a source of stabilization outside themselves." Stability means "finding people who regulate you well and staying near them."

For Lewis, and for many other attachment theorists, human relationships are necessary and life sustaining. We attach to others "in a process that begins before birth and sustains life until its end." Without interpersonal bonds, we literally cannot survive.

**SOURCE** Thomas Lewis, Fari Amini, and Richard Lannon, *A General Theory of Love* (New York: Random House, 2000).

**ADDITIONAL READINGS**

Harlow, Harry F. "The Nature of Love." *American Psychologist* 13 (1958): 673–85.

Hofer, M. A. "Hidden Regulators: Implications for a New Understanding of Attachment, Separation, and Loss." In *Attachment Theory: Social, Developmental, and Clinical Perspectives.* S. Goldberg, R. Muir, and J. Kerr, eds. Hillsdale, N.J.: Analytic Press, 1995.

Kraemer, G. W. "A Psychobiological Theory of Attachment." *Behavioral and Brain Sciences* 15 (1992): 493–541.

Of course, relationships do not always run smoothly, and shared understandings are always open to negotiation. Often, people feel conflicts about their connections with one another. This realization has led to a final view of **relationships as collections of contradictory forces.** Scholars who take what is called a **dialectical approach** see relationships as dialogues between opposing "voices," each expressing a different and contradictory impulse. Although Tony and Tina are happy now, earlier in their relationship they went through repeated periods of uncertainty. Soon after they became close, they both began to feel stifled and trapped in the relationship. However, when they broke up, they realized how much they meant to each other. They felt drawn in two opposite directions, wanting to be both independent and interdependent at the same time. This resulted in an on-again off-again pattern to their relationship. Dialectical theorists know situations like this are quite common. They believe that all relationships are made up of contrasting dialectics that pull us in different directions. In a sense, a relationship is the way a couple comes to terms with these opposing forces.

The four views we've looked at are not contradictory. They each have something important to say about what relationships are and how they work. As we saw in Chapter 1, it's often useful to look at a concept from multiple perspectives. Therefore, instead of offering a formal definition, we'd like to discuss some of the most important characteristics of relationships and show how the four views we've looked at complement each other.

## The Characteristics of Relationships

Despite the lack of a single, clear, all-inclusive definition of relationship, there is substantial agreement on the characteristics that mark most relationships. In this section, we'll see that interpersonal relationships begin in awareness and develop through coordinated interaction; that they are shaped by our own awareness and, in subtle ways, by the presence of outside, social forces. We'll also see that, once in place, they take on a life of their own, exerting as much influence on us as we do on them. Finally, we'll look at the important part communication plays in holding relationships together.

1. *Interpersonal relationships begin with awareness.* When do relationships begin? According to William Wilmot, they begin the moment people become aware that others are aware of them. "People are in a relationship," Wilmot says, "when each has the perception of being perceived—when both persons can say, 'I see you seeing me.'"[12] Wilmot tells a story that is a perfect illustration of this point.[13] One day, he is sitting in a coffee shop, when he notices a young man staring intently at him. In order to avoid the stranger's stare, he turns away, but when he glances nervously around he sees that he is still the object of observation. Wilmot knows that he is being observed, and the young man knows that Wilmot knows. They are therefore in a relationship, although it is clearly one that Wilmot did not choose. In fact, Wilmot is so bothered about this incipient relationship that he quickly leaves the coffee shop. Staying would have been the first step in the development of an unwanted relationship.

2. *Interpersonal relationships develop through coordinated interaction.* Wilmot left the coffee shop because he didn't want to continue the interaction.

Sometimes we act in a similar way: We turn our backs on interaction because we don't want to get involved. In most cases, however, we welcome human interaction because we know it can lead to the development of a deeper relationship.

As we've seen, over time dyadic interactions become interdependent. Each person becomes aware that what he or she does will have an impact on the other person, and each begins to act with the other person in mind. Their behaviors are no longer individual actions but instead are what John Shotter calls **joint actions.**[14] If Matt and Tyrone have a fight, for example, each may believe the other one started it, but that's not what's really happening. The fight does not belong to either one of them—it belongs to both of them. It is something *they* have produced *together,* although it is something that neither one may want. Indeed, one of the paradoxes of joint actions is that they may lead to unexpected ends. As Barnett Pearce points out, "The events and objects of our social worlds—fights as well as helping episodes—are often the aggregate of actions that were not intended to produce them; in fact, sometimes joint actions produce things quite the opposite of what we intended."[15]

One way to understand the unique character of relational interaction is to think of interaction as a game. When two people play a game, they are involved with each other. Within the game, individual actions no longer stand alone. Instead they are "moves" in an interaction sequence. Each move is important because it limits the moves that can follow. In addition, each move affects the outcome of the game by determining who wins and who loses. Interaction is much like a game. As couples interact, their behaviors mesh, and what each does results in joint outcomes. Sometimes the game is cooperative and sometimes it is competitive. Sometimes its results are positive, and sometimes they are negative. But they always change the players. Peter Andersen sums up both the risks and rewards of playing the "interaction game." He says:

*In each relationship we become greater and lesser than we were prior to that relationship.*

## Memory and Relationships

# Eternal Sunshine of the Spotless Mind

Michel Condry, 2004

When Joel (Jim Carrey) finds out that his ex-girlfriend, the quirky, headstrong Clementine (Kate Winslett), has had her memory of him completely erased, he decides to follow suit—by literally putting her out of his mind. But, as the technicians (Mark Ruffalo, Elijah Wood, and Kirsten Dunst) begin the erasure process and his memories begin to fade, Joel realizes that he can't bear to let Clementine disappear forever. The movie traces his desperate attempts to hold on to their relationship. In the process we enter Joel's mind and see how he and Clementine fell in love and how their inability to connect ultimately destroyed their relationship. "Just because you talk constantly," Joel says, "doesn't mean you're communicating." We also come to understand how relationships live on in memory and how our memories of our relationships shape us.

Comic, surreal, and philosophical in turn, the film shows how much we lose when we can no longer bring someone we once cared about to mind. The questions it raises—"Are there people we would be better off if we had never known?" "Can, or should, we rid ourselves of painful memories?" and "How are we changed by the people we once loved?"—are questions that deeply affect how we decide to live our lives.

*We become greater because opportunities for dialogue, intimacy, cooperation, sexuality, disclosure, and reproduction exist in personal relationships. We become lesser because relationships take time, effort, and resources; they constrain our individuality and autonomy; and they create hazards and risks of various sorts.[16]*

3. *As relationships unfold, we begin to analyze and evaluate them.* As humans, we think about our social worlds, and one thing we think a lot about is our relationships. As our relationships develop, we begin to wonder where they are headed. We create mental representations of unfolding interactions, and these mental representations help us identify the kind of relationships we have. The way we construct models of our relationships determines in large measure whether our relationships succeed or fail.

A number of communication researchers have examined the way we keep track of our relationships. James Honeycutt, for example, believes that as we interact we create memory organization packets or MOPs.[17] These changing mental models consist of scenes from the relationship, for example, memories of a first date, an anniversary celebration, or a breakup. MOPs help stabilize our relationships. "Thus," Honeycutt explains, "even though relationships are in constant motion, relationship memory structures provide a perceptual anchor [so that] individuals can determine where they are in a relationship."[18] As we create memories and think about what our relationships are like, we compare our individual memories to the relational prototypes that provide general models of what relationships should be like. When our conception of a specific relationship matches an ideal prototype, we're happy with the relationship. If, however, our relational expectations are too high, we're likely to

**33**

**Blair and Chris's Relationship**
**Label:** friends
**Attributes**
 enjoyment
 fun
 respect
 trust
**Communicative Indicators**
 laughing and joking
 being outrageous
 reinforcing each other

**Blair and Alix's Relationship**
**Label:** friends
**Attributes**
 emotional support
 security
 trust
 respect
**Communicative Indicators**
 being willing to listen
 giving and taking advice
 defending the other

FIGURE 2.2 *How relationships connect us. The relationships we create through communication connect us to one another. Embedded in relationships are cultural norms and individual preferences.*

be unhappy because no "real-life" relationship will ever be good enough.

What's in a relational prototype? According to Wilmot and Baxter, prototypes consist of three things: a natural language label, criterial attributes, and communicative indicators.[19] A **natural language label** consists of the word or words we use to describe a relationship; for example, "acquaintance," "friend," and "best friend" are labels we use to refer to different kinds of friendships. **Criterial attributes** are the characteristics that a relationship must have to be classed by a given natural language label. For example, six common attributes of friendship are *trust, general comfort,*

*respect, security in the other's presence, ease in communication,* and *openness.*[20] Associated with each attribute are **communicative indicators,** the behaviors that display an attribute. *Trust,* for example, might be exhibited by *being willing to self-disclose, keeping secrets, defending one's partner, giving honest feedback,* and so on. Figure 2.2 illustrates how relationships connect us to one another as well as how different dyads create different norms and expectations. As you can see, Blair has a friendly relationship with both Alix and Chris, but the two friendships are somewhat different. A unique characteristic of Blair's friendship with Alix is that it offers emotional support and help.

*Intimate bonds are created and sustained through interpersonal communication.*

Michael Escoffery, *Circle of Love,* 1996

Blair and Alix turn to each other when they want to work out problems or feel the need to open up. Blair's friendship with Chris centers more on having fun. Blair and Chris seek each other out to share activities. In both cases, however, trust and respect are also important.

4. *Our relationships are influenced by outside forces.* If you're an American, the ways Blair, Alix, and Chris define friendship should seem familiar to you because our culture gives us general guidelines about how to be a friend and what we

can expect from our friends. In fact, outside forces have a large impact on what we want from all of our relationships and how we go about creating them. Relationships may feel unique and personal, but they are actually influenced by a number of factors, including (1) cultural norms and media models, (2) the involvement of family and friends, and (3) economic and environmental conditions.

Cultural norms and media models affect the ways we conduct our day-to-day interactions as well as the relational prototypes we use to evaluate relationships. Notions of love, for example, are cultural, not individual, ideals. In modern-day America, we expect to fall in love before we marry. This expectation is passed down to us by our parents and is reinforced in movies, books, love songs, and advertising. In many other cultures, however, love is not a necessary requirement for marriage. The way people in those cultures represent love is quite different from the way we do. In such cultures love is something that may follow marriage—if one is lucky. Indeed, as we will see in Chapter 13, even in America the meaning of love has not always stayed the same. And love is but one example. Our images of family and work relationships are also determined by cultural norms and media representations.

Family and friends also have an impact on how we conduct our relationships and what we expect from them. Parents imposing family rules, close friends urging us to consider their feelings, coworkers giving us their opinions, even therapists, preachers, and attorneys—all can have a say in the way we build relationships. Has a family member ever tried to fix you up with someone who "would be just perfect for you," or has a close friend tried to talk you out of seeing someone "for your own good"? Situations like this happen all the time, and they illustrate how much impact others have on our personal relationships. In this sense, dyadic relationships are seldom made up of just two people: They also include all the other people who feel they have a stake in the relationship.

Another often overlooked factor that affects relationships is their physical and economic environment. Relationships are systems that react to their surroundings. When these surroundings are stressful, the relationship suffers. Long-term relationships don't occur in a vacuum. People get sick, lose their jobs, are pinched for money, and encounter threats and frustrations of one kind or another. When this happens, relationships can falter. An example of the impact of outside stress on relationships occurs in what family researchers call **crossover.**[21] Crossover occurs when stress in the workplace affects the spouse at home. In a study of heterosexual couples, Niall Bolger and colleagues found that when men had arguments at work, they had a tendency to argue with their wives later in the day.[22] They also found that when men were overworked, their wives had to "take up the slack" by doing more work at home. As a result, the wives reported feeling stressed themselves. This is just one example of how environmental forces affect relationships, one that, in Bolger's words, "may also provide insights into why men derive more benefits from marriage than women do."[23] It would appear that when things go wrong outside the relationship, relational partners have to work harder to maintain the relationship.

5. *Our relationships can control us as much as we control them.* As a relationship develops, it begins to take on a life of its own. The relationship that began as a simple acknowledgment between strangers may develop in ways neither party expects or even wants. The sense that relationships develop organically (and the sense that they can sometimes get away from us) is reflected in the way we talk about them. For example, people wonder whether a relationship "can be saved," ponder why it is "out of control," and sometimes try "to escape" from their relationships. These statements show that the very people who created a relationship in the first place may come to feel that the relationship is controlling them.

Indeed, Wilmot argues that relationships are systems that are more than the sum of their parts. He explains:

> When two people have a relationship, there is a "third party"—the relationship itself—which has a life of its own. This synergistic creation is built by the participants yet goes beyond them. As Humphreys says, "There is no such thing as two, for no two things can be conceived without their relationship, and this makes three."[24]

6. *Relationships are constructed and maintained through communication.* If relationships seem as

## Stress and Interpersonal Communication

# How Childhood Relationships Can Make Us Sick

Box 2.1 argued that human relationships are necessary for good health. In "Never Far from Home," Linda Luecken and her colleagues explain the converse: how problematic childhood relationships can result in stress and illness later in life.

The authors believe that negative family relationships influence the amount of attention children give to threat cues in the environment. When too much attention is directed to threat, the ability to cope with stress, regulate emotions, and control physiological responses is disrupted, ultimately increasing vulnerability to physical and psychological illness.

In explaining this connection, the authors show that exposure to high levels of family conflict can cause individuals to perceive ambiguous or even positive events as potentially threatening. In order to protect themselves, children who experience conflict are often hypervigilant, that is, they search for signs of danger and selectively attend to negative aspects of the environment. This tendency to look for threat can follow children into adulthood, impeding their ability to cope with everyday stresses.

Luecken and her research team demonstrate that lack of parental affection and high levels of family conflict are related to poor emotional regulation and poor coping styles later in life. They further show that individuals who have difficulty in self-regulation often experience symptoms of depression, negative mood, anxiety, and disengagement when they become adults.

In addition to psychological effects, there are physiological effects as well. As the authors point out, "daily encounters with potentially threatening situations or stimuli (e.g., conflict with a roommate, traffic jams) are a natural part of life," and overreaction to these chronic minor threats can lead to chronic elevation of stress hormones, which can, in turn, overwhelm the body's ability to function normally. The result can be elevated blood pressure and long-term damage to the cardiovascular system.

The authors say that it is unclear whether positive social relationships or therapy can undo all of these negative consequences of childhood adversity. They show, however, that training in emotion regulation and adaptive coping skills can help and that therapy can effectively reduce negative emotional responses to stress.

This study demonstrates how important it is to create positive interpersonal relationships and how the ability to do so can affect emotional and physical well-being.

Luecken, Linda J., Bradley M. Appelhans, Amy Kraft, and Ana Brown. "Never Far from Home: A Cognitive-Affective Model of the Impact of Early-Life Family Relationships on Physiological Stress Responses in Adulthood." *Journal of Social and Personal Relationships* 23, no. 2 (2006): 189–203.

though they have a life of their own, what keeps them going—their lifeblood—is communication. As we've seen, communication is essential at every point in the development of a relationship. It begins as two people communicate their interest in one another, and it continues as they talk about their desires and needs and work out their interaction patterns. Relationships depend on continuous, high-quality communication. Indeed, relationships are not something we create once; they are something we re-create and refine every time we communicate.

When relationships work well, they contribute to our sense of well-being. When they turn sour, however, they can affect our physical and psychological health as well. The study described in the Research in Review box explains this connection.

# Relational Paths: Intimacy and Distance

The relationships we create take many forms. Some are long-lasting and intimate; in these relationships we come to trust and care deeply about each other. Other relationships are quite distant; we are courteous, but aloof. Most relationships are somewhere in the middle. How do we decide the shape of our relationships? What kinds of issues define our relational profiles? In this section we consider how communication determines the paths our relationships take by looking at some of the dialectical forces that pull us toward closeness or distance.

## Interpersonal Profiles: Private and Public Paths

In his classic article on interpersonal bonding, Arthur Bochner tells us that there are two general kinds of relationships.[25] "On the one hand there is the type of social bond that gains 'coherence from a sentimental bond between persons who are essentially homogeneous'; on the other hand there is the type that integrates complementary differences into 'a practical organization in which mutual sentiments are unnecessary.'" One way to label these two relational paths is to call the first private and the second public.

**Private relationships** are close, personal relationships. Over time they become more and

*Eye gaze often signals the beginning step in the creation of interpersonal communication.*

more personal and unique. In a private relationship it makes a great deal of difference who our partner is. If we lose a friend or lover, we do not substitute someone else easily, for we are closely and interdependently connected. We are affected by each other in important ways, and our ties are very strong. In private relationships we make sense of each other by using unique, particularistic information about each other. In general, the rules of behavior we follow are individualistic, the product of negotiation. On the whole there is a good deal of sentiment involved in private relationships. These relationships are considered to be rewarding for their own intrinsic worth.

**Public relationships** are very different. The members of a public relationship are related in impersonal ways and very little change occurs over time. Members are substitutable. If the clerk who waits on us is replaced by someone else, it will probably make very little difference to us. Instead of being interdependent, we are relatively autonomous. Our connections are slight and easily broken off. In public relationships we

| TABLE 2.1 | A Relational Dichotomy: Private and Public Bonds |
|---|---|

| Private | Public |
|---|---|
| In which we respond to the other in a personal and private manner | In which we respond to the other in an impersonal and public manner |
| Members are IRREPLACEABLE. It makes a difference who the other is. | Members are SUBSTITUTABLE. It makes no difference who the other is. |
| Members are INTERDEPENDENT. | Members are AUTONOMOUS. |
| Their way of knowing the other is PARTICULAR. | Their way of knowing the other is UNIVERSAL. |
| The rules governing behavior are INDIVIDUALISTIC. | The rules of governing behavior are NORMATIVE. |
| The tone of the relationship is SENTIMENTAL. | The tone of the relationship is PRACTICAL. |
| Rewards are primarily INTRINSIC. | Rewards are primarily EXTRINSIC. |
| Examples: sexual pairs, kinship pairs, marital partners, best friends | Examples: strangers, acquaintances, colleagues, work partners |

have little particularistic information about each other; instead, we attend to general class memberships to make sense of each other. The rules governing behavior are socially rather than individually determined—we are courteous and polite. Often the reason for the bond is practical rather than sentimental, and its rewards are extrinsic rather than intrinsic. Table 2.1 presents a model of differences between public and private relationships. We would like to make four points about this relational model.

1. The two types of relationships we have described are extremes, and many variations are possible. As you can see in Table 2.1, we have listed six dimensions that distinguish private and public relationships. Individuals working out a relationship must find a position on each dimension. They must establish, for example, the extent to which they perceive a partner as important and unique as well as the amount of dependence that should characterize their bond. They must also determine how information should be exchanged and what kinds of rules will

be followed during interaction. Finally, they must know how much emotional energy to invest and whether the relationship itself is of primary concern or whether it is simply a means to an end.

In a given culture some kinds of relationships will occur more often than others. For example, people in our culture expect honesty and openness in private relationships and guardedness in public relationships. Couples are expected to share everything, while strangers are to be told very little. Each of us, however, decides how far to go in following cultural norms. This means that although the culture may define only a few basic ways of relating, in reality there are as many kinds of relational paths as there are dyads.

2. *Over time, relationships will fluctuate and change.* Relationships are dynamic. There is constant movement and adjustment along each of the dimensions we have described. While marriage partners are generally dependent upon each other, the degree of autonomy and interdependence they require will vary through their married life.

Constant readjustment of their positions will be necessary. Friends, too, must continually monitor their own behavior, deciding how much dependence and how much freedom should characterize their relationship.[26]

3. *Different skills and sensitivities are needed for different kinds of relationships.* Because we form many different kinds of bonds, we must learn a variety of skills. We need to know how to build private bonds through self-disclosure, but equally we need to know how to maintain a distance from others. Interpersonal competence is often a matter of knowing whether to employ public or private rules of behavior.

4. *Relational profiles are negotiated over time.* How do we settle on the path a relationship will follow? Through communication, both direct and indirect. As we communicate, we constantly send messages about our feelings and needs. Even when the topic of conversation is mundane and trivial, we let the other person know how we feel about him or her and about the relationship. In fact, every time we communicate, we send two different kinds of messages: content and relational. **Content messages** are messages about the topic at hand. **Relational messages** are messages about the relationship itself. For example, when Jack asks Mike a personal question, and Mike answers, "It's quite hot today, isn't it?" the content message is about the weather. The relational message, however, is far subtler and more interesting. By changing the subject as he did, Mike is telling Jack, "I don't feel comfortable answering personal questions. We're not close enough for that." Relational meaning is conveyed as much by *how* something is said as by *what* is said.

Over time, as we communicate, we send each other many subtle relational messages about what we expect and how we are feeling. Through a process of negotiation, we come to an understanding of where our relationship falls on the public/private continuum. Sometimes this process of negotiation is relatively easy, as when two people in love follow the intimacy path. At other times, it can be extremely painful, for example, when one partner wants the relationship to deepen while the other wants to maintain it at a more casual, surface level. Relationships are never stable. Defining and maintaining them always take sensitivity and skill.

## Independence vs. Conformity: A Basic Interpersonal Dilemma

One way to sum up the difference between private and public relationships is to say that private relationships allow us to exhibit uniqueness and independence while public relationships stress conformity and social solidarity. While humans need to feel connected to social groups, they also need to feel separateness. This is why both public and private relationships are necessary and why negotiating relationships is a serious matter.

We live in a society that tends to value the expression of personal individuality. Americans generally dislike dealing with people in terms of social roles. The idea of strangers bothers us; when we meet people, we try almost immediately to "get to know them." We want to interact on a friendly, informal, "first-name" basis right from the start.[27]

We carry this expectation into our long-lasting relationships, believing that over time relationships should increase in "personalness." A relationship that stays in the same place for any length of time is often described as "going nowhere." We expect the same degree of "progress" in our personal lives that we do in the business world. Occasionally this means that we try too hard too soon, not allowing relationships to grow at their own pace.

As a culture we tend to deemphasize public relationships, often losing sight of the fact that people have a need for distance as well as closeness. Public relationships are designed to give us that distance. They are meant to control and pace intimacy, keeping others from making personal demands on us or knowing us too well. Indeed, in public it is our place in the social structure rather than our individuality that defines us. We are identified by formal roles, and we are expected to act formally, following rules of courtesy.

*We never stop communication. Even when we're alone, communication simply turns inward.*

Michael Mortimer Robinson, *Away Thoughts*, 1995

While public relationships may seem undemocratic to some people, they have certain advantages. First of all, they affirm the social order. They remind us of social expectations and duties, making it clear to us that we are part of a collectivity. Second, they actually allow us to develop a sense of separateness. Psychologists tell us that without the ability to create boundaries between the self and others, we would have great difficulty developing a stable identity.[28] Public rela-

tionships also save us a great deal of psychological investment. Think what your life would be like if you were expected to "share thoughts and feelings, reveal intimate information and secrets, extend emotional support, and seek advice"[29] in dealing with everyone you encountered. On a purely practical level, it would be impossible. Although most of our important relationships will be private, there are advantages to public relationships. Box 2.2 gives one author's view of the

BOX 2.2

*Mind Your Manners*

## Some Social Functions of Etiquette

What do you think of rules of etiquette? Are they outmoded signs of a way of life that has disappeared? Are they ways of putting on a false front and deceiving people about your true feelings? Or do they serve some useful social purpose? Judith Martin, who makes her living as Miss Manners, author of advice columns and books on etiquette, believes that manners serve a useful function and that without social codes of behavior people cannot live a civilized life.

Martin recognizes that today most people distrust the idea of good manners. She traces this belief to the philosopher Jean-Jacques Rousseau, who felt that civilization destroys everything that is natural and good in people. She also finds this idea in the human potential movement's celebration of openness and authenticity as ways of life. Martin believes codes of etiquette can be de-structive. They can, for example, be used as a weapon in class warfare. But she also believes that manners are necessary for smooth social interaction. By heading off conflict, social codes allow people with irreconcilable differences to coexist. For Martin, individual freedom has to be tempered by the needs of society. This means that people cannot be free to do whatever they wish. Freedom and equality do not mean that everyone can be completely honest and exactly the same. For Martin, "a complete disregard of any distinctions, a total leveling of all hierarchies results in a kind of universal kindergarten where everyone wears the same playclothes all the time for all occasions and is expected to participate in show and tell all the time."

Martin recognizes that people today believe in being totally open and honest and establishing first-name relationships with as many people as possible. No longer is any distinction made between the ways we treat strangers and the ways we treat intimates. She feels there are dangers in this, one being that the techniques which work in the boardroom are being used in the bedroom. Everything is for sale. If you want to fall in love, she asks, what do you do? "You run a classified advertisement announcing a vacancy and you include a job description with the most detailed skill importance of maintaining politeness in public and of the problems that can occur when we rush into intimacy.

The tension between the need for closeness and distance, the need to be recognized as a unique individual, and the need to be part of a social collective is fundamental. When we work out the nature of our relationships we are working out our answer to this dilemma. Because we believe this is a very important interpersonal tension, we shall return to it a number of times in the course of this text.

# Building Relationships: What Does It Take to Be Relationally Competent?

There's a pervasive myth in our society that relationships—especially intimate relationships—should just happen. In many people's minds, relationships that take work are not good relationships.

STYLISH SF seeks worldly SM for committed relationship, love, and laughter. Photo, please.
Box 556

SHARE THE FANTASY. MWM seeks adventurous female; tall, pretty, funloving, discreet, experimental. Life is short. Why not??
Box 557

GAY WJM. Intense, intelligent, intuitive, seeks nonsmoking monogamous partner to share interest in opera, French cooking, tennis, hiking, new experiences. Ready to take a chance again.
Box 448

realm) and the world of home and family (the private realm). Martin points out a fundamental error in this kind of reasoning: While it may be the goal of business to move along and get things done, the goals of friendship and romance are to "repeat doing the same things and to like being where you are."

Martin believes people are confused about their obligations. She argues that we have to reestablish the dualism of the personal and professional realms so that everyone can have a reasonable portion of each. What do you think?

SOURCE Judith Martin, *Common Courtesy* (New York: Atheneum, 1985). The text was originally delivered as an address at Harvard University under the title "The Question That Baffled Jefferson." An audiotape is available from the Harvard Forum.

ADDITIONAL READINGS

Baldridge, Letitia, and Denise Cavalieri Fiske. *New Manners for New Times: A Complete Guide to Etiquette.* New York: Scribners, 2003.

Martin, Judith, and Gloria Kamen. *Miss Manners' Guide to Excruciatingly Correct Behavior, Freshly Updated.* New York: W. W. Norton, 2005.

requirements." Friends and lovers are hired and fired with the same lack of emotion as employees.

While intimates are being treated like employees, strangers are treated as intimates. Nowadays, being on a first-name basis with your waitress ("Hi, I'm Cherry, and I'll be your server tonight. How 'ya doing?") and having your own personal banker ("You've got a friend at First Federal") seem unavoidable. We no longer make any distinctions between the world of work (the public

Out there somewhere, so the theory goes, is the perfect mate who is everything we want or the perfect friend who will automatically accept and understand us. All we have to do is find that person and the relationship will be perfect. As Steve Duck suggests, this view makes building relationships a little like shopping. We make a wish list of what we're looking for and shop till we drop. If the relationship doesn't work out, it was probably because we made the wrong choice and we can always return the merchandise. Duck suggests another view. To him, relationships are carefully

constructed. "They have to be made—made to start, made to work, made to develop, kept in good working order and preserved from going sour. To do all this, we need to be active, thoughtful and skilled."[30] The process of building healthy relationships Duck calls **relationshipping.** In this section we'll look at what it takes to be good at relationshipping. We'll begin by looking at some of the individual communication skills that will help us make the most of our relationships, and we'll end with a discussion of some of the characteristics of a healthy relationship.

**43**

## Communication Competence
## and Relationships

The model of communicative competence we introduced in Chapter 1 provides an outline of some of the individual skills and abilities we need to relationship successfully. In that model we suggested that to be a competent communicator, an individual must have interpretive, goal, role, message, and self competence. Let's see how this model applies to interpersonal relationships.

- We need interpretive competence to understand and monitor our relationships. Interpretive competence allows us to keep track of what is happening in a relationship. When you're in a relationship, you must be able to assess the relationship, know when it's getting off track, and figure out a way to meet your own and your partner's needs. Insensitivity or carelessness can spell disaster in an interpersonal relationship.

- In addition to interpretive competence, we need goal competence as well. Goal competence is the ability to set and achieve realistic individual goals. When you're in a long-term relationship this involves satisfying your own needs and those of your partner. And, because individuals in relationships occasionally have competing interests, part of relational goal competence is creative problem solving. Willingness to negotiate is key. Being too strategic or too selfish can destroy an interpersonal relationship.

- Role competence is another individual skill that helps us as we build and maintain a relationship. Role competence is knowing when and how to follow social norms and being able to coordinate interactions. When you're in a relationship, it means knowing the parts you and your partner will play in the relationship and developing workable rules and norms. Linda Harris has identified three levels of role competence.[31] **Minimally competent** individuals are inflexible. They can't modify current roles or take on new ones. Instead they either force their partners to take on a particular role, or

they "altercast" (that is, they form relationships only with people who will accept them as they want to be). People who value flexibility, and who are willing to change if they sense the willingness is reciprocal, are called **satisfactorily competent.** Harris believes these people are most comfortable in familiar situations but lack the ability to work out problems in new and creative ways. In Harris's system, the most interpersonally skilled people are those who are **optimally competent.** They know when to adapt and when not to. Because they are aware of the way their interpersonal systems operate, they handle relational problems creatively and effectively.

- Message competence is also necessary in interpersonal relationships. Message competence is the ability to use both verbal and nonverbal message codes effectively. Because relationships are built through communication, when you're in a relationship you need skill in sending and receiving messages. You need to adapt the messages you send to your partner, and you need to be adept at decoding the content and relational messages your partner sends to you. Blurting things out without thinking or reading too much (or too little) into other people's messages can ruin an interpersonal relationship.

- The final kind of individual competence that can help us build relationships is self competence. Self competence is the ability to create and maintain an individual identity and style. People who are sure of themselves and who know who they are are more skilled at building relationships than those who are uncertain or preoccupied with self. They can find a balance between interdependence and independence. Focusing too much on self or too much on the other can damage relationships.

## Some Characteristics
## of Healthy Relationships

Of course, relationships are not owned by only one person. They belong to both parties, and both must be competent if the relationship is to work. That's what makes relationshipping so tricky: The competence must be mutual. In this section we look at competence not as an individual skill but as a characteristic of a relationship. The following discussion is offered as a suggestion, not as a prescription, because each couple is unique, and what works for one dyad may not be suitable for another. We invite you to think about your own relationships and agree, disagree, or add to the list yourself.

1. *In a healthy relationship, there is a shared vision of where the relationship is and where it is going.* Too often, people have very different ideas of the nature of their relationships. In some relationships, couples disagree because their expectations are very different. In other relationships, they're careless, not bothering to think about what is happening until it's too late. In still others, one member is overly concerned while the other ignores the relationship. This is particularly true in traditional mixed-sex relationships, where the job of taking care of the relationship is left to the woman. She takes on the role of relational monitor. She is expected to pay attention to the relationship, diagnose problems, and, when the relationship goes off track, do something to get it back on. But, obviously, she can't do this by herself. As Julia Wood points out, this interpersonal division of labor results in a situation in which women are hyperaware and men are unaware, a situation that can be frustrating for her and suffocating for him.[32] If both parties in a relationship (regardless of gender) pay equal attention to the relationship and are equally willing to discuss it with each other, the relationship stands a better chance of success.

2. *In a healthy relationship, there are clear rules that have been mutually negotiated and that work to the benefit of the relationship itself.* All cultures contain rules, guidelines for the kinds of behaviors that are acceptable. These rules stabilize the culture and help its members live in harmony. The concept of "rule" may seem confining, but actually rules give members of a culture a measure of security and predictability. Rules

*Sometimes we build walls to separate ourselves from others.*

work the same way in the mini-cultures of relationships. Although the rules may be implicit rather than explicit, they are there nonetheless. If they are fair and applied equally, they can help direct the relationship. When rules are unfair, when they are imposed by one party, or when they change from day to day, the relationship suffers.

3. *In a healthy relationship, there is a shared work ethic.* By work we do not mean what happens on the job. The work we are talking about is relational work. As Graham Allan points out in his discussion of friendships, relationships need constant maintenance work. "They need 'servicing.' They need contact; they need involvement; they need a sense of being 'worked at,' whether this is achieved through occasional phone calls or more frequent conversations and shared activities."[33] A healthy relationship is one that encourages both parties to put time and effort into making the relationship the best it can be.

4. *In healthy relationships, metacommunication (communication about communication) is valued.* Sometimes partners work out their problems and reach agreements in subtle, indirect ways. But

often direct talk is necessary. To develop a shared vision, shared rules, or a shared work ethic, people must be willing to engage in relationship talk. In healthy relationships couples develop shared relational symbols and metaphors that allow them to express their feelings and concerns about the relationship in a comfortable way.

# Skill Building: A Preview

In this chapter we've suggested a few of the things you can do to increase your ability to communicate interpersonally. Throughout this book, you will encounter more. At the end of the next chapter, we begin focusing on specific skills that lead to interpersonal competence. While we don't pretend that the skills we've chosen form a complete list, we do believe that mastering them can help you improve your interpersonal competence. In this section we offer you a brief preview of each chapter and its skill-building focus.

Chapter 3 deals with nonverbal message competence. In this chapter we look at the silent messages we send to others. A problem area for most of us is knowing how to express our feelings clearly and congruently, using both verbal and nonverbal channels, so in this chapter we focus on the skill of emotional expressiveness.

Chapter 4 looks at verbal message competence, at how we use talk to build relationships. We also look at the skill of managing conversations, paying particular attention to the most difficult parts of a conversation, openings and closings.

Chapter 5 examines the relational messages that serve to define our bonds with others. It also looks at problematic sequences like spirals and double binds. We believe that many problem patterns could be avoided in relationships if partners had the ability to take each other's perspective and respond empathically. Too often, relationships dissolve because members are not able to see things from each other's point of view.

Chapter 6 examines interpretive competence by looking at the ways we perceive people, relationships, and social events. The skill-building section looks at one of the most important of all interpersonal skills, that of listening. When we think of communication, we often overlook listening and focus on the seemingly more active task of sending messages. In fact, listening is not passive, but rather is an extremely important part of good communication. For that reason it will be the first skill we discuss.

Chapter 7 focuses on role competence, on the social aspects that guide our communication. Often, society encourages us to act in mindless ways, to use tried-and-true social schemata rather than creative approaches to interaction. In this chapter we devote our skill-building section to overcoming stereotyped thinking and communicating creatively.

Chapter 8 talks about the development of the individual self and explains how our self-concept affects communication. We discuss the skill of self-disclosure in this chapter. While most authorities agree that people should reveal themselves to others, doing so is not easy. We look at appropriate and inappropriate ways of letting others know who we are and what we think.

Chapter 9 examines goal competence. It covers some of the ways we make interpersonal communication work for us. Some people have difficulty achieving their goals because they ask either too little or too much. In this chapter we discuss the important skill of assertiveness.

Chapter 10 talks about the family context. While there are many different skills we could focus on here, we believe that comforting skills and active listening are two of the most important. Family members rely on one another for support, and effective members need to know how to give that support.

Chapter 11 explains factors involved in building and maintaining intimate relationships. It also looks at the steps in the dissolution of relationships. Often relationships fail because members don't know how to handle conflict and stress effectively. Because they don't have the skill to fight fairly, their arguments destroy rather than improve the relationship.

Chapter 12 examines interpersonal relationships in the workplace, discussing the kinds of communication patterns that enhance professional relationships. The skill we emphasize here is negotiation.

Finally, Chapter 13 discusses ways in which culture and history influence communication. Every year our world becomes smaller and our chances of communicating across international boundaries increase. We'll end by offering some guidelines on how to make the most out of intercultural contact.

# Process to Performance

## Review Terms

The following is a list of major concepts introduced in this chapter. The page where the concept is first mentioned is listed in parentheses.

situational approach    (25)
developmental approach    (25)
intrapersonal communication    (26)
interpersonal communications    (26)
small-group communication    (26)
organizational communication    (26)
face-to-face public communication    (26)
mediated public communication    (27)
cultural level data    (28)
sociological level data    (28)
psychological level data    (28)
relationships as constellations
    of behaviors    (29)
interdependence    (29)
relationships as cognitive constructs    (29)
relational prototype    (29)
relationships as mini-cultures    (30)
relationships as collections of contradictory
    forces    (31)

dialectic approach    (31)
joint actions    (32)
natural language label    (34)
criterial attributes    (34)
communicative indicators    (34)
crossover    (36)
private relationships    (38)
public relationships    (38)
content messages    (40)
relational messages    (40)
relationshipping    (43)
minimal competence    (44)
satisfactory competence    (44)
optimal competence    (44)

## Suggested Readings

Stewart, John, ed. *Bridges Not Walls: A Book About Interpersonal Communication,* 9th ed. Boston: McGraw-Hill, 2006. This reader contains a broad range of scholarly and popular articles on issues and topics of interest in the area of interpersonal communication.

Wood, Julia T., and Steve Duck. *Composing Relationships: Communication in Everyday Life.* Belmont, Calif.: Wadsworth Publishing, 2005. The authors discuss the routine, everyday behaviors that hold relationships together and shape identities.

**Topics for Discussion**

www.oup.com/us/trenholm

## Observation Guide

**1.** Observe a couple you know for about half an hour. Watch carefully for all of the ways, both verbal and nonverbal, the partners control and influence one another. How do they differ from each other in terms of control? How do they seek feedback, and how do they react to it once they have received it? What inferences can you make about their relationship?

**2.** Think of an interpersonal relationship that is important to you and that has lasted for some time. Graph it on the following chart developed from our model of private/public relationships:

Other is:

*irreplaceable*                      *substitutable*

     1    2    3    4    5    6    7

We are:

*interdependent*                 *autonomous*

     1    2    3    4    5    6    7

The information we use is:

*particularistic*              *universalistic*

     1    2    3    4    5    6    7

The rules we follow are:

*individualistic*                *normative*

     1    2    3    4    5    6    7

The emotional tone is:

*sentimental*                    *practical*

     1    2    3    4    5    6    7

The rewards I get are:

*intrinsic*                       *extrinsic*

     1    2    3    4    5    6    7

Has the relationship always had this profile, or has it changed over time? Were there key incidents that caused the profile of your relationship to change? Is it at the point you want it to be right now?

### Exercises

1. As a class, discuss metaphors for interpersonal relationships. Complete the following sentence: Interpersonal relationships are like _____. Try to think of as many comparisons as possible; then look at what they tell you about the nature of relational bonds. What common themes can you uncover? Open the discussion by considering metaphors that are embedded in our language. For example, consider the following metaphors used to describe love: prisoner of love, bound together, tie the knot, get hitched. What is the central message behind these metaphors? What others can you come up with?

2. Work in twos or threes. Choose a well-defined type of relationship like friendship, romantic love, marriage, and so on. Each person should begin by thinking about how he or she views this relationship. What language labels are used for this relationship? Are the language labels adequate, or do they fail to describe the relationship thoroughly? What criterial attributes would you assign to this relationship (or to different aspects of this relationship)? What behavioral indicators would show you whether someone was living up to the label or not? After each person has had time to think, the group or dyad should share opinions and attempt to come to some consensus about this relationship.

# PART 2

# Sending and Receiving Messages

The way our bodies move through space communicates much about our mood, our interests, what and whom we value, and much more.

Archibald Motley, Jr., *Black Belt*, 1934

## CHAPTER 3

# Nonverbal Competence

In *Under the Tuscan Sun*, American Frances Mayes describes hiring and observing laborers as they renovate the abandoned Italian countryside villa she has recently purchased:

> *Signor Martini sends a couple of friends by. . . . The second friend, Alfiero, gives a surprisingly reasonable estimate. . . . When you don't speak a language well, many of your cues for judging people are missing. We both think he is fey—an odd quality for a mason—but Martini says he is bravo. We want the work done while we are in residence, so we sign a contract. . . .*
>
> *The schedule calls for the work to begin the following Monday. Monday, Tuesday, and Wednesday pass. Then a load of sand arrives. Finally, at the end of the week, Alfiero appears with a boy of fourteen and, to our surprise, three big Polish men. They set to work and by sundown, amazingly, the long wall is down. We watch all day. The Poles lift one-hundred-pound stones as if they were watermelons. Alfiero speaks not a word of Polish and they speak about five words of Italian. Fortunately the language of manual labor is easy to act out. "Via, via," Alfiero waves at the stones and they have at them. The next day they excavate dirt. Alfiero exits, to go to other jobs, I suppose. The boy, Alessandro, purely pouts. Alfiero is his stepfather and evidently is trying to teach the boy about work. He looks like a little Medici prince, petulant and bored as he stands around listlessly kicking stones with the toe of his tennis shoe. The Poles ignore him. . . .*
>
> *Alfiero becomes a problem. He lights like a butterfly on one project after another, starting something, doing a sloppy job, then taking off. Some days he just doesn't show up at all. When reasonable questioning doesn't work, I revert to the old Southern habit of throwing a fit, which I find I can still do impressively. For awhile, Alfiero straightens up and pays attention, then like the whimsical child that he is, he loses his focus. . . . I say that I am malcontenta. I use waving gestures and shake my head and stamp my foot and point. He has used rows of tiny stones under rows of big stones, there are vertical lines in the construction, he has neglected to put a foundation in this entire section, the cement is mostly sand. . . .*

*What neither Signor Martini nor Alfiero realizes is that the Poles let us know when something is not right. "Signora," Krzysztof (we call him Christoforo, as he wishes) says, motioning to me, "Italia cemento." He crumbles too-dry cement between his fingers. "Polonia cemento." He kicks a rock-hard section of the retaining wall. This has become a nationalistic issue. "Alfiero. Poco cemento." He puts his fingers to his lips. I thank him. Alfiero is using too little cement in his mixture. Don't tell. They begin to roll their eyes as a signal, to show us problems.[1]*

Nonverbal messages are powerful, as Frances Mayes's helpful Polish laborers illustrate. In the absence of a shared verbal language, they were able to convey through a variety of gestures what she needed to know about the quality of materials and construction design Alfiero was providing. Despite the verbal limitations, she trusted them far more than she trusted Alfiero, with whom she shared at least a working knowledge of the Italian language and culture.

As we saw in the model presented in Chapter 1, accurate perceptions and knowledge of the self and social system are not enough for effective communication to take place. We must be able to integrate perceptions and knowledge into appropriate verbal, nonverbal, and relational codes. In Chapter 4 we will look at the way we encode messages verbally, while Chapter 5 will assess forms of relational communication. This chapter will discuss the variety of nonverbal channels through which coded messages can be sent and received.

The power of nonverbal codes is striking in cross-cultural situations like the one described here. But we often overlook the importance of more subtle nonverbal messages. For example, studies of small-group communication demonstrate that those who talk more often become leaders while those who actively listen and provide nonverbal feedback seldom get any credit for their contribution. We do, however, give some credit to those who work well in the non-

*Our facial expressions often reveal (and, at times, conceal) our feelings about a person.*

verbal mode. People especially competent at reading others' nonverbal messages are labeled "intuitive," while those who send more nonverbals are called "expressive."

To make it in our culture, a person must first be articulate, then add elements of intuition and expressiveness. We hope that by focusing on nonverbal codes, you will become more aware of their function in everyday communication. You may already know a lot about diagramming sentences and increasing your vocabulary, but how many classes have you had on nonverbal communication?

We share a number of nonverbal signals with other species of animals. The marking of territories, threat displays when territorial bounds are violated, and relaxed, open-mouth expressions that signal approachability are examples of widely shared gestures rooted in a common biology, modified only by environment and culture. These rudimentary forms of communication preceded the evolution of the human brain's neocortex, which made language possible. The tendency to believe nonverbal messages when they contradict verbal ones (as in the opening example) may well be traced to the fact that nonverbal communication has a much longer evolutionary history. Language is, in the scheme of things, the "new kid on the block." Nonverbal communication, having been around, is like an old, trusted friend.

We also use nonverbal communication to initiate most verbal interactions. Breaking into a conversation often involves a complex dance of eye contact, head movement, preliminary gesturing, and vocalized throat-clearing if we do not want to be seen as rude. Greeting friends while walking across campus is preceded by a set of acknowledged approachability cues: eye contact, a flash of the eyebrows, perhaps even an abbreviated waving gesture. These nonverbal cues are not accidental; they are crucial regulators of conversation. For these reasons we think a good starting point for improving our ability to encode and decode messages is to attend to our own and others' nonverbal behaviors. They provide us with a context for interpreting many of the positive and negative connotations of messages. In this chapter, we will define nonverbal communication, describe what makes the nonverbal such a powerful message system, examine in detail each of the nonverbal codes and how they function in interpersonal situations, and then summarize how we use verbal and nonverbal cues together to maintain or alter our interpersonal relationships. We will end the chapter with a discussion of how we can express ourselves better—especially our feelings—through nonverbal communication codes.

# What Is Nonverbal Communication?

Suppose that as you are taking an exam, you notice that the person across the aisle keeps twitching his head and shoulders, then glancing quickly in your direction. Your eyes don't meet and nothing is said, but the other person has a very puzzled look on his face. Would you say that nonverbal communication has taken place?

Many scholars would say yes; others would say no. For the first group, all behavior has communicative potential and therefore should count as an instance of communication. In the preceding example nonverbal behavior has occurred and has been noticed by another person, so some information has been exchanged. Other scholars argue that we have to place some limits on what we call communication. If we don't establish limits, the term *communication* becomes too vague and loses its meaning. To counter this problem, two conditions are attached to nonverbal behaviors before they are considered acts of communication: There must be both some degree of intentionality and some level of consciousness on the part of either the sender or the receiver.[2]

One way to narrow the definition would be to stipulate that nonverbal behavior must be (1) perceived consciously by either the sender or the receiver, (2) intended as a message by the sender, or (3) interpreted by the receiver as intended. Thus, if the twitching behavior of the exam taker was an attempt to signal you for help, we might call it a poor attempt at communication, but an act of communication nonetheless. How would you know it was intentional? You might not know for sure, in which case you'd have to interpret it as an intentional attempt to get your attention and induce a state of guilt, so that you'll help him cheat. If the behavior was simply a sign of nervousness and didn't lead you to attribute it as having any message value, there is no reason to count it as an act of communication.

In a similar vein we can limit the realm of nonverbal communication to those behaviors that are consciously attended to by sender, receiver, or some third party. Frequently, we may not be aware of the nonverbal messages we send to others. As long as no one else is aware of such messages, there is no point in considering them to be communication. For instance, most people are not very aware of how their voice sounds to others. To some, a person whose voice has a nasal quality may sound like whining, while others won't consciously perceive the nasality at all. Those who notice the nasal quality may infer some attitude or personality trait. In this case a message has been received, or "leaked," even though it was not intended or interpreted as intentional.

In his research on the communication of emotion, Ross Buck makes a similar distinction between intentional and unintentional forms of nonverbal communication, but he argues that both forms occur simultaneously and are largely independent of each other. In Buck's view two radically different forms of communication co-exist: a spontaneous and a symbolic communication system.[3] In many ways this distinction is more important than the distinction between verbal and nonverbal codes. In this section we'll discuss Buck's two forms of communication and then examine the communication power of nonverbal codes.

## Spontaneous Communication

**Spontaneous communication** refers to a sender's nonvoluntary display of inner emotional states and a receiver's direct and immediate sensory awareness of those states. According to Buck it is a biologically based signal system that we share with other animals. When we communicate spontaneously, our nonverbal signs (such as gestures or facial expressions) are simply external manifestations of our internal emotions; they are not planned or intentional messages to others. Another person may, however, directly perceive these emotional signals if he or she is "tuned in" to them. It is possible for both sender and receiver to communicate in a purely spontaneous manner, where neither person consciously intends to send or receive the nonverbal signal.

Recent research on the human sense of smell and its relation to interpersonal attraction demonstrates one of the ways that the spontaneous communication system works. As it turns out, our bodies emit signals of genetic fitness via a set of genes known as the major histocompatibility complex (MHC). These genes play a role in immune system functioning and, in evolutionary terms, resistance to disease is greater for offspring if the parents have dissimilar MHC. Natural body odor conveys differences in MHC. In a study where male participants were asked to wear the same undershirt for a full week, Wedekind and Furi found that both males and females who smelled the shirts rated the odor of those with dissimilar MHC genes as more pleasant (!) than the odors of those with similar MHC genes.[4] While colognes and perfumes may mask and thus interfere with this particular spontaneous communication process, the system itself clearly operates beyond intention and conscious awareness.

## Symbolic Communication

Whereas spontaneous communication occurs as a conversation of natural gestures, **symbolic communication** involves the use of arbitrary symbols, socially defined and intended to convey specific messages. While language is the clearest example of symbolic communication, many nonverbal cues are also used symbolically. When you want someone to know that you're glad to see him, you may "put on a happy face" to express that feeling. If you want to gain sympathy, you can produce a sagging posture and a hang-dog facial expression. Humans, unlike other animals, have learned to use symbolic communication to alter some spontaneous expressions. We can, with practice, learn to inhibit many of our natural expressions. For instance, deception involves the conscious control of gestures and facial expressions that would normally indicate emotions we do not want others to see or the manufacture of gestures suggestive of emotions we do not feel. These intentional uses of nonverbal cues are symbolic in nature. They are consciously encoded by senders and decoded by receivers who share the same set of conventional rules for their meaning.

Buck agrees that even though symbolic communication constitutes much of our human communication, spontaneous communication is still very much with us and perhaps more important than we realize. Much of our folk wisdom about "intuition," "animal magnetism," and good or bad "vibes" may be explained as spontaneous communication.

In summary, scholars disagree about how much of our nonverbal behavior can actually be thought of as nonverbal communication. Distinguishing between spontaneous and symbolic communication suggests that we can communicate nonverbally in two very different but equally powerful ways. Sometimes we use nonverbal cues intentionally and according to socially defined rules; at other times we connect with each other on an emotional level that we cannot verbalize or control.

## The Power of Nonverbal Codes

Whether communicated spontaneously or symbolically, nonverbal behavior can evoke powerful messages. We need to be aware that we communicate in unintentional ways, but obviously we have the greatest opportunity to control and improve our use of symbolic (verbal and nonverbal) codes. While nonverbal messages often speak louder than words, they do not necessarily do so at all times. It is really a matter of matching the capacity of particular verbal and nonverbal codes with the nature of the social situation and our own self-identity and relational goals within that situation. To help us make such decisions, we need to understand some of the aspects of nonverbal messages that make them so powerful.

1. *Nonverbal codes are frequently given more credence and are more trusted than verbal forms of communication.* As we have noted, nonverbal codes have been in use longer than verbal ones. And since we live the first 12 to 18 months of life relying totally on nonverbal communication, it is

little wonder that when in doubt, we tend to put our faith in the nonverbal message. Of course, this trust can backfire. Suppose you want to buy an insurance policy. The salesperson's nonverbal communication may seem to indicate a genuine concern for your welfare and may discourage you from reading the fine print of the policy because it's all "mumbo-jumbo." If you relied on the salesperson's nonverbal expression of concern, you might well be relying on the wrong code.

2. *Nonverbal codes are more emotionally powerful.* Nonverbal behaviors tell people about our emotional state. It takes a good deal of practice to hide our true feelings from others—and even then, close friends will often see through our attempts. When we want to convey how we feel about someone, language often fails us. Desmond Morris refers to the myriad gestures that express emotional bonding (interlocked arms, shoulder embraces, hand-holding) as "tie signs" that physically connect people in ways words cannot.[5]

3. *Nonverbal codes, while influenced by culture, do express more universal meaning.* Members of different linguistic groups must spend a lot of time and effort to learn each other's verbal codes, but they can communicate instantly by smiling or wrinkling their faces in disgust. The work of Paul Ekman and Wallace Friesen has shown a number of emotions to be expressed in the same way by members of different cultural groups.[6] Happiness, anger, disgust, fear, surprise, and sadness are all conveyed by using the same facial muscles in much the same way. There are differences, but they occur primarily in the rules that govern *when* it is appropriate to show the emotion in public or *how much* emotion should be displayed. Facial expressions are probably the most universal codes because of their prominence in face-to-face interaction. Other body movements and gestures have multiple and sometimes contradictory meanings within and across cultures, as we shall see later in this chapter. Most of these differences can be explained by Buck's distinction between spontaneous and symbolic communication. The more biologically based and spontaneous a nonverbal code is, the more universal its meaning. Nonverbal codes

used in symbolic ways will express the localized meanings of a particular dyad, group, or culture.

4. *Nonverbal codes are continuous and natural.* Because gestures and body movements flow into one another without obvious beginnings and endings, they seem to be a more natural part of our existence than words. Words are also strung together, but unless you mumble, your words don't slur into one another as nonverbals often do. Nonverbals are immediate—that is, they are physical extensions of our bodies, and their form resembles their message more than words' form does. A gesture signaling someone to "come here" imitates the movement of a body from a far place to a closer proximity. Words, perhaps because they can be written and stored away from the body, often seem more distant and more unnatural.

5. *Nonverbal codes occur in clusters.* Verbal communication is limited to a single channel at a time, but nonverbal communication operates in much the same way as recording studios use multitrack taping systems. Several channels are operating simultaneously and usually in concert. When different nonverbal codes send the same message, the impact is intensified. While you can repeat or rephrase verbal messages to achieve redundancy, it will take more time and still not mirror the intensity of the combined forces of touch and tone, facial expressions, body positioning and movement, and so on.

Given the unique capacity and power of nonverbal codes, we will now examine what they accomplish in everyday interactions.

# The Functions of Nonverbal Codes

We use nonverbal codes to achieve some very specific purposes. While researchers have proposed several ways to classify these functions, we have grouped them into three general types. Nonverbal codes may be used to (1) express meaning in and of themselves, (2) modify verbal messages, and (3) regulate the flow of interaction. Let's look at each of these functions.

## Expressing Meaning

Nonverbal messages are often used to convey how we feel about other people and how we see our relationship to them. Albert Mehrabian suggests that three fundamental dimensions of feeling are expressed through nonverbal communication: liking, status, and responsiveness.[7] It is easy to recognize that nonverbals express **liking** or disliking, as when people smile or turn up their noses at one another. **Status** is conveyed by nonverbal cues indicating how important or influential we think we are in relation to others. Staring at a subordinate may communicate snobbishness or dominance. **Responsiveness** indicates how aware we are of the other person and what level of involvement we feel with him or her. Bursting into tears or laughing heartily would indicate high responsiveness; a blank stare or an ever-so-slight chuckle would represent low responsiveness. In Chapter 5 we'll elaborate on the ways we send each other these relational messages.

## Modifying Verbal Messages

While some nonverbal messages stand on their own, others work in conjunction with verbal messages. Nonverbals can complement, accent, repeat, substitute for, or contradict verbal messages. **Complementing** is the nonverbal elaboration of the verbal message. When friends say they are sick, their flushed faces, unsteady gaits, and pained looks help us determine the extent of their illness. **Accenting** refers to nonverbals that underline or focus attention on a specific word or phrase. Pounding the table with your fist at the same time you say "I've had it!" makes that particular phrase stand out. Sometimes we give a verbal message and then try **repeating** it nonverbally to help the receiver process the total message. For

*Posture, gesture, and facial expression all reveal how we feel about ourselves and others. It is impossible not to send nonverbal messages, although decoding them can be difficult.*

instance, when someone asks a favor, we may say "Yes" and then nod our head to make sure the person knows our response was genuine. At other times we avoid the verbal response altogether, and the nonverbal serves a **substituting** function. A cold stare may say "No!" better than any verbalized refusal could. Some situations require substitution. Deep-sea divers cannot speak, so they rely on hand gestures and other body movements to indicate what they want one another to do.

You may frequently find nonverbal messages **contradicting** verbal ones. When they do, you have a choice to make. One of your professors may say she has plenty of time to go over a quiz with you, but if she remains standing, doesn't offer you a seat, and keeps fidgeting with her watch, you may question the sincerity of the verbal remark. As noted before, we generally believe the nonverbal message when a contradiction oc-

curs. But, this is not always the case. Young children, perhaps because of their fascination with newly acquired language skills, often believe verbal statements, especially in cases of sarcasm.[8]

Other studies demonstrate that some people consistently rely on the verbal channel and others on the nonverbal channel when presented with contradictory cues.[9] One explanation for these channel preferences is that they are learned habits; another is that they are linked to patterns of left-right hemispheric dominance in the brain. The right hemisphere of the brain appears to be highly involved in processing spatial and holistic information, features prominent in most nonverbal codes. The left hemisphere, on the other hand, is better at processing verbal information. In most people, one hemisphere tends to be more active than the other and may affect the channels of communication to which we pay the most attention.

### Regulating the Flow of Interaction

Finally, nonverbal codes function to **regulate** the flow of talk. When two people converse, nonverbals are primarily responsible for the smoothness of taking turns, avoiding long pauses, changing topics, even signaling when it is appropriate to end the conversation. In many professional contexts the function of nonverbal communication is simply the administration of a service or task.[10] Thus, the nonverbal act of holding a patient's arm while the doctor administers an injection functions to make the task easier. A similar behavior in some other setting may function quite differently.

So far we have talked about nonverbal communication in general. We have defined nonverbal communication, seen what makes it such a powerful system, and identified three ways we use nonverbal cues. Now we turn to each separate channel of nonverbal communication. We call each of these channels a nonverbal "code."

# The Structure of Nonverbal Codes: Visual, Auditory, and Invisible Communication

Nonverbal codes are structured in terms of multiple channels. As we've seen, in most instances of communication, behavior from various channels cluster together in order to convey a given meaning. As a result, it is somewhat artificial to talk about each code as a separate form of nonverbal communication, but it is easier to describe each code as if it stood alone. It may help to cluster the codes themselves into groups. Dale Leathers suggests that nonverbal communication be seen as three interlocking systems—as visual, auditory, and invisible communication systems.[11] In Leathers' scheme, the **visual communication system** includes the codes of *proxemics* (use of space), *kinesics* (gestures, body movement, and eye and face behavior), and *artifacts* (physical appearance, clothing, and accessories). The **auditory communication system** involves what is commonly called *vocalics* or *paralinguistics*. Finally, Leathers defined the **invisible communication system** as consisting of *chronemics* (use of time), *olfactics* (smell), and *haptics* (touch or tactile), all powerful but less easily detected codes (see Figure 3.1).

As we review each system and its related codes, keep in mind the functions that have been mentioned, noting how each code is used in combination with others to communicate specific meanings (e.g., attraction, hostility, dominance, anxiety), to modify verbal messages, or to regulate the flow of conversation. For instance, in their review of the nonverbal literature, Laura Guerrero and Kory Floyd described a cluster of nonverbal codes involved in interpersonal attraction.[12] The majority of codes were visual in nature—body type, height, waist-to-hip ratio, proportionality and symmetry of facial and body features, pupil size, and the extent to which one's face retains childlike features. But there is also evidence of auditory and olfaction codes, including a vocal attractiveness stereotype[13] and, as we saw earlier, spontaneous attraction to dissimilar scents.

The first codes we will examine have to do with the visual communication system.

## Visual Communication: Proxemics, Kinesics, and Artifacts

As humans, we are clearly and predominately a visual species. We are much more likely to act on and talk about those aspects of the world that we "see" more than those we "hear" or "feel." This fact is reflected in that visual codes represent the majority of ways we categorize nonverbal interaction.

### Proxemics

Approaching other people is a more delicate proposition than most of us realize. Take the mundane matter of walking across campus or strolling through a busy shopping mall. As soon

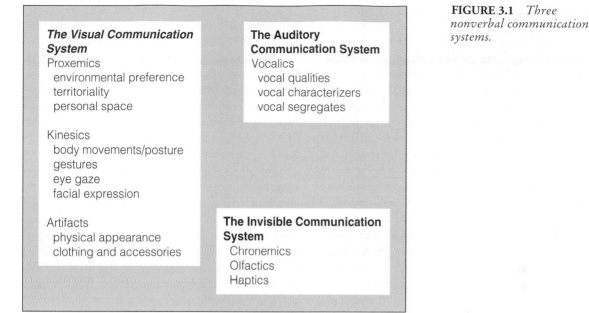

**FIGURE 3.1** *Three nonverbal communication systems.*

as visual contact is made or we sense that another body is nearby, we begin manipulating our own body movements and anticipating the movements of the other in order to avoid getting too close or bumping into one another. Ashley Montagu and Floyd Matson have pointed out that "there are virtually as many rules, customs, and conventions governing the conduct of 'sidewalkers' as there are for car drivers, the difference being that the sidewalk rules are unwritten and tacit and . . . completely unnoticed."[14] The next time you stop to talk to someone, notice how each of you shifts your body back and forth to establish a comfortable speaking distance. Watch when two people move from an open lobby area to a cramped, crowded enclosure such as a hallway, elevator, or cafeteria line. What actions result from this change in distance? People may actually stop talking or change to a more impersonal topic of conversation. Each of these situations is an example of how people use or adjust to changes in the spatial environment. Investigators call the study of messages sent in this mode **proxemics**.

How many ways do we use space to communicate? Architects design interior and exterior spaces to make personal, philosophical, or cultural statements. People grow hedges around the edges of their property to discourage trespassers. And perhaps the most powerful proxemic statements are made during conversation itself, by the simple measurement of how much distance we keep between ourselves and those to whom we talk.

*Environmental Preferences.* While each of us reacts to the environment in some unique ways, we are also programmed genetically and culturally to react in more similar ways. When we feel comfortable in a physical setting, we are more likely to communicate effectively. Or perhaps we should say, when we feel uncomfortable we communicate less effectively and may even attribute these negative feelings to the people in that environment. In a classic study Abraham Maslow and N. L. Mintz asked people in three different environments to rate the same group of photographs of faces (actually negative prints). One room was set up to be "beautiful," another "average," and the third "ugly." People consistently rated the photographs higher in energy and well-being in the beautiful room and lower in the ugly room.[15] This study supports the notion that the environment has a spillover effect on social interaction.

Other factors in environmental spaces can have a dramatic effect on our social behavior as well. Physical features of an environment (such as lighting, color, noise, and extremes in temperature) affect our preference for that environment.[16] In addition, more subjective perceptions (such as familiarity, novelty, and mystery) have been shown to affect whether we will approach or avoid an environment.[17]

According to Albert Mehrabian and James Russell, the combination of these environmental factors and our own predisposed mental sets produces emotional reactions along three dimensions: arousal-nonarousal, dominance-submissiveness, and pleasure-displeasure.[18] For instance, a visit to the Grand Canyon would probably give most people a moderate level of arousal, a submissive feeling, and a strong sense of pleasure, which combine to produce a sense of awe. For some people social conversation is very difficult in a bar or nightclub because they are unable to screen out all the background noise and flashing strobe lights. The level of arousal is so high for them that concentrating on talk is too difficult. Most of us feel more dominant in those settings that are very familiar to us. We are more likely to tell someone what to do when they are on our turf, or territory, than when we are on theirs.

*Territoriality.* The concept of **territoriality** refers to the legal or assumed ownership of space. Lawrence Rosenfeld and Jean Civikly define territoriality as "the assumption of proprietary rights toward some geographical area, with the realization, at least for humans, that there is no basis for those rights."[19] Animals mark their territory by building nests, leaving excrement, and fending off intruders. Humans use a great variety of territorial markers, ranging from where they stop mowing the grass to the placement of personal photographs on otherwise institutional-looking desks.

Stanford Lyman and Marvin Scott have distinguished four types of territoriality in human interaction.[20] *Public territory* is owned by no one and accessible to anyone. City streets, park benches, and plazas exemplify this kind of territory. Each of these may, from time to time, become *interactional territories*, as when a softball team takes over a park to use as a practice field. Other spaces are designed for interaction. These include courtrooms and tennis courts. *Home territories* allow for an even greater degree of privacy. Strangers will rarely intrude on a space they consider to be someone else's home. This includes more than physical violations. A neighbor who constantly peers through your windows is considered rude and will usually not persist if you stare back. *Body territory*, the final classification used by Lyman and Scott, is more frequently referred to as personal space by other researchers.

*Personal Space.* The term **personal space** has been used to describe an imaginary bubble extending out from our bodies, an area considered to be almost as private as the body itself. We react strongly to movement into our personal space—only small children and intimate family and friends are allowed to enter this space without apology. Anthropologist Edward T. Hall has done the most to draw our attention to personal space and other forms of conversational distance.[21] In observations of middle-class Americans, Hall has distinguished four interaction zones:

- Intimate distance (0–18 inches). Reserved for lovemaking and very private conversations.

- Personal distance (18 inches–4 feet). The range at which one is comfortable with friends and acquaintances.

- Social distance (4–12 feet). Used for business transactions and role relations.

- Public distance (12–25 feet). Appropriate for public ceremonies, speechmaking, classroom lectures, and so on.

The actual distance at which you are comfortable talking to others may vary according to your personality and to age, sex, status, or cultural differences in relation to those you interact with. For example, Hall describes a visit to an apartment house in northern Germany. The house had a first-floor studio. From the front porch, the interior of the studio was clearly visible through a large window. While Hall was talking to a young woman on the porch, he could also see and be seen by an artist who was holding a conversation with another person inside the studio. Hall did not know the artist, so he largely ignored what was happening in the studio. A few minutes later the artist came outside and yelled at Hall for intruding without even a sign of greeting.[22] The difference was simply a matter of interpreting space. For the American there was enough space between the two pairs to allow them their separate activities. For the German his space had already been invaded.

Some people simply need more space than others. Unless you are aware of this, you may find yourself trying to move closer to others (to make yourself more comfortable) while they compensate by moving away (to reestablish their comfort zone). Hall points out one problem that may arise: "Since none of us is taught to look at space as isolated from other associations, feelings cued by the handling of space are often attributed to something else."[23] The most likely result is that you will form negative impressions of these people.

Research also demonstrates that those of the same age group stand closer to one another than age-discrepant pairs, and that male pairs space themselves farther apart than opposite-sex pairs, who usually space themselves farther apart than female pairs.[24] Occasionally, the norms for personal space are violated without incident because one of the parties is viewed as a nonperson, as a mere object—for example, waiters, servants, and people in crowded elevators or stadiums.

Stop and think about the communicative functions that proxemics serve. We may use spatial distance or closeness to communicate feelings of liking, or to achieve some sense of privacy, or even to threaten or remind the other person of our status. Can you identify ways we use prox-

emics to regulate conversation or to modify the nature of our verbal statements? For instance, we may stand closer to someone we find physically attractive.

Often the distance we maintain from others is regulated by gestures and other body movements. We turn now to an examination of kinesic interaction behavior.

## Kinesics

The study of body movements such as gestures, posture, and head, trunk, and limb movements is known as **kinesics.** Facial expressions and eye gaze are also considered part of kinesics.

*Body Movements and Gestures.* How we hold or carry our bodies (posture and gait), position them in relation to others, or gesticulate can convey a wide range of meanings. These kinesic behaviors help us determine when people consider themselves to be of equal or different status, want to emphasize a point, and are open or closed to interaction, as well as how confident, nervous, happy, or sad they feel. Research demonstrates that open body positions and leaning in toward the other are perceived as an invitation to interact, whereas folding one's arms or orienting one's body away from the other is often interpreted as being less approachable. Social skill in conversation is often reflected in the combination of relaxed body posture, fewer random body movements, vocal fluency, and effective use of gestures.[25] The use of gestures often seems to occur intuitively and without intent, but understanding what functions they perform can help facilitate smoother conversations. Ekman and Friesen have identified five categories of gestures in terms of their functions: emblems, illustrators, affect displays, regulators, and adaptors.[26]

**Emblems** are gestures that can easily be translated into verbal statements; there is widely shared agreement as to what they mean. When you doubt someone's sanity, you can indicate so by raising your hand to your temple and moving the forefinger in a circle. Almost every culture has developed different nonverbal symbols for saying yes and no. The way someone sticks out

BOX 3.1

# A Nonlinear History of Handshaking

One of the nonverbal gestures that we take for granted is the handshake. It is as common a form of greeting in cultures across the world as one is likely to find. It would seem that such a gesture would have a long history (it does) and a consistent one (it does not).

Historians are not sure when the handshake as a greeting originated. There is evidence that the gesture existed in 16th-century Poland, and was probably widespread in Europe much earlier than that. But from the 16th century to the early 1800s, the gesture lost favor and then returned in a different context and with a different meaning. The decline of the handshake began with the rise of courtly codes of civility among the elite in France, Italy, and Spain. In courtly life, familiar greetings and leave-taking behavior took on the airs of hierarchy and sophisticated manners. The handshake was replaced by the gestures of doffing the hat, bowing, curtsying, and staying to the left of a person of higher rank.

As these codes of civility spread to the middle class, the control of one's body became a preeminent concern. Etiquette manuals, dance instructors, and tutors of all description taught individuals to keep their bodies erect, to walk properly in public, and to avoid gesticulating wildly or crossing the legs while in conversation. These gestures were widely known as the "science of conversing agreeably." But among all the etiquette books, one would not find any advice about shaking hands until a French manual in 1858 finally included the handshake, but restricted its use to the greetings of close friends. How did the gesture reemerge?

Historian Herman Roodenburg notes that the handshake could not make a comeback until the concern with manners began to relax a bit. Even

---

his tongue may indicate that he dislikes you (Rude Tongue), that he wants to be left alone (Concentration Tongue), or that he is flirting with you (Sexy Tongue).[27] In each case the placement or movement of the tongue is the crucial factor. One emblem that has had a very interesting history is the handshake. Box 3.1 describes the evolution of the symbolic meanings associated with this gesture.

Nonverbal behaviors that accompany speech, often emphasizing particular words or painting a picture of what is being said, are called **illustrators**. Hand batons are common examples. When people talk, they may raise a forefinger or wag it at the other person; hold their palms up, down, in front of them, or sideways; thrust their fist through the air, or clasp their hands together. None of these gestures has a meaning in and of itself, as an emblem would. Illustrators depend on, but also add an emphasis to, verbal messages.

While emotions are communicated primarily via the face, **affect displays**, or postural and gestural cues, also work to convey how we feel. A child throws himself or herself to the ground and kicks arms and legs wildly in reaction to parental refusal. Such a tantrum is usually intentional and has a twofold purpose: It spontaneously expresses the emotion felt—rage—and is also a symbolic attempt to annoy or embarrass parents until they give in.

People may also synchronize their actions, consciously or not, to physically demonstrate an affective, or emotional, relationship among themselves. Children imitate the posture and gestures of their parents or heroes; people simultaneously lean forward to hear some choice gossip; and a group of "cool" teenagers mirror one another by leaning casually on one leg and resting their thumbs in their belt loops.

the Dutch of the 17th century, widely acknowledged as an egalitarian society, did not practice the handshake as far as we know. In the meantime, the gesture began its comeback in the neighborhoods of 18th-century Paris and small Dutch towns. But it was not used as a gesture of greeting.

Roodenburg describes the semi-official "extra judicial" institutions that arose in these neighborhoods as a way of settling disputes without having to go before an official court of justice. Each neighborhood had its own informal commissaires who listened to each party and tried to find a way for them to reconcile. Usually one party would admit being in the wrong and would ask for forgiveness. The reconciliation was sealed by the parties giving each other "the hand of friendship." Roodenburg discovered similar rituals for settling disputes within the records of the Calvinist Church, and also noted the similarity between the handshake as a seal of reconciliation and the popular gesture of slapping hands to seal a business transaction in the marketplace. It was not long after these practices emerged that the Quakers began to use the handshake as a simple greeting that denoted a bond of friendship or brotherhood. Addressing each other as friends minimized the elements of hierarchy and class distinction that had previously been characterized forms of greeting in a culture preoccupied with manners and social status.

**SOURCE** Herman Roodenburg, "The 'Hand of Friendship': Shaking Hands and Other Gestures in the Dutch Republic," in *A Cultural History of Gesture*. J. Bremmer and H. Roodenburg, eds. (Cambridge: Polity Press, 1991), pp. 152–89.

**ADDITIONAL READINGS**

Bushman, Richard L. *The Refinement of America: Persons, Houses, Cities*. New York: Alfred A. Knopf, 1992.

Elias, Norbert. *The History of Manners*. New York: Pantheon Books, 1978.

Thompson, E. P. *Customs in Common: Studies in Traditional Popular Culture*. New York: The New Press, 1993.

Nonverbals that help control interaction flow are known as **regulators.** When you want to break into a conversation, you may use preliminary gestures such as leaning forward or tilting your head forward while raising your hand to a position where it may be used as an illustrator. What kinesic cues would you use to tell the other person that it is his or her turn to talk, or to hurry up, or to indicate that even though you have to pause to catch your breath, you have one more point to make before yielding the floor?

This final category includes any body movement designed to manage anxious, emotionally charged, or novel situations. **Self-adaptors** are manipulations of your own body: pressing a hand against your mouth, chewing your nails, crossing your arms, or brushing your hand through your hair. Since touch is often reassuring, we may touch ourselves to calm down or just to feel better. Self-touch may also indicate a desire to withdraw from interaction, to be left alone.

**Object-adaptors** are material objects used in the tension management process. Smoking cigarettes, tapping a pencil on your desk, caressing a stuffed animal, or chewing on a straw are examples. Their only communicative value seems to be that they tell onlookers we're nervous or uncomfortable.

Many kinesic movements (with the exception of emblems) may operate as unconscious messages on the sender's parts. They tell others what we are thinking or feeling. They may also be cues to deception, as the study in this chapter's Research in Review box demonstrates.

*Gaze.* Our eyes aren't just instruments for receiving stimuli; they are themselves messengers. Even the simple act of appreciating physical beauty requires that we proceed with caution. **63**

*Pinocchio's Nose*

# Detecting Deception from Nonverbal Behavior

Lying is an everyday occurrence. In fact, the average person tells one or two lies a day. Given the frequency of lying, it would be useful to be able to detect lies. But is it possible to do so? Do people behave differently when they are lying than when they are telling the truth?

Hand gestures may be one cue to deception. In "The Impact of Deception and Suspicion on Different Hand Movements," Letizia Caso and her colleagues looked at seven kinds of gestures: self-adaptors, emblems, and iconic, metaphoric, rhythmic, cohesive, and deictic illustrators. Iconic gestures reproduce an object or event, metaphoric gestures indicate abstract ideas, rhythmic gestures keep time with speech, cohesive gestures mark the structure of a narrative, and deictic gestures point.

One hundred twenty-eight psychology students from the University of Rome were taken to a lab, given a backpack containing a small object, and asked to look at the object and memorize it. All of the students were told they would be interviewed about the object and about the person who gave it to them. Half of the students were instructed to tell the truth, while the others were instructed to lie. The interview took part in two phases. In the first (the low suspicion phase), the students answered the interviewer's questions by either lying or telling the truth. In the second (the raised suspicion phase), the interviewer pretended to disbelieve the subjects and asked them to repeat their stories. Participants were videotaped and all hand gestures were coded and classified.

The researchers made a variety of predictions. In the first phase, for example, they reasoned that liars would use fewer self-adaptors in order to appear more convincing and more metaphoric gestures because of the cognitive complexity involved in lying. In the second phase, they predicted all subjects would use fewer self-adaptors and more metaphoric gestures as they worked to avert suspicion. They also hypothesized an increase in deictic gestures in an effort to shift the object from themselves to other referents.

Results generally supported the author's predictions, indicating that close attention to hand gestures can be used to detect deception. In interpreting their results, however, the authors underline the fact that no single cue (like Pinocchio's nose) indicates lying. The nature of the situation and kind of lie must be taken into account when trying to detect deception. They also emphasize that being under suspicion influences not only liars, but also truth-tellers. Equating behavioral adaptations with deceit, a technique commonly used by the police, is therefore unreliable. Finally, they point out that cues to deception are more than likely culturally specific. Findings from Italian students may or may not generalize to Americans.

Caso, Letizia, Fridanna Maricchiolo, Marino Bonaiuto, Aldert Vrij, and Samantha Mann. "The Impact of Deception and Suspicion on Different Hand Movements." *Journal of Nonverbal Behavior* 30, no. 1 (2006): 1–19.

Erving Goffman has recommended that we "discipline our eyes" until we have mastered the skill of knowing how to look without appearing to be looking. For a fascinating view of how people in the late 19th century disciplined not only their eye behavior, but controlled their entire bodies to avoid social interaction, read Box 3.2. It demonstrates the extent to which we rely on visual cues to initiate conversation.

One of the first contributors to the literature on visual communication was Adam Kendon, who proposed that **gaze** served three primary functions in communication: (1) expressive, (2) regulative, and (3) monitoring.[28]

*The Expressive Function of Gaze.*   Gaze plays an important role in the communication of emotions. Although identification of most emotions requires the decoding of complete facial cues, the eyes are especially expressive in conveying fear and surprise.[29] Likewise, gaze broadcasts interest in and liking of the other person, and researchers have found that people gaze more when they receive or want to receive approval, especially from someone who is higher in status.[30]

In addition, gazing can frequently create arousal in those being stared at. Imagine eating your lunch alone, enjoying your private thoughts, when you suddenly become aware that someone is watching you. You glance in the person's direction, expecting him to look away, but he doesn't. How do you react? According to P. C. Ellsworth and to Miles Patterson, that depends on the attributions you make. If you sense that the other person's motives are harmless, or you find him interesting in some way, you will probably reciprocate by smiling and looking in that direction again later. If you attribute the other person's behavior negatively, you are more likely to compensate by turning away, giving a nasty look, or leaving the other's presence.[31]

*Using Gaze to Regulate and Monitor Interaction.*   Gaze, along with other nonverbals, serves to regulate and monitor the other's reactions during conversation. Gaze first signals that we're available for communication. Averting our eyes says just the opposite. When you're in a hurry and can't stop to talk, you may pretend not to see the other. Or you may simply opt for the "eyebrow flash"—a common sign of recognition that involves a look, a smile, a raising of the eyebrows, and a nod.[32] It may be used to acknowledge the other without committing yourself to conversation.

Once conversation has begun, eye behavior helps keep turn-taking and transitions flowing smoothly. The general pattern for Americans is to look more when they listen than when they speak, and to very rarely look at each other for more

than a split second. Why do we follow this pattern? When we listen, gaze shows interest in what the other is saying and allows us to receive complementary or contradictory nonverbal cues. When we begin a speaking turn, we are busy concentrating on what we want to say and thus do not look at the other as frequently or as long.

Women, it seems, gaze more than men and are more uncomfortable when visual contact is cut off.[33] Some speculate that this is a function of traditional socialization, which teaches women to be more concerned with social affiliation. A greater difference has been noted in the gazing patterns of blacks and whites. Clara Mayo and Marianne LaFrance have shown that whites look more when listening and that blacks look more when talking and less when listening, just the opposite of whites.

> *The White may feel he is not being listened to while the Black may feel he is being unduly scrutinized. Further, exchanges of the listener-speaker roles become disjunctive, leading to generalized discomfort in the encounter.[34]*

Blacks use more "backchanneling" gestures; that is, they give more verbal and nonverbal feedback to a speaker while he or she is still talking. Because of this, it makes sense that a black speaker would look more while talking: He or she is simply trying to monitor the feedback others are giving. The fact that we use our eyes to monitor feedback has raised the question of where our vision is usually focused during interaction.

*Looking vs. Seeing.*   What do you focus your vision on when you talk to other people? Do you look into their eyes, in the direction of their eyes, or at the whole upper body? D. R. Rutter, in a comprehensive review of visual communication, makes a distinction between looking and seeing.[35] **Looking** refers to gazing in the direction of the other's eyes, whereas **seeing** is defined as visual contact with the whole person. Rutter argues that seeing is more important than looking when regulating and monitoring feedback. It was once thought that people used gaze to signal turn-taking. Now it appears that seeing the

BOX 3.2

## The "Guarded Self"
# How to Avoid Being Seen in Public

Much has been written about the 19th-century movement of the young from American farms to cities. Most went in search of work at one of the many factories that sprang up during the industrial revolution. In any large-scale movement of people there are bound to disruptions of the social order. Perhaps one of the central anxieties faced by these young urban immigrants was the adjustment from life in a community where people were under the watchful eye of neighbors who knew everything about them to an urban life where they were scrutinized by a steady flow of anonymous others. It is not surprising that agoraphobia (an irrational fear of open spaces, of going out in public) became widespread during this period.

John Kasson, in *Rudeness and Civility*, talks about the code of conduct that emerged as a way of managing such fears. "For men and women both . . . the glare of exposure could be over-whelming . . . embarrassment became a normal, even an essential, part of American urban life." Sensitivity to embarrassment was a direct consequence of the lack of communal standards for behavior and a corresponding insecurity about one's own identity. The social webs that nurtured self-identity and held it in check were missing and nothing had emerged to replace them.

Enter the etiquette manual. "Etiquette is the machinery of society," said one New York advice-giver. "It prevents the agony of uncertainty. . . . If one is certain about being correct, there is little to be anxious about." Kasson suggests that etiquette was used as social armor against intrusion, that people needed ways to protect themselves from the scrutiny of others. The self-image of most urban dwellers appears to have been that of a "guarded self" whose maxim was "mind your own business." Body management and nonverbal communication were essential to the maintenance of such a public identity.

To fend off the unwanted gaze of others, advice writers taught the fine art of being inconspicuous. The genteel man or woman avoided flashy clothing; black became the fashion color of choice. Over time, the modern suit emerged for men—a dark, sober, anonymous uniform. In addition, men wore overcoats, full beards, and mustaches, essentially hiding the face and body

whole person is necessary for picking up other turn-taking cues such as nods and gestures. This relegates gaze to a lesser role in regulating interaction. Eye contact (mutual looking) plays an even smaller role. Some research suggests that eye contact happens so rarely that it is probably a random occurrence.[36] We encourage you to test these findings yourself. Keep in mind the distinctions between eye contact (mutual looking), gaze (looking), and seeing (gazing at the whole person). Which occur more often in your own conversations, and what functions do they appear to serve?

*Facial Expression.* One reason for getting a full view of the other person rather than gazing in the direction of the eyes is to pick up entire facial expressions, which may well be the single most important channel of nonverbal communication. People read a lot in our facial expressions. They infer some personality traits and attitudes, judge reactions to their own messages, regard facial expressions as verbal replacements, and, primarily, use them to determine our emotional state. Perceptions of liking and affection, for instance, are tied primarily but not exclusively to facial expressions. In a couple of studies, communicating from others. Likewise, women were advised to avoid "singularity" in their choice of clothing. They were also told to avoid excessive jewelry, strong perfume, or anything else likely to draw attention. In fact, the demand on women was considerably greater than that on men. Women were admonished to avoid going out in public unless absolutely necessary; there were many sectors of the city where an upstanding woman was a rare commodity. When they did venture forth, women were encouraged to travel by carriage rather than risk even a short walk. When walking could not be avoided, she was to step slowly in "a modest and measured gait," always staring straight ahead, never stopping. The rest of the body, for both men and women, was to be stifled. The hands should never touch the face, especially the nose, while in public. Chewing gum, eating, coughing, sneezing—literally anything that drew attention to the body—was to be avoided. Perhaps the greatest act of self-discipline was the reining in of the eyes. Eye contact was seen as an invitation to social discourse, and so had to be guarded against with extreme caution. But even here one could go too far. While it was proper to avoid staring or holding a glance too long, one had also to avoid the other extreme of appearing too shy or fearful.

It was not enough for people of the time to simply manage their own bodies. They were equally responsible for not looking at the indiscretions of others. Said one advice writer: "The rule is imperative, that no one should see, or, if that is impossible, should seem to see, or to have seen, anything that another person would choose to have concealed; unless indeed it is your business to watch for some misdemeanor." In most social situations, 19th-century people simply assumed that what they observed was none of their business.

SOURCE John F. Kasson, "Venturing Forth: Bodily Management in Public," in *Rudeness and Civility: Manners in Nineteenth Century Urban America* (New York: Hill and Wang, 1990), pp. 112–46.

**ADDITIONAL READINGS**

Susman, Warren. "'Personality' and the Making of Twentieth-Century Culture," in *Culture as History: The Transformation of American Society in the Twentieth Century.* New York: Pantheon Books, 1984, pp. 271–85.

Trenholm, Sarah, and Arthur Jensen. "The Guarded Self: Toward a Social History of Interpersonal Styles." Paper presented at the Speech Communication Association of Puerto Rico's annual conference, San Juan, December, 1990.

affection was linked to the extent of facial animation, smiling, head-nodding, eye contact, and greater frequency of illustrator gestures.[37] Since most of the research on facial expressions have focused on emotions, so will our discussion. Here we will examine how six universal expressions are created and controlled and why we sometimes misread facial expressions.

*Universal Expressions.* The study of facial expression owes much to researchers Paul Ekman and Wallace Friesen. The comprehensiveness and quality of their work give us confidence in their findings. They have demonstrated the universality of expression in conveying six basic human emotions.[38] Regardless of culture, the emotional states of happiness, sadness, surprise, fear, anger, and disgust are communicated with remarkable similarity (see Figure 3.2). As Ross Buck would suggest, these facial expressions are recognized universally because they are part of our biological heritage, communicated spontaneously.

Ekman and Friesen identified three separate sets of facial muscles that are manipulated to form these six expressions. These muscles are found in the following areas: (1) the brow and forehead; (2) the eyes, eyelids, and root of the nose; and (3) the cheeks, mouth, most of the nose, and chin. Muscles in all of these facial regions combine in a particular way to produce a representation of a pure emotional state. For instance, surprise is announced by (1) the raising of the eyebrows, (2) the opening wide of the eyes, and (3) the dropping of the jaw and parting of the lips. Look at the other five emotions in Figure 3.2 and identify how they are expressed in each of the three facial regions. You may wish to consult Ekman and Friesen's book *Unmasking the Face* for further practice photos.

A key fact is that facial expressions are often short-lived. We rarely hold a look of surprise for long. If you can't believe the astronomical amount of your phone bill, surprise may quickly give way to disgust or anger. The person with you may see traces of both emotions on your face. The result is called a **facial blend.** Since social interaction usually consists of rapid-fire exchanges, we are constantly changing expressions. What others see are usually blended expressions rather than pure emotional states.

But, you may be saying to yourself, people's facial expressions aren't always genuine. It is true that emotional expressions are universal, but when they are displayed is not. **Cultural display rules** often control this. We know that it is quite improper to laugh at someone who falls down, no matter how funny it strikes us. We are supposed to act surprised when an unannounced party is given in our honor, even though someone spilled the beans earlier. Business practice requires that salespeople show enthusiasm for vacuum cleaners, vegetable dicers, and other products that do not intrinsically excite them. Most people have personal display rules, ingrained early in life, such as "never show your anger in public." These are examples of the symbolic communication system inhibiting and modifying our natural or spontaneous expressions of emotion.

Women, at least in American culture, are generally more nonverbally expressive than men. This is also true with respect to facial expression. Most studies to date show adult women to have significantly more facial reactions and general facial activity than men.[39] Many people, regardless of sex, display a characteristic style of facial expression (see Figure 3.3). Withholders, for instance, may inhibit facial muscle so much that others marvel at how they can talk without moving their mouths.

But controlling the face is not quite as easy as we might think. Professional actors may be regarded as specialists in controlling their faces, but the rest of us don't fare so well. We give ourselves away to the perceptive observer by producing momentary **leakage cues,** unintended signs of our real feelings, which are largely but not completely masked in normal facial management. For example, when trying to maintain our composure in the face of the announcement that a coveted award went to another contestant, we let disappointment leak out when we momentarily turn down the corners of the lips, quickly replacing it with "a stiff upper lip."

*Misreading Facial Expressions.* Even when people spontaneously express an emotional state, we may not perceive it. Norms regarding eye behavior are partly responsible. We look at the other person's face only about 50 percent of the time during conversation. Ekman and Friesen point out that this is due to more than just being polite and not staring at the other. Often we don't want to be burdened with the knowledge of how the other feels. This may reach comic proportions, as when a parent exasperated with a pouting child says, "I'm not looking at you!"

Other reasons for misreading the face include attending to competing verbal and nonverbal channels, not paying close attention to the context of interaction, and not knowing the target person's usual repertoire of facial expressions. When we are concentrating on what the person is saying or distracted by nervous gestures, we are likely to miss the momentary expressions that might reveal how the person really feels. Likewise, failure to perceive the context accurately may cause problems. When a friend or acquaintance is also your interviewer for a job, she may try to neutralize her expressions as much as

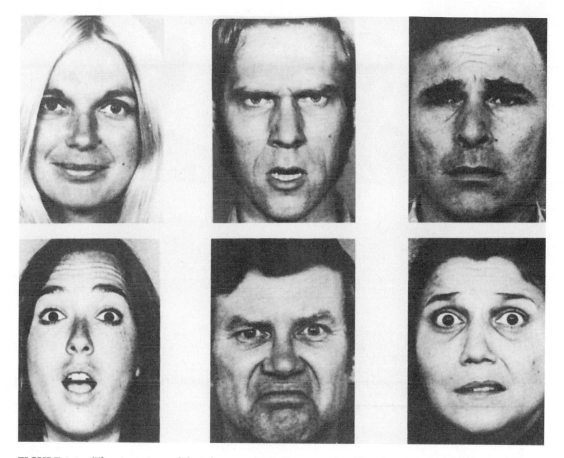

**FIGURE 3.2** *The six universal facial expressions. Can you identify what emotion is being expressed in each of the photographs? Researchers Paul Ekman and Wallace Friesen have studied facial expressions across cultures and have found these six (surprise, anger, happiness, fear, disgust, and sadness) to be universal.*

Paul Ekman and Wallace F. Friesen, *Pictures of Facial Affect* (Palo Alto, Calif.: Consulting Psychologists Press, 1976).

possible so as not to show favoritism. If you think of her as a friend rather than an interviewer, you may read the expressionless face as genuine and think she doesn't want you to get the job. Finally, Ekman and Friesen suggest that you can improve the accuracy of your judgments by learning the idiosyncratic ways the other person uses facial expressions. This means making a concerted effort to record what the person does with his face in various situations, when you know for a fact that his reaction is or is not genuine.

### Artifacts

The final category of visually oriented nonverbal codes is artifacts such as physical appearance and manipulations of that appearance through clothing, jewelry, and other personal accessories. **Physical appearance** alone can be a powerful message. Each culture defines its own particular images of physical beauty, but there are some underlying aspects of body types and proportional arrangements that appear to be fairly universal across cultures.

### Withholder

This person's facial expression doesn't show how he feels. He isn't trying to deliberately deceive; he just shows very little expressiveness.

### Revealer

Revealers tell all with their faces. They are very expressive and often say that they just can't help showing how they feel. You always know when a Revealer does or doesn't like the birthday present you gave her.

### Unwitting Expressor

This person shows emotion without realizing it. He says things like, "How did you know I was angry?"

### Blanked Expressor

Blanked Expressors think they are showing an emotion when in fact they show little if any expression at all. They just have a kind of neutral look on their face at all times. They differ from a Withholder in that the Withholder usually knows that she is not expressive.

### Frozen-Affect Expressor

The Frozen-Affect Expressor constantly shows one emotion (such as happiness) when she is not experiencing that emotion at all.

### Substitute Expressor

These people feel one emotion and think they are expressing it, but most onlookers would say some other emotion is being expressed. The person who feels angry but looks sad would be an example.

### Ever-Ready Expressor

This person almost instinctively shows the same emotion as his first response to any new event. Such a person may express surprise at good news, bad news, or the announcement that he has just been fired.

### Flooded-Affect Expressor

This person frequently displays more than one emotion. One of the emotions is characteristic of the person, similar to the Frozen-Affect Expressor. When another emotion is felt, it is mixed with the old characteristic expression. A person may look fearful, for instance, and thus show both fear and anger when he is angry.

FIGURE 3.3   *Do you have a characteristic style of facial expression? Paul Ekman and Wallace Friesen have identified eight different styles of facial expression in their research. Which one best fits you?*

Adapted from Ekman and Friesen, *Unmasking the Face* (Englewood Cliffs, N.J.: Prentice-Hall, 1975), pp. 155–57. Illustration from Jim Harter, ed., *Men: A Pictorial Archive from Nineteenth-Century Sources* (New York: Dover, 1980), p. 3.

Facial features; beauty, color, length, and style of hair; skin color; the general shape of the body; and posture are among the physical features that people pay close attention to when they first make visual contact. The role of these features in communication depends on our awareness of them and the belief that the sender intended some message by his or her appearance. When a husband puts on a little weight and others notice this fact, communication may or may not be occurring. If you are his wife and you believe that body weight can be controlled, you may interpret his appearance as saying, "I don't care what I look like to you anymore. It's more important that I enjoy myself than that I look good for you."

The communication value of most natural body features is limited. Stereotypes aside, there is no message value in the natural color of one's hair or skin. Thus, we should pay attention to what people do to enhance, display, alter, or conceal their bodies. These are the real messages directed at us, because here the sender has some element of control.

Even so, we rely on these constant features a great deal in deciding with whom to communicate. Research demonstrates that most cultures have strong prototypes of physical beauty.[40] Many people believe that our own culture's prototypes are magnified by the media, influencing the evaluation of and desire to be with other people. One study involved college freshmen who signed up for a computer date to a dance. Pairs were actually matched at random rather than by interest or compatibility. When asked to indicate satisfaction with their date and desire to date again, physical attractiveness was the only predictor of either one.[41] Another study showed how physical attraction serves as a central trait in many of our implicit personality theories. A physically attractive person was consistently rated as more sociable, outgoing, poised, interesting, and sexually warm and responsive than an unattractive one.[42]

We tend to believe that physical beauty is intrinsic and interpreted the same way the world over, but Desmond Morris reminds us how temporary our prototypes are in his comparison of vital statistics of contestants in today's beauty pageants with carved figurines of past epochs:

*If we consider [the Venus of Willendorf] as Miss Old Stone Age of 20,000 B.C., then, had she lived, her vital statistics would have been 96–89–96. Moving forward to 2000 B.C., Miss Indus Valley would have measured 45–34–63, and in the late Bronze Age, Miss Cyprus of 1500 B.C. would have registered 43–42–44. Later still, Miss Amlash of 1000 B.C. would have offered the startling proportions of 38–44–78, but Miss Syria of 1000 B.C., only a short distance away, would have measured an almost modern 31–26–36.*[43]

While the specific features regarded as beautiful have varied across time and culture, research does show some culture-free underlying dimensions. For instance, while different cultures find different **body types** (thin, muscular, plump) attractive, those preferences tend to vary in terms of the relative scarcity of nutritional food. When nutrition is good and food is abundant, cultures tend to prefer thin or muscular body types, but when food is scarce and nutrition is poor, a more plump body type rates as more attractive.[44] It seems that whatever body type the environment makes harder to achieve tends to be more attractive.

Another universal feature of physical appearance is **body symmetry,** or the extent to which both sides of the body (or face) mirror each other. Researchers suspect that members of our species are attracted to symmetrical bodies because they are more likely to be genetically fit. Disease, stress, pollutants, genetic defects, and other environmental extremes often affect the body's development, resulting in a less than symmetrical arrangement of the body's features.[45] Attraction to others is also influenced by **body proportionality** (sometimes referred to as the *phi ratio*), which is the relative length, size, or distance between related physical features.[46] The most notable example of this is the *waist-to-hip ratio* for the female body type (not the absolute measurements, but their relative proportion to one another).

More than perhaps any other nonverbal code, physical appearance demonstrates the tension between the more universal influences of features we can't change and the socially constructed meanings of features that we can modify or adorn. Both influence how and with whom we communicate. Let's look more closely at the communicative impact of material adornments.

People go to great lengths to adorn their bodies. Fashionable clothing and accessories, tight or loose-fitting garments, hair color, earrings, and untied shoelaces are all forms of adornment.

Clothing has been long recognized as a way to communicate social status, group identification, and personality.[47] The popularity of books and magazine articles about what clothing to wear to job interviews and business meetings indicates our concern with the status implications of clothing. In one study, various styles of men's clothing were ranked for social status and then placed on models who had been independently ranked for status according to facial and head features alone. Invariably, higher-ranked clothing increased, and lower-ranked clothing decreased, the perceived status of the models.[48] In many large companies status distinctions are maintained by subtle factors such as suits made of more expensive fabric, while group membership is maintained by similarity in the basic type of apparel (professionals wear dark suits, staff wear simple dresses or shirtsleeves and slacks, maintenance personnel wear uniforms). People often identify with one another by wearing the same or similar clothes. The next time you visit an amusement park, watch groups of people and look for ways they identify with one another through clothing. The most obvious examples will be families where Mom, Dad, and all the kids are wearing T-shirts with the family's last name printed across the back. In what other subtle and not-so-subtle ways do people say they are together?

Finally, dress may convey messages about the self, whether intentional or not. A friend reported turning down a good job offer because she didn't think the people she would have to work with were very stimulating. Her first impression was that "there was beige everywhere. Most of them wore two or three shades of beige, and their faces had a beige cast to them, and I would have to say their personalities were equally as beige." At other times physical appearance may be so eye-catching that the person becomes the focus of our visual field.

The nonverbal codes considered so far have been visual in nature. We now turn our attention to a code that is entirely auditory.

## Auditory Communication

Words are spoken through the medium of the voice, which has characteristics of its own, apart from the content of what is said. These characteristics are called **vocalics,** or paralanguage. *What* is said is frequently less important than *how* it is said. What we convey in our voices can accent, alter, or flatly contradict verbal meaning. For example, sarcasm is often a product of vocal inflection. Our investigation of the vocal channel will begin by looking at the qualities of the human voice that have message potential, followed by an examination of the role these characteristics play in impression formation and emotional expression.

### Vocal Characteristics

While researchers have classified vocalic cues in several ways, we simply want you to be aware of the many components that make up the vocal system.[49] **Vocal qualities** include loudness, pitch, inflection, tempo, rhythm, intensity, articulation, and resonance. **Vocal characterizers** are more specific sounds that we may occasionally recognize as speech acts themselves. Laughing, crying, moaning, yelling, and whining are examples. **Vocal segregates** are sounds that get in the way of fluent speech, including "uhs" and "ums," stuttering, and uncomfortable silences. The combinations of these cues produce the unique voice patterns of each person. You probably know someone whose voice is especially high-pitched or raspy or nasal or monotonic. How do these qualities affect your impressions of such people? People from different cultures or regions within the same culture usually differ from one another in characteristic ways. How do you react to those speakers whose vocal qualities differ from yours?

## Nonverbal Communication and Identity

# Freaky Friday

Mark Waters, 2003

Dr. Tess Coleman (Jamie Lee Curtis) is a harried career woman about to remarry, and Anna (Lindsay Lohan) is her adolescent daughter whose main interest is playing in a rock band. Neither one understands the other: Anna sees Tess as a control freak, while Tess sees Anna as totally irresponsible. Naturally, mother and daughter clash. After one particularly bad argument in a Chinese restaurant, they're given magical fortune cookies, and the next day—Freaky Friday, the day before Tess's wedding—they wake up to find themselves inhabiting each other's bodies.

On one level this comedy is about empathy and the ability to see things from another's perspective; for one day each has to take on the other's identity, and in doing so, mother and daughter learn to value each other. One another level, the film demonstrates the way we express our personalities through our nonverbal behavior. When Tess and Anna wake up in each other's bodies, they are at first horrified. "I look like the crypt keeper," says Anna when she looks in the mirror and sees Tess's body, and Tess is equally upset when she discovers her new body has a pierced navel. Initial dismay aside, to survive Freaky Friday, both women have to learn to manage their new bodies and modify their body language. This film shows how much of who we are lies in our personal nonverbal style and how difficult it would be to change that style.

### Messages in the Voice

The voice is often used to infer personality traits. When you talk to a stranger on the telephone, what image of the person do you form as you listen? David Addington's research on voice types and perceptions shows some of the more common attributions people make about the personality that goes with the voice. An example should suffice. A "breathy" male voice led listeners to infer that the speaker was young and artistic. The same characteristic in a female voice led to a stereotype of a more feminine, prettier, more petite, effervescent, yet shallow individual.[50] The accuracy of such impressions has never been proved. It's more likely that vocal cues are just one more aspect of our implicit personality theories. We factor in the vocal cues alongside others that then trigger a more complete prototypic impression.

We also use vocal cues to infer emotional states, especially when facial cues are unavailable or suspect. One review of the research on vocalics and emotion concluded that two emotions were most likely to be interpreted accurately: joy and hate. The hardest to communicate were love and shame.[51] The ability to judge emotions in the voice does vary, however. Some people are remarkably good at it while others can't make auditory distinctions or don't listen carefully. At certain times the context makes vocal cues more salient. In one study alcoholic patients were more likely to seek additional treatment when a doctor made the referral in an "anxious" voice.[52]

From an examination of the more predominate nonverbal codes involved in seeing and hearing, we now turn to modalities that sometimes stretch our perceptual abilities.

## Invisible Communication: Chronemics, Olfactics, and Haptics

When violations of the social norms regarding time, smell, and touch are obvious, we do attend

*Proxemics and gesture represent means of communicating with others. Here a young man thrusts his hands into his pockets and casts a sidelong glance, indicating his shyness.*

to them. But in our normal everyday existence, they often go unnoticed. Touch is probably the most attended to among these three codes, but it is most often felt rather than seen or heard.

## Chronemics

In our culture, how we spend time matters a lot. Interpreting messages associated with time is called **chronemics.** Time is related to status. A doctor's time is considered more valuable than the patient's time, for instance. The boss often gets to determine what time her employees must arrive at work, when they can take a break, how long lunch is, and when they get to take vacation time. Likewise, we often make judgments of people based on time-related cues such as how fast or slow they talk, the duration of their turns at talk, or the overall percentage of "talk time" they monopolize in meetings.

As we saw in the chapter opening, Frances Mayes experienced cultural differences in the perception of time in her expectation that workers would show up on the day that they scheduled the work to begin, or that Alfiero, the contractor, would spend more time attending to her project once it began. She thought she had regained his attention after throwing a tirade, only to have him "lose focus" and spend even less time on aspects of the project to which she wanted him to attend.

Conflicts in relationships often focus on time. "Why does it take you so long to get ready before we go out? You know I hate being late!" "We eat dinner at 6 o'clock sharp around here, young man!" Jealousy in relationships often prompts close scrutiny of how one partner's time is spent. In his studies of sexual jealousy, David Buss identified one of the strategies for "mate guarding" as monopolizing of the mate's time in order to minimize the partner's opportunities to be unfaithful.[53] On a far more positive note, one of the best methods for indicating intimacy and commitment in a relationship is by simply spending time with one another.[54]

## Olfactics

**Olfaction** has to do with messages we attach to smells emitted by the body. Humans rely on this code much less than other animals and its effects are typically not under our conscious control. Thus, the communicative value of olfaction is limited in that we can be aware of these influences, but not really control them. You may recall the study mentioned earlier in this chapter on olfactic differences in the genetic marker

MHC that is conveyed through body odor. While its impact on attraction is abundantly evident and fascinating, intentional manipulation for purposes of communication is restricted to either masking body odors or not bathing in order to accentuate them. Only a handful of studies exist on manipulations of body odor by use of perfumes and those studies tend to show that people are more attracted to others when they are clean but use no perfume at all or very little perfume or cologne.[55]

## Haptics

From the time we are born, the nonverbal code of touch (**haptics**) is extremely important. Studies of infants have shown how tactile stimulation triggers social, emotional, and even intellectual growth.[56] Advocates of the human potential movement have stressed the need for adults to touch and be touched. In spite of this, we know very little about the role of touch as a message system. According to one reviewer, the research tends to emphasize only the positive role of touch.[57] Few investigators have studied how touch is used to dominate or threaten others. Yet we know from everyday experience that touching conveys a wide range of emotions and meanings.

*Types of Touch.* Touching may be the most ambiguous of the nonverbal codes because its meaning depends so much on the nature of the relationship, the age and sex of the other, and the situation, as well as where we are touched, how much pressure was applied, whether we think the touch was intentional or accidental, and how long the touch lasted. In addition, touch may be applied by brushing, patting, squeezing, stroking, embracing, slapping, kicking, and even tickling. The texture of touch may even be meaningful. Shaking hands with someone whose palm is sweaty is not very pleasant and may be interpreted as a sign of nervousness. The manner in which you place your hand on someone's arm may be the difference between reassuring or patronizing that person. The warmth or coldness of other cues, such as the tone of voice, may add meaning to being touched.

*The Contexts and Functions of Touch.* Touching may be used to signal aggression, status, friendliness, or sexual interest or simply to regulate interaction. But these meanings are mediated by context. Richard Heslin has classified the meanings of touch according to the relational context in which they occur.[58] The *professional/functional* context legitimates any kind of touch necessary to accomplish impersonal ends or services. Doctors and hair stylists are allowed to touch us in ways that other people cannot. *Social/polite* relationships allow for a minimum of touching during greetings, goodbyes, and conversations. A handshake is acceptable, as is a brush on the arm to get another's attention. The meaning of other forms of touch in this setting is more difficult to determine. Brenda Major believes that touch may simultaneously communicate warmth and dominance, but that men and women pay attention to different aspects of the message. When an equal-status stranger initiates touch, men more often see it as an act of dominance; women see it as a friendly gesture.[59] Higher-status individuals seem to have more rights regarding touch. They can initiate touch more frequently, whereas a lower-status person rarely feels comfortable enough to reciprocate that touch.[60]

*Friendship* encourages a number of touching behaviors associated with liking. A shoulder embrace, a greater frequency of brushing the hand or arm, and a slight squeeze are examples of appropriate actions. In *love/intimate* relations, we find more hand-in-hand and arm-in-arm contact, more bodies leaning against one another, and more touching in general. Finally, *sexual relationships* forbid very few forms of touch. But even in sexual relationships, the meaning of touch may vary.

Heslin has proposed a curvilinear relationship between forms of touch and liking. In the initial stages of acquaintance, intimate touch is taboo and should lead to strong dislike. As a relationship becomes defined as loving or sexual, intimate touch becomes pleasurable. There is a danger, however, that the quantity of touching may lead to the view of the other person as a "sex object," reducing, sometimes drastically, the pleasure of touch. Although Heslin didn't include it in his scheme, we would add an *adversarial* relationship context. This could encompass professional wrestlers, some brothers and sisters, and normal folks during the course of an argument. You may grab someone by the shirt collar in an attempt to threaten her, or, if things deteriorate, you may push or shove the person.

Touching is only one of many nonverbal codes. And, as we have reminded you all along, none of the codes stands alone. They operate as a complex, mixed-message system every time we interact with one another. How we can make sense out of and react to the total nonverbal package is the subject of the next section.

# Balancing Nonverbal Codes: Compensating and Reciprocating

Most people in a crowded bus avoid looking at one another or limit their visual behavior to random glances. But what would you think if a stranger kept looking in your direction and, as seating opened up, moved closer to where you were sitting, and then offered someone else his seat and stood even closer to you, occasionally brushing his arm against yours? How would you react?

One way to view this stranger's behavior is to define his advances as increasing the physical and psychological immediacy or closeness between you. Our guess is that unless you were extremely attracted to this stranger, you would probably *compensate* for his behavior by distancing yourself in one or more ways. You might get up and change your seat, turn and look out the window, or bury your head in your newspaper.

We don't always avoid increases in nonverbal immediacy. Sometimes we reciprocate another's invitations. Is there any way to predict when we will compensate or reciprocate? A number of theories attempt to explain how we respond to each other's nonverbal messages.

Most of the theories we will examine are premised on the notion that we enter social situations with expectations about how we and others will or should act. In Chapter 6 we will look at the way in which people form these expectations through cognitive, emotional, and motivational perceptions called schemas. For now, just realize that we form expectations based on a range of sources from biologically hard-wired perceptions to our own personal experience, social and cultural norms, the situational context, and prior interaction with specific relational partners. Whatever the source, our expectations can either be confirmed or violated by the other person's behavior. Different theories predict how we'll respond and offer different explanations for those responses.

## Expectancy Violations Theory

Early theories in this arena simply predicted that confirmations of expectations would likely be seen as positive (leading us to reciprocate) whereas violations would be seen as negative (prompting us to compensate). Judee Burgoon and her colleagues wanted to explain why people might also respond positively when expectations are violated.[61] **Expectancy violations theory** posits that two factors are at work in determining how we respond: (1) violation valence and (2) the reward value of the other person. The combination of these two factors produces an overall assessment of the situation and a behavioral response (compensation or reciprocity). *Violation valence* is simply our perception of the positive or negative value of the violating behavior itself. On the crowded bus, for example, most people find violations of their space uncomfortable but not uncommon (moderately negative valence). Imagine the same behavior if the bus was not crowded at all and you'd probably label it as extremely negative valence. But what if you recognized the person crowding you as a famous actor or you felt that she or he was extremely attractive? Your assessment of this person's *reward value* can change your perception of the valence of the violation.

For the most part, the theory predicts that behavior that conforms to expectations will be viewed positively and behavior that violates expectations will be perceived negatively, but that rewarding communicators have greater flexibility. For instance, Burgoon and Hale found that when a person had an average or low level of reward value, he or she was evaluated more positively when conforming to expectations. For the person initially perceived as having high reward value, she or he was actually judged more positively when engaging in positive violations than when conforming.[62] Focusing more on close relationships, Afifi and Metts catalogued a range of positive and negative expectancy violations that moved the partners either closer together or further apart. Among the more positive surprises were gestures of inclusion, acts of devotion, and escalations of the relationship. Criticism, uncharacteristic behavior, acts of disregard, transgressions against the relationship, and relationship deescalation were some of the more negative violations.[63]

In summary, expectancy violations theory predicts that when attractive, powerful, intimate, or otherwise rewarding communicators surprise us with greater than expected nonverbal immediacy, we are likely to reciprocate and engage in more immediate behaviors in return. When less rewarding people increase immediacy, we will probably compensate, reducing our own immediacy in order to fend off the unwanted increase in physical or psychological closeness. The theory also predicts that when we perceive someone as a rewarding person and they violate expectations in a negative direction (less than expected immediacy), we will try to compensate and return the relationship to a more normal level of interaction. Some research, however, suggests that if the rewarding person continues to send distant or avoidant nonverbal messages, the partner will begin to reciprocate.[64] Thus, at some point, the other person loses

his reward value and we treat him in the same fashion that he is treating us.

## Cognitive Valence Theory

Peter Andersen built on Burgoon's and earlier theories by adding several factors that he believes more fully explain reactions to increases in nonverbal and verbal immediacy (positive expectancy violations).[65] In addition to the immediacy violation itself and the reward value of the person engaging in the behavior, Andersen's theory, **cognitive valence theory,** includes perception, physiological arousal, and a variety of cognitive schema as leading to reciprocal or compensatory responses (see Figure 3.4). Andersen argued that immediacy behavior first has to be *perceived* (even if unconsciously) before another person will respond to it. Perceptions of increased immediacy generally produce some increase in *arousal*. Research suggests that most of the time increases in immediacy produce moderate levels of arousal and are, more often than not, viewed positively. A low level of arousal is a typical reaction when immediacy behaviors are routine (as in exchanging greetings), producing little or no compensation or reciprocity. At the other extreme, a very high level of arousal change is usually indicative of a stressful or fearful reaction and almost always results in the target trying to compensate or resist the attempt to increase intimacy. Stalking behavior represents one rather horrific example of this kind of high arousal immediacy.

Moderate levels of arousal usually facilitate cognitive analysis and the weighing of various interpretations related to the increase in immediacy. As we will see in Chapter 6, people employ a range of *cognitive schemata* or knowledge structures to help make sense of social events. Cognitive valence theory suggests that at least six cognitive schemas are drawn upon to make sense of expectancy violations: cultural appropriateness, personal predispositions (e.g., if I'm a very private person, I may not want to get too close to others), the nature of the situation, the reward

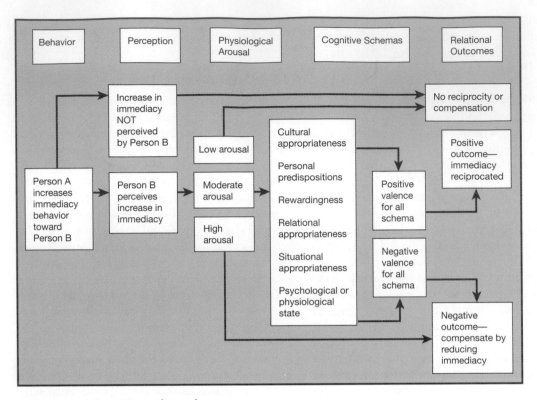

**FIGURE 3.4**  *Cognitive valence theory.*

Adapted from Laura Guerrero, Peter Andersen, and Walid Afifi, *Close Encounters: Communicating in Relationships* (Boston: McGraw-Hill, 2001), p. 273.

value of the other person, relationship expectations, and temporary mood states. In earliest expressions of this theory, Andersen posited that a person needed to interpret all six cognitive factors positively before she or he would likely reciprocate the increased immediacy, but that compensation was likely if even one of the six factors was perceived negatively. More recent research suggests that the six factors have different influences, with relationship expectations and rewardingness of the other being the most consistent influences.[66]

## Compensating and Reciprocating in Everyday Life

How well do these theories explain everyday interactions? If you stop and think about it, we spend a lot of energy trying to find the right balance in our various relationships. One of the principle themes of this text is that communication is used to regulate the tension between feeling independent and feeling connected with others.

When we feel closed in by a relationship, we may compensate by reducing the level of nonverbal involvement. You can probably remember your early teenage years, when you desperately needed to present yourself as an adult, not a child. At that point in life, too much nonverbal involvement with parents, such as holding their hands or staying close to them while shopping, suggests that you are still a child. Compensation becomes a tool for establishing your own identity and your status as an adult.

Understanding the various nonverbal codes we have described is an important part of interpersonal communication. Even more important is understanding how they work in conjunction with one another and with verbal messages. Recognizing how people compensate and reciprocate for increases in nonverbal intimacy can help you manage your nonverbal communication more effectively.

---

# The Interplay of Verbal and Nonverbal Communication

In practice, we seldom communicate solely through nonverbal channels. As we saw earlier, nonverbal codes are used to reinforce, repeat, or contradict verbal messages. At the same time, we often attach verbal labels to our own and others' nonverbal behaviors. The act of labeling is one way that we take nonverbal communication from the realm of the spontaneous to a clearly symbolic level. To illustrate, let's look at the interplay of the verbal and nonverbal in the experiencing of emotions.

Contrary to Ross Buck's assertion that most emotional communication occurs at an immediate and spontaneous level, some scholars believe that emotions, like other concepts, are socially constructed. James Averill, for instance, defines **emotions** as transitory social roles involving one's assessment of a social situation that are experienced as passions rather than actions.[67] According to Averill, the experience of emotions like pleasure or anger involves more than a mere biological or intrapsychic reaction to a stimulus—it is largely dependent upon a system of sociocultural rules that indicate to the individual whether an emotion is proper or appropriate in a given situation. For instance, it is appropriate in our culture to cry at weddings and funerals, so we are much more likely to experience happiness or sadness in those circumstances. We are surrounded by situational cues that prompt our emotions. Yet we do not realize that our emotions are socially defined because part of the social definition is that emotions are passive—they "happen to us" rather than our choosing them. Most of us would rather believe we "fell in love" (uncontrollably) than admit we conspired to follow a socially defined pattern of interactions that eventually informed us that our feelings for each other could properly be called love.

The controversy may be more apparent than real. Buck argues that emotions felt are often but not always communicated spontaneously. Thus, emotions may be socially defined but experienced as inner states that are communicated via natural gestures. And of course, it is possible that emotional states are experienced spontaneously but either denied or modified by cultural display rules, which are socially defined. Perhaps we have become so sophisticated at symbolic communication that many emotions, once experienced at a purely spontaneous level, are now at least partially controlled by social definitions.

What is clear is that the communication of emotion is not always a straightforward process. Richard Buttny has demonstrated how we mix nonverbal affect displays and verbal labeling to hold others accountable for the experience of negative emotions.[68] He suggests that in conversation, relational partners often display and talk about emotions in order to fix blame or responsibility. The most obvious way we do this is by simply showing our feelings through vocalic cues, body posture, and silence or through verbal sarcasm. Another way is by verbally labeling our own negative emotions and implying that the other was somehow responsible. For example, simply stating that you are angry in the presence of a partner can frame events as problematic, as though the other somehow provoked your anger. Finally, we can ascribe a particular emotion to our partner and, in doing so, imply that his or her emotion is excessive, unjustified, or otherwise inappropriate. Note in the following exchange how Lori labels Scotty's emotion (she has just told him that she has to go home to Boston during fall break):

SCOTTY (*with rising intonation*) I'm not gonna take . . . be able to take you to Boston, Lori.

*Nonverbal communication allows us to signal how we feel about others. This satirical painting depicts a middle-class white couple involved in a cultural exchange, reacting both with interest and wariness.*

Gerald Nailor (Toh Yah), Untitled, 1937

LORI  I understand, we'll . . . we'll go another time.

SCOTTY  (*rapid pace, emphatic and rising intonation*) *What* other *time*?

LORI  In the spring . . . I'm gonna have my car up here . . . I'll bring it up after . . .

SCOTTY  Something will come up. (*audible outbreath*)

LORI  Oh *come on*, don't be angry.

SCOTTY  I'm not angry. . . . I just know . . . I . . . I know I just have the feeling that we're not going to get to Boston . . . together.

LORI  We will go another time, Scotty, I promise we will go to Boston together. . . .

SCOTTY  Lori? I'll put money on it . . . right now, that we will *not* go to Boston.

LORI  (*marked increase in volume*) WE WILL GO TO BOSTON! WE WILL . . . BECAUSE WE CAN'T GO NOW WE HAVE springtime to go. . . . I wanted to go just as bad as you did, Scotty, . . .[69]

By telling Scotty not to be angry, Lori is not only labeling his behavior but also framing it as an overreaction to their change in plans. Notice that despite his earlier emphatic statements, he denies being angry and seems willing to modify his emotion as disappointment. She might have been successful had she stopped, but her almost-too-easy insistence that there will be another opportunity seems to provoke a verbal betting gambit ("I'll put money on it"), a fairly clear display of anger.

As this example illustrates, the communication of emotion is a difficult and often unsuccessful enterprise. Even when friends are able to manage the occasional argument or nonverbal battle for dominance in the relationship, their characteristic differences in style and degree of nonverbal expressiveness will likely be an obstacle. Clearly, better understanding and communication of our own and others' feelings would help make relational life a lot easier. With that goal in mind, we turn our attention to some specific guidelines for improving our skills in this important area.

# Skill Building: Communicating Feelings

Managing interpersonal relationships is never easy, but the management of emotional aspects of those relationships is doubly difficult. First of all, there are no simple guidelines. While we will focus here on skills such as how to better express your feelings and how to respond to the nonverbal displays and feeling statements of others, we cannot recommend their indiscriminate use. As much as openness is to be valued in relationships, there are times when emotional wounds are too painful to bear scrutiny. Likewise, some relationships or issues will not be significant enough to warrant bringing out all the heavy artillery to do emotional battle. And sometimes conversations that are direct and forthright can be boring. Can you imagine what it would be like to flirt if all the suspense and ambiguity of meaning associated with it were stripped away?

However, for those times when you desire greater emotional openness in your relationships, you must have some strategies that will help you achieve your goals. Let's focus first on how to

express your own feelings appropriately; then we'll look at how you can help others express themselves.

## Expressing Feelings

Most of us have not been taught how to express our emotions. In our culture, males in particular have difficulty expressing how they feel. The first step in improving our skills is to *become more aware of the emotions we do experience.* Ronald Adler suggests a diary procedure for monitoring your emotional communication.[70] Over a period of several days, you should record incidents in which you experienced a particular emotion such as anxiety, resentment, or pride. Then write a brief description of the situation (events surrounding the emotion), the way you expressed yourself verbally and nonverbally, and the consequences of your behavior (the end results—how others responded). Make sure you record specific nonverbal behaviors and verbal statements. This will indicate the extent to which you are actually expressing your feelings. After several days analyze your diary. Ask yourself which emotions you experience most often, how well you express what you feel, and how others respond to your behavior. By taking inventory in this way, you increase your awareness of your emotional experience and strengths and weaknesses in expressing those emotions.

Another way to increase awareness is to *actively seek feedback about your expressions of emotion from trusted sources.* Ekman and Friesen suggest that people are more internally aware of the specific nonverbal channels from which they have received the greatest amount of external feedback. We learn to pay attention to the nonverbal channels to which others pay attention. Buck calls this the "education of attention," one of the most significant ways we learn to manage our own nonverbal communication.

As you become more aware of your emotions, you can shift your attention to more constructive ways of communicating your feelings. You will want to keep in mind some simple principles to help develop those skills.

A key principle is to *express your feelings in a way that indicates your ownership of them*. Too often we speak of our feelings in impersonal terms, referring to them as if they belonged to the object of our perception or to some objective realm. "The painting isn't a very optimistic one, it depicts a depressing mood" or "Depression has set in again" are examples of failure to demonstrate ownership of feelings. Worse yet, we frequently blame others for how we feel. "You make me so mad" is one of the least constructive ways of talking about our feelings. While we have learned about emotions through a process that is socially constructed, the experience of those emotions belongs to us, not to anyone else. We can indicate ownership of our own feelings by using "I" statements that reflect the influence of both partners' behavior but concede ultimate self-responsibility for our own behavior. "I feel very lonely when you put in such long hours at the office" is much better than "You make me feel invisible." Notice that while the latter statement may have more dramatic impact, it lacks specificity and puts all the blame on the other, which is likely to provoke a defensive reaction, not a constructive one.

A final suggestion is to *match the form of expression with the situation and your own personal and relational goals*. We have three primary options regarding the communication of emotions. We can (1) avoid communicating altogether, (2) express our feelings directly, or (3) express our feelings in an indirect (equivocal) fashion. Each of these options has different consequences, depending upon the situation and our personal or relational goals. Direct expression is appropriate if the timing is right and if the emotion is one that needs to be expressed in order to achieve a personal or relational goal. If you want your friend to know that you value the friendship, a direct expression is probably the most effective way of saying it. On the other hand, avoidance or equivocal communication is sometimes more appropriate. Janet Bavelas and her colleagues define **equivocal communication** as messages that are ambiguous, uncertain, or open to more than

one equally appropriate interpretation.[71] According to Bavelas we should express our feelings in an equivocal manner when all other choices would lead to negative consequences. For example, we are often confronted with a situation in which an expression of our true feelings would most likely hurt the other person. In some cases a painful truth may be the best thing for the long-term health of the relationship; but often it serves no real purpose. The equivocal response is one that expresses more than one truth or skirts the issue carefully. In Jane Austen's *Sense and Sensibility*, Marianne must find a way to state her honest opinion of her sister Elinor's lover without hurting Elinor's feelings:

> *Do not be offended, Elinor, if my praise of him is not in every thing equal to your sense of his merits. I have not had so many opportunities of estimating the minuter propensities of his mind, his inclinations and tastes as you have; but I have the highest opinion in the world of his goodness and sense. I think him every thing that is worthy and amiable.[72]*

Marianne's solution illustrates a classic way of balancing two important considerations: remaining true to her own sense of integrity and preserving goodwill in a relationship that is important to her.

## Reflecting Feelings

In addition to revealing your own feelings, it is also important to help others express theirs. Actively listening to and reflecting what you observe and hear is an important source of feedback to others. We can, for instance, *look for hidden feelings in others' behavior and carefully bring them to the surface*. "It sounds like you like him but can't bring yourself to say it" is an example of a typical reflective feeling statement. We can also *help others clarify their own feelings by pointing out any contradictory or ambivalent (equivocal) expressions*. Watching a friend open the gift you thought he or she would love can often present an opportunity for clarification. At first you notice the bright-eyed anticipation, the excited tone of voice—"Ohhhhh . . ."—and then carefully, with much less inflection, ". . . it's lovely. It's . . . it's just what I wanted." Being polite is, of course, the equivocal response, and you could just let it go at that and try harder next time. But if you really want to know what type of gift will please your friend, it is better to reflect the mixed feelings you heard and clarify them. You might say, "You seemed excited at first, but then a little dismayed. I'd really like to know if you're feeling disappointed."

It's also a good idea to *mention some aspect of the observed behavior first, then search for the feeling.* Consider Bryant, a student who has gone to see his professor about a group project. He has just admitted that his group wasted most of their in-class meeting time.

BRYANT  I didn't want to tell you about all this, I was afraid you'd get angry at me. Now you're telling me that you're not upset, but you're twisting the eraser off that pencil (*behavioral description*). I think maybe you really are mad at me.

PROFESSOR  (*recognizing his anger*) Well, I guess you're right. I am angry, but I hope you realize I'm angry with the whole group, not just you. It irks me that I provide class time for groups to meet and then students find a thousand reasons why they can't make it to class. I set aside time so you won't have to bicker about conflicting schedules and no time to meet, and then this happens. I'm angry at all of you, but I guess I should have realized this would happen.

Bryant bore the brunt of his professor's anger, but at least he helped the professor verbalize and understand his own feelings. Had he not reflected the professor's feelings, Bryant probably would have incurred most of the professor's wrath anyway. At least now, the professor knows what he was angry about and won't direct all the anger at Bryant. He may even be thankful that Bryant helped him recognize a problem in his class that needs to be addressed.

Finally, Lawrence Brammer offers some summary advice for reflecting the feelings of others. He suggests that you (1) read the total message—stated feelings, nonverbal body language, and content; (2) select the best mix of content and feelings to comment on and then occasionally interrupt to reflect those feelings; and (3) reflect the experience and then wait for the other to acknowledge your reflection before moving on.[73] In this way you make sure that the other is able and willing to handle a discussion of those emotions.

Remember, to become more skillful at emotional communication involves more than just learning how to say what's on your mind or showing how you really feel. If you take these principles to heart, you are another step closer to becoming a more communicatively competent person.

This chapter has emphasized the structure and function of nonverbal codes. Nonverbal communication is structured such that messages may be coded in at least seven or eight different channels. We have also mentioned some major functions that these codes serve: modifying the content of a message, expressing emotions, structuring relationships, and managing the flow of conversation. And we have provided some guidelines for improving the way you use and talk about nonverbal communication. Now it's up to you to apply those guidelines to improve your own nonverbal communication.

# *Process to Performance*

## Review Terms

The following is a list of major concepts introduced in this chapter. The page where the concept is first mentioned is listed in parentheses.

**spontaneous communication**  (54)
**symbolic communication**  (54)
**liking**  (56)
**status**  (56)
**responsiveness**  (56)

## Suggested Readings

Ekman, Paul. *Telling Lies*. New York: Norton, 2001. This book presents an engaging look at the ways in which we use nonverbal communication to deceive and read deception in others.

Guerrero, Laura K., and Kory Floyd. *Nonverbal Communication in Close Relationships*. Mahwah, N.J.: Lawrence Erlbaum, 2006. Focusing on relationships with friends, family, and romantic partners, this book provides a synthesis of research on nonverbal communication.

**Topics for Discussion**
www.oup.com/us/trenholm

### Observation Guide

**1.** Make your next trip to the zoo an investigation into nonverbal communication. Visit a large metropolitan zoo where you can observe primates and other species close to humans on the evolutionary scale. What similarities and differences do you see or hear? Organize your observations according to the various codes discussed in the text (facial, gaze, kinesics, and so on). What gestures seem to be used primarily for communication? What functions do they serve? Identify any gestures humans use that might have originated with earlier species. How has the meaning of such gestures changed?

**2.** Specify a particular block of time and try using nonverbal codes as a substitute for verbal ones. When people ask you questions, do not verbalize beyond unintelligible vocalizations such as grunts or groans. Vary the types of responses you make (vocalized only, facial only, combined responses, and so on). Keep track of your nonverbal codes for a couple of days and try to formulate some general principles about when substituting works best.

**3.** Observe people in naturally occurring conversations, recording the specific nonverbal codes used to regulate the flow of interaction. Which cues are more characteristic of smooth turn-taking? Which cues seem to cause awkward transitions or silences? Compare your observations with those of published research (your instructor can recommend journal articles or textbooks that summarize these behaviors).

**4.** It is a rare semester when students are not involved in at least one group project. Take advantage of these opportunities to observe nonverbal interaction more closely. Take a few minutes during each meeting to observe how different group members communicate nonverbally. As unobtrusively as you can, record facial expressions, body posture and movement, gaze, gestures, and vocal characteristics. Also note the situation at hand so you won't interpret nonverbals out of context. What do these observations tell you about the interest level, status relations, and interpersonal competence of group members? What gestures are shared or imitated by other group members? What does this suggest about the bonding of group members together?

### Exercises

**1.** Identify people you think are especially accurate in reading others' nonverbal cues or are very good at getting their message across nonverbally. These should be people who aren't members of your class. Formulate (in class) a set of interview questions to ask these people. You might want to ask what behaviors they attend to most often when they want to know what the other thinks or feels, and how they know when someone is deceiving them. For message sending, ask people how aware they are of their own nonverbals, which codes they use intentionally, and which they think are most important. Would they rather use verbal or nonverbal messages to give instructions or to convey emotions? You should think of other types of messages to ask them about. Interview a dozen people outside of class and compare the answers you get. Prepare a short presentation to the rest of the class, focusing on what you have learned about nonverbal communication competence.

**2.** Assemble groups of four or five. Have each person remove any cash, valuables, and "really embarrassing" items from their wallets. Place the wallets in a basket and give them to your instructor, who will redistribute the wallets to another group. Each group should analyze the contents of each wallet, writing down a brief profile of its owner. The profile should be based only on inferences made from the artifacts found in the wallet. It can include the person's sex, age, personality, appearance, interests. Once the profile of each wallet is written, enclose it in the wallet and return them to your instructor, who will return them to the original owners. Group members may then read the profiles written about them to one another or introduce one another to the class by reading the profiles aloud. Conclude the exercise by discussing the accuracy of the profiles and the particular artifacts that were most influential in communicating those impressions.

**3.** Divide the class into six groups. Each group is assigned one of the following communicative functions: (1) exercising social control, (2) regulating interaction, (3) expressing intimacy, (4) expressing emotion, (5) facilitating service or task goals, and (6) modifying the content of verbal messages. Each group should then compile a list of the ways each nonverbal code helps to accomplish that function. During the week group members should bring to class audiovisual examples of how this is done (family photos, magazine photos, film clips, audiotapes, and so on). Try to find both stereotypic and unusual examples to illustrate these functions. Groups could be given the last 5 to 10 minutes of two or three class sessions to discuss what they have found and prepare a 10- to 15-minute presentation to the class. Presentations could be conducted the following week.

*Language is the medium through which we express our deepest thoughts. In spoken form it connects us to one another; in written form it allows us to cross time and space and enter new worlds of ideas.*

Lily Furedi, *Subway,* 1934

# Verbal Competence

On June 27, 1880, a remarkable woman was born. Although she graduated cum laude from Radcliffe College at the age of 24 and later became a famous author and lecturer, Helen Keller had to battle almost insurmountable odds. Many of you know her story. When she was a child she was struck with an illness that left her both blind and deaf for life. It was impossible for anyone to penetrate her dark and silent world. She developed a crude sign language, but she was constantly frustrated by her inability to communicate, often screaming and crying until she was exhausted.

All of this changed when Anne Sullivan became her teacher. Perhaps you recall the scene from *The Miracle Worker* in which the seven-year-old Helen first learns the meaning of language. She and Sullivan were in the well-house of the Keller home. Sullivan placed Helen's hands beneath the pump and spelled the word "w-a-t-e-r" into them. As she felt the cool liquid spill over her hands, Helen realized for the first time what words were. As she wrote later:

> That living word awakened my soul, gave it light, hope, joy, set it free! . . . I left the well-house eager to learn. Everything had a name, every object which I touched seemed to quiver with life. That was because I saw everything with the strange, new sight that had come to me.[1]

There are two ways to respond to this story. We can dwell on what Helen lacked and the obstacles she overcame. Or we can concentrate on what she gained that day at the well-house. What she gained was language, and with it history, literature, and culture. When she acquired language, she acquired access to the same symbolic world the rest of us inhabit. From that moment on, she didn't have to see or hear the world directly. She could share others' experiences.

This chapter is about what happens to each of us simply because we use language. It's about what language is, how it is put together, and how it affects us. We'll begin by defining language, paying particular attention to the ways the verbal code differs from the nonverbal. Next we'll look at language structure, examining semantic, syntactic, and pragmatic levels. We will then consider how language affects our thoughts and behaviors. Finally, we'll look at ways of over-

**87**

coming language confusion in order to increase message competence.

# What Is Language?

In this section we will compare verbal and nonverbal codes and describe some of the power that comes to us through language.

## Differences Between the Verbal and Nonverbal Codes

One of the major differences between verbal and nonverbal codes is that language is a digital code, while nonverbal is classified as analogic. Before we explain the differences between these codes, see if you can discover them for yourself by considering the examples shown in Figures 4.1 and 4.2. In the first figure, you see a drawing accompanied by a verbal description. Both the words and drawing describe the same subject, using different codes. The way the drawing conveys information is analogic; the way the written description conveys it is digital.

Now look at the second example. Figure 4.2 shows a braille translation of Helen Keller's description of her experience at the well-house. This is in a digital code. Next to it is a still from *The Miracle Worker* in which actors convey Helen's experience analogically. As a third example, think for a minute about the difference between a sundial and a digital clock. A sundial shows time by reflecting the actual movement of the sun across the sky, while a digital clock displays separate numbers that change at fixed intervals.[2]

Try listing adjectives that describe the analogic examples. What do the movement of the shadow on the sundial, the gestures of the actors, and the lines of the drawing have in common? Next, try to describe the digital examples. What similarities are there between the digital readout, the braille letters, and the written words? If, for the

TOADS are found in almost every part of the world. Members of the family Bufonidae, they are squat and fat, have short legs and a warty skin. They secrete a poisonous substance from the parotoid glands behind the eye. They feed on the larvae of harmful insects.

**FIGURE 4.1** *Analogic and digital representation of a toad.*

first set, you came up with words like *natural, continuous, immediate, similar,* or *relational,* you have grasped the nature of analogic codes. If, for the second set, you chose words like *artificial, abstract, arbitrary, separate,* or *logical,* then you've discovered the essence of digital codes.

**Analogic codes** indicate meaning by being similar to what they convey. The actors' movements are like those of real people experiencing real emotions. The lines in the drawing trace the natural shape and form of the object they represent. The movement of the shadow on the face of the sundial mirrors the passage of time. In analogic codes an expression and what it indicates are naturally connected. Many of the nonverbal behaviors we studied in Chapter 3 convey meaning analogically.

In **digital codes** meaning is conveyed symbolically. **Symbols** are units of meaning that are arbitrary and conventional. They're arbitrary because

**FIGURE 4.2**    *Analogic and digital representations of Helen Keller's experience at the well-house.*

I left the well-house eager to learn. Everything had a name, and each name gave birth to a new thought. As we returned to the house, every object I touched seemed to quiver with life.

the relationship they have to the things they represent is artificial rather than natural. Consider the word *joy,* for example. The fact that that particular combination of sounds and letters was chosen to represent the emotion is an arbitrary one. There is nothing particularly joyful in the word *joy*. The word stands for the emotion because people agreed that it should. Symbols are conventional, based on social agreement. We could easily change the meaning attached to the words in our language—if everyone within our language community agreed. Maybe the reason people react so emotionally to language changes is that such changes violate basic social contracts. At any rate, without knowing the conventions used to assign meaning to symbols, digital codes are impossible to understand.

We have seen that the way meanings are expressed differs in the two codes. The kinds of meanings they can express also differ. Analogic codes (especially those consisting of expressive behavior) seem to be best at conveying relationships and immediate emotional states. Digital codes are useful for more abstract, logical meanings. Assume that you don't know the story of Helen Keller. How much of it could you surmise by looking at the picture from *The Miracle Worker*? You could easily recognize that it involves two characters experiencing intense emotion. You might also understand what they're doing and what they feel for each other. What you could not understand is the history of their relationship or their interpretations of it. For this you would have to turn to digital reports.

## Characteristics of the Verbal Code

In Chapter 3 we listed some of the reasons nonverbal codes are so powerful. Language has a different kind of power. Four characteristics of the digital code distinguish it from the analogic code and allow us to act in otherwise impossible ways:[3]

1. *Verbal codes consist of discrete, separable units.* The structure of language is unique. It consists of units of sound and meaning that are discrete and separate. This fact gives language immense flexi-bility, for the units that make it up can be processed and manipulated more readily than those of the nonverbal codes. Words and sounds can be modified, combined in unique ways, and transmitted singly or in combination across time and space. They can be easily saved, stored, and retrieved. This is impossible in analogic codes. Although attempts have been made to break analogic displays into units and to write grammars describing their combinations, most have failed.[4]

2. *Language encourages us to create new realities.* One of the unique things about language is that it allows us to talk about absent or nonexistent things. Words don't need to have actual referents in the physical world. Of course, this is a mixed blessing. Language allows creativity, but it also allows us to deceive one another. In fact, Umberto Eco has defined language as "everything which can be used in order to lie."[5]

3. *Language gives us the ability to think in new and more complex ways.* Abstract nouns, logical words such as *and, or, all,* and *none,* and grammatical markers can't be expressed analogically. Such words allow the development of complex philosophical and mathematical systems. Language enhances our ability to think rationally and logically, although this doesn't mean we always do so.

4. *Verbal codes are self-reflexive.* Language can comment on itself; it allows us to talk about the way we talk. This quality is known as self-reflexiveness. It's what allows us to think about language and modify it when it doesn't work. Without this aspect of language, studying and improving communication would be impossible, for we would have no way to talk about it.

# The Functions of Language

Stop for a minute and think of all the things you normally do with language. Think of as many examples as you can, like commenting on the

## The Transforming Power of Language

# The Miracle Worker

Nadia Tass, 2000; Paul Aaron, 1979; Arthur Penn, 1962

The story of Annie Sullivan and Helen Keller has been told many times, most recently as a made-for-TV movie with Hallie Kate Eisenberg as Helen and Alison Elliott as Annie Sullivan, Helen's teacher. Although the original version is undoubtedly the best—Patty Duke and Anne Bancroft both won Oscars for their stunning performances—the more recent versions are worth viewing as well. All three tell the story of Sullivan's heroic fight to save Helen, blind and deaf for most of her young life, from the prison of her isolation. Sullivan's dilemma is not just to provide Helen with a language, but to make her comprehend what language is. Communication may not always go smoothly, but, no matter how difficult it may sometimes be to express our thoughts, the ability to use language is a miracle. It is impossible to see this film without gaining a new appreciation for the simple fact that we can communicate.

weather, reminiscing with old friends, describing last night's NFL telecast, memorizing facts, cursing, making jokes, talking to yourself, writing poetry, telling white lies, cheering a team to victory. Clearly language isn't just a vehicle for exchanging facts and seeking information. In this section we'll list some of the functions of language.[6]

1. *Language is often used to conquer the silent and the unknown.* We all have a need to escape from silence. When alone in a dark or quiet place, we often talk simply to make noise. Somehow, unbroken silence can be oppressive and frightening—by talking, we defend ourselves against the unknown. We also conquer the unknown by labeling it. Things without names are threatening and mysterious. We can reduce them to more human and manageable proportions by naming them; perhaps we believe something that is named can be controlled. If so, we are not far from a belief in the magical qualities of language.

2. *Language allows us to express and control emotion.* Some talk may simply be an attempt to reduce inner tension. Many psychologists believe that we have a biologically based need to vent emotions. Shouting in joy or cursing in anger are examples of this function. Of course, language can also be used to inhibit emotion. For example, we can talk ourselves into calming down. In a classic episode of *The Honeymooners*, Jackie Gleason's character, Ralph Kramden, repeats, "Pins and needles, needles and pins, the happy man is the man who grins," and then counts to 10, hoping by the time he's finished he'll have forgotten what he was angry about.

3. *Language can reveal or camouflage our thoughts and motives.* What goes on within us remains hidden unless we choose to show it to others. We can discuss inner feelings directly or reveal them more subtly. Freud was one of the first to turn our attention to the meanings of linguistic errors or slips of the tongue. He called these errors *parapraxes* and believed they were caused by inner conflicts.[7] If, for example, a speaker were to say quite sweetly, "We'll do whatever I—I mean you—want," the substitution might indicate a hidden need for control. Although to the trained ear parapraxes reveal inner feelings, they are attempts to hide true desires and designs from both self and other. Of course, we can use language as camouflage more directly; we can hide behind overt lies, evasions, and half-truths.

4. *Language permits us to make and avoid contact.* Language connects us to others. The telephone

company slogan "Reach out and touch someone" reflects this basic function. Telling someone "I just called to hear your voice" is using language to bridge distance. Often when we talk, our language converges, or becomes similar to that of our partners, in an unconscious impulse to connect. The study in this chapter's Research in Review illustrates how one person's politeness transfers to another during conversation. Of course, we can also talk to keep others away, either by using language that excludes them or by talking compulsively. Language can be a wall as well as a bridge.

5. *Language enables us to assert individual and social identity.* Each of us has a unique style; talk enables us to present it and thus an image of how we want to be perceived. At the same time, it also allows us to submerge ourselves in a group. Slang, jargon, and shared language games can signal social solidarity and a sense of belonging.

6. *Language may be used to give or seek information.* It almost goes without saying that language is an important medium for information exchange. It allows us to categorize and interpret the environment. Through language we can state, assert, describe, explain, and demonstrate the order we see around us. We also use language to gather information from others. Even seemingly trivial small talk, or *phatic communication,* can serve as social reconnaissance. Because survival is based on accurate predictions about the world, linguistic means of reducing uncertainty are essential.[8]

7. *Language allows us to control and be controlled by the world. Language is power.* It can be used to influence, regulate, persuade, or dominate. From making a good impression to brainwashing, we use language to control our world. Of course, language also controls us by affecting the way we perceive and think about the world. In many ways we are prisoners of language.

8. *Language can be used to monitor the process of communication.* As we noted earlier, language is self-reflexive; it allows us to *metacommunicate,* to communicate about the communication process. When two people discuss a topic of interest such as politics or religion, they are communicating. When they discuss their discussion, they are metacom-

municating. Metacommunication occurs when we use language to check communication channels ("Did you understand what I said?"), regulate the flow of talk ("Wait a minute. Let me finish making this point"), or comment on language patterns ("I know I change the subject whenever you make a good point. It's just that I can't stand to be on the losing end of an argument").[9]

---

# The Structure of Language: Three Levels of Meaning

Now that we know some of the functions of language, let's look briefly at how language is structured. Language can be analyzed on a number of levels.[10] The three we believe most important to the study of interpersonal communication are the word, the sentence, and the speech act. To understand and use language, we have to understand all these levels of meaning.

## Semantic Meaning: Language at the Level of the Word

Actually, to be technically correct, we should use the term *morpheme* rather than *word.* A morpheme is a linguistic unit of meaning. Although in most cases morphemes are equivalent to words, some word fragments also carry meaning. For example, the *s* that tells us a word is plural has meaning in its own right. Therefore, a word like *dogs* is actually made up of two morphemes: the word *dog* and the plural morpheme *s.*

The study of meaning at this level is called **semantics.** While a full discussion of semantic meaning is beyond the scope of this book, we can at least begin by considering two kinds of word meanings: denotative and connotative.

### Denotative and Connotative Meanings
**Denotative meaning** is public, conventional meaning. It is, in a sense, the meaning that was agreed upon when the language code was

*Please and Thank You,
Two Magic Words That Open
Any Door*

# Politeness Convergence in E-mail Communication

One of the interesting things about the way we use language is that the way we speak is often affected by the way others speak. In fact, according to communication accommodation theory (CAT), it is normal to make behavioral adjustments during conversation. One kind of adjustment, convergence, occurs when people in conversation begin to speak in similar ways. Convergence has been found in speech rate, utterance length, vocal intensity, self-disclosure, jokes, and so on. People have even been known to take on one another's accents.

In "Politeness Accommodation in Electronic Mail," Ulla Bunz and Scott Campbell wanted to see whether convergence could take place in computer-mediated communication. The language variable they choose to examine was politeness.

Bunz and Campbell began by telling their students that a visiting professor was looking for participants to fill out a survey and that this professor would contact them via e-mail with more information. The researchers then constructed four different messages, varying in politeness, which they sent to participants. Message 1 included the verbal politeness markers "thank you" and "please" in the body of the text. Message 2 included structural politeness markers in the opening ("Dear [first name of participant]") and closing ("Regards"). Message 3 included both verbal and structural elements, while Message 4 had neither forms of politeness. One hundred twenty-one students participated. The researchers asked the students to explain, in their replies, their reasons for participating. This was done to make sure there was ample opportunity for convergence to take place. The students' replies were then scored on the basis of the total number of politeness markers they contained.

As predicted, when verbal and structural politeness indicators were included in the message, subjects responded with significantly politer messages. It was found, however, that including both kinds of politeness did not stimulate more polite responses than including only one kind. Factors such as age, gender, and familiarity with e-mail had no effect on politeness responses. Overall, the research shows that although certain social cues may be filtered out by email technology, "politeness indicators are communicated, interpreted, and reciprocated," allowing communicators to build positive impressions online. More research investigating other social cues such as friendliness and personal closeness is currently in progress.

Bunz, Ulla, and Scott W. Campbell. "Politeness Accommodation in Electronic Mail." *Communication Research Reports* 21, no. 1 (2004): 11–25.

constructed. This kind of meaning belongs not to the individual but to the language system itself. To find out the denotative meaning of an unfamiliar word, we simply turn to an authoritative source such as the dictionary. That is why denotative meaning is often referred to as "dictionary meaning." **Connotative meaning** is private, often emotionally charged meaning. It becomes attached to words through experiences and associations. Here, individuals rather than the language system are the

*The desire to bind time by recording spoken communication is universal. The message in these hieroglyphs, written over 3,000 years ago, is accessible today to those who know how to break the verbal code.*

King's Scribe Amenhotep and His Wife Renut, c. 1275 B.C.

final authority. Consider the term *baseball*. Our dictionary tells us that its denotative meaning is

> *a game played with a ball, bat and gloves between two teams of nine players each on a large field centering on four bases that form the corners of a square 90 feet on each side, each team having a turn at bat and in the field during each of the nine innings that constitute a normal game, the winner being the team that scores the most runs.*[11]

While this definition expresses (albeit awkwardly) at least part of the meaning of baseball, it seems curiously flat. There is more to meaning than what is in the dictionary. Part of what is missing is connotative meaning.

We chose this example because we, your authors, have very different attitudes toward baseball. For one of us, baseball is a neutral concept. That author can recall attending only one major league game (when a team called the Senators played in Washington, D.C.). If asked to identify famous baseball players, she could probably list only those whose names are associated with candy bars. For the other, baseball has much stronger and more positive meanings. As a child, he played baseball every day of the summer, using flour from the kitchen to mark out a diamond on a homemade playing field. He memorized batting averages and followed every aspect of fellow Oklahoman Mickey Mantle's career. Even today he shows up at the office at the beginning of spring training wearing a Yankees baseball cap. For the two of us the term baseball has different connotations, as it does for each of you. There are as many connotations for a word as there are unique experiences with it.

### The Importance of Semantic Competence

Mastering the semantics of one's language is important, for no one can communicate competently without an appropriate vocabulary. People who use words incorrectly may talk on for hours without realizing they are conveying messages they never meant.

Lack of semantic competence can also lead to feelings of isolation and rejection. Group membership is often associated with access to special words. If you have ever heard others talk in unintelligible technical terms, you know how incompetent and left out you felt. It's impossible to fit into a professional or social group without mastering the jargon that group favors.

Sensitivity to connotations is also an important part of semantic competence. Many arguments start because one party inadvertently uses a word that has negative connotations for the other. Calling a woman you do not know well "honey" or referring to her as a "girl" are good examples. While some women may not mind, others find this usage belittling. Words like *love* and *commitment* and *responsibility* also carry strong emotional charges. They can cause relational problems if individuals attach different meanings to them. To be fully competent, it is necessary to realize that words call up different reactions in each of us.

## Syntactic Meaning: Language at the Level of the Utterance

Of course, words are rarely used in isolation; they usually occur in phrases or sentences. The study of the process by which words are combined and ordered into grammatical sequences is called **syntactics.**

### Order As Meaning

It's important to be able to order words appropriately. Had the previous sentence been written, "Important it's words appropriately order to be to able," you would have been confused at the very least. Probably you would have decided that your authors were suffering from some kind of mental disorder. Part of a word's meaning is its relationship to the words that precede and follow it.

Although in English a single word may mean several things, context usually makes its meaning clear. *Port,* for example, means something different in the context of "No, not starboard, you fool! Port!" than it does in the context of "Please don't drop that bottle of priceless vintage port."

Consider the difference between the sentences "The ship sails" and "Ship the sails."[12] The words are the same, but their order differs. Meaning based on word order is called **syntactic meaning.** For a more interpersonal example, consider the two sentences "Sam wants to marry Claudine" and "Claudine wants to marry Sam." Although the words are the same, the meanings are not. And it could make a real difference to both Sam and Claudine whether one or both meanings are intended.

### The Importance of Syntactic Competence

Strict rules govern sentence form. If we fail to abide by these rules, most people will react negatively. Syntax is thought to be a mark of social and economic status (which it often is) and also an indication of intellectual ability and moral rectitude (which it definitely is not). Syntax is a product of social learning, not native intelligence. We often believe that people who use "incorrect grammar" (grammar that violates our set of rules) are too "dumb" or "lazy" to use language

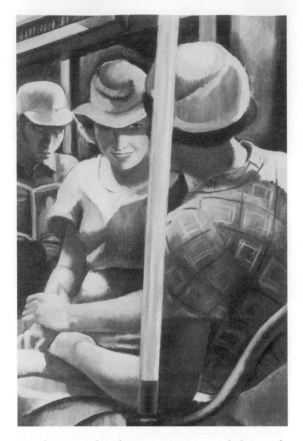

*People use spoken language to accomplish specific goals. One such goal might be the maintenance of a relationship between two friends.*

"the right way," and we let this perception shape our impressions. At the same time, use of so-called incorrect sentence forms among a particular social group can demonstrate the solidarity of group membership. Members of the same social group frequently make the same grammatical mistakes: "We *was* going to her house" instead of "We *were* going . . ." The perceptions attached to syntactic communication determine competence.

## Pragmatic Meaning: Language at the Level of the Speech Act

In order to understand communication, it is necessary to go beyond the semantic and syntactic levels. Having a good vocabulary and knowing the rules of sentence construction will not guarantee adequate communication. We have to know how to use sentences in actual conversation. **Pragmatics** investigates language as it is used in actual interaction.

### Language in Use

People don't generally talk just for the fun of it. When we use language, we use it to accomplish specific goals. The things we intend language to do for us are called speech acts.[13] Examples of **speech acts** are promising, questioning, threatening, praising, declaring, warning, requesting, and so on.

We said earlier that sentences can help us figure out the meanings of words. Speech acts can do the same for sentences. Knowing a sentence's meaning involves knowing its intended speech act. Let's say you've just written a poem. You're not sure how good it is, so you show it to a friend. Your friend reads it, thinks for a moment, and says, "I've never seen anything like it. It's unique." But what does this mean? Puzzling over the syntax and semantics of the sentence won't help you. In order to understand the message, you have to know what your friend was trying to do: compliment you, engage in literary criticism, or weasel out of saying anything at all. To be able to communicate, we must be able to assess the speech acts of others and formulate our own.

### CMM: Interpreting and Producing Speech Acts

How do we know what speech acts mean? And how do we know when and how to use them? A theory called the coordinated management of meaning (CMM for short) helps answer these questions.[14] According to CMM we know how to use language because we follow rules that tell us how to understand and produce speech acts. There are two kinds of rules in CMM theory: **constitutive rules,** which tell us how to recognize speech acts, and **regulative rules,** which identify, in a given context, the speech acts that are appropriate and inappropriate. Before looking at examples of these rules, let's consider how context affects communication behavior.

CMM theory tells us we have different rules for different contexts. What is appropriate in a heart-to-heart conversation is not appropriate at a formal dinner party. What is effective in showing a boss how responsible you are will not be effective in impressing a date. What works at home may not work at school. To communicate effectively, people must take into account the situation, their relationship, their self-images, and relevant cultural rules. Figure 4.3 shows the contexts that CMM identifies as important. The top portion of the figure lists the CMM contexts. As you can see, contexts are nested within one another, with higher levels including lower ones. Let's start near the bottom with the speech act. Speech acts make sense only when we understand the episode in which they occur. An **episode** is made up of a set of speech acts that fit together naturally. If you were to ask communicators, "What are you doing?" their answer would name the episode they're involved in. "Going for pizza," "shooting pool," "buying groceries," "having a barroom brawl," and "closing a big deal" are examples of episodes. Clearly, we expect different speech acts in different episodes—what is appropriate for the barroom may not be for the boardroom. If we know the episode in which an utterance occurs, we can fix its speech act more easily than if we hear it out of context. We'll also know which additional speech acts are appropriate and which would be out of place.

Another important context is the **relationship** between communicators. If you were to ask communicators, "Who are you to each other?" their answer would identify their relationship: student-teacher, husband-wife, boss-worker, and so on. Relationships determine episodes. Episodes such as "discussing one's fears and hopes," "showing affection," and "borrowing money and clothes" are usually appropriate for the relationship we call best friends. But they are not particularly likely if the relationship is professor-student. If we know a speaker's relationship to us, we are likely to understand his or her meanings. We will also be in a better position to do or say the correct thing.

The next context is **life script,** or your sense of self. It answers the question "Who am I or who

do I wish to be?" For example, a person at peace with nature and the universe enters into relationships, episodes, and speech acts that differ from those of an executive determined to make it to the top at all costs. The ways these two individuals interpret the world and the acts they consider legitimate are likely to be diametrically opposed. If we know who someone is, we're in a better position to understand that person's meanings and respond effectively to him or her. Finally, **cultural patterns** affect all other levels, since the groups we belong to determine the nature and function of talk.

## Using Pragmatic Rules in Interaction

How does all of this work in practice? Assume you hear the words "You look terrible today" and you want to know what the speaker meant. To interpret the speaker's intended speech act, you must consult your set of constitutive rules. To pick the right rule, you must use contextual cues; words have different meanings in different contexts.

If the statement is uttered by a physician in the episode of "physical examination," you will probably decide to count the words as a medical diagnosis. If it is uttered by a friend in an episode of "joking around," you will interpret it as the first move in a game of joking insults. Finally, if it is uttered in public by a subordinate who dislikes you, it may be seen as a "challenge to authority." Over the course of our lives, we build up a repertoire of interpretive rules that help us understand communication in a variety of contexts.

To respond to any comment, it is necessary to consult a regulative rule. Regulative rules tell you what speech acts are appropriate given your goals and your understanding of the context. In the case of the physical examination, your goal is probably to get information about your health. Your regulative rule set will tell you that insulting the doctor ("You think I look bad? Have you looked in a mirror lately, doc?") or asserting your authority ("That's quite enough. I'll see you in my office in half an hour") are not appropriate. Of course, these speech acts might be exactly the right thing to do if you are just joking around or if your authority is questioned. Your

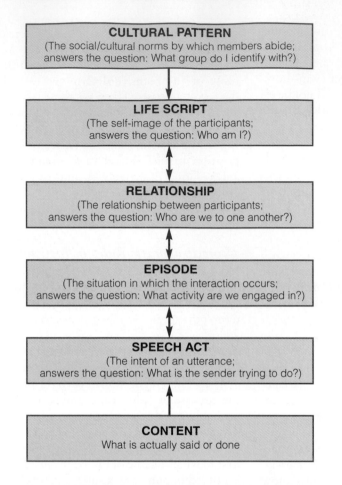

FIGURE 4.3 *Levels of hierarchical meaning in CMM theory.*

CULTURAL PATTERN
(The social/cultural norms by which members abide;
answers the question: What group do I identify with?)

LIFE SCRIPT
(The self-image of the participants;
answers the question: Who am I?)

RELATIONSHIP
(The relationship between participants;
answers the question: Who are we to one another?)

EPISODE
(The situation in which the interaction occurs;
answers the question: What activity are we engaged in?)

SPEECH ACT
(The intent of an utterance;
answers the question: What is the sender trying to do?)

CONTENT
What is actually said or done

|  | (Situation 1) | (Situation 2) | (Situation 3) |
|---|---|---|---|
| **Cultural Pattern:** | Middle-Class American | Middle-Class American | Middle-Class American |
| **Life Script:** | Educated Professional | Wild & Crazy Guy | Cold-blooded Egoist |
| **Relationship:** | Doctor/Patient | Pals | Rivals |
| **Episode:** | Medical Exam | Kidding Around | Business Meeting |
| **Speech Act:** | Diagnosis | Joke | Put-down |
| **Content:** | | **"You look terrible today"** | |

Each level adds meaning to levels above and below. Communication makes sense only in reference to the context in which it occurs.

## Overcoming Language Barriers

# *Spanglish*

James L. Brooks, 2004

Celebrity chef John Clasky (Adam Sandler) and his neurotic wife Deborah (Tea Leoni) aren't doing very well. Their marriage is on shaky ground, they aren't on the same page when it comes to raising their children, and they don't even agree about how to treat the dog. Into their lives come the beautiful Flor (Paz Vega) and her daughter Christina (Shelbie Bruce), who've left their native Mexico to search of a better life in Los Angeles. Flor takes a job as the Clasky's housekeeper and soon finds herself involved in their lives. Although at first Flor can't speak a word of English and must rely on her daughter to translate, she intuitively understands the Claskys better than they understand themselves.

The tagline tells us that *Spanglish* is "a comedy with a language all its own," and in many ways the film is about people searching for language. John and Deborah have lost the ability to talk to one another; in the guise of helping her daughter Bernice (Sarah Steele), Deborah only hurts her; and Christina is so enamored of the Clasky's lifestyle that she (almost) turns her back on Flor. Ultimately it is Flor, the one character without a firm command of language, who manages to help the family solve their problems and find a way to reach out to one another.

rule for the medical episode may read, "Given this context and my desire to get advice from my doctor, the proper speech act for me to perform is a polite request for further information." You then translate this speech act into something like "What treatment do you suggest?"

### The Importance of Pragmatic Competence

Communicating appropriately isn't easy. Embarrassment results when contexts are misinterpreted or rule sets are inadequate. If you have ever burst into a conversation with some trivial remark, only to realize that you interrupted a serious discussion, you know how important it is to label episodes correctly. If you have ever come on too strong too soon with someone, you know how tricky reading relationships can be. If you have ever interpreted an innocent remark as a threat to self, you have seen the way life scripts affect perception. Part of mastering pragmatic competence is being able to identify contextual levels accurately.

Communication is a complex, rule-bound process. If we learn to do it well, our relationships will be easy and rewarding. If we have trouble with pragmatic rules, the world can be a hostile place. In fact, it's been argued that many interpersonal problems result from differences in pragmatics.

# Language, Power, and Politics

Language is a powerful tool. It allows us to express feelings, share information, and achieve goals. Every day we use language to control our worlds. But, if we're not careful, language can control us. In this section we examine the power of language to emancipate and to oppress. We'll begin by discussing one of the earliest formulations of the relationship between language, thought, and action, the Sapir-Whorf hypothesis. We'll then look at how different groups learn to

**99**

use language differently and, as a consequence, come to understand themselves and their actions in unique ways. Finally, we'll look at some recent theories that emphasize the political dimensions of language use.

## Linguistic Determinism: The Sapir-Whorf Hypothesis

The influence of language on thought has been strongly articulated by two linguists, Edward Sapir and Benjamin Lee Whorf.[15] Their analysis of the effects of language on cognition, the **Sapir-Whorf hypothesis,** has two important parts. The first, **linguistic determinism,** says that language determines the way we interpret the world. In the words of Sapir, "we see and hear and otherwise experience very largely as we do because the language habits of our community predispose certain choices of interpretation."[16] The second part of their hypothesis, **linguistic relativity,** follows from the first. If language determines thought, then speakers of different languages will experience the world differently. Thought is relative to language.

Let's look at some evidence for this hypothesis. If you have studied a foreign language, you know that other languages often make distinctions that English doesn't. In English, for example, we simply say *you* when we want to talk to someone directly. In Spanish there are two forms of you, a polite form (*usted*) to be used with older persons, strangers, or those of high status, and a familiar form (*tu*). In Spanish it is grammatically necessary to mark that point in a relationship when participants change from being mere acquaintances to friends.

Not only do different languages tell us how to talk to one another, they also specify what to talk about. Different languages recognize different categories of experience. The words for colors are a classic example. In English there are seven basic colors in the spectrum (purple, indigo, blue, green, yellow, orange, and red). In Bassa, a Liberian language, there are only two: *hui* (which includes our purple, indigo, blue, and green) and *ziza* (which covers yellow, orange, and red).[17]

Another frequently cited example is the fact that Eskimos have many more words for snow than we do. These words enable them to talk about distinctions most non-Eskimos could not perceive. This doesn't mean that Liberians couldn't learn to make fine-color distinctions or that southerners could not learn to see different kinds of snow. It only means that it will be harder to do these things. Without a name for something, it takes longer to distinguish that thing from other things, and the distinctions are less stable.[18] Both the color and snow examples illustrate how our language separates things that are continuous in nature. The color spectrum is just that, a spectrum, not a collection of separate things. As Whorf tells us:

> *English terms, like "sky, hill, swamp," persuade us to regard some elusive aspect of nature's endless variety as a distinct THING, almost like a table or chair. Thus English and similar tongues lead us to think of the universe as a collection of rather distinct objects and events corresponding to words. Indeed, this is the implicit picture of classical physics and astronomy—that the universe is essentially a collection of detached objects of different sizes.[19]*

Some American Indian languages preserve the unity of nature more fully than English. Sentences in these languages don't consist of nouns and verbs. If, for example, an English speaker were to see a light flash in the summer sky, he or she would say, "The light flashed." The action that took place would be indicated by a verb, while that which caused the action would be indicated by a separate noun and article. The Hopi speaker, however, would not divide what was seen into two parts. To the Hopi, the flashing and the light are one and are indicated by one simple "verb," *rehpi.*[20]

The Sapir-Whorf hypothesis tells us that English speakers don't normally see the world the same way Hopi speakers see it. While we may not be complete prisoners of our language, we are deeply affected by its structure. Every language encourages and aids its speakers in some endeavors while making other kinds of thoughts and actions more difficult. Box 4.1 illustrates how the Western Apache use language to comfort and counsel one another.

## Language, Thought, and Action: Language and Naming

The Sapir-Whorf hypothesis argues that language shapes our understanding of the world. The results of this process can be both positive and negative. Language allows us to imagine new worlds and to reflect upon our own behaviors, but it also causes us to distort reality, create stereotypes, and lie. Let's consider some examples of how language affects everyday thought and action.

According to the Sapir-Whorf hypothesis, language allows us to make certain aspects of reality significant by naming them. Conversely, it allows us to ignore unimportant parts of reality by not naming them. Naming has important implications because it is easier to notice and think about a thing that has been named. Consider, for example, two terms that did not exist as part of our language until recently: *sexual harassment* and *date rape*. Although the behaviors associated with these terms have existed for a long time, because they were not named they were not recognized. They lacked legitimacy, and their victims had no way of defining what had happened to them. Once the terms entered our language, it became possible to discuss these problems and work to put an end to them.[21]

In addition to naming things, language also gives things value. Many years ago, a group of theorists called symbolic interactionists pointed out that words consist of action plans. A word not only tells us that something exists but suggests how to think and what to do about it. Consider the object we refer to as a cat. To some it is a *pet*, to some it is merely *food*, and to still others it is a variety of *vermin*. The way we talk about it determines how we think about it and how we act toward it. Or, consider some of the common

terms that refer to women: *Babe*, *broad*, *lady*, *girl*, and *woman* have very different connotations and call for very different actions. The behaviors we are likely to use with a *broad* are very different than those we are likely to use with a *young lady* or with a *woman*.

## Group Membership and Language Use: Discourse and Identity

Our language habits affect not only how we see the world and how we act toward others, but how we view ourselves as well. People who belong to different groups develop different language habits, and these habits have important consequences for the way they think about themselves and the ways they live their lives. Gender and class are two groups associated with different styles of discourse. Box 4.2 gives an example of how both these factors affect language use.

### Social Class and Discourse

British sociologist Basil Bernstein studied the way class membership is related to language usage.[22] He found that working-class language employs shorter, simpler, and more conventionalized grammatical forms, while middle-class syntax exhibits more variety and complexity. Middle-class speakers make more complex grammatical decisions; Bernstein refers to their code as the **elaborated code.** Working-class speakers tend to use grammar in more rigidly determined ways, employing commonly shared forms; for this reason he calls their language code the **restricted code.**

More interesting are pragmatic differences. Bernstein believes that the primary purpose of elaborated codes is to convey information. Elaborated-code speakers try to use language precisely, being careful to fill in all of the details a listener might need. Restricted-code users, on the other hand, emphasize the social aspects of language, using it as a tool for building social identity and binding the individual to the group. They assume listeners don't need to have background information spelled out. The following dialogue is a good example of a restricted code.[23]

BOX 4.1

## Speaking with Names

# An Apache Language Ritual

For those of us who study interpersonal communication, language becomes most interesting when we see people using it to affect one another. Language is important not because it is an immensely complex abstract system, but because people use it to build interpersonal bonds. In an article titled "'Speaking with Names,'" anthropologist Keith Basso describes how the Western Apache of east-central Arizona use a specialized form of speaking to comfort, advise, and support one another.

Basso begins by describing the circumstances under which he first became aware of the language ritual known as speaking with names. A number of friends are seated together in the shade on a hot and dusty late afternoon. Present with Basso are Emily and Louise, Lola and her husband Robert, and their old yellow dog, Clifford. Louise is upset because her younger brother has become ill and has been taken to the hospital. Adding to her distress is the fact that earlier in the month her brother had inadvertently stepped on a snakeskin. Instead of seeking the services of a "snake medicine person" to perform a ritual cleansing, her brother laughed off the incident, thus showing disrespect for traditional teachings and putting himself in some danger of illness or death. Although it is not usual for the Western Apache to disclose personal details like this about their relatives, Louise has mentioned her fears. The following occurs in response. Lola is the first to speak, saying, "It happened at line of white rocks, extending upward and out, at this very place." After a long pause, Emily adds, "Yes. It happened at whiteness spreads out descending to water, at this very place." After another pause, Lola breaks in, "Truly. It happened at trail extends across a long red ridge with alder trees, at this very place." Louise laughs softly as Robert, and then Lola, add, "Pleasantness and goodness will be forthcoming." Louise, much comforted, ends the interaction by turning to Clifford and asking, "My younger brother is foolish, isn't he, dog?"

To most of us, the meaning of this bit of talk is puzzling. We understand the language but cannot fathom its social meaning. All we can tell is that its meaning was clear to the participants and its effects on Louise profoundly comforting. In an effort to understand the web of social understandings in which this conversation is embedded, Basso turned to a native informant, Lola. From her account he was able to piece together the meanings hidden below the words and sentences that had been uttered.

Lola began by explaining, "We gave that woman [i.e., Louise] pictures to work on in her mind. We didn't speak too much to her. We didn't hold her down. That way she could travel in her mind. . . . We gave her clear pictures with place names. So her mind went to those places, standing in front of them as our ancestors did long ago." To understand what Lola means, it's necessary to understand the importance of place names in Apache story-telling. Western Apache narratives are "spatially anchored" to specific locations, and these locations are labeled with descriptive place names. In form, place names provide not only a way of locating a place, but a point from which to view it. When speakers hear a place name, they imagine themselves traveling to that place and standing at the exact location as did their ancestors who first described that place.

Place names evoke with surprising power and clarity all the ancestral events associated with a location. When Apache people practice "speaking with names" they are recommending that their listeners recall an ancestral story and apply it to their personal problems.

When Lola mentioned the first place name, she was trying to do a number of things. First, she was avoiding potentially embarrassing criticism of Louise's brother. She was also shifting attention to Louise herself and showing sympathy and concern. In addition, she was asking Louise to recall a particular story associated with the place name she chose. The situation that had happened at "line of white rocks extends upward and out" concerned a young girl who, while collecting fire wood, slipped and was bitten by a snake. When her arm became badly swollen, a curing ceremony was performed. The girl then returned to her grandmother, affirming that she now knew how to "live right." When Basso asked Louise how she had reacted to the place name, Louise reported that her mind had instantly traveled to that spot and pictured vivid images of the girl. Louise had connected the girl in the story to her brother. Something bad had happened to the girl because she had ceased to think properly, but she was saved and learned from her mistake.

Emily's place name evoked a similar story concerning a young boy who was sick for a long time because he failed to follow ritual demands but who got better and remembered the lesson all his life. Again, Louise received intense images, reporting that she could hear the central character as he talked to his own children. The third place name, mentioned by Lola, was something of a risk, for the tale associated with it was off-color and humorous, concerning a young man who had to walk around clutching his crotch after he became infected because he violated a sexual taboo. Fortunately, Lola's strategy worked,

and Louise laughed as she pictured the young man. Afterwards, Louise commented, "[The boy] was impulsive, He didn't think right. Then he got scared. Then he was made well again with medicine. . . . I've heard that story often, but it's always funny to see that boy holding on to himself, so shy and embarrassed" (p. 240). Robert and Lola, recognizing Louise's change in mood, then spoke to make the message of all these stories explicit by saying, "Pleasantness and goodness will be forthcoming." Louise closed the conversation by addressing the dog Clifford with a gentle criticism of her brother, a comment that told the others, in effect, "Nothing more need be said; you were polite and thoughtful not to criticize my brother, and I thank you for comforting me."

Basso's analysis is fascinating because it shows how much pragmatic meaning can be conveyed by a simple conversation. The ritual of speaking with names performed many functions: it produced a mental image of a location, evoked prior stories, affirmed the value of ancestral wisdom, displayed tactful attention to the face of the participants, signaled charitable concern, offered practical advice, transformed distressing thoughts, and healed Louise's wounded spirits. This example shows us how important a sensitive and caring use of language can be. Basso concludes, "Such powerful moments may not be commonplace in Western Apache speech communities, but they are certainly common enough—and when they occur, as on that hot and dusty day at Cibecue, robust worlds of meaning come vibrantly alive" (p. 244).

**SOURCE** Keith H. Basso, "'Speaking with Names': Language and Landscape Among the Western Apache," in *Rereading Cultural Anthropology*. George E. Marcus, ed. (Durham, N.C.: Duke University Press, 1992), pp. 220–51.

BOX 4.2

*Talking Tough in Teamsterville*

# Male Role Enactment in an Urban Community

Talk is not valued the same in every community. Some cultures encourage talk while others inhibit it. But all develop strict rules about how to talk. In Teamsterville (the label for a blue-collar neighborhood in Chicago) talk is carefully regulated. The men in Teamsterville grow up with circumscribed ideas about the value of talk. Let's look at these ideas.

Teamsterville men know that talking in certain situations will cast doubt on their manliness. For example, self-disclosure or serious talk with women or children is not considered manly. Responding to an insult or to insubordination by talking it out is definitely bad form. The Teamsterville man demeans himself if he responds to a challenge verbally rather than physically. Teamsterville men also avoid talking to status superiors. Talk with authority figures or strangers is mediated through professional speakers like local precinct captains, Catholic parish priests, or union stewards.

When does the Teamsterville man feel free to converse? When he is with his male friends. The place most appropriate for speaking is the street, sidewalk, and, to a lesser extent, porch.

Teamsterville men devalue talk in cases where other men would value it. Compare Teamsterville rules with those followed by white-collar suburbanites or black Americans in urban ghettos. In both of these cultures, being verbal is considered an advantage. The ghetto dweller takes pride in his ability to play word games like the dozens (see Box 13.2). The white suburbanite believes that talking things out is an appropriate way of building relationships.

And the places for talk also differ by culture. Talk in an upper-middle-class suburb takes place in private, sheltered areas such as living rooms or backyards. Visitors are usually from outside a 10-block radius. Adults don't socialize on front porches or in front yards.

It might be tempting for some of us to consider Teamsterville men as linguistically deprived. That conclusion, however, misses the point. All of us are constrained by cultural norms for using language. All of us feel comfortable speaking in some situations and with some people, and uncomfortable elsewhere. The meaning and value of communication are set down for us by our culture.

**SOURCE**  Gerry Philipsen, "Speaking 'Like a Man' in Teamsterville: Cultural Patterns of Role Enactment in an Urban Neighborhood," *Quarterly Journal of Speech* 61 (1975): 13–22.

**ADDITIONAL READINGS**

Hymes, Dell. "Models of the Interaction of Language and Social Life." In *Directions in Sociolinguistics: The Ethnography of Communication.* John J. Gumberz and Dell Hymes, eds. New York: Holt, Rinehart & Winston, 1972.

Philipsen, Gerry. "Places for Speaking in Teamsterville." *Quarterly Journal of Speech* 62 (1976): 16–25.

Gary and George are friends who are discussing their plans for the evening.

GARY  How's about Trucker's tonight?

GEORGE  A little stick, eh?

GARY  Why not?

GEORGE  Okay, mine or yours?

GARY  Oh no! Every man for himself . . . wife, you know.

GEORGE  (*to his new neighbor*) Why don't you come along too?

*The emotional impact of another's words can be far-reaching.*

Bas Jan Ader, *I'm Too Sad to Tell You,* 1970

NEIGHBOR (*with no idea of what he is getting himself into*) Sounds great!

Although our original source didn't give a direct translation into elaborated code, we can imagine that it would go something like this:

GARY  How would you like to go to our favorite country-western bar tonight, the one called Trucker's?

GEORGE  Do you mean to play pool?

GARY  Yes, why not?

GEORGE  OK, let's go together. Should we take your car or mine?

GARY  Oh no, we'd better go separately. My wife wants me to come home early tonight.

GEORGE  (*to the neighbor*) Why don't you come along too?

NEIGHBOR (*understanding completely*) Sounds great!

As you can see, restricted codes are not well designed for use with outsiders. They rely heavily on shared assumptions and expectations, and they encourage social solidarity. They're often found in groups who are, or want to be, set apart from society at large. Prison inmates and adolescents are examples cited by Bernstein. The "dorm talk" college students use with roommates and friends may be another.

Elaborated codes, on the other hand, do little to emphasize group identity. They encourage a more distant approach to communication. While there is a correlation between code and class, code switching can and does occur. Bernstein's point is that the economic and social conditions associated with class make it likely that classes will use language differently much of the time.

Because of these differences, members of different classes may devalue one another's speech. To restricted-code users, those with elaborated codes may seem cold and stilted. Restricted-code users may also feel embarrassed about their language, letting elaborated-code users define the value of their talk. One of the reasons Teamsterville men are so silent is that they view speaking as difficult and their own language style as "substandard." To elaborated-code users, restricted-code speakers may seem illogical and overly emotional, even, perhaps, uneducated or unintelligent. These differences can cause problems in cross-class communication. Think, for example, of how code differences might affect the relationship between a working-class child and a middle-class teacher.

### Gender and Discourse

Do men and women communicate differently? According to folk wisdom and popular belief, the answer is a resounding "yes." It sometimes seems, that when it comes to communication, men and women are from entirely different planets. And until fairly recently, most scholars would have guardedly agreed, for there is a large body of research detailing male/female differences. Studies done in the 70s and 80s argue that men and women's communicative styles differ in significant ways.[24]

*Early Findings.*   Early studies found that gender affects how much we talk as well as how we use talk. When it comes to amount of talk, the nature and goals of the interaction seem to determine whether men or women talk more. *In some situations men talk more, while in others women talk more.* In task-oriented mixed-sex groups, for example, men have been found to talk more than women. In same-sex friendships, however, women appeared to be more talkative.

Early studies also found that *the role of talk in building relationships differs for men and women.* Studies have found that women value "talk for talk's sake" and use talk to build friendships. Men, on the other hand, talk more in goal-directed situations and prefer to bond through shared physical activities rather than through talk.[25] An interesting example of differential bonding styles can be seen in the attitudes men and women hold toward "trouble talk." A number of studies show that males respond to their male friends' problems by downplaying them or giving direct advice, while females respond by exploring the problems in detail and sharing troubles of their own. The stories friends prefer to tell also follow this pattern. Females are more willing to tell stories about situations in which they failed or looked bad, while men prefer to tell stories about successes.[26]

*Men and women also manage conversations differently.* Studies suggest that, in mixed-sex dyads, men interrupt women more and, when interrupted, women give up the floor more readily. Men also use more delayed minimal responses ("Oh" after a brief pause) that may discourage interaction. On the other hand, women's minimal responses ("Hmmm, I see") occur within turns and seem to encourage talk.[27]

Not only do men and women differ in amount and purpose of talk, the actual language forms males and females prefer may also differ. *Men and women have different vocabularies,* in part because social roles focus their attention on different areas of experience. Women, for example, make finer color distinctions than men, while men have greater mechanical-technical vocabularies. It has also been suggested that women are more likely to use words such as *lovely, adorable, precious,* and *fabulous,* adjectives that men avoid. Finally, women have been shown to use weaker expletives and less intense words to express themselves.[28]

*Men and women also differ in the ways they construct sentences.* Researchers have found that women use more **qualifiers** (words like *somewhat, kind of, maybe*) than men do. Women also appear to use more **tag endings** (fragments such as "right?" or "OK?" tacked onto the end of sentences) and **disclaimers** (sentences that ward off criticisms, like, "Well, I may be wrong, but . . ." or "Now hear me out before you say anything").[29] Taken together, these characteristics have been labeled the **female register,** and studies have shown that there is a cost to using this kind of communication. In several studies speakers who used tag endings, qualifiers, disclaimers, and the like were evaluated as warmer and more caring but at the same time less credible, competent, and intelligent.[30] When speakers of either sex use the female register they appear more tentative and uncertain, but the negative effect is larger for women than for men.[31]

Early scholars went beyond cataloguing male-female differences. They argued that differences in communication style could lead to serious misunderstandings between men and women. Linguist Deborah Tannen argued that men and women belong to two different cultures and that male-female interaction can be seen as a case of cross-cultural communication.[32] For example, Tannen reported that men and women use different patterns of disclosure. She argued that men tend to discuss their feelings about relationships only when they feel there is a problem that needs to be fixed and, at other times, prefer to avoid relationship talk; women, however, are often more comfortable discussing feelings and believe that a relationship where feelings are not expressed is problematic. Obviously, if partners in a close relationship follow this pattern, they are more likely to misinterpret each other's communication and work at cross-purposes.

*Recent Criticisms.* While not dismissing early research completely, a spate of recent studies have been more cautious in interpreting gender differences. Elizabeth Aries, for example, points out that the differences that have been found, although statistically significant, are relatively small. We should therefore not give them more importance than they deserve. For example, a study of jury deliberations by Fred Strodtbeck and R. D. Mann is widely cited as showing that men are more task oriented than women. Although men in the study did offer more task-oriented contributions than women, examination of the actual data shows that 79 percent of men's interaction was task oriented, whereas 63 percent of women's was. A difference of 16 percent, while noticeable, is not extremely large, and it should not be used to suggest that women cannot communicate in task-oriented ways. (In this study they did, almost two-thirds of the time.)[33]

Aries also points out that gender differences may occur in one context yet disappear in another. For example, several studies suggest gender differences may be greater in initial encounters or when people interact for short periods of time than in more long-lasting situations where people can get to know one another.[34] As a result of findings like these, Aries tells us, "we need an understanding of the ways gender operates that goes beyond the notion of men and women possessing two contrasting interaction styles" and sees gender "as something people do in social interaction—as the performance of gender-related behaviors in certain contexts."[35]

Finally, Aries notes that many of the differences we see between men and women can be accounted for by other variables, in particular by power and social status; she tells us, "when men and women are placed in the same role or are given the same legitimate authority, many gender differences in behavior are mitigated."[36] For example, Cathryn Johnson has shown that when men and women are assigned to act as managers but given the same amount of authority, their patterns of conversation are quite similar.[37]

What recent critics are suggesting is not that we should throw out older research, but rather that we should interpret it carefully. One of their greatest concerns is that we not draw unfair conclusions. The research on interruptions is a case in point. If we believe that interruptions are always disconfirming indicators of dominance, and if we find out that men interrupt women more than women interrupt men, then we are left with a picture of controlling men and subservient women. If, however, we recognize that some interruptions may signal high involvement and social comfort, then we emerge with a very different picture.[38] Similarly if we interpret tag endings to unfailingly signal uncertainty, then a study that finds women using more tags than men may suggest that women are less confident and more tentative than men. If, however, we recognize that some tags show affiliation and are used to encourage interaction, as recent researchers have, then we draw a different conclusion.[39]

Gender is one of the most important categories we use to understand human behavior, and, because it is used so often, we tend to rely on stereotypes to simplify our thinking. It is therefore important to make sure the stereotypes we use are based on real, rather than contrived, expectations. Drawing conclusions about gender differences is more complex than we once assumed it was. Yet, this complexity can help us to be more fair and accurate when it comes to evaluating one another's communication. By being sensitive to false assumptions, we can avoid damaging stereotypes. And by recognizing true differences and understanding where and when they are likely to occur, we can become more insightful interpreters of meaning.

## Language, Domination, and Freedom

If language is so closely tied to thought and action, then it follows that whoever controls language controls thought and action. This position has been argued by a number of scholars who refer to themselves as **critical theorists.** They point out that whenever we choose words, we choose points of view as well. This choice may be an unconscious acceptance of the assumptions that lie within our class or culture or it may be a conscious attempt to manipulate. Metaphors are one example. Compare the following two newspaper headlines: "Flood of immigrants pours into town" and "Neighbors from across the border join hands with local business people." The effect is entirely different. The first portrays the presence of the immigrants as dangerous and potentially disastrous; the second represents them as a positive addition to the community. The headline writer may be unaware of the political implications of his or her word choices, but they are there nonetheless. The use of euphemisms is yet another example. When a military commander advocates using a "clean bomb" with a minimum of "collateral damage," it's easy to forget that he or she is talking about a bomb that is capable of wiping out whole cities and that the "collateral" damage being discussed is human life.

One of the things that happens when one group controls language is that the experiences of other groups may be ignored or devalued, either overtly (as when racist or sexist terms are common) or covertly (where the devaluation is more subtle.) Critical theorists believe that traditional ways of using language reflect and validate the experiences of dominant groups. One example of this line of reasoning is the feminist argument that traditional academic discourse values logic, abstract thought, argument, and convergent problem solving, qualities more often associated with male experience than with female experience. Such discourse has little space for the more "fe-

male" qualities of emotional expression, concern for process, modesty, and caring.[40] When a subordinate group cannot find a way to express itself in the terms dictated by the dominant group, critical theorists say that group has been silenced. **Muted-group theorists** have suggested that women often feel less comfortable in public situations than do men. Women therefore "watch what they say and translate what they are feeling and thinking into male terms. When masculine and feminine meanings and expressions conflict, the masculine tends to win out because of the dominance of males in society, and the result is that women are muted."[41]

Of course, not all language is harmful or oppressive. It is through language, after all, that we can discuss and critique these problems. Language can be reformed, and newer and fairer modes of expression can be developed. The efforts made to rid our language of sexist bias are a case in point.

## Avoiding Sexist Language

Derogatory attitudes toward men and women can easily slip into language. In fact, it is often difficult to follow normal patterns of talk without reinforcing sexual stereotypes. In this section we'll look at a few of the many examples of sexism in our language and offer some guidelines for communicating in a more fair and equal way. It's important to keep in mind that this analysis looks at just one kind of oppressive language. Racist and heterosexist language patterns also bear the same kind of examination and analysis.

Let's begin with occupations. Occupations tend to be semantically classed as male or female. This is shown by the fact that when a person of the "wrong" sex enters a given occupation, we feel the need to mark that fact linguistically. A woman can be described as a "nurse" with no difficulty, but her male counterpart is usually referred to as a "male nurse." We indicate our surprise in the same way when we find a woman doing a "man's job." Thus, people talk about the new "lady mayor" or report they are seeing a "woman doctor."

Another kind of gender marker is the -ess or -ette diminutive form used in constructions like authoress, poetess, or sculptress. This usage often connotes that the individual being described is not as competent or powerful as her male counterpart. This form singles out women as special cases, as odd exceptions to the rule. We take a poet seriously, but there is something slightly humorous about a poetess.

Terms of address often contain subtle inequalities. It is quite common for a woman to be addressed by belittling terms in public contexts. Clerks or salespersons will much more frequently call a woman "honey," "sweetie," or "dear," than they will a man, who is most often addressed as "sir." And have you ever wondered why the marriage ceremony pronounces a couple "man and wife" rather than "husband and wife"? Wife, after all, is a relational term that defines the bride in terms of her new role, while man is an absolute term. To see this more clearly, consider how meaningless it would be to say, "I now pronounce you man and woman."

What are we to make of the fact that there are more than 10 times as many sexual terms for females as for males, and that many of these terms tend to have negative connotations? Barbara and Gene Eakins tell us that "for women, the act defines the person: as slut, nympho, hooker, trick, whore, and so on."[42] This tendency to talk about women in physical terms is also reflected in our propensity to describe women's physical appearance more than men's. When Vice President Dan Quayle was nominated, the headline didn't read "Blonde cutie gets convention nod," but such ludicrous descriptions are often given of women. Eakins and Eakins cite a few examples:

*A woman running for political office is described as being "a petite grandmother with the figure of a twenty-year-old"; a lawyer being interviewed about her views on the Equal Rights Amendment is described as "well put together"; an artist exhibiting her paintings is portrayed as having a "low husky laugh" and "soft grey eyes"; an athlete is referred to as "a brown-eyed cutie." The women described are not candidates for Miss America or models. . . . . They are women functioning in politics, law, the arts, and athletics.[43]*

Another important way in which language discriminates is through use of the generic "man" forms. On the one hand, when we talk of "mankind" or say that "each person should examine his conscience," we supposedly mean both men and women. On the other hand, as Eakins and Eakins suggest, when someone uses masculine generics "in a general sense and another interprets the word as specifically masculine, there is a miscommunication and females are unintentionally excluded from the idea or statement."[44] Language reflects attitudes toward gender in many other ways. We refer you to Robin Lakoff's classic article "Language and Woman's Place" for an excellent overview.[45] We are not arguing here that language by itself causes sexism—the roots of sexism run much deeper than that. What we are suggesting is that sexist language legitimizes and reinforces sexist thinking and that, without realizing it, we often talk in ways that are insulting and offensive to others. To avoid sexist speech, check yourself against the guidelines for nonsexist language given in Table 4.1.

# Skill Building: Initiating Conversation

Throughout this chapter we have commented on the importance of becoming more competent in all aspects of language. To communicate effectively one must master semantics, syntactics, and pragmatics. While all are important, pragmatics probably plays the key role in interpersonal effectiveness. Language becomes important when we use it to make contact with others. And one

In writing or in speaking, it is easy to perpetuate gender stereotypes without realizing it. As a result, many professional organizations provide guidelines for reducing bias. Listed here are some typical recommendations for using more inclusive language.

1. Avoid the generic use of gendered pronouns.

| Biased | Unbiased |
|---|---|
| A person's facial expression does not always reveal his true feelings. | Facial expressions are not always indicators of a person's true feelings. |
| As someone ages, his financial needs change. | As one ages, one's financial needs change. |

2. Avoid the use of the word man to apply to all people. In general avoid most -man words.

| Biased | Unbiased |
|---|---|
| Mankind | Humankind, people |
| Man-made | Manufactured, hand-made |
| Congressman | Representative, member of Congress |
| Fireman | Fire fighter |
| Policeman | Police officer |

3. Do not presume that people whose gender is unknown or unspecified are male.

| Biased | Unbiased |
|---|---|
| Dear Sir | Dear Colleague, Dear Editor, etc. |
| Nowadays people work so hard that they have no time to spend with their wives and children. | Nowadays people work so hard that they have no time to spend with their families. |

4. Avoid titles, labels, and names whose connotations are not parallel.

| Biased | Unbiased |
|---|---|
| The men and the ladies | The men and the women (or the gentlemen and the ladies) |
| The men in the office bought coffee for the girls. | The men in the office bought coffee for the women in the office. |
| Betty is Mr. Smith's assistant. | Mrs. Bates is Mr. Smith's assistant. |
| Mr. and Mrs. John Andrews | Mr. and Mrs. Andrews (or John and Mary Andrews) |
| I now pronounce you man and wife. | I now pronounce you husband and wife. |

5. Avoid connecting certain professions with only one gender.

| Biased | Unbiased |
|---|---|
| An executive should take *his* subordinates' feelings into account. | Executives should take subordinates' feelings into account. |
| A nurse should communicate clearly with *her* patients. | Nurses should communicate clearly with their patients. |

6. Avoid making unwarranted assumptions about the inherent abilities or characteristics of men and women; make sure that adjectives do not contain implicit judgments.

| Biased | Unbiased |
|---|---|
| Although a woman, she heads up a large corporation. | She is head of a large corporation. |
| Although a man he is sensitive and caring. | He is sensitive and caring. |
| I now pronounce you man and wife. | I now pronounce you husband and wife. |
| The men were aggressive; the women were pushy. | The men and women were assertive. |

of the best ways we make contact is through everyday conversation. Making casual small talk is not a trivial pursuit. It allows us to initiate and maintain relationships, to find out more about the world and ourselves. As noted previously, when a conversation goes well, we feel in tune with the world; when it goes badly, we feel awkward and isolated. In this section we'll look at a special conversational skill: knowing how to initiate conversation.

Talking with friends and colleagues is usually easy. We know and trust each other, and we've already worked out many of the rules of our relational cultures. Talking with strangers is often more difficult precisely because we don't know the rules and so don't know exactly how to coordinate our conversational moves. When we strike up a conversation with a stranger, we are attempting to change our relationship to that stranger, to move from the purely public end of the public/private continuum to the private end. Because a lot is at stake, we may, from time to time, become nervous and tongue-tied. A small amount of apprehension in talking to strangers is natural. Too much may signal the condition of communication apprehension, a kind of long-lasting interpersonal stage fright. People with high apprehension can overcome their fears if they seek help. Communication professors can often recommend a treatment program. Of course, you don't have to be a high-apprehensive to feel awkward in some interpersonal speaking situations—almost everyone has experienced periods of not knowing what to say. If you are like these people, the following guidelines should help make you a more confident conversationalist.

## Initiating Talk

Let's begin by looking at a hypothetical conversation between two strangers, Stacey and Stuart. As the scene opens, Stacey is trying to work up the courage to talk to Stuart.

STACEY (I'm so bad at this kind of thing. I never know what to say. I hope I don't say something stupid.) Hi. Umm, uh, it's really raining cats and dogs out, isn't it? (Oh gosh. I can't believe I said "cats and dogs." He'll think I'm a complete idiot.)

STUART (smiles) Yes. It never rains like this where I'm from. (She seems nice. I wonder if she's new here too.)

STACEY Well, yes, it rains a lot here, especially in the rainy season. (I have no idea what to say next. All I want to do is get out of here.) Umm. (long pause) I have to go. Bye.

STUART Bye. (What just happened?)

What did happen? Stacey made some simple mistakes that could have been avoided: Her self-talk was negative, she failed to pick up on free information provided by Stuart, and her conversational closing was awkward and abrupt. In this section we'll explain these mistakes and look at what Stacey could have done to turn this conversation around. Stacey believed that the conversation would be a disaster, and it was. Her expectations made the outcome inevitable, and the outcome only served to reinforce Stacey's view of herself as a poor conversationalist. If she wants to improve her conversational skills, her first step must be to change her expectations. Stacey's experience would have been quite different had she said to herself, "He looks nice. Since he's all alone, he'll probably be glad to talk to someone. If he is, I may make a new friend. If not, it's not the end of the world. At least I'll have tried." Like Stacey, we should begin by relaxing and by viewing conversation in realistic, positive terms.

## Finding a Topic

Conversations may end before they begin for lack of a topic. Finding a topic, however, is really the easiest part of engaging in small talk. Most people don't expect a brilliant or original opening; they simply want a topic that can act as a springboard for further talk. Stacey's choice of the weather, while not highly creative, was not so bad. Experts in the art of conversation suggest there are three basic kinds of topics you can talk about: yourself, the other person, or the situation. In general, the latter is the best place to start.[46] Here are some examples of situationally generated topics:

> *(in a health club)* Do you use the stairmaster often? What's the best program for a beginner?
>
> *(in a classroom)* What have you heard about this class? Why did you sign up?
>
> *(in a supermarket)* I saw you testing the watermelons for freshness. How can you tell if a melon's ripe?
>
> *(in a private home)* I've been noticing your family photos. They're excellent. Did you take them yourself?

Most environments will suggest a topic, but if they don't the other person will. Here are some examples of topics based on what the other person is doing, wearing, or carrying.

> I notice you're carrying a communication book. Have you taken interpersonal communication? What do you think of it?
>
> Did you get your T-shirt in Beijing? What do the Chinese characters mean? When were you there?
>
> I liked your comment in class today. What do you think people could do to conserve resources? Should the government be more involved?
>
> I've been looking for a place to get my hair cut. Your cut is great. Did you get it around here?

The third possibility, talking about yourself, should be used only in moderation. It's easier to interest others in talking about themselves than in talking about you.

We can sum up this discussion by suggesting a second guideline: *To find a topic, look to the situation or to the other person.*

### Asking Questions

In the examples we've given so far, we've used questions. Asking someone else a question is one of the best ways to start up a conversation. Of course, questions should be used in moderation. You certainly don't want to make the other per-

son feel he or she is under interrogation. Nevertheless, a single well-thought-out question is often a good starting point.

All questions are not equal. The perfect conversational question is one that is interesting and involving to the other without seeming intrusive. In general, open-ended rather than closed-ended questions are preferred. Closed-ended questions ask the respondent to choose a specific response. They usually ask for a one- or two-word answer, for example, "Do you like it here?" "Where are you from?" "How many miles do you jog?" Open-ended questions allow the respondent free rein in answering and usually call for more elaboration, for example, "Why do you like it here?" "What was it like growing up in Philadelphia?" "How did you get involved in jogging?" The latter questions are more involving than the former. Thus, our third guideline for better conversation is *find an involving and interesting open-ended question to ask your partner.*

## Using Free Information During Conversation

A good conversation doesn't stop after one question and one answer. A good conversation flows from one topic to another. An excellent way to get this to happen is to become aware of and use free information. **Free information** is extra information contained in a response, information that can suggest additional topics. In our example, Stuart provided free information to Stacey when he mentioned, "it never rains like this where I'm from." He was, in fact, telling her that he was new to the area and giving her a hint about where the conversation could go. Unfortunately, Stacey did not pick up on this information. If she had, they could have discussed their hometowns, their childhoods, and perhaps even places where they would like to live in the future.

It's important to listen carefully for free information. It is also important to help your conversational partners out by providing them with free information during your turn at talk. If a stranger asks you why you signed up for a class, you should go beyond a minimal response like "it fit my schedule" or "it sounded interesting." Better responses would be "because I'm working at two different jobs, my schedule is pretty tight. I like to schedule all my classes before noon" or "I'm a physical therapy major so learning to communicate effectively is pretty important, and the class sounded interesting." These responses can lead to long conversations on jobs and majors.

## Closing Conversations

The final step in carrying on a good conversation is to know how to close it gracefully. We have cultural expectations for conversational endings. If these are violated, the closing seems awkward and abrupt. Mark Knapp and his colleagues have pointed out that a good conversational closing does three things: (1) It signals inaccessibility by letting the other know that the conversation is nearing an end; (2) it signals supportiveness by showing appreciation for the conversation and hope for renewed contact; and (3) it summarizes the main topics of the interaction.[47] A good closing might go as follows: "I've got to go soon or I'll be late for work. I really enjoyed getting to talk to you about the music industry. If you'd like to hear my tapes, why don't you come by next Thursday. See you soon. Bye." Whether or not the relationship continues in the future, a closing such as this allows both parties to leave feeling good about themselves and their communication.

# *Process to Performance*

## Review Terms

The following is a list of major concepts introduced in this chapter. The page where the concept is first mentioned is listed in parentheses.

**analogic code**   (88)
**digital code**   (88)
**symbol**   (88)
**semantics**   (92)

**denotative meaning**   (92)
**connotative meaning**   (93)
**syntactics**   (95)
**syntactic meaning**   (95)
**pragmatics**   (96)
**speech act**   (96)
**constitutive rule**   (96)
**regulative rule**   (96)
**episode**   (97)
**relationship**   (97)
**life script**   (97)
**cultural pattern**   (97)
**Sapir-Whorf hypothesis**   (100)
**linguistic determinism**   (100)
**linguistic relativity**   (100)
**elaborated code**   (101)
**restricted code**   (101)
**qualifiers**   (106)
**tag endings**   (106)
**disclaimers**   (106)
**female register**   (106)
**critical theorists**   (108)
**muted-group theorists**   (108)
**free information**   (112)

## Suggested Readings

Napoli, Donna Jo. *Language Matters: A Guide to Everyday Questions About Language.* New York: Oxford, 2003. This readable book shatters many of the myths we hold about language.

Tannen, Deborah. *"You're Wearing That?" Understanding Mothers and Daughters in Conversation.* New York: Random House, 2006. Linguist Tannen continues to investigate the hidden relational meanings that lie beneath language choices, this time in the mother-daughter context.

## Topics for Discussion
www.oup.com/us/trenholm

## Observation Guide

**1.** Keep a diary of interactions for half a day. Begin by making brief notes every time you speak to someone, indicating what it was you spoke about. Later, go back and indicate the function each fulfilled. Analyze how you typically use language. How much of your communication is spent in gaining or acquiring information? How much is spent in controlling or persuading others? Is your speech primarily expressive or instrumental?

**2.** Observe people talking in public places. Compare the topics discussed by all-male, all-female, and mixed couples. Compare the ways language is being used. Did you find any gender-related differences? If so, why do you think these differences exist, and how do you think they affect you?

**3.** Choose a recent conversation in which the outcome surprised you in some important way (examples: things turned out really bad, you didn't achieve the goals you sought, things went far better than you had anticipated, and so on). Write a brief description of the situation and your relationship to the other person. Then write the conversation in dialogue form as accurately as you can. Place descriptions of gestures, tone of voice, and so on in parentheses. Next apply the CMM model discussed in this chapter. Identify how you interpreted the various message exchanges in terms of the following:

**a.** the "speech act" as intended by the sender and/or interpreted by the receiver (the constitutive rule)

**b.** the previous and subsequent acts influencing the production of each speech act (the regulative rule)

**c.** your definition of the "episode" and how that influenced message choices or interpretations

**d.** your view of the "relationship" in this situation and how that influenced message choices or interpretations

**e.** the influence of your own "life script" on message choices or interpretations

Follow this up by "taking the role of the other person" and trying to determine how he or she saw the same five elements (a-e). Discuss how this analysis could help you handle similar situations more successfully in the future.

## Exercises

**1.** According to Hayakawa (in Chapter 3 of *Language in Thought and Action*), there are differences between facts, inferences, and judgments.[48] To Hayakawa, a fact can be directly verified; it is a report of something we have seen, heard, or felt. An inference is a statement about the unknown made on the basis of the known, and a judgment indicates an expression of approval or disapproval. Discuss the extent to which the following statements involve facts, inferences, and/or judgments. (See pp. 44–45 of Hayakawa's book for additional examples.)

**a.** She swore, threw the book across the room, and started to scream.

**b.** He was angry.

**c.** She is high-strung and bad-tempered.

**d.** Overweight people should not wear stripes, plaids, or excessively bright colors.

**e.** The grade-point averages of student athletes and student nonathletes are not significantly different.

**f.** Athletes are just as smart as nonathletes.

**g.** Poor people generally have lower morals than middle-class people.

**h.** And Adam lived an hundred and thirty years and begat a son in his likeness, after his image; and called his name Seth. (Genesis 5:3)

**i.** My lover is faithful to me.

**j.** X is the best-looking guy in my class.

**k.** The standard of living in the USA is one of the highest in the world.

**2.** Take a play, situation comedy, or soap opera script. For each line of dialogue, identify the speech act being performed. Indicate when a character switches from one speech act to another and when characters enter new episodes. Analyze how you would portray the character. What relationships does your character have with the others? How would you describe each character's life script? How would you say each line to make clear the meaning of the dialogue? How could nonverbal codes help to increase the effectiveness of your portrayal?

**3.** The following scale is used to measure connotative meanings. According to Charles Osgood, its originator, whenever we come in contact with an object, we (1) evaluate its goodness, (2) judge its potency, and (3) decide how active it is. The first two items on the scale are evaluative, the next three measure potency, and the final three measure activity. By asking people to fill out this scale for any given concept, you can get a sense of what the concept means to them.

Semantic Differential Scale

Concept: _____

For each set of adjectives below, circle the number that best indicates where you would locate the meaning of the concept listed above.

| | | | | | | | | |
|---|---|---|---|---|---|---|---|---|
| good | 1 | 2 | 3 | 4 | 5 | 6 | 7 | bad |
| valuable | 1 | 2 | 3 | 4 | 5 | 6 | 7 | worthless |
| large | 1 | 2 | 3 | 4 | 5 | 6 | 7 | small |
| strong | 1 | 2 | 3 | 4 | 5 | 6 | 7 | weak |
| heavy | 1 | 2 | 3 | 4 | 5 | 6 | 7 | light |
| active | 1 | 2 | 3 | 4 | 5 | 6 | 7 | passive |
| fast | 1 | 2 | 3 | 4 | 5 | 6 | 7 | slow |
| hot | 1 | 2 | 3 | 4 | 5 | 6 | 7 | cold |

**a.** Choose a partner. Think of a number of common activities and objects, for example, tennis playing, mountains, snakes, church, demolition derbies, marriage. Individually, fill out semantic differentials for each concept. Compare your semantic profiles. Discuss how you came to have these associations. How might your meanings affect your interpersonal relationships?

**b.** Take the name of any product, say, "oatmeal" or "potting soil." Ask at least 20 people to fill out a semantic differential scale on the product. Compile the average scores for the evaluation, activity, and potency dimensions. Now plan an advertising campaign for the product. You want to increase those dimensions of meaning on which your product is low. Come up with a plan to give the product more favorable connotations. How could music, color, camera movement, narration, and so on make your product appear better, more potent, and more active?

*Relational messages are often subtle and complex, and not readily deciphered by outsiders. What is being communicated here may be highly charged, yet is enigmatic.*

Emiliano di Cavalcanti, *Five Girls from Guaratingueta*, 1930

## CHAPTER 5

# Relational Competence

The following encounter takes place at a company picnic. The hero is Johnson, who has been with the firm for only a few months. Hardly knowing anyone, he gravitates toward his immediate supervisor. While they are chatting, the vice president for planning, Mr. Bigelow, comes up.

BIGELOW (*ignoring Johnson and speaking directly to the supervisor*) Hope you didn't have any money on last night's game. Did I call it, or did I call it?

(*Our hero stands forgotten as his two superiors discuss the game. When a lull occurs, the supervisor remembers to introduce him.*)

BIGELOW (*with obvious lack of interest*) Nice to meet you, Jackson.

JOHNSON (*wondering if it is appropriate to correct a vice president*) Very glad to meet you, sir. Actually, my name is . . .

BIGELOW (*cutting in*) I've heard good things about you. Keep up the good work. I'm always on the lookout for enterprising young men with fresh ideas. You'll find my door is always open.

JOHNSON (*seizing his opportunity to offer a fresh idea*) You know, sir, one idea I've been considering . . .

BIGELOW Right, fine. (*turning to the supervisor*) What we need is a drink. So how about those Mets! Think they have a chance?

(*Deep in conversation, the supervisor and vice president move off toward the refreshments, leaving our employee feeling distinctly foolish. Just then, Johnson is hailed by a vaguely familiar figure whom he finally places as a fellow worker, Frazier.*)

FRAZIER Hey Johnson, how ya doing? See you got to meet Mr. Big. Did he by any chance tell you (*imitating Bigelow*) "I'm always on the lookout for enterprising young men with fresh ideas"?

(*Both men laugh.*)

FRAZIER Glad to see you. I read your report and, while I think you're dead wrong, I found it interesting. Let me buy you a beer while I give you the benefit of my experience. Your first mistake . . .

JOHNSON (*surprisingly, beginning to warm up to Frazier*) Wait just a minute. What mistake? My plan is excellent. You're going to have to do some hard talking to convince me I'm off base.

The two men spend the next hour arguing, and Johnson leaves feeling he is finally being accepted in the organization.

How did it happen that Johnson felt better about himself when he was challenged than when he was complimented? Why was the cordial conversation with the vice president less pleasant than the argument with the brash young coworker? In this chapter we'll try to answer these questions. We'll look at the kinds of relational messages we send and the way these messages affect us. We'll also examine the way relational patterns define and constrain interactions.

# What Are Relational Messages?

In the previous situation two kinds of messages were being sent simultaneously: content and relational. **Content messages** consist of what is actually said about a topic. They are what we would transcribe if we were recording an interaction verbatim. In the situation with Mr. Bigelow, the content consisted of a compliment. In the conversation with Frazier, it was a criticism. In our scenario, however, something else was happening that was more important to Johnson than content. Relational messages were being sent. Let's discuss what relational messages are, how they are sent, and what they mean.

## The Nature of Relational Messages

**Relational messages** are cues that tell us what sort of a message a content message is.[1] They let us know whether a statement is a put-down, a

sincere overture of friendship, a sarcastic retort, or a joke. They indicate the speech acts behind the content. By telling us how to interpret a speaker's comments, they let us know what a speaker thinks of us. As Paul Watzlawick, Janet Bavelas, and Don Jackson point out, every message "not only conveys information but . . . at the same time it imposes behavior."[2] To understand how relational messages impose behavior, let's turn to another example.

You're at your high school reunion. An old rival sees you. She stares at you for a minute, looks at your brand-new outfit with thinly veiled amusement, and adjusts her impeccably tailored jacket. She glances briefly at her date, shrugs her shoulders almost imperceptibly, and drawls, "Great to see you. Care to join us?" Without saying anything directly, she has indicated her high opinion of herself and her low opinion of you. She has also indicated what she hopes you will do. The unspoken message is clear: "I'm inviting you to join us only because my manners are as well tailored as my suit. I hope, however, you will have the good grace to refuse."

Now let's rewrite the scene, this time supplying you with an old friend. She sees you, her eyes light up, and a big smile crosses her face. She gives you a hug, stands back, and looks you up and down. Keeping her arm around your shoulder, she guides you toward her date. "Great to see you. Care to join us?" This time you know you're sincerely wanted, and you accept with pleasure. Although the content message was the same, there was a world of difference on the relational level.

## Sending Relational Messages

Relational messages are often conveyed indirectly and may therefore escape our attention. They are easiest to read when they signal a change in mood. For instance, when a parent, exasperated by his child's behavior, finally loses patience, the child usually responds to the relational shift. He can tell that this time, when Father says, "Go to bed," there is an additional relational message that says, "And I mean it!"

## Relational Competence and Romance

# Pride and Prejudice

Joe Wright, 2005

When clever, strong-willed Elizabeth Bennett (Kiera Knightley) meets the aloof and snobbish Mr. Darcy (Matthew Macfayden), sparks fly. There is an instant attraction, yet there is also instant antipathy. When Elizabeth overhears Darcy explaining that he will not dance with her as her looks are only "tolerable," she vows to dislike him forever, and, having made up her mind, she is all too eager to accept false rumors about him. Darcy, in turn, has only disdain for her family, and in doing so ruins the budding relationship between his best friend Bingley (Simon Woods) and Elizabeth's sister Jane (Rosamund Pike). The real impediment to their relationship, however, lies in their character flaws highlighted in the title: Both are too quick to judge one another, and both are too easily offended. Darcy hides his hurt pride behind a veneer of reticence and snobbery. Elizabeth hides hers behind a barrage of clever comments. Despite all this, their attraction grows, but their relationship seems doomed, especially after Darcy offers one of the most inept marriage proposals in literary history. The film's tag line summarizes its plot: "Sometimes the last person on earth you want to be with is the one person you can't be without."

Jane Austen's novel, upon which this adaptation is based, is, in part, an exploration of how class and wealth act as impediments to love in 18th-century England. It is also a sensitive examination of the barriers we erect to protect ourselves from being hurt, especially by those we really love, and of the ways our prejudices keep us from seeing people for who they truly are. Part of the appeal of the novel, and of the film, is that the behavior of its characters is so recognizable. As Elizabeth's friend Charlotte (Claudie Blakley) says, "We are all fools in love."

In most cases relational messages recede into the background. If a couple is getting along, their relational messages may acknowledge that fact, saying, in effect, "Our relationship is going fine. Let's keep it as it is." In fact, in most healthy relationships attention is directed to content, and relational meanings are scarcely noticed. Troubled relationships, however, "are characterized by a constant struggle about the nature of the relationship, with the content aspect of communication becoming less and less important."[3]

Relational messages are often sent unconsciously, through nonverbal channels. In their classic work on the subject, Watzlawick and his colleagues equate content messages with verbal statements and relational messages with nonverbal behaviors. While people generally convey relational matters through unspoken dialogue, direct relational talk is possible.[4] When we tell people how much we care, or when we give them direct orders, the relational message is stated directly.

## Relational Messages and Relational Definitions

When relational messages accumulate, they lead to **relational definitions;** that is, they give us an overall sense of who we are to one another. Relational definitions are mental models that label and classify relationships and specify how members should treat one another. As we get to know other people, we let them know what we think about them. We indicate the degree of affection we feel, the amount of attention we expect, and the kind of commitment we're willing to make. These messages define who we are to one another and guide our behaviors.

For example, two individuals may arrive at the following relational understanding: "We are close but not intimate. We feel affection and trust but are not romantically involved. We are friends." Once they define themselves in this way, they will be bound by the norms and obligations of friendship and will try to act as friends should. Their relational definition will direct future behaviors.

The interpersonal literature describes relational definitions in a number of ways. Two of the most important equate relational definitions with cultures and with contracts.

### Relationships as Culture

Culture, in its most general sense, is an acquired set of beliefs, attitudes, and values that people use to interpret their world and guide their actions. As we have seen in other chapters, cultural understandings are necessary for social harmony. While it isn't hard to grasp what culture is, it is hard to decide on the boundaries between cultures. Sometimes we use the term to refer to very large groupings (for example, Western versus Asian culture); other times we use it to refer to smaller groups (for instance, punk rockers or IBM employees). Julia Wood has suggested that if two people develop common orientations and behaviors, they can form their own **relational culture.**[5]

Like larger cultures, relational cultures guide members' perceptions of the world. Members of relational cultures create shared constructs, schemata, and scripts. They develop common language habits and codes of conduct. All the mechanisms that allow larger cultural units to develop work in miniature within relationships. Understanding a relationship, therefore, involves uncovering and analyzing these mechanisms.

### Relationships as Contracts

The cultural metaphor is not the only way to think of relational definitions. A number of theorists, including Robert Carson, have used a contract negotiation metaphor to explain relationships.[6] When people negotiate a legal contract, they state what they expect to receive from one another, indicate mutual obligations, and outline any exceptions or contingency clauses. Carson tells us that the same thing happens implicitly during the negotiation of a **relational contract.** "The members of the dyad never quite state the 'rules' under which they are operating, but the rules are there nevertheless, and they are often followed in an utterly reliable fashion by both parties."[7]

A couple, Amy and Mark, might develop their contract in the following way. Amy tries out a behavior, perhaps by disclosing details of her past and expecting Mark to do the same. He, however, may nonverbally back off, change the subject, or refuse to respond. He wants a clause added to the contract: "There should be boundaries placed on what we discuss. Our pasts should be off limits." Amy may be willing to abide by this rule in most instances, but may wish to add the condition "when a self-disclosure can help us understand or solve a problem, then we should talk about the past." If Mark agrees, the amended version becomes part of their unstated contract.

When this rule is coupled with other rules concerning privacy and involvement, a general definition of the depth-superficiality dimension of their relationship is arrived at. Although Mark and Amy may not realize they have negotiated a contract and may not be able to list its rules, they can usually sum up their general understanding. For example, they may agree that "We respect each other's privacy." In Carson's terms they have negotiated part of an overall "master contract" that defines their relational identity. In Wood's terms one part of the relational culture has been specified. Whatever metaphor we use—culture or contract—the fact remains that couples build up all kinds of unstated rules, normative standards, role definitions, and relational labels.

Our definitions are often strongly influenced by outside sources. For example, we may try to follow religious or community-based images of "good" relationships. And whether we rebel against them or try to follow them, family models are also important to intimate bonds. Regardless of where our original definitions come from, when we enter relationships, we present them to our partners, and they are accepted, rejected, or modified.

# The Content of Relational Messages

For many years we've known that relational messages are varied and complex.[8] For example, Judee Burgoon and Jerold Hale have identified seven major and five minor **relational themes.** Their research indicates that we communicate about the following issues: dominance-submission, emotional arousal, composure, similarity, formality, task-social orientation, and intimacy.[9] Table 5.1 gives examples of these relational topics. We'll examine each in more detail.

## Sending Dominance Messages

Of all the relational messages identified, messages concerned with dominance have received the most attention. These messages focus on control, telling us "who has the right to direct, delimit, and define" the actions of a dyad.[10] They tell us who is in charge. It is common to talk about three types of dominance messages. Those that indicate a desire to take control or limit the action of others are called **one-up messages.** During conversations they often take the form of denials, disagreements, interruptions, topic changes, and the like. Messages that indicate a desire to give in or relinquish one's freedom are called **one-down messages.** Agreeing, acquiescing, giving up the floor, or allowing the other to direct the conversation are examples. Finally, statements indicating equivalence or failing to imply control are **one-across messages.**

Communication researchers often find ...ful to code conversations in order to exa... dominance patterns. Commonly, they indi... one-up messages with a ( ↑), one-down messag... with a (↓), and one-across messages with a (→). Coding dominance isn't difficult. To see for yourself, code the following dialogue. Be sure to consider how what is said relates to the rest of the conversation. To code the interaction, place the appropriate arrow next to each statement.

( ) ALLAN Well, I'd say that you make most of the decisions about household matters.

( ) LOU Yes, I guess I do.

( ) ALLAN Sure you do. You have complete freedom because I trust your judgment.

( ) LOU Yes, I . . .

( ) ALLAN *(interrupting)* For example, when you decided to paint the den green, did I say anything?

( ) LOU No. Sorry about that.

We've made your task easy—the control pattern here is not subtle. Allan's comments are all one-ups. Even though he says that Lou has control, his style belies his words. He takes control of the conversation, interrupts Lou, and finishes Lou's sentences. Allan is clearly saying, "I'm the one in charge." Lou is clearly in the one-down position and appears to be saying, "Go ahead. I'll follow your lead."

Talk, of course, isn't the only way to indicate dominance. Many behaviors demonstrate control. The executive who picks up the chalk at a meeting and stands in front of the blackboard signals a desire to direct the group. Conversely, the person who takes an inconspicuous seat in the back of the room may be trying to avoid taking control.

## Indicating Emotional Tone

In the Burgoon and Hale system, two themes indicate emotion: emotional arousal and composure. *Emotional arousal* refers to how responsive we are to others; it lets others know whether we are excited or bored. People generally find it easy

**TABLE 5.1**   **Types of Relational Messages**

1. **Dominance—Submission**

   "In this relationship I want to take control."

   "In this relationship I want to relinquish control."

2. **Emotional Arousal**

   "I am actively involved in and excited about what is happening."

   "I feel passive and unresponsive."

3. **Composure**

   "With you I am relaxed and in control of myself."

   "With you I am tense and out of control."

4. **Similarity**

   "We are like one another; we have something in common."

   "We are different; we have nothing in common."

5. **Formality**

   "Our relationship is guided by formal, cultural-level rules."

   "Our relationship is guided by informal, individual rules."

6. **Task—Social Orientation**

   "Our primary focus should be on the task at hand."

   "Our primary focus should be on each other and our relationship."

7. **Intimacy**

   "We are closely bound by ties of attachment and involvement."

   "We have little attachment; we are not close."

   a. **Affection—Hostility**

      "I feel positive emotions toward you."

      "I feel negative emotions toward you."

   b. **Trust**

      "I know that you won't hurt me."

      "I fear that you will harm me."

   c. **Depth—Superficiality**

      "I wish you to know personal things about me."

      "I wish to keep myself hidden from you."

   d. **Inclusion—Exclusion**

      "I wish to be with you."

      "I wish to be distant from you."

   e. **Intensity of Involvement**

      "You are a central focus of my thoughts and feelings."

      "You are of no interest to me."

Adapted from Judee K. Burgoon and Jerold L. Hale, "The Fundamental Topoi of Relational Communication," *Communication Monographs* 51 (1984): 193–214.

*These women don't need to say a word to indicate their smug, narrow-minded approach
to life. Their relational messages clearly convey their attitudes.*

Grant Wood, *Daughters of the Revolution,* 1932

to read arousal cues. And often arousal is conta-gious. Talking to someone who is excited can in-crease our excitement level, while trying to tell a joke to an apathetic listener can dampen our enthu-siasm. As Burgoon and Hale point out, arousal messages can "run the gamut from highly manic ac-tivities to complete passivity (as when sleeping)."[12]

*Composure,* the other common emotional theme, indicates self-control. It shows we're ca-pable of calmness and detachment, that we won't give way or fall apart. Sometimes such an atti-tude can seem cold, for it says, in effect, "I can control my emotions and act with poise. Noth-ing you do will cause me to react emotionally." In most cases, however, we value those with composure and draw on their strength. Although composure and emotional arousal may seem to be simple opposites, Burgoon and Hale believe they are separate relational dimensions, for "it is possible for someone to be both highly aroused and highly controlled (as when expressing con-tempt) or nonaroused and uncomposed (as when showing restless boredom)."[13]

## Showing Similarity

*Similarity,* another important relational cue, has powerful effects on attraction and credibility.[14] Although we often hear that opposites attract, research shows that it is more often the case that birds of a feather flock together. People gener-ally seek out others who are similar in appear-ance and actions to themselves. If you doubt this, ask yourself how willing you are to com-municate with someone whose behavior is to-tally different from yours or what your first re-action is to people who look strange. Most people find it difficult to deal with the odd or unusual.

## Defining Episodes

Because we need to know what kinds of rules to follow, we usually scan episodes for *formality* cues. In formal episodes we stick to general, cultural-level rules of conduct, while in informal episodes we can deviate from these rules and act more naturally.

In shared-work situations we must also decide on the level of *task-social orientation* we wish to maintain. We need to let our partners know whether we intend to stick to business or have fun. For example, assume you have been assigned a very attractive lab partner in a tough science course. You must decide whether to concentrate on work or spend time getting to know your partner. This involves some fairly tricky relational negotiations, for if you set the wrong tone, both task and social outcomes can be adversely affected.

## Indicating Intimacy

The relational message with the greatest potential to define a relationship is probably that of *intimacy*. Intimacy messages are central to the growth and development of interpersonal trajectories. Whether our goal is to create a private relationship or to maintain distance, we must control intimacy cues. Perhaps because they're so important, intimacy cues are often hard to express directly. We sometimes become tongue-tied when we try to convey closeness and concern.

Intimacy messages are complex. Burgoon and Hale have wisely broken intimacy down into subcategories, each describing a different dimension of attachment and involvement. Some of the most vital intimacy messages are those that signal *affection-hostility*. Very early in our lives we learn how to identify anger and love. Children become adept at knowing how far their parents can be pushed before affection turns to annoyance. Messages along the affection-hostility dimension are easy to decode, perhaps because they are usually conveyed through a number of channels working in concert.

Another key intimacy dimension is *trust*. People who are trusting are open to risk; they let others know how vulnerable they are and willingly place themselves in positions where they may be hurt. People who are trustworthy won't exploit others' vulnerabilities. We know that relationships don't progress very far toward intimacy unless those involved are both trustworthy and trusting.

*Relational messages can often be read at a distance. This group signals informality, equality, and fun.*

*Depth-superficiality* is another intimacy dimension. It indicates the extent to which partners are willing to give each other access to personal information. In intimate relationships participants engage in self-disclosure. Those who refuse to open themselves to others indicate that they prefer to keep the relationship at a nonintimate public level.

Closely related to depth-superficiality is the *inclusion-exclusion* dimension of intimacy. Messages that fall along this continuum indicate a willingness to associate with others. People generally described as "warm" or "welcoming" are indicating inclusion. Those described as "cold" may be giving off exclusion messages.

Finally, intimacy is signaled by *intensity* of involvement. If you are intensely involved with someone, he or she is central to you, the focus of all your attention. If you are uninterested, unwilling to listen, or inattentive, involvement is minimal.

Intimacy, then, is a complex blend of many factors that can combine in different ways. When people are in love, for example, all of the positive aspects of intimacy work together. Lovers convey affection, trust, openness, closeness, and intensity of involvement. This, however, is only one form of intimacy. Many other combinations are possible. For example, people are sometimes bound together by mutual hostility. Intimacy is not an all-or-nothing affair. To indicate the kind and degree of our intimacy, we send many relational messages.

In our own ways we are always sending relational messages. The way we stand and move, as well as our facial expressions and gestures, let others know what we think of them and want from them. We even send relational messages when we engage in mediated communication. A hastily scrawled note on the back of an envelope sends a different message than a beautifully written letter on scented stationery does. In fact, we can even send relational messages over e-mail or by cell phone, as Boxes 5.1 and 5.2 illustrate.

# How Relational Messages Affect Us

One of the most important aspects of relational messages is that they affect receivers' self-concepts. When we tell others how we feel about them, we can either enhance or diminish their feelings of self-worth. Let's look at some different types of relational messages and see how they affect identity.

## Confirming and Disconfirming Messages

One of the best explanations of the relationship between interpersonal communication and self-concept is given by Evelyn Sieburg. She argues that whenever we communicate with people, we present to them a version of ourselves.[15] Their response invariably tells us something about the success of this self-presentation. Responses that make us value ourselves more are known as **confirming messages.** Those that make us devalue ourselves are known as **disconfirming messages.** Although each dyad is unique, Sieburg felt it was possible to identify responses that confirm and disconfirm most people. Table 5.2 defines and gives examples of these responses.

To understand these responses better, let's look again at the scenario that opened this chapter. Johnson, the new employee, was anxious to make a good impression on his boss by presenting the best self possible. Bigelow's responses served to disconfirm him in several ways. By failing to acknowledge Johnson's presence, Bigelow was being impervious. He told him, in effect, "You are not worth noticing." By failing to match his tone of voice to his cordial words, he confused Johnson. Bigelow's words and actions were incongruous.

Bigelow also interrupted Johnson, cutting him off in mid-sentence. Furthermore, he changed the subject when Johnson began to talk. Because Bigelow minimally acknowledged Johnson's contribution before he took the conversation in another direction, his response was tangential rather than totally irrelevant. Bigelow's tendency to hide behind impersonal clichés was also disconfirming because it kept Johnson at a distance. About the only thing Bigelow did not do was become tongue-tied and flustered, a response that would have signaled incoherence. No wonder Johnson felt unhappy about the meeting. He felt he was being told, "You are unimportant and unworthy."

One of the reasons Johnson liked Frazier was that Frazier used no disconfirmations. Although he disagreed with Johnson, he did so in a way that said, "You are a worthy opponent. I may not agree with you completely, but I respect you."

BOX 5.1

# Netiquette

## Common Courtesy in CMC

Some people manage to be annoying whenever they open their mouths: talking about topics no one else cares about, taking up more conversational space than they should, asking a question that's just been answered, or turning every conversation into conflict. People like this can bring a pleasant conversation to a standstill because they lack common courtesy.

Courteous behavior is necessary whenever and wherever we communicate—including online. In *Netiquette,* Virginia Shea presents some guidelines for avoiding rudeness during computer-mediated communication (CMC). For Shea, the Prime Directive of Netiquette is to *remember that those are real people out there.* This means never saying anything online that you wouldn't say to a person's face. Not only does this rule protect the feelings of others, it protects you from writing something that one day can come back to haunt you.

Communicating always puts demands on people's time. This is equally true in cyberspace, where there is a limit to the system's bandwidth. When you send a copy of a message to everyone on your mailing list or when you accidentally post the same message several times, you are imposing on others. Shea asks you to *recognize the fact that you are not the center of cyberspace.*

Although you may not be aware of it, you create an impression every time you send a message. Although you will not be judged by your clothes, or age, or beauty, you will be judged by the quality of your writing as well as by the content of what you say. Shea urges you to *know what you're talking about and make sense.* Bad information spreads even more quickly on the Net than it does in real life, so take responsibility for your assertions.

If you decide to communicate in discussion groups (either because it is a professional necessity or out of interest) be sure to follow the group's norms. One sure-fire way to embarrass yourself is to be ill-informed. Most discussion groups have FAQs (Frequently Asked Questions) that can give you basic knowledge that others share. And be sure to send messages that are appropriate to a given group. Don't, like the man Shea describes, ask a discussion group of feminists for tips on how to pick up women. Often it's a good idea to *lurk before you leap*; that is, before you enter the conversation, read the comments of others and get a feel for the group.

Violating the rules we've just discussed can lead to flame wars, a series of escalating messages in which individuals attack one another. Prolonged or uncontrolled flaming is not only mean-spirited and hurtful, it can get you a bad reputation. So avoid posting flame-bait (messages that will make others angry) or responding to it. And if you inadvertently flame, apologize

---

As you can see in Table 5.2, a number of responses lead people to value themselves more. These confirming responses include direct acknowledgment, agreement about content, supportive feedback, clarifying responses, and expression of positive feeling. All of these are ways to improve another's self-concept.

How often are disconfirming messages sent and received? The study described in this chapter's Research in Review box provides an answer and lists additional kinds of messages not discussed by Sieburg. As you read it, ask yourself whether you've been guilty of sending discouraging messages recently.

as soon as possible. *Help keep flame wars under control.*

Everyone knows that it is possible to create false identities online. Shea states, "Long-term misrepresentation of oneself in romance discussion groups or chat areas, where the purpose of the interaction is to form a serious relationship, is definitely not acceptable." And *online cheating should be off limits.* Pursuing a romantic relationship with two partners at the same time is as bad form on the computer as it is offline.

For most young people today, the online application of choice is instant messaging (IM). Although IM is a wonderful way to keep in touch, it also has its fair share of problems. Here are a few principles to keep in mind when using IM either for personal communication or in a business environment.

First, *think about what you write.* A poorly thought-out, emotional response can come back to bite you. Whether in a business or personal setting, keep cool. Second, *ask if it's OK to talk.* If the person you want to talk to is available, fine, if not, don't feel hurt. It's unrealistic to expect people to be at your beck and call all the time. Third, *make good use of away messages* to let people know when you're available and when you're not. If you're busy, it's good form to let people know. But don't stay unavailable too long, especially in a business setting. And, if you're using IM for personal ends, avoid going online under a different screen name to spy on your friends.

As for the actual message, *don't use too many potentially confusing acronyms.* Don't assume that everyone, especially those in the workplace, will be up on the latest slang. *Do use emoticons* to make sure your recipient understands what you are saying. And think *carefully when you choose a screen name.* Hotmonkeylove or cyberkitty411 may have seemed appropriate when you picked them in high school, but they may not make the best impression now that you're an adult.

Finally, *consider privacy issues.* Don't, for example, invite a new person into a multiparty IM without checking with the others. And be aware that the recipient might not be alone. It would be embarrassing if the joke you sent to a coworker was received during an electronic presentation or if the target of the juicy bit of gossip you send to a friend is with your friend at the time.

CMC is, after all, just another way for real people to talk. The relational messages we send in CMC are just as significant as those we send during face-to-face interaction, and they demand just as much courtesy.

**SOURCE** Virginia Shea, *Netiquette* (San Francisco: Albion Books, 1994).

**ADDITIONAL READINGS**

Stuart, Anne. "IM Etiquette 101." 2002. Retrieved July 7, 2006, from http://pf.com/articles/2002/06/24304.html.

Thorsberg, Frank. "Instant Messaging Etiquette." 2002. Retrieved July 7, 2006, from http://www.pcworld.com/howto/article/0,aid,99405,00.asp.

Woods, Bob. "Guide to Enterprise IM Etiquette." 2002. Retrieved July 7, 2006, from http://www.instantmessagingplanet.com/enterprise/article.php/10816_1379121.

## Paradoxes and Double Binds

Contradictory messages are called paradoxes, and repeated exposure to them can cause us to doubt the validity of our own perceptions. There are two kinds of paradoxes that can damage the self-image: paradoxical definitions and paradoxical injunctions.[16]

In **paradoxical definitions** speakers present themselves in contradictory ways. A classic example is the statement "I am a liar." If the speaker is really a liar, then the statement must be true. But a speaker who describes himself truthfully cannot be a liar. If this is confusing, you have the idea. Paradoxical messages always confuse us;

**127**

| **TABLE 5.2** | **A Taxonomy of Confirming and Disconfirming Messages** |
|---|---|

| Disconfirming responses | Definition | Example |
|---|---|---|
| Impervious | When B fails to acknowledge, even minimally, A's message | A: Hi!<br>B: (continues working, ignoring A) |
| Interrupting | When B cuts A's message short | A: So then I . . .<br>B: Nice chatting with you. Bye! |
| Irrelevant | When B's response is unrelated to what A has been saying | A: So then he left me.<br>B: I'm thinking of going to Bermuda on break. |
| Tangential | When B acknowledges A's message but immediately takes the talk in another direction | A: I just don't know what to do.<br>B: Gee, too bad. Have you seen my new car? |
| Impersonal | When B conducts a monologue or uses nonimmediate, cliché-ridden, overintellectual language | A: How can I improve my grade, professor?<br>B: Adequate classroom performance is a function of cognitive and affective integration. |
| Incoherent | When B's response is rambling and difficult to follow | A: Tell me what's wrong.<br>B: Well, um, see, it's a . . . gosh, hard to say. |
| Incongruous | When B's nonverbal and verbal messages are contradictory | A: Are you angry with me?<br>B: No. Of course not. Why should I be? (said sarcastically) |

| Confirming responses | Definition | Example |
|---|---|---|
| Direct acknowledgment | When B reacts directly to A's message | A: Can we talk?<br>B: Of course. Come over. |
| Agreement about content | When B reinforces opinions offered by A | A: I've definitely noticed a change in Joe lately.<br>B: Yes. I have too. |
| Supportive | When B expresses understanding and reassurance to A | A: I feel just awful.<br>B: I understand. I think you did the right thing. |
| Clarifying | When B tries to clarify A's message | A: I'm not sure what to do about it.<br>B: So you're confused and upset, is that it? |
| Expression of positive feeling | When B expresses positive feelings about A's message | A: No, I think we should tell him about it.<br>B: Now I know what you mean. Good idea! |

Adapted from Frank E. X. Dance and Carl E. Larson, *Speech Communication, Concepts and Behavior* (New York: Holt, Rinehart, & Winston, 1972), pp. 141–43.

they challenge our belief in rationality and consistency. And what is oddest about them is that although it is the speaker who is being illogical, it is the receiver who feels confused and disconfirmed. Any time a message is delivered that defines a relationship in contradictory ways ("I am your friend but I don't want to be around you," "I respect your ideas but I can't support them"), it can be considered to be a paradoxical definition.

Another kind of paradox, a **paradoxical injunction,** gives us an impossible order, one that must be disobeyed in order to be obeyed. "Stop giving in to me" is a good example. If you obey the command, you are giving in. If you refuse to give in, you are giving in because you are obeying the injunction. Other examples are "Dominate me!" "Be spontaneous," "Disagree with everything I say," and "Love me for myself, not because I ask you to." While paradoxes may be fun to think about if you like brainteasers, during interaction they are much less benign. They undermine our belief in logic and put us in a situation where we're damned if we do and damned if we don't.

Imagine that you are a child whose mother says to you, "I want you to be more affectionate." But when you show affection by trying to touch her, she stiffens and backs off. Or you are a young adult whose father tells you, "I want you to be independent and have a life of your own." But when you do strike out on your own, he develops severe chest pains. Such a situation, where there is no "correct" response, is called a **double bind.**[17] In a true double bind, (1) the relationship between the two people involved must be an intense and important one, (2) the "victim" must be presented with a contradictory injunction, and (3) he or she must have no way of escaping, either by recognizing the paradoxical nature of the message or by withdrawing from the interaction. The victim must react, although reacting "correctly" is impossible.

Imagine being the victim of a habitual double bind, with no way of returning to a more logical world. After a while, this kind of treatment could make you question your own sanity. You might

begin to act in ways normal people would consider "crazy." Even mild cases of contradictory behavior can be upsetting. Some people habitually use sarcasm and jokes so that we're never really sure what they think of us. For most of us, this is disquieting, because we can't be sure whether we are being accepted or not. These kinds of messages are also double binding.[18]

# Pragmatic Patterns and Relational Sequences

While we react strongly to others' relational messages, our own are often invisible. How, then, can we diagnose communication problems? The only real way is to pay more attention to our own actions. You may recall from Chapter 4 that pragmatic communication patterns refer to the way we use speech in everyday interactions—speech acts, episodes, regulative and constitutive rules. By uncovering repetitive sequences of behavior, we can often discover why our relationships are going the way they are. In this section we'll examine the influence of patterns of behavior on interpersonal relationships.

## Looking for Meaning in Patterns

Before we begin discussing pragmatic patterns, there are three points to consider. All three have been implicit in our previous discussions.

1. *Relational definitions are created not by a single individual, but by both members of a relationship working together.* The fact that one person has a domineering personality does not necessarily mean that she will be a dominant member in all her relationships. Her partner has a great deal to do with how dominance-submission patterns are worked out.

2. *To understand relational definitions, we need to become aware of patterns of behavior.*

## "You Mean It Actually Took You This Long?"

# Messages That Discourage

Relational messages can encourage and support or they can undermine. In "Discouraging Messages," Rodney Reynolds investigates messages in which the sender intends to dishearten the receiver. He begins by looking at how frequently these kinds of messages occur and then goes on to describe the kinds of messages that result in discouragement.

In the first part of his study, Reynolds asked 138 upper division communication students, many of whom were working adults, to think of specific kinds of discouraging messages: messages *from* subordinates, supervisors, friends, or people in general and messages *sent to* friends. The students then filled out scales measuring how often they felt these messages occurred, how difficult it was for people to send these kinds of messages, and the extent to which they felt the sender actually knew the messages were rude.

Participants reported that about 15 percent of their conversations involved intentionally discouraging messages. Gender seemed to play a part in these estimates. Men's estimates of the frequency of discouraging messages were higher than those of women. Men were also more likely than women to think that discouraging messages

were easy to send, although both men and women agreed that it was easier for others to send them discouraging messages than it was for them to send this kind of message to others.

In the second part of the study, Reynolds presented participants with 45 different discouraging messages, asking them to sort the messages into clusters based on their similarity. Results indicated six different kinds of discouraging messages. Cluster one (nonacceptance) included instances in which the target's ideas were met with outright rejection. Cluster two (other's failures) occurred when someone the target counted on failed to meet expectations or work hard enough. Cluster three (discrimination) consisted of criticism based on age, gender, or race. Cluster four (questioning character) was made up of comments denigrating the target as lacking character, for example, as being immature, stupid, or not good enough. Cluster five (questioning competence) involved being accused of not trying, not performing, or not getting things done on time. Finally, cluster six (attack and blame) was made up of aggressive and harassing messages making it clear that the target could not possibly succeed and would not be given a second chance.

Reynolds believes that discouraging messages are a special class of hurtful messages. Although they do not occur a lot, they occur across relational types and are frequent enough to be of concern. As relational messages they have the effect of keeping people from developing and reaching their full potential and are therefore particularly damaging.

Reynolds, Rodney A. "Discouraging Messages." *Communication Reports* 19, no. 1 (2006): 16–30.

---

In relationships certain sequences of acts become favored and repeated over time. To diagnose a relationship, we need to uncover these patterns of repeated acts.

3. *It is generally unproductive to blame individuals for the way a relationship progresses.* Although participants often blame the patterns they do recognize on their partners, it is more

*Relational messages serve as context and tone, and they color every interaction.*

productive to place any blame on co-created patterns.

These points are part of a perspective developed by researchers known as the **Palo Alto group**.[19] These researchers, primarily psychotherapists, wanted to learn why some relationships were so destructive. They felt the answer could be found in communication patterns. While our interest is with a more normal range of behaviors than those investigated by the Palo Alto group, the insights they provide can quite easily be applied to everyday interaction.

## Patterns vs. People: The Locus of Dyadic Communication

The Palo Alto group argues that when people enter a relationship, it is the relationship itself that most affects them, not their individual personalities. With some people we are relaxed and happy; with others we are at our absolute worst. Does this mean our personalities change when we are with different people? The Palo Alto group says no. What changes is our communication system. To understand relationships, we must understand the behaviors that make up the dyadic system.

But how do we go about looking at behaviors that are usually invisible? What should we look for? First, we should look at sequences rather than individual acts. Unless we know how an in-

dividual act is connected to other behaviors, we cannot understand its relational meaning. Let's take an example. Suppose you hear a laugh. Can you assume that it means someone is happy? Of course not. It all depends on what happened before. The laugh may have been an appreciative response to a good joke. Or it may have been a scornful response to a desperate request. The smallest unit to carry relational meaning is not a single act, but at least two acts in sequence, or what is called an **interact**.[20]

To understand a relationship fully, we must often look at a number of interacts. Let's assume that the laugh we heard followed an apology. To understand this interact's relational meaning, we must connect it to other interacts. Perhaps the following scenario applies. Lee habitually gets mad and insults Adam. When this happens, Adam usually responds by threatening to leave Lee, who, terrified that Adam will make good on the threat, begs for forgiveness. At that point Adam scornfully laughs at Lee, which causes the whole process to start over. The laugh takes on a sinister aspect in this scenario, for the sequence clearly is a disturbed one. Of course, this unpleasant pattern is not the only explanation for the apology-laugh. Perhaps when tired, Lee acts irritable but usually realizes it and apologizes immediately. Adam, understanding this, laughs good-naturedly to let Lee know everything is OK. A very different meaning can now be assigned to the laugh. The point here is that we can understand and control relationships best by looking for patterns. If necessary, we can then intervene to break the pattern.

## The Problem of Punctuation

Even among people who can identify dysfunctional patterns, there is often a stumbling block to changing them: the tendency to punctuate sequences inappropriately. In grammar, punctuation marks are ways of dividing words into units that belong together. In punctuating a sentence, we use a capital letter to show where it begins. In a relational sequence **punctuation** serves essentially the same purpose: It lets us know when the sequence begins.

Let's consider an example that occurs often in real life, although the position of husband and wife may be reversed. A couple is locked in a pattern in which the wife, feeling ignored, nags her husband. The husband responds to this attack by withdrawing. The more he withdraws, the more she nags, and the more she nags, the more he withdraws. They are enmeshed in a self-perpetuating pattern.[21]

Even if they recognize what's going on, they may spend all their energy arguing over who started it. The wife punctuates the sequence by saying it was the husband's fault. The husband punctuates it by saying he withdrew only because she began it all by nagging. Of course, none of this does any good; the conflict only worsens.

## Types of Patterns

Although each dyad works out its own relational patterns, some occur with enough frequency that they can be labeled and described. Common relational patterns include (1) complementary and symmetrical, (2) evolving, and (3) unwanted repetitive.

### Complementarity and Symmetry

One of the easiest ways to classify patterns of interacts is to consider whether they are similar or different in relational meaning. When the acts in a sequence are relationally opposite, we have what is called a **complementary pattern.** A sequence characterized by a repeated pattern of one-ups followed by one-downs would be so labeled. A pattern consisting of acts that are similar is called a **symmetrical pattern.** If such a pattern consists entirely of one-ups, it is considered to be an example of **competitive symmetry.** If it includes only one-downs, it is **submissive symmetry.** Look at the following conversations and see if you can tell which is complementary, which is competitively symmetrical, and which is submissively symmetrical.

### Conversation 1
JOAN  Let's begin by defining the problem.
JANE  OK, that's fine.

JOAN  We'll make a chart showing all the negative forces.
JANE  Sounds good. Should I . . .
JOAN  No, I'll do it. Hand me that paper.
JANE  OK.

### Conversation 2
JOAN  Let's begin by defining the problem.
JANE  We did that last time; we don't have time now.
JOAN  We need to review it. I'll make a chart . . .
JANE  You can do that later. Anyone have any solutions?
JOAN  Wait a minute! Who made you the expert?
JANE  Don't be a jerk!

### Conversation 3
JOAN  How would you like to begin?
JANE  Whatever you suggest is just fine.
JOAN  I'll agree with whatever you say.
JANE  No, really, you decide.
JOAN  I'd be happy to go along with what you think.
JANE  I really have no preference.

It's not very difficult to label these conversations. Conversation 1 is complementary. Joan takes control and Jane acquiesces. Their control behaviors are opposite and therefore complement each other. Conversation 2 is characterized by competitive symmetry. Here both Joan and Jane want to direct the activity. Such a conversation may signal a fight for leadership. Conversation 3 illustrates submissive symmetry. Although the two seem agreeable, they are actually in a contest to see who can force the other to take control.

Is one sequence better than the others? Not really. Although the complementary relationship shows the least amount of disagreement, it's not necessarily the best. Habitual complementarity can trap participants in rigid roles. When we are young, it is natural for our relationship with our parents to be complementary. But how natural would it be if we still let Mom and Dad make all the decisions when we were 30?

While on the face of it symmetrical patterns seem to be negative, since they are characterized by struggle, there are times when they can be positive. The clash involved in competitive symmetry can sometimes motivate partners to be more creative. And sometimes the willingness to give in characterized by submissive symmetry can signal care and concern. What is unhealthy is any pattern so rigid it cannot change. If, for example, a dominant member in a complementary relationship becomes ill and can no longer make decisions, it may be necessary for the submissive member to take over. If the members cannot make the switch, severe problems of adaptation are possible.

### *Evolving Patterns: The Problem of Spirals*

Over time, relational roles may become more and more extreme. When the actions of each party intensify the actions of the other, we have a **spiral**.[22] Spirals often arise where there is competitive symmetry. Assume you and a friend are competing for a prize. The harder you work and the better you do, the harder she works and the better she does. As you near your goal, you redouble your efforts, and she does the same when it looks like you are about to win. While healthy competition may lead you to reach your potential, unchecked competition may spiral out of control and become an obsession.

There are times when intensifying a relationship makes it better. If by showing affection you increase a friend's confidence so that he acts more lovable, you will probably feel even more affection. The relationship can develop in a positive direction. This is a progressive spiral. Unfortunately, the opposite can occur. If, for example, you lose trust in a friend, that friend may decide that it is useless to act in a trustworthy manner. He may therefore violate your trust, and the relationship will degenerate. This is a regressive spiral.

William Wilmot believes that most relationships are characterized by alternating spirals that fluctuate between being progressive and being regressive. He argues that most couples place limits on how high or low a spiral can go. When a spiral reaches one of these limits, it must change directions or the relationship will dissolve. Our nagging wife and withdrawing husband cannot keep up their regressive spiral for long. It will have to reverse if they are to stay together.[23]

### *Unwanted Patterns: Controlling URPs*

If relational patterns are negotiated, you would think that people would steer clear of destructive sequences. Unfortunately, many patterns are undesired and undesirable. In **unwanted repetitive patterns (URPs)** participants feel out of control. Have you ever known someone who just rubbed you the wrong way? Every time you got together, a fight would inevitably ensue. If so, you have experienced an URP. In most URPs the following conditions will occur: (1) A clear sequence of alternating messages will inform each participant exactly what comes next; (2) the URP will be recurrent; (3) it will occur regardless of topic or situation; (4) the sequence will be unwanted; and (5) the participants will both share the perception that it could not be avoided. They will feel a compulsion to see it through to its conclusion.[24]

It is not completely clear why URPs occur. They appear to be an immediate reaction to "triggering" messages. Participants respond automatically, without considering the consequences. They touch off simplistic, almost childish, responses in each other. Perhaps these responses are somehow connected to core beliefs about the self.

What can be done about URPs? The first step is to recognize them for what they are and to try to overcome the tendency to punctuate them inappropriately. The next step is somehow to break the sequence. Wilmot offers five suggestions for stopping spirals that seem applicable to all kinds of URPs.[25]

1. *Change your behavior.* For example, if a partner is afraid of commitment and your

*People with a history can read each other's relational messages at a glance.*

Dale Kennington, *Cocktail Party II*

insistence is only making her more fearful, perhaps you should stop asking for commitment and instead treat the relationship more casually. Wilmot suggests that if doing more of the same doesn't work, doing less of the same might.

2. *Use third parties.* Friends, counselors, or relatives can all provide new perspectives and break problem patterns.

3. *Reaffirm your relational goals.* If your partner is very important to you, try to recall how the relationship developed and what your original goals and commitments were. If the person is a casual acquaintance, think about why it is necessary for you to work together. Discuss this with your partner.

4. *Try to spend either more or less time with the person.* You may succeed in breaking the pattern either by sharing more of yourself or by taking time out to be alone.

5. *Try changing an external situation.* Maybe a change of location, even a vacation together, may succeed in upsetting relational

habits and providing new patterns of behavior.

# Skill Building: Empathy and Perspective-Taking

This chapter has emphasized how relational messages influence the way people interpret the content in each other's messages and, over time, define the nature of their relationship. While relational messages are occasionally verbalized, we have seen that most of the time they are conveyed nonverbally and indirectly. Since relational messages are often communicated spontaneously, the ability to manage them hinges on our becoming more aware of those relational messages we send to and receive from others. We already saw in Box 5.1 how being unaware of relational messages can cause problems online. Box

5.2 shows some of the inadvertent negative messages we send when using cell phones. Whether by phone, computer, or face-to-face, we can improve relational competence through mindful perspective-taking and sensitive empathy.

Traditionally, social scientists have defined empathy in one of two ways: (1) as an individual's ability to experience how another person feels or (2) as the ability to predict accurately another person's verbal descriptions of herself, her situation, or her own emotional state.[26] We prefer to separate these definitions, referring to **empathy** as the ability to spontaneously identify with another on a direct emotional level and **perspective-taking** as a more cognitively oriented appraisal of how the other perceives himself, his situation, and his emotions. These two skills are closely related but not identical. Empathy is probably experienced and communicated at a spontaneous level; perspective-taking is more symbolic in nature.

While empathizing with another certainly helps us understand that person's feelings, empathy alone will not necessarily result in effective communication. Perspective-taking is often required to see the situation more completely and respond appropriately. An example may help clarify this distinction. Let's suppose that your best friend, Samantha, has been rather depressed lately. You know her so well that even when she tries to cover it up, you sense how she feels. In fact, you are so in tune with her that after only a few minutes of interaction, you feel as depressed as she does. You clearly empathize with her, but your getting depressed is not quite the prescription for cheering her up. Empathy alone does not provide much comfort. On the other hand, if you engage in perspective-taking, you are attempting to see the situation from her vantage point and make some sense of it. You try to identify what aspects of the current situation she has focused on, what goals she might have had in mind, what from her perspective must have gone wrong, and why she reacted as she did. In short, you're not just feeling as she feels, but trying to cognitively understand what the whole situation looks and feels like to her. In doing this, you also take into account such things as how she views your relationship and what she expects or hopes a good friend will do in a situation like this. As a result, you might realize that what she needs is your understanding and your gentle reassurance that things will improve. The last thing she needs is the burden of having to help *both of you* recover from depression. Keeping the distinction between empathy and perspective-taking in mind, let's look at some ways that we can improve both of these skills.

Perhaps the single most important thing you can do is *remind yourself to pay attention to the spontaneous emotional expressions of others.* Tests of nonverbal receiving ability indicate that people vary widely in their sensitivity to the nonverbal cues of others. However, researchers have also discovered that when instructed to pay attention to nonverbal cues, most people improve significantly.[27] The implication should be clear—empathy (sensing another's emotional state) results from being aware of his or her nonverbal indications of emotion, but we have to remind ourselves to be attentive. No one else is going to do it for us.

Empathic ability can also be improved if you *communicate in a more expressive manner yourself.* Ross Buck has argued that empathy is not really an individual skill because it is strongly influenced by the expressive communicative qualities of both sender and receiver. According to Buck, "by being expressive, a person encourages the other to reciprocate, so that an expressive person in effect goes through life leaving a trail of emotional expression in his or her wake, while a nonexpressive person leaves the reverse."[28] If our own expressive behavior prompts others to be more expressive and we pay attention to the wider range of nonverbal cues they display, we should be more accurate in reading others' emotional state. Greater empathy will be the result.

Empathy is important in that it provides an emotional connection and a motivation to understand and help others. But greater cognitive awareness of another's point of view requires

BOX 5.2

## Can You Hear Me Now?

# Cell-Phone Etiquette

Whenever a new technology develops, people have to work out social norms to govern its use. When the elevator first became popular, for example, people had to figure out how to deal with being in a confined area with strangers. Thus, the norm: Please face the front of the car. When land-line phones came into vogue, rules for where and when to call, how to negotiate party lines, and how to begin and end calls were needed. Today, it is the cell phone that challenges our social competence. Most of us realize how frustrating and disruptive cell phones can be, but we are only beginning to figure out how best to use them.

In "On the Mobile," cyber researcher Sadie Plant points to some of the challenges individuals must face when using cellular phones.

*The mere presence of a cell phone can be disquieting.* Almost everyone realizes that the constant ringing of a cell phone can be disruptive, but it turns out that just being in the presence of a cell phone can lead to tension. Knowing that a call could intervene can "siphon concentration, demanding attention even when it is not in use," which is why, "for many couples, its presence can be as powerful and distracting as that of a

third person." Cell phones can also intimidate by sending messages about status and power. A number of the people Plant interviewed admitted to being inhibited if a companion displayed a mobile that had more state-of-the-art features than theirs.

*Taking calls can disrupt face-to-face conversation.* Most people know it is bad form to interrupt during normal conversations. Yet, when their cell phones ring, this knowledge flies out the window. People stop in mid-sentence to answer a call without realizing that they are putting their copresent friends "on hold." Having to sit and listen to one side of a conversation is embarrassingly like being an eavesdropper. It is unsettling because one is "neither fully admitted nor completely excluded" from the social space created by the call. An important skill necessary when using cell phones in social situations is deciding how to divide attention between those who are copresent and the person on the other end of the line.

*Cell conversations can be intrusive in public.* Because of the feedback systems in cell phones, people have a tendency to speak louder than they realize. Overhearing a stranger argue with his wife or describe every minute of his (boring) day is bad enough; if his conversation takes place at top volume, it is even worse. Loud conversations are especially disturbing in places where escape is blocked. Many public places are now introducing "mobile-free" zones, where cell phone use is discouraged. In New York City, for example, an ordinance exists that forbids the use of cell-phones in theaters and museums. Unfortunately,

more than just an emotional connection. It requires us to infer how the other person's social-cognitive framing of a situation differs from our own.

One important way we can enhance perspective-taking ability is to *resist our own egocentric tendencies to define the other's experience in our*

*own terms.* This means we must be able to suspend our own view of a situation before we can see another's perspective on the same situation. It may be useful to take inventory of the personal constructs, stereotypes, scripts, and rules that we typically associate with a particular situation and

that doesn't seem to stop everyone. If you think that annoying cell-phone behavior isn't such a big deal, consider the fact that "in 1998, a German businessman died in a fight provoked by what was perceived to be ill-mannered use of his mobile." Rude cell behavior can be dangerous to your health.

*Context is important.* More and more cell phones are being used in the workplace. The fact that their use is approved, however, does not mean they can be used in any way at any time. There are still rules to follow in order to avoid making cell phone faux pas. One you may not have thought of is choosing a professional-sounding ring tone. The latest pop hit or a simulation of Tarzan's yodel may be cute in private, but it sends an entirely different message when you're trying to convey a professional image.

*How to avoid rude behavior.* People are beginning to reach consensus on the social norms governing cell phones. Listed here are some rules that have been suggested for using cell phones appropriately. Read them and see if you agree.

Think twice about taking calls when with other people. *In general, in person relationships should always take priority over phone calls.* So learn when to turn your cell phone off; your caller can always leave a message. If you are expecting an important call, always inform the person you are with ahead of time.

*When in public show concern for others.* Keep your volume under control. If possible maintain a distance of at least 10 feet from other people. And never talk in elevators, museums, libraries, restaurants, places of worship, theaters, concert halls, or classrooms. If you've set your phone to vibrate and a call does come in while you're in a public place, don't answer it. Leave and call the person back from a more appropriate location.

*Don't multitask.* Most writers on cell-phone etiquette agree that making calls while conducting business is a "don't" because it holds up other people. Give your full attention to the task at hand. And never drive while talking on your cell unless your car has a "hands free" setup. Cell phones are increasingly becoming a safety hazard.

Finally, *remember that your phone is sending a message about how seriously to take you.* So avoid loud, lengthy, annoying, or cloyingly cute ringtones in professional situations; keep that sequined cell case at home; and remember that having the latest gadgets doesn't make you better than those around you.

**SOURCE** Plant, Sadie. "On the Mobile: The Effects of Mobile Telephones on Social and Individual Life." Retrieved July 7, 2006, from http://www.motorola.com/mot/doc/0/234_MotDoc.pdf.

**ADDITIONAL READINGS**
Krotz, Joanna L. "Cell Phone Etiquette: 10 Dos and Don'ts." Retrieved June 4, 2006, from http://www.microsoft.com/smallbusiness/resources/technology/communicaitons/cell_phone.mspx.

"Mobile Etiquette." 2006. Retrieved June 4, 2006, from http://phoneybusiness.com/etiquette.html.

"The LetsTalk.com Cell Phone Etiquette Guide." 2003–2006. Retrieved July 7, 2006, from http://www.letstalk.com/promo/unclecell/unclecell2.htm.

then explore alternative ways of defining that situation. Interacting with people whose ethnic or social background differs from your own is another way to gain a different vantage point. Make it a practice in such conversations to place your own opinions and perceptions on hold and listen carefully to how others talk about events and people. Try to identify how the other's cognitive framework (personal constructs, scripts, attributions) differs from your own.

You can also increase your perspective-taking ability if you *ask others to verbalize their per-*

*spectives and then probe for details.* While this may be awkward in some situations, it simply represents an extension of the normal process of getting to know someone. People regularly share their opinions with one another but do not always explore one another's views in much detail. Since most people are willing to talk about their own egocentric views of the world, why not take advantage and learn as much about their perspective as you can? The more you practice perspective-taking, the sharper your skills will be when you need them.

# *Process to Performance*

## Review Terms

The following is a list of major concepts introduced in this chapter. The page where the concept is first mentioned is listed in parentheses.

content messages    (118)
relational messages    (118)
relational definitions    (119)
relational culture    (120)
relational contract    (120)
relational themes    (121)
one-up message    (121)
one-down message    (121)
one-across message    (121)
confirming message    (125)
disconfirming message    (125)
paradoxical definition    (127)
paradoxical injunction    (129)
double bind    (129)
Palo Alto group    (131)
interact    (131)
punctuation    (131)
complementary pattern    (132)
symmetrical pattern    (132)
competitive symmetry    (132)
submissive symmetry    (132)
spiral    (133)
URP    (133)

empathy    (135)
perspective-taking    (135)

## Suggested Readings

Spitzberg, Brian, and William R. Cupach. *The Dark Side of Interpersonal Communication*, 2nd ed. Mahwah, N.J.: Lawrence Erlbaum, 2006. In this new edition, the authors examine how people deal with communication that is "difficult, problematic, challenging, distressing and disruptive."

Stafford, Laura K. *Maintaining Long-Distance and Cross-Residential Relationships*. Mahwah, N.J.: Lawrence Erlbaum, 2005. In addition to discussing long-distance romantic relationships, Stafford also looks at military families who are parted during active service.

## Topics for Discussion
www.oup.com/us/trenholm

## Observation Guide

**1.** Think of a situation in which you were disconfirmed by someone. Describe the disconfirmation. How did you feel about it? How was the situation resolved? Now think of a situation in which you felt confirmed. What was done or said to give you that feeling?

**2.** Have you ever been in an URP? If so, describe the pattern in detail. What was the sequence? How did you feel? What did you do about it? If the URP was resolved, how was this accomplished? If it was not resolved, what do you think might have worked? If you have never been in an URP, you have probably observed one. Answer the same questions as previously about an observed URP.

**3.** Think of a current relationship. What is your relational definition? How did you arrive at it? What kinds of agreements and norms characterize the relationship? Think of a rule that took some negotiation and describe this process. If the negotiation process was easy, what made it so? If difficult, why? What could have been done to ease the situation?

**Exercises**

**1.** Take a play, a recording of a favorite TV show, or a tape of a real-life conversation. Working with a partner, choose a segment and code it, using the following system:

Dominance ( ↑ + ) : An attempt to severely restrict the freedom of the other.

Structuring ( ↑ ) : An attempt to control the other while leaving him or her some options.

Equivalence ( → ) : An attempt at mutual identification or equality.

Deference ( ↓ ) : A willingness to follow while retaining some freedom.

Submission ( ↓ + ) : An extreme willingness to be led by the other.

Discuss the coding until you agree. If possible, record your discussion on a portable tape recorder. What kind of pattern do you see? Is it complementary or symmetrical or mixed? How would you sum up their relationship? (To make this even more interesting, go back and listen to the tape of your own interaction. Together, analyze the control dimension that occurred between you during this exercise.)

**2.** This exercise is designed to give you practice in sending and receiving relational messages. Begin by forming groups of four or six. Turn to the 12 relational themes identified by Burgoon and Hale. Take a pack of 3 × 5 cards and print the names of each relational theme on a separate card, making cards for both positive and negative expressions of a theme (that is, make one card for dominance and another for submission, one for affection and one for hostility, and so on).

Now shuffle the cards and deal an equal number to each member. The person who begins chooses a card from his hand and acts out the relational message. The only words that can be used are the letters of the alphabet recited in order. As a player acts out the message, each member of the group should write on a scrap of paper the message being conveyed. After all members have made their guesses, they should compare answers.

Award five points to the player if he manages to match at least one group member; award five points to all who guessed correctly. Once the points have been awarded, the current player discards the card that was played, and the next person acts out one of her cards. Continue until all the cards have been played. In case of a tie, have the players involved play a runoff round.

Discuss how difficult it was to convey the messages. Are you an emotionally expressive person? Why or why not? Are you sensitive to others' messages? Why or why not?

# PART 3

# Interpersonal Processes

Good communication involves paying careful attention to the social world you occupy, as well as listening closely to those around you.

Franklin McMahon, *Irish Pub*, late 20th century

## CHAPTER 6

# Interpretive Competence
## Perceiving Social Worlds and Listening to Others

"I can't believe you're writing this down," Adam says to his father, who is furiously scribbling the words "milk" and "Pop Tarts" on a scrap of paper. "I just don't want to forget what I need while we're out," his father replies. Adam laughs at his dad and exclaims, "Man, you are old before your time!"

Some forms of short-term memory loss are the direct result of physical impairment in the brain, often caused by a stroke or accident. Adam may have a legitimate concern about what he perceives as premature symptoms of aging demonstrated by his father. But recent research suggests that episodes like this are just as likely the result of social perceptions perpetuated within a culture.[1] Adam's perception linking memory loss to getting older represents a prominent cultural stereotype, as does his father's perception that he needs to make a list in order to "not forget" the two items he plans to purchase.

Social psychologists Becca Levy and Ellen Langer examined the effect of cultural stereotypes about aging on the ability to remember social information.[2] They showed photographs of several elderly persons and described an activity each person had engaged in to two different age groups (15- to 30-year-olds and 59- to 91-year-olds) from each of three cultures, telling participants that they would later meet these individuals. Participants were mainland Chinese, members of the American Deaf community, or hearing members in the United States. Subsequently, participants were shown the photographs again and asked to provide the activity associated with each person. As expected, the younger participants performed equally well on the memory test, regardless of their cultural background. For the older age groups, there were significant cultural differences. Both the Chinese and Deaf elders had better memories than the hearing members of American culture. Why such significant differences?

Levy and Langer chose participants from China and the American Deaf community precisely because neither culture had much in common other than their reputed high respect for their elders. In contrast to Americans who do not have a hearing impairment, the American Deaf are largely insulated from conversation with the hearing and from media fare where negative stereotypes of the elderly might be learned. In fact, when all three groups were asked, "What are the first five words or descriptions that come to mind when thinking of somebody old?" the American hearing sample listed significantly more negative traits than either of the other groups did. As you might expect, negative stereotypes correlated strongly with poor performance on the memory test. This suggests that after years of encountering and internalizing such negative stereotypes, including the expectation that one's memory will fail as one ages, elder Americans live up to those expectations. Elders who have much more positive views of the aging process do not seem to experience the same level of short-term memory loss.

This study dramatically illustrates the fact that our perceptions of the world (and of our place in it) are based on culturally shared assumptions. We see what our cultures and communities tell us to see and we fail to notice what they feel is unimportant. Often we act as though we were on automatic pilot, relying on old habits that keep us from seeing what is really there. Obviously, this kind of cognitive carelessness can affect the accuracy and effectiveness of our interpersonal encounters.

Langer refers to our tendency to interpret social worlds habitually as **mindless interaction**.[3] After more than two decades of research on the subject, Langer has come to view this mindless form of perception in terms of three characteristics: entrapment in old categories of thought, inability to attend to new signals, and reliance on single perspectives. In contrast, a more mindful approach permits us to create new categories for examining social worlds, open ourselves to new information, and see the world from multiple perspectives.[4] Of course, we cannot and need not be mindful of every aspect of perception. If we did, we'd never be able to get to on with the business at hand. Instead, we need to be selectively mindful, replacing cognitive habits that have outlived their usefulness.

In this chapter, we'll look at the many ways that people make sense of social life. As you

learn about the various ways we perceive social situations and listen to one another, you'll want to keep asking yourself these questions: "Do my perceptual habits encourage me to be more aware or less aware of what is happening around me?" and "Can I alter my perceptual habits in ways that give me more options for interpreting and acting with others?"

In addition to a general discussion of perception, two other themes will emerge in this chapter. One is an emphasis on listening. Many textbook authors devote separate chapters to perception and listening. But if you stop to think about it, listening is a rather obvious extension of our ability to perceive and interpret the behavior of others. Unless we perceive the world intelligently, we cannot possibly be very successful as listeners. The second theme is the importance of the role of emotion in the perceptual process. New research on the neuroscience of the brain has repeatedly demonstrated that our emotions represent a significant "alert system" that motivates us to attend to both incoming stimuli from the social environment as well as the state of our own internal environment. We will draw upon some of this research as we proceed and conclude with a discussion of emotional intelligence, our ability to listen to emotional information.

# The Process of Perception: An Overview

Interpreting the world is a complex process of constructing meaning, one that is influenced by many factors. What we experience in the present, for example, is tied to what has happened in the past and is affected by what we anticipate will happen in the future (see Box 6.1). It is also a function of our emotional state, our motivations, and the social cognitive structures we inherit from our cultures. A first step in gaining more control over our perceptions, and thus becoming more interpretively competent, lies in recognizing and appreciating their complexity.

## The Perceptual Trio: Emotion, Motivation, and Cognition

The process of constructing perceptions is also affected by an individual's emotional, cognitive, and motivational state.[5] What we attend to and how we interpret it depends upon how we feel (emotional states), our ways of categorizing the social world (social cognitions), and our momentary and long-term goals and objectives (motivations).

### Emotion and Perception

For a long time, the dominant view of emotion could be summed up in the phrase, "Don't let your emotions get the best of you." Emotional reactions were seen as clouding our judgments rather than facilitating them. Research over the last several decades has seriously challenged this view. In fact, it is now fairly well established that emotional responses work hand-in-hand with our capacity to reason and make effective decisions. Emotional arousal appears to be the body's way of signaling various brain systems to "pay attention" to incoming stimuli, facilitating both the processing of information and its storage in long-term memory.[6] In biological terms, emotions are all about our survival as organisms. Emotions allow us to react to external conditions. As such, emotions produce *feelings* that influence our perceptions of the people and things around us.

Because all humans share a biological heritage, our brains and bodies are hardwired to experience emotional reactions to stimuli in largely preset ways. This does not mean that individual experience and culture have no role to play. All three forces—nature, culture, and individual experience—work together to shape the link between emotional states and perceptions.

Of all the potential objects in the environment that might induce emotion, only a few are hardwired in. When we see anything resembling a snake or other predator we act instinctually—we

jump or freeze and then feel afraid (in that order!). But we react emotionally to lots of other objects because of the social or cultural meanings attached to them or because of individual experience. Most of us have had the experience of having a strong visceral reaction (negatively or positively) to a person we've never met before. Chances are that there is some facial feature, tone of voice, or aspect of her or his posture that unconsciously reminds us of someone we strongly dislike or totally adore that triggered such a response, but we may never recognize the reason for that perception.

As one example, Elizabeth Phelps and her colleagues have shown in several brain-imaging studies that there is a tendency for people to have a more enhanced recognition for unfamiliar faces of members of their own race and a more fearful reaction to unfamiliar faces of other races, as measured by activation of the amygdala, the brain system involved in responding to fear. The higher participants scored on a measure of racial bias, the higher the level of fear activation.[7] This tendency is called the **same-race advantage** for facial recognition. It is more pronounced for white Americans than African Americans, presumably because members of a minority group have more contact and experience interacting with those in the majority than the majority does interacting with members of minority populations (the **contact hypothesis**). Demonstrating further support for the contact hypothesis, the activation of a fearful response disappears when participants are shown faces of other-race persons whom they know.[8] This demonstrates one of the ways that cognitive and emotional circuits influence our perceptions and also shows how experience can modify those same categories.

Emotions can also be induced by specific memories of events or people, which in turn affect how we perceive a current situation or person. Memories often appear "out of the blue" and into our conscious thoughts. When they do, they not only influence how we feel, but can have a spillover effect on how we perceive and are perceived by others. When strong emotions

BOX 6.1

## The Power of the Present

# Memory, Perception, and Imagination

As humans, we live in some combination of three worlds—the past, present, and future. All three impinge on each other in complex ways. Psychologist Daniel Gilbert describes *perception* as the faculty that allows us to see the present, *memory* as the means of seeing the past, and *imagination* as our capacity to render the future. Interestingly, he notes that all three share similar shortcomings that inevitably lead us to misremember the past, misperceive the present, and misimagine the future. The key factor in all three processes is the brain's incredible power to manage the billions of bits of data encountered moment-by-moment.

**Memory.** Our brains are essentially data compressors that reduce incoming perceptions to a few key features, compare those features to preexisting categories, and store snapshots of the whole experience. Thus, our memories are not full-featured or faithful representations of past events. They are "constructions assembled at the time of retrieval," and they are assembled from a maddening array of sources: (1) partial information abstracted and stored during the original experience; (2) emotional feelings associated with the original event; (3) other bits of relevant information already stored in the brain, but not specifically attended to in the original experience; (4) information acquired after the experience; and (5) thoughts and feelings present at the time when the stored memory is being retrieved (Moskowitz, 2005). Actually, retrieving is not a very appropriate term for how we reconstruct a memory. We fabricate memories, in the weaver's sense of that term, by piecing together or reweaving the array of sources involved. Researchers now know that what we remember says as much about our present circumstances as it does about the past, including our current motivations and emotional states. Gilbert uses the term *presentism* to note that our present perceptions tend to dominate both memory and imagination. We remember in ways that fit our present circumstances, particularly our current motivations. For instance, couples whose relationships have deteriorated tend to remember the entire re-

are experienced during a social encounter, they often amplify the memories of that episode by releasing hormones from the adrenal gland that strengthen memory traces.[9] Support for what is known as the **mood congruity hypothesis** indicates that memories are more easily retrieved when there is a match between the emotional state at the time the original memory was formed and when it is retrieved. This is why we are more likely to be flooded with unpleasant memories when we are sad or have an abundance of great memories when we are very happy. Our current mood not only enables us to recall episodes involving similar emotions, but also influences how we reconstruct past memories.[10] If Grant gets an-gry at Amy because she left the apartment unlocked, and he recalls other times when she forgot to do important tasks, he may remember having been angry in those previous episodes even though at the time he felt her forgetfulness was endearing or cute. Thus, memory is not only fallible, it appears that we "remember" in ways that facilitate our current emotions and motivations.

## Motivation and Perception

Recent research on brain functioning has rekindled interest in how individual motivations affect the way the brain processes information, including our perceptions of situations and impressions of others.

lationship as an unhappy one, not just the fact that it ended badly (Holmberg and Holmes, 1994).

**Perception.** We also tend to misperceive (or perhaps we should say partially perceive) present circumstances, not because our brains are trying to dupe us, but because representing everything that is happening around us in full detail would simply take too much time and tax the brain's processing systems, resulting in paralysis and an inability to act. We don't realize the extent to which we see limited aspects of the whole and actually fill in other details based on knowledge structures such as stereotypes.

**Imagination.** Likewise, we project into the future. Where is this relationship going? How will I feel about my friend five years from now? Should we continue to see each other? Perception and memory are intertwined, each affecting the other. When we imagine what our future will be like, the same kind of complex interaction occurs. For example, we tend to underestimate the amount of novelty that is likely to occur in the future and overestimate how similar to today the future will be even when the future we anticipate is only a few minutes away. In a study, students were asked to take a simple five-question test and choose whether they would prefer to learn the correct answers or to receive a candy bar as a re-

ward, but not learn the answers. Those who were asked to choose before the test chose the candy bar. Those who were given the choice after the test opted to learn the answers. A third group did not take the test, but was asked to predict what choices they would make both before and after taking the test. The third group consistently chose the candy bar in both cases; they were simply unable to imagine how the curiosity generated by the experience of taking the test would trump the appeal of the candy bar (Loewenstein, Prelac, and Shatto, 1998).

**SOURCES** Daniel Gilbert, *Stumbling on Happiness* (New York: Knopf, 2006).

Gordon B. Moskowitz, *Social Cognition: Understanding Self and Others* (New York: Guilford Press, 2005), p. 22.

D. Holmberg and J. G. Holmes, "Reconstruction of Relationship Memories: A Mental Models Approach," in *Autobiographical Memory and the Validity of Retrospective Reports*, ed. N. Schwarz and N. Sudman (New York: Springer-Verlag, 1994), pp. 267–88.

G. F. Loewenstein, D. Prelac, and C. Shatto, "Hot/Cold Intrapersonal Empathy Gaps and the Under-prediction of Curiosity" (unpublished manuscript, Carnegie Mellon University, 1998), cited in G. F. Loewenstein, "The Psychology of Curiosity: A Review and Reinterpretation," *Psychological Bulletin* 116 (1994): 75–98.

Gordon Moskowitz has argued that a considerable degree of human goal-seeking operates automatically, outside of conscious awareness.[11] Motivations that operate outside of our awareness are called **auto-motives**. Automatic processing can take over once goal-oriented behaviors become habitual. Many skills, such as driving a car or fielding a baseball, once learned sufficiently well, can be and are engaged in by means of automatic processing. This is the brain's way of maximizing efficiency. Such automatic processing often produces a "perceptual readiness" to attend to, judge, and act in accordance with certain individual motives or values, particularly those to which one has made a long-standing commit-

ment. Goals related to our sense of self, to our professional commitments, or to our image of what a given type of relationship should be like are examples of motives that may have been initiated consciously, but over time have become habitual. For instance, a professional interior designer may have had an intuitive feel for principles of good design as a young child, and then made a conscious effort (i.e., was motivated) to learn those principles by enrolling in art school. After several years of study, internships, and work in a professional design firm, the motivation to redesign the world around her has no doubt been internalized to such a degree that she doesn't stop to think about it, except when a client needs a rationale for why she creates a particular design. She is motivated to perceive the visual world in terms of design principles.

Another striking feature about our motivations is that they can influence our perceptions of situations that may seem irrelevant to that particular motive. Research suggests that if that motivation is "primed" (i.e., engaged or made conscious) in one context it can have a carryover effect in other unrelated contexts.[12] Take our professional interior designer's habitual motivation to be concerned about design elements in her visual world. We wouldn't be surprised that her townhouse was exquisitely furnished or that the backyard garden could be featured in *Better Homes and Gardens*, or that she forms impressions of other people by how well they coordinate their clothing. Those contexts seem relevant to principles of good design. But we might be surprised to find out that her habitual readiness to see design principles in visual perception sometimes influences the way she judges conversations or how she feels about her relationships with others. Having contemplated a particularly difficult design problem all day, she may be primed to interpret a conversation with her friend that evening as poorly designed or reflecting that the pattern of their lives is out of joint. And she may not even realize that she's drawing upon a design yardstick to measure their relationship. At other times, she may feel that the design aspects of her life are overwhelming and be motivated to turn off that interpretive framework for a while.

If motives operating at the edges of our awareness can have this kind of impact on our perceptions, it is equally or even more likely that motives we are consciously aware of will impact our perceptions. One study compared the perceptions of people who were explicitly asked to adopt a goal ("form an impression" of a target person from a list of behaviors the person had performed) with others who were implicitly "primed" to adopt the same goal by subtle exposure to words suggestive of the idea of impression formation. Both groups recalled a greater number of behaviors the target had performed than did a third group that was simply asked to remember the behaviors.[13] Having the goal of

"forming an impression" enhanced what people recalled, whether or not the participants were consciously aware of the goal.

Recall from the chapter opening Adam's concern about his father making a grocery list for the two items he needed to purchase. Adam's perception of his father's forgetfulness could be shaped by both his emotional connections ("Even though I won't admit it in public, I do care about my father's mental health") and his own motivational goals ("Why does he always forget the Pop Tarts?"), as well as the cognitive schemas he carries around in his head ("Old people are forgetful"). Next we take a closer look at some of those cognitive schemas.

## Social Cognition and Perception

**Social cognition** refers to the study of the cognitive structures and processes that influence our perceptions of people and social events (see Table 6.1 later in this chapter). The stereotype is perhaps the most common example of a cognitive structure that influences how we communicate with others. As we've seen, when we meet a new person the brain cannot map every detail of the person's physical appearance or behavior, and people certainly do not reveal everything about themselves in the first few minutes of interaction. But the brain does pick up on salient features of the other's behavior and compare them to preexisting categories. As a result, we "fill in" a lot of the missing details automatically by applying categorical thinking and form an increasingly more complete (but alas, not always accurate) image of the other. This tendency to rely on categories of thought as much or more so than specific details from the current situation has been called the **principle of least effort**.[14] In the section that follows, we will explore a wide range of cognitive schema or ways that human brains categorize social life.

Before discussing the specific processes, let's ask ourselves why social cognitive, emotional, and motivational schemata play such an important role in interpersonal communication. We think there are four connections. First, *social cognitions affect how we receive and interpret others' messages and the emerging patterns of interaction.* Our cognitive and emotional categories create expectations for how people will or should behave or how social situations are supposed to unfold. Second, *social cognitions guide our actions.* In order to be socially appropriate and personally effective, we need to know how to frame a given situation and thus know what rules apply. Third, *examining the appropriateness of the social cognitions we employ can enable us to reassert some measure of control over social situations.* We can easily fall into routines that are no longer productive or even counterproductive—recall Langer's notion of mindless interaction—and need to be adjusted. Understanding that social cognitions are templates for behavior, we can choose to change the template. Finally, *communication with others can alter our social cognitions.* At its core, communication is a creative process, with obvious potential to change our social worlds. While some aspects of cognitive processes are probably hard-wired, the *contents* of our cognitive schemata are the product of many prior communication experiences and can be modified by further communicative interventions. Langer might tell us that mind*less* interaction tends to reproduce existing schema, whereas mind*ful* interaction has the potential to modify those same schema. For a really good example of how this can play out in serious, everyday situations, see this chapter's Research in Review.

As we examine specific schema, keep in mind that the use of these cognitive categories is driven as much by our motivations and emotions as it is by the categories themselves.

# The Structure of Social Cognition

Before we can fully understand how our social cognitions influence the way we communicate, we need to have a basic understanding of how such processes work. We start by examining a variety of cognitive structures or schemata and then note how these schemata operate in interaction.

## Types of Cognitive Structures

Many different kinds of cognitive structures influence our social behavior. Cognitive psychologists have created the term *schemata* as a general label for these mental models. A **schema** is a cognitive structure that helps us process and organize information.[15] It is a cluster of abstract knowledge containing typical features, qualities, behaviors, or other expectations based on our experience with specific people, places, or events, but those specific people, places, or events may or may not be part of the mental representation.[16] These expectations, in turn, enable us to comprehend and make sense of novel events.[17] Researchers disagree about how such mental categories are actually organized. For instance, some argue for a **prototype model** of schema organization, with a prototype being a typical category member or a cluster of the most common features associated with a given category.[18] For instance, each of us probably has a mental image of a person we'd call a "used-car salesperson"— for me, it's someone with shiny, slicked-back hair, a multicolored suit, a plastered-on smile, and a smooth tongue. Other researchers believe that schemas are organized in terms of an **exemplar model**.[19] This model posits that our mental categories are composites of specific examples of actual people, places, or events we've experienced, not abstracted features, but whole people, actual car lots, and real slices of sales presentations. As Cantor and Kihlstrom suggest, it is likely that we use both prototypes and exemplars in some blended fashion to organize our perceptions.[20] Either way, we use cognitive schemas in two ways to generate information related to perception: (1) to fill in missing information or gaps in our knowledge and (2) to make inferences, or generate additional information beyond what we've actually seen or heard.[21]

Researchers study schemata by exposing people to social events and then testing how they

## When Being Mindful Really Matters

# Making Accurate Decisions in a Cockpit Crisis

Discussions of mindfulness can seem dry and academic, but the ability to think actively and creatively and to share that thinking with others can have life-and-death consequences. Consider an airline crisis. Here pilot and copilot must make split-second decisions. Although having two people in the cockpit should cut down on human error, in some instances, error actually increases. In "Shared Mindfulness in Cockpit Crisis Situations," Janice Krieger argues that only when both pilot and copilot operate in a condition of shared mindfulness will they be able to handle crises effectively. Shared mindfulness is a state of mindfulness that is cooperatively achieved so that both individuals are continually open to incoming data.

But how is shared mindfulness achieved? What kind of communication inhibits it? To find out, Krieger videotaped 10 dyads, made up of experienced aviation students, as they responded to crisis scenarios. To make the situation more realistic, they deliberated under severe time pressures and environmental distractions. Krieger used what is called grounded research. That is, instead of having preconceived ideas about what

she would find, she allowed her findings to emerge from the data. As she looked at the tapes, she identified key factors that either enhanced or inhibited shared mindfulness.

Four factors were found to be related to shared mindfulness: (1) reasoning from a positive perspective; (2) using a kaleidoscopic perspective; (3) verbalizing thoughts and feelings using precise, confident, and conditional language; and (4) acknowledging each other's contributions. In other words, when dyads focused on what could go right rather than what could go wrong, saw the problem from different perspectives, talked aloud as they thought, and listened actively to their partners, they were able to achieve shared mindfulness. Factors that inhibited shared mindfulness were (1) precognitive commitment, (2) nonpositive reasoning strategies, and (3) overt dominance. That is, when dyads made up their minds early, when they focused on obstacles to solving the problem, and when one dominated the other, they were unable to act mindfully.

Krieger found that the dyads that made the best decisions also used more mindful communication, whereas dyads that were trapped in scripted thinking made poor, life-threatening decisions. Interestingly, if one partner acted mindlessly, even if the other was mindful, the dyad as a whole was unable to make an effective decision. Krieger admits that the study needs to be replicated in more realistic conditions, but she feels that her study gives initial support to the idea that mindfulness is often shared and that it can affect crisis decisions.

Krieger, Janice L. "Shared Mindfulness in Cockpit Crisis Situations: An Exploratory Analysis." *Journal of Business Communication* 42, no. 2 (2005): 135–67.

remember what they have experienced. As we've seen earlier in this chapter, people do not reproduce memories, they reconstruct them. The difference between what actually happened and

how it is remembered is taken to be an indication of the expectations associated with cognitive schema. Current summaries of the research on cognitive schemata point to several general types:

personal constructs, person and group stereotypes, role and relational schemas, self-schemas, and event schemas.

## Personal Constructs

A **personal construct** allows us to describe things in greater detail and make judgments about them. Constructs are mental yardsticks for deciding how two things are similar yet different from a third thing.[22] They answer the questions, "What are its characteristics?" and "What do I think about it?" For instance, you might judge members of the Hell's Angels and Guardian Angels to be violent and dangerous in contrast to members of the Los Angeles Angels of Anaheim baseball team. Another person might perceive the Guardian Angels and Los Angeles Angels to be positive role models, with the Hell's Angels serving as negative role models. A third person, not being a baseball fan, might construct the differences in terms of how boring it would be to be on the baseball team versus how exciting it would be to join the other two groups. The terms *violent, dangerous, positive* versus *negative role models*, or *exciting* versus *boring* are examples of personal constructs. We will look at other examples of personal constructs in person perception later in this chapter.

## Person and Group Schemas: Stereotypes

A **stereotype** is a cluster of expectations or beliefs about the probable behavior of members of a particular social group.[23] Stereotypes have a certain sense of "allness" to them, as if every member of a group always behaves like other members. Thus, stereotypes answer the question, "What can I expect this kind of person to do?" Several studies have shown that people, especially when distracted or multitasking, often rely on stereotypes and thus misremember whether statements heard or behaviors observed were actually performed and by whom. In one study, participants watched a videotape of two women, one described as a Democrat, the other as a Republican, each making statements about their political beliefs. Both speakers made statements

*The way we identify people and their social roles helps to determine whether or not we choose to communicate with them.*

that were consistent with the general stereotype of beliefs held by their political party, but they also made some statements that are not generally believed to be held by members of their party (e.g., a Republican making a pro-choice statement on abortion or a Democrat favoring stricter measures on immigration). Some participants had been instructed to think about how they felt about the statements being made (self-focus), while others were told to focus on what the speaker felt about the statements (other-focus). When participants were later asked to recall which woman made which specific statements, they tended to attribute statements to the source suggested by the stereotype rather than to what each woman actually said. Older adults and those with self-focus instructions were the most likely to misattribute statements.[24] Other studies have shown similar error tendencies, with friendly behaviors more likely to be attributed to a priest and unfriendly behaviors to a "skinhead"[25] or assertive statements attributed to a person believed to be of higher status than her or his conversational partner.[26]

We know that any cognitive category is an abstraction and a partial summary of our past experiences, so we would expect that stereotypes, like other schemas, may be more or less accurate when applied to a given person. They may outlive their usefulness and they are often unfair to

## Stereotypes and Social Identity

# *Mean Girls*

Mark Waters, 2004

Newcomer Cady (Lindsay Lohan) knows all about survival of the fittest. She was raised in Africa by anthropologist parents. What she doesn't have a clue about is surviving an American high school and maneuvering her way through a world where everyone is judged by the people with whom they hang out. Cady's first friends (Lizzy Caplan and Daniel Franzese) are social outcasts, but it's not long before Regina (Rachel McAdams), the most popular girl in school, asks her to become a member of the Plastics. At first, Cady joins as a lark, but as she spends more time with the mean girls, she starts to change, and soon her inadvertent actions plunge the school into chaos.

*Mean Girls* satirizes the caste systems that determine high school popularity. Loosely based on Rosalind Wiseman's book *Queen Bees and Wannabes: Helping Your Daughter Survive Cliques, Gossip, Boyfriends, and Other Realities of Adolescence,* the film is more than just another high school comedy. It is also a clever commentary on how easy it is to embrace stereotypes and how often we allow flawed models to determine the way we see ourselves and others.

individuals, but they do make the world more organized and predictable. Culture is a major source of stereotypes, many of which are simplistic and prejudicial to members of fringe groups. We will explore communication patterns related to prejudice in Chapter 13.

### Role and Relational Schemas

In addition to mental models of personality types or members of specific ethnic or cultural groups, we also draw upon cognitive structures that organize our expectations about roles that people play and the types of social relationships that we can have with others. A **role schema**, for instance, is an internal representation of the rules, norms, and behavioral expectations associated with social roles such as occupations, gender, age, and so on. Like most children, Adam (the Pop Tart lover in our opening story) shares a cultural image and expectations about the role of fathers in general and measures his own father's behavior against that image. Such role schemas may involve sophisticated subcategories, such as cool or uncool fathers, dead-beat dads, and so on. Adam may be wondering why his caring father has such a difficult time remembering Adam's need for sustenance.

Although not a direct test of cognitive role schemas, Phillip Zimbardo's classic study of a simulated prison illustrated how quickly volunteer college students adopted role-specific behavioral expectations. Students assigned to be "guards" quickly became authoritarian and employed psychological abuse tactics to divide and conquer the student "prisoners" as they began to make alliances and resist the guards' violent tactics. The study, originally planned to last two weeks, had to be called off after six days because, as Zimbardo put it, "our guards became sadistic and our prisoners became depressed and showed signs of extreme stress."[27]

**Relational schemas** are "cognitive representations of typical interaction patterns"[28] and indicate interpersonal expectations as opposed to expectations based exclusively on one person's role or personality. Relational schemas are thought to organize a range of information about specific types of relationships (e.g., typical patterns of interaction, thoughts and feelings about relationships) and to trigger emotions associated with those relationships. Specific types of relational schemas include mother-daughter, romantic partners, best friends, business partners, and so on. Recent research suggests that relational schemas emerge, at least in part, on the basis of one's experiences with significant attachment figures in infancy and childhood. For instance, Collins and Read identified three dimensions related to attachment experiences: comfort with closeness, ability to depend on others, and anxiety about being unloved or abandoned.[29] Every time we interact, we use a relational schema to guide our own message production. If we want to maintain a friendship, for example, we will behave in accordance with the relationship rules we associate with the schema of "good friends" and may even avoid behaviors that we think of as those belonging to merely "casual friends." If our desire is to move the relationship even further, say toward that of "best friends," we will rely on our conception of behaviors that fit that schema.

## Self-Schemas

One of the most amazing feats of the human brain is that it not only enables us to perceive, organize, and act on information about the social environment but also provides us with the sense of personhood or agency—that there is a "me" doing the perceiving, remembering the past, imagining the future. The fact that we have this capacity has puzzled philosophers for ages and has only recently led to speculation by the neuroscientific community as to how this ability we call consciousness evolved in our species' history.[30] Nonetheless, cognitive psychologists have demonstrated that our sense of self operates on the same basis as other schemas. **Self-schemas** can be defined as information about ourselves that is organized, linked, and includes abstractions such as aspirations, values, attributes, preferences, and behavioral routines.[31] Hazel Markus

*Particular social situations call for particular modes of behavior and communication. We use scripts to guide our everyday actions.*

pioneered the study of self-schemas and has noted that people make self-schema judgments about themselves rather easily and quickly, make predictions about their own behavior consistent with their self-schema, and, interestingly, are highly resistant to learning information about themselves that contradicts their self-schemas.[32] We will explore more about the self-concept and self-schemata in Chapter 8.

## Event Schemas: Scripts and Episodes

**Event schemas** register our beliefs and expectations about different kinds of social situations. We associate different behaviors as typical of a fraternity party versus a dinner party. For instance, we may expect beer to be served at one and wine at the other. Or we may expect people to act in a more spontaneous and raucous fashion at one and to be dignified and reserved at the other, and so on. Some social events seem to invoke scripted behavior, while others allow us to interact in a more flexible or open-ended fashion.

**Scripts** are guides to action. A script is defined as "a coherent sequence of events expected by the individual either as a participant or an observer."[33] Scripts answer the questions, "What can we do together?" "How shall I proceed?" and "What do I do next?" Many scripts—such as those for attending a traditional wedding or going to a Catholic Mass—are well defined and make it easy for us to know what to do next. Unscramble the following list of behaviors associated with a "restaurant" script, and place them in the usual sequence:

- The waiter takes your order.
- You pay the bill.
- You go to the salad bar.
- You look at the menu.
- You leave a tip.
- The host seats you.
- The waiter brings your meal.
- The waiter brings drinks or appetizers.
- You ask about the special.

Chances are you know the script pretty well. What other situations do you know that are highly scripted? Robert Abelson noted that we typically choose to engage in scripted behavior when certain *preconditions* (features present in the social environment) exist and we have developed an *action rule* indicating that it is appropriate to invoke that particular script.[34] But we don't always choose the scripted route. In these cases, we rely on more general event schemas called episodes. **Social episodes** are "internal cognitive representations about common, recurring interaction routines within a defined cultural milieu."[35] Episodes are typically less scripted and define expectations in broader, more general terms—hanging out, going shopping, gossiping, studying together, attending a lecture, watching TV. Specific, sequenced routines are replaced by a range of possible behaviors, as long as they don't stray too far from the overall content of the episode. We will explore more about social episodes later in this chapter.

Personal constructs, stereotypes, role schemas, relational and self-schemas, and event schemas illustrate the many ways that our brains organize social information and assist us in perceiving and interacting with others. Each of these schemas, summarized in Table 6.1, directly affects our interpersonal communication. We interact differently with different types of people in different situations. We may even have a script for testing the "best-friend" potential of a new and emerging relationship. Such a script might suggest that certain best-friend behaviors ought to occur before others. For example, an invitation to an all-day shopping spree might precede spending a weekend at the family's summer camp, since the first is of shorter duration, limited to a single activity, and doesn't involve contact with one's family. As we interact we use personal constructs to make mental notes about the relational implications of each other's messages. Some of these impressions may even alter our relational schemas, changing the way we approach similar others in the future. Once we have formed a basic impression of a type of person or relationship, our stereotypes help us anticipate how the other is likely to behave. And as long as we don't mindlessly employ these schemata, but also remain open to new possibilities as they emerge, our communication can be both efficient and effective.

## Cognitive Schemas and Perception

Clearly, our perceptions of situations and other people are influenced by our own motivations, emotions, and cognitive structures such as schemas and scripts. We do not simply perceive the social world as it is, but construct that world and the people in it by organizing and interpreting incoming information in light of mental models or cognitive structures developed from previous experience. We are "active" processors of information, adjusting it to fit our preconceptions. The way we do this and the confidence we have in our perceptions is nothing short of amazing. In this section, we look at (1) how we convince ourselves

| TABLE 6.1 | What Do Cognitive Schema Help Us Do? |
|---|---|

| Type of Schema | Help Us To | Example |
|---|---|---|
| Personal constructs | Define the characteristics of a person, object, or event | Physical: thin-bulky<br>Interaction: talkative-quiet |
| Prototypes<br>Exemplars<br>Role schema<br>Relational schema<br>Self-schema | Identify what kind of person, relationship, or object we're dealing with | Person: nerd or gearhead<br>Role: interviewer-interviewee<br>Relational: All-American couple, bosom buddies<br>Self: optimistic-pessimistic |
| Stereotypes | Develop expectations for the behavior associated with a persona or social event | Blondes have more fun; Greeks are stuck-ups; engineers are boring |
| Event schema<br>Scripts<br>Episodes | Know what to do in a particular situation | "greeting script," "first-date script," "knock-down, drag-out argument" |

that our perceptions are accurate and meaningful rather than biased and arbitrary and (2) under what conditions our perceptions are likely to be derived from automatic versus more conscious processes.

### Naïve Realism: Seeing What We Believe

Cognitive psychologists and neuroscientists have repeatedly demonstrated the extent to which subjective biases influence our perceptions of people, objects, and events. Our brains are primed by context, our momentary and more enduring goals, and emotional states to capture a relatively small number of crucial visual or auditory cues and "fill in" the rest of the information from preexisting cognitive categories to form a perception of the object, person, place, or event at hand. We go well beyond the information given, allowing our interests to dictate what we pay attention to and giving greater weight to emotional aspects of our experiences. We experience what we perceive, and to a lesser extent what we remember, as though they were complete and accurate representations of the world. Cognitive psychologists refer to this tendency as

naïve realism.[36] Our perceptions feel real to us, and, by and large, they are accurate enough to enable us to do what we need to do. We do not realize that what we are seeing and hearing are *interpretations* of the world and thus we treat what we see "as if" it were objective and real. Paraphrasing William James, we "make" our experiences more than they make us.[37]

How do we essentially fool ourselves into thinking that we see the world as it really is? One critical factor is that the basic mechanisms operating in naïve realism would have had considerable survival value as our species evolved. Evolutionary psychologists believe that survival was much more likely for organisms whose brains could process information quickly based on minimal but highly significant cues. Thus, our ancestors who *acted* prior to identifying all the details about a potential predator lived to see another day. Likewise, much of our social knowledge is in the form of cultural values and norms that have been internalized to the point that we don't question them. They serve as internal, but largely invisible, frames of reference and guide our perceptions in ways that we simply need not doubt (unless we encounter someone who does not share those norms and values). Finally, we become so accustomed to our own cognitive schemas and scripts that we do not realize we are employing them. It feels to us as though we are seeing things "as they are."

What are the consequences of naïve realism? How does it impact our social judgments? One major consequence is that we just don't recognize our own biases, even when they are pointed out to us. In one study, researchers asked students to rate how considerate they were toward others in comparison to the average person on campus. Then participants were told about previous research demonstrating that 70 to 80 percent of people rate themselves as above average in similar types of comparisons. When asked if they had exhibited this bias in their earlier ratings of consideration, 63 percent of participants still said their earlier ratings were accurate. Another 13 percent thought they had previously underestimated how considerate they were![38] Other consequences are that we typically assume that similar others "think like I do" (false consensus), but that opponents who interpret the same information differently than we do must be reflecting a bias. Coming as no surprise to media reporters, research even indicates a tendency to see neutral parties who disagree with our perceptions as biased against us.[39]

### Dual Processing and Impression Formation

As the concepts of mindless interaction, naïve realism, and the principle of least effort suggest, people have a marked tendency to rely on categorical thinking in their judgments of others, but typically fail to realize it. However, there is evidence that we can and do overcome this tendency on many occasions. The fact that we can engage in both automatic and mindless interaction and in more mindful assessments of details about others has been captured by what social scientists call **dual-process models** of impression formation.[40] Researchers refer to our reliance on schemas and other categories by various terms:

*automatic, mindless, heuristic, top-down* or *theory-driven processing*. When we exert greater effort and break out of this mindset, researchers speak of *controlled, mindful, systematic, bottom-up,* or *data-driven processing*. Dual-process models attempt to outline the conditions in which we are more likely to exert effort and look closely at the data available to us about the other. We can summarize this dual processing of perceptual cues in terms of three steps: (1) attention and identification, (2) controlled categorization, and (3) personalization.

*Attention and Identification.* The first step in any perceptual process is that we take notice of some stimulus in our environment—whether an object or another person—and identify or categorize it. This initial process of attention and identification takes place almost exclusively at an automatic, preconscious level. If the stimulus is another person or several persons as competing stimuli, **selective attention** will influence which of the many possible stimuli we will focus on. To some extent selective attention is driven by our preconscious goals and motivations, as we saw in our discussion of the carryover effects of motivations from one context to another. But there are also aspects of other people's features and behavior that "grab" our attention. We are more likely to attend to **salient features**, those that are most prominent and difficult to ignore. Research suggests that we selectively attend to features or behaviors that are intense, novel, complex, and sudden or changing.[41]

Once specific stimuli about a person have garnered our attention, the identification process continues by automatically triggering any one of a number of schemas (e.g., social categories such as age, sex, ethnicity) whose frequent use makes them easily accessible. Processing is likely to remain at the automatic level unless the perceiver has a self-relevant reason to begin evaluating the other in a more systematic way. We "know" that a certain kind of person is in our field of vision, but have no need to make them the subject of our thoughts. This explains why we often treat "waitstaff" in restaurants or hotels as nonpersons. Once we have categorized them in terms of their role, they become irrelevant to us as individual persons and we rarely need to process additional information about them.

*Controlled Categorization.* When we do find another person relevant to our purposes, we abandon our purely automated mode of processing and initiate a more systematic evaluation of him or her. This does not necessarily mean that we avoid stereotyping or other cognitive schemas. Marilynn Brewer argues that at this stage, we make a conscious decision as to whether or not we need to know the other on a personal level.[42] If we do not, we will continue to categorize in a top-down fashion, drawing upon schema-based expectations such as stereotypes or roles. The person is relevant to us, but in a way that is appropriate to a given social category. At work, for example, our boss's behavior is highly relevant to us, but we probably utilize a schema for boss-employee relationships instead of feeling a need to get to know the boss on a personal level. But what if the boss consistently behaves in a manner atypical of bosses in general? Does this mean we develop a more personalized impression of her? Probably not, according to Brewer. Her research suggests that if the person doesn't fit the existing category, we may engage in a process of **individuation**, where we decide that the boss is an exception to the rule and we assign her as an extreme or special instance of the category. Thus, the social categories we draw upon can be quite nuanced. Within the social category of "teachers" we might differentiate among a *prototype* (the typical teacher), an *exemplar* ("the best teacher I ever had"), and special cases (unconventional teachers, or the most bizarre). By differentiating we are being more mindful in our perceptions, yet we are still constrained by categorical thinking.

*Personalization.* There are times when the combination of our own interests and the behavior of others suggests that category-based processing is not appropriate or useful. Brewer calls

this the **personalization** stage because the perceiver becomes actively involved in organizing information around the individual person, free of stereotypes or other categorical expectations.[43] What conditions lead us to make more personalized impressions? You shouldn't be surprised to learn that emotional and motivational factors are the most influential. If we sense that our own personal goals can be enhanced by learning more about the other person, we are far more likely to drill for information from the bottom up. Personalization may be triggered by the inadvertent discovery that you and the other person have similar goals (e.g., you both plan to participate in professional tournaments involving the card game *Magic: The Gathering*). Likewise, if you have recently experienced a significant emotional loss and want to fill the void, you are more likely to seek out and make the effort to personalize another person than if you met that same person at a time when your emotional life was full and satisfying.

In summary, our perception of others is driven both by our own biases as naïve realists and by salient features that others bring to the table. As we've seen, the perceiver's own motives and purposes play a key role in determining when automatic processing gives way to more controlled or mindful processing of information.

# Four Processes in Interpersonal Perception

To interact with others successfully requires a wealth of social knowledge. You must be able to trust your intuitions (i.e., automatic processing based on your cognitive schemas) or attend with greater mindful effort to information in your social environment in order to form good solid impressions of events, people, and relationships (i.e., what Brewer calls controlled processing).

This is no easy task. To help, we've tried to simplify the problem by highlighting four perceptual processes that people engage in before, during, and after social interaction (see Table 6.2). These include identifying (1) what the situation is, (2) who the other person is, (3) who you are and what kind of relationship between self and other is implied, and (4) why patterns unfold the way they do. Let's examine each of these processes more closely.

## Sizing Up Situations

The more we know and make use of information about the particular situations in which we interact with others, the more likely we are to produce effective messages. We have to say this with some caution because research demonstrates that although people know a lot about situations, they tend to underutilize that information when explaining communication behavior.[44] To counter this tendency, we propose four useful ways to become more mindful of situations: (1) identifying types of episodes, (2) using scripts to guide interaction, (3) recognizing the consequences of following scripts, and (4) thinking about situations in more complex terms.

### *Orienting Ourselves: Episode Identification*

At one time or another, we have all been in situations where we didn't know what was going on or what to do. Visiting a foreign culture or being initiated into a secret society are examples of situations we might not understand as well as we'd like. Within the boundaries of our own social circles, we are much more adept at recognizing the nature of a given situation and the behavioral expectations associated with that situation. In its simplest form a situation is "a place plus a definition."[45] When we enter a specific environment, our first task is to orient ourselves and get our bearings. "Where am I?" "What is happening here?" Where we are determines to a large extent what we can do socially. But identifying the place alone is not enough. The definition of a situation implies constraints on our interaction behavior.

| TABLE 6.2 | The Four Social Cognition Questions |
|---|---|

**For any given conversation or social interaction:**

1. How does each participant view the situation? What type of event or activity does each think he or she is participating in?

2. What impressions do the participants have of each other?

3. What kind of relationship have the participants enacted? Do they both view the relationship as having the same status (for example, friends or casual acquaintances)?

4. What explanations do the participants provide to account for their own and each other's behavior?

For instance, a church building can serve as a place for worship, weddings, ice cream socials, even bingo. We would not expect to behave in the same way in each of these episodes. To communicate appropriately requires that we recognize both the physical and the social cues that define the episode or activity that is taking place. Each culture has an array of social episodes that enact what it means to be members of that culture. For example, there are lots of different "biker" cultures (e.g., Harley motorcycle clubs, outlaw bikers, biker women, sober bikers, bikers for Christ) who differentiate themselves by the types of activities they engage in or avoid. Members hang out at bike shops or participate in "bike week rallies" such as the Sturgis Motorcycle Rally held every August in Sturgis, South Dakota. We define our relationships, in large measure, by the kinds of episodes that we engage in with each other (e.g., going to a movie, shopping, dining out, kayaking, talking politics, planning a garden, taking a vacation). Individuals maintain their self-identities by the kinds of social episodes they choose to enact and the types of people who are invited or excluded from participation.

Often we have a particular episode in mind when we initiate a conversation with someone. Perhaps you know someone who likes to "pick fights" or tease a brother or sister in order to get him or her riled up. Often an episode is a process of negotiation—one person suggests an activity, only to have the other counter with another option, as in this conversation:

LAURA  I noticed that Kmart is having a sale on lawn mowers.

VINCENT  This is the only evening I'm free all week. I don't want to spend it shopping for a lawn mower. Besides, the Battle of the Mack Trucks is going on at the fairgrounds tonight.

Social interaction is a continuous dance in which participants accept and decline each other's invitations to enact different episodes. For instance, when two old friends have a chance meeting on the street, the question, "Can I buy you a drink?" is an invitation to engage in the episode of "talking over old times." Refusing the drink because you are not thirsty would be missing the point—it would reflect a failure to recognize the other's definition of the situation.

### Using Scripts to Guide Interaction: Open, Closed, and Defined Episodes

When people play out an episode, they may also follow a script. As we have seen, a script is a highly predictable sequence of events. Some classroom learning episodes are highly scripted; others are not. For example, you may be able to predict (from experience) that every Wednesday morning your history professor will call the roll, hand out a quiz, collect the quizzes, lecture for 20 minutes, and end the class with a humorous anecdote. The more predictable the sequence of events, the more scripted the interaction is. Another class may be taught so differently that you never know for sure what will happen in a given class period. Both examples are classroom episodes, but only the first one follows a clearly identifiable script.

Scripts and episodes are useful guides to interaction. Identifying the episode narrows the range

of possible actions and reactions. Knowing the script makes social life even more predictable. Michael Brenner has proposed that the vast majority of social episodes fall into one of three types: closed, open, and defined.[46]

*Closed Episodes.*  When a situation is almost completely scripted, it is a **closed episode.** Rules for proper behavior are well known in advance and govern the flow of interaction. Rituals such as greetings and religious observances are closed episodes. Many business organizations tightly script interactions by training their personnel to follow carefully devised sets of procedures. If you've ever applied for a loan at a bank, you have probably participated in a closed episode. You have a standard set of questions you want answered (the loan rate, fixed or variable, length of repayment, and so on) and so does the loan officer (income, collateral, address, credit references, and so on). Other, less formal, interactions are also somewhat scripted. An episode of "small talk" has a limited range of topics, although the sequence in which these topics are discussed may vary.

*Open Episodes.*  When participants enter a situation without any preconceived plan or with a very general one, they are involved in an **open episode.** In such situations there is greater freedom to create new forms of interaction and to change episodes midway through. Episodes such as "hanging out with friends" are sometimes scripted, but not always. When almost anything can be introduced as a topic of conversation or an activity to perform, the episode is an open one. An orchestra performing a John Philip Sousa march is clearly following a musical script, but a group of musicians having a "jam session" is not. The freedom to improvise or break the rules is typical of an open episode. Some open episodes may be unsettling, since there is no clear idea of what should be done next. Perhaps you have been in situations where nobody seemed to know what to do. We know of an instructor whose routine on the first day of class was to walk into the room, assume the lotus position on top of his desk, and say nothing for the first half of the class. His point was to show how communication is used to define ambiguous situations. Eventually, students would begin talking to one another, trying to figure out what he was doing. From the students' point of view, this was an open episode.

*Defined Episodes.* While closed episodes are known to be such in advance as a result of expectations, many situations are defined "in progress" as participants follow their own personal goals and plans to achieve a working consensus. Even so, the consensus is often temporary—definitions of the situation may fall apart as quickly as they develop. A **defined episode** is an open episode in which the participants are trying to negotiate some closure. The difference is that open episodes are experienced as creative and liberating; defined episodes are competitive attempts to control the activity. Brenner suggests that defined episodes are often ambiguous and unstructured interactions because each partner may be proposing alternative directions for the episode. For example, a not-very-good salesperson might initiate a "sales episode" but eventually succumb to a clever-but-unwilling-to-buy customer's definition of the situation as "shooting the breeze." A romantic evening can be spoiled quickly when a candlelight dinner becomes redefined as an episode of "stilted conversation" or "talking about the kids." In closed relationships people may spend a lot of time just deciding what episode to enact next. We know of four friends who, in the course of one evening, proposed over 20 different activities for that evening. Needless to say, they ended up doing nothing but talking about what they could be doing. Chances are none of the persons involved planned to spend the evening that way, but our observations lead us to believe that these two couples frequently end up playing this "what do you want to do tonight" episode.

Although we may think that closed episodes are too limiting and value open ones for the freedom they provide, stop and think how chaotic social life would be without any well-defined or scripted episodes. The important thing, of course, is that we recognize the types of episodes others propose so that we can accept the invitation or decline gracefully.

## Thinking More Mindfully about Situations

We have previously defined the nature of a situation in terms of the idea of context—a physical place plus a social definition. It is clear from research that people are mindful of situations and use information about the situation to help them interpret the meaning of events and messages, but they also tend to underappreciate how much the situation constrains and explains our interaction with others. There are several reasons for this, the understanding of which can help us become more mindful about the power of the situations to influence interpersonal communication. (1) *Situational forces are often invisible to us*—we tend to notice the behavior of persons in situations more than the situational constraints themselves because our attention is drawn to people doing things, not to the situation that frames and informs what and why they are doing it. (2) *Situations involve multiple dimensions of activity.* For instance, in a given situation, we may be involved in performing one or more tasks, while at the same time attending to and deciphering the interaction behavior of the other person and processing details about the physical environment (which may be stable or changing). (3) *The presence of a difficult task can cause greater cognitive load,* impairing our ability to attend to other details of the situation. Researchers have frequently demonstrated that giving people a difficult task to perform while simultaneously asking them to form impressions of other people results in less mindful, more automatic processing of information about the environment and the people in it.[47] (4) *Other people are part of the situation* and are reacting to situational constraints as much as we are (e.g., following similar or different scripts). Thus, situational expectations can shape the emerging patterns of interaction between people without either one recognizing this fact. In effect, we have to monitor both our own understanding of the situation as well as taking the perspective of the other and imagining how they perceive the situation, what their situational goals might be, and how all of that is affecting the unfolding pattern of interaction.

## Sizing Up People

As we interact, we come to an understanding of what other people are like. Knowing how to size up the individual is another way to reduce our uncertainty about communication. In studying the process of impression formation, researchers have discovered several factors that influence our judgment. We will discuss four of these factors: (1) the use of personal constructs, (2) implicit personality theory, (3) self-fulfilling prophecies, and (4) cognitive complexity.

### The Use of Personal Constructs to Judge Others

Earlier in the chapter, we identified personal constructs as mental yardsticks for evaluating objects, events, and people. Here we focus on how we use those constructs to form impressions of those people with whom we communicate. Since constructs are "personal," no two people will use them in exactly the same way. You and I may both observe Bill eating a sandwich in two bites, mustard dribbling down his chin. You may think he is "aggressive" while I argue that he is "messy" and "impolite." What we see in others is a combination of their actual behavior and our personal construct of their behavior. These constructs say as much about you and me as they do about Bill.

Even though we each use different constructs to judge others, we do use them in similar ways. Steven Duck has noted a typical pattern in the use of four different kinds of constructs.[48] The four types are:

- Physical constructs (tall-short, beautiful-ugly)
- Role constructs (buyer-seller, teacher-student)

- Interaction constructs (friendly-hostile, polite-rude)
- Psychological constructs (motivated-lazy, kind-cruel)

Our initial impressions are frequently based on physical attributes—we take stock of how people are dressed or how attractive they are. These are quickly followed by the formation of role constructs as we try to make sense out of each other's position in the social world. As we talk, we may focus attention on interaction constructs, or aspects of the other's style of communication. Finally, we use these observations to infer what makes the other tick (psychological constructs)—we begin to guess at motivations and build a personality for the other. When we reach this last stage, we have gone beyond simply interpreting what we see and hear; we've begun to assume that we know things about the person that we can't see.

### Implicit Personality Theory: Organizing Trait Impressions

We don't simply form isolated opinions of other people; rather, we organize all of our individual perceptions into a more complete picture by filling in a lot of missing information. One of the ways we do this is through what is referred to as an **implicit personality theory.** This is the belief on our part that certain individual traits are related to other traits. If we observe a trait that we think is part of a cluster, we will assume that the person also has the rest of the traits in the cluster. Each of us has our own notions of what traits go together. For some, the traits (or constructs) "intelligent," "quiet," and "friendly" may cluster together.[49] If we observe behavior that we interpret as friendly and quiet, we may then attribute intelligence to that person without any firsthand evidence. The formation of trait impressions depends on several factors: (1) the perception of central traits, (2) the order in which traits are observed, and (3) the influence of prototypes and stereotypes.

*Central Traits.*   Some traits may carry more weight than others in forming impressions and can be described as central traits. When present, a central trait changes the way we perceive the whole cluster of traits. In a classic study, social psychologist Harold Kelley presented two groups of students with the following list of adjectives describing a new instructor they were about to meet. One group was told the new instructor was "*warm,* industrious, critical, practical, and determined"; the other group was told the instructor was "*cold,* industrious, critical, practical, and determined."

Which description do you think led students to form a more favorable impression? If you said the first description, you are in agreement with most of the students in this study. The central trait (warm-cold) changed the way the perceiver judged the other traits, which in turn affected the overall impression.[50]

### Primacy vs. Recency Effect

Another factor that makes some traits stand out is when they are first perceived. The tendency for first impressions to be lasting ones is known as the **primacy effect**. When more recent observations change our initial impression, we have the **recency effect**. Which effect is more likely to prevail? Generally, the primacy effect rules—we tend to form impressions quickly and hold on to them. For example, you attend a social mixer and see Pete, whom you do not know, placing a whoopee cushion on the chair of some unsuspecting person. You surmise that he must have gone to a lot of trouble to bring the cushion to the party and wait for the right moment to play his practical joke. You quickly form an impression of him as a "clown," and you are not overly impressed by such people. Your impression is likely to stick, even if he spends the rest of the evening in a rather docile mood. The primacy effect is directly linked to the widely observed principle of least effort noted earlier in this chapter. It is clearly less effort for us to sieze on one or two salient behavioral observations and fill in the rest by employing an implicit personality

schema than to hold off making a firm judgment until more evidence is in. If this is the typical case, under what conditions does the recency effect kick in? As we saw earlier in this chapter, we are more likely to make a greater effort when we have a motive to do so. Research shows that people who strive to be more accurate or think they will be held accountable for their assessments of others are less swayed by initial information and allow more recent information to influence their impressions.[51]

## Sizing Up Relationships

As we read the situation and form impressions of the other, we also face the perceptual task of determining what aspects of self fit the situation and how the emerging relationship between self and other should be interpreted.

### Self-Monitoring: Deciding Who to Be

We will consider the self-concept and communication in Chapters 7 and 8; for now, it is important to realize that our self-concept is frequently connected to both our sense of the situation and our relationship to others in that situation. The awareness of images of self and the ability to adapt these images to the situation at hand has been referred to as **self-monitoring**.[52] A high self-monitor tends to read the social situation first and then present an appropriate face, as opposed to simply presenting a consistent image of self in every situation.

Mark Snyder characterizes the difference between a high and low self-monitor in the form of the question each might ask in defining the situation:

> *The high self-monitor asks, "Who does this situation want me to be and how can I be that person?" In doing so, the high self-monitoring individual reads the character of the situation to identify the type of person called for by that type of situation, constructs a mental image or representation of a person who best exemplifies that type of person, and uses the prototypic*

*Daily situations can involve multiple dimensions of activity: performing tasks, attending to the behavior of another person, and processing details about the physical environment.*

*person's self-presentation and expressive behavior as a set of guidelines for monitoring his or her own verbal and nonverbal actions. [The low self-monitor asks,] "Who am I and how can I be me in this situation?"*[53]

Instead of calling on a prototype to guide his or her actions, the low self-monitor behaves in accordance with an image of his or her "real" self.

Our culture often sends us mixed messages. For instance, we are told to "be ourselves" and "don't ever change"—messages that seems to endorse the low self-monitor's position. On the other hand, we're also told to "be flexible" and "avoid getting in a rut." Research demonstrates that being adaptable (being a high self-monitor) is one of the keys to social success. It is probably best to recognize that either extreme can be lim-

iting. If we always try to maintain a consistent self-concept, we will be less versatile and won't experience as much of the full range of human emotions. But if we are always changing to fit the situation or someone else's conception of us, we may compromise important standards and values. The best course is to ask ourselves what is more important in a given situation—being adaptable or being consistent.

### *The Impact of Relational Schemas and Specific Relational Definitions*

When people interact, each presents an image of self to the other. These images are, however, usually quite fluid. We are responsive to the feedback of the other and begin quickly to negotiate a definition of the relationship between us. Thus, one important perceptual process is the identification of the type of relationship that applies in a given situation. Office workers at a company picnic may perceive that the supervisor-subordinate relationship with the boss no longer applies during a game of softball. But what if the boss assumes he or she is still in charge and gets to decide who should pitch? The difference in perceptions may lead to negative feelings that were never intended.

This process of identifying a relational definition can take the form of automatically applying a relational schema (outside our awareness) or more consciously drawing upon relational scripts typical of interaction with a specific person in the past. In terms of schemas, researchers have found that relational schemas can be invoked automatically, particularly when a person has been "primed" to activate a specific schema. In one study, college women were asked to visualize their parents or a group of friends during the initial phase of the research. Later they read a sexually permissive story and were asked to rate it for enjoyablility. It mattered which type of relationship schema had been activated, as the women who were primed to think about their parents rated the sexual story as significantly less enjoyable.[54] In other studies, people primed to think about their relationship with a critical, hostile, or unpleasant person were more self-critical when performing a task, judged ambiguous information as more hostile, or avoided persons who physically resembled the person who was unpleasant.[55] Such priming of relational schemas occurs in our daily lives as well as in the research laboratory. Virtually any environmental cue, if significant enough, can activate a relational schema. Getting a phone call from an old friend, catching a whiff of a familiar perfume, or hearing an old song on the radio can activate a relational schema and unconsciously establish a framework for our next encounter.

There is solid evidence that our thoughts are populated with relational schemas of significant others. We hear our parents' voices as we contemplate a decision. We can envision how our boss will respond to our request to extend a vacation. We are more likely to attend to and recall information that is consistent with the opinions of someone they will be conversing with later.[56]

Mark Baldwin has argued that relational schemas operate as interpersonal scripts or "if-then statements."[57] A husband might come to a conclusion about arguments with his wife: "If she gets angry and I don't respond, she will be annoyed, so I'd better say something to show I'm involved." A student might learn from prior interaction with professors that "If I ask how I can improve my paper instead of complaining about the grade, my professor will at least listen to my concerns or might offer an extra credit assignment."

Sally Planalp found that student-professor prototypes not only guide students' and professors' interactions but often help them survive these interactions intact even when the actual pattern of interaction varies from the schema. She asked students to read different versions of conversations between a student and professor in which the student asked to add the professor's class, make up an exam, or change a grade. In the different versions, the professor made dominant, neutral, or submissive statements about the student's request and the student responded in a submissive, neutral, or dominant manner. One week later, students were asked to identify whether the conversation they had read the week before contained the dominant, neutral, or submissive statements. As expected, students "remembered" (incorrectly) having read statements that were more in line with prototypical expectations than with the actual dialogues the students had read.[58]

Robert Carson has used the term **master contract** to refer to the worked-out definition of a relationship that guides the recurring interaction of any dyad.[59] This means that as a relationship develops, perceptions that were originally guided by a schema give way to an understanding based on verbalized agreements or silent acceptance of established patterns of behavior. We will have more to say about relationship patterns in the remaining chapters of this book. For now, it is important to recognize that identifying the type of relationship you're involved in may be just as crucial as knowing the situation or forming a useful impression of the other.

## Explaining Behavior: Attribution Theories

When all is said and done, we are frequently left with the question, "Why did he (or she) do that?" or "Why did I do that?" Most of the time we are quick to offer some type of explanation, create closure for ourselves, and move on. At other times, we are asked to account for our behavior and offer an explanation. Theories concerned with how we infer the causes of social behavior have been called **attribution theories**. Before we examine the research on attributions, let's look at a conversation and try to explain what we observe in the behavior of the participants.

Imagine that you've been visiting your friends Angela and Howie for a few days. You are sitting at the kitchen table with Howie when Angela comes home from work. She looks very tired. The following conversation ensues:

HOWIE (*looking up from the plastic model car kit he has been putting together*) Hi, honey. How was work?

ANGELA (*after saying hello to you, she scans the room*) Howie! You haven't done the dishes yet? They're left over from last night. Can't you do anything you're asked to do?

HOWIE It's been a busy morning. I just haven't had time.

ANGELA No time! You don't have a job. You're not looking for work. And you can't find 15 minutes to do a dozen dishes?

HOWIE I've been looking through the classifieds, for your information.

ANGELA Did you send out any resumes?

HOWIE No, not really . . .

ANGELA Here we go again. Do I have to physically force you to sit down and write letters of application and send your resume out?

HOWIE I'll do it. I'll do it.

ANGELA You'll do what? The dishes or the resumes?

How would you explain the communication behavior of your two friends? Is Angela the kind of person who constantly nags and belittles others? Or did Howie provoke this tirade? What other explanations could there be?

Attribution theorists have discovered several ways you and I infer the causes of each other's behaviors. Consistent with the dual-process models of impression formation, attribution researchers have concluded that people operate on the basis of a two-step process: (1) They make initial, automatic inferences about the causes of behavior and then under certain conditions (2) adjust those assumptions by engaging in more thoughtful, controlled processing of the information available. People tend to attribute cause to one of two forces: either the person or the situation. Our perceptual capacities typically direct attention to the person behaving; thus attributions tend to overemphasize personality and other person-related causes (e.g., momentary goals). But there are times when situational forces are unmistakable—most people would behave anxiously when told that a family member has been rushed to the emergency room. We would be less likely to attribute their behavior to having an anxious personality in that situation.

Studies have shown that people can make adjustments to their initial attributions by employing either a discounting rule or an augmenting rule. The **discounting rule** suggests that if people are given information suggesting that the situation promotes the type of behavior observed, they will adjust an initial attribution that the person caused the behavior. Likewise, if the initial judgment was that the cause was situational and the observer receives information indicating that the behavior is associated with a personality disposition, the observer then discounts the role of the situation to some extent. The **augmenting rule** focuses on inhibiting factors. If a situation would normally constrain the behavior observed and the person exhibits the behavior anyway, the cause must simply be the force of his or her personality. Imagine that you are eating dinner in a very classy restaurant, and you hear a person talking at very loud volume throughout the meal. You are probably annoyed and no doubt think of this person as highly inconsiderate. The situation clearly calls for more moderate behavior. The augmenting rule also applies when a personality trait normally inhibits a given behavior. A shy person, for example, would not be expected to act in a really expressive manner, such as yelling and screaming at others. We are more likely to correct an initial assumption that there is something wrong with the person and look for a more situational explanation.

Next we summarize the research on attributions in terms of four biases in how we explain our own and others interpersonal behavior.

### Attribution Bias #1: The Anchoring Effect

First impressions have a lasting impact. When someone is instructed to focus on a task in a certain way or asked for his or her initial judgment on an issue, that first snap judgment tends to have a lasting impact. In terms of attribution theory, the **anchoring effect** refers to the fact that a person's final judgment about the cause of another's behavior is almost always biased in the direction of his or her initial point of view.[60] This does not mean that the initial judgment will not be corrected in some way, but that whatever adjustments the perceiver does make will not be neutral. They will be adjustments that deviate from that starting point, and often they do not move very far, as we'll see in the next section.

### Attribution Bias #2: Overestimating Personality

One of the most powerful tendencies in explaining the cause of another person's behavior is to assume that the person not only intended the behavior, but that a personal disposition—honesty, friendliness, arrogance, and so on—is the primary reason underlying the behavior. Research demonstrates that this tendency can occur automatically without our being aware that we are doing it. Moskowitz calls these **spontaneous trait inferences** (STIs) and notes that such snap decisions about others serve to anchor our judgment and are hard to change.[61] Why do we do it? One reason is clearly cultural. Those of us in Western cultures are taught that individuals are the primary makers of their own success. We are doers. Our heroes are individuals who make things happen. We make sense of the world through these kinds of stories so often and so effortlessly that it becomes routinized. We reach for the trait explanation first and then back off that explanation only if there are other more compelling reasons to change our minds. In some other cultures, most notably in Asian cultures, relationships take precedence over individual preferences, often resulting in situational or relational attributions. In one cultural test of these assumptions, Matthew Lieberman and his colleagues found that while U.S. and East Asian college students made similar automatic trait attributions, the East Asians were much more likely to "correct" their initial assumptions and identify situational causes of behavior than were the U.S. population, even under conditions that typically enhance trait dispositions.[62]

Our ability to read personality into situations is illustrated by a fascinating study conducted by Sam Gosling and his colleagues. They took participants to 94 offices in five office complexes and asked them to form impressions of the people who occupied each office by examining the artifacts and condition of the office (the occupants were not present at the time of the visits). The personality ratings made by the participants were compared with similar ratings made by coworkers of the office occupants and showed remarkable consistency.[63] Participants were able to make relatively accurate assessments of personality traits even though they had never met the persons whose offices they examined.

### Attribution Bias #3: Underestimating the Situation

Underestimating situational causes and overestimating personal ones go hand-in-hand. While people readily concede that situations influence behavior, they aren't very good at recognizing this in practice. As we saw in the section on sizing up situations, the influences of the situation are often subtle. In fact, some research even suggests that focusing participants' attention on the situation leads them to strengthen their assumptions that the person, not the situation, is responsible for the behavior. Daniel Gilbert and colleagues showed participants silent videotapes of a person sometimes talking about anxiety-provoking topics and other times about non–anxiety-related topics. Half of the participants were given the additional task of memorizing the topics of discussion as they watched the tapes (high cognitive load). Even though those participants were focused on memorizing information about the situational constraints, they failed to adjust their initial dispositional attributions. Those not experiencing cognitive load were able to consider the situation and make adjustments.[64]

### Attribution Bias #4: Perspective Matters

Finally, attribution theory research has demonstrated a clear tendency for actors to invoke more situational explanations than observers do. When we're asked to explain our own behavior, we are much more likely to recognize how much the situation impinges on what we do. If I throw a shoe at the television, I can explain that it was because of tension built up at the office, a stupid call by the referee, or the loose morals of Hollywood producers. There are several reasons why actors tend to overattribute behavior to situational factors. In the case of negative behavior, blaming it on the situation can serve as an excuse or justification. Another reason is that we simply have more information about our own past and present experiences than an observer would. We know if we had a bad day; an observer probably doesn't. Finally, our visual vantage point makes a difference. When we behave, we don't see ourselves performing the action. What we do see is other people and external circumstances. It's

*Listening is a complex, multistage process. When we listen well, we enhance our ability to communicate.*

Claudio Bravo, *Oleo Sobre Lienzo*, 1979

much more likely that we will reference the situation as the cause for our behavior.

We also tend to cut some slack for members of our own social groups. We explain the behavior of members of our own *in-groups* (friends, associates, our own ethnic group) more charitably than we do the behavior of highly stereotyped *out-groups* (groups to which we do not belong).

BOX 6.2

Interpretive Competence

# *Making Sense by Using Reflections and Interpretations*

The process we have dubbed as interpretive competence is all about making sense out of social situations, the people involved, and the messages they send or give off. One way to improve interpretive competence is by practicing two feedback tools that make possible interpretations more obvious. When we use these two talk tools, others can confirm or redirect our interpretations, if need be. Psychologist Gerald Goodman suggests two specific "talk tools"—reflections and interpretations—that help produce better sense-making. *Reflections* are feedback messages that attempt to mirror or register another's meaning. There is no bid to add new meaning or analyze or judge; we just try to re-present the other's message in a somewhat condensed version. It's trying to get the essence of what another means. A good reflective statement is the kind that elicits a response like "exactly" or "absolutely."

One easy way to learn how to provide reflections is to listen to group discussions and think of ways to summarize the different points of view being expressed. Goodman calls this a *roundup*

*reflection.* Here's an example from an episode of *Donahue.* A 20-minute debate on parental discipline of children has been relatively one-sided, with both the panel expert and most of the audience expressing the sentiment that parents should be more assertive and less permissive with their kids. A number of different points have been made about being tired of kids talking back to their parents, the parents feeling inferior to "experts" (e.g., child psychologists), or feeling guilty for possibly damaging a child's self-esteem, and even the idea that a good smack now and then gets and keeps a child's attention. Phil Donahue, consummate talk show host, sums several minutes of talk with a concise reflection that rounds up the fragmented comments: "It's as if we're almost afraid of our own children . . . afraid to assert our own authority . . . everything is the parent's fault and there's a lot of guilt inflicted on them."

Donahue's summary statement crystalizes the sentiment and also implicitly invites others to express an opposite point of view, which they do. But the dissenters, who argue that kids need more reassurance, that guilt is a way of making parents more aware, and that physical punishment indicates a lack of communication skills and can easily lead to reliance on absolute force, are being shouted down by the majority. Once again, Donahue draws out the essence of the minority argument: "In some quarters of this room is the suggestion that if we use words like 'firmness, reasserting control,' what we allow some parents to do is . . . use absolute force without any kind of sensitivity toward the wishes of a child. . . Force works only for a little while."

In general, researchers have found that we attribute positive behavior by in-group members to their personalities, while negative behavior is explained in terms of situational factors. We explain the behavior of out-groups in exactly the opposite manner. Positive behavior is explained away, as situationally produced, while negative behavior is seen as the product of personality or group culture.[65]

Can we overcome these tendencies to discount the situation when observing other people's behavior, especially those whom we do not

As Goodman notes, Donahue's use of roundup reflections "brought balance to the issues."

*Interpretations,* on the other hand, are attempts to remake another's message, to add new meaning, and to redirect the process of sensemaking. Interpretations are much more assertive than reflections. As a result, they are risky ventures, but they demonstrate that interpretive competence is as much a process of constructing meaning as it is one of discovering it. Interpretations can actually help another person see his or her actions in a new context—they can add new meaning to one's understanding. Goodman illustrates this with a lengthy phone conversation between long-time friends Jean and Claudette, both single and in their thirties, complaining about the lack of nonsexual relationships with men of their own age:

CLAUDETTE  I've never even had those *semi-*friends that some women make out of men.

JEAN  That's been true all the years I've known you, Claude. I've always seen you that way. But it's been so easy for you to attract all sorts of lovers. You beat us all at capturing men.

CLAUDETTE  Big deal—all I have to do is make myself up and catch their eye . . . But why can't men see us as more than just their sexual conquest? . . . Am I to blame 'cause I was born beautiful? (*they both laugh*) But really, what the hell did I do to deserve this treatment?

JEAN  (*mock cowgirl drawl*) Not a thang, honey. Pretty little thang like you . . .

(*Back to regular voice*) Uh, maybe you *can* do, you know, something about the way you talk to men. Claude, I have to tell you, over the years I've seen you contribute to the problem just the way you communicate . . . It might be partly your fault that guys look at you as sexually available.

Goodman notes that Jean offers two interpretations in this brief excerpt from their conversation. The first is her classification of Claudette as highly successful at developing sexual relationships with men. It's meant and taken as a compliment. The second interpretation is considerably more risky. Jean suggests to Claudette that she is partly to blame for not having male *friends* because she communicates in a way that suggests she wants a *sexual* relationship. The conversation continues with Claudette resisting but not necessarily rejecting Jean's interpretation. While no definitive conclusions are drawn, Jean has successfully created new meaning for Claudette to ponder. In this example, Jean has not only made sense of Claudette's original message, she has also sized up her friend and gently offered Claudette another way of sizing up her own situation.

SOURCE Gerald Goodman, *The Talk Book: The Intimate Science of Communicating in Close Relationships* (Emmaus, Pa.: Rodale Press, 1988).

**ADDITIONAL READING**
Cherney, Marcia, and Susan Tynan. *Communicoding.* New York: Donald I. Fine, 1989.

know well? While difficult, it is possible for observers to engage in **perspective-taking** and to learn to see things from the actor's point of view. Some studies have demonstrated that when participants are asked to take the perspective of the other, observers generate more situational explanations and actors become more dispositional in their attributions.[66] Taking the perspective of the other almost always enhances interpretive competence. Specific strategies such as using and responding positively to reflections and interpretations are described in Box 6.2.

# Listening: Interpreting Verbal and Nonverbal Messages

So far we have looked at how social cognition and perception work and how they allow us to make sense of our worlds. In this section we will show how they are related to communication through the process of listening. **Listening**, according to the International Listening Association, is "the process of receiving, constructing meaning from, and responding to spoken and/or nonverbal messages."[67] As the definition suggests, listening is not the same as hearing. **Hearing** is a physiological process that occurs when sound waves are processed by the central nervous system. Listening is a social cognitive activity that is affected by past experiences and future expectations. Listening also differs from hearing in that listening is not limited to sound but involves data from all of the senses. When we listen we must hear, but we must also see and feel. To be effective interpersonal listeners, we must be able to hear the words our partners utter, but we must also be able to pick up on the nonverbal cues that tell us what they actually mean.

Listening is an absolutely essential part of communication, yet it is often overlooked. When most people think about improving their ability to communicate, they think about developing their sending skills: They imagine themselves giving more effective public presentations or speaking to those around them with more confidence and clarity. They seldom think about improving their ability to listen to what others have to say. Yet studies have shown that listening is a vital skill in both personal and professional settings. In fact, listening has been linked to leadership effectiveness, managerial competence, and the development of rewarding relationships.[68] Many of the communication problems we face, both personally and professionally, are directly related to faulty listening.

*Our ability to react emotionally to things we hear in conversation is shaped by nature, culture, and individual experience.*

## The Listening Process

As the definition of listening suggests, listening is a complex, multistage process. When we listen we attend to, interpret, evaluate, and respond to messages. First, we direct our attention to that part of a message that is relevant and screen out irrelevant details and distractions. Next, we use appropriate schemata to make sense of what we hear and see. We also evaluate the message, asking ourselves if it is believable and complete. Finally, we respond in appropriate ways. Although these steps seem simple, they are actually quite difficult and call for complex social knowledge and conscious effort. It is easy to let attention wander, to misinterpret meanings, to accept content without thinking, and to respond in ways we are not aware of. Have you ever drifted off during a class discussion so that when you did start to pay attention you had no idea what anyone was talking about? Have you ever turned an assignment in late or missed an appointment because you got the dates mixed up? Have you ever believed what you were told or accepted a faulty argument simply because you didn't bother to think about what was said? And have you ever been accused of not listening when, in fact, you actually were? These are common examples of poor listening. They happen every day, and they can interfere with effective communication.

## Types of Listening

We listen for many reasons and in many ways.[69] Sometimes we listen simply to discriminate between stimuli. For example, we struggle to identify a scary sound heard in the night; we listen carefully to determine whether our guests are coming "today" or "Tuesday"; we try to decide whether our boss's smile is sincere or feigned. This kind of listening, called **discriminatory listening**, is basic to all other forms of listening. We succeed in this kind of listening by accurately recognizing message elements.

Sometimes we listen for the sheer pleasure of the activity. For instance, we listen to our favorite CDs; we hear and see a stage production of a new play; we watch a classic movie and appreciate the director's cinematic skill. In all of these cases we are engaging in **appreciative listening**. Experiences such as these can challenge us mentally (e.g., when we listen to a new or more intricate form of music or when we encounter a complex work of art) and can affect our moods (e.g., when we listen to our favorite bands or watch a TV show simply to relax). We succeed in this kind of listening if we enjoy and recognize the value of the listening experience.

Much of the listening we do involves receiving and remembering new information. For example,

we listen as our accountant explains the new tax laws; we concentrate as our child tells us what he wants for his birthday; we watch and listen as a friend tells us how she feels about a family crisis. In these situations, we are involved in **comprehensive listening**. We succeed if we understand and can accurately re-create the intended meaning.

We also listen to make judgments. For instance, when we see a commercial, we listen to determine whether to buy the product; when we hear a politician talk, we decide whether we support her views; when a friend asks to borrow money, we try to evaluate our chances of being repaid; and when a child says he doesn't care about being cut from the team, we listen carefully to decide whether or not he is in distress. These are examples of **evaluative listening**. When we listen evaluatively we make judgments about the intentions and competence of a source and about the completeness of the information. Here we do not succeed by simply understanding the message; success involves making sound decisions about it.

Finally, we listen to help others. When a child cries uncontrollably, we try to find out what is wrong and comfort and calm him; when a friend's most important relationship breaks up, we lend a sympathetic ear; when an acquaintance needs to talk about a decision, we help uncover options. In these cases we are taking part in **empathic listening**. When we listen empathically, we allow our partners to talk out their problems. We refrain from giving advice or being evaluative; instead, we respond in ways that encourage them to find their own solutions. We offer support and send the message that we care. Success in empathic listening occurs when others are better able to understand or cope with a problem.

## Effective Responding

Imagine the following: You are sitting at your computer playing FreeCell. Your roommate is obviously upset and starts to tell you how stressed and anxious she is. You listen, but, as you listen, you keep looking at the computer screen and continue to play. Your roommate suddenly stops, says, "Never mind!" and storms out, slamming the door behind her. Or imagine this. You go to your 9 A.M. class barely awake. You prop yourself against the back wall and sit, motionless. You let the rest of the class answer your professor's questions, while you stare blankly ahead. Your professor gives you a disapproving look. What did you do? In both cases you may have comprehended what was being said, but you failed to respond adequately. Listeners must do more than collect and store information; they are expected to respond verbally or nonverbally to what they process. Responding so that speakers know that you are listening is called **active listening**. You respond actively by maintaining eye contact, by nodding and smiling, by asking for clarification when it is necessary, and by encouraging the other person to express his or her thoughts. In the scenarios described here, you failed to listen actively, and, in doing so, you sent unintended messages. Your lack of focus told your roommate that you didn't care about her problem, and your low responsiveness told your professor that you were bored and uninterested. In both cases you carelessly sent disconfirming messages.

## Emotional Intelligence and Listening

To respond effectively, listeners must be sensitive to nuance. They must be able to gauge the feelings of their partners and often they must read between the lines, uncovering the relational message hidden in the content. People who lack the ability to understand the emotional messages of others or who are unaware of their own emotions will have great difficulty maintaining relationships. People such as these lack a form of intelligence called emotional intelligence.

What makes a person intelligent? Traditionally the answer has been the ability to understand abstract ideas, to analyze complex problems, and to reason logically, the kinds of abilities that make for success in high school or college and that are tested by standard IQ tests.[70] More recently, this view has been challenged. A number of psychologists now argue that we have "multiple intelligences," different abilities that help us solve different kinds of problems and adapt effectively to our environments.[71] One set of adaptive abilities, a set closely related to communication competence, is called emotional intelligence.

**Emotional intelligence**, or **EI**, is the ability to process emotional information. The individual who is emotionally intelligent is able to reason about emotions and to use emotions to improve thinking. John Mayer and Peter Salovey, the psychologists responsible for much of the current interest in EI, believe that EI consists of four factors or "branches." The first, *perceiving emotions*, is the ability to recognize emotions in others' faces and bodies. Knowing when a friend is unhappy or recognizing that your mother is becoming exasperated are examples of the perceiving branch of EI. The second branch, *facilitating thought*, involves understanding that moods and feelings can enhance other kinds of thinking. Knowing that you'll do a better job of planning a birthday party if you're happy and that it is probably unwise to make an important career decision when you're feeling depressed and anxious are examples of facilitation. The third branch, *understanding emotions*, involves the ability to analyze emotions and understand how they are connected. Knowing that if you break a promise to someone close that person will feel hurt or understanding that frustration often leads to aggression are examples of understanding. Finally, the forth branch, *managing emotions*, refers to the ability to regulate emotions in order to "promote emotional and intellectual growth." Being able to "count to 10" rather than getting angry or knowing how to cheer yourself up when you're feeling down are examples of the fourth branch of EI.[72]

There has been considerable hype surrounding the concept of emotional intelligence. People whose primary goal is to sell books and promote workshops have equated EI with everything from moral character to "motivation, confidence, mental stability, optimism and 'people skills.'" And they have claimed that, simply by hiring an "EQ" coach, we can all become wildly popular at home and at work.[73] Obviously, these claims are overblown. However, there is a growing body of scientific research that shows that there are positive outcomes to being emotionally intelligent. There is evidence that subjects high in EI are rated as more caring by their friends and have fewer roommate conflicts than those who lack EI, that emotional intelligence may "help people more successfully navigate their relationships with spouses and romantic partners,"[74] and that "as EI rises, so does academic performance, measures of relatedness, [and] the ability to communicate motivating messages."[75] Although EI research is still in a formative stage, it reminds us that there is a close connection between emotion and thought and that to adapt effectively to our social worlds we must be able to manage our emotions.[76] It also lends support to the idea that interpretive competence is necessary for effective communication.

What is the relationship between emotional intelligence, listening, and communication competence? We believe that good communicators are good listeners. And good listeners are emotionally intelligent. Remember that not all of the meaning of a message is in the words. To truly understand what others are saying, you need to be aware of the feelings that lie beneath the words, and that takes the ability to perceive emotions and to understand their meaning. To listen effectively, you also have to be in the right frame of mind. It is impossible to attend to a message when you are distracted by your moods, and it is difficult to give others the attention and understanding they need if you are anxious or unhappy. Thus, the ability to facilitate thought and the ability to manage emotions are also related to good listening. If you want to become a better listener, you need to attend to and manage emotions.

# Skill Building: Becoming a Competent Listener

Each of the kinds of listening we have discussed involves different skills. We end this chapter by discussing ways to improve comprehensive, evaluative, and empathic listening.

## Improving Comprehension and Evaluation

Although comprehension and evaluation are important in all settings, they are particularly crucial in one-way settings like lectures or public presentations. Because these situations do not allow a great deal of interaction, listeners must take special steps to ensure that they understand what is being conveyed. And because these kinds of presentations are often persuasive in nature, they must also be extremely critical as they listen. At their annual conference in 1984, members of the Speech Communication Association adopted a list of skills essential for listening in these kinds of settings.[77]

To listen comprehensively, they believe, listeners must be able to do the following:

- Recognize main ideas
- Identify supporting details
- Recognize explicit relationships among ideas
- Recall basic ideas and details

To critically evaluate what a source is saying, listeners must:

- Attend with an open mind
- Perceive the speaker's purpose and organization of ideas
- Discriminate between statements of fact and statements of opinion
- Distinguish between emotional and logical arguments

- Detect bias and prejudice
- Recognize the speaker's attitude
- Synthesize and evaluate by drawing logical inferences and conclusions
- Recall implications and arguments
- Recognize discrepancies between the speaker's verbal and nonverbal messages

## Improving Empathic Listening

While all types of listening are important, the one most closely related to improving interpersonal communication is *empathic,* or therapeutic, listening. It is especially important when emotions are involved. To improve empathic listening requires many of the same skills for comprehension, plus the following four important guidelines or rules:

1. *Respect the other's point of view.* To respect another's point of view means that we must want to listen; we have to care about what the other person thinks and feels. This is especially difficult during interpersonal conflicts because we become so preoccupied with our own ideas and emotions that we don't take time to think about our partner's views. We are also quick to dismiss what others say if it differs from what we believe. We tend to close down the perceptual process when encountering something with which we disagree. It is essential to explore the other's point of view rather than avoid it.

2. *Make sure you fully understand what the other has said before responding.* Most people spend more time preparing their own messages than listening to others' statements. This leads to the rule of understanding before you speak. Think how many times you have interrupted someone before he or she was finished in order to make an objection or correction. As a result, you may think you disagree when you don't. Interruptions rob you of information and serve to disconfirm others.

3. *Check your understanding by paraphrasing.* Once you think you understand what the other

is saying, you should check it out by paraphrasing. To **paraphrase** is to state in your own words what you think the other person means. Paraphrasing isn't a matter of repeating what has just been said. Instead, you should describe your understanding of the comment in your own way. If a friend says to you, "I hate my physics class. Everyone is smarter than I am. I know I'm going to fail. I don't know why you hang around with a dummy like me, anyway," check to make sure you understand what your friend is really trying to say. A paraphrase might go something like this: "Let me see if I understand. You're having trouble in class and it's making you doubt your competence. You're afraid I'll think you're dumb if you do badly." In social cognition terms you're trying to recognize the personal constructs the other is using or the script he or she seems to be following.

Most people's first instinct is to comfort rather than paraphrase. "Nonsense, you'll do fine. Don't worry" is a good response only if your friend is not serious. If she is really upset, such a response dismisses her fears, saying in effect, "You have no right to feel the way you do." A paraphrase allows you to make sure you know what is bothering her. When you're not used to doing it, paraphrasing can seem odd. Try to vary the opening line of a paraphrase. It sounds trite and awkward to start off every statement with "What I think I hear you saying is . . ."

4. *When paraphrasing, make sure you express relational as well as content meaning.* In many interactions feelings are more important than words. If your partner says, "You know, you forgot my birthday, not that it's that important, really," you should check out the feeling behind the statement. Some people have difficulty expressing feelings overtly, so they hint instead. A good listener will try to read between the lines and will help others say what they really mean.

While listening to others means trying to see the world from their point of view, we must not become completely other-centered. To improve our perceptual awareness we must also listen to ourselves. We can employ the same skills by focusing inward to discover the world as we have constructed it. Ask yourself questions as to why you seem more comfortable in some situations, with certain people, or in specific types of relationships. Don't simply accept your first explanation; try paraphrasing your own views. You may discover that you really feel different or you may convince yourself that there are other ways of looking at the circumstances or people involved.

This chapter has provided you with a lot of information about the perceptual process and some of the cognitive schemata that people use to make sense of their social world. We have tried to simplify what you need to know by structuring this information around four cognitive processes that influence interpersonal communication: how we size up situations, people, and relationships and how we explain the causes of social interaction. Finally, we have suggested how you can improve your listening skills in order to better understand your own and others' cognitive frameworks. Understanding social cognition processes is the first step to improving interpersonal communication because so much of the meaning we assign to messages depends on our *perceptions* of the social context and the persons involved.

# Process to Performance

## Review Terms

mindless interaction   (144)
same-race advantage   (145)
contact hypothesis   (145)
mood congruity hypothesis   (146)
auto-motives   (147)
social cognition   (148)
principle of least effort   (148)
schema   (149)
prototype   (149)
exemplar   (149)
personal construct   (151)

stereotype   (151)
role schema   (152)
relational schema   (152)
self-schema   (153)
event schema   (153)
scripts   (154)
social episodes   (154)
naïve realism   (155)
dual-process model   (156)
selective attention   (156)
salient features   (156)
individuation   (157)
personalization   (157)
closed episode   (159)
open episode   (159)
defined episode   (160)
implicit personality theory   (161)
primacy effect   (162)
recency effect   (162)
self-monitoring   (162)
master contract   (164)
attribution theories   (165)
discounting rule   (165)
augmenting rule   (165)
anchoring effect   (166)
spontaneous trait inferences   (166)
perspective-taking   (169)
listening   (170)
hearing   (170)
discriminatory listening   (171)
appreciative listening   (171)
comprehensive listening   (171)
evaluative listening   (171)
empathic listening   (171)
active listening   (172)
emotional intelligence   (172)
paraphrase   (174)

## Suggested Readings

Csikszentmihalyi, Mihaly. *Finding Flow: The Psychology of Engagement with Everyday Life*. New York: Basic Books, 1997. The author provides a set of prescriptions for "reclaiming ownership" of our emotional lives by becoming more fully engaged in everyday tasks.

Gilbert, Daniel. *Stumbling on Happiness*. New York: Alfred A. Knopf, 2006. Gilbert demonstrates that we rarely know what really makes us happy because of typical failures associated with memory, perception, and imagination of the future. In particular, he shows how our perceptions of the present dominate both the past and the future, restricting our ability to perceive what is possible.

## Topics for Discussion
www.oup.com/us/trenholm

## Observation Guide

**1.** Watch a half-hour episode of a situation comedy or other television program that consists primarily of dialogue. If you can, audio- or videotape the program so you can play it back several times. Choose an interesting segment, such as a misunderstanding, and write down the essence of each message exchanged. Then write down the perceptual factors that best account for why that message was produced or interpreted the way it was.

**2.** Conduct your own study of attributions. Look for newspaper or magazine accounts of some event that two or more people perceived differently. Write down a brief description of the situation, the behavior in question, the actor's account, and the target's explanation. What biases do you find in the results? Are they consistent with those reported in this chapter? If not, can you explain the differences?

## Exercises

**1.** This exercise is designed to measure the way you construct your interpersonal world and form impressions of others. It is based on George Kelly's Role Repertory Construct Test. The end result will be a list of several of your own *personal constructs*. Follow these steps:

   **a.** Look at the following list of role titles and place in the blank the name or initials of someone you know personally who fits that category. Choose a *different* person for each category. If you can't think of anyone for a particular role, then name some other important person in your life and describe the role he or she plays in relation to you.

| Role Category | Name or Initials of Person |
|---|---|
| 1. Mother | _____ |
| 2. Father | _____ |
| 3. Boyfriend (or girlfriend) | _____ |
| 4. Brother (or someone like a brother) | _____ |
| 5. Sister (or someone like a sister) | _____ |
| 6. Best same-sex friend | _____ |
| 7. Best opposite-sex friend | _____ |
| 8. A teacher you like | _____ |
| 9. A teacher you dislike | _____ |
| 10. Most intelligent person you know | _____ |
| 11. Someone you pity | _____ |
| 12. A boss or superior | _____ |
| 13. Someone who threatens you | _____ |
| 14. A new acquaintance | _____ |
| 15. Yourself | _____ |

   **b.** Now think about three of the persons you listed (your mother, sister, and someone who threatens you) and compare them. Try to think of some important ways that two of them are alike but different from the third person. For instance, you might say that two of these people are friendly while the other is more cold-natured. On a sheet of paper, list as many "constructs," or similarities and differences for these three people as you can. Your list might look like this:

friendly–cold-natured

good-looking–unattractive

talkative–quiet

   **c.** Repeat step b for each of the following role sets:

     1. Father, your boss, a new acquaintance

     2. Boyfriend, best same-sex friend, best opposite-sex friend

     3. Liked teacher, disliked teacher, yourself

4. Brother, sister, most intelligent person

5. Best opposite-sex friend, mother, sister

6. Girlfriend, father, mother

Your list should be rather long by now. This should give you a pretty good idea of the personal constructs you typically use to form impressions of others. Compare your constructs with those of your classmates. How similar or different are they? Which constructs that other people use seem unimportant to you? Why do you think people see the world so similarly or differently?

2. Throw an impression-formation party. As a class, design a set of 5–10 questions that you can ask strangers in order to get to know them a little better. Then assign several class members to interviewing teams (one interviewer and one camera person). If you can, secure a portable video camera unit and videotape interviews with people of different ages and ethnic or social backgrounds. Make sure you film each person for about 10–15 seconds before you begin asking the questions (we'll explain why later). If you cannot get video equipment, use audiotape recorders and take several snapshots of each person. Bring the recorders and/or snapshots to class on the designated day. Replay the videos in class, stopping once before any verbal communication takes place and then again at the conclusion of the interview (or look at the snapshots before you listen to the audiotapes). Have each person in the class write down his or her impressions, based first on the nonverbal cues alone, then on the total verbal-nonverbal image. Compare your impressions and talk about the perceptual factors that affected those impressions.

3. Work in small groups of four. Listed here are statements one friend might make to one another. Each person in the group should choose

one of the statements and devise a "back story" that explains what prompted the statement and what the speaker's concern really is. Without divulging the story, each group member in turn should take on the role of speaker, while the remaining group members offer responses. The speaker should then divulge the scenario and discuss whether or not group members' responses were helpful or not. After each person in the group has had an opportunity to take on the role of speaker, the group should discuss why different responses were or were not useful. If paraphrasing was not used, then the group should work on coming up with a paraphrase for each situation that sounds natural and encourages communication.

a. I don't know what to do. I stopped going to my math class at midterm, and now it's almost finals and I'm in real trouble. I'm on probation as it is. I just can't really get excited about general education requirements or anything else for that matter.

b. My girlfriend won't talk to me. I call and leave messages with her roomates but they don't pass them on. They tell me she is not in when I know she is because I've seen her. I know if I could actually talk to her, everything would be OK. I've left notes on her car and I've left countless messages on the answering machine. It's not as though she doesn't love me, I know she does.

c. I'm so frustrated. I think I'm not cut out for college. I have to work so much harder than everyone else. Everyone else seems to have a great time and go out, while I've got so much to do. I have no social life. I must just be too stupid for college.

d. I hate my boss. She's on a power trip, asking me to do stupid things that aren't even in my job description. I'm just a little late and you'd think I started World War III. I think she has it in for me. She doesn't seem to treat anyone else that way. I can't quit, though, because I need the money.

*Virtually every interaction comes embedded
with social rules.*

Marcel Duchamp, *Sonata*, 1911

## CHAPTER 7

# Role Competence
# Adapting to Social Expectations

A very young child does not know what an "address" is. He knows that he has a home and that he lives there with his sister and his dog, and he may even be able to repeat "47 Pratt Street" when his grandparents ask him where he lives. But he doesn't understand the idea that his home has coordinates and can be located in relation to other people's homes.

Slowly, however, the idea of "address" takes shape. The child learns to differentiate his friends' homes from his own. He knows what it means to go to Grandma's or to visit cousins in New York. Eventually, he will understand much more. He will learn to locate the homes of everyone he knows on a map. Where formerly a letter to a cousin was simply addressed "To Kerry," now the envelope carries quite specific directions: "1200 Elm Street, Newfield, New York, U.S.A., The World, The Solar System, The Universe." The child becomes fascinated with the world and his place in it. As sociologist Peter Berger tells us, "This locating of oneself in con-

figurations conceived by strangers is one of the important aspects of what, perhaps euphemistically, is called 'growing up.'"[1]

Berger points out that as children mature they continue to accumulate addresses—ones locating them on a social rather than a geographical map. "I'm seven years old"; "My dad and mom are divorced"; "I go to second grade, but I'm not very good at spelling"; "My mom is a secretary"; "When I grow up I'm going to learn to fix cars and drive a Trans-Am." As children learn their position on the social map, they also begin to understand just what they can expect out of life and what life expects out of them. They adapt themselves to a larger social system. What this adaptation means for identity and for communication will be the topic of this chapter and the next. In this chapter we will look at some of the ways society shapes and controls us. In the next chapter we will consider how, despite these social pressures, we manage to create an identity that is uniquely ours.

# Being Part of the Group: Following Social Rules

One of the fundamental facts about us is that we are social animals. The fantasy of the loner, living a solitary life and answering to no one, may fascinate us, but most of us will spend our lives following rules others have made. To live a "civilized" life means we must be willing to live up to the expectations of others. The competent communicator is one who follows social rules. In this section we'll look at what social controls and pressures to conform we are exposed to and examine how social roles work and how they constrain our communication.

## Social Control and Conformity Pressures

Why does society place such a high premium on conformity? One reason is that in order to operate effectively, members of social groups must coordinate their activities. Each member must complete assigned tasks and follow rules. Since we belong to many social groups, we are subject to many levels of social control. Berger asks us to think of ourselves at the center of a series of concentric circles, each representing a system of control. These circles represent social coordinates; they stand for the "many forces that constrain and coerce one."[2]

The forces that constrain us are many. Formal economic and legal sanctions control our actions in obvious ways. In addition, more subtle pressures affect us: the desire to uphold the standards and moral customs of our community, our fear of ridicule, our fundamental need for inclusion. Whatever the reason, we are, to a large extent, what our culture wants us to be. Anthropologist Ruth Benedict expresses it this way:

*The life history of the individual is first and foremost an accommodation to the patterns and standards traditionally handed down in his community. From the moment of birth the customs into which he is born shape his experience and behaviour. By the time he can talk, he is a little creature of his culture, and by the time he is grown and able to take part in its activities, its habits are his habits, its beliefs his beliefs, its impossibilities his impossibilities.*[3]

While we feel that individuals have a bit more room to maneuver than Benedict allows them, we also believe that a large part of who we are and how we communicate is determined for us by social norms. One of the most powerful limits to our freedom comes from social roles. The study abstracted in this chapter's Research in Review section illustrates how strong commitment to a role affects communication.

## The Nature of Social Roles

Every day we face new situations. If we had to stop and decide how to act in each case, we'd have a difficult time of it. Luckily, we act appropriately without very much thought. This is because we know implicitly how someone in our position should behave: We have learned what sociologists call a role, one of the strongest forms of social control.

To understand what a role is, we have to begin by understanding the concept of position. A **position** is a social label that tells people who we are, what our duties and rights are, and where we stand in comparison to others. Some of the positions a society recognizes are occupational (butcher, baker, candlestick maker). Others refer to placement in the family (grandparent, parent, son, or daughter). Still others indicate age, sex, prestige, or associational groupings.[4] In all cases positions indicate location on the social map.

Positions are not just empty titles. People are expected to take their positions seriously. Children and adults do not amuse themselves in the same ways. A professional politician and a professional wrestler will address their publics differently. Each

## "Guys Can't Say That to Guys"

# Male Role Enactment During Comforting

Both men and women agree on the type of support they want when things go bad. Both rate person-centered messages, messages that acknowledge feelings and encourage talk, as more effective than messages that give direct advice or avoid the problem. Nevertheless, men are less likely to use these kinds of messages when called upon to comfort others. Why are men so reluctant to use person-centered messages? In "'Guys Can't Say *That* to Guys,'" Brant Burleson and his colleagues hypothesize that person-centered messages are viewed as "feminine" and are therefore avoided by men, especially when in the presence of other men. This is particularly true for men who are gender schematic, that is, who have strong needs to enact masculine roles.

The authors undertook a series of studies to test this idea. In the first, they asked 387 college students to read transcripts of conversations in which a helper offers comfort to a friend. The transcripts varied in terms of sex of helper and target as well as in person-centered language. Subjects evaluated how realistic they thought the scenarios were, as well as how much they liked the helper. They also filled out a scale measuring their own gender schematicity.

Results showed that when the male characters used person-centered language, male subjects judged the conversation to be less realistic and felt less liking for the helper than in other conditions. This pattern was stronger for men with high gender schematicity.

In a second study subjects were asked to judge the importance of four different comfort strategies—*solace* (giving the distressed person the opportunity to talk), *dismissing* (getting the target's mind off the problem), *escape* (avoiding or ignoring the problem), or *advice* (suggesting a solution) —while in a third study subjects were asked the likelihood of using each of these strategies. In both cases, male subjects rated *solace* lower and *dismissing* and *escape* higher in scenarios involving male characters. Finally in a fourth study subjects were asked to produce comforting messages, which were coded for use of person-centered language. Once again, use of person-oriented messages was related to gender, although in this case whether the individual in distress was responsible for his own problem mediated the results.

Overall, this set of studies lends support to the idea that men fail to use person-oriented messages not because they can't, but because they feel that person-centered messages are inappropriate to male role enactment. It illustrates that sometimes, living up to one's role gets in the way of communication effectiveness.

Burleson, Brant R., Amanda J. Holmstrom, and Christine M. Gilstrap. "'Guys Can't Say *That* to Guys': Four Experiments Assessing the Normative Motivation Account for Deficiencies in the Emotional Support Provided by Men." *Communication Monographs* 72, no. 4 (2005): 468–501.

position carries with it a set of behavioral guidelines. These guidelines are what we call **roles:** sets of expectations that govern how persons holding a given position should behave. We know several things about roles: (1) They are learned; (2) they are general; (3) they affect our identities; and (4) most of us play multiple roles.

1. *Roles are learned.* We aren't born with a knowledge of roles. We learn to meet social **181**

*We are asked to play many roles in society, and sometimes it leads to role conflict.*

expectations in much the same way we learn to ride a bicycle or play the accordion. We learn by observing others, by receiving instruction, by practicing, by experiencing praise or criticism. All of the principles that affect learning in general affect role acquisition. Box 7.1 shows one of the many ways we learn roles: through imitative play.

2. *Roles are generalized guidelines for behavior.* While roles give us a general idea of how to perform in a given position, they don't spell out every move. We are often left to our own devices when it comes to working out the details of our

performances. Most college students, for example, need time to figure out how to be a student. Being a student entails more than enrolling for classes; students must act, dress, and even think in particular ways. Freshmen or returning students may have a hard time of it at first, since these issues are rarely addressed in the college catalog. A role is a generalized and idealized model for behavior, not a fully developed script. Competent role performance, therefore, involves experimentation, improvisation, and adjustment.

3. *Roles affect beliefs about self.* It takes time to learn a role, but after a while the strangeness wears off. Eventually, people stop noticing their roles. A first-year teacher, for example, may initially feel ambivalent about her authority. But it will probably not be too long before she begins to believe in a teacher's right to instruct and discipline. She may even begin to consider rebellious students as unruly or ungrateful. Similarly, a soldier newly promoted to the rank of officer may be slightly embarrassed by accompanying signs of deference. He will soon become accustomed to being saluted, however, and will begin to resent insubordination.

Enacting a role over a prolonged period may affect one's personality and identity. **Role rigidity** occurs when a role takes over one's identity. Most experts believe it is psychologically necessary to separate self from role. People whose commitment to a single role is too rigid tend to lose perspective. They may find it increasingly hard to relate in any other way. Teachers, for example, may become so used to the role of instructor that friendly conversations turn into lectures. Military officers may treat their children like little "noncoms."

4. *People have multiple roles to play.* People fill a number of positions simultaneously. This means they must be nimble in moving between roles. An intern in a hospital, for instance, must be a number of different people: At work he or she is a doctor; at home, a husband or wife; at a

party, a friend or neighbor; and at town council meetings, a citizen. Our intern must be sensitive enough to recognize the varying demands of each role and flexible enough to adapt to them, for each role calls for a slightly different form of communication. Meeting the communication demands of all of these situations involves a great deal of role versatility. The number of roles an individual can successfully play is called a **role repertoire.** Clearly, the larger the role repertoire, the more communicative flexibility one has.

Most of the time people switch roles easily. Sometimes, however, they experience **role conflict.** This occurs when two or more roles make opposing demands. Workaholics, for example, often find that professional and personal demands conflict. Attention directed to family concerns is attention taken away from their businesses, and vice versa. Resolving this kind of dilemma is no easy matter; it may ultimately lead to painful choices.

Role conflicts also occur in times of social transition. In the period before an old role has become obsolete and a new role fully accepted, people are often pulled in opposite directions. Our changing understandings of what it means to be male or female and current redefinitions of the shape and purpose of the family are good examples.

# Choosing Our Roles

If it is true that we play multiple roles, how do we decide who to be in a given situation? How, indeed, do we know who we are? George McCall and J. L. Simmons address this question in their role identity model.[5] In order to get through life, they believe, we have to decide which identities to assume. In a sense we are like circus performers, juggling commitments and role demands, trying not to slip off the tightrope that defines our passage through life.

While we have many role identities, some are more important than others. What determines the salience of a role? McCall and Simmons believe there are three sets of factors: (1) the degree of support we receive for playing a role, (2) the amount of commitment we feel toward it, and (3) the kinds of rewards we receive from it. Let's look at each of these factors.

## Social Support and Role Identity

If those around us support our efforts, we are more likely to embrace a role than if they ridicule us. It is a fact of life that we are constantly being evaluated. Assume, for instance, that you dream of becoming a marathon runner. If your family and friends give you support and encouragement, you will go on with your dream. If they laugh at your lack of speed and stamina, you may not believe enough in yourself to keep on.

### The Looking-Glass Self
A number of social scientists besides McCall and Simmons have stressed the importance of social support in defining and maintaining a role. Charles Horton Cooley, for example, believes that others act as mirrors, reflecting back at us who we are and how we're doing. Cooley expressed this idea in a two-line poem: "Each to each a looking glass/Reflects the other that doth pass." The **looking-glass self** is the self that comes to us from others.[6] Think about it for a moment. No matter how strong-willed and self-assured you are, if everybody you encounter treats you as incompetent, you will question your abilities. Or even worse, suppose everyone ignored you completely. You'd probably begin to wonder if you were dreaming. It would be like looking into a mirror and failing to see your reflection.

### Social Comparison Processes
Social support is essential to most of us. Why? Leon Festinger in his **social comparison theory** gives one reason.[7] He believes that people have a basic need to know how they're doing; they need

BOX 7.1

## They Just Like to Be Not the Same as Us

# Play Patterns and the Development of Sex Role Identities

In *Boys and Girls: Superheroes in the Doll Corner*, elementary school teacher Vivian Gussin Paley describes how kindergartners' play contributes to sex role development. Paley tells us that by kindergarten age, children have a strong need to define what it means to be boys and girls. Younger children are not concerned with gender. Three-year-olds, for example, fail to distinguish between male and female behaviors. A three-year-old playing the role of a policeman may also

cook the food and feed the baby, while one playing a mother may put on a man's vest and hat. Boys may tell you they are fathers and girls that they are mothers most of the time, but occasionally they will say the opposite without feeling uncomfortable.

Around the age of four, children begin to play gender-based roles more frequently. Girls start enacting family dramas, assigning themselves the roles of mother, baby, or sister and preferring that boys be fathers, plumbers, carpenters, or firemen. Although the girls are sometimes willing to exchange their domestic roles for those of Wonderwoman or Supergirl, it is the boys who specialize in being monsters or superheroes.

By age five or six, gender-based play is firmly established. Not only do the children fantasize sex-based roles, they invent rituals to separate themselves. Although society helps to create the shape of play by providing Barbie dolls and Star Wars action figures, the children themselves often elaborate on gender themes in creative ways. In the group Paley observed, for example, boys

to know how their opinions and abilities stack up. Since it's hard to find objective scales to measure beliefs and talents, most of us must turn to other people for feedback.

We don't turn to just anyone, however. People who are similar to us provide us the most useful comparisons. A beginning tennis player would be foolish to compare herself with Martina Navratilova; it would make more sense to look at another beginning player. Similarly, college students gain little insight from knowing they're more educated than kindergartners; they need to know how they rate against other college students. Most of the time we compare ourselves with those we believe are in our league or who

are slightly better than we are. Because our need for social comparison is so strong, most of our associations will be with people who are similar.

What Festinger is suggesting is that the need for social comparison leads to conformity pressures. We choose as friends people who are similar enough to reinforce role identities. If unexpected changes in identity are discovered in a relationship, efforts will be made to reestablish similarity. Have you ever been shocked and disappointed when a friend turned out to hold unexpected opinions? If so, you probably exerted subtle pressures to change your friend back into someone with whom you felt more comfortable. Have you ever been uncomfortable because your abilities hopped to get their milk, while girls skipped to the paper shelf.

What does typical play look like in a kindergarten class? Let's watch the boys play in the doll corner. Jeremy begins. He drags the play oven to the middle of the floor, announcing, "This is the computer terminal." The other boys quickly begin arranging the rest of the spaceship. Andrew talks into a silver dress-up slipper, "Pilot to crew, pilot to crew, ready for landing. Snow planet down below." Suddenly the boys sight Darth Vader. Andrew takes two sticks, runs over to the paint corner, and asks Mary Ann for red paint to transform them into light-sabres. Then, before rushing into battle, he says gallantly, "Thanks, miss; I won't forget this."

Meanwhile, the girls have decided to build a zoo from blocks. They take four rubber lions and name them Mother, Father, Sister, and Baby and place them in a two-story house. Paley observes, "Girls tame lions by putting them into houses. Boys conquer houses by sending them into space."

Paley notes that the stories boys and girls tell at this age are also very different. Girls tell stories of "good little families" of kings and queens, princes and princesses. Boys prefer tales with bad guys. Paley once asked the girls why boys never told stories about princes. The girls responded that princes are too "fancy" for boys. Boys like characters who are rough. One of the kindergartners, Charlotte, summed up the discussion: "Here's what I think. They don't want to be fancy because girls do. They just like to be not the same as us."

**SOURCE**  Vivian Gussin Paley, *Boys and Girls: Superheroes in the Doll Corner* (Chicago: University of Chicago Press, 1984).

**ADDITIONAL READINGS**

Paley, Vivian G. *Bad Guys Don't Have Birthdays: Fantasy Play at Four.* Chicago: University of Chicago Press, 1991.

Paley, Vivian G. *You Can't Say You Can't Play.* Cambridge, Mass.: Harvard University Press, 1988.

Stein, Sarah Bonnett. *Girls and Boys: The Limits of Nonsexist Childrearing.* New York: Scribner, 1983.

were above or below your friends'? Some people will pretend to be better than they are, while others will play dumb, just to fit in. We try to be what our comparison groups tell us we should be.

## Commitment and Role Identity

The amount of material and the number of psychological resources invested in a role also determine how significant it will be. Perhaps you have always admired a runner. Ever since you were a child, you wanted to be like her. Your commitment will be so great you may persevere even in the face of discouraging feedback. This effect will be doubly strong if you've made a financial investment, say, by buying expensive running shoes and hiring a coach. Commitment and investment are important factors in determining role salience.

Daryl Bem offers a theoretical explanation of why commitment and investment make certain role identities more salient.[8] His **self-perception theory** maintains that one way we learn about who we are is through self-observation. Bem believes that often it is hard for us to tell directly what we are thinking and feeling. In order to get a clearer idea of our emotions or attitudes, we observe our external behaviors. What we see ourselves doing often helps explain ambiguous emotions or attitudes.

This theory may seem odd to you. Most people think they have direct access to emotions and attitudes. Bem's point, however, is that internal sensations are often hard to identify. Think about it for a moment. How do you feel when you're in love? Does your heart race? Do your palms sweat? Does your breathing rate increase? Now think about what you experience when you are scared to death. Aren't the sensations pretty similar? One way to tell the difference is to observe external cues. If these sensations occur during the middle of a crucial job interview, it is probably fear you are feeling. On the other hand, if they occur during an intimate candlelight dinner, love is the likely culprit.

Bem also believes external cues give us information about our attitudes and values. If we observe ourselves spending a great deal of time and effort doing something, we will probably decide it is important and worthwhile. People often say things like "I must really like the food here; look at how much I ate," or "It must have been a great party; I stayed till dawn," or "I spend all my time training for the marathon; it must be the most important thing in my life right now." The more time, effort, and money we spend on something, the more likely we are to believe we value it.

### Rewards and Role Identity

Both intrinsic and extrinsic rewards also determine how important a role becomes to us. The average person who runs a marathon is unlikely to be motivated by extrinsic rewards, for runners are not usually highly paid. A runner may receive important intrinsic rewards, however. Amateur runners often feel a sense of pride in accomplishing what few others can do. This feeling of competence goes a long way toward strengthening role allegiance. On the other hand, a runner who fails to complete a race, who experiences painful leg cramps, and who is going broke paying entrance fees may reconsider the importance of running.

McCall and Simmons believe that all of the factors we have discussed interact to determine reactions to roles. Throughout our lives we try on the different roles society presents to us. Those that fit are retained, while those that don't are rejected until we build up a repertoire of roles we're willing to play.

---

# How Social Roles Affect Communication

The reason roles are of interest to us is that they affect our communication with one another. Embedded in every role are instructions for how to talk and what to talk about. In this section, we investigate how roles guide interactions and how all of the social roles we play turn us into performers.

## Communication as Performance

Of course, gender is not the only role that affects interaction. Children and adults speak differently, as do members of different occupations and members of different social groups. When we take on a role, it is almost as though we are handed a script which maps out our social performances for us. Roles tell us how to play our parts in the social drama of everyday life.

### *Creating the Ideal Character: Face-Work*
Like stage actors, social actors want to make an impact on an audience. We want to create characters who will be admired and accepted. McCall and Simmons believe that "one of man's most distinctive motives is the compelling and perpetual drive to acquire support for his idealized conceptions of himself."[9] Gaining the approval of an appreciative audience is one way to acquire support for the idealized self, and one way of doing this is to create a character who embodies the values of society.

Sociologist Erving Goffman uses the term **face** to describe the part of self presented to others for their approval.[10] As we mentioned in Chapter 1, an individual's face embodies social values; it is an approved identity. **Face-work** is effort spent in presenting face to others. Although the term *face* may seem odd at first, Goffman is actually following common usage. For example, we say that a person who violates social values has "lost face." We describe efforts to avoid embarrassment as "saving face." And some college students refer to time spent impressing others as "face time."

During communication we present face by taking a **line.** Our lines consist of the verbal and nonverbal behaviors we use during a performance. We must be very careful to take appropriate lines. If we act in ways that aren't "in line" with our position on the social map, others will reject us. The middle-class social climber who tries to pass as a member of the social register or the rich industrialist who tries to relate to his factory workers by acting like "one of the guys" are both out of line. Both will be ridiculed.

During communication we must be careful to preserve our own face and protect that of others. Not only must *we* make a good impression, we must help *others* to make a good impression too. If, for example, we are at a formal dinner party and one of the other guests commits a faux pas, we generally look away, politely pretending not to see that he or she is using the wrong fork. If the social error committed is so obvious that it cannot be ignored, we may try to redefine or diminish it. If our guest unknowingly insults the hostess, we may treat the comment as a joke.

In actively working to maintain our own face, we try to steer clear of situations we feel we can't handle. If someone brings up a topic we're ignorant about, we may change the subject to avoid embarrassment. If we inadvertently offend someone, we can save face by apologizing for our insensitivity or by offering to make amends.

Goffman believes that interpersonal communication is a risky business. We must continually be on our guard for threats to face and line.

*Role performances require constant adaptations ranging from observing others to being observed.*

*An unguarded glance, a momentary change in tone of voice, an ecological position taken or not taken, can drench a talk with judgmental significance . . . There is no occasion of talk so trivial as not to require each participant to show serious concern with the way in which he handles himself and the others present.*[11]

The image presented by Goffman is that of nervous individuals doing their best to avoid disaster. While Goffman may exaggerate the dangers of interpersonal communication, there is certainly some truth to the idea that we are motivated by social approval. Unless you're a completely free spirit, you're probably careful not to do odd or embarrassing things in public. And unless you are completely uncaring and insensitive, you try to keep others from making fools of themselves. Stop and think about it for a minute. You may be surprised to find how much communication centers on protecting face and line.

### Getting Ready for the Play: Other Aspects of Self-Presentation

When we go to a play, we expect costumes, lighting, and sets. When we interact in everyday life, we also expect a proper background.

*Sets, Costumes, and Props.* Goffman divides the arena where our everyday performances take place into two parts.[12] The public part, the stage, he calls the **front.** There are two aspects to front: setting and personal front. **Setting** includes all of the scenery and props that make the performance possible. **Personal front** involves costume, makeup, physical characteristics, gestures, and the like.

When our front is creatively designed, we can give an effective performance. If we don't maintain a convincing front, however, our performance may crumble. Executives of major corporations know the value of sumptuous surroundings. They spend a great deal of money on impressive office furnishings and artifacts, in the belief that a visitor who spies an original Picasso on the mahogany wall of the reception area is bound to be impressed by their power and wealth. If they're also wearing a $1200 suit and are surrounded by a large and respectful entourage, the effect will be increased. Their front acts as a frame for the business drama about to unfold.

All of us are viewed against the backdrop of our own front regions. If our personal surroundings are warm and inviting, we're likely to make friends easily. If we have to communicate in a cold and forbidding atmosphere, we will have to work harder to overcome its effects. The way we set the scene for encounters can affect their outcome. You might find it interesting to analyze what your surroundings say about you and how they affect the ways that you communicate.

*Backstage Behavior.* If actors had to remain on stage for more than a few hours, they would probably lose touch with reality. Luckily, between acts they can retreat backstage, where they are no longer on call; they can relax and be themselves. The private area where social actors can escape the critical eye of their audience is called the **back region.** "The faculty lounge, the members-only club, the executive washroom, and the rehearsal studio are examples of back regions."[13] Goffman believes that dedication to role is not always absolute; most of us need a place where we can slip out of our roles and simply be whoever we want.

The back region answers our need for privacy. By entering it, we escape the rigors of role enactment. But what if we don't have a physical space to flee to? Then we must rely on psychological space. We find a way to let others know the roles we are playing do not completely define us. Goffman calls this **role distance.**[14] Every situation we enter, he says, puts demands on us. Occasionally, we resent these demands and try to let others know that there is more to us than meets the eye.

Goffman did much of his research in the medical community, where roles are very well defined. The role of intern is a particularly demanding one. Although interns are expected to be dedicated to their profession, an intern's status in the hospital isn't high. Interns may therefore feel the need to exhibit role distance. There are a number of ways they can do this. They can use a slightly amused facial expression designed to show the absurdity of their position. They may take longer than necessary to obey a request, forcing others to ask twice. They may flirt or joke, reminding those present of other roles in the outside world. This borderline rebellion allows them to fight back without actually violating role demands. Think back to your school days. How did you and your classmates rebel against your status as schoolchildren? We're willing to bet you used similar tactics.

## *Narrative and Identity*

# *Big Fish*

Tim Burton, 2003

William (Billy Crudup) never had a true picture of his larger-than-life father, Edward Bloom (played by Albert Finney as an adult and Ewan McGregor as a young man). As Edward lies dying, William looks for the facts behind his father's improbable fictions. In reliving Edward's mythic tales of witches, giants, and werewolves, he begins to see how stories can sometimes reveal a truth that can't be told in any other way. By the film's end, William has come to accept is father's tall tales and to see their meaning in Edward's life. "A man tells his stories so many times," he tells us, "that he becomes the stories. They live on after him and in that way he becomes immortal."

This touching film explores how, both as a culture and as individuals, we use narratives to make sense of the world. By incorporating elements found in folk and fairy tales, Burton invites us to think about the functions of cultural narratives. By showing us how Edward and William's relationship is defined through stories, he shows us the importance of family narratives. And, by allowing us to see the gradual emergence of Edward the man from Edward the mythic hero, he shows us how we all use stories to create an image of the person we are and of the person we wish we could be.

*Ensemble Acting.* Most plays are not one-person shows—the success of the performance depends on teamwork. Social actors are in much the same situation. Along with roles come **role sets,** others who help put on a given performance. The role set of a defense attorney includes clients, prosecuting attorneys, judges, law clerks, and office staff. The role set of a rock star may include band members, agents, managers, bodyguards, roadies, an astrologer or two, and, perhaps, groupies. These are the people who make performances possible. With them, individuals can become stars; without them, they convince no one.

Members of a role set must exercise loyalty, discipline, and circumspection.[15] A politician's family is a good example of a role set. One of their functions is to back up the candidate's performance, presenting an image of wholesomeness and dedication. They must be careful not to give away the act by revealing the candidate's flaws. They must stay in character, never deviating from the party line and never showing anything but delight with their lot in life. And they must never hog the spotlight by seeking personal publicity. According to Goffman, being a particular kind of person is not necessarily a personal matter; it involves a high degree of teamwork.

It is clear that the members of a role set must work together. If members refuse to coordinate their acts, chaos is likely. There are several ways to ensure a cohesive performance. One is to choose relational partners who will play their parts reliably. The politician who chooses a spouse merely to further a career uses a method called **altercasting.** While most of us are not that cold-blooded, we often choose friends who will support our definition of self. Morris Rosenberg has said, "Friendship is the purest illustration of picking one's propaganda."[16]

Another technique we can use to ensure smooth performance is that of **mirroring.**[17] Mirroring is the flip side of altercasting. Here we achieve

**189**

*Cultural understandings shape the way we view gender roles.*

coordination by following the lead of our partner. While both altercasting and mirroring can
assure a coordinated performance, they are not
very satisfying, since in either case it is one partner who makes all of the decisions. A more satisfactory technique, from the relational point of
view, is **mutual negotiation.** Here both partners
work together to construct roles that are mutually satisfactory. To do this successfully we must
have the kind of maximal competence we discussed at the end of Chapter 2.

## Communication and Story-Telling

Whereas Goffman sees humans as performers in a
social drama, other theorists view humans as
story-tellers. **Narrative theorists** believe that we
make sense of our world by making up and sharing stories about it. These stories may be addressed to ourselves, for example, when we create
a personal identity by constructing an autobiography, or they may be directed to others. Families, businesses, and even whole nations share

stories that reflect their sense of who they are and "provide a communal focus for individual identity."[18] The social roles we choose to play are reinforced and maintained through narrative forms including legends, stories, jokes, and myths.

Story-telling begins at a very young age. Vivian Paley has written a number of charming books that describe how children play. In *Bad Guys Don't Have Birthdays*, she shows how children work out their own personal fears and conflicts and learn to cooperate by making up stories as they play.[19] In constructing stories about good guys and bad guys, Care Bears and monsters, children make sense of their lives, figure out their place in their families, and express their needs and concerns.

As adults we continue to tell stories, both in private and in public. Psychologist Jerome Bruner has written about the importance of the autobiographies we create for ourselves. Bruner agrees with other narrative theorists that reality is not immediately given but instead socially constructed. He argues that we understand our own identities by telling stories about ourselves. These stories, once constructed, can determine how we live our lives. They become so real that they begin to "achieve the power to structure perceptual experience, to organize memory, to segment and purpose-build the very 'events' of a life." Bruner believes that, in the end, "we *become* the autobiographical narratives by which we 'tell about' our lives."[20] What Bruner means is that as we experience life, we constantly think about and reinterpret it. Over time, we begin to take these interpretations as absolute facts, and we may even start behaving like the characters in our stories. A person who views himself as a victim may begin to act like a victim, whereas someone who sees herself as a bold and courageous character takes on that identity. If you were to write out the autobiography you have created in your mind, what form would it take? Would it be a comedy, or a drama, or a farce? What would its major themes and moral lessons be?

Although autobiographical narratives can be idiosyncratic, they usually follow the story-telling conventions of the author's culture. In creating individual identities, we are actually following social guidelines. The social aspects of narrative are more clearly seen when we look at group narratives. Families, for example, often create stories that they tell and retell over the years. Often these stories embody family values. For example, a story about how Dad walked 10 miles through the snow to get to school is designed to teach children to value the advantages they have and to admire hard work and perseverance. Stories can also establish family roles. The story about how naughty Jane was and what a little angel Tommy was suggests that Jane is the "black sheep" of the family, while Tommy is the model child.

Larger groups also use stories and jokes to build cohesion and socialize members. In large businesses, certain stories become part of the corporate culture. Stories about how great the founder of the business was give voice to the values of the organization. Jokes let employees know what kinds of behaviors are permissible and what kinds are ludicrous. Even countries use narratives to build social cohesion and construct shared versions of reality. At a national level, we often participate in mythic story-telling. A **myth** is an anonymous shared story of "origins and destinies." National myths explain the nature and goals of a country and reflect the qualities and values admired by its citizens. Politicians may retell and add new elements to national myths in order to appeal to voters. President Reagan, considered one of the most effective communicators of his time, used mythic story-telling repeatedly. The story he had to tell was one that appealed to many Americans looking for national identity and validation. To Reagan, America was a "chosen nation, grounded in its families and neighborhoods, and driven inevitably forward by its heroic working people toward a world of freedom and economic progress."[21] This is an enormously appealing and self-justifying story, but it is, of course, only one of the stories that can be told about America. Other Americans, with different experiences and

BOX 7.2

# When Is a Man a "Real Man"?

Like most of the concepts encountered in this book, "manhood" is a social construction, a human invention that carries with it a long and varied history. Acknowledging that fact makes the search for what is universally "male" a rather futile one. In examining the evolution of American manhood, historian E. Anthony Rotundo tells us that the concept has passed through at least three significant historical rewrites.

Colonial men, who were thought to be more virtuous and sexually restrained than women, defined themselves primarily as heads of households and emphasized their duties to family and community more than any individual achievements they might have accomplished. Reason and control of the emotions were considered traits of manliness. Rotundo refers to this era as an age of communal manhood.

In the early years of the 19th century, this view began to give way to a concept of self-made manhood as the new market economy merged with a still relatively young republican form of government. As the market philosophy of individual in-terest began to take hold, a man's identity and social status as a person who had achieved success in business and politics began to mirror the economic philosophy. Ambition, rivalry, dominance, aggression, and freedom from authority defined "the new man." Even so, these new passions were not unambiguously praised. A man had to demonstrate that he had these desires under control.

Slowly, toward the end of the 19th century, another transformation began to take shape. The felt need to control the passionate side of manhood began to disintegrate. Competitiveness and toughness were exalted as ends in themselves, while the male body's appearance and athleticism became important components of manhood. Rotundo calls this the emergence of passionate manhood. These passionate tendencies became so strong that many men exchanged what would today be called love letters.

Rotundo's examination of the transition from boyhood to manhood in the 19th century reveals some fascinating communication practices that marked the move from one social role to another. For most middle-class boys, the first three to four years of life were lived in the largely female world of the home (including the wearing of female-style gowns). Mothers instilled in their sons the strong moral values of good character (self-restraint and self-denial) that would later be needed to control the passions that dominated the marketplace world of adult men.

different belief systems, construct stories with different sets of heroes and villains.

Narratives allow individuals, group, and nations to make sense of the world. Much of our understanding of who we are, what we are here for, and how we should behave is communicated to us in story form. It's a good idea to pay attention to the stories you hear every day. They are more than just ways to pass the time. They are cultural constructions that shape our lives.

# Skill Building: Becoming More Mindful

In both this and the previous chapter, we've stressed how easy it is to let routines take over our communication. We've seen that people perceive the world and others in it by filtering

By the age of six, boys found freedom from a female world perceived as constraining in the free play of their peers. This "boy culture" was wild, careless, primitive, violent, and almost totally devoid of adult supervision. Rotundo describes it as "mutual nurture combined with assault and battery." Their play was dominated by rituals that emphasized the values of stoicism (suppressing feelings of pain or tenderness), daring (high risk-taking), loyalty, the mastery of new skills, competition, and—most of all—independence. The worst fate for a young boy was to be called a "mama's boy." It meant that he stayed too close to the values of home. In contrast, young girls remained in the confines of the home, under the watchful eyes of their mothers and older sisters.

The transition from boyhood to manhood was anything but clear-cut. Young men struggled mightily with the twin uncertainties of love and career. "Boy culture" did little to prepare them for either, so they had to turn to each other for support. They did so by creating their own clubs and organizations in which they debated, ate, drank, and sang. In effect, they replaced the physical assaults of boy culture with verbal assaults that taught them the value of a quick wit, a good argument, and abstract thinking—all skills they would need in the workplace. In transition to the world of romantic love, these young men developed romantic friendships that would to-day be easily mistaken for homosexual relationships. They frequently slept in the same bed, sometimes held each other for warmth as well as an expression of affection, and confided in each other in great detail about their personal hopes and fears. Since females were largely an enigma to young men, their male friendships served as a kind of rehearsal for marriage that allowed them to test feelings of intimacy without a lifelong commitment at stake. Such romantic relationships were widely accepted among both young men and young women. For women, these types of relationships would last throughout life; for young men, they represented but a passing phase on the road to manhood. In fact, these same highly charged emotional relationships in youth became rather stoic and distant friendships in adulthood.

**SOURCE**  E. A. Rotundo, *American Manhood: Transformations in Masculinity from the Revolution to the Modern Era* (New York: Basic Books, 1993).


**ADDITIONAL READINGS**
Henley, N. M., and C. Kramarae. "Gender, Power, and Miscommunication," in *Miscommunication and Problematic Talk*. N. Coupland, H. Giles, and J. Wiemann, eds. Newbury Park, Calif.: Sage, 1991, pp. 18–43.
Wood, J. T. *Gendered Lives: Communication, Gender, and Culture*. Belmont, Calif.: Wadsworth, 1994.

their perceptions through socially constructed schemata. We've also seen that there are many pressures on us to play socially approved roles and to follow socially appropriate scripts. What this means is that it is possible to get through life on automatic pilot, to carry out our lives in a mindless way.

There are some benefits to mindless action. When we rely on distinctions from the past, we don't have to stop and think about everyday activities. When we automatically follow social roles, we can easily fit in. Life seems very simple when we are acting mindlessly. At the same time, acting mindlessly presents some real dangers. When in a mindless state, we lack creativity, exhibit emotional and cognitive rigidity, and find it impossible to adapt to new communication situations. Our relationships lack flexibility and originality. In this section we'll look at some ways you can gain more control over your perceptions and actions by becoming more mindful. This basic interpersonal skill will allow you to create more rewarding relational cultures.

## Mindfulness and Open-Mindedness

Mindfulness and mindlessness are basic cognitive states. According to psychologist Ellen J. Langer, **mindlessness** is a state of reduced attention. The individual is trapped in categories devised in the past. **Mindfulness,** on the other hand, is a state of "alert and lively awareness" involving active information processing and encouraging the creation of new categories and distinctions.[22]

The mindlessness/mindfulness dichotomy is similar to Milton Rokeach's distinction between closed- and open-mindedness. Rokeach believed that people could be categorized according to the rigidity of their cognitive systems. For Rokeach the basic characteristic that defined a person's openness is "the extent to which the person can receive, evaluate, and act on relevant information received from the outside on its own intrinsic merits, unencumbered by irrelevant factors in the situation, within the person, or from the outside."[23]

Closed-minded people, when compared with those who are open-minded, tend to be less able to learn new information. They have more difficulty discriminating between information and the source of that information so that they tend to accept whatever authorities say is true. They also tend to have problems in resolving conflicts, refusing to compromise because they equate compromise with defeat.

While followers of Rokeach have often treated open- and closed-mindedness as relatively enduring personality characteristics, Langer emphasizes that mindfulness and mindlessness are mental states and that people can be encouraged to switch from one to the other. She argues that mindlessness is not a personality characteristic, that we are all capable of both mental conditions.

Langer also denies the common belief that it is easier to be mindless than mindful. Psychologists used to believe that we resist mindful activity because being mindful takes too much effort. Langer proposed that "effort is involved in switching from a mindless to a mindful mode, analogous to the force required to change the direction of a moving object," but that the mindful state, once we have switched into it, is no more tiring than the mindless state. Being mindful can be effortless and even energizing.[24]

## Increasing Mindfulness

When we are in a mindless state, we are, by definition, unaware and uncritical. The first step in reducing mindlessness, then, is to *become aware of the extent to which perceptions and behaviors are socially determined.* Most people fail to realize that their perceptions and behaviors are largely socially constructed. The social rules we follow as a matter of course seldom have the "feel" of rules. We believe our behavior is freely chosen rather than socially controlled.

Unfortunately, much of our conduct is triggered by habit. We eat not because we're hungry but because the clock says it's noon. We go to a party not because we particularly want to but because all of our friends are going. We dress appropriately because it wouldn't be right not to. When we do all of these things, we are letting the social situation control our responses. In order to become more mindful, we must *become aware of the contextual triggers that govern our behavior.* There may, in fact, be nothing wrong with following social rules, but we can't decide until we recognize that these acts are rule-governed.

When we are in a state of mindfulness, we can critically evaluate our options. We may decide to follow the norms and act out our roles, or we may decide to transcend the system; what's important is that we make a conscious decision. One test you might want to apply in deciding whether to conform to social expectations is to tack a "because clause" onto a description of your behavior. You should say to yourself, "I'm going downtown tonight because . . ." If you can't think of any good reason for your action, maybe that action bears more thought.

Often we do things in noncreative, rigid ways because we come to premature closure. Once we've thought of one way to do something, we don't go further and try to think of other possible ways to do it. This closure can occur in our process of enacting role requirements or in our efforts to solve problems. For instance, a teacher may teach the same way he or she has always taught without bothering to ask if there's a different way to teach. Or a group may make mediocre decisions because the members stop as soon as they've found a solution without asking themselves whether it is the best solution. What both of these examples suggest is that we should make a real effort to *examine thoughts and actions critically, looking for new solutions and perspectives.*

One way to increase creativity is to make sure that we *don't engage in self-censorship or premature cognitive commitments.* One of the biggest blocks to creativity is our fear of being judged. We hold back potentially interesting ideas and commit to dull but safe solutions because we're afraid original ideas and actions may seem silly. This tendency to self-censorship is so strong that we must often use artificial means to change it. Techniques such as brainstorming, where individuals are encouraged to express all ideas no matter how insignificant or ridiculous they may at first appear, are specifically designed to help us overcome our own fear of creativity. While brainstorming is often used in formal organizational contexts, it can be used by single individuals to solve interpersonal problems. Remember that to get along with someone else, you must be flexible, adaptable, and creative. In relationships don't be afraid to try something new.

Another way to increase creativity is to *take multiple perspectives.* Much of how we react to the world we learned as children. As we grow up we learn to take on new perspectives so as not to be trapped in childish patterns. But even

as adults we can benefit from trying our best to see the world in as many different ways as possible. Piper and Langer did an interesting study in which they asked people to watch a soap opera from several different perspectives—that of a politician, a director, a psychologist, a lawyer, a doctor, and a child.[25] This mindful viewing allowed subjects to see the characters as more complex and less stereotypic than did a control group of mindless, single-perspective viewers. Subjects got more out of the show when encouraged to take multiple perspectives. The same might be true of real-life experiences if we were to work hard at seeing things in multiple ways.

All of us could benefit by spending more of our time in a mindful rather than a mindless state. The best way to do this is to become more aware of the situations in which we act mindlessly and to be critical of our own behaviors.

# Process to Performance

## Review Terms

The following is a list of major concepts introduced in this chapter. The page where the concept is first mentioned is listed in parentheses.

**position** (180)
**role** (181)
**role rigidity** (182)
**role repertoire** (183)
**role conflict** (183)
**looking-glass self** (183)
**social comparison theory** (183)
**self-perception theory** (185)
**face** (186)
**face-work** (187)
**line** (187)
**front** (188)
**setting** (188)
**personal front** (188)

## Suggested Readings

Dow, Bonnie J., and Julia T. Wood, eds. *The SAGE Handbook of Gender and Communication.* Thousand Oaks, Calif.: Sage, 2006. This book of readings provides insights on how gender affects all aspects of communication, including intimate relationships, organizational communication, public address, mass communication, and intercultural communication.

Paley, Vivian G. *A Child's Work: The Importance of Childhood Play.* Chicago: University of Chicago Press, 2005. This highly readable book explores the ways children use language in role-playing and story-telling in ways that carry through into their adult lives.

**Topics for Discussion**

www.oup.com/us/trenholm

## Observation Guide

**1.** How controlled are you by simple social norms? How willing are you to sacrifice face or line? Choose a simple social norm and violate it. Don't do something outrageous that would offend others; simply do something that is slightly odd or atypical. For example, wear an article of clothing that is not quite appropriate. Or sit by yourself instead of joining your friends as you usually do. Carefully note reactions. Be specific. What kinds of pressures were placed on you? Describe your own feelings about doing this. Was it hard to do? Did you feel awkward and uncomfortable? Are you too much or too little affected by social norms? Relate this experience to the social comparison process.

**2.** Analyze your own style of self-presentation from a dramatic point of view. Think of a particular communication incident where you were trying to make a good impression. What face were you trying to present? What line did you take? How did your setting and personal front either help or hinder you? Describe in detail all relevant props, furnishings, and costuming decisions. Was this a solo performance, or did you count on others to help you put on your front? If the interaction was successful, how much was attributable to front? If the interaction didn't quite work out, how would you redirect it if you had the chance?

**3.** Collect the stories and jokes you hear during the next few days. Write them out so that their details are clear to you. Now analyze these stories in as much detail as possible. Try thinking of yourself as an anthropologist or folklorist who has stumbled upon a collection of stories from a foreign culture and is trying to reconstruct and make sense of that culture. What lessons and values are implicit in the stories? What does that tell you about the culture from which they were collected? Did any parts of their content surprise or even offend you? Why?

## Exercises

**1.** Working with a partner, list all of the roles you have assumed during the last week. Try to determine the communication expectations for each role. Write out at least three rules of communication behavior for each role you identify.

**2.** Work with an opposite-sex partner. Plan a skit showing a male-female interaction embodying typical sex roles. Present it to the class, but take the sex role opposite to your own; that is, if you are male, play the female part, and if you are female, play the male part. As a class, discuss the portrayals. What behaviors were used to portray the opposite sex? Were the portrayals accurate? How did you feel while portraying your part, and why? Was this hard or easy? Embarrassing or fun?

*Many artists use the self-portrait to provide a window to their own sense of identity.*

Edvard Munch, *Self-portrait with a Wine Bottle*, 1906

## CHAPTER 8

# Self Competence
# Establishing Individual Identities

"Don't call me that! My name is Toby," says an irritated three-year-old, responding to his father's attempt to dub him with some clever nickname. The act of naming carries great social significance for us. As we learn to categorize the world around us, we also learn our place within it. Our name usually sets us apart from other human beings and is one of the most significant ways that we remind ourselves of our uniqueness—of our individuality. In fact, new theories about the evolution of the human mind and of language suggest that the very things that make us human, such as self-consciousness and personal memory, are not necessarily innate. These abilities seem to be derived from the use of language itself during the very early years of childhood.[1] Our own American culture and language use in particular recognize and emphasize the uniqueness of the individual person.

Interpersonal communication influences the development of this unique personal identity. Since we cannot "see" ourselves (except in mirrors, in photographs, and in our mind's eye), we rely on others' impressions of us and feedback to us to form our own opinions of self. As this sense of self begins to develop, we are confronted with one of the most enduring dilemmas of social life: whether to conform to social expectations and present ourselves as "one of the group" or to deviate and be seen as an individual who stands "apart from the crowd." When we conform to standard roles and rules, we are taking on a **social identity** defined by and borrowed from society; when we resist standard roles or make our own rules, we are forging a **personal identity.** To be fully human means to develop and express the self in terms of both social and personal self-identities. In the previous chapter we looked at forces that encourage conformity and the development of our social identities; in this chapter we explore the factors that foster independence and individuality, or personal identity.

The tension between conformity and independence is probably felt to some extent in all cultures, but it is particularly strong in our culture. **199**

In collectivist cultures such as Japan and China there is a greater tendency to conform to social expectations—expressions of individuality are seen as disrespectful and self-centered. Pressures to conform are present in our own culture as well. Chapter 7 demonstrated that people adapt to the social roles and situations defined by their culture. The starting point for social life is the inheritance of complex signs and symbols from previous generations. The family you were born into had already established roles, rules, and customs long before your arrival, as did the schools, churches, political parties, and other institutions you may have joined later.

We begin this chapter with a brief historical overview of how the modern image of ourselves as unique individuals came about. This is important because we have a very strong tendency to think of "the self" as being a fundamental aspect of human nature, as something that has always existed regardless of culture or the passing of time. Once we understand that the concept of self is a historical construct, we will spend the bulk of this chapter looking at how researchers today have defined and studied the concept of self, how it changes over a lifetime, and how it relates to our interpersonal communication practices.

# The Self in History

The concept of personal identity or self-concept is a recent historical development. During most of recorded history, people defined themselves according to their place or rank in society (lord of the manor, servant, merchant, peasant, and so on). Certainly people recognized their own individual existence, and frequently thought of themselves as having "souls," but they did not dwell on the unique differences between one soul or self and another. The first recorded use of the word "conscious" to denote awareness of internal thoughts and sensations dates from the late 16th century, while the word "self-conscious" doesn't make its appearance until over a hundred years later.[2] Several historians have observed that as cultures change, so does the language that describes the self.[3] Different historical eras, it is argued, generate their own "modal selves." A **modal self** refers to an idealized type of person whose existence is viewed as essential if the prevailing social order within a culture is to maintain itself.[4] This conception of self also rests on the assumption that when cultural change occurs, it demands a change in the types of people who inhabit the culture. For instance, the kind of person who knew his place and drew his identity largely from being the "head of a household" fit very well in the hierarchical society of colonial America. We might call the modal self of that time a "communal self" because playing out the role you were dealt by gender and birth was essential in re-creating the moral and social order.

The cultural vision of self began to change as the industrial revolution and the new American democracy took hold. Prior to the revolution in machinery and methods of work, most people worked from their homes. The home and the workplace were one and the same. The concept of a private self apart from the community had little significance since everything one did was closely scrutinized by family and community leaders. But the proliferation of shops and factories caused a division between public and private spheres: The public arena became the world of commerce and politics, and the home a refuge from that world. In a world where men left the home to work and where the household was becoming more of a feminine domain, it was difficult to sustain the male identity as "head of the household." In addition, the new economy required employees who were punctual, loyal, honest, and hard-working. These requirements were the driving force for the creation of what historian Warren Susman has called a "culture of character" and a corresponding modal self defined by various attributes of *character: being conscious of duty, a good citizen, honorable, moral, well-mannered, and a doer of good deeds.*[5]

Late in the 19th century, another transformation occurred. The modal self built around character began to give way to the even more individualized concept of *personality*. Where a self-image based on character was accomplished by living up to a well-defined social standard of morals and values, a self-image defined by having a personality meant to be *different, fascinating, stunning, magnetic, creative, dominant, or forceful.*[6] How did this shift in modal selves happen? Susman believes that several factors were at work, but two stand out. One is the fact that more and more Americans moved to urban areas to find work. There they lived constantly in a crowd, and developed the need to feel significant or different from everyone around them. In diaries, journals, and advice books of the time, people repeatedly stressed that "personality is the quality of being Somebody."[7] A second major change was a move from a producer to a consumer society. A person of good character fit in well in a society that needed to make things, but not in an economy more and more designed around people "buying things." With an image of self as a unique personality, one would be more inclined to buy accessories and decorate the home in a way that reflected one's individual traits. By the beginning of this century, all the elements were in place to support our modern notion of who we are.

Certainly one factor affecting self-identity today is the rise of new media that give us more venues than ever before for self-presentation. The study described in this chapter's Research in Review explores some of the paradoxes involved in contemporary self-presentation. Box 8.1 also takes up this theme. In it Kenneth Gergen argues that we are in the midst of a great social transformation and that our image of the self as a stable, enduring construct is beginning to crumble.

# Self-Concepts: Gaining Independence from Social Roles and Rules

As we saw in Chapter 7, a smoothly running society depends on our following socially assigned roles and rules. We also saw that roles do not totally define us. We exercise some choice in the matter of adopting which of several possible roles to play in any given situation. We play some roles more frequently than others and may become very good at a few of them, internalizing them as part of who we are. But we also distance ourselves from some roles and avoid others as much as possible. The choices we make concerning what roles we play and how we play them reflect a growing independence from our cultural inheritance. This independence from cultural rules eventually culminates in one or more rather stable self-concepts, which we use to determine when we should conform to social rules and when we should resist following them. In order to understand how self-concepts emerge and stabilize, we need first to define them.

## What Is the Self-Concept?

In our modern era, the **self-concept** is defined as each person's own subjective view or image of himself or herself as a person.[8] While we often use the terms *self-concept* and *personality* interchangeably, they are not the same thing. Most scholarly definitions of **personality** assume each of us exhibits organized, enduring, and characteristic ways of behaving *as measured by psychological tests*. The difference? Personality refers to how psychologists see us; the self-concept refers to how we see ourselves. Although others (including researchers) are entitled to their own opinions about us, and may disagree with one another about what kind of person we really are, our self-concept remains our own private view of ourselves.

## Presentation of Self in Cyberspace

# Blogs as Mediated Interpersonal Communication

Blogging is a relatively new phenomenon. Many weblogs consist of online editorial commentary by professional journalists or political analysts. But anyone can create a blog. In "Presentation of Self on the Web: An Ethnographic Study of Teenage Girls' Weblogs," Denise Bortree looks at some of the challenges teenage bloggers face as they look for ways to use this mass medium as a tool for interpersonal communication.

Bortree points out that personal bloggers address two audiences at once: close friends and anonymous readers. This can present problems. When communicating with strangers, for example, people usually inflate claims about the self; but with friends, they try to be honest. In addition, self-disclosure is risky with strangers, yet it is necessary to build relationships with friends.

Because the majority of bloggers are young and female, Bortree decided to focus on teenage girls. She began by logging on to Blogspot.com, reading the blogs she came across to get a feel for how they were used. Eventually she narrowed her investigation to six teenage girls. These girls established interpersonal relationships by telling stories and sharing intimate thoughts, "including their frustrations, their disappointments, and, at times, their despair." They also posted IM conversations and the results of Internet personality quizzes (What kind of virgin are you? Which Harry Potter candy are you?) Bortree believes these latter postings were a way of communicating personal values and characteristics: an indirect form of self-presentation.

The girls felt that communicating online helped them discuss issues they would have felt uncomfortable addressing offline. Yet, while they used their blogs to establish interpersonal closeness, they were also aware they were communicating with strangers and that they had to be careful about what they said. Thus, they were torn between trying to project a public image and honestly disclosing thoughts and feelings.

The girls presented themselves in several ways. By mentioning all the people they spent time with, they portrayed themselves as socially competent and ingratiated themselves with those they mentioned. By posting the results of internet surveys, they offered a kind of personal profile of themselves, sometimes in a self-deprecating way. By adding design elements to the templates offered by their providers, they signaled their originality and creativity.

Bortree points out that their blogs were just one way the girls communicated, but one that fulfilled a significant function. "Unlike other forms of communication typically used by teenage girls . . . weblogs allow the girls to maintain a journal about their lives, keep a record of their thoughts and feelings on a daily basis, and at the same time give others access to those thoughts and feelings."

Bortree, Denise Sevick. "Presentation of Self on the Web: An Ethnographic Study of Teenage Girls' Weblogs." *Education, Communication & Information* 5, no. 1 (2006): 25–59.

*Pensive self-reflection is one way we contemplate the self and our interactions with others.*

Elaine De Kooning, Self-portrait, 1946

As we will see, some perspectives on the self emphasize the behavioral (personality) dimension, while others take more of a self-concept approach. In this section we look at five different ways of thinking about the self: self as narrative, self as cognitive schema, self as a set of behavioral indicators, self as relational achievement, and self as internal dialogue. Although each perspective differs from the others in significant ways, they also complement each other and capture different aspects of our self-understanding.

## Self as Narrative

Talk about reinventing the wheel. One of the most recent approaches to defining the self is a restoration of the oldest form of human knowledge, that of knowing ourselves through myth and story. From this perspective, the self-concept is fashioned over time as a narrative with ourselves as the main, heroic character. In Chapter 7, we touched on this briefly, noting that the human propensity for narrative includes telling stories about biographical selves. We make and re-make the story of our lives, each time struggling

BOX 8.1

## The Saturated Self

# Will You Still Be You Tomorrow?

Social psychologist Kenneth Gergen believes that we have already entered an era of profound social change. In his book *The Saturated Self*, he contends that modern transportation and communication technologies (e.g., international travel, television, telephones, electronic mail) are propelling us toward a new type of self-consciousness, which he labels a postmodern or *populated self.*

Noting that communication defines social reality, Gergen argues that different historical eras produce different kinds of self-identities. The modern era (dating from the late 19th and early 20th centuries), with its rational, scientific viewpoint that constructs the world as composed of fundamental, essential properties, makes it natural to think of the self as a thing-in-itself, as a fundamentally stable entity. And as long as most relationships are based primarily on face-to-face or written communication, and most of those relationships last a lifetime, the self-identities formed and maintained through social interac-

tion with well-known others are likely to seem very stable indeed. As a result, most people in Western cultures think of themselves as having a "true self," a stable interior identity that remains essentially consistent despite changes in fads, location, relationships, and so on.

But Gergen, and many others, believe that the modern era may be coming to a close. A crisis in the social and natural sciences has raised doubts as to our ability to know anything objectively. Many scholars now believe that even the language with which we express our so-called objective viewpoints does not reflect or mirror reality; it is tainted through and through with social and ideological bias. Moreover, Gergen points to the "enormous proliferation of relationships" that new technologies make possible. We are much more likely than previous generations to have friends and acquaintances all over the geographical map. Many of these relationships will be fleeting, but nonetheless provide opportunities to interact with "different" others and to try on new self-identities. Radio, television, and newer forms of electronic communication have dramatically expanded the range and variety of relationships we are able to witness and participate in. We no longer form our opinions (or self-identities) based solely on an immediate audience of parents, peers, and local community values. It is not uncommon for people to think of themselves as having relationships with media celebrities, or to actually talk with them on television call-in

to give it more coherence. According to psychologist Dan McAdams:

> We are all tellers of tales. We each seek to provide our scattered and often confusing experiences with a sense of coherence by arranging the episodes of our lives into stories. This is not the stuff of delusion or self-deception. We are not telling ourselves lies. Rather, through our *personal myths, each of us discovers what is true and what is meaningful in life. In order to live well, with unity and purpose, we compose a heroic narrative of the self that illustrates essential truths about ourselves.*[9]

Constructing the **narrative self** is a complicated and ongoing task. McAdams argues that we spend most of our childhood gathering the shows. The combination of computer desktop publishing and electronic modems gives people the chance to "become direct agents in their own self-multiplication" (the capacity to have a significant presence in more than one place at a time).

Conversations with unknown others via the Internet or 900 numbers is now a 24-hour-a-day possibility. Gergen believes that these new forms of relationship are accelerating at the same time that traditional relationships are undergoing radical transformation. He describes all-too-typical family interactions as "microwave relationships" because of the vastly differing schedules of parents and children that make the family sit-down dinner a rare event. Such relationships are being defined by "intense heat for the immediate provision of nourishment." The idea of spending "quality time" with our children is one indication that the amount of time devoted to such relationships is changing.

Gergen calls this the social saturation of identity. With a greater variety of relationships, either fleeting or in a constant state of disruption, stability in relationships and in personal identities will become harder and harder to maintain. The result is "a populating of the self" with many different possible identities, many of which contradict each other. As more voices enter the fray, the question "Who am I?" becomes more difficult to answer. The self that seems rational within one set of relationships may seem absurd from another viewpoint. While this splitting of the self in many different directions makes us candidates for a permanent identity crisis, it may have some liberating features as well.

One possibility that Gergen envisions in the emerging postmodern self is a greater emphasis on relationships over individual concerns. Instead of asking, "How should I live my life?" we may be more inclined to wonder, "What will my family do with its life?" or "How will my marriage go today?" or "How will my team of coworkers get by this week?" While it seems odd to make relational terms the center of attention and to push the self to the periphery, neither social unit is more "natural" than the other. For most of human history, the community or social group has been the dominant social unit. The ideology of individualism has risen to prominence only in the last three centuries, and even then, only in Western cultures. If Gergen is right, the next hundred years may be very interesting indeed.

**SOURCE** Kenneth J. Gergen, *The Saturated Self: Dilemmas of Identity in Contemporary Life* (New York: Basic Books, 1991).

**ADDITIONAL READINGS**

Giddens, Anthony. *Modernity and Self-Identity: Self and Society in the Late Modern Age.* Stanford, Calif.: Stanford University Press, 1991.

Lash, Scott, and Jonathan Friedman, eds. *Modernity and Identity.* Oxford: Blackwell, 1992.

primary materials out of which we will eventually fashion a relatively coherent personal myth. What are the most significant of these primary elements? They include but are not limited to:

- *Our earliest bonding experiences, which influence the emotional tone of the self-narrative.* During the first year of life, the interaction between infants and their caregivers results in a form of attachment that ranges from highly secure to ambivalent or avoidant. The more secure the level of bonding, the more likely the child is to develop a sense of optimism. The eventual self-narrative emerges with an underlying hopeful tone, reflected in the basic belief that the world is trustworthy, predictable, and good. An insecure parental attachment is more likely to spawn a pessimistic narrative, in which the central character is frustrated, does not succeed, or faces difficulties that are beyond his understanding. McAdams is careful to note that individuals can overcome such inauspicious beginnings, but the odds are not in their favor. The pessimistic tone is repeatedly reinforced by expectations of disaster, distrust, or deception.

- *Culturally available themes and images, experienced primarily in childhood fantasy and play.* Throughout the preschool years, we collect an amazing array of images from bedtime stories, books, comics, television shows, action figures, and movies, not to mention the larger than life characters and situations invoked at family gatherings, religious services, and school playgrounds. The wicked witch, the mighty hero, the dastardly coward, and the cuddly cousin all strike us in different ways, perhaps in keeping with the narrative tone that defines our emerging outlook on life. Some of these images are frightening; others intriguing; still others less impactful. We identify with and adapt many of these images to suit our own momentary purposes and longer term interests. Out of these early identifications, many options for self-discovery and self-making emerge.

- *The recurring motives and ideological strivings of late childhood and early adolescence.* In the elementary years, a child's behavior and thought processes become more organized. Motives begin to emerge as internal dispositions that play out across different situations and relationships. Some begin to seek power and control more than affection or caring or inclusion. Although motives clearly vary according to situation and relationship, some motives may begin to take center stage and show up more frequently in the accounts we offer to explain our accomplishments or diffuse responsibility. As we enter adolescence, self-identify becomes an even more central question. Physical changes associated with puberty and an increased facility for abstract

thinking conspire to raise serious questions about who we are, what life is all about, and whether the beliefs we have inherited are the only options. McAdams notes that theories, creeds, and other systematic beliefs begin to have more appeal than the simpler stories of childhood. It is in this ideological context that the personal self-narrative begins to be more consciously constructed, debated, and logically analyzed. New directions are contemplated and explored, but serious identity commitments are put on temporary hold. McAdams refers to this process of trying on new identities without playing "for keeps" as a **psychosocial moratorium** (a term borrowed and modified from the renowned psychologist Erik Erikson).

From the resources outlined here the maturing adult begins to construct a self-narrative that represents his or her commitments to a particular persona with particular motives and beliefs about the world and the people who populate it. These commitments are much firmer than those of the adolescent who is trying them on for size, but are not set in stone and are still open to further negotiations. In fact, as our own (highly competent) biographers, we are prone to modifying our self-narratives from time to time as different parts of our story come into sharper focus or as new events prompt us to make sense of earlier events in new ways.

Understanding the self as a constructed narrative highlights interpersonal communication as a prominent site for self-development. In the earliest stages, interaction with caregivers shapes the emotional landscape. Later, others are invoked as partners in episodes of play or as sources of lasting images. But equally important is the fact that self-narratives are shaped and reshaped in the telling of our story to others. As the relational perspective developed in Chapter 2 suggests, to whom we tell our story is not an insignificant fact. We often adapt our stories and ourselves to achieve a better fit with the criterial attributes of a given relationship.

## Self as Cognitive Schema

Cognitive psychologists present another way to understand the experience of self. They refer to **self-schemata** as cognitive structures that organize and guide the processing of self-related information.[10] People use different organizing principles to make sense of their collection of self-concepts. Hazel Markus has identified several of them. For some people, independence or dependence is the central principle in their self-schema; for others, masculinity or femininity may be dominant.[11] Whatever the organizing principle, it affects how we perceive ourselves and our social world. For instance, someone whose self-schema is based on the organizing principle of "being competitive" is likely to remember more incidents in which she was competitive and fewer in which cooperation occurred. Evidence also suggests that such a person is likely to hold the view that "everyone is competitive" as a way of justifying her own competitiveness.

Sometimes an organizing principle becomes elaborated into a **life script,** or a relatively fixed way of thinking about the self and relating to others. Eric Berne originated the concept and defined four very general life scripts: "I'm OK, You're OK," "I'm OK, You're not OK," "I'm not OK, You're OK," and "I'm not OK, You're not OK."[12] Each of these scripts represents a basic view of self and others and influences how we perceive social situations. Barnett Pearce and Vernon Cronen offer an extended definition of a life script as "that repertoire of episodes that a person perceives as identified with him/herself."[13] The life script of a practical joker, for example, would entail a number of episodes such as "hiding things from people," "placing a thumbtack or whoopee cushion on another's chair," and other, similar escapades.

While most people no doubt adopt life scripts that they believe will result in positive public images, on some occasions a life script can be used as an excuse for a potentially negative self-presentation. A person who fears that he won't

*Early attachments affect our ability to form future relationships. The sense of belonging and companionship shared between this father and child suggests that the child will be secure later in life.*

be capable of performing a new dance step may decline an invitation to dance by invoking his life script of "A real man doesn't . . . " He may thus be using his life script as a **self-handicapping strategy.** In their research on this subject, Steven Berglas and Edward Jones defined a self-handicapping strategy as a technique for manufacturing protective excuses ahead of time to prevent possible failure in the future.[14] The research has shown that some people will talk or act in ways that protect them from bearing the brunt of future failures. They'll offer excuses in the event that they fail an exam, make a mistake in a financial report, or miss a crucial free throw. Supposedly, the excuse planted ahead of time ("I had to work," "Company came over," "The old wrist is acting up again") takes the heat off the individual and places the blame on the circumstance.

As should be apparent, the basic notion behind the self as cognitive schema is that the human brain organizes information (including information about self) in patterned ways that enable us to be somewhat predictable to ourselves as well as to others. Critics of this perspective argue that envisioning the self as cognitive structure is too psychological and does not acknowledge the considerable influence of interaction with others. But many psychologists would agree that the content of our cognitive schemas is socially constructed and therefore reflects social interaction to some degree. It is clearly possible to imagine how self-schemas, life scripts, and self-handicapping strategies could serve a role in constructing our self-narratives.

## Self as Behavioral Indicators

Whereas self-narratives and cognitive schemata help us understand how a sense of self emerges and changes over time, we must not forget the role that our physical behavior plays in shaping who we are. In fact, the relationship between our self-identity and our actual **behavioral self** is a reflexive one. That is, the self-understanding we bring to a situation shapes the way we communicate, and in turn, the way we communicate can influence and revise what we think about ourselves.

For example, a young woman enters her boss's office during her first week on the job to talk about how to approach her first real client. She has had considerable sales experience in a previous position with another company. She sees herself as an "aggressive and competent salesperson." This identity shapes the way she communicates with her boss. She walks into the office with confidence, engages in a little small talk, and then proceeds to lay out her plan for snaring the client. Along the way, however, she uncharacteristically stumbles over her words, forgets a major step in her proposal, and almost knocks the boss's coffee cup off the desk. While these behaviors do not completely shatter her competent salesperson image, they do crumble it a bit around the edges. The feedback she receives from observing her own behavior plus the boss's reaction modifies her immediate sense of self-worth; she won't see herself in quite the same way the next time she enters the boss's office. One instance like this may only be seen as a temporary setback, but two or three rocky episodes in a short period of time could begin to call into question her sense of self. This reflexive relationship between self-identity and communication should make us realize that our self-concept is always under construction, and therefore subject to change.

You may recall, from Chapter 7, Daryl Bem's **self-perception theory** to explain how many of our self-definitions come about and are changed. Bem suggests that we come to know who we are by observing our own behavior "after the fact" and then inferring what kind of person we must be.[15] Suppose you're cleaning your apartment and notice that your garbage can is full of paper and aluminum cans. On a whim you decide to take them to a recycling center. Later that day as the temperature drops below zero, you think about turning the heat up but decide against it. Finally, you catch yourself just as you are about to toss a gum wrapper out of your car window. You put it in the ashtray instead. As you take stock of your behavior, you may be led to the conclusion that you are fast becoming a "conservationist." This may also happen when friends point out aspects of your behavior that you have overlooked. In effect, you may say to yourself, "I did give money to the college fund. I do stop to help people who have flat tires. I must be a charitable person."

In short, a significant part of our self-identity is defined by the behaviors that we routinely engage in and reflect upon. There is an obvious chicken-and-egg question here. It is never clear whether we behave in ways consistent with our preconceived self-image (e.g., to fit the self-narrative) or alter our sense of self as a way of accounting for our own behavior after the fact. But whatever the case may be, behavioral indicators are important aspects of self-identity. Clearly, others attend to our behavior and draw conclusions about us from what they observe. In fact, it is our interdependent, joint behavior with others that leads to a fourth perspective called the relational self.

## Self as Relational Achievement

It should already be clear that we are not alone in the process of defining who we are. We inherit a limited range of possible selves from the cultures that envelop us or which we seek out. We discover additional possibilities in media and new communications technologies (see Box 8.1). But our most significant self-defining opportunities are embedded in our closest relationships. As we discussed in Chapter 2, a close relationship becomes a third entity (you, me, and us). In our ongoing efforts to develop and maintain a relationship, we inevitably adjust and modify our individual self-identities. Thus, the **relational self** refers to the particular self-identity we normally display in a given relationship. William James once said that every person "has as many different social selves as there are distinct groups of persons about whose opinions he cares." Even with the relatively small number of close relationships most of us have, it should strike us as amazing that we are able to sustain a sense of self-unity in the face of multiple selves for multiple relationships. Although we may employ different self-concepts in a variety of different relationships, we do not necessarily experience these multiple selves as fragmented. We are able to compartmentalize our relationships in such a way that we do not perceive any incongruity between how we act as the tyrannical boss or the loving husband. Charles Horton Cooley explained how we come to view the self differently

*What we tell about ourselves can differ, depending on which presenting self is providing the narrative.*

in the presence of different people. You may recall Cooley's *looking-glass self* introduced in Chapter 7. Cooley identified three essential elements in the self-concept: (1) how we think we appear to the other person, (2) how we think that person judges our appearance, and (3) how we feel about ourselves in reaction to the other's perception of us. Cooley shows how we might come to feel that we are not the same person from one relationship to another when he says that "we are ashamed to seem evasive in the presence of a straightforward man, cowardly in the presence of a brave one, gross in the eyes of a refined one, and so on."[16] Perhaps if we met all three of these people in the space of five minutes we would feel a little uncomfortable with who we really are. But we ordinarily have some breathing space between encounters that enables us to shift gears and establish an appropriate persona.

While interacting with very different kinds of people can occasionally test our sense of self, this is not always the case. Our self-concept can appear to us as relatively stable when we are equally comfortable in a variety of different relationships. For instance, a person may feel just as comfortable being "herself" with her parents as she does with her best friend. In each case, however, she perceives herself in somewhat different ways. With her parents she sees herself as independent, serious-minded, and caring. With her friend she may still see herself as caring, but also as witty, playful, and carefree. "I am occasionally serious with my friend, but for the most part I am like a kid who never grew up; for my parents I grew up years ago to avoid being treated like a child." The type of relationship we have with another person inevitably affects who we are in that relationship.

In spite of the fact that we behave differently in various relationships, the limited range of those relationships can reinforce our sense of a stable self-identity. Several researchers have noted that the choices we make in terms of whom to spend time with and what types of situations to enact can provide consistent feedback to reinforce a single, preferred self-concept. Anthony Greenwald has drawn an analogy between the self and a totalitarian political organization, in that we can be so intent on the survival of a particular image of self that we surround ourselves only with people who reinforce that image and pay attention only to feedback we want to hear.[17]

## Self as Internal Dialogue

At least some of the personal narratives that we construct about ourselves actually take place as internal dialogue. The self can be conceived of as a system of selves that engage one another in "intrapersonal" discourse.[18] Such self-talk can take many forms. In some cases, people spend time in self-reflection, meditation, or prayer, which may be directed at self-improvement. In other cases, people actually talk to themselves. Linda Lederman conducted an interesting study in which she asked people the extent to which they engaged in self-talk, how they addressed themselves, and when such interactions were likely to take place.[19] Participants in the study indicated that they did indeed experience conversations among their multiple "selves," and that they spoke in the various voices of the critic, the supporter, or some internalized other (e.g., a parent or best friend). Although people occasionally referred to themselves by name, most spoke to themselves as a "You," as in "How could you get yourself in this mess?" Dialogues were conducted silently or out loud. Some talked to themselves constantly, others when feeling low, when nobody else was around, or when going through a difficult period. Self-talk can be a way of organizing one's thoughts, as well as working out issues, as one self debates another on the merits of a potential course of action. One participant described the experience as being "like an internal 'Muzak.' It just goes on and on and I don't even know it's there until I stop and listen to what I am saying to myself about me." Lederman also found that people generally saw themselves as relatively harsh self-critics, but were equally capable of ignoring their own advice. In short, self-talk functions much like other forms of interpersonal communication.

Lederman characterizes the individual self as a system of selves, and the internal dialogue as equivalent to relationships between or among various selves. She labels the particular self that steps forward in any given interaction and engages another person as the **presenting self.** From this perspective it is easy to see that the narratives we tell ourselves and others about the self may well differ, depending upon which presenting self is telling the story. Is it any wonder that figuring out who we are is a complex and frequently perplexing endeavor?

The five perspectives on self that we have reviewed—self as narrative, as cognitive schema, as behavioral indicators, as relationships, and as internal dialogue—more than hint at the complexity involved in making sense of ourselves. Each of these perspectives reflects our cultural assumptions about the existence, or at least the construction of, an entity called "self." For a rather intriguing alternative, you can read in Box 8.2 about a cultural approach that values eradication of the notion of self. No one perspective provides a comprehensive picture, but together these perspectives can help us better understand and explain how we acquire and nurture our sense of self. In the next section of this chapter, we take a look at how the self-concept influences our communication with others.

# Individual Differences and Interpersonal Communication

At the outset of this chapter, we drew a distinction between research into the self-concept and the personality, respectively. The self-concept is usually measured by asking an individual to describe his or her private view of self, allowing the individual to highlight what aspects of self are perceived as relevant to a given situation. An assessment of personality, on the other hand, is typically based on an individual's response to a series of questions generated by researchers and deemed by them to be an important predictor or explanation of behavior.

Since most of the research on personal dispositions and communication behavior has used personality measures, we report some of those results in this section. Our own bias is that self-concept measures are a better indicator of the link between personal identity and interpersonal communication for two reasons. First,

self-concepts are probably "activated" by the individual's perceptions of a given situation or relationship, and the individual is usually in a better position than the researcher to describe his or her own perceptions. This means that even though a person scores high on a particular measure of personality (say, assertiveness), that aspect of self may not be highly relevant in a given context (waiting in line to see a movie) or within the rules of a specific relationship (a best friend). Second, personality tests are often wrongly regarded as the final word in describing the ontological status of the individual. The idea that "If I scored high on the Machiavellian scale, then I must be Machiavellian" seems inadequate to describe the complexities of a given human personality.

Nonetheless, research conducted from the personality approach can be both interesting and informative if placed in proper perspective. Sometimes an aspect of one's personality may be tacitly influencing behavior, even though the person is not consciously aware of it. Some research indicates that implicit or nonconscious motivations (such as personality traits) are better predictors of spontaneous behavior, whereas consciously attributed motivations (such as the self-concept) better predict how we will respond when we anticipate a particular situation.[20] As you read this section of the chapter, keep in mind that specific findings are most likely to apply when a particular personality orientation has been activated and is represented as a self-concept.

Like the self-concept, personality traits have been shown to influence how we communicate verbally and nonverbally. In this section we review the research on five communication-related personality traits: (1) communicator style, (2) rhetorical sensitivity, (3) communication apprehension, (4) attachment style, and (5) intimacy motivation.

## Communicator Style

The concept of **communicator style** has been defined by Robert Norton as "the way one

BOX 8.2

## Zen and the Art of Selflessness

# "What Is Your Original Face Before Your Mother and Father Were Born?"

Our culture values people as isolated, separate individuals. We spend a great deal of our time reflecting on who we are. But not every culture attaches so much importance to the individual and ego involvement in social life. In fact, in Japanese Zen Buddhism, practitioners strive to eliminate self-identity altogether, to achieve a sense of *mu*, or nothingness. They reject the idea that a person's essence or being can be an object of thought.

The ideal of personal activity in Zen is "non-doing," or what some call a "state of no-mind." According to T. P. Kasulis, the author of *Zen Action, Zen Person*, it is the ability to be "unselfconsciously responsive," or in harmony with the surrounding social context and interpersonal relations. Lao-tzu, the founder of Taoism, once suggested that the ideal person was like water—responsive and yielding, but not fatalistic. By yielding (or being in harmony with the situation), water follows its path and eventually wears away the rock obstructing it (thus it is not fatalistic).

Of course, this philosophy is quite complementary with much of Japanese culture. Social situations are highly defined in Japan, so that knowing one's role and being in harmony with the situation is much easier than it is in our own culture. The self is defined to a much greater extent by social relationships with parents, children, husbands and wives, and in-laws.

All these important relations or "betweennesses" are stripped away when a person enters a Zen monastery. The result, if Zen training is suc-

verbally, nonverbally, and paraverbally interacts to signal how literal meaning should be taken, interpreted, filtered, or understood."[21] Norton identifies nine prominent communication styles that not only color the meaning of messages but establish personal identities as well. One's style may be dominant, dramatic, contentious, animated, impression-leaving, relaxed, attentive, open, or friendly. Table 8.1 defines and provides examples of each style.

A style is usually established by the simple repetition of behaviors associated with that particular style. Others soon begin to expect the person to interact that way on a regular basis. A person who repeatedly turns a clever phrase or states her observations in offbeat ways may be

regarded as having an impression-leaving style. The more she uses that style, the more likely it is that others will associate it with her personality. She doesn't always have to be clever or offbeat to maintain the style. Once established, it is likely to affect the expectations of those who know her. You may hang around just in case she says something striking.

According to Norton, people don't usually rely on a single communicator style, but instead develop what might be called a "style profile"—a combination of style variables. One person may tend to communicate by blending a dominant style with a friendly and attentive style. Another may be equally effective combining a dominant style with some aspects of the impression-leaving cessful, is a person whose self-definition has been essentially erased, since there is little sense of a private self to begin with. Rinzai, a well-known Zen master, refers to this achievement as becoming "a true person of no status."

According to Zen philosophy, the self is a social fiction that gets in the way of truly experiencing life. Kasulis describes the process of writing at his desk, including the pen, paper, and other paraphernalia around him: "These are not merely things in my experience; they *are* my experience. My self does not relate to these things, my self is these things." Contrary to our Western view of a person apart from, yet moving through, one context after another, the Zen view is that an individual is a person only insofar as he or she is *in* one of these contexts. Private feelings may exist, but the individual's meaning as a person is predominantly public—and observable in relationship to others. Like a chess piece without a chessboard or a rulebook to play by, the solitary person has no meaning. Kasulis contrasts the two views in the following example of two people exchanging apologies:

For Westerners, the discourse would go something like this:

A: *Oh, excuse me.*

B: *Oh no, excuse me.*

For the Japanese, the emphasis would be not on the individual who is responsible, but on the relationship, or the "betweenness" of the two:

A: *The indebtedness does not end.*

B: *Oh no, the indebtedness goes this way.*

There is little doubt that the self is one of our many socially constructed realities. But for us, it is one that seems so natural we can hardly imagine living without it. For a Zen person, the self is *the problem* that distorts perception of events and relationships. The Zen master poses the problem in one of the most popular koans in Zen training: If identity is so fundamental, "What is your original face before your mother and father were born?"

**SOURCE** T. P. Kasulis, *Zen Action, Zen Person* (Honolulu: University Press of Hawaii, 1981).

and contentious styles. You might want to inspect Table 8.1 and see if you can discover your own style profiles. Which one style or combination of styles do you use most frequently with your best friend? When interacting with your instructors or an employer? Can you identify situations in which the style you use may not be the most effective one? Think of a particular situation, such as telling a friend about one of your recent accomplishments. To what extent do you conceive yourself in terms of a particular communicator style in that situation? Which style does your self-concept encourage? Which ones does it prohibit or discourage? A useful exercise is to practice using different communicator styles until you can turn them on and off at will. Then

you can manage your style rather than having it manage you.

### Rhetorical Sensitivity

In the view of Donald Darnell and Wayne Brockriede, there are three basic types of communicators: (1) Noble Selves, (2) Rhetorical Reflectors, and (3) Rhetorical Sensitives.[22]

### The Noble Self

The person who has a self-schema that emphasizes consistency above all else is a **noble self.** Darnell and Brockriede defined these people as ones who "see any variation from their personal norms as hypocritical, as a denial of integrity, as a

| TABLE 8.1 | Communicator Styles and Their Manifestations |
|---|---|

| Communicator style | Verbal and nonverbal manifestations |
|---|---|
| Dominant | Tends to come on strong, take charge of social situations, speak frequently, and otherwise control conversations. |
| Dramatic | Likes to act out the point physically and vocally. Tells jokes and stories and often exaggerates to make the point. Speech tends to be picturesque. |
| Contentious | Loves to argue, quick to challenge others, precise about defining things, and often insists that others show proof to back up their arguments. Once wound up, hard to stop. |
| Animated | Expresses self nonverbally: constantly gestures, using a wide variety of facial expressions; face and eyes usually reveal emotions and feelings. |
| Impression-Leaving | Says things in a memorable fashion. People usually don't forget such a person easily. |
| Relaxed | Comes across as calm and collected during interaction, especially under pressure. The rhythm and flow of speech are rarely affected by feelings of nervousness. |
| Attentive | Listens to others very carefully and lets them know it by giving nonverbal feedback such as eye contact and nodding. Shows empathy and can usually repeat back exactly what others said. |
| Open | Readily reveals personal information. Openly expresses emotions. |
| Friendly | Gives positive feedback to recognize, encourage, and reinforce other people. |

Derived from Robert Norton, *Communicator Style: Theory, Application, and Measures* (Beverly Hills, Calif.: Sage, 1983), pp. 64–72.

cardinal sin." A Noble Self who has an organizing principle of honesty may struggle frequently with issues such as how to respond to a friend who asks, "Do you think I'll get the job?" or "How do I look?" The Noble Self will feel a strong obligation to say exactly what he thinks, no matter how it affects the other person.

### The Rhetorical Reflector

At the other extreme are **rhetorical reflectors,** persons who "have no Self to call their own. For each person and each situation they present a new self."[23] This kind of person is most concerned about being "appropriate." She will fol-

low the social rules of the situation or will try to be the kind of person the other wants her to be. In response to the friend's question, "How do I look?" the Rhetorical Reflector will say what she thinks you want to hear.

### The Rhetorical Sensitive

In contrast to these two extremes, the **rhetorical sensitive** has a much more complex self-schema. Roderick Hart and Don Burks characterize this kind of person as an "undulating, fluctuating entity, always unsure, always guessing, continually weighing . . . the values, attitudes and philosophical predispositions of others."[24] Once he understands the complexity of the situation, the other, and the self, he "swims in a sea of probabilities" before actually communicating. Such a person

- Realizes that there is no "single self," that any situation will require one of several selves
- Avoids communicative rigidity and does not try to be overly consistent or arbitrarily follow social conventions
- Avoids forming messages without regard for the other, yet doesn't simply try to placate others
- Realizes that there are times when an idea should not be communicated
- Seeks a variety of ways to communicate ideas and feelings[25]

Being rhetorically sensitive requires that we think about the way we communicate before, during, and after we interact with others.

It should be clear from this discussion that a rhetorically sensitive communicator is one who can monitor situations, determine which self would be most appropriate, enact an effective communicator style, and make any necessary adjustments. No doubt we would judge such a person as highly competent. And of course, now that we know what to do, we can work at becoming rhetorically sensitive ourselves. All we need to do is practice. There may, however, be one major obstacle in our path that practice alone will not overcome: a debilitating anxiety known as communication apprehension.

## Communication Apprehension

**Communication apprehension** refers to "an individual's level of fear or anxiety associated with either real or anticipated communication with another person or persons."[26] According to the research of James McCroskey, as much as 20 percent of the U.S. population can be categorized as highly apprehensive.[27] Most of us are anxious about communicating in one situation or another: public presentations, job interviews, first dates. Being apprehensive in these situations is

fairly normal. Those people who are highly apprehensive tend to feel anxious in a wide variety of communication situations, including talking to people they already know.

When communication apprehension strikes, the results are very predictable. All our knowledge about communicating effectively goes out the window. For instance, even though we know that a more dramatic communicator style would grab an audience's attention and give us a better chance of being heard, the feeling of fear strangles our expressiveness. Fortunately, researchers have discovered several facts about this anxiety that make it much more manageable.

Communication apprehension is not an innate disability, but a learned reaction to physiological arousal. When we're called upon to perform an important task, the body begins pumping more adrenalin into the blood to provide energy. Physically, we feel an increase in arousal; cognitively, we label that arousal as fear.[28]

The fear of communicating can be overcome, first by labeling the arousal as energy rather than fear, and then by focusing on the potentially positive rather than negative outcomes of any communication transaction. Although you shouldn't expect an overnight transformation, you can begin to approach communication situations with a different perspective, one that puts you (and those you interact with) in mutual control of social forces, rather than letting the forces control you.

## Attachment Styles

Another communicative predisposition grows out of our early relationships. Researchers have investigated different **attachment styles** that develop in infancy but continue to influence communication and relationship behavior throughout life.[29] As we saw earlier in this chapter, infants form an early mental image of self and others based on interactions with primary caregivers. Attachment theory holds that infants develop different styles of attachment depending upon the positive or negative nature of these mental images. Kim Bartholomew has elaborated on four styles of adult attachment that stem from these early interactions. If the images of self and other are both positive, a **secure style** of attachment emerges that fosters highly sociable behavior. The individual becomes comfortable with both intimacy and autonomy. When both images are negative, however, a more **fearful style** results. The child with a low regard for self is more dependent on others for acceptance, but may have trouble gaining favor because of a lack of trust in others. Hypersensitive to social approval, but fearing rejection, he or she is likely to avoid social situations and close relationships. Desiring intimacy, but seemingly unable to achieve it, one who is fearful of attachment is often anxious and ambivalent around others. A third style results when a person has a low opinion of self, but a generally positive view of others. Bartholomew calls this a **preoccupied style.** Like someone with a fearful style, this person is highly dependent upon others who will reinforce feelings of self-worth. When a preoccupied person finds someone who makes him feel good, he can become very obsessive about the relationship. Finally, a person with a **dismissing style** tends to deny any need for attachment. Such a person has a very positive self-image, but a markedly low opinion of other people. As a result, she values her autonomy and asserts that relationships are not all that important, preferring to spend time and energy on the more impersonal arenas of work and individual leisure pursuits. Compared to the people who exhibit the three nonsecure styles, those with secure styles are much more likely to have romantic relationships that last longer and to report greater satisfaction and stronger perceptions of intimacy, commitment, and trust in those relationships.[30] They also tend to engage in more expressive and supportive behaviors and in less verbal aggression or withdrawal when interacting with others.[31]

## Intimacy Motivation

The need for intimacy has been studied in a way that mirrors our concern in this chapter about the personality/self-concept distinction. D. P. McAdams defines the **need for intimacy** as a "recurrent preference or readiness for experiences of close, warm, and communicative exchange with others—interpersonal interaction that is seen by the interactants as an end in itself, rather than a means to another end."[32] Research suggests that the need for intimacy is a largely nonconscious preference for spending time in dyads as opposed to group situations, and for engaging in higher levels of eye contact, smiling, and laughter that seems to promote self-disclosure in others.[33] Those high in the need for intimacy also engage in a greater percentage of interactions with women.[34] These people seem to have an almost intuitive sense of how to carry off a socially intimate performance.

Judy-Anne Craig and her associates measured another form of this need that reflected people's conscious concern for achieving intimacy. They referred to this as a *self-attributed need for intimacy*. They found that this orientation led people to engage in a greater number of total interactions with many different people rather than just close dyadic partners. They speculated that this conscious awareness of self as needing intimacy was more focused on achieving an *outcome* (making a friend, self-disclosing to further a relationship, and so on) rather than being engaged in a less conscious *process* that naturally exhibits characteristics of intimacy.

It should be clear by now that the way we think about ourselves can either limit or expand our ability to communicate. We cannot overemphasize the importance of giving ourselves options for communicating in a world where the only question about change is how fast it will occur, not if or when. To manage our communication in such a world requires that we increase our awareness of the self we present to others and discover ways to balance the tensions between conformity and individuality. We conclude this chapter by exploring how we can put our knowledge of self-concepts to work for us.

# Skill Building: Improving Competence Through Self-Disclosure

Feeling good about ourselves—having a good self-image—is an essential component in effective interpersonal communication. It is difficult to appear competent if you do not feel competent. It is hard to like others and be liked by others if you do not like and respect yourself. While the development of your self-concepts was hardly under your control as a child, at this stage you are not a finished product. You have just as many opportunities as an adult to surround yourself with the kind of people who will hold up the mirror for you and help you fashion a general life script and self-concepts appropriate to various situations and relationships. Just as your parents played a key role in providing a stable environment for the development of your childhood self-concept, the significant others in your current social networks (and those in your future) play, and will continue to play, key roles in helping you become a well-rounded, communicatively competent adult. Meeting new people and negotiating changes in our ongoing relationships means that our self-concepts always remain under construction. Knowing this should lead us to further develop any skills related to presenting and managing the self. One of the very important and often misunderstood communication skills that we need to master is self-disclosure.

## What Is Self-Disclosure?

**Self-disclosure** is usually defined as any information you reveal about yourself that others are unlikely to discover from other sources. This covers a wide range of territory, from the simple revelation that you like country music to the highly risky disclosure that you spent six months in a juvenile detention home as a teenager. When and how we choose to reveal aspects of our per-

The self-concept is always under construction. Even in our quietest moments, self presentations may be made to an imagined audience or defined in part by the particular scene or stage directions we believe to be appropriate.

Alexej von Jawlensky, *Head Kopf*, 1920

sonal history can make a lasting impression on others—to our benefit or to our detriment. Our disclosures can strike a chord of empathy in another person or cause him or her to recoil from us. Disclosures are often risky, and when they are, they place us in a vulnerable position. For example, admitting that tears welled up in your eyes during a particularly sad movie scene may cause a new acquaintance to perceive you as overly emotional, out of control, or weak. But exposing vulnerability by such disclosures is one of the very few ways that people in our culture establish trust with one another. Without trust, solid friendships and close, intimate relationships are not possible; without one or two of these relationships, there is no support system for ongoing elaboration of our system of self-concepts.

There is a danger, of course, that some people will go to extremes, becoming avid self-disclosers in hopes of developing hundreds of close relationships. A frequent problem for very lonely people is that when they get the opportunity to disclose, they overdo it. You have no doubt been victim to grandpa's stories about the good old days or to a new acquaintance who took you seriously when you said, "Tell me a little about yourself." These types of episodes are called *flooded disclosures* because the individual needs to "get it all out" and may not think he or she will ever get another chance. Most of us (especially males) don't have to worry about going too far—we are underdisclosers, typically revealing far less than our relational partners would like to hear. Another typical problem is *premature disclosure*, which occurs often in a dating context. Because of a person's strong desire to make a good impression and get to know the other, the individual reveals intimate details too quickly and unexpectedly and not in the normal flow of conversation. The result is the opposite of what was hoped for: The individual is often perceived as troubled or deviant, and is not seen as attractive or likable.[35] Researchers have been studying the process of self-disclosure, and some of the general principles they have formulated can help us manage our self-disclosures and avoid some of the pitfalls just described.

## General Rules for Revealing the Self

Learning to self-disclose requires an understanding of the communication process and a careful balance between conforming to socially appropriate rules and breaking the rules in creative ways. In this section we'll begin by looking at some general rules that should guide your use of everyday self-disclosure. Then we'll consider how to handle one particular kind of disclosure: the coming out process.

**1.** *Make sure that disclosures are appropriate to the topic at hand and fit the flow of conversation.* This rule is so general that it could apply to any message, not just self-disclosures. But it is also a rule easily overlooked. Conversation between two new acquaintances is supposed to reduce anxiety, not cause it. That's why we usually follow the rules of small talk and say things that are safe. We want to make a good impression, so we try to sprinkle the conversation with interesting information about ourselves, but such revelations need to fit the conversation. If what we reveal to another person seems a little weird or poorly timed, it's all that other person has to work with in making a judgment about us. Once we become acquainted, we tend to get sloppy in applying the rule. You might decide ahead of time to reveal something at the next opportunity and then force the disclosure in an irrelevant way or at an inappropriate time. If it's important for the other to know and the conversation isn't moving in that direction, you can always steer things a bit. You can, for instance, nonchalantly move a discussion about last night's episode of *Frazier* to a previous episode that dealt with an issue that reminds you of something you did two years ago (which was what you wanted to reveal in the first place). The key is to make the flow of topics as natural as possible. If you force it, the other will probably feel that he or she has been set up. Once a relationship gets on its feet, you can relax the rule a bit. As long as someone feels comfortable with you, that person can deal with an occasional disclosure out of the blue.

**2.** *Begin with safe, nonrisky disclosures.* When disclosures do not involve high risk, you put less of yourself on the line should the disclosure fail to leave the desired impression. The safest disclosures are *descriptive* ones that reveal factual information about yourself (your hometown, your major, occupational plans). While safe and nonthreatening, however, these disclosures are not always the most captivating. Ideally, you want your initial disclosures to be safe but a little tantalizing. They can say to the other, "There's a lot more to talk about . . . when we're both ready." You should realize, however, that even descriptive disclosures say a lot about you. The revelation that you plan to be an accountant implies a lot (even if stereotypic) about your personal qualities, future lifestyle, and so on.

**3.** *Disclose in small doses.* To avoid the problem of burdening another person with a flood of unwanted disclosures, it is usually best to reveal a glimpse of yourself here and there. Flooded disclosures may make us feel good ("Whew, it feels great to get that off my chest"), but they seldom sound as good to the embattled listener ("Ouch, stop! Please stop, I can't take any more!"). Small doses keep things manageable and also give the other person an opportunity to disclose, which leads to the next principle.

**4.** *Match the level and amount of the other's disclosure.* Otherwise known as the "norm of reciprocity," this rule monitors the process of opening up by making sure the relationship does not become a one-sided affair. It's easy to get caught up talking about ourselves and forget to give the other person a chance. By matching disclosures, we virtually guarantee that we both approve of the way things are going. If the other person's disclosures become briefer or revert to an earlier level of safe topics, that's a good sign that he or she isn't ready to move on. It also indicates that you should slow down the pace of your own disclosure. For some people, too much disclosure can be overwhelming. It's not that they don't like you or want to know more about you, they just need to catch their breath and let things unfold more slowly. The matching principle is probably the single most important rule of disclosure because it reveals the state of the relationship between two people.

**5.** *Remember that style of disclosure is as important as substance.* How you disclose your feelings and opinions and how you receive another's disclosures can encourage or discourage the whole process. Your nonverbal manner itself should signal openness and reinforce the verbal message. Trying to self-disclose in an indirect manner ("beating around the bush") may suggest that you feel uncomfortable, don't really trust the other person, or have to be very careful how you say things. Any one of these nonverbal messages could undermine the attempt at verbal openness. Likewise, showing little enthusiasm for the other person's disclosure attempts can reduce the chances for further disclosure. Barbara Montgomery's research on open communication indicates that most people pay more attention to the style of disclosure than to the actual content being revealed.[36]

**6.** *Reserve your most important disclosures for significant, ongoing relationships.* People who self-disclose indiscriminately do not understand that self-disclosure is an integral part of what makes intimate relationships so special. The escalation of disclosure from small, reciprocated, safe topics to largely unrestricted and risky revelations requires the safe confines of a trusting and committed relationship. As we saw earlier in this chapter, strong bonds of attachment serve as the primary context for nurturing a stable personal identity that is open to change. While on rare occasions people successfully reveal a great deal about themselves to total strangers, such as pouring out their soul to a fellow passenger on a five-hour train ride, such occurrences are not the norm. They generally occur as a result of unusual circumstances (will never see the person again, seeking out the help of a professional counselor, and so on).

While these rules serve as general guidelines for managing self-disclosure, you may discover that sometimes you want to risk breaking one of these rules. Because creative efforts are often appreciated in our society, you may occasionally be successful in such ventures. One way of increasing your chances in these situations is to use aligning actions to manage perceptions of deviance from the norm. An **aligning action** is a statement that tries to minimize the perceived deviation from the norm by pointing out special circumstances or reasons why the deviation should take place. Imagine that you've just arrived at your fifth freshman orientation session on your second day on campus. The host pairs you off with yet another student to get acquainted. (You've only been through this routine about 150 times already.) Under these circumstances you might say something like, "You'll forgive me, I hope. I've only met a hundred people in two days and we've said the same things to each other a hundred times over. I'm sure you've experienced the same thing. Maybe you wouldn't mind if we talked about something more substantial than all the parties we've attended?" Chances are the other person does feel the same way and would gladly agree. Without the aligning action, however, you could have launched into an episode of flooded disclosures and probably scared the person away for good.

## A Case Study in Disclosure: The Coming Out Process

Disclosures run the gamut from the fairly mundane to the deeply personal. Although it is true that every time we disclose to others we may be misunderstood or rejected, in most cases self-disclosure is relatively easy. But there are some disclosures that are potentially more difficult. Unfortunately, one of these occurs when gays, lesbians, or bisexuals reveal their orientations either to parents or to friends. Although results of such a revelation can be—and often are—acceptance and affirmation, they can also result in rejection and hostility. Because people who decide to come out can never know for sure what the reaction to their disclosure will be, coming out must be handled carefully. This kind of high-risk disclosure presents unique communication challenges.

Before we discuss how to handle this kind of disclosure, both as sender and as receiver, let's define **coming out**. Communication professor Robert Owens describes it in the following way: "*Coming out of the closet* or simply *coming out* or *outing* oneself is a developmental process, a

self-affirming rite, through which lesbian, gay and bisexual individuals first recognize their sexual orientation" and then share the news of that orientation with another person.[37] Psychologist Ritch Savin-Williams sees coming out as involving two related tasks: coming out to self and coming out to others. In the first case, the individual moves from nonrecognition of his or her sexual orientation to self-recognition and acceptance. In the second, the individual decides to disclose this same-sex orientation to peers, family, and society at large.[38] The process of coming out can be difficult and confusing, yet most mental health professionals see it as a positive act that leads to increases in self-esteem and decreases in feelings of loneliness and alienation.[39]

### Coming Out to Others: How to Reveal Same-Sex Orientation

In interviewing hundreds of lesbian, gay, and bisexual youngsters, Owens found first-hand evidence of the risks associated with coming out. For example, the parents of one lesbian teen he interviewed refused to continue paying for her chemotherapy after her disclosure. Other young people have lost all their friends, been physically harassed, been thrown out of the house or disowned, and, as the case of Matthew Shephard illustrates, even been killed. Given these risks, why would a gay or lesbian person decide to come out? For the teens Owens interviewed, the answers are clear. The coming out process allows one to reveal one's true self to others.

Because discussion of sexuality is so highly charged in our society, coming out is not a topic that can be handled casually, even if one anticipates a positive response. Most experts agree that disclosure of same-sex orientation will go more smoothly if the communication is carefully planned. The first step in this planning is *choosing the manner of disclosure*. Generally speaking, the more important a self-disclosure, the greater the importance of it taking place face to face. Sometimes, however, that is impossible and it may be necessary to write instead. Mary Borhek, in *Coming Out to Parents*, advises: "Write the

## Disclosure and Self-Knowledge

# Big Eden

Thomas Bezucha, 2001

New York artist Henry Hart (Arye Gross) left Big Eden years ago, but, when his grandfather, Sam (George Coe), has a stroke, Henry returns to this small Montana town to care for him. Henry has never told anyone in Big Eden that he's gay, but that doesn't seem to matter, since everyone, including Sam, already knows. In fact, Henry's return starts off a round of matchmaking as all the cowboys who hang out at the general store watch to see who Henry will end up with. The plot of the movie revolves around whether Henry's unrequited attraction to his old high school friend Dean (Tim DeKay) will keep him from seeing how much Pike (Eric Schweig), the bashful owner of the town's general store, cares for him. The movie is also about whether Henry will keep running from his past or finally come to terms with who he is and where he belongs. In a touching scene, old friend Grace (Louise Fletcher) tells him, "Listen, you know what they say when you get lost in the woods? If you stay put, stay in one place and don't wander. They'll find you. And I was just hoping you'd let yourself be found this time. I was hoping you'd let us find you."

*Big Eden* illustrates how hard it is to find the words to talk about the things that really matter and how the secrets we are afraid to share may not be secrets to anyone except ourselves. This warm-hearted romantic comedy also shows us what it might be like to live in a world where being different is perfectly OK and where the people who love you just want you to be happy.

letter and put it away for a week or longer, then get it out and reread it. . . . Cut out all words or sentences that sound angry, sarcastic, or joking." She also urges the writer to include expressions of love and concern and to set up a time to get together and talk.[40]

If it is possible to talk directly, the next stop is *deciding where and when the conversation should take place.* One of our students was on the phone in his dorm's hall when his brother came out to him. Unfortunately, while the student was trying to think of what to say to his brother, an exuberant crowd of students returning from a football game was running up and down the hall. Obviously this was not the optimal time and place to have a serious discussion. As a result, the interaction did not go very smoothly. Fortunately, our student was able to call his brother back later and have a good conversation. As this story illustrates, if you decide to come out, you should choose a quiet, private place free of interruptions and allow time to discuss the topic fully. If the news must be conveyed over the phone, make sure the recipient is in a situation that is comfortable and private. E-mail is never a good alternative.

Once you've chosen the time and place, how should you begin? Don't apologize, and don't leave the other person to guess the news. Beginning with either, "I'm sorry. I've got something terrible to tell you," or "Well, I . . . I don't quite know what . . . maybe you already know that . . . You know, don't you?" is an extremely poor way to open the subject and conveys that you are uncertain or ashamed. If so, then you're not ready to make this disclosure. A better approach is short and direct. Therapist Betty Berzon suggests: "There is something **221** about me I want to tell you because I care about you, and I want to be able to share more of myself with you."[41]

*Being prepared to deal with negative reactions* is another important part of the process. It may take the recipient of the disclosure time to get used to the idea that a close friend or family member is gay, lesbian, or bisexual. In our society, most people assume that everyone is heterosexual. Hearing that someone they are close to is one of the estimated 5–10 percent of the population who are not may be a shock. Be patient. After all, you took time to develop your sexual identity; it stands to reason that it will take others time to get used to the news.

Negative reactions can run the gamut from shocked silence to active opposition. If silence is the response, offering the recipient an opportunity to say what's on his or her mind is useful. Saying something like, "How do you feel, now that you know?" or "Are there any questions you'd like to ask?" may encourage talk, but it's not a good idea to force the conversation. If, after being given the opportunity to respond, the other person remains silent and uncomfortable, calmly withdrawing for the time may be the best bet. "I know this is a lot to think about. I'm ready to talk whenever you are," is one way to close the conversation.[42]

Sometimes the recipient of a coming out disclosure may try to argue or talk you out of being gay or lesbian. As absurd as this sounds, it happens frequently. Rather than being drawn into an argument, the best reaction is to calmly let the person know that you are sure of your sexual orientation and that, although there are challenges in being different, being gay or lesbian does not condemn one to an unhappy or lonely life. Anger or sarcasm must be avoided, no matter how sorely you may be tempted. Even if you are extremely disappointed in the other person's reaction, it's important to leave the door open for further dialogue. In that regard, several days after announcing one's sexual orientation, it is a good idea to drop in or phone to let the recipient know that you are concerned and care to continue the relationship.

Studies show that coming out to friends is generally easier than coming out to parents.[43] Coming out to parents presents greater risks because parents control both emotional and financial support. Robert Owens counsels gay teens who are coming out to parents to consider the worst-case scenario and have plans for alternative housing and other support if necessary. He also suggests examining one's own motives. Because coming out, like all disclosures, can be used as a weapon, it's important to *resolve anger and ambivalence ahead of time and make sure coming out is based on caring and respect.*

He and other experts liken parental reactions to a grieving process. Shock, denial, anger, and guilt are common parental reactions, and even the most understanding parent may grieve over lost expectations. In fact, it takes most parents two years or longer to fully accept same-sex orientations. Throughout the process, parents will fluctuate between acceptance and grief and will have many questions. You should therefore *anticipate questions and have well-thought-out answers* even before you initiate the coming out process.

### Receiving Coming Out Disclosures: What to Say When a Friend Comes Out

Serious disclosures often leave recipients uncomfortable and embarrassed, wanting to respond in the right way but not knowing what to say or do. In the case of same-sex disclosure, the recipient, no matter how accepting, may be surprised or shocked and completely at a loss for words. After all, we all feel awkward when discussing "taboo" topics, and sexual orientation, in our society, certainly qualifies as taboo.

What, then, should you say if a friend comes out to you? Well, first of all, rather than panicking you should feel honored. Your friend would not tell you if he or she did not trust and respect you. Perhaps the first thing that you can do, regardless of how you feel about the announcement, is to *thank your friend for trusting you* with such personal information and let your friend know that you admire his or her courage and level of self-knowledge.[44] Although friends come out to friends because they want to strengthen the relationship by being honest, their biggest fear is that the disclosure will destroy the relationship. Therefore, it is also important to *reassure your friend that the relationship will not change.*

If you feel uncomfortable, say so directly, and *ask for time to adjust*, then use that time to *become more informed.* Most Americans are ignorant when it comes to matters of sexual orientation, and, no matter how sophisticated you may be on other topics, you probably carry some false beliefs and stereotypes. Now is the time to correct those beliefs. The most obvious way is to ask your friend questions, but, if that is too direct, another way is to read books or articles on same-sex orientation. Your friend may be willing to recommend some sources, or you may wish to consult some of the materials provided by P-FLAG (Parents and Friends of Lesbians and Gays), a national organization that provides sensible, down-to-earth advice and support for people coming to terms with a friend or relative's sexual orientation.[45]

If you can't accept the fact that your friend is lesbian, gay, or bisexual, then at least *take responsibility for your feelings.* Acknowledge that *you* have a problem that you have to deal with and decide whether the issue is worth losing a good friend over. Do not try to compartmentalize your feelings, accepting your friend while rejecting his or her orientation. As Owens states, "acceptance by parents, friends, and siblings cannot be selective. Parents and friends cannot accept only a part of an individual while denying another.[46]

Openness about sexual matters is a fairly recent event. This means that there are no hard and fast rules for handling coming out, either as the person who is disclosing or as the recipient of disclosure. Each of us must improvise, and the process may not be easy. But with some thought and sensitivity this form of disclosure can strengthen interpersonal bonds.

As this chapter has stressed, our identities are constructed in the process of communicating with others. Whether we see the self as a biographical narrative, a cognitive construct, a behavioral entity, or as several partners in a relationship with others or within our own self-system, one thing is for sure: We manage the self through messages exchanged with others. We can become more self-competent by increasing our repertoire of message options: verbal and nonverbal strategies, a working vocabulary, the range of communicator styles we can use comfortably, and so on. In the following chapters we'll encounter a number of communication tactics that will serve us in this regard. The important thing for you to do at this point is to make a commitment to yourself to develop your ability to use a wide range of communication strategies. You might begin now by making a list of some specific communication behaviors or skills that you don't perform as well as you'd like. Seek out opportunities to work on these skills so that you can add them to your repertoire and call on them when you need them. By doing so, you will be building the kind of identity that is adaptable enough to enjoy the best of times and survive the worst of them.

## Process to Performance

### Review Terms

The following is a list of major concepts introduced in this chapter. The page where the concept is first mentioned is listed in parentheses.

**social identity**   (199)
**personal identity**   (199)
**modal self**   (200
**self-concept**   (201)
**personality**   (201)
**narrative self**   (204)
**psychosocial moratorium**   (206)
**self-schemata**   (207)
**life script**   (207)
**self-handicapping strategies**   (207)
**behavioral self**   (208)
**self-perception theory**   (208)

### Suggested Readings

Grodin, Debra, and Thomas Lindlof, eds. *Constructing the Self in a Mediated World*. Thousand Oaks, Calif.: Sage Publications, 1996. This book is a collection of essays by 14 highly respected authors on subjects ranging from women's identities in self-help literature to identities in virtual reality to advice on conducting relationship therapy in a postmodern world.

Langer, Ellen J. *On Becoming an Artist: Reinventing Yourself Through Mindful Creativity*. New York: Ballantine, 2005. Langer looks at the barriers that keep us from achieving creativity, including the fear of making mistakes. This book makes us aware of the ways that self-censorship keeps us from developing the self we'd like to be.

---

### Topics for Discussion

www.oup.com/us/trenholm

---

### Observation Guide

**1.** For this exercise you will rely on the observations of at least two other close friends. This is called the 20-Questions Statement Test. The objective of the exercise is to discover aspects of your self-concept that are "consistent" or at least apparent both to yourself and several of your friends. You should write down 20 two- or three-word statements about yourself by completing the following phrases:

   **a.** "I am . . ."

   **b.** "I like . . ."

   **c.** "I have done . . ."

Ask your friends to complete the same statements about you. Now compare lists, identifying those self-concept statements that appear on all or most of the lists. What similarities or discrepancies surprise you the most? Are most of the statements self-identifying ("I am . . ."), evaluative ("I like . . ."), or behavioral ("I have done . . .")? What does this tell you about your self-concept(s)? Conclude your observations by writing a brief analysis of your self-concept in each of the relationships involved. Why do you think you appear the way you do to each person?

**2.** Visit a day care center or early childhood learning center, or observe a series of mother-infant interactions. Look for examples of self-concepts in development. Record examples of verbal or nonverbal communication that reflect the child's awareness of his or her own intentions, motivations, or sense of self. Watch how adult caregivers structure interaction or conversation to lead a child to a greater sense of accomplishment or self-awareness. Ask questions of the older children, such as, "Who's your favorite hero?" or "Who do you like to be when you play?" What do their answers tell you about their developing self-concepts? What behaviors or roles are reinforced by playmates or attending adults? Ask your instructor if you can present some of your findings to the class.

### Exercises

**1.** This exercise should be conducted in groups of four. Initially, two people will role-play a conversation while the other two act as observers. Later you will reverse roles. The objective of the exercise is to improve your ability to enact a wider range of communicator styles. You should follow the steps listed here. Step a may be done prior to class to save time.

**a.** Individually, write down your own ideal communicator style profile for meeting new people. Write down how you would like to come across in terms of the styles described in Table 8.1. Also write down a style you feel is very difficult for you to enact and a situation in which you would like to be able to use this style.

**b.** Decide who will role-play and who will observe first. One observer should record the behavior of role player 1, and the other role player 2. Observers should make a list of the nine communicator styles and write down examples of each style they witness during the role-play. Plan to provide feedback at the conclusion of the role-play.

**c.** The first role-play is a conversation between two strangers. After exchanging greetings, you will hold a two-minute conversation about your choice of topics: sports, movies, careers, campus or world events, and so on. Throughout the conversation, role players want to enact their ideal communicator style profile. Don't tell the observers what that style

is, just try to come across in the preferred manner. Begin the conversation.

**d.** After a couple of minutes, cut the conversation off and let the observers provide feedback to each role player. Compare style observations with what the role player was trying to do. Suggest ways to improve the enactment of each aspect of the style profile.

**e.** Switch roles and repeat steps b, c, and d.

**f.** If you have time, continue the exercise by working on the difficult situation and style profile that each person has written down. Conclude the exercise by talking about how you can improve your range of styles in actual situations.

**2.** Bring to class examples of media messages that reinforce how people in our culture think about the self, in terms of either their social or their personal identities. Look for examples in magazine advertisements, television commercials, song lyrics, newspaper advice columns, radio or TV talk shows, and so on. In what ways do these messages affect how we see ourselves? Is there any truth to the argument that a society (in our case, a consumer society) creates the kind of people (in our case, consumer-oriented selves) it needs to keep the system going?

*Through everyday interactions we affect one another in profound ways. Something as small as a glance away during a conversation can be a subtle message that affects our sense of self, our opinions and beliefs, and our views of what is right and wrong.*

Edward Mortelmans, *Reflections,* 20th century

## CHAPTER 9

# Goal Competence

Early on a Friday morning in 2005, Brian Nichols, a prisoner facing rape charges in an Atlanta courtroom, seized a deputy's weapon, opened fire, and killed three people before fleeing. At about 2:30 A.M. on Saturday morning, after allegedly gunning down a fourth victim, Nichols forced his way into the apartment of 26-year-old waitress Ashley Smith. Nichols tied her up and threatened to kill her. But this time Nichols didn't shoot. Instead, for seven hours, he and Smith talked. At some point, Smith, whose husband had died four years earlier, asked him to let her go so she could see her little girl. "I told him that if he hurt me, my little girl wouldn't have a mommy or a daddy." Although he refused, she later reported, "I could kind of feel that he started to—to know who I was." Smith slowly began to earn his trust. "I talked to him about my family. I told him about things that had happened in my life. I asked him about his family. I asked him why he did what he did." Gradually their talk turned to religion. Nichols reportedly told her he felt lost and that God had led him to her. Smith repeatedly tried to convince him to turn himself in, telling him that per-

haps he needed to be caught so that he could share his faith with other prisoners. At 9 on Saturday morning, he let her go. Later, when the police arrived he gave up without a fight.[1]

Ashley Smith acted heroically. Her ability to stay calm and her willingness to reach out to Nichols probably saved both their lives. Through talk she earned his trust, created a relationship, and convinced him to turn himself in. Through conversation, he was transformed. Of course, not all talk is this dramatic. But all talk, no matter how trivial it appears, has the potential to create relationships and to effect change. In this chapter we will look at ways people use communication to influence one another in order to achieve interpersonal goals.

When we think of influence, we generally think of intentional persuasion like cult recruitment, political rhetoric, TV or print advertising, public service messages, and the like. Although these are certainly arenas for persuasion, the most important and potent site of influence is interpersonal communication. Every day we are surrounded by a sea of interpersonal influence. Sometimes influence messages are obvious: A friend argues a point, a family member asks for a favor, an acquaintance tries to convince us to change our behavior. But much of the time interpersonal influence is more subtle and harder to recognize. A raised eyebrow in response to a statement, an unstated obligation to a friend or family member, an account accepted or rejected, a bit of gossip that illustrates good or bad behavior—we may not realize it, but all of these are examples of interpersonal influence. They are subtle messages that affect our sense of self, our opinions and beliefs, and our views of what is right or wrong. Through everyday interactions we affect one another in profound and important ways.

In this chapter we'll look at some of the ways individuals influence one another in interpersonal contexts. We'll begin with an overview of the influence process. We'll then consider some principles that allow individuals to influence one another, and we'll look at ways to construct effective influence messages. Finally, in the skills section at the end of the chapter, we'll consider ways to gain one's goals while respecting the rights of others.

# The Nature of Strategic Interaction

The field of speech communication has traditionally been concerned with the study of strategic interaction—with explaining how people use communication to change the opinions and beliefs of others. Certainly not all influence is conscious. As we'll see later in this chapter, we can influence one another without even knowing we are doing so. But much of the time when we engage in influence we do so with conscious intent. In this part of the chapter we focus on strategic influence. We'll look at what influence is and how it is affected by culture. We'll then consider

some of the issues influence agents must balance and discuss a few of the skills that communicators must draw on in order to achieve their goals.

## What Is Influence?

Influence, like communication, has been defined in many ways. And, like communication, these definitions can be broad or narrow. In this chapter we will use a broad definition, using the term **influence** to refer to any act of communication, whether consciously intended or not, that is capable of affecting attitudes or behaviors. Influence is, in a sense, an umbrella term that covers a wide range of communicative behaviors.

### Types of Influence

If influence is a general concept, what communication behaviors does it include? Robert Sanders and Kristine Fitch identify three types of influence behaviors: simple directives, compliance-seeking behaviors, and persuasion.[2]

**Directives** are straightforward statements or requests that influence simply by providing information. If Thalia wants Calvin to pass her the salt, all she has to do is ask. Assuming that Calvin and she are getting along, he will probably comply; no argumentation is needed. In **persuasion,** on the other hand, communicators use evidence and reasoning to get others to comply in cases where direct requests might meet with resistance. When Calvin's doctor explains three medical reasons why Calvin (who is somewhat of a couch potato) should exercise regularly, the doctor is using persuasion. **Compliance-seeking behaviors** lie somewhere in the middle. Here communicators use strategic interaction to achieve their ends. Pregiving is a classic instance of compliance-seeking. If, for example, Calvin's friend Janelle decides the best way to get Calvin to lend her money is by doing Calvin a favor before asking, Janelle is using a compliance-seeking strategy. Other strategies that have been identified as compliance-seeking include hinting, being strategically friendly, inducing guilt, being unpleasant until the other gives in, and the use of threats and promises.[3] As we will see later in the chapter, communication scholars have identified a wide range of strategies people use in order to influence others and achieve goals.

## Culture and the Persuadable

Before we consider how people use these forms of influence to achieve their goals, we should take a minute to acknowledge the part culture plays in influence. The theories and principles we will discuss have, for the most part, been developed by American scholars to explain the behavior of middle-class Americans in the late 20th and early 21st centuries. They are not universal. Other cultures approach influence differently. Culture, then, is an important force in influence, determining not only *how* it is possible to convince people, but also *what* it is possible to convince people of.

Within any culture or community, some ideas and actions are so firmly accepted that they are not open for discussion. Because they are widely believed, persuasion is completely unnecessary. In contrast, other beliefs and behaviors are so strongly rejected that any arguments in their favor would be dismissed out of hand. In such a case persuasion is simply not possible. In the middle are what Kristine Fitch calls **persuadables,** topics that can be argued, issues on which change is possible. Fitch believes that the range of persuadables differs from culture to culture.[4] What is taken for granted in one culture (or in one historical period) may be unthinkable in another, yet open to debate in a third. The rights of women is one such topic. In some countries the idea that women deserve equal protection under the law is so patently absurd that no amount of influence will lead to its acceptance. In others, no one would ever question it, so influence is unnecessary. In still others, for example, in countries in a period of transition from traditional to modern values, this topic is persuadable.

To take another example, in the United States copying someone else's work and passing it off as one's own is considered stealing. Students can, in fact, be dismissed from school if they are caught. In other countries, however, where rote memory

is a common way of learning and tradition is valued, copying is likely to be seen as a mark of respect, not as a crime. The proposition "copying another's work is wrong" would be difficult, if not impossible, to argue in the latter countries. It is simply not a persuadable, in part because in those countries it is not buttressed by cultural assumptions or supported by a vocabulary that encodes those assumptions. In a culture that does not value originality, does not believe in the private ownership of ideas, and does not have a word like *plagiarism,* how could one argue convincingly that copying ideas is wrong?

Cultural differences like these remind us that influence must be built on agreement about what it is possible to talk about and about the form talk should take. This is as true for relational cultures as it is for larger cultural groupings. All influence attempts must be built on shared values and a shared vocabulary. What is remarkable about the story that opened this chapter is that Ashley Smith found common ground with Brian Nichols. Once she found that they shared a common faith and common experiences, she was able to speak in language that he could understand.

## Issues in Influence

From all reports, Ashley Smith did three things in the hours she spent with Brian Nichols. She let him know who she was, she established a relationship with him, and she presented arguments about why he should let her go and give himself up. We believe that all three were important factors in her survival.

Ruth Anne Clark and Jesse Delia have suggested that whenever we talk we too simultaneously address three different issues.[5] One is the **instrumental issue.** We address this issue when we attempt to achieve a specific goal through talk. In most cases of influence the instrumental issue is primary. However, at the same time we behave instrumentally, we also send relational and identity messages. As we work to build shared understandings of who we are to one another, we address the **relational issue.** And as we

## Changing Attitudes and Paying Respect

# Paper Clips

Elliot Berlin, Joe Fab, 2004

In the late 1990s, the teachers at Whitwell, a small school in rural Tennessee, were faced with a problem: how to teach their predominantly white, Christian middle-school students about diversity. The answer: Study the Holocaust. *Paper Clips* documents the true story of how a simple social studies project turns into a life-changing experience for the entire town.

In researching the Holocaust, the students discovered the fact that during the Nazi occupation, many Norwegians attached a paper clip to their shirts as a subtle symbol of resistance. (In fact, Norway was where the paper clip was invented.) When one of the students admitted having a very hard time visualizing the enormity of the number who died in the Holocaust, the class decided to collect one paper clip for every life lost. Their simple project gained momentum when two German reporters publicized their efforts. Soon people from all over the world responded, sending personal letters and mementoes as well as tens of millions of paper clips. Eventually the students tracked down one of the original rail cars used to transport Jews to the death camps and had it shipped to Tennessee in order to create a museum to honor the dead. In one of the film's most moving scenes, several Holocaust survivors travel to the school to share their stories.

Can a tragedy of such enormity be communicated? Is there a way to make what happened so many years ago in Europe relevant to a group of American youngsters in rural Appalachia, some of whom who had never seen a German or a Jew? The students and teachers at Whitwell found a way. Not only did they devise a personal method of visualizing a moment in history, but they did it in a way that included the entire community. This film shows that with enough creativity and tenacity it is possible to make an impact on the world and, in so doing, change one's own attitudes and values.

---

confirm or reject each other's self-presentations, we address the **identity issue.**

It is tempting to assume that, during influence, the instrumental issue is the only one that counts. But that's not the case. The three issues are so interrelated that each affects the other. If, for example, Randy wants to persuade an acquaintance to accept his reasoning, it is not enough for him to argue convincingly. He must also build rapport and create an impression of competence. His most brilliant arguments will be ruined if his relational and identity messages fail. Competent communicators know that the ability to align one's actions with those of a partner and to present oneself positively is just as important as the ability to plan strategically. All three issues are involved in goal achievement.

## Skills for Goal Achievement

Influence calls into play many communication skills. Two of the most important, we would argue, are sensitivity to face and the ability to role-take. Both involve a willingness to step outside oneself and anticipate the effect of one's messages.

### Face and Interpersonal Influence.

As you may recall from Chapter 7, whenever we communicate we run the risk that our social identity, or face, will be rejected. For most people, losing face is humiliating and embarrassing.

In fact, even imagined slights can cause serious distress. Scholars who study face-work commonly talk about two kinds of face.[6] **Positive face** refers to our need to be approved of and appreciated by others. This aspect of face can be threatened by insults or criticism or by any statement that implies we are not as good as we could be. If Bob says to Bill, "How could you have done something so stupid?" he threatens Bill's sense of competence. If, on the other hand, he says, "Well that's not what I would have done, but I can understand why you did it," he lessens the threat considerably. **Negative face** refers to our need to remain autonomous and unconstrained. Statements that constrict our freedom of action, for example, orders, are threats to negative face. If Bill tells Bob, "Go get my car right now," he conveys the idea that Bob has no choice. If he says instead, "If you've got a minute would you mind getting my car," Bob feels less like his behavior is being controlled.

Intentional influence can threaten both kinds of face. Direct advice like, "You should give up smoking" suggests that the recipient is less than perfect (Smoking is bad, and you're a smoker) and tries to control the recipient's behavior (You must stop). It's no wonder that advice is often viewed as inappropriate and less than helpful.[7] In fact, people often respond defensively or become more resistant when they are aware that someone is trying to change them. This reaction is known as **psychological reactance,** and it explains why reverse psychology can sometimes be a tool of influence, especially with young children. If you order a child in the "terrible twos" to eat his carrots, for example, you may get resistance. If, on the other hand, you says, "I'm not going to give you any carrots; I'm giving them all to your sister," the child may demand his share and ask for more. Whether you label this reaction reactance or a threat to negative face, it is based on the human need to avoid having choices restricted.

Communicators who want to influence others must find a way to lessen the threats to face that are inevitable in any influence attempt. The communicator who blurts out criticisms and requests without thinking about how they will be received is going to have a difficult time achieving goals.

### Symbolic Role-Taking

Sensitivity to others' face needs implies the ability to put aside one's own concerns and focus on the needs and feelings of another. Although most people know, on a cognitive level, that everyone reacts to the world in slightly different ways, in practice these differences are often ignored. People create messages on the basis of what makes sense to them, not necessarily what makes sense to others. Competent communicators overcome this difficulty by engaging in **role-taking,** the act of see things from the perspective of the other.

Role-taking is not automatic. It takes time to develop. The strategies very young children use to get their way show that they have not yet learned to role-take. At the beginning they assume that others can read their minds; it never occurs to them to explain their needs. Later, they begin to understand that it is important to ask for what they want, but it is only in later stages of development that they come to understand that a request should be accompanied by a reason and that the best reasons take others' needs into account.

Role-taking is necessary not only for children but for adults as well. It allows us to identify objections others may raise to influence attempts, and it allows us to choose the most effective line of action in a given situation. Most importantly, it allows us to understand others' needs.

# Theories of Influence: Understanding Others' Needs

In our discussion so far, we've indicated that to influence others you must be able to understand their needs and goals. This is no small task; human needs are complex and varied and not easy to predict. Still, some widely shared needs seem to apply across many situations. In this section we'll investigate ways communicators can influence others by taking advantage of their needs for rewards, consistency, and identity.

## The Need for Rewards

One of the most influential theories in all of psychology is learning theory. Basically, **learning theory** holds that people act so as to maximize rewards and minimize punishments. Actions that are associated with positive outcomes will be repeated, while those resulting in negative outcomes will be avoided. Most of the time, this makes sense. People are usually better off if they seek pleasure and avoid pain. But any strong need can form the basis of strategic influence, and the need to maximize rewards and avoid punishment is no exception.

We are willing to bet, in fact, that your parents used principles of learning theory to control your behavior when you were young. By praising you for being good and grounding you when your behavior was less than perfect, they were using learning theory. It may not have worked all the time, but it undoubtedly taught you that the consequences of behavior can be either pleasant or painful and at least made you think twice before you did something that would get you into trouble.

All learning theorists believe that behavior consists of stimulus-response chains that follow one another in a never-ending series. Whenever organisms encounter a **stimulus,** or unit of sensory input, they react to it with a **response.** When you hear a loud noise (stimulus) you may jump (response). Or when someone praises you (stimulus), you may work harder (response). Learning theorists believe that behavior can be changed by manipulating either stimulus or response.

There are several models of learning: Classical conditioning, operant conditioning, and social learning are three of the most important. The classical conditioning model focuses on the stimulus; in particular, it looks at what happens when two stimuli are paired. The operant conditioning model focuses on the response; it looks at how the consequences that follow responses control those responses. And social learning focuses on observational learning. Figure 9.1 compares these models.

### Classical Conditioning

Pleasant stimuli naturally call forth positive responses, and negative stimuli lead to negative reactions. For example, most people wince when they get an injection. There is nothing very surprising about this. What is more surprising is that the response to this stimulus can be transferred to another stimulus. Just reading about getting a shot or just passing a doctor's office may be enough to make some people cringe. When two stimuli are paired so that the response to one becomes attached to the other, **classical conditioning** has taken place. In our example, the actual shot is what is called the **unconditioned stimulus;** because it is painful it elicits a negative response, called the **unconditioned response.** Catching sight of the doctor's office is the **conditioned stimulus;** because it has been paired with getting a shot, over time it too begins to elicit a negative response, the **conditioned response.**

Many of you are no doubt familiar with I. P. Pavlov's experiments in classical conditioning.[8] Pavlov knew that without any conditioning, laboratory dogs salivate when given meat powder. The unconditioned stimulus of meat powder is naturally followed by the unconditioned response of salivation. His experiments demonstrated the effects of associating a new stimulus, a ringing bell, with the meat powder. After a number of trials the bell alone began to cause the dog to salivate. The dog learned to respond in a new way.

Classical, or associational, learning plays a large role in interpersonal situations. Many of our responses to others are based on associations. As we mentioned in Chapter 6, it's not unusual for people to feel instant dislike for a stranger simply because he or she reminds them of someone they dislike. It's also not uncommon to let responses to context color impressions. People often dislike people they meet under trying or uncomfortable conditions and are overly

## Classical Conditioning

**situation:** As a child, every time Tim made funny faces, his friends and relatives laughed and he felt good. Clowning was associated with praise and laughter.

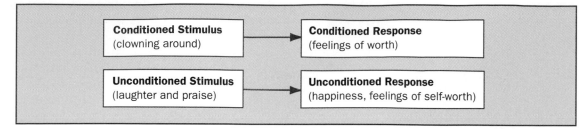

## Operant Conditioning

**situation:** In high school, Tim enters the talent show; audience response determines his future responses.

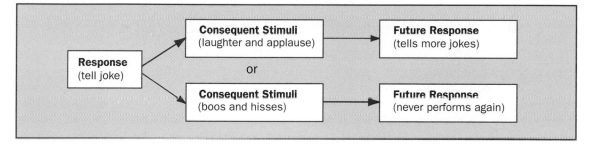

## Social Learning

**situation:** Tim observes the success of a famous comedian; he imagines himself becoming famous, too. He imitates his hero.

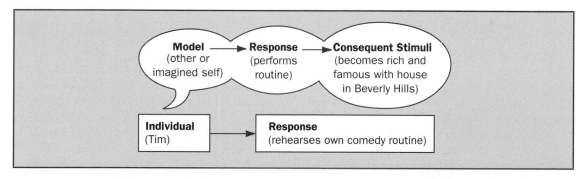

**FIGURE 9.1** *A comparison of three learning theories.*

BOX 9.1

Weapons of Influence

# Mental Shortcuts That Trigger Compliance

Most of us use mental shortcuts to guide us through life. When we don't have the time or information to make informed decisions, we fall back on *heuristics*, simple rules that don't take much thinking. Although following these mental shortcuts works for us most of the time, they can be turned against us by compliance professionals. Psychologist Robert Cialdini identifies six of these weapons of influence.

*The rule of reciprocation* says that "we should try to repay, in kind, what another person has provided us." If the Joneses invite us to dinner, we owe them a return invitation. If the Smiths give us a gift during the holidays, we hurry out to buy them something, too. The rule of reciprocation involves us in a "web of indebtedness." Although this can lead to positive social consequences, it can also be used to influence us. Free samples, for ex-ample, may not be so free if they make us feel obligated, and unwanted favors can trap us into doing things we would not ordinarily do.

*The commitment rule* says that once we make a choice or take a stand, we should behave consistently. Cialdini gives an interesting example of how consistency can get us in trouble. Before Christmas, the airwaves are full of advertisements for toys. In response to their children's entreaties, many parents promise they'll buy the toy their child wants. Yet, when they get to the store, the toy is out of stock. The parent compromises, buying a substitute, often from the manufacturer of the desired toy. In January, the original toy magically reappears. And what do most parents do when their child says, "But you promised"? They buy their child a second toy. The toy company doubles its profits because parents don't want to break commitments.

*The social proof rule* says that behaviors are correct if others perform them. Have you ever stood outside with a group of friends and looked up at the sky? Chances are that if you do, pretty soon other people will also look up, in a case of "monkey see, monkey do." Influence agents use social proof by making things look popular. Those long waiting lines outside certain night-clubs make it look like the place must be extra-impressed with those they meet in luxurious surroundings.

An interesting example of classical conditioning is the **luncheon technique.** Many years ago distinguished psychologist George Razran, who was one of the earliest translators of Pavlov's work, ran a series of studies showing that subjects are more positive about the people and things they experience while eating. Robert Cialdini explains that it is not a long step from Pavlov's study to Razran's luncheon technique.

*Nor is there a long step from the luncheon technique to the compliance professionals' realization that all kinds of desirable things can substitute for food. . . . In the final analysis, then, that is why those good-looking models stand around in the magazine ads. That is why radio programmers are instructed to insert the station's call letters jingle immediately before a big hit song is played. And that is even why the women playing Barnyard Bingo at a Tupperware party must yell the word* Tupperware *rather than* Bingo *before they can rush to the center of the floor for a prize. It may be Tupperware for the players, but it's* Bingo! *for the company.*[9]

How powerful are associations such as these? Very. In addition to being a staple in the arsenal special; of course, often this is merely a ploy and there is actually plenty of room inside. When the number of people who have contributed to a celebrity telethon is flashed on the screen, it signals home viewers that they should give. After all, if everyone's doing it, it must be a good thing.

*The liking rule* points out that people generally like and comply with people who are friendly to them. While it's easy to turn down the request of a stranger, it's pretty difficult to turn down a friend. This is why neighbors feel compelled to buy unwanted boxes of Girl Scout cookies or band candy. Cialdini warns us to be wary of strangers who try to hard to be friends, especially if they have something to gain.

*The authority rule* is based on the idea that the best course of action is to obey people in power. Of course, this rule works if the person in power is actually an authority; unfortunately it is far too easy for people to pass themselves off as authoritative when they are not. Titles, clothing, even automobiles can demand undeserved respect and deference. In an interesting study, researchers found that motorists waiting for the car in front of them to go through a green light would wait considerably longer before honking their horns at a luxury car than an economy model.

Finally, *the scarcity rule* tells us that scare resources are more valuable than resources that are easily obtained. In the case of diamonds, this may be the case. In other situations, it may not. When salespersons tell you, "The floor model is the last one we have. When that's gone, there won't be anymore," if you're like most people, you'll be more likely to buy. After all, if you don't, you may never have a second chance.

Under normal conditions, these rules work. It's only when they fall into the hands of people who have something to gain that they become weapons of influence. In some ways we are caught on the horns of a dilemma. If we rely on these rules we can be fooled; but often we *must* rely on them because we live in a world where we seldom have the time or energy or cognitive resources to completely analyze a situation. What should we do? Cialdini says that when we encounter someone who falsifies, counterfeits, or misrepresents a situation then we need to fight back: by boycotting, complaining, threatening, or reporting the offense.

**SOURCE** Robert B. Cialdini, *Influence: Science and Practice,* 4th ed. (Boston: Allyn & Bacon, 2001).

of advertisers, classical conditioning principles are used in cult recruitment. Cult recruiters are often attractive and friendly people who seem sincerely happy, vital, energetic, and unconditionally accepting both of one another and of the target. They may invite the target to a picnic where simple games like dodgeball, tug-of-war, and red rover are played. Songs and chants and cheers evoke the atmosphere of summer camp. All of these stimuli are associated with childhood, where simple obedience was expected and rewarded. In a sense they regress the target and make compliance responses more probable.[10]

The lessons we can learn from classical conditioning are not new, nor are they revolutionary.

They are partially summed up in the old saying, "You can catch more flies with honey than you can with vinegar." But they are important. If you want to be more successful at influencing others, then you should create positive associations. If, on the other hand, you want to resist influence, then be aware of how your surroundings influence you and be wary of anyone who appears to be using associations to manipulate your mood. Box 9.1 offers warnings about some other ways influence agents may prey on unwary targets.

## Operant Conditioning

Associational learning is not the only way rewards and punishments affect people. Actions are

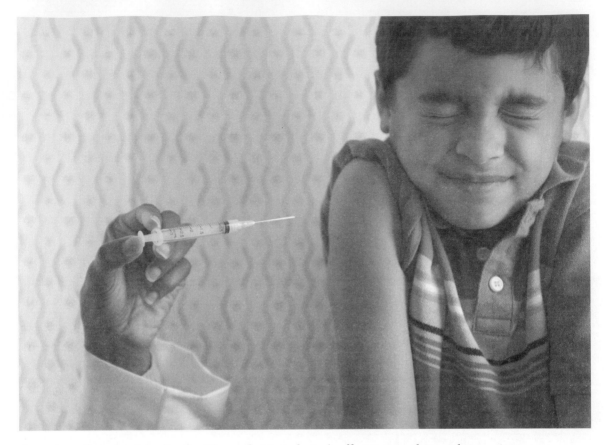

*Sometimes the mere thought of getting a shot in a doctor's office is enough to make us cringe.*

also controlled by their consequences. According to **operant conditioning,** if a response's consequences are rewarding, the response will be repeated; if punishing, it will cease.[11] Controlling the consequences of an action is called **reinforcement.** But what kinds of consequences provide the best reinforcement? The answer isn't easy. Whereas money and power are effective reinforcers in our culture, even they don't work with everyone. The only way to know whether a reinforcer will be successful is to try it. If it increases or decreases a target behavior, it is a reinforcer. If it has no effect, then it's not.

For most schoolchildren, a teacher's scolding is a negative reinforcer, while a teacher's praise is positive. But not always. The class clown is a good example of someone who may be encouraged by disapproval. The more the teacher shouts and scolds, the more likely it is that the clown will continue. Because people find different stimuli appealing, the first step in operant conditioning is to find out what stimuli will be effective reinforcers.

Acts of interpersonal approval or disapproval, called **social reinforcers,** are usually potent forms of influence. Cult members dispense smiles and praise freely whenever a visitor agrees with them, but when the target shows doubt, these reinforcers are withdrawn. In order to keep receiving positive reinforcement, a prospect may censor his or her uncertainty. This reaction is not so unusual. Think for a minute about what happens when people you value criticize or tease you. You probably change your behavior. It takes a very unusual person to keep on doing things that others obviously dislike.

## Social Learning

So far we have looked at learning that results from active exposure to positive and negative stimuli. **Social learning theory** emphasizes indirect learning, learning that involves anticipation and imagination.[12] According to social learning theory one of the most important ways we learn is by observing others being rewarded or punished. This kind of learning is called **modeling** or **vicarious learning.** What happens to someone else shows what may happen to us. If a schoolchild sees a classmate punished for acting out in class, she learns that such behavior leads to trouble. If she sees her friend gain popularity as a result, however, she may decide to follow suit.

Not all models are equally influential. We are most influenced by models similar in attitude, gender, or age. In addition, models who are reliable and competent, who are of high status, or who are attractive will have greater impact. Finally, the more people we see being rewarded for a given behavior, the more likely we are to try that behavior.[13] These principles help to explain why cult recruiters are so successful, for they are usually young and attractive.

Another way people learn is by rewarding themselves when goals are met. This is called **self-reinforcement.** A person who tells himself, "As soon as all my work is done, I'm going to treat myself to dinner in a good restaurant" or "I'm going to keep rehearsing until I can play this piece perfectly, no matter how long it takes" is using principles of social learning to control his own behavior. Punishments and pleasures may be actively self-imposed.

A final way we learn is as a result of symbolic representations of consequences. Social learning theory is based on the belief that humans are thinking beings. Through our ability to reason, we can imagine an action's consequences. We can

also respond to others' persuasive arguments. Rewards and punishments mediated through thought and talk are a powerful mode of control.

## Learning and Interpersonal Exchange Processes

Learning theories have been used to explain a number of interpersonal processes, among them the reasons relationships form and dissolve. **Social exchange theory** is a learning model that states that if given a choice between two relationships, we will choose the more rewarding one.[14] Most people give up on relationships when the punishments begin to outweigh the pleasures. In general, people avoid costly relationships although they may endure a short string of losses if they believe they'll get a return on their investment in the long run. According to social exchange theory, while every successful exchange may not involve a large profit, it should at least allow us to break even.

Every interaction involves relational messages, or cues indicating how a specific message should be interpreted. In exchange theory, objects or actions that carry relational meaning are called **relational currencies.**[15] Gifts, favors, time, access rights, and so on are all examples. Even food can carry relational meaning. When you visit home after an absence, a special meal may be prepared. What is significant is not the food itself, but the affection conveyed by the action.

Exchange can be very complicated. Like economic currency, relational currency can become devalued or inflated over time, partners can fail to agree on appropriate exchange rates, and relationships can even go bankrupt if the exchange is mismanaged. If, for example, one of the parties feels she is doing all of the giving and receiving nothing in return, trouble can result. If Melanie was brought up in a family that expresses love through expensive gifts and Carlos wasn't taught to value material goods, there may be conflict. She will think he doesn't respect or care for her, while he may think her shallow and grasping. Neither will get adequate rewards, and the relationship may fail. When we think of the effects of rewards and punishments on behavior, we must remember to include relational currencies.

## The Need for Consistency

A second basic need, one that has been a cornerstone of many of the most important theories of influence, is the need for consistency. Feelings of inconsistency are troubling to most people. We feel uncomfortable, for example, when people we know act erratically. We are taken aback when friends disagree with us or when enemies suddenly take our side. We feel embarrassed when we catch ourselves doing things that contradict our values and beliefs. And once we've made a decision, we feel uneasy going back on it. In brief, we want others to act consistently and we want to act consistently ourselves.

But is this need strong enough to affect behavior? In the words of psychologist Robert Cialdini, "There is no question about it. The drive to be (and look) consistent constitutes a highly potent weapon of social influence, often causing us to act in ways that are clearly contrary to our own best interests."[16] Cialdini argues that principles like consistency gain their power because they usually work to our advantage. Most of the time, consistency promotes stability and predictability. Without consistency our lives would be disconnected and chaotic. In fact, so strong is our need for consistency that we attach negative labels to people who are inconsistent, calling them "two-faced" or "hypocrites."

Like all strong needs, however, consistency can be used as the basis for influence. Just as our need for rewards can open us to influence attempts, so too can our need for consistency. Have you ever heard yourself say any of the following things: "I don't want to but I promised"; "I've spent so much time on it, I can't give up now"; "I had to do it—after all it's the kind of thing people like me do"? If these statements sound familiar, then you've been influenced by the need to avoid inconsistency. If you have, don't worry. You're not alone. Consistency appeals are very powerful forms of influence.

### Cognitive Dissonance Theory

There are a number of theories that can be classed as **consistency theories,** but perhaps the most influential is cognitive dissonance theory.[17] Like learning theory, it has percolated into popular consciousness and has become an accepted explanation for behavior. According to **cognitive dissonance theory,** cognitions can be either consonant (consistent), dissonant (inconsistent), or irrelevant. *I like snow* and *I'm moving to Buffalo*, for example, are consonant cognitions. *I hate the cold* and *I'm moving to Buffalo* are dissonant. *I love kung fu movies* and *I'm moving to Buffalo* are irrelevant. Although most of us hold dissonant cognitions without even noticing, when we become aware of the fact, we feel uncomfortable. This discomfort is called **dissonance,** and, according to dissonance theory, when we become aware of dissonance, we do our best to reduce it.[18]

### Ways to Reduce Dissonance

Robert Gass and John Seiter provide examples of some of the ways people work to reduce dissonance. Assume, for example, that immediately after having vowed to cut back on junk food, you find yourself going to the vending machine and buying a Coke and a package of chips. Suddenly you realize what you've done and begin to feel dissonant. What can you do to reduce this dissonance? Robert Gass and John Seiter discuss six ways to deal with inconsistency: denial, bolstering, differentiation, transcendence, modifying one or both attitudes, and communicating.[19] As you read through these examples, ask yourself how often you've used them in similar situations.

**Denial** involves ignoring the inconsistency. "What problem? There's no problem," would be an example of denial. **Bolstering** means rationalizing one's decision, for example, by convincing yourself that "I really need some quick energy so that I can study better." **Differentiating** entails redefining the decision so that it is no longer dissonant, for example, by saying, "It's not as though I'm eating a candy bar. After all chips are made from corn, and corn is really healthy." **Transcendence** is focusing on larger issues: "Worrying about calories is so unimportant in the wider scheme of things." **Modifying** one or both attitudes is another option, for example, by deciding, "It's OK if I eat junk food, as long as I only do it once or twice a week. It's not necessary to cut it out completely." Finally, **communicating** involves gaining social support. Telling yourself, "I know my friends will agree with me when I explain that concerns about junk food are overblown," is an example of using communication to reduce dissonance. Why not simply admit, "I'm doing something I just vowed not to do?" Because doing so would be admitting to inconsistency, and most of us hate doing that.

## Commitment and Consistency

Dissonance theorists have shown that **commitment** is a key factor in determining how likely we are to avoid appearing dissonant. The more we commit to a line of action, the more difficult it is to go back on it, without experiencing a great deal of dissonance.

Commitment is used in all kinds of influence. When high schools ask students to sign "prom pledges," they are using commitment, as are religions when they offer members opportunities to testify to their faith. The politician who asks you to sign a petition is asking you to make an initial commitment, as is the salesperson who asks you what you like about that new car you are thinking of buying. And the lawyer who asks a potential juror, "If you were the only person who believed in my client's innocence, could you withstand the pressure of the rest of the jury to change your mind?" is hoping to use commitment to influence future deliberations.[20]

Commitments differ in the power they have to induce consistency needs. The most powerful commitments are ones that are *public, effortful,* and *voluntary.* Let's return to the example of the dissonance raised by eating junk food. In the example, the vow to avoid junk food was made in private. But what if you had stood up in front of a room full of people and made the same vow?

Research shows that you will be much less likely to succumb to temptation if your commitment is made in *public.*

Commitments that involve *effort* are also highly influential. This explains why social groups often institute difficult and demanding initiation ceremonies. Fraternity hazing, for example, can involve beating, exposure to cold or extreme thirst, eating disgusting food, punishment, and threats of death—in some cases with tragic results. Why, despite the efforts of outsiders to ban these activities, do organizations insist on them? Because they know that going through this kind of hazing increases one's commitment to the organization and the value that is placed on it. Having gone through such brutal treatment, it would feel inconsistent to say, "It wasn't worth it."[21]

Finally, to be influential, commitment must be *voluntary.* If you agree to something because someone has a gun to your head, you will stop agreeing as soon as the threat is no longer there. Similarly, if you agree to something because you are paid to, it is unlikely you will feel any internal need to agree. But if you agree to something in the absence of an external force you will have to accept inner responsibility for agreeing, and that will make it more likely that you will keep on agreeing.

Understanding how consistency and commitment work can make people more successful influence agents. A very easy way to influence others is to point out that their current behavior or attitudes are inconsistent. "Would a person who cares about the environment do that?" may be enough to make someone stop wasting energy. This appeal begins by labeling the target, and then points out that he or she is not living up to the label.

Very subtle uses of consistency also have big payoffs. For example, when telephone solicitors ask individuals, "How are you feeling tonight?" and receive favorable replies, their success rate can almost double.[22] Evidently, once having admitted that one's own life is going well, it's harder to turn down a request to help other people. And getting people to agree to a small request usually means that you will be better able to get them to

*An act of interpersonal disapproval can be a potent form of influence.*

agree to a later, larger request, a strategy known as the **foot-in-the-door technique.**

Not only is it useful for people who want to influence others to understand consistency theories, knowing how these theories operate can help people resist unwanted influence. The next time you feel backed into a corner, ask yourself if you are being ruled by what Cialdini calls a need for foolish consistency. And if you are, walk away.

## The Need to Establish Identity

We have nearly finished our discussion of the forces that motivate action. There is one more we should look at, however, and that is the need to have our identity validated. A number of theorists hold that people need to respect themselves and be respected by others.

### Value Theory

In his **value theory** Milton Rokeach tells us that the self-concept is a powerful guide to behavior.[23] Each of us has an identity we try to live up to. For Rokeach, the clearest reflection of people's identities is their values. A value is simply a belief that some goals and paths to goal achievement are better than others. For example, some people believe that altruism is more worthwhile than self-interest; they therefore act with kindness and charity. Others believe it is important to achieve personal success. They may value ambition and material security above everything else. Table 9.1 lists some of the values Rokeach believes are basic to all people. If you were asked to rank these, which would you consider the most important?

Rokeach believes people can be influenced by appeals to their value systems. If, for example, bravery is high in your hierarchy of values, you may undertake very foolhardy actions in order to avoid being labeled a coward. You may be highly influenced by challenges or dares. If you believe that stealing is wrong, anticipated guilt may stop you from shoplifting. Values are key parts of our life scripts. One of our strongest motivations is to remain true to what we believe is right.

Not only do we need to be true to private images of self, most of us also need to present favorable public images. Young children may begin smoking in order to appear older and more sophisticated to their peers. They may even get together and practice until they can smoke without feeling sick or looking foolish. For them, smoking is a form of self-presentation. What kind of interpersonal appeal will discourage them? Probably not rational arguments about health hazards. A better approach might be to convince them that smoking is unattractive and unsophisticated, that it makes them look silly and juvenile.

Value theorists believe that people often engage in unrewarding and inconsistent behaviors simply to act out a valued life script. The "macho" man, for example, may have to do a lot of unpleasant things to prove himself. Think about

| TABLE 9.1 | Terminal and Instrumental Values |
|-----------|----------------------------------|

| Terminal values—<br>preferable end states of existence | Instrumental values —<br>preferable modes of conduct |
|---|---|
| A comfortable life (a prosperous life) | Ambitious (hardworking, aspiring) |
| An exciting life (a stimulating, active life) | Broad-minded (open-minded) |
| A sense of accomplishment (lasting contribution) | Capable (competent, effective) |
| A world at peace (free of war and conflict) | Cheerful (lighthearted, joyful) |
| A world of beauty (beauty of nature and the arts) | Clean (neat, tidy) |
| Equality (brotherhood, equal opportunity for all) | Courageous (standing up for your beliefs) |
| Family security (taking care of loved ones) | Forgiving (willing to pardon others) |
| Freedom (independence, free choice) | Helpful (working for the welfare of others) |
| Happiness (contentedness) | Honest (sincere, truthful) |
| Inner harmony (freedom from inner conflict) | Imaginative (daring, creative) |
| Mature love (sexual and spiritual intimacy) | Independent (self-reliant, self-sufficient) |
| National security (protection from attack) | Intellectual (intelligent, reflective) |
| Pleasure (an enjoyable, leisurely life) | Logical (consistent, rational) |
| Salvation (saved, eternal life) | Loving (affectionate, tender) |
| Self-respect (self-esteem) | Obedient (dutiful, respectful) |
| Social recognition (respect, admiration) | Polite (courteous, well-mannered) |
| True friendship (close companionship) | Responsible (dependable, reliable) |
| Wisdom (a mature understanding of life) | Self-controlled (restrained, self-disciplined) |

Terminal values are associated with life goals; instrumental values define appropriate means for achieving these goals. Both guide action.

Reprinted with permission from Milton Rokeach, *Beliefs, Attitudes, and Values* (San Francisco: Jossey-Bass, 1968). Copyright 1968 by Jossey-Bass.

it. Have you ever sacrificed rewards because getting them would involve violating a value? Have you ever done things that were irrational and inconsistent in order to act out a social role? If so, you may agree with value theory.

### Relationships and Self-Validation

Although Rokeach points out that people are motivated by a need to live up to their values, he doesn't have much to say about how people make identity statements to one another. Nor does he take into account the fact that identity may not be

something one person shows to another, but rather something that is negotiated during interpersonal communication. Walter Carl and Steve Duck, however, offer us a better understanding of the process by which identity needs are achieved thought everyday talk.[24] As we pointed out at the beginning of this chapter, every time we talk we send messages about identity and relationship issues. Sometimes we address these issues in very conscious ways; at other times, however, we are less aware that we are doing so. Nevertheless, a great deal of interpersonal communication centers

## "Wait 'Til You Hear What I Heard"

# Gossip as Strategic Interaction

Are gossipers mean-spirited individuals out to ruin reputations and destroy relationships, or are they simply engaging in a healthy social activity that strengthens group bonds while it entertains? The answer may be a little of both. Gossip is a very complex activity; past research has shown that it can be a way of covertly asserting one's status, a way of working out relationships within social groups, and a technique of social control. It is also an intrinsically interesting form of talk.

In "Gossip as Strategy: The Management of Talk About Others on the Reality TV Show 'Big Brother,'" Joanna Thornborrow and Deborah Morris analyze how gossip is used as an influence strategy in episodes from the British version of the *Big Brother* TV series. What is interesting about communication on *Big Brother* is that players must achieve two different strategic goals at once. Their talk must please both their housemates, who can nominate them for eviction, and the viewing public, who can vote them out of the house.

Within the house, gossip allows players to forge alliances. By accepting an invitation to gossip, the receiver shows solidarity with the person who initiates the gossip and tacit opposition to the person being gossiped about. In a game that is "essentially about getting on with other people," deciding to initiate or accept gossip is a matter of strategic importance. Aligning with an unpopular player can result in negative perceptions by other players and by the public at large, whereas aligning with a popular player can have positive results. The authors show how gossip works as a useful but risky strategy that, when used skillfully, can help players manipulate the way other players and members of the public see them and can serve as a way of damaging the character of their opponents.

Although the producers of the show would have us believe we are eavesdropping on reality, we are, in fact, watching a game in which contestants are consciously acting in strategic ways. Despite this fact, the techniques the authors identify do seem to be used, in less extreme forms, in everyday life. This study offers an interesting illustration of the social work that can be accomplished through gossip when the stakes are high. As to whether everyday gossip works the same way, we'll let you be the judge.

Thornborrow, Joanna, and Deborah Morris. "Gossip as Strategy: The Management of Talk About Others on the Reality TV Show 'Big Brother.'" *Journal of Sociolinguistics* 8, no. 4 (2004): 246–71.

on influencing others to accept views of self and definitions of relationships. In fact, Carl and Duck argue that "everyday talk is a matter of continuously seeking confirmation of a self in relation to others." They believe that even the most pedestrian discussion serves to "take a position, to espouse beliefs, and to promulgate attitudes and opinions."[25]

Imagine, for example, someone who tends to complain a lot. If you were to ask that person if he or she was engaged in interpersonal influence, the response would more than likely be a denial. Yet, in regularly voicing trivial complaints—"My neighbor is too noisy," or "My son never calls home," or "The clerk didn't give me the correct change"—the individual presents a view of self:

in this case a self who is constantly being put upon by everyone. By bringing up these topics, our complainer asks others to validate this view of self. For Carl and Duck, relationships are places in which individuals advance and negotiate their understanding of themselves and of the world. As such, they argue, interpersonal influence is going on all the time both explicitly and implicitly.[26] When we inform others of accomplishments, offer accounts and excuses for our behavior, gossip with one another, or even just comment on the news, we are attempting to validate our sense of self and align ourselves with others. In this sense, we are always engaged in interpersonal influence. The study cited in this chapter's Research in Review shows how gossip can be used strategically during influence.

We will return to the notion that identity is something that is negotiated in relationships when we look more closely at message strategies. For now simply keep in mind that people have a strong need for others to accept their self-presentations, and they express this need both consciously and unconsciously.

### Summary: Choice and Motivation

As we have seen, learning theories hold that people are motivated by the rewards and punishments accompanying their behaviors, consistency theories state that people need to make their belief systems stable and consistent, and value theories tell us that people act so as to create favorable images. But which theory is right? It's possible that they all are. At various times we may try to fulfill all of these needs. Daniel Katz believes that people form and maintain attitudes for several different reasons.[27] He identifies four functions of attitudes: adjustment, knowledge, value expression, and ego defense. The first three correspond pretty closely to learning, consistency, and self-validation theories, respectively. The last reflects the individual's need to defend the ego from psychological threat and is based on psychoanalytic theory.

Katz makes two important points about motivation. The first is that people are motivated at various times by various forces. Although Katz doesn't explain why our motivations shift, it's possible that people have different motivational schemata that guide actions. When the reward-punishment schema is uppermost, we tend to judge an action in terms of gains and losses. When a value schema is in place, we take a more noble stance. And when the consistency schema is being used, we try to act rationally. If this is true, then part of being a successful change agent involves calling up the correct schema in our audience. There are things a persuader probably can do to switch a target from concern with reward attainment to concern with value exemplification. Think about it. What would you do to change the focus of a target's attention from self-interest to self-sacrifice?

Katz makes a second point worth considering. Different methods must be used to change different kinds of attitudes. If a behavior is driven by a need for adjustment, then it can be changed by promises or threats. If it helps the individual maintain a stable worldview, then rational arguments should be used. Katz tells us that interpersonal influence must be flexible and varied.

## Source Characteristics

While an understanding of target needs plays a major role in interpersonal influence, it's not the whole story. As we've seen, a source always makes some identity declaration during interaction. Communication scholars have known for a long time that not all speakers are equally persuasive and that who the speaker is may be as important as what he or she says. While Aristotle was the first to recognize that a speaker's character, knowledge, and goodwill are a significant part of persuasion, others since him have noted the importance of the attributions receivers make about sources.[28] Think of all the ways we have of describing persuasive speakers; we refer to their credibility, expertness,

*One of the many types of interpersonal influence is assigning expert power to someone whose special knowledge or skill is something we wish to learn.*

dynamism, charisma, and the like. Clearly, the characteristics a public speaker manages to convey to an audience provide him or her with a great deal of power. Source characteristics are probably even more important in the interpersonal context, where the relationship between sender and receiver is a close and personal one. Let's examine these ideas more closely.

## Power and Interpersonal Influence

Power and influence go hand in hand. A powerful person is one who can control a situation, and this control can come in many ways. John R. French and Bertram Raven believe there are five kinds of power: reward, coercive, expert, legitimate, and referent.[29]

A source perceived as controlling rewards has **reward power.** The employer determining who gets a raise, the political boss deciding on the next candidate for governor, the guy in the bar buying drinks for his buddies, or the teenager lending out the latest CDs are all wielding reward power. When people own things we want or need, they become important to us, and their importance is in direct proportion to our need. Control of physical or emotional resources is a prominent aspect of power.

Of course, the ability to dispense rewards is not the only base of power. The person who can inspire fear has **coercive power.** Most people comply with the requests of an armed criminal or a burly bully. On an interpersonal level, fear of being excluded or unmasked can lead to psychological coercion. People often rule with threats as well as promises.

Sometimes a source is influential because he or she has special knowledge or skill. This influence base is called **expert power.** In an age in which it is impossible to know everything, people must rely on specialists. We seldom question the recommendations of physicians or engineers or scientists.

While intelligence and training are significant sources of power, sheer attractiveness can also lead to influence. The people we admire have **referent power.** Rock stars have their groupies, gang leaders their faithful lieutenants, and teenagers their adoring kid brothers and sisters. In each case these figures embody some moral or physical attribute others admire. Imitation is not only the sincerest form of flattery but an indication of interpersonal influence.

Of course, sometimes the actual characteristics of a source are not as important as his or her symbolic characteristics. When people become representatives of social institutions, they take on **legitimate power.** Most law-abiding citizens obey a police officer without question. Compliance has almost nothing to do with the officer's personality or ability; rather, he or she represents the power of the state and therefore has the "right" to control actions. While you may question the fairness of a particular assignment your professors make, you seldom question their right to make assignments. The academic setting legitimizes teachers' requests.

## Self-Presentation Strategies

Having a power base is all very well, but it counts for nothing unless others know about it. Power is largely a matter of attribution. How, then, do you make sure others know you're powerful? One way is by employing self-presentation strategies to translate power bases into observable behaviors. Edward Jones and Thane Pittman have described five methods of strategic self-presentation used in interpersonal influence situations: ingratiation, intimidation, self-promotion, exemplification, and supplication.[30]

According to norms of reciprocity, we generally like those who like us. It is hard to mistreat people who appreciate us; indeed, we often feel we owe them something in return. This suggests that we can influence others by appearing to like them and by being pleasant and friendly. This strategy is called **ingratiation.** The ingratiator uses charm, helpfulness, and flattery to control others.

While many people are sincerely nice, the ingratiator is strategically nice. In practice this is somewhat tricky. If the ingratiator is too nice, the target will become suspicious, and the strategy will backfire. The classic case of the ingratiator is the "yes man" who tells others whatever they want to hear in order to curry favor. While this is an extreme behavior, most of us have been taught that we should be pleasant if we want to influence others. As the saying goes, you can catch more flies with honey than with vinegar.

People who use **intimidation** aren't at all concerned with being nice. Instead, they want to appear dangerous. We generally give in to people who get ungovernably angry or violent. Young children often throw tantrums to get their way, while older people bully and threaten. Sometimes the destruction the intimidator threatens is self-destruction. Having an asthma attack or a dizzy spell whenever we are crossed is one way of controlling those around us.

**Self-promotion** is another strategy. Self-promoters want to be perceived as competent. They emphasize expert power. Others are so impressed with their training and experience that they have little choice but to agree. The dilemma facing the self-promoter is how to present an impressive list of credentials without seeming to brag. One way is to ensure the aid of a friend who can enthusiastically describe the promoter's accomplishments, allowing the promoter to look modest and slightly embarrassed. While self-promotion can be carried to extremes, most people try to appear as competent as possible. We all like to look as though we know what we're doing, especially in public situations. Every time we attempt to build credibility, we are engaging in mild forms of self-promotion.

BOX 9.2

## Caveat Emptor

# Techniques of Confidence Tricksters

Professional confidence tricksters rarely use a "hard sell" when setting up their marks. In fact, it is often the mark who begs to be let in on the deal, believing he's putting something over on the con artist. Con artists know that getting their targets to persuade themselves is their most effective technique. Two things are essential in a well-run con game: The mark must believe it's possible to get something for nothing, and the con must seem absolutely trustworthy. How do con artists manage to make their marks believe their unbelievable tales? By knowing the mark's weaknesses and by putting on a credible front.

One of the most imaginative and stylish of all confidence tricksters was "Count" Victor Lustig. Early in his career he managed to sell the Eiffel Tower, not once, but twice! Throughout his life he assumed many identities and created many unusual "business opportunities" for gullible investors.

A classic example was the "money machine" he sold to a hardheaded businessman for $25,000. In the winter of 1925–26, Lustig turned up in Palm Beach hoping to find the perfect mark, someone whose greed was equaled by his need for status. Lustig's first step was to acquire an appropriate front. Hiring a chauffeur-driven Rolls-Royce, he checked into an expensive suite at one of the finest hotels and waited. Before long, opportunity presented itself in the person of Herman Loller, a self-made millionaire frustrated by his lack of social importance. To someone like Loller, knowing a cultured European aristocrat was extremely flattering. As they became friends, Loller confided some business setbacks. Lustig reluctantly revealed that he, too, had had money

Another way to influence is through **exemplification.** Exemplifiers control others by personifying the values they admire. They project so much integrity that others feel either admiration or guilt. Think of the influence wielded by religious prophets or saints; they are extreme examples of exemplifiers, people whose goodness is power.

Most of us don't go that far, although we do use exemplification in many influence situations. The child who acts like a "little angel" to impress his folks, the student who asks the teacher for extra reading assignments, and the employee who is always willing to work late if the boss needs her are all using this presentational strategy. Of course, exemplification doesn't always lead to popularity. Students have highly uncomplimentary labels for other students who try to impress

teachers; exemplifiers make everyone else look bad in comparison.

The final strategy outlined by Jones and Pittman is called **supplication.** Here the presentation is that of helplessness. The supplicator appears so weak and defenseless that others feel a duty to act as protector. Not so long ago, women were taught that men resented strong women. Advice columns urged women to play dumb if they wanted to get a man. Women had to pretend to be bewildered by machines, too weak to carry anything heavier than a handbag, and too scatter-brained to balance a checkbook. A competent man would then step in and solve all of the problems. Through helplessness women achieved a certain kind of influence. Most of that has changed now, and most people feel the change is a healthy one, for the supplicator often pays the problems but that they had been solved by his "money-making machine," a box that would duplicate any paper currency so accurately that no bank could tell the difference. To "romance" the story, Lustig revealed that the machine had originally been developed by the Germans to undermine Allied currencies during World War I. It had fallen by chance into the hands of a Romanian friend. It was, of course, the only one of its kind in the world.

Loller begged for a demonstration. Lustig showed him a beautiful mahogany box into which he placed a $100 bill. Six hours later, he removed two damp bills, identical to the last detail. They looked perfect, as they should have, since both were completely genuine. Lustig had merely altered the threes and eights of the serial numbers on one bill to make it identical to the other. He calmly suggested that Loller take each bill to a bank to make sure it was genuine.

Loller was hooked. He begged for a copy of the box. Lustig demurred. When Loller offered $25,000, he reluctantly gave in. Loller was so taken by Lustig's story that when the box failed to work, he convinced himself that he was operating it incorrectly. It was almost a year before he began to suspect and went to the police.

If you feel that Loller must have been particularly gullible, consider the fact that Lustig pulled off the same scheme again, selling his machine to a sheriff for $10,000 and the chance to escape from jail. It appears that people will believe just about anything if they really want to.

**SOURCE** Colin Rose, ed., *The World's Greatest Rip-Offs* (New York: Sterling, 1978).

**ADDITIONAL READINGS**

Mackay, Charles. *Extraordinary Popular Delusions and the Madness of Crowds.* New York: Farrar, Straus & Giroux, 1932.

Wade, Carlson. *Great Hoaxes and Famous Imposters.* Middle Village, N.Y.: Jonathan David, 1976.

price of diminished self-worth. People who play helpless for too long, whether male or female, may come to think of themselves as helpless, and that is not a particularly good feeling. "Learned helplessness" is the label given to people who have actually lost particular abilities or skills because of fear or long-term supplication.

While all of these strategies can be unhealthy if carried to an extreme, we probably all use modified forms of them. Think about it for a minute. When you want something from someone, do you ever use these techniques? Probably. They are common ways of influencing others. You might find it interesting to consider whether you know people who are ingratiators, intimidators, self-promoters, exemplifiers, or supplicators. Most of our students have no difficulty thinking of examples from among their friends or acquaintances.

## Influence as Self-Persuasion

We hope we haven't given you the impression that influence is something a source does to a target. We don't want you to think that clever sources have complete control over their targets. Keep in mind that sources can set up conditions that will enhance influence, but it is receivers who ultimately convince themselves. Box 9.2 gives a good example of how receivers participate in their own persuasion.

**Cognitive response theory** stresses the large part played by the receiver during the influence process. It states that during persuasion, receivers generate cognitions about the messages they hear. Receivers search their cognitive files for preexisting attitudes, knowledge, and feelings and try to make sense of a source's message in

| TABLE 9.2 | Verbal Influence Strategies |
|---|---|
| Direct request | "Can you give me a lift home?" |
| Hinting | "I'm not sure how I'll get home. I guess I can take the bus." |
| Bargaining | "If you give me a ride home, I'll fill up the tank." |
| Pregiving | "Remember when I gave you a ride last week. Well . . ." |
| Deception | "The last bus has left and I'm stranded." (Even though it hasn't.) |
| Ingratiation | "You look great today. I'm lucky to have a friend like you. Oh, by the way, can I have a ride home?" |
| Moral appeals | "Friends should help each other out, don't you agree?" |
| Manipulation | "It takes me two hours by bus to get home and I'm not feeling well." |
| Distributive communication | "You're thoughtless and selfish. You never do anything for me." |
| Aversive stimulation | (Burst into tears) |
| Withdrawal | (Gives the silent treatment until the target asks, "What's wrong?") |
| Threats | "If you don't give me a ride, you'll be sorry." |

Material adapted from Linda K. Guerrero, Peter A. Andersen, and Walid A. Afifi, *Close Encounters: Communicating in Relationships* (Mt. View, CA: Mayfield Publishing Co. 2001), pp. 291–96.

light of what they already know. Messages supported by prior beliefs will probably be accepted; unsupported messages may have a negative or boomerang effect. Influence targets are active generators of information rather than passive receivers. In a real sense we cannot influence others; we can only hope they will influence themselves in ways we want them to. Like all communication, influence is an active transaction between source and receiver.

## Message Strategies

In the previous sections we have looked at general explanations of how influence works and have noted that source characteristics are power-ful factors in persuading and influencing others. But how does all of this translate into actual communication behavior? When faced with actual influence situations, what does the competent communicator do? If you were in situations like the following, what influence strategies would you use?

*Your aunt who lives nearby and with whom you are close has a large basement with a finished recreation room. You have a very tiny apartment and would like to have a big party in your aunt's basement. However, she can be finicky about cleaning and sometimes minds noise.*

*You are going away for a weekend and need someone to take care of your cat. You have spoken to your neighbor, Marty, once or twice in the past year. He seems to be home most weekends. You want him to feed the cat while you are gone.*

*Your car has stalled out and the battery is dead. You need to call the service station to get your car jumped but do not want to leave the car. A teenager approaches. You want her to call the service station and report where you are.*[31]

These situations represent just some of the cases studied by researchers interested in an area of interpersonal influence known as compliance gain or, more currently, **compliance-seeking research.** These researchers investigate the conditions in which communicators will use different kinds of message strategies.[32] In this section we begin by looking at the kind of messages that are frequently used to seek compliance. We also consider how they are employed during actual interaction.

## Compliance-Seeking Strategies

Over the years, a number of social scientists have compiled lists of compliance-seeking strategies. One of the earliest was developed by Gerald Marwell and David Schmitt.[33] More recently, Laura Guerrero and her colleagues have described the kinds of verbal influence ploys we use on a day-to-day basis.[34] Table 9.2 summarizes and gives examples of these verbal methods of gaining compliance.

**Direct requests** (or directives) are the most common strategies used to influence others. Simply asking for what you want in a direct, nonconfrontational way is the simplest method of obtaining one's goals. And it is also the most frequent strategy in relationships marked by high levels of satisfaction.[35] Despite the effectiveness of direct communication, however, we often shy away from direct expressions and instead use compliance-seeking strategies to get our way. **Hinting** is one such strategy. If, instead of directly asking if he can borrow Aubrey's notes, George casually mentions the fact that his own notes are incomplete in the hope that Aubrey will offer to lend him hers, his hint acts as an indirect request. Hinting is more face-saving than asking because it avoids the possibility of a direct

refusal (which would threaten George's face) and it doesn't impose on Aubrey (which would threaten her negative face.). If Aubrey doesn't want to give George her notes, she simply ignores the hint, and both parties save face. Of course, this strategy depends on the receiver's ability to pick up on subtle hints. People differ in their ability to process indirect requests, and there are cultural differences in preference for direct or indirect responses.[36]

In situations where asking or hinting appears ineffective, **bargaining** may be tried. Here the parties work out a *quid pro quo*. For example, Alice agrees to help Joey find a birthday gift for his Dad if Joey takes her out to eat afterward. In successful bargaining, both parties get something they want. An interesting twist on this strategy is called **pregiving**. As we've already seen, in pregiving, Joey does something nice for Alice prior to making his request. Alice then feels obligated to reciprocate. Of course, bargaining and pregiving won't work if the parties have nothing to exchange.

Not all the strategies are positive. **Deception** can sometimes be used to influence others. In a bargaining situation, it is possible to make a false promise in order to get one's way. For example, Gina can promise to pay back the money she borrows from Marla, then conveniently forget her promise. Or Billy can tell his Dad that he needs the car to go to the library, when he actually intends to use it to ride around with his friends. As Guerrero points out, use of deception tends to undermine relationships and thus can easily backfire.

As we have seen in our discussion of self-presentation strategies, **ingratiation** can work as an influence ploy. It is hard to turn someone down who is being particularly pleasant and complimentary. Of course, ingratiation has to be subtle. If the receiver guesses that the compliments and flattery he found so appealing are actually false, then he will obviously not be persuaded.

Sometimes individuals decide to use **moral appeals** to convince others. They point out what a good (or bad) person would do in a given situation. For example, "A good sister would spend time with her brother" can be used to influence Selma to spend her Saturday babysitting rather than going out with her friends. Similarly, "Anyone who ignores a friend in need is heartless" may make Stan realize he needs to help Abe with his problems. Of course, the success of this kind of strategy depends on whether Selma or Stan accepts the moral appeal as valid.

Use of moral appeals is not specifically intended to cause guilt; rather, it is intended to remind people of their moral obligations. **Manipulation,** on the other hand, is an attempt to make a partner feel bad: jealous, guilty, or ashamed. Thus, Chris may decide to make Pat jealous in order to get Pat to pay more attention. Or Jessica's mother may point out how lonely she feels in order to make Jessica feel guilty for not calling home more often. Sometimes a partner may use **distributive communication,** in which he attacks his partner verbally. Name-calling, insulting, or blaming the other are overtly negative ways of gaining one's ends. Guerrero believes that tactics such as these "usually are ineffective and often lead to escalated conflict."[37]

Manipulation and distributive communication appear to be special cases of **aversive stimulation,** a strategy that involves using punishment or negative reinforcement to get one's way. Whining, sulking, crying, or being generally unpleasant are examples of aversive stimulation. Children often use this technique when they want their parents to buy them a new toy. Although this may work for children, it may not work for adults. In fact, people find it one of the most unpleasant of all the compliance-gaining strategies.[38] People can take only so much punishment before they decide the relationship is not worth the pain and suffering.

**Withdrawal,** leaving the field and refusing to communicate, is considered by most people to be even more unpleasant than aversive stimulation. For example, Rosario may refuse to talk to Phillip when he doesn't do what she wants him to do. This disconfirmation can be very punishing, and, in order to get the relationship back on line, Philip may feel he has no choice but to give in. However, because withdrawing is a kind of disconfirmation, Philip will end up feeling bad about himself, and the relationship will probably be a troubled one.

Finally, **threats** are sometimes used to get one's way. As we have already seen, the bully who threatens to harm the other kids on the block if they don't cough up their lunch money may be successful in the short term, but may eventually suffer retaliation. And the use of threats in a close relationship only leads to the dissolution of the relationship.

It is important to think about the kinds of self-presentation and compliance-gaining strategies you habitually use. As we have seen, some are ineffective and destructive, even though they may be frequently used. The further we digress from direct, positive strategies the more damaging are the results. Unfortunately, people often "specialize" in certain kinds of persuasive ploys, relying on familiar scripts rather than thinking about the effects of their actions. The bully, for example, may automatically use threats and aversive stimulation because he lacks more effective methods of influence. It is important to remember that honesty and directness work best (at least in our culture) and that "readily doing favors and granting requests may be part of the recipe for keeping relationships happy."[39]

## Strategies in Interaction

Identifying types of strategies and looking at their success in particular contexts is just one way to approach the study of compliance-seeking communication. Another is to look at how individuals actually employ these strategies in talk. Robert Sanders and Kristine Fitch have argued that interpersonal influence involves more than just assessing a situation and choosing one's favorite strategy. In practice, compliance-seeking episodes are complex, incremental, and interactive.[40]

Sanders and Fitch tells us that "rather than deploy a strategy, it is more accurate to say that compliance seekers, with the cooperation of target persons, strategically work out what inducements to offer."[41] Assume, for example, that Lea wants to ask Chris, who has a truck, to help her move her furniture. She begins by introducing the topic of moving to see how Chris will respond. Chris, however, doesn't pick up on the topic, so Lea makes an indirect request, commenting on how easy it would be to move if she had a truck. Chris still doesn't offer to help, so Lea changes the topic while she figures out the best approach. Later, she reintroduces the topic, and they negotiate until Chris decides that it's time to acquiesce.

The conversation between Lea and Chris is fairly typical of the way people use influence strategies in everyday conversation. Most interactions of this kind proceed in small increments and involve complex estimates of the social meanings associated with making and giving in to requests. Throughout the conversation, both parties are concerned with how their behaviors look to the other. In addition to these relational considerations, a large portion of influence-centered interaction is devoted to working out practical arrangements.

In their research on how people go about influencing one another, Sanders and Fitch found that "compliance seeking is not adversarial, but involves efforts by both parties to accommodate the other's needs, while avoiding or minimizing cost to themselves. The result [is] often a complex 'dance' through talk about the practicalities of the matters at hand."[42] Influence, like communication in general, is not something a sender does to a receiver, but rather something that sender/receivers do together. The more partners are willing to hear one another out and discuss their needs cooperatively and the more willing they are to compromise and problem solve, the easier compliance-seeking will be.

When people are not able to follow a cooperative script, "confrontation, abrupt termination, or both are likely to ensue."[43] That may be why so many of us hang up on telemarketers. Despite their attempts to establish personal ties by asking us how our day has been, they aren't actually trying to establish dialogue. The fact that they are pursuing a strategy and reading from a script removes most people's willingness to engage in

the incremental and interactive process that leads to compliance.

## Interpersonal Influence and Goal Competence

Interpersonal influence is a complex process that takes a great deal of sensitivity and awareness. In order to persuade others, the competent communicator must understand the theoretical principles underlying social influence processes. These principles are not hard to apply. There are certain basic ways to enhance influence that cut across all theories. First of all, communicators should be aware of their own bases of power. Others respond to us according to the attributions they make about us; we want those attributions to be favorable. The persuasive speaker should build credibility; the interpersonal communicator should present himself as attractively as possible.

Second, it is important to frame appeals that take into account the needs and desires of others. If we know people are motivated by rewards, we can convince them by offering rewards. If we know they are troubled by inconsistency, we can show that our proposals will lead to stability. If we understand their values, we can appeal to them. The competent change agent matches technique to receiver needs.

Third, we should realize that if we can get receivers to influence themselves, our work will be done for us. Encouraging a target to behave in ways related to our proposals is a cardinal influence principle. If we can get someone to try our product, to act on our ideas, to testify to our beliefs, we have gone a long way toward persuading him or her. Only the incompetent communicator sees persuasion as a one-way process.

Fourth, we should recognize how pervasive influence is in interpersonal relationships. Not all influence is intentional or conscious. Not all involves the framing of complex appeals. A lot of

*Our ability to set and achieve goals depends on interaction with those we look up to.*

Robert Delaunay, *Runners*, 1924–1925

interpersonal influence occurs through mundane, everyday talk as we negotiate meaning and present versions of self to others.

In summary, competent communicators must be sensitive to the context, to their own self-presentations, and to the target's needs and vulnerabilities. They must then be able to translate this sensitivity into rhetorically acceptable message forms. While we cannot list all of the ways to do this, we can urge you to observe what works and what doesn't and to form your own theories of interpersonal influence.

# Skill Building: Becoming More Assertive

Ellen has had a long week and needs some privacy. She wants to write some letters, watch a video, and just relax. Just when she's settling in, her friend Scott knocks on the door. He's had another fight with his girlfriend and, for the third time this week, wants Ellen to analyze his relationship. Ellen likes Scott a lot, but she's tired of playing counselor. Although she'd like to tell Scott to leave, she doesn't know what to say. After all, he's upset and she really wasn't doing anything important. So she sighs and spends the evening attending to his needs rather than to her own. Later she feels disappointed with herself and resentful of Scott. Ellen has a problem in being assertive.

In many ways Steve is the opposite of Ellen. When people like Scott ask him for help, he's likely to insult them, yelling at them to get out and leave him alone. Although his style is very different from Ellen's, Steve and Ellen share a problem in being properly assertive. Neither Ellen nor Steve knows how to attain goals effectively. Ellen is nonassertive; she gives up when she should stand up for her rights. Steve is aggressive; he is inappropriately abusive when he perceives his rights as being threatened. Both need to learn how to express their needs clearly and firmly in a way that shows respect both for themselves and for others. In short, both need to learn how to be assertive.

While you may not share either Ellen's or Steve's interpersonal styles, you too may sometimes have problems in being assertive. Regardless of how confident you are most of the time, in some situations you probably find it hard to achieve your goals. Ask yourself if you find any of the following behaviors difficult: expressing your viewpoint when others disagree, expressing negative emotions when you honestly feel them, expressing positive feelings like affection or empathy, disagreeing with authority figures, asking people to explain things you don't understand, making requests, or denying a request from someone you care about. If you do, you may benefit from becoming more assertive.

The first step in improving your ability to get your needs met is to *know the difference between nonassertive, aggressive, and assertive responses.* **Nonassertiveness** is a dysfunctional behavior in which individuals do not stand up for their rights when those rights are infringed upon. It is "self-denying, generates anxiety and negative feelings toward oneself and others, and leads to strained interpersonal relations." **Aggressiveness** is a dysfunctional behavior in which individuals ignore the rights of others by using offensive and hostile behaviors. It "generates negative feelings—such as guilt, remorse, fear of consequences, and alienation—causes constant confrontation with others, and leads to shallow emotional ties." **Assertiveness** is "standing up for one's own rights, without infringing upon the rights of others. It is adaptive behavior because it is functional in a given context, is self-enhancing, generates positive feelings toward oneself and others, and leads to smooth interpersonal relations."[44]

Suppose Elisa borrowed Jodi's notes and did not return them as promised. Now Jodi needs them and wants Elisa to bring them to her. Elisa is busy and says she'll do it tomorrow. A nonassertive response would be, "I really need them tonight. If it's too much trouble, I guess I can take the bus over to your house and pick them up." An aggressive response would be, "Elisa, I'm sick and tired of your thoughtlessness. This behavior is so typical of you. Just don't expect me to ever do you a favor again. In fact, don't bother to talk to me again." An assertive response would be, "Tomorrow will be too late. I've set aside time to study tonight. I know you're busy, but I'm sure you can spare the half-hour it will take to drive over. I'll expect them by seven."

To improve your ability to achieve goals, take time to *examine your attitudes toward your own and others' rights.* The key to assertiveness is standing up for your rights without violating those of others. It takes some thought to find the ideal balance point between self-respect and respect for others, especially when rights come into conflict. If you're not sure whether you are overstepping your rights or selling yourself short, talk it over with a friend.

Talking with a friend brings us to another way of becoming more comfortable with assertive behavior: *Get feedback about your behavior.* One way to judge your behavior is to try to look at it from the outside. If, for example, you are in a restaurant where the service is terrible, and you're not sure whether to complain, ask yourself what a reasonable person would do in the situation. If you agree that a reasonable person would complain, then go ahead. You can also get feedback by directly asking others. If an employee has come in late for the third time in a week, you can check your behavior by asking a friend to listen to what you intend to say and evaluate its assertiveness. You can even get feedback from your employee. "I'd like you to make sure you get here by eight. When you're late, it inconveniences the rest of us, because we have to wait to get into the office. Do you think this is an unreasonable demand?"

If assertiveness is something you'd really like to work on, *consider keeping a diary in which you record responses to problem situations.* If you decide to keep a diary, record what triggered the situation, how you felt, what you actually said or did, and what you would like to have done. The written record should provide you with a clearer idea of situations that cause you problems, and by writing down what you wish you'd said, you can practice assertive behaviors. In addition to writing down appropriate responses, you can actually *rehearse correct responses by role-playing them*. Unfamiliar responses are more difficult than those that are familiar. If you're not used to being assertive, you need to rehearse until assertive responses become natural. And when you do handle a situation just as you wanted to, *give yourself self-reinforcement*. Congratulate yourself, let a friend know what you did, or even give yourself a treat. You've mastered a new skill and you deserve to be rewarded.

Finally, *know that sometimes you may choose not to be assertive*. Not everyone is reasonable, and not everyone will respond appropriately to your decision to be assertive. Sometimes you may decide not to be assertive. Harold Dawley and W. W. Wenrich tell us

> the governing factor in your decision should be the evaluation of the seriousness of the potentially negative consequences of your assertive behavior. If in a particular situation you believe that the liabilities of an assertive act far outweigh the possible rewards, you may choose—and wisely so—not to assert yourself. But the key word here is "choose."[45]

# Process to Performance

## Review Terms

The following is a list of major concepts introduced in this chapter. The page where the concept is first mentioned is listed in parentheses.

influence (228)
directives (228)
persuasion (228)
compliance-seeking behaviors (228)
persuadables (229)
instrumental issue (229)
relational issue (229)
identity issue (230)
positive face (231)
negative face (231)

psychological reactance (231)
role-taking (231)
learning theory (232)
stimulus (232)
response (232)
classical conditioning (232)
unconditioned stimulus (232)
unconditioned response (232)
conditioned stimulus (232)
conditioned response (232)
luncheon technique (234)
operant conditioning (236)
reinforcements (236)
social reinforcer (236)
social learning theory (237)
modeling (237)
self-reinforcement (237)
social exchange theory (237)
relational currencies (237)
consistency theories (238)
cognitive dissonance theory (238)
dissonance (238)
denial (238)
bolstering (238)
differentiating (238)
transcendence (239)
modifying (239)
communicating (239)
commitment (239)
foot-in-the-door technique (240)
value theory (240)
reward power (244)
coercive power (244)
expert power (245)
referent power (245)
legitimate power (245)
ingratiation (245)
intimidation (245)
self-promotion (245)
exemplification (246)
supplication (246)
cognitive response theory (247)
compliance-seeking research (249)
direct request (249)
hinting (249)
bargaining (249)

## Suggested Readings

Gass, Robert H., and John S. Seiter. *Persuasion, Social Influence, and Compliance Gaining.* Boston: Allyn & Bacon, 2003. This popular text gives a comprehensive overview of theories of influence.

Pratkanis, Anthony, and Elliot Aronson. *Age of Propaganda.* New York: Owl Books, 2001. The authors investigate the tactics that people use to get us to comply, why they work, and how we can combat them.

## Topics for Discussion

www.oup.com/us/trenholm

## Observation Guide

1. Schools are in the business of influencing people. What are some of the ways the institution you now attend tries to influence you? How did they get you to come? How do they control you once you're here? How will they affect you once you are an alumnus? Don't forget things like architecture and interior design of dorms and classrooms, layout of campus, college handbooks and advertising materials, peer influences, course selection, and so on. How successful is this influence?

2. Analyze your own power. When you want others to do things, how do you go about it?

What bases do you use? How could you improve and increase your power bases? Outline a plan to become more powerful.

3. Observe people you know who are ingratiators, intimidators, self-promoters, exemplifiers, and/or supplicators. Describe in detail how they go about achieving power. Describe your feelings about them. Do you find yourself using any of these techniques? What is the outcome?

## Exercises

1. Bring a number of popular magazines containing advertisements to class. Form small groups and look through the magazines to find examples of each theory of influence. Keep looking until you have uncovered uses of learning theories, consistency theories, and value theory. A single ad or article may use several theories at the same time. Once you have found examples, report to the class. Which of all the examples do you think was the most effective? Why?

2. Form groups of four or five. You have just been hired to mount a campaign to improve the image of the city of Mudville. Think of the worst city you can imagine; Mudville is at least that bad. Its civic leaders have decided to try to improve the morale of its citizens and the image it projects to the rest of the world. Your group is to come up with a public relations campaign. Report your plan to the rest of the class, explaining the theories behind each technique. (Make up any information about Mudville itself that you feel you need.)

3. Choose a partner. Individually rank the terminal and instrumental values given in Table 9.1. Give a rank of 1 to the value most important to you personally, a rank of 2 to the second most important value, and so on. Once you have finished, think about what these rankings say about you. Are you altruistic or egoistic? A realist or an idealist? Discuss your rankings with your partner. Explain why you feel the way you do. (This is also a good exercise to do with people who are close to you. It will allow you to examine one another's value structures.)

4. Work in dyads. Each member should think of three situations in which a message has to be delivered that is a potential threat to face. Exchange situations. Each person should think of two ways of delivering the message: one in which both positive and negative face are threatened, the other in which the speaker delivers the message in a way that saves both positive and negative face. Once you're done, discuss your answers with one another. If time permits, discuss situations in which you felt your own face was threatened and how you felt.

# PART 4

# Relational Contexts

The family, while consisting of individual
members, is far more than the sum of its parts.

Honore D. Sharrer, *Tribute to the American
Working People*, 1951

## CHAPTER 10

# Family Interaction Patterns

*We are a family that has always been very close in spirit. Our father was drowned in a sailing accident when we were young, and our mother has always stressed the fact that our familial relationships have a kind of permanence that we will never meet with again. I don't think about the family much, but when I remember its members and the coast where they lived and the sea salt that I think is in our blood, I am happy to recall that I am a Pommeroy—that I have the nose, the coloring, and the promise of longevity—and that while we are not a distinguished family, we enjoy the illusion, when we are together, that the Pommeroys are unique. I don't say any of this because I'm interested in family history or because this sense of uniqueness is deep or important to me but in order to advance the point that we are loyal to one another in spite of our differences, and that any rupture in this loyalty is a source of confusion and pain.*[1]

So begins John Cheever's short story "Good-bye, My Brother." This description of the fic-tional Pommeroy family is striking in its por-trayal of the mixed emotions of family life. Here is a man who views his family as close, perma-nently bonded, and loyal. At the same time, he admits it is undistinguished, built on illusion, and not a frequent subject of his thoughts.

Families are indeed a varied lot. They can be as quiet and inconspicuous as the Pommeroys or as public and powerful as the Kennedys. Even people who have no shared bloodlines often consider themselves family. Organizations as varied as churches, clubs, even businesses de-scribe themselves as "one big happy family." Politicians haggle over whose party best repre-sents "traditional family values."

From the perspective of this book, the family is a social construction, both a product of com-munication and a context in which communica-tion takes place. In fact, it is one of the richest sources of communication patterns that we have. In order to better understand the impact the family has on our communication, in this chap-ter we'll examine the family as a system, its his-torical evolution, and some of the communica-tion patterns found within the family system.

*Being part of a family—even a troubled one—can provide us with a sense of stability in a changing world.*

## Maintaining Family Ties

As you read this chapter, you may find yourself looking for some magic formula, some specific set of communication patterns or skills that will enable you and your family to reach the zenith of family life. You should know by now that you won't encounter any such formula in this book. The interpersonal communication patterns that lead to success or failure are many, and their creation and variety should be a source of celebration as much as sorrow. In fact, many family therapists and researchers agree that the myth of the "ideal family" is a problem in itself.[2]

What is the myth? You probably know it well. The ideal family inhabits a home where stress rarely occurs. Members of the family can and do talk to one another about almost anything, regardless of differences in age, sex, or viewpoint. They smile comfortably at one another even when they disagree. They don't yell or scream. They hug a lot. They listen to one another with ears pricked for maximum reception—something

an expert might call "total listening." They frequently sit and look at one another for long periods of time—just thrilled to be a family unit. They indulge in practical jokes and other forms of good, clean fun. In short, they play, pray, stay, say "hey," and are A-OK together.

So maybe we exaggerate a little. But the fact is that "normal" families don't always get along. They have built-in differences in perspective and conflicts of interest. There are typical stages in family life that produce crisis points. Outside interests of family members and socioeconomic changes require adaptation and change by the family as a unit. Yet for all the difficulties any family must face, it is perhaps the best-equipped social unit in society. Families are conservative by nature, providing a buffer between a rapidly changing society and the individual's need to maintain a stable identity. The family, even a troubled one, can provide a sense of permanence in an otherwise changing world. The family is our first "social reality" and the source of many of the communication patterns and types of relationships we will repeat later in life. Virginia Satir has characterized the family as a "factory" where different kinds of people are made.[3] It is the family as a factory that we wish to investigate here.

As a producer of persons, communication patterns, relationships, and other social realities, any family can be judged as doing its job very well or quite poorly. In some cases the results may appear to speak for themselves, as when one family turns out several productive citizens while another family consistently produces social deviants. In most cases the results are mixed, and many other socioenvironmental factors have to be considered. Rather than identify any one "ideal" family type, this chapter will describe the family as a system of elements that operate together, producing communication patterns that enable its members to either adapt to, or resist, outside influences and typical crises within the family system. Once you understand the processes underlying family interaction, you should be a better judge of your family of origin (the family that produced you) as well as any family you help produce in the future. In fact, once you understand the patterns of interaction that were forged in the family you grew up with, you may be surprised to find yourself repeating many of those same patterns in your current intimate relationships (see Chapter 11). Let's begin by looking at the system of relationships we call a "family."

# The Family as a System: Structure and Function

Scholars differ on the precise definition of what a family is. Some prefer to emphasize the traditional values of our culture and define the family in terms of marriage and biological kinship. We prefer to use a somewhat broader definition that includes groups of people who think of themselves as "family" even though they may not be related by blood or marriage. Kathleen Galvin and Bernard Brommel define the **family** as "a network of people who live together over long periods of time bound by ties of marriage, blood, or commitment, legal or otherwise."[4]

Social scientists are fond of describing families as "systems" because this metaphor draws our attention to how some members of an organized unit are affected by changes in one or more of the other parts of the system. Like most human systems, a family can be seen as a relatively organized collection of interdependent parts (e.g., mom, stepdad, brother, sister, baby, and wacky aunt) that act together as a whole unit.

Family rules and interactions may be observed at the level of the whole unit ("As a family, we always had a big Sunday dinner at Grandma's—she was the only one with place settings for 24") or at the level of one of its many subsystems ("Annie and Chris always fought over whose turn it was to do the dishes"). **Subsystems** may vary from the husband-wife, parent-child, or brother-sister dyad to tempo-

rary coalitions formed by one group of family members against another.

Something to remember about a family as a system is that each family member is one of its parts. And even though each part is a unique individual, he or she is also a functioning component of the whole system. As in any mechanical system, there must be some working order among the individual parts. In a human system we would call the working order between any two parts their "relationship." The various working orders developed by the entire family could be called the **family structure.** The structure of the family keeps it functioning smoothly, coordinating the efforts of its various subsystems. The family system can also be analyzed in terms of its **family functions,** that is, the services it provides for its members and the society at large. The most obvious functions of a family are to provide socialization, food and shelter, and emotional support for its members. For society, the family serves as a major means of passing on cultural beliefs to succeeding generations.

Finally, every human system goes through a process of **evolution.** No family system remains static. The evolution of the system refers to how the family adapts to the developmental changes and personal needs of its members as well as to the changing social and economic needs of the culture. We will look at each of these aspects of the family system in turn.

## Family Structures

A family may have as many different structures as it has events or issues to deal with. There may be a power-authority structure for dealing with family discipline problems, a decision-making structure for determining how the family will manage impending changes or make use of its free time, and perhaps an interaction network that indicates which family members are more likely to talk to one another about problems, share secrets, or form coalitions in order to increase their influence. In each of these structures family members play different roles and relate to other family members in unique ways. These roles and relationships are built up as members repeat patterned episodes of communication.

### Power-Authority Structure

Each of us learns a great deal about how to handle and express authority by observing how it worked in our own family. Ronald Cromwell and David Olson define **power** in the family as the "ability (potential or actual) to change the behavior of other family members."[5] In most families power is legitimately held by one or both parents. Parents are allowed to discipline their children, but not vice versa. However, as most parents know, children quickly develop their own power bases. Little Johnny knows that putting on his "cute face" will usually make his father laugh rather than punish him, and he also knows that crying will wear his mother down until she allows him to have some ice cream.

Some families establish very clear lines of authority, others allow individual members to determine how much influence they want to exert. Basil Bernstein refers to the first type of family as having a **positional structure;** the second type he calls a **person-oriented structure.**[6] In a positional family, lines of authority are hierarchically arranged. In a traditional family, power may ultimately rest with the father. In his absence the mother takes charge, and in her absence temporary power is passed on to the oldest child, and so on. Some research indicates that positional families make greater use of restricted language codes (see Chapter 4). In other words, there are limited opportunities for children to verbalize their own opinions, since they don't have much influence. Person-oriented families, on the other hand, rely to a much greater extent on communication as a means of influence. All members of the family are usually allowed to state their opinions and to defend or explain their actions prior to any discipline. As a result, these families teach their children to use elaborated language codes, a skill that enables them to adapt to a wider variety of social circles. Not every family can be labeled as positional or person-oriented. Bernstein describes the two types as being at opposite ends of a spectrum. Your family probably falls somewhere in between. Later in this chapter we will find out how a family's authority structure influences the development of a child's cognitive and communicative abilities.

### Decision-Making Structure

In some families the power and decision-making structures may be almost identical. This would be the case if the parents make all of the family decisions, set the rules, and are the only ones who enforce them. In person-oriented families, however, a variety of **decision-making structures** are possible since children are allowed greater opportunities to influence one another and their parents. In any given person-oriented family, a more verbal and expressive child or spouse may play a larger role in decision making than less verbal members.

As part of its decision-making structure, a family is likely to develop a particular decision-making style or use a different style to handle different kinds of decisions. Ralph Turner has identified three common family decision-making styles: consensus, accommodation, and de facto.[7] Perhaps one of them fits your family. The least common, but most admirable, style of decision making is **consensus.** A family reaches consensus when its members try to make a unanimous decision, seeking input from all members, negotiating differences of opinion or values, and finding a solution that everyone feels is satisfactory. This method requires a great deal more talk than the other two styles. In many cases true agreement among family members is an almost impossible task. However, the process of trying to reach consensus may well be more important than the actual outcome.

A more common style of decision making is **accommodation,** a process in which less articulate or less dominating members of the family give in to those who hold the power or are more persistent. Decision by vote is a form of accommodation. Turner suggests that members usually accommodate because they don't see the value of further discussion. They see the "handwriting on the wall" and figure it isn't worth their time to argue when others leave no room for negotiation. In the long run this style may have a negative impact on family life, especially if the same few members are allowed to dominate decision making and "discussion" becomes a meaningless term. Using this style also tends to avoid conflict, which means that problems may not be aired and tensions may resurface more often. However, this need not always be the case. An accommodating style can be managed successfully if everyone gives in on occasion, so that each family member has a sense of being able to influence the rest of the family when an issue is important to him or her.

When neither of the first two methods works, many families resort to de facto decision making. A **de facto decision** is one in which a single member of the family acts alone or the matter is decided by events, usually after a period of unproductive discussion. A typical example of this style occurs on family trips. A 20-minute discussion about where to stop for lunch seems to be resolving nothing. After passing a dozen fast-food restaurants, the driver finally pulls over in exasperation: "We're eating here!" Or a sign along the interstate warning "Last services for 50 miles" makes the decision for them.

No doubt one of these styles characterizes the way most families make decisions, yet you may find that your family has one or more unique patterns of communication when making decisions. If you can describe that pattern and its outcomes (who it favors, how satisfactory it is to most family members, and, most important, what quality of decisions it produces), you will be in a better position to understand and change the process when necessary.

### Interaction Structure

Another way to look at the structure of the family is to describe the communication channels that are most frequently used within it. Some family members may spend more time with one another; some may talk to one another more than they do to other family members. The typical patterns of interaction within a family (who talks to whom most frequently) are its **communication network.** The structure of family networks may vary a great deal. A family with a *centralized* network has a single member who interacts a great deal with all the members and may or may not pass information along to the rest of the family. This central member acts as a go-between, keeping family members in touch even though they may not actually speak to one another very often. In an extended family a parent or grandparent may play this role. Sons and daughters living away from home may phone their parents rather than one another, since they know they'll find out what's happening that way.

Families that are highly cohesive tend to reflect a decentralized network, one in which frequent interaction is likely to occur among all or most family members. Extended families of this type may have large phone bills, since everyone wants to hear the news from the source. When something exciting happens to one member, he or she shares it with everybody, not just the central figure.

Look at the diagrams of different communication networks in Figure 10.1 and see which one best represents your own family network. In fact, your family may have more than one network. Many families alter their communication patterns in order to deal with different situations or events. Since individuals have different likes and dislikes, one or more members may be automatically left out of the network when certain types of information are being exchanged. The prudish sister who thinks gossip is a form of evil is more likely to be the subject of the family rumor mill and less likely to hear about it. The brother who eschews sports is not included in the summer-long discussions of the pennant race, even though he may often be within earshot of those discussions. Younger children, especially, are often told to go outside and play when a family problem has to be dealt with. They are not yet a part of the problem-solving network.

Let's take a look at some of the structures we've been talking about in a hypothetical family,

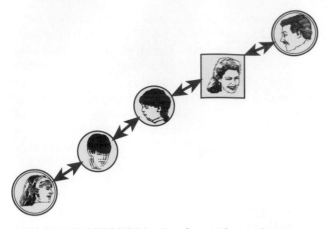

THE CHAIN NETWORK. *Family members relay messages to one another via a series of other family members. It is typically used when members see each other occasionally but are rarely all together at once. Messages are, however, prone to distortion as they are passed along.*

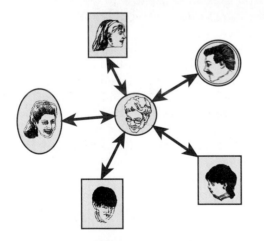

THE WHEEL NETWORK. *A highly centralized network found in families that communicate through one key figure. Most members do not talk directly to one another. They find out about each other from the central figure.*

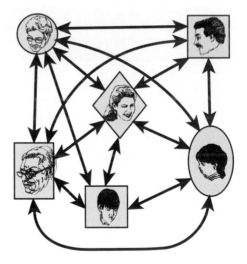

THE ALL-CHANNEL NETWORK. *The most decentralized network of all. It is characteristic of families that spend a lot of time together as a unit and in separate dyads. All or most of the communication channels are open and utilized.*

**FIGURE 10.1** *Three family communication networks.*

the Clicks. At the simplest level the family role structure consists of a father (Bic, age 38), a mother (Barbara, age 36), an elder daughter (Brenda, age 15), a middle son (Buck, age 12), and the "baby" (Binky, age 6). The power structure in this family is a positional one, with the father and mother having the most influence, followed by Brenda, with less influence exerted by Buck and Binky. Although no one has ever stated the power structure, the children "know" that Mother is more likely to enforce rules regarding table manners and foul language, whereas Father makes sure everyone does assigned chores. In the parents' absence Brenda is allowed to enforce rules, but she cannot actually punish her brothers.

The decision-making structure is a little different. When important decisions are made, such as where to go on vacation, everyone gets to make a pitch for where he or she would like to go. Buck has developed the habit of researching his places of interest (this year he wants to visit several historical museums and see a Red Sox game), so he is often more persuasive than his brother and sister. Although the parents tend to rule out some places because of expense or distance, a family decision is usually reached by majority vote. Most family decisions are made this way. (This decision style reflects a mix of consensus and accommodation.)

Finally, the interaction structure in the Click family is an interesting one. Brenda is very close to her father, primarily because she's interested in his work as a race car mechanic. She's always asking him questions about how things work. She's also very protective of Binky and hates Buck's guts. Buck is the isolate in the family. He reads a lot about history and loves baseball. He talks extensively about his interests, but not to anyone in particular. If pressed, he would say he gets along with Binky better than anyone else in the family. Binky is his mother's favorite. They frequently form a coalition in the family decision-making process. The three Click family structures are depicted in Figure 10.2.

The structured relations of the Click family are not necessarily typical of most families.

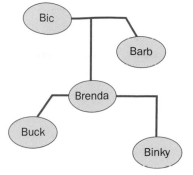

**a. Power–Authority Structure**

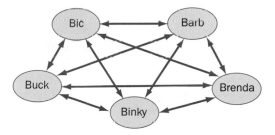

**b. Decision-making Structure**

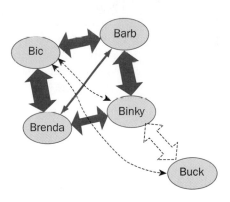

**c. Interaction Structure**

FIGURE 10.2  *Three family structures—the Click family.*

Every family establishes its own patterns and means for handling recurring situations. You may want to analyze your own family's structures and see whether they've changed since you were younger.

## Characteristics of Family Structures

Family structures evolve over time as family members establish and repeat patterns of interaction. These structures have a number of characteristics in common, including the differentiation of members into roles, the creation and maintenance of boundaries, and the coordination of subsystems.

*Role Differentiation.* In a given family structure, members perform different tasks in relation to one another. In an efficient family structure these roles are complementary. When a parent disciplines, a child is supposed to obey. This ideal isn't always achieved, of course, but the system won't function very well if the ideal is rarely achieved. Tension often arises in families when two members compete for the same roles, as when one parent intentionally counteracts the authority of the other: "I don't care what your mother said, you can't go!" The point here is that there must be enough complementarity of roles for the system to function, yet not so much specialization of roles that the family cannot adapt to the absence of the member who usually plays a particular role.

*Boundaries.* According to Salvador Minuchin, a noted family therapist, a family must establish and maintain clear boundaries among its members and between itself and the outside world. The **boundaries** of a subsystem consist of "rules defining who participates and how."[8] Inside the family there are often physical boundaries such as separate bedrooms, toys, or clothing, and corresponding rules for who is allowed to enter such spaces and play with or wear such belongings. Parents may even impose boundaries on themselves to give their children room to breathe or grow or simply to avoid being overwhelmed by

demands. Not interfering as two younger children settle their own dispute or telling them "I can't help you out—you'll have to solve this problem yourselves" is an example of setting boundaries. It says, in essence, "No adults allowed."

Likewise, families may regulate the extent to which the outside world is allowed to penetrate the family's day-to-day world. David Kantor and William Lehr identified three basic types of families that differed largely in how they deal with the society at large.[9] An **open family** is one that encourages its members to experience a wide variety of social life and then share those experiences with the rest of the family, providing a constant source of new ideas. This kind of family adapts to changes in the culture and is typified by the prototypic parent/chauffeur rushing children off to dance class, piano lessons, baseball practice, and the movies before taking in an adult education course at the local community college. The boundaries between family life and the rest of life are quite flexible, each influencing the other.

A **closed family** reacts to the larger society with a little more suspicion or indifference. "The family that plays together stays together" is a maxim that expresses the values of the closed family. Many outside activities are restricted or participation is monitored very closely by the authority figures in the family. At any rate, family always comes first in relation to outside activities. Boundaries are often reflected in different sets of rules—one for appropriate behavior with family members, another for behavior in the presence of strangers.

In contrast to the close-knit relations and high degree of sharing in both open and closed families, the third type of family is much more independent and unpredictable. This type may go months without much interaction among family members and then suddenly spend the next three weeks in constant companionship. Plans for a family get-together may be made and then changed several times because of the fluctuating interests of family members. Because life is so unpredictable in such a family, Kantor and Lehr called it a **random family.** The boundaries in random families are not very clearly drawn and may be a frequent source of misunderstanding and dispute.

Minuchin describes the boundaries of a family system along a continuum that ranges from "enmeshed" at one end to "disengaged" at the other extreme.[10] An **enmeshed system** is one that sacrifices the autonomy of its members in order to experience a great deal of cohesion. Family members feel close to one another, but the family doesn't develop clear boundaries around each person's identity. As a result, privacy and independent thinking are discouraged. A **disengaged system,** on the other hand, promotes independence at the risk of not developing a sense of family loyalty. The boundaries around individual subsystems are too rigid, and in the extreme case members are unable to provide each other with social support. It is important to remember that these boundaries may be true of the family as a whole or that individual subsystems in the family may be enmeshed or disengaged. In stepfamilies, boundary issues can be especially confusing, as the research described in this chapter's Research in Review section demonstrates.

*Coordination of Subsystems.* In one sense, family life isn't much different from life in the corporate world. This is especially true of a large or extended family. Just as businesses are organized around teams of individual employees with different skills trying to coordinate their efforts to produce a product, so a family unit is organized into subsystems of individuals whose efforts must be coordinated in order to produce its products (reasonable facsimiles of persons, values, chores, and so on). Later in this chapter we'll look at the typical communication patterns of the various family subsystems. For now, it is important to realize that these subsystems do overlap and have to be coordinated. The husband-wife dyad cannot act in isolation. Whatever spouses do as husband and wife will also influence their roles in the parent-child subsystems they are a part of. A prime example of this is reflected in the tension many parents feel about both spouses working and being away from their children. While the parents may be convinced that they need the money, they may be equally concerned about how the children will handle (and interpret) being left alone or with a sitter. Careful explanation may be necessary in order to enable these subsystems to adapt to the change without damaging the more permanent family relationship.

## The Functions of the Family

The structured relationships that emerge through repeated episodes of communication do so for a number of reasons. When we examine the reasons for these communication patterns, we are really asking what their function or purpose is within the family unit. Communication within the family works in two very broad ways: (1) Internal functions keep the system running and serve the individuals who make up the family unit; (2) external functions or services are provided to the larger society. We shall look at each of these in turn.

### *Internal Functions*

Families provide such basic necessities as shelter, warmth, and care. In addition, the family may also fulfill the following psychosocial functions: socialization, intellectual development, recreation, and emotional support.

*Providing Care.* The human infant is one of the most helpless creatures on the face of the earth. Unable to provide for himself, he exists in an extended state of dependence on adults. Thus, the most basic needs such as food, shelter, clothing, and caretaking become the first function that the family fulfills. This function has the status of moral, if not legal, obligation in most societies. In the United States the courts may take a child away from his parents if he is not adequately cared for.

*Socialization.* Beyond simple provisions, the family is also one of the primary teachers of what

## "You're My Parent but You're Not"
# Dialectics in Stepfamily Communication

Stepfamilies are complex. Not only do they consist of the currently married couple and the children who live with them, but they also include the ex-husband or wife and extended family members. As Dawn Braithwaite and Leslie Baxter point out in "'You're My Parent but You're Not,'" the nonresidential parent is a very real presence in the family. To the children, in particular, the nonresidential parent is "a presence-and-absence" that makes family communication difficult.

Using the relational dialectic approach discussed in Chapter 2, Braithwaite and Baxter set out to identify the contradictions inherent in communication between college-age stepchildren and their nonresidential parent. Using a semi-structured, focused interview, their research team interviewed 50 college-age stepchildren about communication in their stepfamilies. After supplying descriptive information, the respondents told a story about typical communication and discussed the story with the interviewer. They then described challenging aspects of communication with their parents.

Braithwaite and Baxter found that two contradictions were central to the experiences of the students. The first dealt with parenting. On one hand, the students wanted their nonresidential parent to be actively involved in parenting; on the other, they resisted it either because they found it too disruptive of their daily lives, because it caused conflict and dual loyalties, or, if the nonresidential parent sided with the stepparent, because it created an adult coalition against the child.

Closely connected was a second contradiction focusing on openness. The students expressed a desire for intimate communication, but, at the same time, found it difficult to talk to the nonresidential parent. Sometimes this difficulty was because the absent parent was unfamiliar with the child's everyday life. At other times open communication was resisted in order to avoid hurt feelings or angry or jealous responses. Overwhelmingly, the respondents handled this dialectical tension by segmentation: being open about some topics but closed about others.

The authors point out that the two contradictions identified in this research "form a totality, or knot of interdependence." In choosing to be closed about some topics, the students limited the amount of parenting that could take place. In being open, they gave up their freedom. They feel that the contradictory nature of this kind of communication should stand as a warning to separated adults who are coparenting children to listen carefully to their children and to encourage and support them as they work out these dialectics. Simple advice like encouraging the child to talk more openly may be adding to, not alleviating, problems.

Braithwaite, Dawn O., and Leslie A. Baxter. "'You're My Parent but You're Not': Dialectical Tensions in Stepchildren's Perceptions About Communicating with the Nonresidential Parent." *Journal of Applied Communication Research* 34, no. 1 (2006): 30–48.

it means to be human, male or female, moral or immoral, polite or impolite. As children we learn what sort of behavior is deemed appropriate for boys and girls as a result of the sexual stereotypes provided by our family. The results of socialization are so ingrained that by the time we are near adulthood, many of our patterns of thought and behavior seem "natural" to us and are hard to change. A child who is socialized to be patriotic may have a hard time understanding how anyone could not show respect for our national symbols. We have a friend whose mother required her children to stand at attention every time they heard the national anthem, regardless of whether they were at a parade or watching a baseball game on TV. Many of us have been socialized in similar ways.

*Intellectual Development.* Many parents spend a great deal of time, money, and anxiety to make sure that their children have ample opportunity and rewards for academic achievement. The learning environment is loaded with educational toys, magazines, and special cable TV selections. Communication often takes the form of reciting the ABCs, counting, or responding to a battery of questions: "What's your name? How do you spell it? Where do you live? What's your phone number?" Kindergarten is preceded by educational day care, and so on. At the other extreme, many parents neglect early intellectual development, hoping the schools will do the job later on. Or they openly reject it, saying things like "I hope my child doesn't grow up to be smart. Who needs it?"

*Recreation.* Play is one of the major forms of childhood activity. Every family has its own repertoire of family games and traditions. Not every family plays together, but they can find ways to just "do nothing" together, which is essentially what the recreation function is all about.

*Emotional Support.* Probably the most important of the internal functions is the ability of the family to provide a sense of belonging—love, affection, kinship, companionship, acceptance, and inner resolve. This is especially important in terms of individual self-esteem, in which the strength drawn from the family serves as a springboard for confidence in dealing with the external world.

A number of social critics have lamented the fact that many of the functions once provided primarily by the family are now being taken over by the larger society (child care, schools, nursing homes, and so on). Christopher Lasch argues that, as a result, we expect the family to be primarily a refuge of emotional support.[11] Such an overemphasis on any one function may be asking too much of the system.

### External Functions

The family serves the culture as much as it serves its individual members, in two primary ways: (1) passing cultural values to its younger members and (2) accommodating cultural change.

*Transmission.* The family is the first and perhaps the most important transmitter of cultural values from generation to generation. Parents relay the cultural myths and guidelines they learned when they were young by reading the same stories, legends, and fairy tales to their children. They perform the same function when they reinforce the values their children glean from television. Many people overestimate the influence of TV programs on young children and underestimate parents' ability to influence how children interpret what they see and hear. Parents play a vital role in this process. The attitudes and values that children hold are directly related to those of their parents, at least early in life and usually for much longer.

Straw polls taken in fourth-grade classrooms invariably show that children vote for the same presidential candidates as their parents. Parents are the ultimate authorities from a child's perspective, and the ultimate message from parents to children is how to belong to their own social circles and the larger culture. Every culture

BOX 10.1

### A Better Place to Live

# How the Built Environment Shapes Family and Community Life

Winston Churchill reportedly said, "We shape our buildings and then they shape us." Social scientists have for some time documented the effects of overcrowded homes, the lack of privacy, the aesthetic design of rooms, lighting, decor, and many other features of the environment on human perception and behavior. And now, architects are beginning to take seriously the design of neighborhoods that foster interaction among members of a community. Given what we know about the mutual influence of people and their environment, it's surprising that we don't exercise more control in shaping the homes and communities that shape us.

In *A Better Place to Live*, author Philip Langdon has chronicled what is wrong with the design of typical American suburbs and what a handful of architects and developers are doing about it. Langdon argues that suburban living not only has contaminated the environment (e.g., excessive automobile emissions), but has also been bad for us as individuals and as communities. The suburban mode of life fragments people and communities because it separates where we live from where we work, shop, and play. It also raises the cost of living unnecessarily. The average two-car family must work three months—

after taxes—just to support its annual automobile expenses. Furthermore, most suburbs are exclusively residential, with few parks or other public places where people can congregate and interact. Grocery stores and other daily amenities are generally located well beyond walking distance on congested commercial strips. The overall effect is that most suburbs are not inviting enough for people to make a permanent commitment to live in them. High turnover results as nearly one-fifth of Americans change their address each year. It is no wonder that people are reluctant to develop relationships with transient neighbors. The lack of socialization within a community can lead to a sense of isolation, which erodes mental stability (Etzioni, 1991) and places additional strain on marriage partners who have no one to turn to but themselves to satisfy their varied social needs.

For the past decade, architects Andres Duany and Elizabeth Plater-Zyberk have been designing new urban communities along the lines of the 19th-century small town. They call on city governments and town planners to follow several principles of neighborhood design that will encourage social interaction and turn neighborhoods into safe, full-functioning communities:

- Each neighborhood should have an identifiable center that will attract people and a well-defined set of boundaries that enable people to identify "the neighborhood" without totally separating them from other neighborhoods.

- The neighborhood should be small enough (a quarter to half-mile radius) for people to walk from the center to the edge in 5–10 minutes. (A neighborhood that is walkable promotes interaction and gives people a sense of ownership.)

- It should contain a mixture of different sizes, prices, and types of housing to accommodate people of different income levels and different stages of life. Houses should be in proximity to one another (on relatively small lots). This enables a wider range of diversity and fulfills developer Henry Turley's admonition that "democracy assumes—no demands—that we know, understand, and respect our fellow citizens."

- Each neighborhood should have a network of interconnected streets and sidewalks that make it easy to get from one place to another without getting lost or feeling fearful. Duany and Plater-Zyberk argue that streets should be seen as outdoor "public rooms" so people can enjoy spending time in them. To make the streets more amenable to humans, garages would be moved to the back of the lot, making them accessible from alleyways.

- Each neighborhood should have a number of "civic" buildings (a meeting hall, a church, a school, a day care center, etc.) where people can congregate.

- The best neighborhoods should also have what sociologist Ray Oldenburg calls "third places" (cafés, pubs, beauty parlors, etc.) where people can socialize without feeling compelled to invite others home with them.

- More small businesses should locate within or near neighborhoods so people can work close to home. Alternatively, larger corporations should continue the trend of allowing many employees to telecommute from their own home.

These principles are being applied in towns and cities across the country. Seaside, Florida, is one example of a walkable community. Most of its streets are a narrow 18 feet wide and paved with a brick-like material that forces motorists to slow down. Every house has a generous front porch and is located close enough to the sidewalk to encourage small talk with passersby. Streets are laid out in a grid pattern, but are anything but dull-looking. Langdon describes them as "visual knockouts" because of the narrow, steepled houses that line them and the frequent pavilions, gazebos, and sculptures that break up the flow. Charleston Place in Boca Raton, Florida, has garden courts and brick walkways with rose-covered walls between backyards. Its "outdoor public rooms" are so inviting that residents can be seen outside on every block during the evening hours.

Communities designed for interpersonal communication ultimately support family life by providing safer neighborhoods and a wide-ranging support system. When parents and children feel less isolated from the social world around them, they may not have to solve all their problems within the confines of the home—and who knows—they may be a bit less likely to get on each other's nerves.

SOURCE  Philip Langdon, *A Better Place to Live: Reshaping the American Suburb* (Amherst: University of Massachusetts Press, 1994).

**ADDITIONAL READINGS**

Etzioni, Amitai. *A Responsive Society: Collected Essays on Guiding Deliberate Social Change.* San Francisco: Jossey-Bass Publishers, 1991.

Lappé, Frances Moore, and Paul Martin DuBois. *The Quickening of America: Rebuilding Our Nation, Remaking Our Lives.* San Francisco: Jossey-Bass Publishers, 1994.

Oldenburg, Ray. *The Great Good Place: Cafés, Coffee Shops, Community Centers, Beauty Parlors, General Stores, Bars, Hangouts, and How They Get You Through the Day.* New York: Paragon House, 1991.

teaches its young to be patriotic, to value their own way of life in comparison to other cultures. In our own culture this means that parents must pass on values such as liberty, the pursuit of happiness, and, usually, material wealth, democratic rule, religious freedom, individualism, expansion of horizons, and so on.

*Accommodation.* In addition to the passing on of unchanging cultural values, the family also encourages its members to adapt to many of the changes that any society goes through. Our own culture has undergone major social changes in the last 25 years. The role of women has been redefined, civil rights have been granted, or at least promised, to many minorities, and battles for freedom of sexual preference rage on. But these changes become real only when major social institutions such as the family, the church, and the corporation begin to accommodate them. In the family, old rules about what is women's work or which toys and games boys and girls should play with are gradually replaced. Now is a good time to assess how your own family has or has not adapted to some of these major cultural changes.

On a more mundane level, families ensure cultural change by competing with other families in the pursuit of a more elaborate lifestyle. "Keeping up with the Joneses" is an American middle-class tradition. American technology creates computers and video recorders; American families accommodate by purchasing them and making changes in daily routines and lifestyles so that they get their money's worth. Eventually, these superficial changes may result in changes in one or more family structures. For instance, the child who masters a computer language may be consulted more frequently and earn a more prominent position in the family's decision-making hierarchy.

The degree to which family life is separate from or integrated into a local community also teaches children about their proper roles as citizens. It is significant that much of the social interaction in our neighborhoods has moved from front porch stoops and parlors to family rooms and backyards in the past few decades. Box 10.1 shows how some architects and social planners are rethinking the isolation of American families in the traditional suburb.

# The Evolving Family: Calibrating Change

Families are not static social units. From the time two people decide to marry or start a family, they can expect change to play a major role in their affairs. Some of these changes are highly predictable; others are not. The successful family will be the one that learns to manage the typical stresses and strains of family life. The chances of being successful can be increased by understanding the dynamics of change and by developing some useful coping strategies. Let's look at each of these processes in more detail.

## The Dynamics of Change in the Family

The sources of change in family life are many. Among the most predictable changes are those associated with the family life cycle and stressful contact with outsiders. In addition, there are unpredictable crises such as illness or death, divorce or desertion. Each of these events may cause either a temporary or long-term upheaval in family structures, rules, and the boundaries drawn among family subsystems.

### The Family Life Cycle

Over the years researchers have pieced together the typical stages of the family life cycle. These stages represent the most likely sequence of events in family life. Most scholars would agree with the following seven **life cycle stages** adapted from the work of David Olson and Hamilton McCubbin.[12]

- *Stage 1:* Young married couples without children

- *Stage 2:* Families with preschoolers
- *Stage 3:* Families with school-age children
- *Stage 4:* Families with adolescents
- *Stage 5:* Launching families—sending young adults into the world
- *Stage 6:* The empty nest—life after the children
- *Stage 7:* Retirement years

While each of these stages is highly predictable (assuming a couple does have children), the degree of stress and strain associated with each stage will vary from family to family. The more a young couple anticipates how their life may change with the birth of a first child, the easier the transition may be. Many people now make elaborate plans for retirement; others wait until they "get the golden parachute" before concerning themselves with the inevitable changes. Knowing what's ahead may not make for completely smooth sailing, but it does help one to prepare psychologically for impending changes. Talking about such changes in advance helps a family to negotiate and coordinate the future rather than react to events as they happen.

Perhaps the most significant change in a couple's life is the onset of the first pregnancy. For most people this stage represents the transition to being a family. Researchers have found that even in the most egalitarian of relationships, the birth of the first child engenders a return to more traditional sex roles. In part this is due to the lack of role models for being egalitarian parents—and so we typically fall back on our own parents (who were likely to be traditional mothers and fathers) as role models. In two recent studies couples who defined their relationship as egalitarian and companionate had the greatest difficulty adjusting to the birth of their first child. On the other hand, couples whose relationship already had clear sex-role divisions found the adjustment to be much smoother.[13] In another study J. H. Meyerowitz and H. Feldman found that having a baby tended to improve the relationship between spouses during the early weeks

following birth. After five weeks, 85 percent of couples said things were "going well" in their own relationship. Within four months, however, the percentage dropped to 65 percent. At the same time, many of the husbands had taken on most of the family decision making, and both spouses reported a decline in the amount of time spent talking to each other.[14] Further cementing a return to traditional roles, many women reported that their pregnancy helped them to feel more accepted by their husbands and even their own parents.[15]

Another key transition period in the family life cycle is the "launching period"—when young adult children go away to college, move to their own apartment, or get married and leave home. In most marriages this is a characteristic low point in marital satisfaction, spousal companionship, and consensus on roles within the marriage.[16] One of the most significant factors during this period is the void that departing children create in the family system. Stephen Anderson characterizes the changes with the following example:

> The physical departure of a child whose day-to-day familial role included the regulation of emotional distance in the parents' relationship (for example, misbehavior when marital tension rises, serving as referee during conflicts, or as a coalition partner supporting one parent against another) could precipitate the need for parents to deal more directly with one another or to triangulate another child into the vacated role.[17]

In comparing families in which a child left home for college versus families in which the child stayed home and commuted to a local university, Anderson found that perceptions of the amount of personal communication between spouses actually increased when the child commuted but decreased when the child went away to school.[18] Presumably, this result was due to the continued presence of the son or daughter as an indirect source of communication between parents.

*Family subdivisions, such as those between sisters, can significantly alter other relationships within the family.*

The study of changes in communication patterns across the family life cycle is in its infancy. These initial results suggest that many interesting discoveries await us.

### Stressful Contact with Outside Sources

Just as the family life cycle produces change from within the family unit, so may other factors impose change from the outside. Every family member belongs to numerous groups and social institutions, all of which may produce stress that is brought home. The most obvious of these institutions are the school and the workplace. When a parent loses a job or a child is sent home from school for disciplinary reasons, the effect reverberates throughout the family system. Even more subtle stresses, such as a bad day at the office, may precipitate an argument between the spouses, which may be overheard by a child, who thinks it is her fault that her parents argue. Likewise, an entire family may experience stress from a neighborhood that disapproves of their barking dog or the junkyard appearance of their property.

### Illness or Death of a Family Member

Every family has to anticipate the developmental changes inherent in the family life cycle as well as the impact of everyday contact with the outside world. But other crises such as death, major illness, or handicap are not so predictable. In one sense the crisis stage is inevitable; every family knows it will suffer loss in some form. But few families can prepare themselves in advance for such crises. There is a strong taboo in our society against talking about death. Perhaps it is a tribute to the power of the verbal code. We are afraid of the "magical" aspect of language, that words let loose may somehow escape our control and unleash dark forces.

Our unpreparedness, combined with the emotional pain, makes the family system especially vulnerable during such crises. In addition, the physical loss or diminished capacity of a family member means that the system must change—someone else must function in the roles formerly played by that person. This is rarely an easy adjustment. The loss of a spouse may require that the remaining spouse get a new job, be both mother and father to the children (or, if the children are older, the spouse may become dependent on them), or force the oldest child to take over household and babysitting chores, and so on. Some members of the family may resent anyone who tries to fill the shoes of another ("You're not my mother—you can't replace her!"). In some cases the cohesiveness of the family may suffer, especially if the deceased member was the primary source of affection. In other cases a slightly disengaged family may strengthen its bonds as everyone pulls together to offer reassurance and keep the system functioning.

### Divorce or Separation of Family Members

Another major crisis in family life involves the deterioration, temporary or more permanent, of the relationship between two or more family members. Although the term *divorce* is usually reserved for the termination of a spousal relationship, it could just as easily be applied to any relationship within the family. Two older brothers who have not spoken to each other in years, a runaway child, a son or daughter who marries just to get away from home—all represent a breaking of ties that bind. In each case the crisis requires a readjustment in the family system. Most divorces, especially those involving children, are essentially a matter of redefining relationships rather than a total termination. In today's society, termination of a marriage does not usually result in the termination of parenting roles. Ex-spouses tend to maintain some kind of relationship, even if it is indirect contact where the children serve as the channel for communication. Even so, a recent study shows that few ex-spouses have frequent contact with each other, and what contact there is tends to be less than harmonious. While most ex-spouses agreed that their relationship should be based on norms of politeness, 41 percent of them admitted that they did not treat their ex-spouse as well as they should.[19]

Ex-spouses who have coparenting status rarely talk to one another or about their children. This prompted one researcher to redefine coparenting as "parallel parenting" in which there is little if any consistency in the rules and in disciplining the child from different parents.[20] The lone exception to this trend seems to be in some dual-career families in higher socioeconomic circles.[21] Apparently, in situations where the woman is financially self-sufficient and does not have to rely on the ex-spouse for support, the relationship with the ex-spouse is more harmonious. This allows both parents to put their relationship behind them and concentrate more on their roles as parents.

Is there a predictable pattern that families follow in dealing with unexpected losses such as death or divorce? According to a number of scholars, there is. Kathleen Galvin and Bernard Brommel have synthesized the work of these scholars into four basic **crisis stages**.[22]

- *Stage 1:* Shock resulting in numbness or disbelief, denial
- *Stage 2:* Recoil stage resulting in anger, confusion, blaming, guilt, and bargaining

- *Stage 3:* Depression
- *Stage 4:* Reorganization resulting in acceptance and recovery

These stages are normal, perhaps even necessary, for a successful adaptation to changed circumstances. At each stage communication is crucial, if only for family members to express the emotions of denial, anger, and depression. Obviously, they can express these feelings to one another, but it may also help if their social network of friends and acquaintances lends a supportive ear. Well-meaning friends may avoid the family in their time of grief or distress, cutting off valuable assistance. What should you say in such situations? The best evidence suggests that a simple expression of sympathy and a willingness to listen are the best responses. Knowledge of the typical stages the family is going through should help you to understand (and not judge) what you hear.

## Strategies for Coping with Change

Since nothing is as permanent as change, it is wise to start developing strategies your family can use in managing its own life cycle as well as handling unexpected events.

### Anticipating Change

Everyone develops a basic philosophy or outlook on life. Some people expect their lives to be settled by the time they are 25 or 30. They expect to develop a routine and live that way ever after. Others are frightened by such prospects. While we do not advocate a chaotic lifestyle with no goals, expectations, or ritualistic patterns, we do suggest that you come to terms with the fact that just when you think you've got it all together, a major change is probably right around the corner. One way to improve your forecasting ability is to read extensively about individual and family life cycles. These changes happen to most families, and it is unlikely that yours will be the exception.

### Encouraging Family Cohesiveness

Families that develop and maintain at least a moderate amount of cohesiveness are more likely to survive stressful times than those that become too disengaged. When members lose touch with one another, providing emotional support in crisis situations becomes more difficult. Most families probably think of themselves as having strong bonds simply because they are family. Clichés like "Blood is thicker than water" and "Family comes first" reinforce the cultural stereotype of what it means to be a family. Yet a family needs to exhibit *observable* signs of cohesiveness—interdependent behavior patterns—that it can call on in times of need. Look for evidence of cohesion in your family's everyday interaction. What family rituals seem important to all or most members? What activities will members sacrifice if a family emergency arises? If some family members are away at college or live in another city, how regular are the phone calls or letters? These kinds of interdependent actions are probably the best indicators of cohesiveness.

### Maintaining Adaptability

Family interaction can easily get into a rut, following routine patterns of decision making, assignment of chores, times and places to talk, and so on. When a family encounters stress or the loss of a member, some of these routines may actually become dysfunctional. A family that has always emphasized logical thought in its decision making may be unable to think clearly in an emotional crisis. Logic may not even be the best course of action in such situations. To be adaptable means that a family system has *alternative* ways to handle even the most routine problems.

How can you encourage adaptability? One way is to force the family to deal with minor changes on occasion. Successful management of small problems can increase coping power in the face of larger ones. Another simple activity is to ask family members to think of new solutions to typical problems, even while "the old way" is still working. In business these are called contingency plans, and it is considered a cardinal sin not to have any.

### Building Social Networks

The old adage "no man is an island" could be applied to families as well. A family may be quite self-sufficient in good times and may have tremendous inner resolve during tough times, but it never hurts to have the support of neighbors, church members, or friends of the family. In troubled times nothing may seem very stable within the family unit, and that's when a stable social network (of which the entire family is a member) can serve as a safety net. Members of this network can provide a perspective that is often missing in a time of stress.

# Families in History

Earlier in this chapter, we talked about the myth of the ideal family. Today many fear the loss of traditional family values and lament the statistical death of the nuclear family. Taking into consideration a 50 percent divorce rate, the high rate of teenage pregnancies, the increasing number of single-parent and stepfamilies, and the fact that almost one-fourth of all American households are single individuals, we seem to have cause for great concern. But if we consult our own history, we find that the family has undergone several radical transformations that easily rival what we are witnessing today.

In *Domestic Revolutions*, historians Steven Mintz and Susan Kellogg recount three such transformations in what could be called the modal, or most frequently occurring, type of family structure and lifestyle. Beginning with colonial times, the *godly family* gave way in succession to the *democratic family* of the early 19th century, and the *companionate family* of the mid-20th century.[23]

The **godly family** of the colonial era has also been described as "a little commonwealth" because every facet of social life was centered in family activity—the family was a microcosm of the larger society. The family household was the site of economic production, a place of religious instruction, and as head of the household, the

*By providing care and emotional support families protect and form their children.*

Gerrit Greve, *Celebrating the Birth of Jake,* last quarter of the 20th century

father was its legal and political representative to the wider community. Family relations were very formal and the authority structure was unquestionably patriarchal and hierarchical. The male head of the household had sole possession of the family's resources of land and expertise in a craft or trade. As a result, he could command the respect and deference of his children, who were considered to be miniature adults in need of discipline more than nurture. Child-rearing was but one of many functions of the family, and a secondary one at that. Infants could be "put out" to wet nurses for breast-feeding so the mother could devote more time to household chores. Older children were frequently sent to live with other families where they could be more properly

disciplined. The entire community supported family discipline in this way. Given the strong Calvinist belief in original sin, moral instruction to rid the child of evil influences was much more important than any notion of building the child's self-esteem. But by the end of the 18th century, a new industrial economy was gearing up to weaken the father's all-encompassing authority and signal the end of the godly family.

In its place, a new **democratic family** structure developed. This new modal family was less formal, less hierarchical, and more tender. As work moved outside the home, the family became a more private institution. Marriage and parenting acquired a startling new emotional significance as the home, no longer a microcosm of

BOX 10.2

## Childhood in the 18th Century

# What Shapes the Family That Shapes Us?

William Hogarth, artist and political satirist in early 18th-century London, is said to have produced "the most significant single body of hard facts about English manners of his age." His drawings, published in the popular broadsheets of London, were well known. At the time, London was a collection of merging villages, not yet the great metropolis it would become in the 19th century. Hogarth's sympathies were with the oppressed lower classes, beleaguered servants, and innocent children corrupted by the city. His satire was directed at the whole social structure (customs, laws, government, and church) that failed to protect the children who were sent from the countryside to find work. He saw the family, and especially the child, as victims of a corrupt society—one he hoped the moral commentaries in his drawings would help reform.

According to art historian David Kunzle, "Hogarth's perception of the child was as an essentially parentless creature in a society which reneged upon parental responsibility within both the private nuclear family and the public family formed by social institutions." A good deal of his work as an artist was devoted to criticizing a society that allowed such things to happen.

One of Hogarth's most important ventures was a series of five drawings, produced in 1730, known as *A Harlot's Progress.* This box shows the first and last of these drawings, depicting Hogarth's view of the treatment of the family and its members by the very social institutions

FIGURE 1

FIGURE 2

created to support the people. In the first plate (Figure 1) we see an innocent young country girl, Kate Hackabout, arriving in London to stay with her cousin Tom and find work as a servant. But there is no family to meet her or protect her from the procuress (foreground) who seeks out and lures young women into prostitution. Note the other young girls in the wagon (background), who are under the watchful eye of a minister, seemingly protected from harm. The inadequacy of the church is seen, however, as the minister offers no assistance to the young Kate. Meanwhile, a variety of lecherous characters abounds (note the man in the doorway, hand in his pocket, believed to symbolize a Colonel Charteris, who was on trial for rape at the time of this drawing).

In the intervening scenes Kate "progresses" from the role of servant girl to that of a prostitute, is arrested and sent to a women's prison, where she receives inadequate care. In the final plate (Figure 2) she has died a premature death, leaving an illegitimate child (center, in front of the coffin). The young child, alone and ignored by the "mourners," is no doubt doomed to a miserable life himself.

What Hogarth has shown us in these remarkable renderings is the role of larger social forces (whether corrupt or not) in shaping family life at a given point in history. We might do well to look at our current social structures (patterns of work, legal system, government intervention, therapy professions, and so on) and contemplate how they shape roles and communication patterns within the various forms of the family as we know them today.

**SOURCE** David Kunzle, "William Hogarth: The Ravaged Child in the Corrupt City," in *Changing Images of the Family*, Virginia Tufte and Barbara Myerhoff, eds. (New Haven: Yale University Press, 1979), pp. 9–140.

society, became a protective shell keeping the cut-throat world of work at bay. Children were now recognized as unique individuals in need of love and attention, as well as preparation to be successful citizens and laborers. Child-rearing became the full-time job of the mother, who assumed more of the moral authority within the home. The goal of a mother shifted from breaking the will of a sinful child to shaping his or her character to face the temptations of life. The goal of a wife was to reform her husband, who faced constant temptation in the public sphere, and to promote moral reform of the society as a whole. Box 10.2, which portrays the bankrupt moral society of urban London almost three hundred years ago, illustrates the need for moral reform that became widespread in the era of the democratic family.

The values of self-denial and character development defined the democratic family. But family values would undergo another domestic revolution in the early 20th century with the emergence of the **companionate family.** Paralleling and promoting the shift from a self-concept based on character to one celebrating personality (see Chapter 8), the companionate family extolled the virtues of spouses as "friends and lovers" and parents and children as "pals." Permissive child-rearing practices were believed necessary to foster self-expression, self-fulfillment, and mutual happiness. Smaller family sizes and the abundant wealth of the nation made it possible for many (but certainly not all) to invest heavily in the idea that one's children should experience a better lifestyle than that of the parents.

In contrast to the rather clear modal families of the past, Mintz and Kellogg describe our modern era as "a society without a clear unitary set of family ideals and values." It is likely that we are in the midst of yet another historical transformation, but it is not yet clear whether a single modal type of family will take center stage, or what roles, characteristics, and values will define it. In the section that follows, we will do our best to make sense of the research on the family communication patterns that characterize our own time.

# Family Communication Patterns

Without adequate communication, family structures of any age would fall apart, internal and external functions would be impaired, the continuity of culture would be disrupted, and the idea of "family" would devolve into a useless social concept. In this section we want to direct our attention to many of the communication patterns that keep modern families functioning, as well as some that threaten to tear at the fabric of family life. Some of these patterns are characteristic of the family as a whole; others are typical of subsystems within the family unit.

## Interaction Patterns in the Family as a Whole

Family systems interact in ways that make their life together more than the sum of the individual members. Two broad categories of interaction will be considered: (1) the creation of specific rules to guide family communication and (2) the development of more general family themes and identities.

### Family Communication Rules

For a family to function adequately, the behavior of its members must be at least partially coordinated. This coordination can be achieved through the establishment and enforcement of family rules. You may recall that in Chapter 4 we introduced two types of communication rules: regulative and constitutive. You will find that family life is full of both types.

*Regulative Rules.* These rules serve as guides for action. Regulative rules describe what kinds of actions define one as a member of the family. From an individual or a family perspective, these rules may be seen as *obligatory, prohibited, appropriate,* or *irrelevant.* As you read the following examples, think about the regulative rules that operate in your own family.

An obligatory rule is one that is usually verbalized as "you must" or "we have to." Some obligatory rules are blatant: "As long as you live under this roof, you will keep your room clean" or "Always be on time. Nothing is worse than being late." Others are the result of subtle, often nonverbal, example-setting and reinforcement: "From the time we were very young, we always hugged and kissed each other before bedtime. No one said you had to, but Mom got this hurt-puppy look on her face if you forgot."

Most children probably think the world is populated with rules for what you "can't" or "shouldn't" do. "Don't raise your voice to me—or your father!" "Don't you dare go out of this house looking like that!" These rules generally describe behavior that may be OK for members of other families, but not this particular family. Occasionally, a rule statement may be a combination of *obligation* and *prohibition:* "I want you to be honest with me—but you don't have to tell me everything you do!" A wide variety of family rules can be described as simply *appropriate.* These rules don't carry the force of an obligation but are deemed "good" behavior for a family member. Being polite to strangers and sharing toys with a brother or sister might be considered appropriate actions. Any time a behavior is met with a response like "That was a good thing you did. I'm very proud of you," it probably reflects a rule or guide for appropriate communication.

Finally, some regulative rules are *irrelevant* as far as family membership is concerned. Those actions a person performs that neither embarrass other family members nor evoke a response of pride can be considered irrelevant. For some families a child's participation in extracurricular activities at school might be thought of as simply filling time; for another family it might be an obligation.

*Constitutive Rules.* While regulative rules guide action, constitutive rules determine meaning. For some families a given behavior or communication pattern may have positive connotations, while others view the same pattern as negative. The following statements are examples of family members offering *interpretations* of behavior: "Helping your brother with his chores means that you care," "Talking to strangers is dangerous," "Going to X-rated movies is a sin," and "A real man stands up for himself." Constitutive rules may have implicit regulative rules associated with them. When a person says, "Making snide remarks is a sign of disrespect," he or she is probably implying that you shouldn't make snide remarks to people. But that may not always be the case. If someone is acting stuffy, you may follow the regulative rule "A stuffed shirt deserves no respect."

Think for a moment about the constitutive rules that distinguish your family. Are there actions that your family interprets differently than most? What regulative rules are associated with them? Make a list of which rules in your family are well known by everyone, which ones are unwritten, and which ones cause the most misunderstanding or conflict. Are there some things you can't talk about as a family? Are there other things that, while taboo in most families, are discussed openly in your own?

### Family Themes and Identities

The family communication rules we just looked at apply to specific behaviors and instances. When we look at the overall pattern of family rules, we are likely to discover some general themes that influence the specific rules we follow. **Family themes** are recurring attitudes, beliefs, or outlooks on life shared by the entire family. Many families thrive on competition, subscribe to a particular set of religious beliefs, or view "togetherness" as the key to a happy life. Some families are anxious; they worry about everything. In contrast, other families have an overall outlook that "life is a gamble; take a risk." This family theme influences many of their everyday rules. They have fewer prohibitive rules than most families, and they always make themselves available for new experiences.

When family themes are prominent and the family unit is cohesive, a **family identity** emerges. Just as each individual develops a self-image, so members of the family share a group image, a sense of who they are as a unit. When you hear family members describe themselves as "fun-loving," "high achievers," or "responsible citizens," they are putting into words the constructs or images that govern their behavior as a group. We know an extended family that has labeled themselves as "sojourners" because none of them stays in one place very long. One member moved his family three times in one year. Another has moved from New England to the Southwest and back five times in six years. Most family members start getting "itchy" after two years in the same place.

Based on interviews with members from a wide variety of families, journalist Jane Howard summarized 10 characteristics of "good families." As you read her list you'll notice specific family themes, rules, roles, and communication practices. According to Howard, good families:

- *have a chief, heroine, or founder.* This person is the magnet who draws family members together and inspires someone in the next generation to carry on the family traditions.

- *have a switchboard operator.* This person always knows what everyone is doing and keeps the others posted.

- *are cohesive but not stifling.* Membership in the family means a great deal to all, but does not prevent members from pursuing outside interests.

- *are hospitable.* Their homes are places where other people's children like to spend time.

- *deal directly with their problems.* Members do not avoid confrontation or hope problems will go away. They find a way to work through conflicts.

- *prize their rituals.* They celebrate holidays, special events, and everyday life in unique and sometimes cornball fashion. Members anticipate the regular Sunday brunch or the summer reunion at the lake.

- *are openly affectionate.* Members share how they feel about one another, although in a wide variety of ways.

- *have a sense of place.* Whether it is "the old country," "the old homestead," or a new home housing old family symbols, members share a definite sense of belonging tied to those symbols.

- *build connections to posterity.* Through children or extended family, members see themselves as linked to something purposeful and enduring.

- *honor their elders.* Respect for the family heritage is embodied in intergenerational communication.[24]

How would you describe your own family's identity? What makes yours a "good" family? What themes or communication rules are associated with the family identity?

## Interaction Patterns in Family Subsystems

Every family consists of one or more subsystems. In this section we will describe several different family dyads, including the husband-wife, the parent-child, and the sibling subsystem.

### The Husband-Wife Subsystem

The first subsystem in a family is the husband-wife relationship. Prior to the birth of the first child, this relationship is the focus of family life. Studies indicate that the quality of communication between the spouses is the single best predictor of satisfaction with the marriage.[25] How much satisfaction they experience depends, in part, on what type of marital relationship they negotiate and how they handle recurring issues such as control, togetherness and freedom, and expression of affection. Mary Anne Fitzpatrick and her colleagues have studied how congruent couples are in their relational definitions along three conceptual dimensions: autonomy-interdependence, conventional-nonconventional ideology, and conflict engagement-conflict avoidance. As a result four very different types of couples have emerged from these studies: traditionals, separates, independents, and separate traditionals.[26]

**Traditional couples** are highly interdependent, share conventional views of marriage and family life, and engage in conflict on a fairly regular basis. They are also very expressive in their communication styles, and sharing information is a high priority with them. **Separate couples,** on the other hand, tend to be more autonomous—spouses give each other more room, they aren't as expressive, and while they hold fairly conservative views on marriage, they don't feel as strongly about their views as traditionals. In addition, they tend to avoid conflicts as much as possible. They deal with conflict situations by taking on complementary roles—one person decides what to do, and the other follows. **Independent couples** differ from the others in that they subscribe to more nonconventional values and views about relationships. They are not as autonomous as separates, but are only moderately interdependent. Spouses are very expressive emotionally and do not avoid conflict with one another. In fact, independents have the highest levels of self-disclosure observed among all couple types. Fitzpatrick reports that 60 percent of the couples she has studied fall into one of the first three types. The remaining 40 percent are "mixed types," which means that the couples disagree in their definition of the relationship or in their views about marriage. **Separate/traditional couples** are the most distinct of these hybrid types. Spouses have the most conventional sex roles of all types, self-disclose very little, ask fewer questions, and yet score consistently high on all ratings of marital satisfaction. One study reported that wives in this type of relationship have a more accurate understanding of their husbands than in any other type.[27] Of the four types, traditionals and separate/traditionals seem to be the most satisfied with their marriage, while independents and separates report the least satisfaction.

Regardless of the type of relationship, research indicates that satisfaction with the marriage tends to level off over time, and especially after the birth of the first child. The decline in

satisfaction is usually compensated for by the satisfaction derived from the new role as a parent.[28] Research, as we have already seen, shows a marked increase in traditional values and sex-role stereotyping once children arrive on the scene.[29] Thus, the transition to parenthood may lead to changes in the spouses' definition of their relationship. Another potentially detrimental change with the advent of parenthood is that partners begin to spend more time in parental roles and less time with each other. Family therapists often advise spouses to check their talk when they are finally alone to make sure that, even then, they don't talk about the children. Ask yourself what rules you think a family should establish to increase the likelihood that the parents will have at least some "alone time" as a couple.

The maintenance of a positive husband-wife subsystem depends in part on what they do talk about when they are alone. We have already seen that the type of relationship spouses have affects their willingness to self-disclose and their frequency of communication. Research also indicates that, in general, men and women perceive the importance of certain types of communication quite differently. Linda Acitelli reports that husbands tend to value "talk about their relationship" only when they perceive it to be necessary (for instance, to resolve a conflict). Women, on the other hand, value relationship talk even when things are going smoothly.[30] This preference by men to avoid routine relational talk and women's preference for it can place a strain on the husband-wife relationship, especially when so much interaction time is devoted to children and other matters.

Furthermore, wives tend to have much more vivid memories of significant relational conversations or events such as a first date or a recent argument. This can lead wives and husbands to misconstrue that such events were less important to the husband. However, the research showed no relationship between ratings of an event's importance and ability to recall the event in vivid detail.[31]

There is also evidence that how spouses communicate depends on generational and life-span influences. In a study of the conversations of young, middle-aged, and retired married couples, Paul Zietlow and Alan Sillars found that middle-aged and older couples were generally less expressive than younger couples.[32] Younger couples used communication as an outlet for releasing tensions and also as a vehicle for negotiating needed role changes. The middle-aged couples also communicated to adjust roles but seemed less urgent in their need to confront conflicts. Older couples demonstrated a uniquely cordial style of interaction (characterized by casual conversation and small talk) when conflicts were not very important to them, but were noticeably bitter and complaint-oriented during conflicts. They seldom communicated to resolve conflict as the younger couples did. The older couples were seen as subscribing to a vision of the spousal relationship as one that "can minimize conflict and, at the same time, create incompetence in addressing those conflicts which are not resolved by conformity to external role standards."[33]

While some of these patterns reflect generational differences in values and relational definitions, the importance attached to conflict issues may well reflect different stages of the family life cycle for these couples. Younger couples tend to be faced with many more adjustments, especially if children are involved. Thus, they may have to confront more conflicts than older couples. In contrast, the middle-aged and older couples, having weathered many storms, could afford to be more relaxed and less expressive about conflict issues.

### The Parent-Child Subsystem

The function of the parent-child subsystem is one of mutual socialization. An infant needs to be cared for, be offered emotional support, and have appropriate behavior shaped through an imaginative blend of example and discipline. There is no question that the messages parents send a child influence the development of the child's personality and moral code. What parents struggle with is trying to determine precisely which communication patterns will lead to the desired outcomes.

Experts differ widely in their specific advice to parents, and even a sampling of different views would be beyond the scope of this book. What does seem to be generally agreed upon is that affection and support messages are the first priority of parenting, with control and discipline a close second. Research suggests that to gain the compliance of a child, a basic bond of *affection* must be established first. **Support messages** from parents such as praising, approving, encouraging, and showing affection are linked to higher levels of self-esteem in children and greater conformity to authority.[34] Desmond Morris has suggested that all children under two years of age need basic care and unconditional love; when they reach age two, restrictions and discipline should begin.[35]

The forms of discipline available to parents are not much different from the compliance-gaining strategies introduced in Chapter 9. In the parenting literature they are referred to as **control messages:** power assertion, love withdrawal, and induction.[36] **Power assertion** refers to a parent's use of physical coercion, unexplained demands, restricted privileges, and so on. Consistent use of coercion tends to make children feel rejected by their parents and leads to aggression, dependency, and less internalization of moral standards. **Love withdrawal** also involves a strategy of threatening negative consequences if the child fails to comply. Love withdrawal occurs when a child's failure to obey results in a parent withholding expressions of affection, ridiculing the child, or displaying the proverbial cold shoulder. **Induction** is the strategy of reasoning with a child about his or her behavior in an effort to help the child *understand* why they should follow certain rules ("You can't play with the train because you might break it") or why a given behavior is wrong or hurtful ("How would you feel if Sally did that to you?"). Most parents use a mixture of all three types of discipline. In fact, researchers have known for quite some time that any type of discipline can be effective when

## Fathers and Sons
# *He Got Game*

Spike Lee, 1998

Jake (Denzel Washington) is in prison for killing his wife (Lonnette McKee) when the warden (Ned Beatty) makes him an offer that's hard to refuse: Jake's sentence will be reduced if only he can convince his son Jesus (Ray Allen), the nation's top high school basketball player, to attend Big State University. But to do so, Jake will have to reestablish his relationship with the son who hasn't spoken to him in over six years.

Jake is not the only one putting pressure on Jesus. Sensing that the boy can be the next NBA superstar, everyone around him, including his girlfriend (Rosario Dawson), tries to get a piece of the action. Without any true support, pressured from every side, Jesus has to make a decision that may well be the most important one in his own life and that of his father.

On one level the film is a satiric look at the temptations that await talented athletes in a game that can be more about big business than about sport. On another level, the film addresses the complex relationship between a father and a son. When Jesus was a child, Jake saw basketball as his son's only chance to have a better life, and he placed the child under unrelenting pressure. But in driving his son to greatness, Jake also drove him away. This film is a good springboard for thinking about how difficult it sometimes is for parents and children to connect and about how important it is to forgive.

the overall relationship between parent and child is warm and affectionate.[37] Researchers have been particularly interested in the effects on a child's moral reasoning capabilities when one disciplining strategy is used more frequently than the others. In their review of this research, Gene Brody and David Shaffer found that greater parental use of inductive strategies is closely associated with a child's ability to internalize ethical standards and apply them even when parents or other authority figures are not present. Frequent use of power assertive strategies, on the other hand, tends to produce an external moral orientation, where the child is more responsive to the probability of rewards or punishments and less likely to internalize and think in complex ways about moral issues. The results when parents use love withdrawal have been more problematic, with no clear indication of its effect on moral reasoning.[38]

Interestingly, mothers appear to be the primary disciplinarians in most families. Given their less active role in actually dispensing discipline, effective fathers seem to influence their children's moral development more indirectly as "competent role models" whose moral values rub off on their children.[39] Another possibility is that fathers tend to specialize in power assertive strategies but use them sparingly while mothers do the bulk of the disciplining using more inductive strategies. The evidence for such a view stems from the fact that many mothers of father-absent children use more power assertive strategies, presumably because they have to do the work of both parents.[40]

There is also evidence that parental use of inductive strategies not only influences a child's social-cognitive and moral reasoning, but also directly affects the child's own communication skill development. Children of mothers who used inductive, person-centered strategies are more effective than children of position-centered or power assertive parents at a host of communicative tasks, including persuading others, giving instructions, taking the perspective of the other, and offering comfort to someone who is distressed.[41]

Obviously, inductive strategies are unlikely to work until a child is old enough to respond to them with some degree of understanding. And as children get older, other influences besides the parents (television viewing, peer culture, other adult role models) begin to make inroads. By this point, parents hope that their children will have internalized the family's values at least to the extent that they influence the child's choice of friends and how they respond to alternative values expressed on television or by teachers and other adults. One area of concern for many parents is establishing regulative rules regarding the amount and type of TV programming a child is allowed to watch. Also related is the generation of constitutive rules regarding the meaning and morality of televised violence and sexual behavior and the distinction between reality and fiction. Several studies have examined the role of television as a source of conversational topics between parents and children and the role of parental mediation or explanation of television form and content to children. **Parental mediation** refers to a parent viewing television with the child, discussing specific programs before or after they are seen, and talking about TV in general. Roger Desmond and his colleagues have identified three general categories of parent-child talk about TV: (1) *criticism,* in which parents make evaluative comments about specific programs or commercials; (2) *interpretation,* in which parents explain TV as a medium or calm a child's fears about violence or unusual behavior observed; and (3) *rule making and discipline,* in which parents encourage the viewing of certain programs, as well as limiting others.[42] In regard to rule making, these researchers report some interesting results. A child's comprehension of what he or she watches is closely related to the type of parental mediation that occurs. The abil-

*One external family function is cultural transmission. Here, grandparents keep a tradition alive by teaching their grandson the art of origami.*

ity to distinguish reality from fiction, for instance, was enhanced when (1) the family controlled television viewing, (2) both positive and negative rules were enforced, (3) strong discipline was utilized, and (4) the amount of TV watched was relatively low. In addition, comprehension of specific program plots was related to the adherence to TV rules, positive communication between mother and child, and frequent explanations of TV content by parents. Since viewing television is often associated with greater passivity, the researchers suggest that "one of the most important functions of family mediation may be to elevate some children's amount of invested mental effort or attention during viewing."[43]

As adolescence approaches, parent and child often experience a great deal of apprehension about and stress in their relationship. Increased influence by peers and attempts to establish a more autonomous relationship with parents often result in strained interactions. But new studies demonstrate that these difficulties do not reflect the total relationship between parent and child. William Rawlins and Melissa Holl report that adolescents tend to view both parents and friends as important conversational partners, but target them for discussion of very different topics and needs. Parents are seen as important sources on issues that require a historical perspective—something the parent has been through before and would know about. On the other hand, if input is needed regarding current issues or problems, adolescents turn to their friends. Another important and encouraging difference was the perception that although parents are seen as more judgmental than friends, they are also seen as more caring. There is a realization that parental criticism usually emerges from a real concern for the child.[44]

Another interesting change in parent-child relationships occurs during the launching years. Stephen Anderson found significant gender differences when a son or daughter leaves home. Mother-son communication improved after the son went away to college, whereas the mother-daughter relationship was better if the daughter remained at home and commuted to college.[45] Anderson hypothesizes that the son's departure from home gave him enough distance to reestablish a stronger familial bond. In contrast, daughters were better able to manage the mother-daughter relationship and establish their own identity at the same time.

As we noted in a previous section of this chapter, the companionate family that dominated the earlier part of this century seems to be undergoing a new transformation. New family structures, such as a blended family with one stepparent and/or one or more adopted children, have introduced new elements into parental communication practices. Mark Fine and Lawrence Kurdek found that in stepfamilies, the biological parent and the stepparent often follow very different parenting scripts. Biological parents engage in, and believe they should engage in, more parenting behaviors than their stepparent counterpart. Differences occurred in regard to control (disciplining behaviors), but were especially strong in terms of showing warmth. The authors surmised that natural parents, because of their greater biological investment in the child, were much more likely to spend time with and communicate support to the child.[46] These findings demonstrate the ambiguity that continues to abound regarding appropriate roles in newly emergent family forms.

## The Sibling Subsystem

Sibling relationships are perhaps the most interesting relationships in a family. When siblings are young and close in age, they are a primary source of imagination and ingenuity. Twins frequently create their own private languages, and other siblings are almost as imaginative. An older sibling may socialize a younger brother or sister almost as much as her parents. Mix in a little sibling rivalry and you have relationships as rich as any other.

Siblings are peers and thus have a more egalitarian relationship with one another than with their parents. Since they can be more assertive with one another, siblings usually are. Their interaction is characterized by physical aggression and other forms of antisocial behavior. As children get older, they mature and engage in more social behavior, cooperating to play games and so on. Cooperation increases more between same-sex siblings than it does between brothers and sisters, due no doubt to emerging sex-typed identities. Younger children tend to imitate one another a lot, but this behavior also decreases more between opposite-sex siblings as they grow older.

Several other age- and sex-related tendencies have been borne out by research: Younger children tend to like and revere their older siblings, and their liking is not reciprocated to the same degree; older brothers and younger sisters tend to have the most conflict-ridden relationships;

and the older sister-younger brother relationship usually has the least conflict.[47]

Like other subsystem relationships, the sibling relationship changes over the life span. A. Goetting summarized these changes as occurring in three stages: (1) childhood-adolescence, (2) early and middle adulthood, and (3) old age.[48] During all three periods siblings tend to provide one another with companionship and social support, although physical proximity is greater during the childhood period. In childhood an older sibling is likely to function occasionally as a caregiver and to teach social and other skills to the younger sibling. In adulthood the frequency of interaction may decline, especially if siblings are geographically separated, but relationships are often maintained via telephone and family reunions. In their review of research on sibling relations, Victor Cicirelli and Jon Nussbaum note that even when interaction is sparse, adult siblings maintain a symbolic relationship by identifying with one another and recalling shared incidents.[49] Older siblings tend to provide services to one another such as occasionally lending money, baby-sitting one another's kids, sharing concerns, and caring for elderly parents. Finally, in old age, the relationship may take on greater significance as friends and other family members die. Older siblings also help one another review life events and face current ones. The range in types of elderly sibling relationships is also interesting. D. T. Gold characterized five types of relationships as intimate (14 percent), congenial (30 percent), loyal (34 percent), apathetic (11 percent), and hostile (11 percent), respectively.[50] The percentages reveal the relative strength and importance of sibling relations as people get older. It is also interesting to note that sisters are an increasingly important target of interaction for both males and females as they age. Cicirelli and Nussbaum speculate that the greater expressiveness of females and their traditional role as nurturers lead both males and females to seek out sisters for emotional support and physical aid.

Clearly, communication patterns within the various family subsystems change in number, frequency, and function over time. Even so, family relationships have a kind of permanence seldom experienced outside the family. Indeed, most romantic relationships develop outside the family boundaries but soon become enmeshed within the extended family via marriage and childbirth. We often take for granted the closeness and emotional support that family members traditionally provide one another. But we have only to be reminded of the pain of child abuse, abandonment, and other forms of family violence to realize that the ideals are not always achieved. Acknowledging the dark side of family life should encourage us to develop the communication skills necessary for building and sustaining positive personal and family relationships. To assist in that endeavor, let's revisit the model of communicative competence introduced in Chapter 1.

# Communicative Competence and the Family

As you may recall, we defined communicative competence in Chapter 1 as consisting of five subskills: interpretive, role, goal, self, and message competence.

## Family and Interpretive Competence

Interpretive competence involves attention to context. When we are mindful of how a current family conversation or dispute relates to the family's history, its important rituals or values, and its place within a larger kinship or community network, we exhibit interpretive competence. In Chapter 6, we discussed cognitive schemas such as relational prototypes and scripts. These operate in families as well. Family members often develop similar prototypes of how a family should interact, but these may be countered by peer group and media influences. Whatever our prototypes of the ideal family, even if they are myths, they establish expectations and channel what we desire to happen. When actual interactions do not live up to the ideal, we can be unreasonably harsh critics of our family unit. In addition, our expectations (and those of other family members) are subject to change, especially in these turbulent times when the companionate family ideal appears to be evolving toward some as yet unknown new modal family. Questions arise in such a complex world. Should we judge older rituals and scripts as out of date and in need of modification? Do we cling to the companionate ideal and judge our current patterns of interaction in light of its values? Attention to these issues helps us assess the appropriateness of family identities, rules, and disciplinary strategies as well as the significance of everyday roles and conversations.

## Family and Role Competence

Families have much to teach us about role competence. We tend to think of roles as "job descriptions" and being able to play them competently as simply learning a few sets of rules and skills. Yet if we take the concept of the family system to heart, we will realize that the roles we play are interlocked and thus always changing. Systems theory tells us that there is no husband role without a wife, no child without a parent role, and no way to be a brother or sister without someone cast in the opposite role. Family therapists tell us that problems in families never belong to individuals alone, but are symptoms of the roles parents and children play in relation to one another. Acting out the role of "rebellious teenager," for instance, often involves a triangle of roles: an overinvolved mother, an underinvolved father, and the rebellious son or daughter.[51] Just as professional actors must master ensemble relationships to pull off a successful part, developing role competence within the family means learning all the parts different members play and how they are interwoven. Knowledge

of typical communication patterns associated with different role relations and the realization that alternative patterns can be negotiated help us become more proficient at role competence.

## Family and Goal Competence

The range of possible family types, roles, rules, and communication strategies offer us plenty of goals to pursue within the family context. We may want our family to be more like the "good families" described by Jane Howard or desire greater involvement of family members in the neighborhood or community. But identifying goals for family communication and achieving them are two different things. Sometimes we have to be more realistic about what's possible. While we might prefer to live in a community like Seaside, Florida (see Box 10.1), where the physical environment is designed to harmonize families and neighborhoods, we have to make do with the families, houses, and communities in which we actually live. It might be surprising to know that on average, people living in the Bronx, New York, have more positive feelings and greater hope and faith in what the future holds for their families and communities than people of far greater wealth and social status living in Beverly Hills.[52] Achieving our goals for better family communication is more likely when we approach them realistically—improving one interaction at a time, one relationship at a time.

## Family and Self Competence

As Virginia Satir puts in, our families are "peoplemaking factories."[53] The communication patterns established early on between the primary caretaker and an infant do much to shape the self-concept, self-esteem, cognitive development, and even the attachment style by which the child will relate to others much later in life.[54] Not only are the foundations for self competence laid in infant-parent communication, the process of self-development continues throughout the family life cycle. Self-identity is influenced by communication patterns in sibling as well as intergenerational relationships. In turn, emerging or faltering levels of self competence feed back into the family system. An individual's problems affect the entire family system, often in complex ways. As we change, the family system must adapt and reconfigure itself.

### Family and Message Competence

Our families are also laboratories for message making. We not only learn the meanings associated with verbal, nonverbal, and relational acts at home, we are also given the opportunity to try out new words and gestures and test the relational implications of new communication strategies before attempting them in the larger social world. A brother or sister is often the first to hear and critique a request for a first date or an apology soon to be offered to a friend. Parents listen patiently while we polish a speech for a fifth-grade class or rehearse lines for the school play. In daily interaction with family members, we test compliance-gaining strategies, practice gender displays, and learn how to give or receive feedback. It is not, of course, just practice. As we saw in Chapter 5, relational messages in families have serious consequences. Family members are sometimes victims of "double binds" in which a spouse or child simultaneously receives confirming and disconfirming messages and doesn't know how to respond appropriately. Message competence is both learned and tested within the family.

In many ways, our families affect our communicative competence. For almost all of us, the family will be a lifelong context in which we operate. Sometimes soothing us, occasionally antagonizing us, family members remain a significant part of our lives long after the family of origin gives way to the creation of a new family unit through marriage and childbirth. Family members are often our line of last resort when things get tough.

In closing this chapter we turn our attention to one of the skills that enables family members and friends to count on one another in times of need: the skill of comforting.

# Skill Building: Communicating to Comfort

One of the most essential forms of communication within the family is the emotional support function. Parents provide emotional support when they show affection for and acceptance of their children and each other. This not only fosters cohesiveness within the family unit but also serves as a key component in a child's development of a positive self-image and feelings of self-worth. Many of the communication skills associated with this function (such as active listening, empathy and perspective-taking, and expression of feelings) have been discussed in earlier chapters. Another closely related skill is that of comforting one another during times of emotional upheaval and distress. Keep in mind that while this skill is essential in spousal and parent-child relationships, it is also helpful in other contexts, such as developing and maintaining friendships and intimate relationships.

Brant Burleson defines the act of **comforting** as trying to alleviate, moderate, or salve the distressed emotional state of another person.[55] There are numerous ways to offer emotional comfort, but researchers have identified several important distinctions among the messages that most people use and the ones that tend to be successful. We have drawn three general principles from this research to help improve your competence when trying to comfort others.

The first step in successful comforting is to *adopt an other-centered approach.* This means that you must listen carefully to understand how the distressed other sees his or her situation and what feelings he or she has experienced. Your response will be more sensitive if you acknowledge the validity of the other's viewpoint and feelings ("I know how much you wanted your relationship with Jeff to work out. It really hurts when you put so much into a relationship only to see it fall apart"). In contrast, most people become speaker-centered and either give advice ("Why don't you try . . .") or tell the other how he or she should feel ("You can't let things get to you like this. You've got to be tough"). In one study researchers asked bereaved parents and spouses what kind of comforting messages they found to be most "helpful" and "unhelpful." Giving advice, minimizing their feelings, encouraging their recovery, and forced cheerfulness topped the list as unhelpful messages. In contrast, simply expressing concern, providing an opportunity to ventilate feelings, and just being there were seen as most helpful.[56]

Another way to comfort effectively is to *compose messages that are evaluatively neutral.* This strategy involves describing the other's feelings and the situation giving rise to those feelings in general rather than specific terms. Thus, you should avoid mentioning too many specific details or evaluating the personalities involved. In comforting a friend who just broke up with her boyfriend, you will probably inflict more pain if you mention how difficult it must have been to return his ring or to give up some cherished ritual (spring break vacations) that the two shared. Negative evaluations such as berating the boyfriend ("He was no good for you") are usually ineffective as well. Keeping things at a general level shows that you care; getting too specific implies a kind of opportunistic voyeurism— as if you can't wait to explore what went wrong.

You can also improve comforting messages by trying to *help put events and feelings in perspective for the other.* This is probably the only form of advice-giving that a distressed person will tolerate because it may help the person better understand his or her own feelings. Sometimes this means offering alternative explanations of the events that have taken place. If a friend feels that she didn't do well in a job interview, you can, after acknowledging her feelings, propose that she look at it as a learning experience. If she can identify aspects of the interview that didn't go well, she'll know what to work harder on next time. Or you can reverse the perceptions. Maybe the interview was not successful because it was

not a company in which she could fully display her talents. Perhaps she prevented a greater calamity down the road: working for a company that would not appreciate her. Because stressful situations are often emotionally overwhelming, Burleson suggests that many distressed people fail to develop cognitive explanations of their feelings—explanations that might produce some psychological distance from the emotional trauma.

James Applegate has proposed that in attempting to provide comfort, people use strategies that differ in terms of how much of the perspective and feelings of the other are acknowledged and elaborated on. The least effective strategies are those that condemn, deny, or ignore the feelings and perspective of the other. Somewhat better are those strategies that at least *implicitly* recognize the other's perspective and feelings by diverting attention to other topics, simply acknowledging how the other feels, or attempting to "explain away" those feelings. Finally, the most sophisticated and successful comforting strategies *explicitly* confirm the other's feelings, elaborate on or explain the feelings, or help the other gain another vantage point regarding those feelings.[57] Most people, most of the time, tend to use denial or implicit strategies rather than the more explicit strategies, even though research has confirmed that the more explicit strategies are perceived as more effective.[58]

Comforting messages seem to work best when we take the perspective of the other and demonstrate an acceptance of his or her feelings. While the skills involved in comforting are demanding, we can, with patience and practice, learn to be more competent at providing solace and encouragement to those whose well-being is important to us.

Throughout this chapter we have identified some of the structures, functions, and communication patterns that typically emerge in American families. Knowledge of these patterns is certainly a good first step in improving your ability to function effectively as a member of your family. But your family is bound to be different in some ways from the "norms" described here. Thus, it is essential that you develop the ability to recognize and describe the patterns of interaction that your family actually follows. This task may take a considerable amount of your time, but it will be worth it. You might keep a journal in which you write down the communication behavior you observe in all of the subsystems of your family as well as those times when you are all together. Try to abstract the communication rules and family themes present in the observations you have recorded. Try to predict the evolution of your family system by imagining how things might change at the next step in the family life cycle or in the event an unexpected crisis occurs. Once you have described the way things are in your own family, you can begin to explore other alternatives. Ask friends how they handle similar situations in their families. Next time you read a novel or watch a film, pay attention to scenes involving families. What rules, themes, or identities do they project? What we are suggesting here is not an easy assignment. But it may well be the best way to improve your knowledge and your ability to help create or revitalize your own family.

## Process to Performance

### Review Terms

The following is a list of major concepts introduced in this chapter. The page where the concept is first mentioned is listed in parentheses.

### Suggested Readings

Galvin, Kathleen M., Carma L. Bylund, and Bernard J. Brommel. *Family Communication: Cohesion and Change*. Boston: Pearson Allyn & Bacon, 2004. This is a new edition of a highly comprehensive and readable introduction to communication in the family.

Gottman, John. *Raising an Emotionally Intelligent Child: The Heart of Parenting*. New York: Simon & Schuster, 1997. Gottman argues that much of the communication between parent and child involves "emotion coaching." He offers strategies for coaching children so that they learn to master their emotions.

## Topics for Discussion
www.oup.com/us/trenholm

### Observation Guide

**1.** Write a brief paper describing the evolution of your own family. Start as far back as possible, relying on interviews with older members of your family (grandparents, great-aunts and -uncles, and so on). Try to determine which family themes have survived the generations and which ones have characterized each successive generation.

**2.** Observe different television families—single-parent, extended, nuclear, and blended (those created by adoption or remarriage). Look for common threads. Which commonalities are essential to the concept of "family" and which ones are just currently fashionable?

**3.** In the same vein as the previous activity, choose a fictitious television or film family and study several episodes of family interaction. Identify the family themes, regulative and constitutive rules, and other recurring communication patterns in evidence in the family and its subsystems. Compare the fictitious family with your own and other families you have known. Which themes, rules, boundaries, or patterns are unrealistic? Are TV families similar to or different from real ones? What expectations do TV families engender in real ones? Are there any dangers in the depictions of families on television?

### Exercises

**1. a.** Divide the class into several groups, varying in size from two to six. Each group will be a family unit for the duration of one week. Either the group or the instructor can decide who will play the roles of mother, father, oldest child, and so on. You may want to assign different ages to each of the children.

**b.** Once roles are determined, the "parents" should meet to discuss the values and rules that they want to use as guides to raising their children. At the same time, the siblings may meet and develop their own personas for the week.

**c.** Next, each "family" should meet as a group to plan two or three outings for the coming week. These may include trips to the park, shopping excursions, a family dinner. Plans should be tailored to fit the ages of the children. Childless couples will, of course, plan their own events. These outings should be planned and carried out during the week.

**d.** Parents should make the "rules" for the week clear to each of the children. Some parents may insist that a child phone one or both of them for permission to go out at night, for example. (The instructor may wish to set some ground rules to prevent abuse. For instance, role playing might be limited to specific hours of the school day.) In the spirit of the exercise, family members should reluctantly follow some of the rules they don't like and, on occasion, try to see what they can get away with.

**e.** Each family member should keep a journal of thoughts, feelings, and observations of communication in the family. A short paper might be required in which family structures, functions, identity, rules, decision-making style, and so on are evaluated and commented on. A class discussion at the end of the week should be enlightening.

**2.** Divide the class into seven groups. Each group is responsible for researching one of the stages in the family life cycle and making a 10-minute report to the rest of the class. Research could focus on identifying (1) the major issues in each stage, (2) typical communication patterns, and (3) the most common family problems. Groups can use skits, role-plays, and other audiovisual means for depicting family communication in each stage.

*Fashioning an intimate relationship is one of our most fascinating human creations.*

John Carroll, *Two Figures*, 1929

## CHAPTER 11

# Intimate Relationships
# Creating Dyadic Identities

A young man approached the instructor of his interpersonal communication class and revealed the following dilemma:

> I've dated the same woman several times, and it seems like we've got a pretty good thing going. I mean, we talk about things pretty openly and we get along really well. But last week she stumped me. We were talking along and she said something about what a "goofy relationship" we have and then she laughed pretty hard. I asked her what she meant, and she said, "Oh, nothing, really; sometimes we just strike me as being funny together." For the life of me, I don't get it. If we really have such a good relationship, then I guess she's just joking and I should take it in stride. But maybe she's trying to tell me something. Maybe the so-called joke is her way of telling me she's not so hot on this relationship anymore. Should I believe what she says or what I think she means? I sure wish I knew.[1]

This young man's experience is not unique. At one time or another, most of us have been in a similar situation. We have faced those awkward moments in a relationship where we're not sure which carries more weight: the messages being exchanged at the moment or the definition of the relationship we thought we had prior to that exchange. As students of communication, we realize that relationships are constantly being defined and redefined through the communication process. We know that in the beginning of a relationship most of the messages we exchange are based on cultural scripts or limited knowledge of the other's social status and group memberships. To get to know someone on a personal level is a more complicated process.

In this chapter we want to explore how we move relationships away from the public level and toward the more personal. We'll begin by briefly examining how intimate relationships have evolved historically, then we'll define intimacy as we think of it today and its two major forms: friendships and romantic couples. Next we'll look at two ways these relationships can be created: through conscious planning and rational awareness of relational messages or through a slower, less conscious process of creating interdependence and other conditions for intimacy.

Then we'll investigate the various ways people are attracted to one another over time, culminating in a review of the typical stages of development, maintenance, and decay in friendships and then in romantic relationships. We will also examine what it means to be communicatively competent in our close personal relationships. Finally, we'll consider two important communication skills that help us keep a close relationship together: managing conflict and stress.

## Have People Always Had Intimate Relationships?

To even ask this question may seem puzzling to many. We feel certain that people, no matter what culture or century they lived in, must have always felt the basic human emotions of love, closeness, and sharing intimate secrets. How could it be otherwise? But historians have long known that what counts as love, intimacy, or closeness has varied significantly from one place and time to another. Howard Gadlin chronicled the changing meanings of "intimacy" from colonial America to the modern era. He noted that colonials thought of intimacy in terms of physical rather than psychological closeness.[2] Married couples interacted with one another in a way that we would find aloof and disconcerting. Richard Sennett tells us that in 18th-century Europe, people courted one another using a fixed system of ritualized lines. The same "phrases" were used from one affair to the next, as though they had no particular meaning for the specific partners involved.[3] Romantic love, with its emphasis on knowing the innermost thoughts of a partner, seems clearly to have been an invention of the 19th century.

Communication theorist Timothy Stephen has speculated that the modern tendency to define close relationships as *jointly created worlds*

*Intimate relationships allow prolonged gazing and close contact.*

Edouard Manet, *Chez Le Pere Lathuille,* 1879

*of shared meaning* would not have made sense in earlier eras where basic values, beliefs, and lifestyles were widely shared and men and women had distinctly different roles to play in society. Under those conditions, a relationship based on the creation of a "unique dyadic world" would likely have been seen as a threat to the stability of the social order. But as our society became more pluralistic, the need to choose among alternative value systems and self-identities has created the conditions for close relationships that serve as a bond for reinforcing those values and identities.[4] This brief look at the history of intimacy should help us realize that the types of relationships we value today have not always been so important to people. That realization should serve as a reminder that in the future, intimate relationships may take yet another historical turn. Indeed, new technologies are even now offering us new opportunities to form new kinds of relationships, as the study abstracted in this chapter's Research in Review shows.

# How Are Intimate Relationships Formed Today?

Intimate relationships normally begin just like any other social relationship—governed by rules and conventions of politeness, by the adoption by each person of a culturally provided face and line, and so on. But at a certain point these impersonal roles and rules are abandoned and replaced by a new, more personalized system of interaction. How does this happen? What are two people moving toward when they begin to create a private interpersonal relationship? Let's turn our attention to how private relationships develop.

## Defining Private Bonds

In Chapter 2 we outlined how private bonds tend to differ from public ones in our culture. It might help to think about each of the dimensions mentioned as *criteria* by which we judge a relationship to be more or less intimate. For instance, we said that private relations tend to place a greater emphasis on *who* the persons involved are (irreplaceable criterion), and on *how* they structure their everyday lives around shared activities (interdependence criterion), share more unique information about themselves (particularistic criterion), negotiate unique rules to guide their relationship rather than follow social norms (individualistic rules criterion), allow emotion and affection to play an important role in their interaction (sentimentality criterion), and finally, derive more rewards from the relationship itself as opposed to what the relationship can do for each person individually (intrinsic reward criterion).

We do not believe that every intimate relationship will fulfill all of these criteria or that the criteria represent some sort of ideal of intimacy. But we do conceptualize modern intimacy as exhibiting more of these criteria, more frequently, than public relationships do. For instance, people, such as members of a surgical team, who work together on tasks that are highly interdependent may actually spend more hours in a day together than each spends with significant others. However, they probably wouldn't classify their work relationships as intimate unless they also exhibited several of the other criteria mentioned above. We can define **intimacy** in our own time as a unique bond created by two people through some combination of highly interdependent actions, individualized rules, and personal disclosures, and viewed by both parties as relatively affectionate, intrinsically rewarding, and irreplaceable.

A central feature of all relationships is that they are not static. Thus, an intimate relationship may be more or less interdependent or sentimental or individualistic from day to day, or even from moment to moment. In fact, many intimate relationships dissolve. In one study college students were asked to identify and report on their closest relationship. Nine months later, 42 percent of these close relationships had crumbled.[5] As for those relationships that do survive, we might even say that they are created and re-created by repetition of familiar episodes with consistent roles and rules. They may also be renegotiated and changed through the introduction of new episodes or modified roles and rules. For example, two friends constantly rebuild their relationship by engaging in favorite episodes such as "going to the movies," "cross-country skiing," or "exchanging recipes" with each other. A married couple may reaffirm their intimacy through regular episodes of "recounting the day's events" and "talking about future plans." Or they may increase their intimacy by adding some new episode such as "camping in the woods" to their repertoire. Or they may shift the basis of their intimacy. They may become more autonomous (he takes cooking classes and a separate vacation; she

## Sharing Words Online

# Trust and Self-Disclosure in Online Friendships

Early experimental research in computer-mediated communication (CMC) was based on the notion that reduced communication cues made CMC intrinsically impersonal. Yet more recent research has found that, in many cases, online communication feels deeper and more personal than face-to-face communication, an effect known as *hyperpersonal* communication. Yet, how do communicators establish deep and trusting relationships with people they have never physically met? In "'I've Never Clicked This Much with Anyone in My Life,'" Samantha Henderson and Michael Gilding investigate sources of online trust.

Like many of the studies we've reviewed, the researchers used qualitative, in-depth semi-structured interviews. One half of the interviews were conducted online and one half offline. Respondents were asked to tell the story of one of their online friendships and to discuss 10 of their closest friendships.

All of the respondents identified characteristics of online communication that could reduce trust: limited cues that allowed unrealistic self-presentation, lack of accountability, and more scope for deceit and betrayal. Yet, the vast majority of the respondents commented on the fact that these characteristics also provided opportunities for the development of trust. Online communication, for example, "fast-tracked" self-disclosure by removing the discomfort sometimes associated with open communication. The asynchronous nature of communication allowed respondents to think carefully about what they wanted to say, resulting in higher-quality communication. And the lack of accountability invited risk-taking. A surprising finding was the extent to which the self-disclosure of one party encouraged a "leap of faith" and reciprocal self-disclosure in the other. The most important aspect leading to trust was the degree to which CMC encourages performance, or "the sharing of words." The authors emphasize the fact that online relationships are "pure" in the sense that they are unprompted by anything other than intrinsic rewards. And pure relationships encourage communication, self-disclosure, and risk-taking.

The authors end by noting that, in addition to factors inherent in the nature of the medium, situational factors, like the importance of establishing intimacy, make it possible to establish trust with strangers. If "trust is a bet about the future contingent actions of others," today we are willing to make that bet—especially online.

Henderson, Samantha, and Michael Gilding. "'I've Never Clicked This Much with Anyone in My Life': Trust and Hyperpersonal Communication in Online Friendships." *New Media and Society* 6, no. 4 (2004): 487–506.

joins a fitness club and starts "bowling with the girls") and compensate by increasing the amount of self-disclosure with each other.

From these examples we should realize that an intimate relationship isn't something we make and then put on a shelf to look at and admire. Relationships are a lot like driving the same way to work or school every day. We know there are other routes, but we continue to follow the familiar path. In the same way, we keep rebuilding the same relationship day in and day out by engaging in the same familiar episodes. Intimate relationships, then, only seem stable to us because we repeatedly glue together the familiar parts (interacts, episodes, and so on) or replace them with new ones that are similar in some way. And frequently, they aren't very stable at all, as events signal changes on some or all six of the dimensions of intimacy.

In our culture the most common types of intimate relationships tend to be romantic couples, friendships, and family members. In a study of college students' closest relationships, Ellen Berscheid and her colleagues found that nearly half identified a romantic relationship, while 36 percent nominated a friendship and 14 percent mentioned a relationship with a family member.[6] Since we discussed family relationships in the last chapter, we will devote most of this chapter to a discussion of friendships and romantic couples.

## Friendships and Romantic Relationships

On the surface the differences between friendships and romantic relationships seem obvious. Rules for sexual behavior mark the distinction for some people. For others, mutual expressions of passionate love indicate romance, whereas friendship is based on strong liking or companionship. Others think of romance as short-lived, giving way to friendship if the relationship is to last. Try your own hand at defining the difference between friends and lovers. It's not as easy as you might think.

There probably are other, more subtle differences such as our expectations about where each type of relationship should fall on the six dimensions we've mentioned (how much sentiment should be expressed, how much and what type of interdependence is allowed, and so on). For example, some theorists argue that behavioral interdependence among friends is normally voluntary; they don't usually make demands on each other's time without asking first.[7] In a marriage such interdependence may be expected and even taken for granted. Thus, while both types of relationships may be considered intimate ones, they tend to differ in one major respect. As relations develop over time, friendships tend to retain their voluntary nature, while romantic relationships show a tendency to build obligations and commitments into their bond.

Even within the same type of intimate relationship, such as marriages, we know that people work out their relationships in vastly different ways. For instance, any one intimate relationship might be characterized as highly irreplaceable, interdependent, and sentimental; moderately individualistic and intrinsic; not especially particularistic. In such a relationship neither person may be able to conceive of living with anyone else, even if one partner died. They may do almost everything together, from working in the same office to attending the same social events to going to bed at the same time. They may be very expressive in their affection for each other.

Or they may have both grown up in a subculture that dictated most of the rules for how partners are to relate to one another and thus developed only a few rules that are truly unique to their own relationship. They may also have been taught to marry the right kind of person for reasons of social status or economic security, and so they derive as many extrinsic rewards from the relationship as they do intrinsic ones. And finally, they may enjoy talking about topics that many of us would consider impersonal, such as world and civic events, the weather, and what's on television, so much so that they spend little time talking about and revealing private attitudes and feelings. And they may be very satisfied with their relationship.

## Influences in Defining Intimacy

We have defined intimacy as a flexible concept, fluctuating along several dimensions of behavior and meaning. We have also seen that the meaning of intimacy changes from culture to culture, from family to family, and from time to time within cultures and families. Let's look at the influence of family and cultural messages on how we define our own intimate relationships.

### *Family Messages*

In the last chapter we discussed some of the types of long-term relationships that couples develop.

Such relationships are often influenced by family interaction patterns learned earlier in life. Thus, each of us may bring into a relationship quite different impressions of what intimacy means. Perhaps you can recall verbal or nonverbal messages you heard as a child that suggested to you what "ideal" relationships were like. These differing perceptions of intimacy no doubt influence how we come to define any current relationships.

### Recent Cultural Messages

Likewise, our views of what intimate relationships should be like can be influenced by changing cultural messages. In a review of popular magazines from the 1950s to the early 1970s, Virginia Kidd chronicled a major shift in perceptions of and advice given about interpersonal relationships.[8] The 1950s and early 1960s vision of relationships was described by Kidd as a single standard of self-sacrifice and avoidance of conflict (Vision I). Every effort was made to keep your partner happy. This view eventually gave way to a second vision in the late 1960s, one in which self-sacrifice was replaced by self-fulfillment and conflict avoidance was replaced by a norm of open expression of feelings, friendly or hostile (Vision II). A follow-up study in 1993 by Diane Prusank, Robert Duran, and Dena DeLillo found that a third vision had made its way into women's magazines since the 1970s.[9] Vision III seems to suggest a middle-ground approach to the choice of self or other orientation by encouraging sensitivity, and negotiating when and how to be open while still protecting the partner's feelings. Couples are advised to schedule time for discussing different issues, such as how frequently to have sex and how to achieve equality in the relationship. Table 11.1 identifies some of the major differences in these three visions.

## The Creation of Intimate Relations

Some researchers believe that intimate relationships develop because, like the Marines, people are constantly looking for a few good ones. The process is portrayed as resembling shopping for a good pair of shoes. You keep trying pairs on until you find one that fits. This approach assumes that people are highly cognizant of their own behavior and the implications of their interactions with others. Other social scientists point out that intimate relations often seem to just happen and can't be predicted very well in advance. The conventional wisdom here is that you just never know when love is going to hit you. Furthermore, many relationships develop slowly, almost imperceptibly, mixing elements of both the personal and impersonal. Both views are probably true at times, since communication patterns and their meanings are often seen more clearly in retrospect.[10]

### Planning for Intimacy

Some analyses of how intimate relations develop attribute a lot of strategic planning to the partners involved. Initial interactions are described as "auditions for friendship," and interactants are thought to be consciously evaluating each other's behavior in light of how well the other matches some ideal partner. In this view most of the communication between two newly-mets is in the form of testing the other's credentials for intimacy: "Are you my type?" "Do you measure up to my standards?" "Here, take this test. Let's see if you can pass it."

But how frequently or to what extent do we actually test the intimacy potential of a new relationship? Certainly we sometimes take stock of our lives and realize that our intimate relations are few and far between. First semester, freshman year may be one of those times. We meet dozens, even hundreds, of new people, only a few of whom will become close friends. We may be very conscious of how we select them and they select us. Dating is another example of the kind of situation in which we may be highly aware of the potential of a relationship. We are taught to use the dating game as a means for finding the right person; it is not usually seen as an end in itself, an activity to be enjoyed outright. The cultural messages we receive may encourage us to be more aware of the process. In our culture the number of self-help books on achieving intimacy suggest that it is a prized possession. We may start to look at relationships as "commodities"—products to be purchased. If we

**TABLE 11.1**   **A Comparison of Interpersonal Ideologies in Three Eras**

| Vision I<br>1950s–early 1960s | Vision II<br>mid-1960s–early 1970s | Vision III<br>mid-1970s–late 1980s |
|---|---|---|
| SINGLE STANDARD is the norm for relational behavior, defined in terms of appropriate male-female behavior. | CHANGE is the norm for relational behavior; model marriage is a myth. | PREDICTABLE CHANGE is the norm for relational behavior; relationships go through phases. |
| Relational meanings are PRECONCEIVED. | Relational meanings are FLEXIBLE, negotiable. | Relational meanings are NEGOTIATED within certain boundaries. |
| Deviation from norms is akin to EMOTIONAL PROBLEMS. | Deviation from norms can be seen as CREATIVITY, a way to negotiate new types of relationships. | Deviation from norms reflects GROWTH of INDIVIDUAL SELVES; knowledge of own and other's self can help the relationship adapt to these changes. |
| Competence is creating an image resembling the cultural IDEAL. | Competence is OPENNESS; relationships are a way to express the unique self. | Competence is TAKING CARE OF THE RELATIONSHIP, balancing concern for self and others. |

**Major prescriptions for communication**

| | | |
|---|---|---|
| SELF-SACRIFICE—make others happy. | BE YOURSELF—express your own feelings. | FOCUS ON THE RELATION-SHIP—make it work through negotiation. |
| AVOID CONFLICT or causing discomfort; conflict is negative. | COMMUNICATE. Failure to communicate is negative; "Suffering is not the worst thing in life . . . indifference is." | SHARE YOUR FEELINGS, BUT SEEK PERMISSION FIRST. Draw boundaries around when and where to deal with conflict. Schedule time for it. |
| TOGETHERNESS. Simply being with each other is most important; "You won't even want a night out alone." | AUTONOMY. Togetherness is important as long as it doesn't interfere too much with own freedom. | EQUALITY. Couples achieve their own sense of balance in the relationship. This balance is defined by the couple, not easily understood by outsiders. |

Adapted from two sources: Virginia Kidd, "Happily Ever After and Other Relationship Styles: Advice on Interpersonal Relations in Popular Magazines, 1951–1973," *Quarterly Journal of Speech* 61 (1975): 31–39; Diane Prusank, Robert Duran, and Dena DeLillo, "Interpersonal Relationships in Women's Magazines: Dating and Relating in the 1970s and 1980s," *Journal of Social and Personal Relationships* 10 (1993): 307–20.

adopt this view, we may indeed pay more attention to our shopping habits, making sure that we're good consumers of relationships.

In summary, there do seem to be occasions when we are highly aware of the intimacy potential of a new relationship. We may even plan encounters in advance, hoping that the relationship will move in the direction of intimacy. But there is no indication that we are always so conscious of where a relationship is going. In fact, many relationships survive for years on a relatively impersonal basis before they develop toward intimacy.

### Conditions for Intimacy

Intimate relationships are not always planned; proposals are not always rehearsed. There is not always a pursuer and a pursued. But neither does an intimate relationship spring itself on the parties in full-fledged form. The development of such a relationship is part of the communication process. But for one reason or another, the partners involved have not perceived (or have ignored) the intimacy potential in the messages and activities they have shared. Researchers point to a number of factors that may be combined and either gradually or suddenly make us aware of a relationship's potential for intimacy.

One of these factors, **physical proximity,** simply increases the likelihood that two people will communicate more frequently with each other. This factor alone seldom leads to intimacy, unless there are few other people available for interaction. More often, proximity sets the stage for other factors to interact. Perhaps one of the most common and often overlooked sources that lays the groundwork for possible intimacy is the frequency of **shared episodes.**

An episode is shared when two people engage in an activity that neither could do alone. Thus, when two people work closely together, or go mountain-climbing together, or engage in any shared activity repeatedly, they increase their interdependence. At first, partners develop behavioral interdependence. Their initial investment is simply an exchange of coordinated behaviors. Harriet Braiker and Harold Kelley point out that the normal pattern of development in close rela-

tionships is a movement from (1) behavioral interdependence to (2) the creation of rules and norms for joint action to (3) interdependence in personal attitudes and characteristics.[11] This suggests that establishing behavioral synchrony, while it does not in any way guarantee intimacy, certainly paves the way for future development should it be desired or encouraged.

Earlier we mentioned that dating is usually seen as a precursor to a more serious relationship, although it could be viewed as an end in itself. Parents and teenagers often view the process differently. A teenager, seeing the date as just an activity, tells her parents not to worry, "It's nothing serious." The parent, perhaps intuitively recognizing the potential of such behavioral interdependence, admonishes, "Don't go out with anyone you wouldn't want to marry."

Other situational factors can influence movement toward intimacy. Times, places, and dates can affect how we feel and create what Mark Knapp calls a "state of **intimacy readiness.**" Valentine's Day, spring fever, and the senior year of high school or college all qualify as intimacy producers.[12] Likewise, finding yourself in a situation that is normally defined as intimate may induce feelings of intimacy. You go to a dance with several friends and acquaintances; as the evening wears on, most of your friends drift off, leaving you alone in the company of the only other person in your party—one who happens to make an attractive partner. Fate strikes again—with consequences no one could have predicted. In these circumstances it doesn't matter so much who the partner is—what matters is that there is a partner. The relationship may be off and running before you've even had a chance to assess it.

**Romantic feelings** are another situational factor that influences movement toward intimacy, perhaps the most common factor in our culture. Most of us require that "falling in love" feeling before we legitimize a relationship as intimate. In their analysis of romantic love, Warren Shibles and Charles Zastrow identify three primary components: (1) an event that brings two people together, such as a date; (2) positive self-talk, an inner dialogue in which you convince yourself that the other is attractive; and (3) an emotional response or feeling of arousal (increased heart rate, nervous excitement, and so on).[13]

Interestingly, the absence of one component changes the nature of the feeling. Arousal and attraction without the event lead to romantic fantasies; the event and arousal without the attraction produce avoidance; the event and attraction but no arousal suggest friendship but not love; and so on. The most fascinating component, however, is the emotional response. A number of studies have demonstrated that any emotion, including love, consists of two things: physiological arousal and a cognitive label, such as love, hate, fear. The cognitive labels are produced by cultural and social definitions of the situation.[14] In one study, three groups of men experienced different levels of arousal before viewing videotapes of women they were told they would get to meet. Those who had higher levels of arousal were more attracted to beautiful women and more repulsed by less attractive women than those men who had been exposed to lower levels of arousal.[15]

Regardless of the type of intimate bond or our level of awareness about how it was created, researchers have long known that intimate relations rarely get off the ground without some form of attraction. People who find each other attractive communicate more frequently, giving their relationship the opportunity to develop in a more personal direction.

# Interpersonal Attraction: Opening the Door

We may "like" a lot of people, that is, develop a positive impression of them through self-talk, without ever pursuing a more personal relationship with them. In some cases this may be "liking from afar" (without any interaction to speak of); in other cases we may continue to interact with a person on a cultural or sociological level. Richard Sennett has referred to this type of interaction as **civility,** or "an activity which protects people from each other and yet allows them to enjoy each other's company."[16] We are likely to be attracted to a lot of people in this way. Many of the same factors that attract people to form civil, impersonal relations also lay the groundwork for more personal relationships should both partners desire to pursue one. In fact, one theory of attraction suggests that we begin almost immediately to evaluate others as potential friends or romantic partners. From the entire pool of people we meet, we begin a process of "filtering out" those who have little potential and taking a closer look at those who show promise. Let's discuss this theory in more detail.

## Duck's Filtering Theory of Attraction

Steven Duck's **filtering theory** of attraction explains when and how we use the verbal and nonverbal cues of others to determine their attractiveness as a relational partner. He suggests that people use a distinct and sequentially ordered set of criteria to evaluate each other's attractiveness.[17] We assess the attractiveness of a new acquaintance and of people we have known for some time differently. Attraction is determined by different criteria as a relationship moves in a more personal direction. These criteria act as filters, sifting out those people who are not likely to fit in one of our social circles. According to Duck the sequence of filters goes something like this: (1) sociological or incidental cues, (2) other pre-interaction cues, (3) interaction cues, and (4) cognitive cues.

### Sociological or Incidental Cues
The first criterion of attraction is that people must have an opportunity to observe each other. Thus, such factors as the proximity of homes or work sites, the frequency of interaction, and the expectation of future encounters encourage the development of attraction.

### Other Pre-Interaction Cues
Once we know that we're likely to meet a person again, we begin to scrutinize his or her behavior

from afar. Physical cues such as height, weight, beauty, clothing, and other surrounding artifacts become useful as a basis for attraction. These cues may be used to infer the person's social status, income, and lifestyle. Perceptions of how similar or different we are may be inferred, but they are limited in scope. We may, however, use this information to determine whether we want to initiate a conversation and what topics of conversation might be appropriate.

### Interaction Cues

Much more information becomes available to us once interaction begins. The topics of conversation we both enjoy, the length of time each person talks, smoothness of turn-taking, as well as duration of eye contact and interaction distance, may all be cues that help us determine liking. Some behaviors of the other may turn us off immediately, while others may take several interactions to evaluate. According to Duck the more we interact, the less important the sociological and pre-interaction cues will become as a basis for attraction.

### Cognitive Cues

Eventually, interaction behaviors enable us to form impressions of the other's attitudes, beliefs, and personality. Once these are formed, attraction is more likely to be based on assessments of these cognitive characteristics than on group memberships, clothing, or specific behaviors.

## Interpersonal Magnets: Factors That Pull Us Together and Push Us Apart

The filtering process we have just described tells us how people assess attractiveness in a very general way. A lot of research has been conducted on more specific factors that draw people together and create attraction or repulsion between them. This research finds that people are often attracted to each other for one or more of the following reasons: perceptions of physical beauty, important similarities, reciprocated liking, complementary needs, and anticipated costs or rewards. We will

look briefly at what this research suggests about the interpersonal dance of approach-avoidance.

### Physical Beauty

As filtering theory suggests, **physical beauty** is often the most important basis for attraction *initially*. In Chapter 3 we talked about physical appearance as a nonverbal code. We also noted that most cultures identify prototypes of male and female beauty, which influence our perceptions of physical attractiveness. This information suggests that we would most likely pursue relationships with those people we consider the most physically attractive. However, several research studies support a slightly different view, called the **matching hypothesis.** According to this research the decision to interact and pursue a more personal relationship is often based on the perception that we are relative equals in terms of physical attractiveness.[18] Many people assume they don't have a chance with someone they think is better-looking than themselves. As a result we often evaluate the attractiveness of both self and other to see if we match up.

### Similarity

How many times have you heard it said that "birds of a feather flock together" or that two people are "kindred spirits"? Common sense tells us that people are attracted to each other because they have key **similarities:** They like the same food, the same politics, and the same kind of people. They share many of the same personality traits. Most of the research that has tested the similarity hypothesis finds some measure of support for it.[19] Even so, a clear understanding of the relationship between similarity and attraction has been elusive. For all the ways that two people can be similar, there are just as many, if not more, differences between them. In fact, recent research suggests that the most important similarities related to attraction may be outside our awareness altogether.

Brant Burleson and his colleagues have found that similarities in cognitive complexity (see Chapter 6) are strongly related to attraction. In one study, married couples were much more similar in their levels of cognitive complexity than randomly generated pairs of males and females.[20] In the same study, the married couples were tested for similarity in their ability to accurately perceive the intentions of their partner during a discussion of a marital problem. Interestingly, couples who possessed similarly low skill levels were equally satisfied with their relationships as were the highly skilled couples. Burleson believes the results indicate that similar levels of cognitive and communicative ability lead to enjoyable interactions. For highly complex and skilled individuals, engaging in accurate and sensitive communication and feeling understood may be a good test of a valued relational ability. For less skilled individuals, concern about innermost feelings and nuances of meaning may be seen as "obsessive, boring, and hair-splitting." Similar results were found in studies of friends and dating partners, where similarity in value attached to emotional forms of communication (ego support, comforting, and conflict management) predicted attractiveness of partner and satisfaction with the relationship.[21]

## Reciprocal Liking

We are often attracted to another person for the simple reason that he or she has demonstrated **reciprocal liking,** or an interest or observable liking for us first. Several studies confirm that expressed liking will usually be reciprocated.[22] If you think about it, it's only natural to like those who like us. After all, if someone is capable of recognizing what a wonderful person you are and enjoys *your* company, she must be a half-decent person herself. Likewise, the person whose face registers disgust when he sees you enter the room is likely to elicit the same response from you.

Some research shows that expressed liking may often be enough to offset initial perceptions of dissimilarity. Benjamin Broome found college students to be more attracted to a foreign student who was quoted as saying Americans were easy to get along with, well informed, and interesting to talk to.[23] In this case the expressed "liking"

was for Americans in general; it wasn't even directed at the target.

While the reciprocal-liking hypothesis may seem natural, it doesn't always hold up. Under some conditions we tend not to respond positively to those who show liking for us. The basic premise of the reciprocal-liking hypothesis is that each person likes himself. If, however, a person has a negative self-image, he may have a hard time convincing himself that others really do like him and may view expressions of liking as polite insincerity. This may be called the Groucho Marx syndrome ("I wouldn't join a club that would have me for a member"). Such a person thinks there must be something *wrong* with someone who would like him. Also, the expression of liking must be situationally appropriate. If there is any indication that the behavior of the other is patronizing or manipulative in some way, we may not reciprocate.[24]

## Complementary Needs

According to psychologist William Schutz, each of us has differing degrees of three basic interpersonal needs: inclusion, control, and affection.[25] As a relationship develops, the degree to which one person's needs match or **complement** the other's may make them more or less attractive to each other.

The **need for inclusion** refers to how strongly we desire to be in the presence of other people. Obviously, there are times when each of us wants to be alone, but some people may have a greater need for privacy. Schutz described such a person as an *undersocial.* Likewise, an oversocial person is one who seems to constantly need people around. This need takes two forms: (1) the need to include others in your own activities—a reaching out to others—and (2) the need to be included in activities initiated by others—as when others invite you to join their group or club. For a pair's inclusion needs to be complementary, they must be fairly similar.

The second interpersonal need, the **need for control,** refers to a characteristic desire to control the behavior of others or have others control our behavior. The person who likes to control others is called an *autocrat;* someone who prefers to let others decide is labeled an *abdicrat.* Control needs are complementary when one person likes to take charge and the other doesn't mind or actually prefers that someone else be in control. Since most people prefer to have some degree of control in their relationships, control needs often have to be worked out through negotiation.

Finally, people may differ in their **need for affection.** This refers to the degree to which an individual feels she must express affection or closeness to others or have others express affection for her. This differs from inclusion needs in that we may like to have a lot of people around us but feel no particular motivation to get very close to them. Or we may not care for the company of a lot of people but want to be very close to those few we do include in our social circle. Obviously, when two persons' needs for affection differ greatly, they won't be able to fulfill those needs for each other. As a result, attraction may wane when such needs go unfulfilled over a long period of time.

### Costs and Rewards

According to one perspective on attraction, people exchange resources as they interact. These resources are often referred to as relational currencies (see Chapter 9) and may be economic in nature (money, goods, services, and so on) or more or less *intimate* (time, friendship, love, and so on).[26] The outcome of any exchange of resources between two people can be viewed in terms of losses and gains. According to exchange theory, as interpersonal communication takes place, the ratio of costs to rewards derived by each person is a good predictor of how attracted each person will be to the relationship. One of the difficulties in testing this hypothesis has been identifying what communication behaviors and episodes are most rewarding or costly to a particular individual *prior* to interaction. It is still possible, of course, that people do base their attraction for one another on this kind of analysis, at least some of the time.

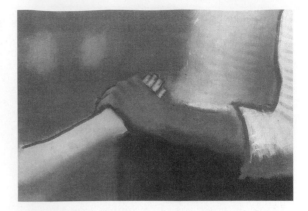

*During the integration and bonding stages, friends and lovers signal the nature of their relationship to the world, often through nonverbal means.*

### Other Sources of Attraction

Researchers are unlikely to ever identify all of the sources of attraction that bring people together. Attraction may be based on important qualities of conversation itself (above and beyond what it suggests about underlying similarities, complementary needs, and so on). We can only speculate that such factors as humor or witty repartee, nonverbal behavior reminiscent of a previous relationship, and a host of other idiosyncrasies may be frequent bases for attraction. It may be a good idea to try to identify the things that you find most attractive about the content and manner of *talk* experienced in the various relationships you have already established.

Remember that the factors we have isolated as leading to attraction aren't as static as they may sound. Interaction affects our perceptions of similarity, complementarity, costs and rewards, and so on. We create these factors *in talk*. We cannot overemphasize this fact. Two people may have similar needs, but unless they make each other aware of their similarities, there is no basis for attraction. Self-perception theory (see Chapter 7) suggests that we may communicate with others in such a way that we later determine we *must* like them. Some research confirms that this

| TABLE 11.2 | A Comparison of Two Models of Relationship Development | |
|---|---|---|

| Friendship development (Rawlins) | Stage | Romantic development (Knapp) |
|---|---|---|
| Role-limited interaction | 1 | Initiating |
| Friendly relations | 2 | Experimenting |
| Moves toward friendship | 3 | Intensifying |
| Nascent friendship | 4 | Integrating |
| Stabilized friendship | 5 | Bonding |
| Waning friendship | 6 | Differentiating |
| — | 7 | Circumscribing |
| — | 8 | Stagnating |
| | 9 | Avoiding |
| — | 10 | Terminating |

Adapted from William K. Rawlins, "Friendship as a Communicative Achievement: A Theory and an Interpretive Analysis of Verbal Reports," unpublished dissertation, Temple University, 1981, and from Mark L. Knapp, *Interpersonal Communication and Human Relationships* (Boston: Allyn and Bacon, 1984).

frequently happens when people disclose personal information to relative strangers.[27]

As we interact with people, we may discover a number of ways we are attracted to one another that could serve as a basis for developing a more personal relationship. Next we turn our attention to how relationship development typically takes place.

# The Closer the Better: Revealing Self to Other

As the filtering theory of attraction suggests, being attracted to someone initially doesn't automatically move the relationship toward intimacy. Even though a person meets all the criteria for

being an attractive "casual acquaintance" or "conversational partner," there may be little evidence that he or she would be "a good friend" or "romantic partner." For relationships to move in the direction of intimacy, qualitatively different communication patterns must be initiated and repeated. Researchers studying these changes in communication generally refer to the development as occurring in stages. In this section we will describe the typical stages of relational development, first for friendships and then for romantic couples, paying close attention to the communication patterns that typify each stage. Table 11.2 offers a comparison between the stages of development for friends and the stages typical of romantic relationships.

## Stages of Development in Friendship

The study of friendship has been sorely neglected by social scientists—romantic relations seem to

*People who become friends often share common interests and enjoy doing particular activities together.*

have garnered most of the attention. Nonetheless, interest in how friendships take shape is increasing. One of the most comprehensive models of friendship development has been proposed by William Rawlins.[28] A typical friendship progresses through six stages: (1) role-limited interaction, (2) friendly relations, (3) moves toward friendship, (4) nascent friendship, (5) stabilized friendship, and (6) waning friendship.

### Role-Limited Interaction

Friendships start out like any other relationship. Initial interactions are characterized by the adoption of social roles and rules such as those described in Chapter 7. We have described these as public interactions governed by the rules of civility. Although some friendships may be forged quickly as the result of participation in an unusual set of circumstances (for example, life-threatening situations or isolation from others), these are the exceptions.

### Friendly Relations

As we indicated earlier, role interactions can be carried out in a number of ways. An adviser-advisee or employer-employee relationship may be characterized by businesslike attention to detail or may include overtones of positive sentiment. In completing a loan application, there is no *necessity* that banker and client exchange humorous anecdotes or friendly chit-chat. In many such situations the friendly behavior pattern is to be enjoyed in its own right; it is not necessarily an invitation to further friendship. Nonetheless, friendly relations do establish the groundwork for a potential friendship to be built.

### Moves Toward Friendship

When people interact in roles, their behavior is dictated by cultural rules and their reason for being together is "obligated" to a large extent. We would consider it rude and outrageous if a loan officer suddenly complained of being tired and cut short our banking transaction. Yet it is this very obligation of role playing that is a barrier to friendship and other intimate relations. Rawlins suggests that one of the fundamental defining elements of friendship is its voluntary nature. Friends may, with much greater success than the loan officer, complain of tiredness and be released from an ongoing activity. In the moves-toward-friendship stage, invitations to engage in episodes that are less role-bound are extended and voluntarily accepted. Many of these activities may be short in duration so neither party feels obligated to continue the interaction. Third parties may be included to avoid undue strain in these tentative explorations. Other activities may proceed in a kind of open-ended time frame. Since participation is voluntary, either party may decide when he or she wants to conclude the episode; neither party has a right to place demands on the other's time. "Going to a movie with several others" is a good example of a short-term third-party episode. The possibility of extending the evening at a favorite watering hole typifies the open-ended time frame.

Qualitative changes also occur in the content of interactions during this stage. Rawlins's research indicates that people begin creating "jointly constructed views" of the world during this phase. Talk may initially focus on similarities in attitudes and values and gradually change to explorations of differences in opinions. When consensus results in the altering of viewpoints held prior to interaction, a jointly constructed view emerges. Friendship is often characterized by voluntarily spending time together and enjoying highly relaxed forms of nonverbal communication.

## Nascent Friendship

Once moves toward friendship become repetitive, a pair may begin to think of themselves as "becoming friends." Friendship is crystallized in this stage. Significant changes in communication take place. Role interactions that once characterized the relationship are now seen as inappropriate. Rawlins refers to this as the development of "negative norms"—forms of communication that are now out of bounds. Even though the

voluntary nature of friendship remains a constant feature, emerging friends often *choose* to participate in a wider range of activities and topics of conversation.

## Stabilized Friendship

The establishment of friendship is rarely celebrated in our culture. There are few, if any, bonding rituals such as "becoming blood brothers." As a result, the bonds of friendship are often very fragile. Verbal legitimacy may be obtained by calling each other "friend," but the meaning of the term is weakened by overuse. Casual acquaintances often call each other friends, in spite of the fact that they know very little about each other. Immigrants to this country often have difficulty adjusting to how loosely we use the term. "I'm having 20 *friends* over for a party—why don't you join us?" is a real contradiction in terms for many non-natives.[29]

How, then, do we know when a relationship has become a stable friendship? Most writers emphasize the importance of developing trust. Obviously, trust doesn't just materialize at a single stage of relational development. The process unfolds slowly, involving two related types of behavior. **Trusting behavior** refers to any behavior that increases one person's vulnerability to another. Anyone who voluntarily enters a dangerous situation with another person or reveals very personal information to another is engaging in trusting behavior. Police officers routinely place themselves in the trust of their partners. **Trustworthy behavior** is a response to trusting behavior that protects the vulnerability of the other. A friend who lets a secret slip out to a third party has failed to exhibit trustworthy behavior. The development of trust is a delicate process and takes considerable time as friends expose their vulnerabilities one by one, often with extreme caution.

Another way that individuals maintain friendships is through assimilation of each other's attitudes and beliefs. In other words, we sometimes adjust our own beliefs to be more in line with those of our friend. One study, however, revealed a tendency in cross-sex friendships to estimate the other's opinion on an issue by assuming that they agree with us more than they really do.[30] This suggests that we may maintain stability under somewhat false pretenses.

Many people distinguish among types of friends or levels of friendship. Paul Wright differentiates *superficial* friendships, in which partners enjoy each other's company, from more *developed* friendships based on mutual concern and recognition of the other's uniqueness and irreplaceable qualities.[31] While researchers seldom agree about the precise number of levels of friendship, a common distinction is to differentiate among casual, close, and best friends. Casual friendships fall into the superficial category, while close and best friends would qualify as more developed relationships. People generally have several close friends but only one best friend.

Robert Hays asked college students to keep a daily record of their interactions with one close and one casual friend for a week. He found that close friends interacted more frequently, across a greater range of settings, and perceived their talk to be more exclusive and more emotionally supporting than did casual friends. Having fun and feeling relaxed with each other were strong predictors of relational progression.[32]

Suzanna Rose and Felicisima Serafica studied the strategies that different types of friends used to keep or end their relationships.[33] For casual friends frequent interaction was an important aspect of maintaining the relationship. A lack of interaction, whether by design or happenstance, seems to threaten such relationships. The maintenance of close and best friendships was more dependent on the quality of interaction, especially demonstrations of affection. Such relationships were more likely to end if arguments, betrayals, or boredom lowered the level of perceived affection. Interestingly, less frequent interaction was more threatening to close than to best friends. As one woman put it: "You have to work harder at a close friendship than a best one. It requires more effort. You can't take a close friend as much for granted."[34]

### Waning Friendship

Like any relationship, a friendship does not maintain itself. It requires effort on each person's part to keep in touch and to explore new activities and interests. Friendships may begin to wane as a result of neglect, lack of support from significant others, major violations of trust, deviance from important relational norms, competing demands on time, and a host of other possible factors. In terms of communication patterns, a waning friendship may be revealed by a growing increase in restraint where candor once existed and in autonomy where togetherness was once the rule. When this is undesirable, we should probably be concerned but avoid overreacting. Most friendships will go through periods like this. We all have friends who seem to disappear—no cards, no letters, no phone calls—only to resurface months later, fill us in on all the news, and go on as though there had been no interruption.

Many of the stages and communication patterns in friendship development are similar to those encountered in relations we define here as romantic couples—dating partners, spouses, long-term live-in partners. In fact, many couples describe themselves as "best friends" in addition to being romantically involved. Yet there are essential differences in the way romantic relationships develop and the communication patterns that constitute that development. We will look at these relationships next.

## Stages of Development in Romantic Coupling

Romantic relationships progress in many of the same ways that friendships do, and the same issues of trust, candor-restraint, and autonomy-togetherness have to be worked out. Since we have already discussed many of these issues, our review of the stages of development for romantic pairs will be somewhat brief. We'll try to point out the major differences between relationships that are moving along a friendship trajectory as opposed to those on the romantic path.

Although many models of the development of romantic intimacy are available, we will use one of the more popular ones, developed by Mark Knapp.[35] Five stages depict the "process of coming together": initiating, experimenting, intensifying, integrating, and bonding. While these stages may not reflect the development of every romantic relationship, they do describe a typical path. Later we will look at the process of relationships coming apart.

## Initiating

This stage is similar to the "role-limited interaction" stage of friendship. Communication at this point largely consists of greetings and other types of contact required by the situation. The first day on a new job or the first day of a new semester present us with numerous opportunities to initiate relationships. Communication is extremely stylized to allow people to interact with little knowledge of one another. Initial filters of attraction may be applied and judgments of communication competence made.

## Experimenting

If a relationship survives the initial contact, the pair may continue to use standard formulas of interaction to engage in small talk. People who are skilled at initiating and maintaining conversations (see Chapter 4) manage relationships at this level quite competently. Small talk and other interaction rituals enable a person to present a desired self-image, form impressions of the other, and isolate similarities for further exploration. A norm of politeness rules these interactions.

For most of the past century, the experimenting phase was the domain of males. It was generally assumed that a male would make the first move to initiate a date. (However, this was not the case in the 19th century. See Box 11.1 for a historical exception to the rule.) In today's climate of equality, of course, female-initiated dating has made a return. But with what results? In a recent study, 90 percent of the males questioned had been asked out on a first date by a female. In less than half the cases, however, was a second date initiated by the female. It appears that once a dating relationship begins, subsequent dates are either mutually negotiated or initiated by the male. In spite of that fact, males had positive perceptions of a female initiator (versus a woman who waited to be asked out or hinted

to the man). The direct female initiator was perceived as more flexible, truthful, extroverted, more of a feminist, and more socially liberal.[36] The researchers speculated that the perception of the female-initiator as a feminist may change the nature of the script a male draws upon to guide actions on a first date.

Flirting is another interesting way in which both males and females experiment with relationship potential. However, flirting behavior is easily misinterpreted. This was illustrated in a study where students completed a questionnaire measuring their beliefs about flirting and were then shown one of eight different versions of a conversation between a male and female student waiting outside a professor's office. In four of the video segments, a male initiated the conversation and exhibited nonverbal cues characterized as "friendly," "flirting," "seductive," or "neutral." In the other four versions, a female initiated the conversation. No matter how intimate the nonverbal display, when the man initiated the conversation, he was rarely perceived as seductive or promiscuous. For the female, on the other hand, the mere fact that she initiated the conversation was enough for her to be perceived as "somewhat seductive." The authors concluded that perceptions of the female would probably be even stronger had the setting been in a bar or some other "marketplace" location.[37] Thus, flirting behavior, while clearly an option as a tool for experimenting, still appears to be problematic in terms of the gendered messages drawn from its occurrence.

During the experimenting phase, individuals are very concerned with showing themselves off to their best advantage by using what Robert Bell and John Daly have called **affinity-seeking strategies.**[38] These include behaviors like giving gifts; taking charge of situations; acting in a warm; empathic manner; doing favors; and the like. High self-monitors and highly assertive and responsive individuals appear to be better able to use a full range of behaviors to generate liking than are most people, while those who are highly apprehensive about communicating have a more limited repertoire.

BOX 11.1

## Playing the Dating Game

# A Social History of Courtship

In every culture and in every age, people meet and fall in love. When it happens, it seems to be the most natural thing in the world. In reality, falling in love is not as personal and spontaneous as it appears to be; rather, it is part of a culturally constructed courtship system that is connected to social as well as individual concerns. In *From Front Porch to Back Seat*, Beth Bailey examines the history of this system in America and shows its connection to issues of power, money, and gender identity.

In the late 19th century conventional heterosexual courtship took the form of "calling." When a young woman reached marriageable age, she was allowed to receive male callers in her home, under the watchful eye of a chaperone. The entire calling system was controlled and regulated by women and took place in their sphere.

Only if he were expressly invited by a young woman or her mother was a young man allowed to pay a call. It was considered highly unsuitable for a man to force his attention on a lady by initiating contact.

By the mid-1920s an entirely new system of courtship—the date—had emerged. Although the word "date" was originally associated with prostitution (making a date was a code for buying sexual favors), it soon became an accepted term for a new courtship pattern. Couples who dated no longer sat together in the front parlor of a private home. They went out to theaters, restaurants, and dance halls. This move into the public sphere gave couples unprecedented freedom. It also transformed power relations between the sexes. Men, who controlled the public sphere, now controlled courtship, and women were forbidden to take the initiative. According to mid-20th-century advice manuals, girls who "usurped the right of boys to choose their own dates," who refused to respect "the time-honored custom of boys to take the first step," would "ruin a good dating career." Bailey argues this role-reversal occurred because "going out" cost money—men's money. Both men and women recognized that dating involved an economic exchange. A young man with lots of

### Intensifying

Most relationships don't move beyond initiating and experimenting. As in friendship, intimates-to-be make overtures to each other that signal a new intensity to their interactions. Knapp notes a number of changes in verbal communication patterns: increased informality in forms of address, increased use of the pronouns we and us, the creation of private codes and verbal shortcuts, and so on. But these do not occur overnight. The process involves a good deal of testing. Affinity-seeking strategies, for instance, are subtle ways of indicating our own relationship-readiness, but to determine the feelings and perceptions of the other requires even greater subtlety. Research shows that talking about the state of a relationship is generally taboo, so people resort to more indirect tests. Leslie Baxter and William Wilmot call these "secret tests." Apparently, when a relationship has "romantic potential," partners rely most frequently on indirect suggestions, separation tests, endurance tests, and triangle tests.[39] **Indirect suggestions** include such things as jokingly referring to the relationship in more serious terms and flirting. This allows the initiator a chance to see how the other money could afford a beauty queen; a poorer man had to settle for a less attractive partner. Expensive flowers or fine restaurants were symbols that said "for the man, 'See what I can afford,' and for the woman, 'See how much I'm worth.'"

Bailey points out that the rise of dating coincided with the rise of consumption and competition as cultural ideals. Whereas courtship was about marriage, dating was about competition. Before World War II, American youth used dating as a way to demonstrate popularity and self-worth. One won the dating game by the number, variety, and quality of the dates one could get. While no girl wanted to date a "semigoon" or "spook," even an unappealing date was better than nothing. At dances, popularity was measured by the number of different partners one danced with. To be left with the same partner for more than one dance was a girl's worst nightmare and a source of embarrassment to her escort whose own worth fell if his date was not a sought-after commodity.

After World War II, couples began to value stable and safe relationships rather than conspicuous popularity. Nevertheless, competition was still involved. Young people felt great pressure to make the "best catch" possible. A 13-year-old who did not date was considered a "late bloomer," and by 15, teens were expected to have "steadies." The college woman who reached graduation without her MRS degree often felt her education had been wasted. No one wanted to be left behind in the marriage sweepstakes.

Regardless of whether young people went steady or dated multiple partners, the relations between the sexes remained the same. Girls were advised to demonstrate submissiveness, never to take the initiative, and to avoid seeming to be smarter than their boyfriends. As a teenage boy from Shaker Heights said, "I don't mind if a girl knows more than I do . . . I just like her to act like she knows a little less."

Today the values and assumptions associated with dating seem slightly ridiculous. Since the sexual and feminist revolutions courtship has changed dramatically. Modern relationships are characterized by more freedom and equality as well as by more uncertainty and complexity, as couples work out difficult issues of independence, control, and gender identity.

**SOURCE** Beth L. Bailey, *From Front Porch to Back Seat: Courtship in Twentieth-Century America* (Baltimore: The Johns Hopkins University Press, 1988).

responds. If he or she takes it as a joke, things likely will remain at the more superficial level. **Separation tests** involve such things as not seeing the other for brief or extended periods of time (to see if the other makes contact or seems to have missed us), whereas **endurance tests** increase the costs associated with the relationship to see if the other is willing to remain. Asking a person to go out of his or her way to do a favor is an example. Finally, **triangle tests** include going out with others to test for jealousy and mentioning someone else you think the other might be interested in to see his or her reaction.

James Tolhuizen also studied strategies that partners use to transform a casual dating relationship into a more serious and exclusive one.[40] While many of the same affinity-seeking strategies used during experimenting were also employed at this later stage, Tolhuizen found a greater tendency for partners to talk about and negotiate relational issues, to make direct requests for a more serious relationship, and to show affection through more casual touching, verbal expressions of affection, and increased sexual intimacy. Although there were very few gender differences, females did engage in more relational negotiation and more often waited for the male to press for greater commitment. In most situations the person who wanted a more serious relationship used a combination of strategies, usually coupled with increased contact or reward-giving.

## Integrating

At this stage, partners in romantic couples begin to organize their everyday lives around each other. Interdependence becomes more and more visible to others. As with friendship, jointly constructed views of the world emerge, plans are made with the other in mind, and social circles begin to overlap. In fact, one study of romantic relationships demonstrated just how important communication with the other's social network is. Malcolm Parks and Mara Adelman interviewed 172 college students, asking how frequently they talked to their dating partner's family and friends and how much those people supported the relationship. Interviews three months later showed that those who were more involved with their dating partner's social network were more likely to still be dating. In addition, they also felt they had a better understanding of their partner's behavior, attitudes, and feelings.[41]

Integrating may occur in a number of other ways. Some people make small purchases together that become common property. Others may change some of their habits so they can spend more time together. For example, a divorced mother invites a potential stepfather to have dinner with her and her children. Integration can also be achieved symbolically. Leslie Baxter defines **relational symbols** as "concrete metacommunicative 'statements' about the abstract qualities of intimacy, caring solidarity . . . which the parties equate with their relationship."[42] She describes five types of symbols that couples often associate with their relational identity and how they are used:

- *Behavioral action symbols:* interaction rituals, games, nicknames, or inside jokes that are frequently and exclusively used by the couple

- *Events/times:* references to the first date, first kiss, or a particular weekend that holds significance for the couple
- *Physical objects:* gifts that signify important steps in the relationship
- *Symbolic places:* references to places that have special meaning
- *Symbolic cultural artifacts:* songs, books, or films the couple views as "their own"

Many of these relational symbols are used as integrating mechanisms to indicate the exclusivity of the relationship, seclusion from the outside world, shared activities, and growing intimacy. In short, they signal partners' integration as a couple.

Integrating the lives of two separate individuals is no easy task. The process is fraught with difficulties, and most relationships must endure a lot of conflict to survive this far. Many people find their differences are too significant to encourage further development. As a result, they terminate the relationship or reestablish a greater degree of independence and lessen the intensity of their involvement. For those who forge ahead, the role of interpersonal conflict is crucial. Social scientists are gradually learning the significance of conflict in the development of close relationships. Avoiding conflict may prevent people from discovering potentially rewarding aspects of a relationship. Overreacting to conflict or mishandling it can make continuing the relationship painful. Successful management of conflict often leads to greater understanding and commitment to a relationship.

## Bonding

Once two people's lives have become intertwined to their mutual satisfaction, private commitments are often formalized. The bonding stage is really one that institutionalizes the relationship. At some point, the two parties have a serious discussion about their level of commitment to each other. Robert Fulghum calls this **covenant talk**—"two people working out what they want, what they believe, what they hope for each other."[43] While marrying, buying a house together, or making some other public commitment cements the bond and gives it a public image, Fulghum advises couples to pay more attention to their covenant talk because it's "the real wedding." Although the typical intimate relationship in our culture reaches the bonding stage by integrating two selves through reciprocated self-disclosures, this is not an absolute necessity. Close bonds are frequently created among members of sports teams, youth gangs, musical groups, and groups supporting some cause. These group members may feel bonded out of a sense of brotherhood or sisterhood, as opposed to knowing very much about one another's personal feelings or psychological profiles. Some unique professional dyads, such as ice-skating duos, dancers, and trapeze artists, develop a kind of intimacy based more on complex behavioral interdependence than on knowledge of the psyche. Yet we would be hard-pressed to classify these relationships as simply based on sociological or cultural knowledge of each other.

Although relationships don't stop developing at this point, there is often a "honeymoon" period in which the emotional bond between two individuals seems to carry the day. This period rarely lasts very long, but let's hope it will last long enough for us to introduce the next section of the chapter.

*Holding and touching are signals of a highly intimate relationship.*

# Two Close for Comfort: Relational Maintenance and Dissolution

Once the bonds of friendship or romance are viewed as a long-term involvement, a new issue comes into play. Partners must negotiate how each can reestablish a sense of identity and more clearly define the boundaries between the self and the relationship to promote harmony. In this section we'll focus on these issues, as well as examine the stages a deteriorating relationship passes through.

## Balancing Self-Identity and Relational Identity

When two people form a close relationship, they give much of themselves to it. Accommodations are made by both parties so that the new relationship can fit into their already busy lives. Other relationships may suffer from lack of attention, as may some personal pursuits. Obviously, what's given up is replaced by much that is new and exciting and that promises to offer future rewards. At the same time, the bonding process can frequently lead to a feeling of being engulfed by the relationship. Intimates, especially those who live together, spend many of their nonworking hours in close physical proximity. And for those who subscribe to the "openness in communication" school of thought, the psychological intimacy can be overwhelming. The self-identity can get lost in the shuffle.

How do people deal with the problem of investing themselves in an important relationship while maintaining a strong sense of self? This is probably the major issue in managing close relationships. Some people react by becoming virtually self-less, contributing most of their energy to the relationship. Others place the emphasis on self-growth, maintaining close relationships so long as they don't stifle that growth.

Most of us, however, must learn to creatively manage the tension between self-identity and relational identity. Researchers characterize this tension in friendship as one of learning how to balance (1) the need to be expressive versus the need to be protective, (2) the need for autonomy versus the need for togetherness, and (3) the need for predictability versus the need for novelty.[44] For long-term romantic relationships, we see these three tensions occurring as well, but we add a fourth tension, that of balancing traditional and nontraditional gender roles.

### The Expressive-Protective Dialectic

When two people learn to trust each other, they're usually more willing to disclose both positive and negative personal information. The focus on trust reveals what William Rawlins calls **expressive-protective dialectic.** Friends share a desire to be expressive, to reveal personal thoughts and feelings. At the same time, however, too much openness may reveal areas of vulnerability. This leads to a need to be protective of each other's weaknesses. Protectiveness works in two ways. First, there is a need to protect the self. Each of us has vulnerabilities or old wounds

we don't like to open. A relationship that extols the virtues of total openness may put undue stress on us. Second, we must be sensitive to similar vulnerabilities in our close friends. This means learning not to pry into certain areas.

Candor and restraint are both necessary to maintain a stable relationship. In fact, Rawlins argues, friends have to negotiate "necessary conditions for closeness." This tension is experienced on a topic-by-topic basis as friends and lovers decide which issues are ripe for candid disclosure and which are best handled with restraint.

### The Autonomy-Togetherness Dialectic

This issue isn't limited to friendships, but it is an especially sensitive issue since the bond of friendship is such a voluntary one. The **autonomy-togetherness dialectic** states that friends must be careful not to assume that the other will automatically participate in any given activity. They cannot always take each other's time for granted. However, it's awkward to repeatedly ask each other about activities that we do together on a routine basis. The ability to balance this tension is the hallmark of good friendships. This tension also exists within romantic relationships. In fact, it may be more crucial because the amount of time spent together is usually much greater. Each partner in a relationship should realize that the more time they spend together, the greater the need for freedom is likely to become. And since no two people are alike, one partner may reach that threshold more quickly than the other.

These relational issues, themes, boundaries, and patterns are worked out by couples in much the same way that families work them out (see Chapter 10). In fact, our family of origin may contribute a great deal to what we see as the possible ways to work out these tensions.

### The Novelty-Predictability Dialectic

A major aspect of developing a relationship is establishing regular patterns of interaction that the couple comes to view as distinctively its own. According to the **novelty-predictability dialectic,** over time, the relationship takes on a life of its own and partners become quite predictable to each other. With this level of predictability comes the risk of boredom or the feeling that the relationship has turned stale. In a study of this phenomenon, Leslie Baxter found that most couples prefer the basic nature of their relationship to remain predictable but would like their conversations and daily activities to reflect greater novelty.[45] "You never surprise me anymore" is a good sign that the daily routine is too predictable.

### The Gender Role Dialectic

As we already saw in Chapter 7, roles, and in particular gender roles, are very important determinants of how we behave as individuals, as well as of how our society deals with continuity and change. When we follow traditional roles we transmit stable cultural values. When we design new roles, we adapt to a changing world. The **gender role dialectic** focuses on the tension between accepting traditional gender definitions and finding new ways of being masculine or feminine.

Traditional gender roles are related to the traditional assumption that eventually most of us will pair up with someone of the opposite sex and produce children, and the female will act as the children's primary caregiver. Therapist Betty Berzon describes this traditional arrangement in the following way:[46]

> *In order to accomplish this [the female] is trained to be nurturing, emotionally expressive, and skilled in homemaking. In order to keep her at home, she is conditioned to be submissive and dependent. . . . The male, on the other hand, is considered to be the primary provider of the material support that makes the female's caregiving possible. He is expected to be assertive, in control of his feelings, independent, and in charge.*

Berzon points out that these roles, originally developed to be complementary, stay with us, even when the assumptions that are their foundation no longer hold. Nowadays the female partner in a heterosexual dyad may put her child in day care and take a job. This decision can lead to stress, especially for traditional couples. If, for example, Julia wants to stay home with the children, but instead finds herself working outside the home for financial reasons, she may feel extremely guilty about "failing" her children. Her husband Joe may also feel guilty because she has to work. Or, to take the opposite scenario, what about Sam who would like nothing better than to stay home with the kids, and Sarah, who would love a high-powered job? If they decide that Sam will become the primary caregiver and Sarah the primary wage-earner, they may have to face social pressure from friends and family who feel this arrangement isn't quite right. In both cases, problems stemming from a failure to resolve the gender role dialectic may make both couples miserable, trapping them in expectations that don't match their personalities and preferences.

So far we've looked at opposite-sex dyads, ones in which men pair up with women. But we know that men also pair up with men, and women with women. Here different problems can arise. In same-sex dyads, complementary roles based on gender don't work. Although this might seem to be ideal solution, freeing the couple from constricting roles, partners must still figure out how to allocate their obligations and prerogatives.[47]

Jeanne Marecek and her colleagues suggest three ways traditional gender roles may affect the way roles are assigned in same-sex relationships.[48] In the first, practical factors determine who does a given task, and subsequently, additional behaviors that are part of the same gender role will be assumed. For example, if David works late, Dan (who likes to cook) may take over meal preparation. Later on, Dan may find himself doing other "similar" tasks, for example cleaning, shopping, and other household tasks. This may suit both men, but it can become a problem if, over time, Dan begins to wonder why he has to do all the housework and comes to resent a role he took on without realizing it. In a second pattern, the more dominant member or the member with higher status may lay claim to the masculine role because in our society the masculine role is often seen as more valued and more rewarding. If Stella, for example, makes more money than Sue, she may feel this entitles her to make major decisions. As a result, Sue is expected to be more dependent and more passive. Once again, this division of labor can trap partners into rigid roles they may tire of. Finally, a third possibility is that roles may be assigned by how closely each partner identifies with traditional gender roles. The more male-identified of the partners may take on traditional male roles, while the more female-identified may take on traditional female roles. Note that in all three situations, traditional gender roles intruded into the relationships.

Although it is possible to free ourselves from gender role playing, it is difficult. Like it or not, we internalize the gender messages we see around us and have a hard time moving beyond gender. Berzon cautions us that for both heterosexual and homosexual dyads, "the real problem is about patterns getting set and then becoming doorless rooms from which there is, it seems, no exit."[49] In both same- and opposite-sex dyads, roles should be designed that take into account both partners' interests, skills, and personalities. These roles should be periodically revised as partners' needs and interests change. A combination of careful negotiation and sensitivity to each other's needs is the hallmark of resolving the gender role dialectic.

### Working Out Dialectic Tensions

Baxter studied how couples managed the first three of the dialectic tensions we've examined. She found that couples managed the tensions by utilizing six different strategies.

- *Selection:* The couple opts for one of the extremes. You may recall from Chapter 10 that "separates" in married couples chose to spend much of their time apart (preferring autonomy over togetherness).

- *Cyclic alternation:* The couple cycles through periods of togetherness, followed by another period of autonomy (or cycles of highly predictable, then novel activities).

- *Topical segmentation:* The couple chooses autonomy or closedness in some activities, togetherness or openness in other arenas.

- *Moderation:* The couple might compromise or dilute both polar extremes. For instance, small talk that is open but superficial would dilute the pull toward either openness or closedness.

- *Disqualification:* The couple manages the tension through equivocal or indirect means, for example, by hinting at problems rather than discussing them openly.

- *Reframing:* The couple transforms the issue so that it is viewed as having a different level of meaning. Autonomy could be redefined as enhancing the time spent together (and no longer defined as the opposite of togetherness).

Baxter found that a majority of couples managed the autonomy-togetherness dialectic through cyclic separation, while segmenting or moderating openness-closedness. Segmentation was also frequently applied to manage the predictability-novelty issue. Couples tried to introduce novelty at the level of their activities while maintaining predictability in talking about their relationship, remaining faithful, and so on. Couples also went through periods of interacting predictably, then introducing some novelty (cyclic alternation).

A lot of couples balance candor-restraint tensions, almost unconsciously, by mismanaging interpersonal perceptions. Partners buffer themselves by occasionally using ambiguous or tangential communication. For example, they often talk around the edges of an issue they disagree on. They may phrase their views in such a way that the other can interpret some agreement if so desired. As long as the issue isn't crucial to their everyday interaction, they can engage in restraint. The success of long-term relationships often depends on how well a couple works out basic relational dilemmas such as autonomy or togetherness.

In an insightful review of research, Allan Sillars and Michael Scott identified several perceptual biases that develop and are reinforced in intimate relationships.[50] Specifically, they found that individuals in intimate relationships tend to (1) perceive their own relational communication (such as instigating conflict) as more positive than their partner does, (2) overestimate the similarity between their own and their partner's attitudes, (3) differ in their perceptions of who makes important family or relational decisions, and (4) describe relational problems in general rather than specific terms (for example, referring to each other's general traits rather than focusing on specific behaviors). These tendencies frequently lead intimates to blame each other for conflicts and to attribute their partner's behavior to personality traits, and their own behavior to situational factors.

Sillars and Scott offer some interesting explanations for these perceptual biases. For one, they argue that *familiarity* increases our confidence that we understand our partner's feelings and attitudes. This confidence, based initially on self-disclosures and efforts to understand, may soon expand to areas that haven't been so thoroughly investigated. Thus, we only *think* we understand each other. Mind reading, often referred to as a cardinal sin in interpersonal relating, may actually serve an important function from time to time.

Emotional involvement is also a leading candidate for perceptual bias according to Sillars and Scott. Intimates are at once each other's "most knowledgeable *and* least objective observer."[51] Overall, positive sentiment for one's partner may bias interpretation of messages in the direction of **assimilation,** or greater presumed agreement than actually exists. On the other hand, during periods of stress or conflict, messages may be interpreted on the basis of **contrast,** or greater presumed disagreement. Likewise, research indicates that when people experience emotional stress, their abilities to process information decline and they rely on more simplistic, stereotypic ways of thinking. Obviously, this can lead to perceptual biases.

## Relational Maintenance Behaviors

It is important to balance dialectical tensions. But how do we do so? One way is to enact what are called **relational maintenance behaviors**. These are the mundane everyday routines we use to shape our relationships. As we pointed out in Chapter 2, relationships need to be maintained. Most of us understand how necessary it is to keep the physical objects we own in good repair. We take our cars in for servicing; we mow the lawn and weed the garden; we even get periodic health checkups. But when it comes to relationships, we often forget how important routine maintenance is. Yet without relational maintenance, most relationships can't survive. Communication scholars Linda Guerrero, Peter Andersen, and Walid Afifi have reviewed some of the behaviors that couples report they use to keep their relationships on track. These are reported in Table 11.3. As you can see, couples use a variety of ways to keep their relationships healthy. And these methods appear to work. Guerrero and her colleagues report that college-age couples who use constructive maintenance strategies show a greater likelihood of staying together and are more satisfied with their romantic relationships than those who do not.[52]

Of course, different kinds of relationships are maintained in different ways. And different kinds of maintenance strategies are called for at different stages in the life of a relationship. For example, married couples make more use of task-sharing and social networking than dating couples.[53]

As Table 11.3 shows, we hold relationships together through everyday interaction. We talk about nothing as though it were important, we anticipate and perform requests before we are asked, or we read the Sunday paper without speaking. Sometimes, we intentionally or unintentionally misread or misunderstand one another in order to maintain the perception of agreement. When couples are unable to engage in this kind of interaction because they are separated from one another, they must other find ways to hold their relationships together, as Box 11.2 shows.

| TABLE 11.3 | Common Relational Maintenance Behaviors |
| --- | --- |

**Openness and Routine Talk**

Talking and listening to one another; for example, self-disclosing, talking about the relationship, asking about each other's day

**Positivity**

Making interaction pleasant; for example, complimenting, acting cheerful, accommodating the other's wishes

**Assurances**

Giving assurance about commitment; for example, saying that you still care, showing commitment, talking about the future

**Supportiveness**

Giving social support and encouragement; for example, comforting, sacrificing, being there in times of need

**Joint Activities**

Doing things together; for example, going places together, visiting each other's homes, working out together

**Task-sharing**

Doing routine chores together; for example, sharing housework, planning finances together, helping each other with tasks

**Romance and Affection**

Expressing positive feelings; for example, saying "I love you," giving each other gifts, flirting, having a romantic dinner

**Social Networking**

Spending time with each other's friends and family; for example, acting as a couple in front of others, going to family functions together

**Mediated Communication**

Using mediated channels to communicate; for example, calling each other, sending text messages, writing letters, communicating through IM

**Avoidance**

Avoiding conflicts by *not* communicating; for example, giving the other privacy, avoiding issues that lead to trouble, planning some separate activities

**Humor**

Using personal jokes and humor; for example, teasing each other, giving gag gifts, making each other laugh

**Balance**

Making the relationship fair; for example, putting the same amount of effort into the relationship, returning favors, making sure both parties are rewarded equally

**Antisocial**

Using manipulative or coercive behaviors; for example, pouting to get attention, making the other feel guilty, creating jealousy

Adapted from Laura K. Guerrero, Peter A. Andersen, and Walid A. Afifi, *Close Encounters: Communicating in Relationships* (Mountain View, Calif.: Mayfield, 2001), pp. 230–31.

BOX 11.2

## Seeing Our Partners Through Rose-Colored Glasses

# Long Distance Dating Relationships

There's no doubt that long-distance dating relationships can be difficult to manage. The expense of phone bills and travel, the difficulty of evaluating the relationship from a distance, the uncertainty and jealousy that can arise when negotiating relationships in the new environment, and the stress of deciding how to use one's limited time together all place a burden on partners.

Despite these difficulties, long-distance relationships may not be as problematic as you might think. There are actually advantages to being apart, among them time to focus on school or career and feelings of freedom and autonomy. In her review of research on the subject, Laura Stafford says that "most studies have found equal or even high levels of satisfaction, commitment and trust in LDDRs [long-distance dating relationships] compared to geographically close ones." In fact, in cases where partners end up moving to be close to one another, it is not unusual for them to miss their former freedom, to feel that the relationship is no longer as interesting or exciting as it had been, and to have problems in adjusting to being together.

Couples in face-to-face interaction often experience conflict, but they have time to grow accustomed to one another's flaws, to work out their conflicts, and to negotiate relational dialectics. Couples in long-distance relationships who are suddenly reunited must confront the same problems as their face-to-face counterparts, but because they have not had time to become accus-

tomed to one another, conflicts may come as a surprise, and they may have fewer strategies for managing disagreement.

Stafford argues that a key aspect of long-distance dating relationships is the tendency to idealize one's partners. Although positive distortions are often an important part of courtship even when partners are together, and although some degree of "benevolent misconception" is necessary in long-term relationships, it is important to find a balance between idealism and illusion. Because partners who are separated have less of a chance to see and adapt to one another's failings and because, when they are together, they tend to be on their best behavior, their views of one another may be highly romanticized and inaccurate. Indeed, long-distance partners "may have little idea of how idealized and inaccurate their images are." This is one reason why reuniting can be an especially stressful time.

What can help couples who have been apart make a smooth transition to being together? Stafford suggests that partners recognize the fact that they have been looking at one another through rose-colored glasses. Because "depth of acquaintanceship" is an important and reliable predictor of relational stability, she sees the primary task facing reunited partners as getting to know one another through everyday interaction. In addition, she argues that it is important to engage in and manage conflict, for in confronting difficult issues, partners will find out whether or not their relationship has a future.

**SOURCE** Laura Stafford, *Maintaining Long-Distance and Cross-Residential Relationships* (Mahwah, N.J.: Lawrence Erlbaum Associates, 2005).

**ADDITIONAL READING**
Goodwin, S. A., and others. "The Eye of the Beholder: Romantic Goals and Impression Biases." *Journal of Experimental Social Psychology* 38, (2002): 232–41.

Despite our best efforts, not all relationships last. Sometimes we are unable to keep the relationship going the way we want it to and it becomes clear that it is starting to decay. In the next section, we turn our attention to the stages that characterize relational decline. As we describe these stages of coming apart, remember that they aren't necessarily irreversible. Relationships are frequently rebuilt after short periods of decay. Although, naturally, rebuilding becomes more difficult when deterioration is the result of long periods of neglect or extremely painful conflicts and violations of trust.

## Stages of Relationship Dissolution

Mark Knapp's model of relational change includes five stages of deterioration: (1) differentiating, (2) circumscribing, (3) stagnating, (4) avoiding, and (5) terminating. Steve Duck describes the process a bit differently by focusing on the locus of action as it moves from the internal thoughts of a single person (*intrapsychic phase*) to interaction between the partners (*dyadic phase*) to announcements to the wider social network (*social and grave-dressing phases*).[54] In addition, research demonstrates that the sequence of relationships coming apart as depicted by researchers fits very closely with the prototypic sequence of events that people associate with de-escalating relationships. James Honeycutt, James Cantrill, and Terre Allen found that individuals tend to agree on the rank order sequence of the 11 behaviors as indicative of a relationship coming apart (see Table 11.4).

### Differentiating

When relational partners begin to remind each other that they are separate individuals and that they have other concerns besides their relationship, they have begun the process of differentiating. Often episodes of differentiating are triggered by seemingly innocuous events. A close friend—we'll call her Mary Ann Marker—described receiving a piece of junk mail shortly after her marriage to a man named Jones. The letter was addressed to "Mary A. Jones." At first she didn't realize who the letter was meant for. When reality sank in, she said, it almost destroyed her identity. She didn't know who she was. She promptly informed her husband that she wanted to keep her maiden name. The emergence of two-career families, with the necessity of dealing with competing time constraints and goals, has made this stage more commonplace than it might once have been. This stage may be more accurately referred to as a stage of relational maintenance, since most intimate relationships cannot avoid periods of differentiating. Many couples may engage in a repetitive cycle of breaking up and making up, as partners move from bonding to differentiating, back to integration and bonding, and so on.

### Circumscribing

Deterioration becomes more serious when intimates begin to restrict their communication with each other on a regular basis. This may occur as a result of major violations of trust or increasing uncertainty about the quality of the relationship. Sally Planalp and James Honeycutt studied events such as deception, changes in personality or values, competing relationships or extramarital affairs, and confidence betrayal—all events that increased uncertainty about the relationship. Over one-quarter of the relationships ended as a direct result of such an event. Another one-third felt that their relationship was never as close after the event took place.[55] Knapp indicates that conversations in this phase are shorter in duration, limited to safe topics for fear of touching a raw nerve, and almost totally devoid of any new self-disclosures. The only time a couple seems happy is when the partners are putting up a front for their friends.

Much of the dissolution of the relationship at this point can be internal to one partner. Steve Duck describes an *intra-psychic phase* in which one partner begins to doubt the other or finds him or her lacking in terms of relational performance. The partner considers the costs associated with withdrawing from the relationship as well as the positive benefits in pursuing alternative

| TABLE 11.4 | Prototypic Behaviors in De-escalating Relationships |
| --- | --- |

| Knapp's stage of deterioration | Duck's phase of dissolution | Prototypic behaviors in de-escalation |
| --- | --- | --- |
| Differentiating | | |
| Circumscribing | Intrapsychic | 1. Stop expressing intimate feelings |
| | Dyadic | 2. Disagree about attitudes, opinions |
| | | 3. Argue about little things |
| | | 4. Verbal fighting and antagonizing other |
| Stagnating | Social | 5. Spend less time together |
| Avoiding | | 6. Avoid other in public settings |
| | | 7. Trial rejuvenation |
| | | 8. Talk about breaking up |
| | | 9. Become interested in others |
| | | 10. Start seeing others |
| Terminating | Grave dressing | 11. Final breakup |

Males ranked "arguing about little things" before "disagreeing about attitudes and opinions" and placed "spending less time together" before "verbal fighting."

Source: James Honeycutt, James Cantrill, and Terre Allen, "Memory Structures for Relational Decay: A Cognitive Test of Sequencing of De-escalating Actions and Stages," *Human Communication Research*, 18 (1992): 528–82.

relationships before coming to the conclusion that he or she would be justified in breaking off the relationship. There may also be aspects of what Duck refers to as a *dyadic phase* of confrontation over relational transgressions or failures. The partners may make attempts at repair or reconciliation, which if successful result in a new commitment or bond. If these attempts are not successful, the parties may openly discuss their intentions to sever the relationship.

## Stagnating

This stage is apparent when both members have developed such an expectation of unpleasant and unproductive talk that they feel there is little left to be said. Relationships that are based primarily on extrinsic rewards may continue for many months or years at this stage. While there is little interaction between partners at this stage, Duck indicates that some partners enter a more active *social phase* in which they initiate gossip and offer their respective accounts of the impending doom to select members of their social networks. By doing this, they signal to each other that the relationship is inevitably coming to its end.

## Avoiding

Physical avoidance soon follows. The partners begin rearranging their lives to avoid the necessity of face-to-face interaction. Separate bedrooms, different work shifts, and trial separations are examples of the behavior characteristic of this stage. The pain of interaction simply isn't worth it anymore.

## Breaking Up Is Hard to Do
# High Fidelity

Stephen Frears, 2000

*High Fidelity* is an engaging comedy that explores why some relationships work and others don't. Rob Gordon (John Cusack), who, with his friends Dick (Jack Black) and Barry (Todd Louiso), runs a used record store in Chicago, has just broken up with his girlfriend Laura. This isn't Rob's first romantic failure—in fact as far as he's concerned Laura doesn't even make his "Top Five All-Time Breakups."

As the movie unfolds, Rob decides to visit his ex-girlfriends—from his first sweetheart to the beautiful but shallow Charlie (Catharine Zeta-Jones)—to find out why he's so hopeless at relationships. Anyone who's ever experienced the pangs of lost romance, feared commitment, or done amazingly embarrassing things in the name of love will identify with Rob.

### Terminating

The final stage of interaction prior to physically and psychologically leaving a relationship consists primarily of talk that prepares each person for the impending termination. Often situational factors are responsible for the death of a relationship, as when one party has to move to another city or a college senior has to leave friends behind. Even under these conditions, people frequently disassociate themselves from their friends a few weeks before the move is made. Presumably, this makes the actual termination easier.

Duck aptly defines this as a *grave-dressing phase.* Talk takes the form of emphasizing benefits of the future ("It's off to the real world. Several interviews. Things are looking great!") or denouncing the past ("I'm getting out of this stinkhole. Four years—what a waste!"). Postmortem retrospection can even be somewhat positive as partners take stock of what they once had, but this is usually tempered by the need for each partner to tell publicly his or her own version of the break-up story. Odds are high that each will claim responsibility for initiating the break-up and attribute significant blame to the other party.

Many organizations schedule "exit interviews" when their employees leave the company, in hopes of finding out why they quit and what can be done to prevent others from following the same course. This wise practice has not yet become routine in interpersonal relationships. Perhaps a few valuable lessons could be learned if we adopted such a policy.

Managing the stages of relational growth and decline calls for considerable communicative competence. Let's look more closely at how we can improve our competence in relationships.

## Warning Signs: Gottman's "Four Horsemen of the Apocalypse"

While it may seem inevitable that most close relationships will ultimately enter a state of decline, we do know from experience that many people develop committed relationships that work well over the long haul. Perhaps the best evidence to date of what makes these relationships successful can be found in research of John Gottman and his colleagues at the University of Washington.[56] Gottman has studied the interaction patterns of more than 2,000 couples over two decades and his work has produced some startling insights into how couples in all kinds of close relationships can maintain the quality of their communication and fend off the initial signs of relational decay.

*Keeping It Together*

In Chapter 10, we noted that researchers such as Mary Anne Fitzpatrick had found that very different forms of marital relationships (traditionals, separates, independents) could be successful. Gottman's work mirrors that conclusion. He identifies three different styles of successful coupling based largely on how the partners manage conflicts: validators, volatiles, and avoiders.[57] **Validating couples** communicate frequently and have developed a pattern of listening carefully and reinforcing each other's right to different opinions and emotions even when they disagree. Because the partners show each other a great deal of mutual respect, they do not have as many arguments as other couples. Interestingly, many of the arguments they do have center around the autonomy-togetherness dialectic as they try to balance their need for independence with their shared life as a couple. A common conflict pattern for these couples is one in which they spend some time expressing and validating each other's opinions or emotions, then move to a second phase of trying to persuade the other to move toward their own position, followed typically by some kind of negotiated compromise. **Volatile couples,** on the other hand, argue frequently and spend very little time validating each other's opinions during the heat of an argument. They bypass the validating stage and move directly into passionate attempts to persuade each other of the correctness of their own opinions. Even so, the partners usually manage to resolve their differences because they value honesty and independent thinking—and see themselves as equals. They also balance their frequent arguments with more laughter and affection than other types of couples. **Avoidant couples** build a strong relationship based on the similarities they share while largely minimizing or compartmentalizing their differences. When they do argue, they

rarely resolve anything. Gottman characterizes many of their fights as "standoffs" and notes that, more often than not, the partners tread very lightly around the issues where they disagree, failing to explore the nature of their conflict in any real depth.

The amazing finding in Gottman's research is that, despite major differences in their interaction styles, couples in successful marriages share one notable pattern of interaction. They all maintain a healthy balance between the amount of time spent expressing positive versus negative feelings and actions for one another. Gottman points to what he calls "the magic 5:1 ratio" of positive to negative interactions among couples whose relationships are thriving. For example, where volatile couples engage in more negative interactions than the other two types, they make up for it with a greater intensity and frequency of positive interactions. Avoidant couples experience far fewer conflict episodes, but the ratio of notably positive episodes where they show a great deal of passion and affection does not typically exceed the 5:1 ratio. More of their interactions can be characterized as "neutral" in terms of passion. Across all of these couple types, Gottman found that couples expressed positive feelings for one another in a wide variety of ways, including showing interest, being affectionate, acting in thoughtful or appreciative ways, showing concern, being empathic, joking around, sharing excitement, and being responsive and accepting of each other even when disagreeing.[58]

Relationships that are coming apart, however, demonstrate a number of signs that negativity is on the rise and threatening to throw off the 5:1 ratio. Here Gottman identifies two types of couples whose relationship patterns typically end in rapid decay and ultimately in divorce. The first type he calls **hostile/engaged couples.** Like volatile couples, they fight frequently, but their interactions are peppered with insults, sarcasm, and overall contempt for one another. A second type, **hostile/detached couples,** are not as overtly abusive in what they say to each other, but experience emotional distance in their interactions. They fail to really listen to each other, rarely look in each other's direction, and often react defensively at the slightest remark.

In both of these types of unstable relationships, Gottman's research shows another pattern, one that he describes as "tumbling down the marital rapids."

> *Unhappy marriages resemble each other in important ways. True, each has its own personality and idiosyncracies, but they share one overriding similarity: they followed the same, specific, downward spiral before coming to a sad end. This spiral includes a distinct cascade of interactions, emotions, and attitudes that, step by step, brought these couples close to separation, divorce, or an unhappy, lonely life together. . . . The first cascade a couple hits as they tumble down the marital rapids is comprised of "The Four Horsemen of the Apocalypse," my name for four disastrous ways of interacting that sabotage your attempts to communicate with your partner. In order of least to most dangerous, they are criticism, contempt, defensiveness, and stonewalling. As these behaviors become more and more entrenched, husband and wife focus increasingly on the escalating sense of negativity and tension in their marriage. Eventually they may become deaf to each other's efforts at peacemaking. As each horseman arrives, he paves the way for the next.*[59]

## Criticism

Every relationship has its stresses and strains, and, as we've seen, successful couples learn how to manage or at least minimize the problem areas in their relationship. Couples in stable relationships complain to and about each other frequently. The first significant relationship-threatening pattern that Gottman reports is when complaining turns into criticism. Gottman sees a big distinction between complaining about a partner's actions and criticizing his or her character. **Criticism** leaves the realm of specific, iden-

tifiable behaviors by attacking the other's personality in a broad, almost undefinable manner. Complaining about a specific action can lead to healthy results. It airs a grievance that can be addressed. Criticisms tend to be generalizations that carry implicit blame. "You always do that," "You never support me," and "I should have known I couldn't count on you" are tell-tale phrases of criticism. It's easy to see how criticism by one partner can evoke a similar response from the other. Frequent episodes of mutual criticism can quickly drown any desire to praise or make affirmative character statements about one's partner, making it less likely that the couple will be able to maintain the 5:1 ratio that typifies stable relationships. Learning to complain more effectively can defeat criticism. Effective complaining requires identifying one specific action by your partner that you are unhappy with and not allowing yourself to generalize the issue beyond the behavior in question.

## Contempt

When episodes of criticism begin to dominate a relationship, it's not difficult for contempt for one's partner to set in. Gottman defines **contempt** as "the intention to insult and psychologically abuse your partner" and as an "immediate decay of admiration."[60] Contempt is expressed in the form of insults, name calling, hostile humor, sneering, rolling of the eyes, and other gestures of disgust. Another disastrous form of contempt is when one partner mocks or ridicules the behavior of the other, as if to say, "I don't respect or trust a word you're saying." The only antidote to contempt is for couples to make conscious efforts to refrain from engaging in the practices listed earlier and to rediscover and acknowledge their partner's positive attributes.

## Defensiveness

Defensiveness is a very common reaction to contempt. It "feels" natural to defend oneself when under attack, so that's exactly what we do. We engage in **defensiveness** any time we experience fear in response to a perceived threat or attack, whether in the form of a partner's complaint, criticism, or expression of contempt. We defend our innocence or deny our own responsibility for whatever charge is being levied at us. Typical defensive behaviors include making excuses, whining, shifting the blame, or countering with a criticism of our own. The problem is that defensive reactions only escalate a conflict and make matters worse. Being defensive does nothing to address the issues at hand; it simply wards them off and makes your partner even more angry. Defensiveness is often interpreted by others as an effort to evade the issue, thereby implying that you are guilty as charged, but can't face up to it. What's the remedy? Because defensiveness is almost always associated with a feeling of being overwhelmed emotionally, the first step is to regain composure or to calm down before reacting. A second step is to learn to listen and speak nondefensively. Gottman argues that we need to ignore what's being said about us (granted, difficult to do when being called a lying weasel) and learn to hear our partner's negativity as an attempt to underline how strongly she or he feels about the problem and what desperate measures are being employed to get us to pay attention. In order to speak nondefensively, you need to be conscious of your own body language and avoid letting your own complaints escalate into criticism or contempt.

### Stonewalling

**Stonewalling** refers to at least one partner engaging in a habitual pattern of stony silence or emotional distance from the immediate interaction and the overall relationship. As the name suggests, the stonewaller becomes so nonresponsive that it is like talking to a stone wall. Some stonewallers actually believe they are helping matters by remaining "neutral" rather than responding negatively. They do not seem to realize that their so-called neutral message is being read in no uncertain terms as one of the most powerfully negative statements possible. Gottman's research shows that nearly 85 percent of stonewallers are men and that typically a wife's heart

rate rises dramatically when her husband is stonewalling.[61] Men do not seem to respond as negatively to being stonewalled by their wives. While this suggests that stonewalling is primarily a problem wives have with their husbands, the important point is that once stonewalling becomes a frequent occurrence—no matter who the stonewaller is—the relationship is in serious trouble. One of the simplest methods of resisting the tendency to stonewall is to make conscious efforts to replace your blank stares with **back-channeling,** which is the use of head nods, brief vocalizations (such as ("uh huh," "ok," or "yeah"), or other gestures to indicate that you are listening and have not withdrawn emotionally.

Gottman's research is the most definitive evidence to date about the specific signs of relational decay and, more importantly, what successful couples do to avoid or minimize the tendency to fall victim to patterns of criticism, contempt, defensiveness, and stonewalling. Obviously, managing the stages of relational growth and decline calls for considerable competence in every aspect of communication. Let's look more closely at how we can improve our competence in close relationships.

# Communicative Competence and Intimate Relations

Many scholars believe that our modern era has been dominated by an **ideology of intimacy,** although some think this may be changing.[62] Such an ideology implies that intimacy, or psychological closeness, is the yardstick by which we should measure all of our relationships. Relationships in which we have not yet shared personal information are often referred to as "mere" acquaintances or "superficial" relations, as though they have not progressed very far. We saw that

*Work relationships are often characterized by a lack of sharing of personal information, but intimacy is not necessarily a yardstick by which to measure all our relationships.*

ritual introductions to strangers can feel remarkably like "auditions for friendship." Our expectations for close friendships and romantic relations are so naturally tied to sharing intimacies that we often regard low levels of intimacy as indications of a stalled or failed relationship. The assumptions we make about intimate relationships will affect how we process information, play out our roles, establish goals, define the self, and construct messages. In turn, all of these communicative competencies will influence how a particular close relationship develops over time. Let's look at how intimacy and the various forms of communication competence are related.

### Intimacy and Interpretive Competence

Interpretive competence involves our ability to pay attention to and integrate important contextual information such as social setting, time, appropriate relational prototypes and scripts, and so on. As this chapter has shown, friendships and romantic relations tend to develop in a somewhat scripted sequence of phases. Knowledge of these typical phases and ability to recognize relational

message cues that signal potential for movement from one phase to the next are important components of interpretive competence. Perhaps the greatest indication of our perceptual competence is our ability to pick up subtle cues and attend to the feedback of the other. No one wants to be too obvious or to be seen as begging for a more intimate relationship. A classic case of perennial misreading of perceptual cues involves the characters of Sam and Diane from the sitcom *Cheers.* Despite their obvious attraction for one another, they work from very different prototypes of what an intimate relationship ought to be like. Sam expects an enjoyable physical relationship and a quick jaunt through the phases of relationship development. Diane, on the other hand, wants charm, wit, and intellectual stimulation to accompany their path to psychological intimacy. A good deal of the humor in the show was based on the reliable fact that each would interpret the other's "scripts for intimacy" as entirely the wrong way to do it.

### Intimacy and Role Competence

The roles that we expect a friend, lover, or marriage partner to play and the roles that actually evolve in a relationship are often quite different. Gender roles obviously play a big part in close, heterosexual relations. Competence in this regard reflects our ability to adapt our roles to one another. Our culture creates expectations that gender roles in marriage, for instance, should be relatively equal in terms of who does the housework, gets the meals, and who is allotted free time for leisure pursuits. Yet in the vast majority of cases, even where they work outside the home, women still perform a disproportionate share of household duties while males assume and get more leisure time once the workday is completed.[63] The unresolved tensions surrounding such role definitions can be a real test for a close relationship. Likewise, role definitions in friendship can influence perceptions of intimacy. If one partner has a role expectation that a best friend will drop everything in order to attend to a friend's need and the other views being physically present as a voluntary act, role competence will not likely be displayed in the case of a minor crisis. In this way, role competence in relation to intimacy is not only relationship-specific, but may also be situation-specific. We can work to improve our role competence by talking about our expectations or deciphering each other's expectations from discussions about past relationships. We can also probe for reasons when a partner seems disappointed in us. Often disappointment is related to unfulfilled role expectations. Role negotiation is never easy in close relationships. The dialectic tensions discussed in this chapter reflect deep-seated role expectations about appropriate levels of autonomy, openness, and novelty in a relationship. Role competence requires an ability to recognize when a relationship is experiencing too much autonomy, for instance, and to respond with behaviors that will enhance togetherness.

## Intimacy and Self Competence

As we have already seen, the construction of a highly enmeshing relational identity can sometimes threaten our sense of self apart from the relationship. The fluctuations in sacrificing or empowering the self as seen in the transition from Vision I to Vision II type relationships (see Table 11.1) demonstrates how we have culturally dealt with this dilemma. With the emergence of Vision III in the late 1970s, we appear to have found a way out. By promoting both mutual self-development and working on the relationship as important goals, we try to enhance both rather than choose between them. Of course, these admirable goals are easier stated than achieved. The odds of maintaining or building self competence are enhanced when we choose relational partners who are similar to ourselves, especially in terms of social skills or cognitive complexity, as Burleson's research discussed earlier in the chapter suggests. However, given our propensity for selecting partners on the basis of physical attractiveness or social approval of others, we may frequently place ourselves in relationships where the balance is harder to achieve.

The typical phases of relationship development and our modern emphasis on falling in love may also make things more difficult. While there is great pleasure in the feelings associated with romantic love, the high expectations of oneness, togetherness, and emotional arousal actually create the inevitably temporary honeymoon state. This letdown makes the reassertion of self-interest appear as the first step down the road to dissolution. In fact, our tendency to view relationships as ever-changing (going through stages) while holding to a concept of self as essentially stable (the true self) may make us feel that we are compromising self every time we enter a relationship. Perhaps this explains why so many are afraid to commit themselves to a close relationship. Self competence cannot be viewed in isolation from the other elements of our model of competence.

## Intimacy and Goal Competence

Failure to identify specific relational goals is one reason why close relationships do not always turn out the way we would like. Knowing that we want a good or close relationship is often too ambiguous. The better we understand what we want out of a relationship, the more likely we are to translate the goal into effective messages. When we encounter a relational problem, such as a conflict or a serious transgression, our tendency is to focus first on what we need to *do* in order to manage the conflict or whether to reveal, conceal, or confront the other about the broken promise. Focusing too quickly on the message or action itself means we will probably do whatever we have done in the past in similar situations and usually involves a limited range of options and unpredictable or unsatisfactory outcomes.

Taking the time to ask ourselves what we want as an outcome can lead to more precise or more creative message choices. For instance, knowing how much and what kind of autonomy you want in a relationship helps you better decide which activities to pursue and which to decline. By not assessing your relational goals adequately, you may solve the immediate situation only to realize that what you really wanted was to redefine the relationship itself.

## Intimacy and Message Competence

Clearly achieving intimacy is affected by the messages we intentionally and inadvertently use to entice, enthrall, manipulate, mollify, adulate, anger, help, or hurt one another. We demonstrate message competence when we express ourselves in ways that our relational partner can comprehend and that also reflect an understanding of the social situations, roles, goals, and desired self-images in which we carry out our relationship.

Message competence depends a great deal on the other competencies, but does not necessarily follow from them. We may know exactly what needs to be done to repair a faltering relationship, for instance, but fail miserably due to our inability to find the right words or demonstrate nonverbally just how earnestly we want to change. How do we improve message competence in close relations? One way is to pay closer attention to our partner's reactions to the words and actions we already perform. We may discover emotional trigger words (or actions) that have predictably positive or negative effects. For those situations that can be anticipated, rehearsing what we want to say and imagining how the friend or partner might react can be helpful. Another way to improve our message making is to practice particular skills such as those discussed at the end of most chapters in this text.

Managing intimate relationships requires a variety of perceptual and communication skills. At the outset we must present ourselves in a favorable light and develop our repertoire of positive relational messages and affinity-seeking strategies. Through the subtle use of secret tests, we can better judge when to pursue a relationship and when it might be better to hold off. The relationships we do pursue can be integrated and so-

lidified by developing meaningful relational symbols. As a relationship matures, we must carefully negotiate ways to handle the inevitable tensions of autonomy-togetherness, candor-restraint, and predictability-novelty. The maintenance of such relationships also depends on our ability to confront major problems that we are unable to handle through subtle hints and suggestions. This makes the management of conflict one of the most important communication skills for partners in an intimate relationship. We turn our attention now to this crucial skill.

---

# Skill Building: Managing Interpersonal Conflict and Stress

Even in the best of relationships, we occasionally go through periods of conflict and stress. Conflicts are a normal and expected part of everyday life. While communication can't magically erase basic differences in values, goals, and expectations, it can help us manage relational problems if used realistically and skillfully. In this section we'll look at some rules for getting the most out of conflict. We'll consider what the positive aspects of interpersonal conflict are, discuss how conflict is often mismanaged, and look at how you should go about communicating during a conflict episode.

## Positive Aspects of Interpersonal Conflict

In general, **interpersonal conflict** occurs whenever goals are blocked. Interpersonal conflict occurs when the goals or actions of two people are incompatible, that is, whenever they cannot negotiate a mutually satisfactory outcome.[64] While conflicts can make us angry and irrational, they are not always bad. Well-managed conflict should be welcomed rather than avoided, for it can be healthy for a relationship. Here are several specific positive characteristics of conflict.

1. *Conflict means interdependence.* Conflict is a sign that two people are involved in each other's lives. If people were entirely autonomous, they could not experience conflict. The fact that people fight means that they still care.[65] While repeated conflict may be a sign of relational disintegration, fighting means a relationship has not entered the stagnation stage. When conflicts are successfully managed and resolved, the aftermath is often an increase in cohesion—many partners feel closer after a well-managed conflict.

2. *Conflict signals a need for a change.* While change can be frightening because it disrupts familiar patterns, it can also be healthy. Without the ability to adapt, a system will eventually run down. Conflict is an opportunity to become more adaptable and creative. A productive conflict allows participants to find new ways of relating to each other.

3. *Conflict allows problem diagnosis.* Many people tend to deny rather than acknowledge problems. Overt conflict can provide information about mutual needs and expectations. It also acts as a safety valve by keeping problems from building up. A relationship in which no conflict ever occurs is unnatural. Its members may be engaging in unrealistic denial.

## Mismanaged Conflict

One of the reasons we fear conflict is that most of the time we manage it very badly. Let's look at some of the things we all do that make conflict destructive rather than productive. One way to mismanage conflict is to try to escape it. Individuals or couples undergoing intense conflict may sometimes experience "a mental paralysis which leads to no action at all."[66] They appear uninterested and unconcerned although they are really experiencing intense emotion. The ultimate outcome may be literal escape—the partners walk away from each other and allow the relationship to dissolve. While it may be inevitable that a relationship will end, escape doesn't give it a chance to succeed.

The opposite way of mismanaging conflict is by being too aggressive. Instead of ignoring the problem, the couple fights. While fighting isn't necessarily a bad thing, there are destructive ways to fight. George Bach and Peter Wyden discuss several.[67] One way to ensure that a fight will be harmful is to time it badly. Try not to begin a fight as your partner walks through the door after a busy day or right before dinner guests are scheduled to arrive. People should be prepared to deal with conflict; adequate time should be set aside for the process.

Fights should also be kept up-to-date. If a fight is continually postponed, it may get out of control when it does occur. Failing to confront problems as they crop up is known as **gunnysacking.** It's as though you stick all of your grievances into an old gunnysack, which gets heavier and heavier until finally it bursts.

Gunnysacking can lead to another unfair tactic, **kitchen-sinking.** In a kitchen-sink fight every possible argument (everything but the kitchen sink) is thrown in. For example, Mary and Janet, two neighbors, may start arguing because Janet hit Mary's garbage cans while backing out of her driveway. In the course of the fight, however, they will use any weapon they can lay their hands on. Janet may call Mary a troublemaker, and Mary may counter by calling Janet selfish and reckless. Janet will then up the stakes by calling Mary's children names, and Mary may respond by insulting Janet's husband. And so on. Before long, the original topic has been forgotten; the goal now is to draw as much blood as possible.

Another unfair tactic mentioned by Bach and Wyden is labeling, or **stereotyping.** If Janet were to say to Mary, "Of course you're inconsiderate. New Yorkers always are," she would be guilty of stereotyping, a practice that will only lead to more conflict.

## Effective Feedback During Conflict

Simply avoiding negative tactics is not enough. To manage a conflict successfully, you should also express yourself clearly and directly, letting the other person know exactly what you are feeling. In the skill-building sections of both Chapters 3 and 4, we stressed how important it is to know your own feelings and express them directly and clearly. Here we offer some specific guidelines for feedback during conflict.[68]

1. *Own your own message.* Let's say you are extremely annoyed with your mate over his or her failure to cut the grass. Instead of working in the yard as promised, your partner has settled down in front of the TV to watch roller derby. Which of the following is the best way to bring up your feelings? Should you say, "You know, it doesn't really bother me, but the neighbors are beginning to complain. Everyone on the block thinks the grass is too high"? Or should you say, "I'm angry. You promised to cut the grass, but you haven't done it"?

If you're the one who is angry, it is dishonest to attribute the anger to someone else. Besides, telling someone that "everyone" agrees that he or she is inadequate leaves that person feeling defensive and helpless.

2. *Don't apologize for your feelings.* If you keep apologizing, you put all the blame on yourself. Would you take the following comment seriously? "I'm sorry, I hate to bring this up, and I probably have no right to feel this way, but it kind of bothers me when you talk like that."

3. *Make your messages specific and behavioral.* Your partner needs to know exactly what is upsetting you. Of the following two statements, which is best? "I think you've got a really rotten attitude" or "You just interrupted me. It makes me angry because I feel that you aren't interested in hearing what I have to say." Most experts agree the second gives more information and is therefore more helpful. Changing one's entire attitude is a pretty tall order; being careful not to interrupt is a much easier task. Often people sim-

ply don't realize they've been doing something offensive, and they are happy to change when they get specific feedback.

4. *Make sure your verbal and nonverbal messages match.* If you try to appear calm and controlled while telling someone how angry you are, you are sending a mixed message. Similarly, if you use sarcasm to express your feelings, you disconfirm your partner. "I just love it when you do that" said in a sarcastic and biting tone is confusing and ineffective feedback.

5. *Avoid evaluating and interpreting your partner.* What can someone do in response to a statement like "You are just about the most egotistical, narcissistic person I've ever met"? Very little, except to feel inadequate and insulted. Instead of describing a behavior, you have attacked a person.

## Conflict Containment

When conflict gets too large, it spins out of control. One way to keep it manageable is by **fractionating,** or breaking it up into small, easily managed units. Trying to change everything overnight isn't the answer. Working on one small thing at a time is.[69] Let's say you're in one of those momentary states when everything looks bad, when you hate your entire life. Try to fractionate your feelings. If you find out that you dislike your job, hate your neighborhood, and are less than thrilled with your social life, work on these problems one at a time. If you and your boss aren't getting along, sit down and try to list your grievances in simple, behavioral terms. Now you have an idea of where to begin. Through a process of negotiation, you may be able to reach agreement about how to resolve your conflict.

One technique that helps in fractionating is **negative inquiry.**[70] If your boss tells you she's unhappy with your performance, instead of becoming defensive, try asking for as much information as possible. Say something like "Could you tell me exactly what I'm doing that is below standard?" After she responds, go one step further: "Is there anything else you can think of? Are there other things I could do to improve my performance?" You show your willingness to improve and you gather useful information at the same time.

It's also important to plan your approach to conflict and to analyze each conflict after the fact. Conflicts are usually stressful, and we know that under stress our thinking becomes very simplistic and stereotypic. That's why you should evaluate conflict strategies when your thinking is clearest.

There is no magic cure for relational problems, but there are ways to manage them more effectively. In this chapter we've emphasized the positive aspects of conflict and we've looked at some of the things that can go wrong when our communication gets out of control. In the skill-building section at the end of the next chapter, we'll return to this topic. We'll give you some hints on how to choose an appropriate conflict style and how to improve your negotiating skills.

# Process to Performance

## Review Terms

The following is a list of major concepts introduced in this chapter. The page where the concept is first mentioned is listed in parentheses.

intimacy   (297)
physical proximity   (302)
shared episodes   (302)
intimacy readiness   (302)
romantic feelings   (302)
civility   (303)
filtering theory   (303)
physical beauty   (304)
matching hypothesis   (304)
similarity   (304)
reciprocal liking   (305)
complementary needs   (305)

need for inclusion   (305)
need for control   (305)
need for affection   (306)
trusting behavior   (309)
trustworthy behavior   (309)
affinity-seeking strategies   (311)
indirect suggestions   (312)
separation tests   (313)
endurance tests   (313)
triangle tests   (313)
relational symbols   (314)
covenant talk   (314)
expressive-protective dialectic   (316)
autonomy-togetherness dialectic   (316)
novelty-predictability dialectic   (316)
gender role dialectic   (317)
assimilation   (319)
contrast   (319)
relational maintenance behaviors   (319)
validating couples   (325)
volatile couples   (325)
avoidant couples   (325)
hostile/engaged couples   (325)
hostile/detached couples   (325)
criticism   (326)
contempt   (326)
defensiveness   (326)
stonewalling   (327)
back-channeling   (327)
ideology of intimacy   (327)
interpersonal conflict   (330)
gunnysacking   (331)
kitchen-sinking   (331)
stereotyping   (331)
fractionating   (332)
negative inquiry   (332)

## Suggested Readings

Cupach, William R., and Brian H. Spitzberg. *The Dark Side of Relationship Pursuit: From Attraction to Obsession and Stalking*. New York: LEA, Inc., 2004. This book looks at current research on obsessive relationships.

Guerrero, Laura K., Peter A. Andersen, and Walid A. Afifi. *Close Encounters: Communication in*

*Relationships.* Mt. View, Calif.: Mayfield, 2001. A thoughtful and complete review of theory and research in relational communication. Chapter 3, on social attraction, is especially useful in understanding intimate relationships.

---

### Topics for Discussion

www.oup.com/us/trenholm

---

### Observation Guide

**1.** Think of a long-standing relationship you've been involved in (either a romantic relationship or a friendship). Use Duck's filtering theory to examine how your relationship got to the point it did. What sociological or incidental cues made it possible for you to get to know each other? What preinteraction cues stood out when you first met? As you look back on the relationship, has the importance of these cues changed over time? What, specifically, was it about the way you communicated initially that allowed you to deepen your relationship? Try to list at least five characteristics that made your interaction rewarding. Finally, how have cognitive cues worked to cement your relationship? Are there any benefits, attitudes, or values on which you disagree? If so, how do you negotiate these differences? If possible, ask your partner to do the same. Compare your answers.

**2.** Choose a close friend or romantic partner and ask his or her permission to tape record several conversations. Analyze your conversations in order to determine (1) what stage the relationship appears to be in and (2) what communication behavior tends to maintain the relationship in that stage or encourage further development or differentiation. Instead of tape recording, you could use a transcript of IM conversations, but make sure you have your partner's permission.

**3.** Choose at least two close relationships (for example, two close friends, two family members, a romantic partner and a friend). Keep a journal for one week and record examples of how you handle the four dialectic tensions (expressiveness vs. protectiveness, autonomy vs. togetherness, predictability vs. novelty, and traditional vs. flexible gender roles) in each of these relationships. At the end of the week review what you've written and ask yourself whether you handled them successfully. Write down some things you could have said or done to improve your management of these tensions.

### Exercises

**1.** Bring to class as many examples of cultural messages about attraction and ideal images of intimate relationships as you can find. These can include magazine and television advertisements, personal advice columns or talk shows, or music videos or lyrics. In small groups take some of these examples and rewrite or revise them to fit Vision I of Virginia Kidd's relational ideals (see Table 11.1). What other visions are possible? Create ads or responses to advice column questions that would reflect these different visions. Talk about ways to evaluate and respond to cultural messages.

**2.** Your instructor will give you a copy of William Schutz's FIRO-B scale to complete before coming to class. This scale measures the interpersonal needs for control, inclusion, and affection. In class your instructor will create several dyads, some pairing people with very different scores on the different needs, others pairing people who are similar on one need or another. Role-play the following situations assuming that you and your partner have an intimate relationship:

**a.** deciding whether to establish separate or joint checking accounts

**b.** establishing rules for when and how often nights out with the "guys" or "girls" will be allowed

**c.** deciding what forms of public displays of affection you should engage in

You may think of other situations as well. Then discuss as a class the impact of interpersonal needs, complementarity, similarity, and the negotiation of differences in needs.

3. Break into groups of three. Your task will be to write an article entitled "Five Ways to Keep Long-Distance Relationships Healthy." Begin by discussing your own experience with long-distance relationships. Then make a list of the challenges this kind of relationship presents. Finally, agree on ways you can overcome these challenges.

*The ability to communicate well is essential to workplace success, helping us to create good relationships with our colleagues and allowing ideas to flow freely and productively.*

## CHAPTER 12

# Professional Relationships Communicating with Colleagues and Other Strangers

Adrienne Richmond is walking to work. It is the first day of her new job with a new company in a new city. Within the past three weeks she has moved into a new community, leased and furnished an apartment, stocked it with food and fish (in her new aquarium), and generally oriented herself to her new "digs." She found a great apartment close enough to work that she can walk five blocks through what she is hopefully describing as "my little community." Today she participates in another kind of orientation—a full day of learning about the company she has joined, signing up for benefits, and meeting her new boss and coworkers. She is understandably anxious and preoccupied as she walks to work, but not so much that she fails to notice things about her new community. She offers a tentative "hello" to people she passes on the sidewalk, unsure whether they are predisposed to greeting strangers or just prefer to be left alone. She picks up her ritual morning newspaper and exchanges a few words with the man she knows only as Jack, of Jack's News, a small kiosk on a busy street corner. In the next block, she can't help but notice as four or five people engage in animated conversation while sipping their morning coffee at an outdoor coffee bar. A sign outside a small townhouse and art studio designates it as a historical preservation site, built in 1844, and she notes its aged clapboard siding. For whatever reason, the historical marker and the site of dozens of people walking down the street captures her imagination. What must it have been like to walk this same street a 150 years ago? She tells herself that, as a woman, chances are she would not have been walking alone, on her way to work.

As Adrienne nears the regional headquarters and the world that awaits her at Zeos Bank of the Americas, her thoughts shift to what the day holds. She left her previous position at another global banking facility to begin duties as an audit officer with Zeos. She is excited because the new position involves considerably more responsibility, a greater chance to use her college minor in Spanish, and travel to Mexico and throughout Latin America. It also comes with a substantial raise in salary! But she's also a bit apprehensive. What will her new *coworkers be like? What topics will the two-day company orientation cover? How many other new employees will be involved? Will her boss, whom she met on the occasion of her previous interviews, be as forthcoming and supportive as she appeared to be during the interviews?*

Whether she realizes it or not, Adrienne's 10-minute walk to work and the day she anticipates there are filled with an almost unceasing frenzy of public and professional communication encounters. She has met strangers on the street, a casual acquaintance in the owner/operator of Jack's News, and will meet throughout the day with new coworkers. The relationships she is developing and will continue to develop are unlike most of the interpersonal relationships we've explored in earlier chapters. Because of their public nature, interactions like those Adrienne has with members of her neighborhood community—grocers, café waitstaff, the owner of Jack's News, and many others—are often overlooked. While not considered "serious" relationships worthy of contemplation, they are the social glue of a community. Because of the number of hours we spend at work, and due to their impact on our career path, the communication that constitutes our work relationships gets a great deal of care and attention. In this chapter, however, we explore a wide range of such "public" relationships.

# Interpersonal Communication in Public Situations

Only a handful of our relationships can be considered friendships or intimate relationships. We simply don't have the time or the need to develop every relationship into an intimate one. This means that most of our relationships remain in the impersonal, public sector of social interaction. To better understand how public interpersonal situations work, let's consider a little history on the subject. Then we'll examine how we manage public interactions and professional relationships today and what factors lead to success in such interactions.

## Public Realms in History

In the opening scene of this chapter, you'll recall that Adrienne pondered the past as she made her way to work. She not only questioned whether a woman of her age would be taking such a walk, but she also tried to imagine how her interaction with people along the way might have been different. Would she have said more than "hello" to casual passersby? Would a woman like herself have felt safe? Would she have been allowed to walk alone? What kind of work would she have been permitted to perform?

The public realm of impersonal roles and civil communication has been a far more important place in other historical periods than it seems to be today. As we have already seen, many earlier eras were less individualistic and more communal (Chapter 8). Public spaces were often designed for interaction, even though the kinds of interactions allowed might have been proscribed by gender, class, or other social characteristics. In 15th-century Italy, for instance, architect Leon Battista Alberti wrote, "The People, by thus meeting frequently together at publick Feasts, might grow more humane, and be closer linked in Friendship one with another. So I imagined our Ancesters instituted publick Shows in the City, not so much for the Sake of Diversions themselves as for their Usefulness."[1] Public life in the Rennaisance and throughout much of history was highly "theatrical" and intended to result in feelings of benevolence, goodwill, expansiveness, jubilation, and generosity of spirit.[2]

In fact, the rising influence of print in the 18th century was seen as a threat to public discourse. Because reading meant spending time in isolation from others, it was not uncommon to hear diatribes against mad, fantasizing writers and readers.

Historian Warren Leland believes this anxiety that reading and writing might minimize the significance of oral discourse led to an ironic explosion between 1650 and 1800 of more than 200 essays, manuals, and books urging a more conscious use of conversation.[3] When performed correctly, conversation was seen as a sifter of Truth. One writer noted that "The primitive and literal Sense of this Word [conversation] is . . . to *Turn round together;* and in its more copious Usage we intend by it, that reciprocal Interchange of Ideas, by which Truth is examined, Things are, in a manner, *turned round,* and sifted, and all our Knowledge communicated to each other."[4] The assumption, now challenged by modern communication theory, was that language contained the Truth, and that in speaking, the Truth would win out. Certainly, the American Revolution was sparked by much oral debate among ordinary citizens. But too much solitary reflection or private, nonpublic discourse raised the threat that fantasy would obscure the Truth. Conversation performed without care could be equally harmful. The 17th century witnessed the rise of coffeehouses and salons in France and England devoted almost exclusively to the practice of public conversation. Of course, the next three centuries observed the slow evolution of a private sphere, first within the home and later within the self-concepts of persons themselves. With that evolution, private forms of conversation began to dominate. Today, the public sphere has receded in importance to the point where there are fewer and fewer public spaces where serious conversation among strangers or acquaintances is likely to take place. Nonetheless, truncated forms of public communication do still exist in our neighborhoods, workplaces, and via the ever increasing numbers of interactive electronic media (as you may recall from Box 5.1 and Box 5.2).

## Interacting in the Public Realm Today

Every relationship begins as an encounter between strangers and therefore starts out as a public rather than a private matter. In Chapter 2, we introduced Miller and Steinberg's concepts of cultural and social level data as being the basis for these kinds of public interactions.[5] Once members of dyads become more familiar with one another they may develop more individual ways of interaction, but this does not mean that people in close relationships abandon cultural or social level rules altogether. Even in our closest relationships, we sometimes treat each other in terms of social role expectations. Colleagues who are also friends may preface their remarks at work with statements like, "I need your opinion on this issue as my colleague, not as my friend" so that their friendship does not place undue stress on their working relationship.

At the other extreme, it seems that our culture has placed less and less stock in nourishing the resources for cultural and social level interaction. Richard Sennett has described much of contemporary society as dominated by an "ideology of intimacy" in that we tend to measure the quality of cultural- and social-level encounters by the same yardstick that we use for intimate relations: psychological closeness.[6] We quickly become impatient and bored with others if they do not seem to have the qualities of a potential friend. But most public interactions don't measure up very well on that yardstick, leading us to devalue them as inferior forms of communication to be avoided or hurried through. Such an attitude can make the public realm an empty and barren space in our social lives.

A more positive approach to interpersonal communication in the public realm would be to recognize the value that cultural- and social-level relationships have in sustaining our sense of community, decency, and respect for diversity. To make public situations work, people invent and nourish standard ways to interact and reduce uncertainty. We have identified the following criteria that seem to govern public interactions and enable people to be effective in them: (1) the interaction should involve appropriate roles and scripts; (2) interactants should be respectful of each other; (3) interactions should enable both participants to achieve their practical goals; and

*Showing respect to those around us can include something as simple as paying close attention to them when they are speaking to us.*

William Gropper, *The Senate*, 1935

(4) interactions should allow some room for the expressive behavior of individuals.

### Enacting Roles and Scripts

Becoming personally familiar with every sales clerk, stockboy, or cashier we encounter would be impracticable and inefficient. To save time, protect our privacy, and make social interaction more predictable, members of our culture have worked out scripts and roles for most conceivable public interactions. Recall that a script (discussed in Chapter 6) is a highly predictable sequence of behaviors or events; it tells us what should happen next in a given situation. Roles (discussed in Chapter 7) define the expectations each person has of the other; they tell us who should perform each part of the script. A cashier would be baffled if you offered to pay for a shirt you had not yet picked out (because you messed up the sequencing of the script). Likewise, you cannot ask the sales clerk to "try the shirt on and see if it fits" (because that's not part of the sales clerk's role). Any interaction is more difficult when you don't know the roles or the lines of action, but public interactions are virtually impossible without them.

### Showing and Deserving Respect

Even though our private lives are shielded from those we interact with in public encounters, we are still people and not simply automatons. In fact, the hallmark of social interaction is the giving and receiving of respect. Rom Harre, a noted social psychologist, argues that "the deepest human motive is to seek the respect of others."[7] Role interactions can become dehumanizing for one or both persons involved, but they need not. Very few social roles are designed to belittle those who play them. The problem usually arises because people don't understand the complementary nature of social roles—for example, no one can properly be identified as a doctor without having patients. Likewise, role interactions may go bad when a culture develops a misguided sense of individualism. According to some observers our culture has been experiencing a long-term trend toward narcissism—a kind of self-interest that devalues any relationship that doesn't help a person get in touch with the private, personal self.[8] When this happens, a large portion of the social world (strangers and casual acquaintances) becomes unimportant to us, unless we can quickly transform them into intimates.

The result is a lack of respect for the vast majority of people we come into contact with.

When social roles are properly valued, respect is achieved by the use of some subtle social mechanisms. Erving Goffman has identified two such mechanisms that help people maintain **deference** or respect: avoidance rituals and presentational rituals. He has also shown that in order to be worthy of the respect of others, a person must show proper demeanor.[9]

*Avoidance Rituals.* People show respect by purposely allowing one another the right to privacy. **Avoidance rituals** refer to the cultural norms for appropriate personal distance, as discussed in Chapter 3. You may have experienced discomfort when an overeager salesperson pounces on you as you enter a store and hovers too close, even though you protest, "I'm just looking, thanks." Another avoidance ritual is the use of formal titles and surnames rather than first names, a sign of respect that many fear is disappearing from the American sense of etiquette. Younger people seem to prefer the informality of first names and associate the use of formal ad dress with snobbery or aloofness. Older Americans, on the other hand, are often offended at such familiarity. Can you think of other ways that people avoid trespassing on one another's privacy? Which ones do you think are most acceptable today?

*Presentational Rituals.* Avoidance rituals show respect by identifying out-of-bounds role behavior. **Presentational rituals,** according to Goffman, show respect in a more positive vein. These rituals include salutations, compliments, provision of minor services, and invitations to participate in group activities. Notice how each of these rituals shows respect in a typical morning at the office. Upon arrival at work, coworkers greet one another in a friendly manner, but they don't take a great deal of time to do so ("Good morning, Mr. Whitmore," "How are you, Ms. Pendergrass?" and so on). If one of them has been away on vacation, the greeting is usually much more expressive ("Well, what do you know! Look who's back from the tropics. Did you enjoy your vacation?") and a little longer in duration. This doesn't mean the parties are better friends; it is simply a matter of showing respect. To greet the returning vacationer in the same way that you greet the associate you saw yesterday would be disrespectful, as though his or her absence was not recognized. Even when you dislike the other person, the show of respect simply maintains civility.

Throughout the day colleagues may compliment one another on the way they are dressed, or how they handled a client, or for the promptness in providing needed information. Or they may symbolize respect by providing small, unrequested services such as pouring an extra cup of coffee or delivering an important piece of mail. Finally, respect can be shown by including everyone, even the office lowlife, in group activities. If a few people are stopping off for drinks after work, an invitation to anyone in earshot is an appropriate sign of respect. The invitee should be allowed to decline: It is the invitation, not the acceptance, that symbolizes respect.

Goffman notes that avoidance rituals and presentational rituals are in constant tension. To invite a colleague or acquaintance to join you is trespassing on his or her right to privacy. "A peculiar tension must be maintained, for these opposing requirements of conduct must somehow be held apart from one another and yet realized together in the same interaction: the gestures which carry an actor to a recipient must also signify that things will not be carried too far."[10] Thus, the importance of offering invitations without expecting compliance, doing small rather than large favors (that might imply escalation of the relationship), and not overdoing the greeting ritual should be recognized.

*Demeanor.* To be civil means that you show respect toward others and behave in a manner deserving of respect. Every culture defines the qualities of a decent person a little differently, and cultures change over time. Goffman identifies the characteristics of **demeanor,** or of a properly "housebroken" human being: discretion and sincerity, modesty, sportsmanship, reasonable command of the language, control of body movements, control of emotions, appetite, and desires, and poise under pressure.[11] Perhaps you can add or delete items from this list to capture the state of proper demeanor people expect in today's world.

### Giving Priority to Practical Goals

People interact in public for one of two primary reasons: to accomplish some practical end such as the purchase of goods and services or simply to enjoy the company of others through role playing. Our top priority is often the practical. We go to the market to buy food and related items, not to visit with the personnel. This criterion may seem so obvious that it need not be mentioned, yet you have no doubt encountered people who have temporarily forgotten the purpose of a transaction. A customer who wants to return a defective product may get so annoyed at waiting in line that he barks at the clerk (whose ultimate goal is to provide customer satisfaction). In turn, the clerk reacts to the customer's rude behavior by saying, "I don't have to take this, sir. You can return your product when you get a new personality!" The customer storms away, shouting the equivalent of "I will never shop here again!" Only later do they both realize that they failed to achieve their practical goals.

### Making Room for Expressive Behavior

The other primary reason for public interaction is often overlooked. We usually assume that practical goals are the major reason for interacting with people we don't know very well. But Richard Sennett suggests that for most of our history, people have reveled in the opportunity to "playact" in public.[12] **Playacting** simply means to try on new roles, to be someone you've never been before, to hide behind a mask and enjoy the company of strangers. Many public places exist where such behavior has a higher pri-

ority, but there are fewer now than in the past. People congregate and get lost in the crowd at concerts, sporting events, and large New Year's Eve parties. In these places people can increase their repertoire of identities and can literally be anybody they want to be. We can still playact to a certain degree in groups of strangers, as when one stranger convinces another to join in an impromptu dance during Mardi Gras. Friends are more likely to engage in some scripted routine from a favorite movie, and do it in front of a group of strangers as a form of entertainment. In short, some public interactions allow us the opportunity (at least) to be expressive, to enjoy life, to act the fool, and to give others some enjoyment by participating with us or playing the role of audience.

Now that we have seen some of the criteria that govern public interactions, we want to look more closely at interactions in the context of work. First, we'll describe patterns characteristic of professional dyads. Then we'll investigate the interpersonal communication processes in small work groups and large organizations.

# Communication in Our Communities

## Space and Place: Community Design and Communication

Author James Kunstler makes the point that the design and symbolism of the buildings that populate our public spaces speak a language of either public engagement or uncivil isolation. He argues that the facades of public buildings serve as "walls of a large outdoor room" and that these "public rooms" can either be inviting or profoundly uncivil. In Kunstler's terms, the symbolism of a blank brick wall says, among other things, "[This] street has no meaning. . . . The

## Community and the Third Place

# Barbershop

Tim Story, 2001

Calvin (Ice Cube), a man with big dreams, feels stuck running the barbershop he inherited from his father. What Calvin doesn't realize is that the barbershop isn't just a place to get a haircut, it's part social club, part classroom, part political forum, and part home away from home—the cornerstone of a tightly knit community on Chicago's south side. The barbershop is inhabited by a diverse group, including a know-it-all college boy, Jimmy (Sean Patrick Thomas); a reformed two-time loser, Ricky (Michael Ealy); a white Jewish homeboy, Isaac (Troy Garity); a spurned but spirited young woman, Terri (Eve); and last, but certainly not least, a provocateur

and elder statesman, Eddie (Cedric the Entertainer). The barbershop is not only a place to hang out, it's a place where anyone can say anything, as Eddie proves in his irreverent comic takes on Rodney King, O. J. Simpson, Rosa Parks, Martin Luther King, and Jesse Jackson. When Jimmy calls him out, he responds, "Wait, hold on here. Is this a barbershop? Is this a barbershop? If we can't talk straight in a barbershop, then where can we talk straight? We can't talk straight nowhere else."

The main story line centers on Calvin's growing recognition of what the barbershop means to the community and his attempts to get it back after he foolishly sells it to a loan shark, while a subplot follows the attempts of two bumbling thieves (Anthony Anderson and Lahmard Tate) to figure out what to do with the ATM machine they've stolen but can't seem to open. While these story lines lend the film narrative structure, what's really important and what makes this film remarkable is the conversation. *Barbershop* is a perfect example of a "third place," where locals can interact and where community is built. The film illustrates how important such a place is and how much would be lost without it.

public realm has no significance and what goes on there doesn't matter. . . . We don't care what goes on outside our building."[13] He suggests that:

*When buildings fail to define public space at a scale congenial to humans—as along any commercial highway strip—people cannot be there in safety and comfort. They will not walk there. They will not pause and mingle there with other people. They will not communicate there.*[14]

By way of contrast, a building with mighty columns or a graceful entrance opening onto the

town square honors the street and the people in it. Such design invites us to revel in our roles as citizens of a republic who care about the common good.

Likewise the design of our neighborhoods can invite or discourage interaction of a public nature. Drive or walk down any residential street and pay close attention to the size and orientation of front porches or stoops. Are the porches large enough for their owners to sit out and close enough to the street for them to speak casually to passersby? Or like many modern homes in suburbia, is the front porch so small as to be nonexistent? Sometime around the 1960s, home designs began to emphasize the private patio,

**343**

moving the center of social life to the backyard rather than the larger neighborhood. (For more on the design of neighborhoods, review Box 10.1 from the chapter on family communication.)

### Third Places: Connecting with Your Community

In her walk to work, Adrienne Richmond's attention was drawn to a lively conversation at an outdoor coffee bar. Sociologist Ray Oldenburg has studied what the presence or absence of such places means to a community.[15] He argues that sustaining community requires **third places** beyond the home and the workplace, where conversation is the dominant activity and which are populated by a wide range of people, including "regulars," "casual drop-ins," as well as relative strangers. Oldenburg identified eight criteria that seem to distinguish "third places" from other places that fail to nourish a sense of community: (1) the place is considered "neutral territory," not "owned" by any one social group; (2) patrons are seen as having relatively equal status; (3) conversation is the dominant activity (in other words, loud music and other entertainments do not derail conversation); (4) it has accessible hours and is located within walking distance for most of the patrons; (5) it has a recognizable group of "regular" patrons, but is frequented by many others; (6) an unimpressive décor; (7) a playful mood; and (8) a "home away from home" feeling about the place.

Places that typically measure up well in light of Oldenburg's criteria include corner groceries, beauty parlors, pubs and cafés, donut shops, and similar places located in or near a residential neighborhood. One problem in the United States is that zoning laws often prohibit such mixing of business and residential establishments. It is ironic that laws designed to preserve neighborhoods often actually contribute to their decline. Oldenburg's point is that the absence of such places makes it doubly difficult for people in a community to establish and maintain relatively impersonal but much needed social (as opposed to personal) relationships.

Thanks to the writing of critics like Kunstler and Oldenburg and a rethinking of the social ramifications of architectural designs by architects such as Duany and Plater-Zyberk (see Box 10.1), there is hope that our communities may once again become communication-friendly spaces. In the meantime, let's turn our attention to another place where people engage in cultural, social-, and occasionally individual-level interactions—the workplace.

# Interpersonal Communication in the Workplace

Adrienne Richmond will engage in a multitude of conversations during her first weeks on the job at Zeos Bank. She has no other way of learning about the organization that she has joined other than by gleaning information from the variety of communication encounters that await her. These include face-to-face interactions with coworkers and customers, group meetings, performance appraisals with her supervisors, memos, e-mails, internal newsletters, and other corporate documents such as annual reports or mission and vision plans, as well as corporate training videos and in-house news broadcasts. The ubiquity of communications in organizations has led James Taylor (the organizational communication theorist, not the musical lyricist) to argue that "conversations are the stuff of organizations." Taylor sees organizing and communicating as synonymous: conversations lead to organizational narratives which structure the way people interact. An organization is "a text produced by a set of authors, through conversation."[16] For new employees especially, learning all the nuances of this "text" can be a daunting task. But any member of an organization needs to understand how to read between the lines and sharpen his or her own contributions to the corporate storyline. Among the stories employees co-author are ones about (1) the organizational culture itself; (2) the various teams that plan, produce, and promote its products; (3) how to deal with status and supervision; (4) how to relate to and serve customers; and (5) how to draw the lines between one's work and personal life.

## Sizing Up Organizational Cultures

Just as individual selves are shaped by national and regional cultures (Chapter 8) and dyads develop relational cultures (Chapter 5), so does each organization form its own unique culture. An **organizational culture** can be defined formally as a system of shared meanings and beliefs expressed through symbolic forms such as rituals, stories, and myths which function to hold a group of people together.[17] More colloquially, organizational members might define it as "the way we do things around here." It is the culture of an organization that gives meaning to messages and events, making them understandable to insiders, but possibly confusing to those unfamiliar with the culture. We know that cultures differ at the societal level. But culture is often more invisible at the organizational level. We tend to think of American organizations as sharing essentially the same beliefs about what it takes to be successful. It is only when we transfer from one organization to another that we begin to find different beliefs about the importance of hierarchy and authority, different expectations about working overtime and weekends, tendencies to stifle or thrive on the creative ideas of employees, and so on.

Most scholars recognize organizational cultures to be communicative creations. Differences such as those cited here are not inherent in certain industries or types of organizational tasks. Rather, they emerge from the hundreds of conversations and nonverbal displays that members exchange every day. Karl Weick, a noted organizational theorist, likes to compare organizations to spider webs. Each day employees collectively spin the various webs of power, reward, and or-

ganizing structures as members interact with one another. At night, when employees go home, the webs fall apart. The next day they are spun again, probably in much the same fashion as the day before, but also exhibiting a few subtle changes so that the structure continues to evolve.[18] Recognition of the influence of organizational culture as a context for shaping meaning is a crucial factor in building one's competence as an organizational communicator.

### Fitting in and Standing Out

When a new employee joins an organization, two socializing processes are set in motion: The organization tries to indoctrinate the new recruit, and the new recruit tries to "learn the ropes" and "make her mark" on the organization.

From the organization's perspective the new employee must be taught the values and rituals of the organization's culture. In other words, socialization processes teach one how to be a good employee. Written materials, canned presentations, and informal insights about the beliefs, values, and behaviors expected are the focus of socialization efforts. While some of this socializing is through formal training and company publications, most of it comes from coworkers and supervisors. But the process is not an automatic one. As Daniel Feldman reports, a certain degree of trust and friendliness has to develop before the "regulars" will share vital information with a new recruit: "Until incumbent employees felt they could trust recruits, they withheld information about supervisors' preferences and personalities, making the recruits less competent in the eyes of the supervisors."[19]

Typically, new recruits are fresh from college or an intensive training period and are eager to show what they have learned. It is infinitely wiser, however, to remain a student for a while—learning from coworkers, conforming to standards you may not really like, and earning trust. This kind of compliant behavior will open the doors to inside information that, according to Fredric Jablin, "helps the new employee decode and interpret the scripts and schemas that prevail

**BOX 12.1**

# The Conversational Organization

In this chapter we have introduced the idea of organizations as conversational texts. More and more, the everyday world of work is being seen as a place where interpersonal and group conversations and relationships matter. Rather than thinking of *organizations* as "things" already made and structures like the chain of command, departments, and job descriptions as stable, this view focuses on *organizing* as an ongoing activity conducted in and across many conversations. In her book *The Business of Talk,* Deirdre Boden characterizes this process as a "lamination" of conversations whereby many different conversations involving many different players become knit together and shape one or more understandings of the organization as a whole.

Other writers about organizations emphasize how globalization and new communication technologies have made the pace of change overwhelming. According to Iain Somerville and John Edwin Mroz, corporate leaders "find themselves ill-prepared and increasingly frustrated in dealing with the changing rules of the game. Managing in the old way is not working, yet the new way is difficult to comprehend" (p. 65). Their research points to seven new core competencies that are emerging as critical for success in today's high-speed, global organizations: (1) commitment to a higher purpose, (2) every employee needs to manifest leadership, (3) multidisciplinary teaming, (4) organic partnerships, (5) knowledge networking, (6) global search for models of success, and (7) embracing change. It is striking how much each of these core competencies requires conversation not only to share information, but also to shape responses to changing patterns and sustain working relationships and knowledge networks.

*Commitment to a higher purpose.* Somerville and Mroz note that almost every organization has a mission statement, but very few have discovered how to translate that mission into everyday action by employees. Part of the problem is that mission statements are often developed in isolation by top management rather than encouraged to emerge from the interwoven talk of employees. Somerville and Mroz cite as an exception the mission of Herman Miller, Inc., the manufacturer of furniture for workplaces and other unique environments. Their mission is to "improve the quality of our customers' lives and become their reference point for quality and service." The key is to make organizational conversations the site where important thinking and decisions happen and to ask employees to help continually create and sustain the higher purpose of the organization.

*Instilling responsible leadership.* For a "higher purpose" to emerge, employees have to feel responsible for its origin and its care and feeding on a daily basis. For the organization to respond quickly and smartly to new problems or opportunities, all employees in the organization need to think of themselves as leaders and be ready to act when the situation calls for it. But how will one know the appropriate reaction to situations that are hard to define in advance? The answer is to be involved in daily conversation about your unit's mission, the organization's mission, the changing landscape in which the organization operates (e.g., customer needs, competitive challenges, emerging technologies). Only when one is part of a network of overlapping ("laminated") conversations, can one hope to know how to manifest leadership when a particular situation arises.

*Encouraging multidisciplinary teaming, forging organic partnerships, and promoting knowledge networking.* All three of these competencies require ongoing conversation and the development of working relationships that keep employees, clients, and industry experts connected and "in the know." Somerville and Mroz say that today's organizations "must find a way to make the spontaneous forming and re-forming of high-performing multidisciplinary teams a natural way of working" (p. 71). This means "thriving on diversity" rather than just tolerating or celebrating it and using multiple perspectives to solve problems. It also means breaking down barriers and blurring traditional boundaries in order to focus on what needs to be done and how best to do it rather than which department or professional discipline is responsible. Forming organic partnerships refers to extending the conversation into alliances with other organizations or agencies outside the organization. Many organizations now partner with one another, combining their unique expertise to co-produce a product or service. Small biotechnology firms routinely partner with a larger pharmaceutical giant whose sales force can promote a new drug discovered by the smaller firm and jointly tested by the two companies. Such partnerships cannot happen unless organizations encourage employees to be in conversation outside the boundaries of their organization, creating and sharing knowledge through the networks of cutting-edge industry experts, academic researchers, marketing and consulting firms, and so on.

*Fostering global search and embracing change.* To be truly on the cutting edge, Somerville and Mroz argue that organizations have to change the way they view the larger world as a resource. Rather than assuming that Western approaches to organizing and solving problems are naturally superior and should be exported to other less developed economies, organizations must expand their search for "best practices" to a global scale. According to Somerville and Mroz, "Global search means that all levels of the organization will embrace the effort to seek markets, competencies, and resources from the farthest corners of the globe. . . . Weaving this global search mentality into the fabric of the organization will demand instilling values and rewarding people for thinking globally, searching globally, and acting globally—even if the organization and its customers are all domestic" (p. 75). How do we do that? We have to be prepared to converse across cultures, across industries, across many more lines of division than we may have previously been comfortable doing.

When the Berlin Wall fell in 1989, it was more than a political event. It was a metaphor of things to come. Today's "Berlin Walls" are falling because organizations are learning that conversation is a powerful way to scale those walls and wear them down.

**SOURCES** Deirdre Boden, *The Business of Talk: Organizations in Action* (Cambridge, England: Polity Press, 1994). Iain Somerville and John Edwin Mroz, "New Competencies for a New World," in *The Organization of the Future.* Frances Hesselbein, Marshall Goldsmith, and Richard Beckhard, eds. (San Francisco: Jossey-Bass, 1997).

in the organization."[20] Then, once you're accepted as one of the group, you can begin making your mark.

### Attending to Organizational Stories and Ritual Practices

If the work, politics, and performance of an organization is structured by the many conversations and other "texts" co-authored by its employees, it makes sense to pay attention to the symbolism inherent in our everyday work conversations. These symbols are prevalent in a variety of forms: in the vocabulary and metaphors employees use; in the narratives and stories told; and in ritualized practices of all kinds.

The vocabulary of a workforce speaks volumes about its culture and the expectations that employees have for themselves and others. That each organization has its own vocabulary goes well beyond the idea that there might be special terms or phrases used in describing its products and services. By an **organizational vocabulary** we mean the various ways of speaking and interpreting messages or the metaphors that dominate the talk of the whole organization or one of its subcultures. For example, in one organization, a "machine" metaphor may punctuate the talk of management and employees. "Let's get *the wheels turning* around here!" "You don't want to become *a cog in the wheel . . .*" "Let's not have a *breakdown* in communication." "Everybody's got a *function* to perform, but none of us are *irreplaceable parts.*" When this kind of talk dominates, people create and respond to expectations that fit the metaphor. Their behavior may become more machine-like in a variety of ways: punching the clock (rather than sticking with a job until it's done); performing work assignments according to instructions (rather than figuring out better ways to perform); and so on. Gareth Morgan has explored a number of metaphors that are used to structure the work and communication flow in organizations—organizations seen as machines, organisms, brains, garbage pails, psychic prisons, political systems, and so on.[21] Morgan points out that metaphors

have paradoxical effects. Any metaphor can illuminate and inspire employees in some ways and restrain or debilitate them in other ways. The prominence of a "military" metaphor may be helpful in that there are clear *lines of authority* and *rules for engagement,* but the landscape may also be littered with *minefields* and employees forced to *watch their flank* for someone with a new *battle plan* or an effort to *take out a strategic target* (you!!). One of the adjustments Adrienne Richmond must make in moving from her previous organization to Zeos Bank (or even within subcultures of the same organization) is to recognize the subtle ways that employees talk and how the dominant metaphors shape expectations and action.

### Narratives and Stories

We humans are notorious story-tellers and the workplaces we inhabit are full of stories. Not only do we tell stories, but many scholars are coming to the conclusion that story-telling is the primary means by which Homo sapiens become human beings. W. Barnett Pearce argues that "narrative structures, plots, roles and the like comprise the templates in which we live our lives."[22] Our brains are structured such that we look for a way to fit any new piece of information into an existing storyline (recall our discussion of cognitive scripts in Chapter 6). When we can't find a story to fit the facts, we create a new one. When we look to the future, we imagine how the story of our career, our family life, or our role in next week's staff meeting will play out.

In organizations, the range of stories can be truly amazing, but most of them are embedded in larger stories that give some coherence to the whole. When coworkers tell each other stories about why the last advertising campaign failed or what to do when the boss confronts you about your expense vouchers, these stories may be seen as connected to a larger story about the leadership of the department or team. If the storyline on the boss is that he "micromanages" everything, then his tweaking of the ad campaign and his incessant worrying about how every dollar is spent are part of a larger story. Furthermore, the story of his selection as manager may be linked to an even larger story about top management's "tight reign" or "top-down control" of things. Not surprisingly, organizational metaphors are intricately bound up in these stories.

### Rituals and Practices

While stories give meaning to organizational interaction, they are expressed through a variety of ritualized social practices. Some rituals fall into the category of "standard operating procedures." These can be proscribed ways of performing certain tasks or they may just be patterns of interaction that have emerged and been sustained by employees over a long period of time. Other organizational rituals might be considered as celebratory practices. Rituals of this type include formal or informal ways of recognizing outstanding performance or long years of service. Examples include annual dinners to honor retirees or monthly lists of the top sales agents posted in prominent locations. Some rituals have specific stories associated with them. There is an oft-told story about a manager in a high-tech manufacturing firm who wanted to reward an engineer who burst into his office late one evening with the solution to a problem that had stumped the best engineers in the company. Unable to think of an appropriate way to recognize the achievement, the manager gave the engineer a banana he had not eaten for lunch. Years later, the company still awards a "Golden Banana" each year to employees who help solve perplexing problems.

It is also important to realize that not all of the metaphors, stories, and rituals in any organization mesh or are shared by everyone within the organization. Whatever the dominant organizational culture may be, there are always subcultures that resist some of the practices and interpret them very differently. There are always competing stories about what things "really mean." One way of sorting out these differences is to look at the patterns of interaction that constitute various communication networks within the organization.

*The stories we tell each other at work help give meaning to organizational interaction.*

### Participating in Communication Networks

For individual stories to become chapters in the "text" that is an organization, they must be shared and gain currency among the larger body of employees. While a few stories are sanctioned in official company communications such as newsletters, memos, or in-house news broadcasts, most stories circulate the old-fashioned way—by word of mouth—through various communication networks.

There are actually many different kinds of communication networks in large organizations, most of them formed informally by people with a need for information that isn't available through regular, formal channels. Some networks, like the grapevine, have been named and are recognized by almost everyone. Others are almost invisible, and even the members of such networks may not realize they exist. An informal network exists whenever members who do not formally report to one another exchange information on a somewhat regular basis. They may talk about almost any informational topic. An "innovation" network, for instance, might include people who share an interest in technology or ideas even though they are located in a variety of units and talk only when they happen to run into one another. Often they find out about new product lines and other techniques months before they are reported in company newsletters and internal memos. A network can be considered an informal group, even though all of its members rarely meet at the same place and time. Since most members communicate regularly with at least some of their network partners, important messages usually get to all of the members in a relatively short time.

The **grapevine** is perhaps the most interesting and certainly the most researched of the networks. People are curious about the action behind the scenes and often talk about what they know or have heard in the hallways, beside the water cooler, or over coffee. Many people rely on the information gleaned from the grapevine to increase their own understanding of the organization, predict future changes, and consolidate their own power by being in the know. People who fail to tune in to the grapevine are often likely to be the subject of rumors. Research verifies that most people have a negative image of the grapevine but would rather have possibly misleading information than no information at all.[23] The most interesting findings, however, are those that dispute popular opinion about the grapevine. Contrary to what most people think, the grapevine is amazingly accurate. One study estimates that nearly 80 percent of the information acquired through the grapevine is basically accurate.[24] Several studies have found that information passed via the grapevine was distorted less than most messages passed through formal channels.[25] Astute managers know the value of the grapevine and frequently use it to spread information that their people need to know but that is too sensitive to be commented on publicly.

In organizations, information is power, and the lack of it can weaken your position in the company. We recommend that you view the grapevine as a viable channel of communication, though always taking what you hear with a grain of salt. Try to cultivate other informal networks as well; you never know when such contacts will pay off. In addition, you'll be the kind of informed employee who can be a true asset to the organization.

## Making the Team

While Adrienne Richmond is beginning to see important distinctions in organizational culture between her previous employer and her new one, and knows that over time she needs to tap into the larger communication networks at Zeos, her most immediate concern is fitting in and finding her place in the local department or work group where she will spend most of her time on the job. Eventually, she may be asked to serve on other project teams as well, so her group communication skills and her understanding of group dynamics will be tested repeatedly throughout her career. Furthermore, she wants her coworkers and supervisors to see her leadership potential, so she wants to look for opportunities to demonstrate leadership without coming on too strong this early in the game. In building our understanding of how communication creates a sense of teamwork, we'll examine four dynamics: leadership, group roles and skills, group norms, and group cohesion.

### Leading the Team

In most organizations the leadership role in a task or decision-making group will be formally assigned. As a leader you will be expected to motivate, direct, evaluate, correct, and work with the group in an efficient manner while ensuring high-quality production. What makes for effective leadership? For years researchers thought that leadership could be predicted by identifying the **personality traits** of leaders. They hoped to discover the consistent stuff of

## Communication in the Business World

# Lessons from The Apprentice

Is it possible to learn strategies for business success from a reality television show? Although many critics would answer no, millions of young viewers form their initial perceptions of the business world by watching *The Apprentice*. What lessons are they learning as they observe contestants' workplace communication?

Katherine Kinnick and Sabrena Parton decided to find out by analyzing the first season of this popular TV show. Their study used what is called content analysis. Three independent coders were trained to watch the show, note the communication skills needed for each weekly challenge, and record any time a team or individual was praised or blamed because of his or her communication competence.

Results showed that the communication skill most frequently called upon in weekly challenges was persuasion. In the authors' words, "the business world as presented on *The Apprentice* is one whose ultimate goal is persuading others." In critiques, both by Trump and his associates and the other contestants, competitors' communication skills were frequently mentioned. Poor leadership and inadequate interpersonal skills were seen as important barriers to business success. Contestants (mostly the males) were consistently criticized for failures of leadership (not taking charge, failing to address problems head on, using nondemocratic leadership styles, and micromanagement). On the interpersonal front, contestants (mostly the females) were criticized for being too emotional, being too confrontational, talking down to clients, and blurting out inappropriate responses. Finally, compared to the bottom five, the top five finalists were evaluated by their coworkers as using more even-tempered, diplomatic, and collaborative communication styles. It is interesting that Mr. Trump did not praise any of the contestants for being good communicators, but he was quick to criticize those with poor communication competence. It is also remarkable that instances of unethical behavior were barely noticed, perhaps sending the message that "the mentality of 'win at all costs' is still the rule in business."

The authors believe the show illustrates the importance of communication in business settings. Admitting that *The Apprentice* is far from a realistic image of the corporate world, they believe that "the ability to work cooperatively on a team, to lead a team, to meet deadlines, and to deliver on assigned tasks is an undeniably real demand of today's workforce."

Kinnick, Katherine N., and Sabrena R. Parton. "Workplace Communication: What *The Apprentice* Teaches About Communication Skills." *Business Communication Quarterly* 68, no. 4 (2005): 429–56.

leadership: intelligence, charisma, sociability, and so on. But the correlation between personality and leadership has proved elusive. After more than 750 studies, the attempt to construct a profile of leader characteristics has been largely written off, and researchers have turned to other approaches.[26]

Today, **leadership** is more and more viewed as a communicative achievement. Leaders are thought to be "managers of meaning" who invite others to share in defining and building a shared vision of the group or corporate future. The study described in this chapter's Research in Review shows that it is not just academics who see communication as an important aspect of leadership; this opinion is shared by most people in the business world. Indeed, the ability to communicate clearly and persuasively can mean the difference between success and failure.

Leadership is the product of a leader-follower relationship, not the act of a single individual. Many organizations have redefined the role of managers, moving away from the notion of a manager as one who controls, supervises, or tells others what to do. In today's "team-based" organization, a manager is more often thought of as a resource person—someone who has the responsibility of locating and providing support knowledge and materials so that employees can perform their jobs at a higher level of excellence. Max De-Pree, chairman of the board at Herman Miller, an innovative furniture manufacturer, describes the role of leader as "a servant" whose only success is the performance of the followers. For DePree, the qualities of leadership are all relational. A leader has an awareness of the human spirit that fosters integrity, intellectual curiosity, comfort with ambiguity, the courage to trust followers, and the realization that to lead one must be present—available to listen and talk with employees.[27]

Leadership can be seen as a group relationship as well as a series of dyadic relationships. **Dyadic linkage theory** challenges conventional business wisdom that leaders should treat all of their subordinates in the same manner to avoid giving the impression of playing favorites or treating some employees unfairly. Some recent research calls this view into question. The dyadic linkage model of leadership suggests that every dyadic relationship is unique in some ways and that effective leaders adapt their style to fit the person. This means that, as a leader, you might use a more autocratic style with those subordinates who respond well to direction, prodding, or an occasional kick in the pants. Likewise, you

would be prudent to give more latitude to highly competent, go-it-on-their-own employees, and to use a more participatory, equal-status style with workers who perform the most critical functions in your unit.

In short, leadership requires sensitivity to followers' needs and a rather flexible package of communication options. Think about your most recent work experience. Imagine yourself as the leader of that group. How would you adapt your leadership style to each individual member? What would you do to motivate each one?

### Building Teamwork Skills

Experts agree that for a group to work well together, members must take on different roles and reinforce one another for role performances. Most also agree on five specific roles that are most essential: task leader, social leader, information provider, tension releaser, and devil's advocate. The important thing to remember here is that in playing group roles, members need to achieve a delicate balance of complementarity and duplication. In other words, group interaction is most effective when the role each person plays complements rather than competes with the roles of other group members. For instance, when Gibson provides the group with information about projected sales figures (information provider), Gerber questions the validity of the figures (devil's advocate). In turn, Gibson provides additional information about how the figures were arrived at. Their actions are complementary because together they have increased the group's confidence that the information they have is accurate; they have advanced the group toward its goal. Sometimes role behavior is not complementary. When an argument gets out of hand, Gruber (tension reliever) breaks the tension with a joke. If Gerber follows with another joke, his behavior is competing with Gruber's, not complementing it (unless, of course, the first joke failed to ease the tension successfully).

Role specialization can be taken too far, however. Group members need to be able to play a variety of roles to cover for a group member who is absent or not up to par on a given day. It might be helpful to think of group members as having primary and secondary roles. Primary roles are the ones they play most frequently; secondary roles are the ones they are capable of performing when the regular performer cannot. It takes time for roles to develop in a new group, so you should expect competition for leadership and other key roles to take place until members find their niche. Roles that are not assigned formally will develop as a result of the positive or negative feedback the group provides to each member's communicative efforts.

*Establishing Norms.* Group roles refer to behavioral expectations the group has for specific individuals. Group norms, on the other hand, are expectations the group has of *all* its members. Without norms a group has no identity, no way of distinguishing itself from all the other work groups in the organization. And it has no way of governing the behavior of the whole group. A group can develop norms for high or low productivity, or members may establish a pattern of pulling practical jokes on one another.

Communication is the key to establishing good group norms and maintaining them or changing outdated ones. Members of effective groups tend to talk to one another about the standards they follow and reinforce one another for performing well. The job satisfaction of individual workers has been traced to their working with colleagues who express positive attitudes about their jobs.[28] Most groups have key members, sometimes known as "opinion leaders," who are the most influential in changing the norms. A good leader will seek these people out when he or she wants to change the internal standards of a work group.

*Developing Cohesion.* While roles and norms are necessary for effective group functioning, cohesiveness makes group life enjoyable and fulfilling. It provides members with a more complete sense of group identity and a sense of belonging. Simply defined, **cohesion** refers to the degree to which group members like one another and want to remain in the group. There are a number of factors that relate to cohesion: the expression of similarities in attitude, beliefs, and values; the use of group-related pronouns such as we, us, and ours instead of yours and mine; the development of trust; inside jokes, unusual rituals, traditions, or stories; survival of difficult times together; and so on. When a group begins to exhibit this kind of behavior, it is becoming more cohesive.

As much as cohesiveness is valued, experts point out the pitfalls of becoming too cohesive. When a group becomes too tight-knit, members tend to try to maintain group relations at all costs. The result is a phenomenon known as **groupthink:** Critical thinking is sacrificed in order to promote group agreement.[29] Group members begin to think of themselves as incapable of making mistakes. Instead of basing decisions on careful analysis of the facts and the alternative courses of action, they become sloppy and overconfident. They end up making bad decisions or defective products. Because of this tendency, experts recommend that groups be cautious about letting loyalty to the group become too important.

To promote effective group relations, it is healthy to develop communication patterns that reflect complementary roles, clear-cut norms, and a moderate degree of cohesiveness. Think about the groups you've worked with in the past. What were the roles, norms, and forms of cohesion of the most successful ones?

In addition to good relations between supervisors and subordinates and among work groups, it is also important to become adept at managing organization-wide communication channels. We will explore these channels next. In the following section we look at how organizational cultures develop and at some of the ways workers can adapt to the role demands of complex organizations.

### Surviving Supervision and Status

Most organizations rely on some type of formal hierarchy of authority, where some members have legitimate rights over others. These rights include the assignment of work, supervision, and evaluation of job performance. Research indicates that supervisors spend roughly one-third to two-thirds of their time in direct communication with their subordinates, usually providing information about organizational policy and practices, the goals of the company, job instructions, rationales behind instructions, or feedback about performance. Subordinates, for their part, tend to provide their superiors with information about themselves, job-related problems, tasks that need to be done, current work, and information about policies and practices requested by the supervisor.[30]

### Status Differences in Communication

The key attribute of the supervisor-subordinate relationship is that of status. Since supervisors have higher status by virtue of their position, they also seem to have initiation rights. Supervisors are freer to start and stop discussions and to interrupt a subordinate; superiors can also choose to stand closer, touch casually, and use an informal mode of address; for a lower-status employee to reciprocate would be a sign of disrespect. In addition, superiors regularly expect subordinates to disclose information that makes them potentially vulnerable. For example, if you admit to your boss that you find it difficult to work with another employee, such information could be interpreted negatively and could affect your chances for a raise, promotion, or good evaluation. Given these problems, it is little wonder that supervisors and subordinates are often wary of one another.

Yet research also confirms that developing an effective relationship with your supervisor is one of the best predictors of job satisfaction.[31] How can you build a quality supervisor-subordinate relationship? Obviously, the supervisor is in the best position to set the tone for the relationship. He or she can make a concerted effort to avoid the negative effects of the status barrier. The subordinate can also do a lot by maintaining respect for those of higher status without sacrificing personal integrity. As you read about the keys to su-

pervising effectively and directing communication upward, try to think of ways that status differences help or hinder communicative efforts.

### Effective Supervisory Communication

In a comprehensive review of research on supervisor-subordinate communication, Fredric Jablin reports that more research has been focused on characteristics of effective versus ineffective supervisors than on any other topic.[32] The most complete list of characteristics related to effectiveness was provided by Charles Redding.[33] He suggested that better supervisors

- are more "communication-minded"—they enjoy talking with subordinates
- are willing to listen and take appropriate action in response to employees' suggestions and complaints
- tend to "ask" or "persuade" employees more frequently than "telling" or "demanding" them to do things
- are sensitive to subordinates' feelings and ego-defense needs, careful to reprimand in private, and so on
- are more open in passing information along to subordinates, giving advance notice of changes, and explaining rationales behind policies and regulations

There are problems with simple lists like this one, however. A number of situational factors can influence effective leadership. Take the characteristic of being open with subordinates, for instance. As we have seen, the organizational culture socializes its employees (supervisors and subordinates alike) to use particular communication styles and avoid others. A manager with an open style of communication may not last long in a "closed-mouth" organization. In addition, Jablin has shown that subordinates are more likely to respond to an open style when their supervisor is less involved in organizational politics.[34] Perhaps subordinates don't trust a superior who is likely to move on up the ladder as much as they do one who "stays home" and

## Alienation in the Workplace

# Office Space

Mike Judge, 1999

Since Peter Gibbons (Ron Livingston) started working at Initech, every single day of his life has been worse than the day before. He sits in a cubicle all day long, updating software and trying to avoid all eight of his managers, including the smarmy Bill Lumburgh (Gary Cole). When Peter asks a hypnotherapist to help him like his job, the therapist puts him into a trance, tells him to stop worrying, and then drops dead before the hypnosis can be reversed. No longer filled with anxiety, Peter tells the company consultants exactly what he thinks, including the fact that he spends most of his week staring at his desk pretending to look busy. But instead of getting him fired, his new attitude gets him a promotion.

As the plot unfolds, Peter falls in love with a waitress (Jennifer Aniston) who's in danger of losing her own job because she doesn't show enough "flair" by wearing more than the minimum of funny buttons on her uniform. Along with his two best friends (David Herman and Ajay Naidu), Peter also gets embroiled in a scheme to siphon money from Initech's account into his own. But the story line is less important than the way this smart and funny film satirizes American business practices. Peter knows that "human beings were not meant to sit in little cubicles all day, filling out useless forms, and listening to eight different bosses drone on about mission statements." It would appear that some corporate managers aren't so sure.

---

seems more loyal to his or her subordinates. Also, such politicking may actually increase the perceived status differences between superior and subordinate. Furthermore, the maturity level of an individual or group of subordinates can alter a supervisor's style. A supervisor is more likely to be successful by being demanding and less open with a group that demonstrates few work-related skills and a low motivation level.

Building effective supervisory, coworker, and team relationships is critical to the functioning of any organization. But we must not forget that all of those relationships are designed to produce quality products and services for customers or clients.

## Serving the Customer

Another common interaction is the one that takes place between customers and clerks. These roles are sometimes called "boundary-spanning" roles because the individuals who fill them interact primarily with people who are not members of the work organization. Typical roles include sales representatives, purchasing agents, public relations personnel, real estate agents, table servers, delivery persons, postal clerks, bank tellers, financial advisers, and so on.

In some ways these relations are more difficult to manage because the status distinctions are not so clear-cut. Supervisors and subordinates know who the ultimate authority is, and professionals are expected to know more than those who seek their help. But the customer-clerk relationship has not been so neatly defined. Some customers view the role of a clerk as essentially a servant, and many businesses instruct their personnel to put the customer first. Other people recognize the relationship as one of mutual dependency and grant customer and clerk fairly equal status. Still other customers place themselves in a submissive

*Customer relations are often impersonal and sometimes unfeeling.*
*Note the bureaucrats hiding behind rules and regulations in this*
*eerie evocation of modern organizational life.*

George Tooker, *Government Bureau*, 1956

role to the salesperson ("When you get the time, could you please show me the Nikon 35mm camera? I would really appreciate it. Thank you ever so much. No, that's OK, I'll wait").

In spite of these differing assumptions about the nature of customer relations, there are some general guidelines. Perhaps the most important thing for a salesperson to remember is that different customers respond to different approaches. Just as in other contexts, here people have learned different rules for appropriate or preferred interaction with sales representatives. When shopping, some like to browse and don't want to be bothered by salespeople—and they

give off unmistakable nonverbal cues: not making eye contact, turning away from approaching salespeople, and so on. Other people desire special attention and will wait for the clerk to approach them, demonstrate merchandise, or offer advice. Asking questions about their preferences is a subtle way to find out whether advice is desired. A clerk must always be sensitive to the customer's nonverbals—they will tell you if your rules are not their rules.

Most customers will respond to simple, courteous behavior and a pleasant but not overly friendly manner. In positions where repeat business is important, a clerk should find out the customer's name and remember to use the appropriate form of address (Mr., Ms., Dr., and so on). Many salespeople go out of their way to provide regular customers with a little extra attention, such as a card or phone call in advance of a sales promotion. That little extra often results in customer loyalty.

## One-to-One Marketing

Traditionally, most business organizations have viewed marketing to and communicating with customers as a one-to-many proposition. For any given product or service, the goal is usually to increase "market share" or the total number or percentage of customers. With the advent of modern communications technology, many organizations now target individual customers and seek to build "customer share," or selling a greater number of the company's products and services to an individual customer over her or his lifetime.[35] Don Peppers and Martha Rogers describe the basics of this approach in their book *The One to One Future: Building Relationships One Customer at a Time.* Their prototypical case is that of a man who remembers it is his mother's birthday at the absolute last moment. He calls a flower shop in his mother's home town and begs them to deliver a bouquet within a couple of hours. Not only does the company honor his request, they use a computer database to automatically send him a reminder 48 weeks later not to forget his mother's birthday again and suggest several products that he might consider purchasing.[36] This approach, also called **relationship marketing,** involves organizations developing "information-rich" relationships with individual customers and then attempting to serve that customer across a wide range of products over many years. You can imagine the owner of the flower shop providing convenient service to ship many different seasonal items for different holidays and anniversaries, each time asking the customer about other potential needs she can fill. As the owner becomes more knowledgeable about the client's interests and needs, she aims to become

the one-stop provider of choice. Because she has more information about this particular customer, she has a huge competitive advantage over other providers. She is also banking on the fact that if she provides excellent service, the customer will not go elsewhere. As a customer, why change providers when the current one anticipates and fills your every need? Some customers may become uncomfortable knowing that an organization is building a rather elaborate personal information file on them, but as long as the trust involved in such a relationship is not broken, many customers welcome the attention and service.

## Internal Customers Matter

Another form of customer service occurs within the boundaries of the organization itself. Many workers do not have direct contact with external customers. For instance, if your job involves producing computer chips in Taiwan that will be shipped to Houston, Texas, and installed in a computer, you are not likely to ever have contact with the ultimate end-user. Many companies now train employees to think of the person who will add the next component to a product or integrate your report into a larger one as an "internal" customer. Kathleen Reardon and Ben Enis refer to the process of training employees to think in these terms as **persuasive internal marketing.**[37] Even if the organizations you ultimately work for do not use this terminology, it is still an excellent way to think about your own role in any organizing process. If everyone performs their part in such a way that they make the next person's job easier, better informed, or of higher quality, the final product or service will be outstanding. Obviously, pleasing internal customers requires information-rich communication to establish and maintain a good understanding of their needs.

## Drawing the Line on Relationships

One of the difficulties that employees like Adrienne Richmond face is how to manage close interpersonal relationships that develop in the workplace. Since Adrienne has recently relocated to a city where she has no family, friends, or even acquaintances, she will most likely develop much of her social circle at work. The spark of romance may even come her way in the workplace.

## Framing Friendship in the Workplace

Researchers have long realized that the workplace in modern industrial societies has become a primary source of community for many of us. In the days before we became such a highly mobile society, it made some sense to employees to compartmentalize their lives and form collegial relationships at work and maintain friendship circles within the stable communities they had grown up in: The dictate "don't mix business and pleasure" had some grounding in a world with distinct boundaries. But those days are long gone. For many people, the workplace *is* their most significant community, and it is where they meet and make new friends.

It is still the case that the majority of relationships with coworkers remain at an acquaintanceship or "friendly relations" level.[38] But it is far from uncommon for very close friendships to develop among colleagues. While the incidence of friendship in the workplace is on the rise, it is surprising how little research has been conducted on these types of relationships. In one of the few studies to examine the developmental pattern of such friendships, P. M. Sias and D. J. Cahill found many of the same factors that account for friendship development in other contexts: physical proximity, perceived similarity in attitudes, self-disclosure, and increased discussion of more intimate topics. Closely associated with the transition from acquaintanceship to friendship was having worked together on shared tasks, introduction of non-work-related conversation topics, increased socializing outside the workplace, and reduced caution in sharing some opinions. Cohesion in a work group was often a contributing factor as well. A move to an even closer "best friends" relationship category typically involved

discussion of even more intimate topics and further reduction of caution in what was shared.[39] Conditions in the workplace itself often served as a catalyst for friendship development. Critical incidents such as a conflict with a supervisor or some other work-related problem often led coworkers to seek social support from each other, which in turn led to sharing of other problems and the development of trust.[40] One of the outcomes of developing close friendships that Sias and Cahill reported was a reluctance on the part of an employee to leave the job, even if other aspects of the job were not very pleasant.[41]

## Managing the Office Romance

Traditional wisdom has held that business and pleasure do not mix. For most of this century, organizations have discouraged the pursuit of romantic relationships in the workplace. Many companies had strict policies forbidding both husband and wife from working for the organization or at least from working in the same unit. But such attitudes are changing, primarily because people have relaxed their attitudes about sexual activity in general, more women have entered the workforce, and the organization has become more central to many people's lives.[42]

In the past, when romance flourished in the office, organizational policies often called for one partner (usually the woman) to quit or be transferred. The rationale usually focused on the perception that working intimates might allow their romantic problems to affect their work, or that such relations would serve as a distraction to other workers. In addition, it has often been charged that employees might use romance, or sex at least, to further their chances of career success. James Dillard conducted a study in which he asked both participants and observers of office romances to describe the motives for such a relationship and its effect on the workers' productivity. Surprisingly, he found that only 17 percent of participants and observers thought the relationship had a harmful effect on the employees' job performance. The majority (62 percent) felt that the relationship made no difference at all, while 21 percent thought the relationship actually had a positive effect on performance. The most disturbing (but not surprising) finding was that gender bias remains alive and well. Females who were perceived to be using the relationship to enhance their careers were the subject of negative talk on the organizational grapevine. On the other hand, males who were perceived as forming the relationship because they were really in love were greatly admired by grapevine participants.[43]

Patrice Buzzanell asked 326 members of many different organizations how they had experienced romantic relations at work and how they managed them. She found that those who had actually participated in an office romance were much more positive about the relationship than those who had not had one. In terms of managing the relationship, Buzzanell discovered that when romantic partners were careful to maintain their professional demeanor and patterns of information sharing with coworkers, their relationship was either ignored, supported, or encouraged by others.[44] Some writers on the subject have asserted that the negative consequences of office romance are more pronounced in organizations that restrict the emotional expressiveness of their employees, forcing them to sneak around, act guilty, or exhibit sexual tension.[45] The preoccupation with not getting caught may affect their work more than the problems in the relationship itself. Some have argued that relaxing concerns about romantic relationships at work will provide a better context for all kinds of male-female relationships. When colleagues are not worried about how a cross-gender relationship will be perceived, they may be more likely to form close platonic friendships and more effective working relationships with the opposite sex. Box 12.2 certainly illustrates the need for males and females to better understand one another's communication tendencies.

## Deciphering the Boundaries Between Home, Work, and Community

Earlier in this chapter, we encountered sociologist Ray Oldenburg's notion of three "spaces" in which we live the bulk of our social lives: home, the workplace, and the "third places" of community. Traditionally, many social relationships were compartmentalized into one of these spaces, with the greatest overlap between home and community. Conventional wisdom suggested that we keep these spaces isolated from one another, with the most solid lines of demarcation between work and home. We were told not to bring office problems home or take domestic troubles to work. Some organizations advocated that employees be involved in community activities to create a sense of corporate goodwill, but rarely did community issues become high priorities in the corporate boardroom. Today, however, the boundaries have become hopelessly blurred. Workplaces are communities. As we have seen, friendships and romantic relationships blossom there. People work from home. They take work home with them. Organizations can no longer afford to ignore the effects their policies have on local communities. Managing relationships that cut across these boundaries is full of challenges.

Linda Harris once posed this analogy: if "work" was a husband and "home" was his wife, what kind of relationship would they have?[46] Would the organization be a traditional dominant husband who treats home as a submissive wife? Whose needs get recognized as the priority? How does a father choose between a late meeting at the office or attending his daughter's first soccer game? What would an egalitarian relationship between work and home look like? Many organizations now have policies for flextime and family leave, but according to a study by sociologist Arlie Hochschild, very few employees take advantage of these policies, raising questions about how the policies are interpreted within the organization's culture.[47]

BOX 12.2

## "Sorry, I'm Not Apologizing"
# Conversational Rituals Between Women and Men at Work

Much of our everyday conversation is ritual. We repeatedly ask others how they are doing without any expectation that they will take us literally and give a full account of their recent medical history. We say and hear things in a mindless fashion because what's really important is that our words serve as a social lubricant. What we say is far less important than the fact that we are still talking to one another. Deborah Tannen, in her book *Talking from 9 to 5,* says that while we often exchange significant content messages about the work we do, "the meat of the work that has to be done is held together, made pleasant and possible, by the ketchup, relish, and bun of conversational rituals" (p. 41). When a ritual is

recognized, both parties know not to take the words literally. Problems arise, however, when coworkers use different rituals and fail to recognize the appropriate category of talk. One example is the ritual use of the words "I'm sorry."

The British are well known for "saying sorry." They say it to each other perhaps 20 or 30 times a day. When a London sidewalk is crowded and people inadvertently bump each other, a near chorus of "sorry" can be heard. Its function is merely one of maintaining a sense of decency while being jostled about on a busy street. In America, saying "I'm sorry" can easily be misunderstood, especially in the world of work, where most of the jostling has to do with image and status. To be successful in business, women have been frequently advised to avoid apologizing and other forms of so-called powerless speech. Softening criticism with praise, thanking people for routine services, and asking others for opinions instead of asserting your own are forms of speech often seen as submissive. They are also behaviors that women tend to engage in more than men. Misunderstandings often occur because men fail to recognize them as ritualistic, and women do not realize that men will take them literally.

Tannen tells of a well-known columnist who gave her a private phone number, only to have

To be a well-rounded communicator, you must manage public, impersonal relationships just as well as you do intimate ones. You also have to manage the ambiguities that define the boundaries between these kinds of relationships. In this chapter we have described the major criteria that shape public encounters. These criteria can serve as general guidelines when other, more specific information is not available. Next we want to look at how the issues we've discussed in this chapter translate into the model of communicative competence that we have stressed throughout the text.

# Communicative Competence and Professional Relationships

Competence in professional and public relationships requires different sensitivities than those called for in family and personal relationship contexts. Public interactions utilize civil discourse that relies on ritualized knowledge instead of

Tannen lose it. When asked if she would provide the number again, the woman instantly responded with "Oh, I'm sorry—it's . . ." In this case, and in many others, "I'm sorry" is not really an apology; it's a way of saving face for the other person or expressing regret or understanding. In the same way, saying "thank you" even when the other person has not provided any service, can be a ritualized way of closing a conversation. But all rituals depend on mutually shared assumptions. If women at work often say they're sorry and men never do, the imbalance probably reflects ritual versus literal interpretations.

Women tend to use compliments and give praise at work much more than men do at work, but are reluctant to criticize directly. Men, on the other hand, like their criticism straight and tend to keep quiet when someone is doing a good job. The result: Men often miss the indirect criticisms given by women and women feel ignored or taken for granted because they are seldom told if they are doing a good job. Another ritual difference is the kind of small talk used as conversational filler. Women, according to Tannen, often complain about problems in relationships as a way of showing that they are on equal footing (neither is perfect). If taken literally, this kind of talk can be interpreted as chronic complaining.

Equally confusing to some women is the ritual sports talk banter engaged in by most men and, increasingly, by many women.

While there are gender differences in conversational style and ritual use of language, the important point is that taking ritualistic language literally can lead to problematic perceptions of others. Since we tend to be unaware of many of the ways that we ourselves use language ritually, it should not surprise us when we interpret the rituals of others in a literal fashion. And since the American workplace was shaped largely by the language rituals of men, it may still take us a while to learn and appreciate the full range of rituals available to us.

SOURCE Deborah Tannen, *Talking from 9 to 5: How Women's and Men's Conversational Styles Affect Who Gets Heard, Who Gets Credit, and What Gets Done at Work* (New York: William Morrow & Company, 1994).

**ADDITIONAL READING**

Conrad, Charles. *Strategic Organizational Communication: Toward the Twenty first Century.* Orlando, Fla.: Harcourt Brace, 1994. See especially Chapters 12 and 13 on strategies of accommodation in managing gender, race, and ethnic diversity in organizations.

personal knowledge about others. To demonstrate competence in this context means balancing a friendly but aloof demeanor so that we can enjoy each other's company without prying or burdening the other with issues in our personal life. In family and intimate relationships we are expected to do just the opposite.

## Professional Relationships and Interpretive Competence

Many people who are excellent at deciphering others once they get to know them seem hopelessly inept at initial encounters with strangers. Such people probably have well-developed cognitive schemas relevant to showing empathy, managing conflict, and reading personal motivations, but need to have extensive personal knowledge of the other before they can put their social skills to work. Ours is a culture that values the personal and tends to devalue impersonal relationships as if they were somehow inferior and unsatisfying. Perhaps that is why we refer to such interactions as small talk. We don't expect big dividends, so we spend little time elaborating or practicing social scripts that go beyond the first two or three minutes of interaction and yet remain at an impersonal level. We seem to have lost what earlier generations referred to as "the art of conversation." However, we do have very efficient scripts for moving interaction in a personal direction. One study of conversational expectations indicated that Americans are predisposed to reveal quite intimate details about themselves within the first 30 minutes to an hour of conversation.[48] Thus, it appears that we have plenty of room for improvement in our interpretive competence at this level but few models to follow.

## Professional Relationships and Role Competence

Another consequence of the infusion of the personal into the public realm is a confusion of roles. Where earlier eras provided clear-cut social roles and codes of etiquette to manage cultural transitions, our age has made informality its badge of honor. But this often blurs role distinctions, as when financial institutions advertise themselves as "your friend" in the community. As Judith Martin (otherwise known as "Miss Manners") has pointed out, if your banker is your friend, you would certainly be understanding and forgiving if a bank officer forgot to process your new home loan until after interest rates had gone up a half-percentage point. The officer meant well. How could you be angry at a friend who was just trying to do his or her job? Role competence is hampered when we don't know the rules for enacting the role. Sometimes the rules are clear to anyone with experience in a given role. The simple remedy in such cases is to learn the role by observing those who are good at it. But in times of profound social change, public roles are often challenged.

One such role undergoing dramatic change today is the role of professional caregivers in the field of human services. Since the rise of the welfare state, social services agents have been trained as professionals whose role was defined as problem solvers for the poor and disabled. The com-plementary role cast for the client of social services was a "victim"—too weak and powerless to help him or herself. Critics of the welfare state have charged that these role assumptions created a vicious cycle of learned helplessness. Today, many social service agencies are moving toward a model where clients are seen as untapped sources with a capacity to solve their own problems when empowered and given a shared role in making decisions about what resources they really need.[49] Obviously, what counts as role competence for both caregiver and client have changed significantly. Role competent behavior will continue to change as our culture struggles to define our public roles in relation to one another.

Changes in work roles have also challenged our communication competence. Gone are the days when an employee could be successful by not making waves and being loyal to the company. The new rules stress taking risks, being willing to make mistakes, asking for more responsibility, working faster, and shooting for total quality.[50] Being role competent is not getting any easier.

## Professional Relationships and Self Competence

While role competence makes sense in work or public settings, concern for self competence may seem oddly out of place. In fact, our discussion of interpretive and role competence implies that there is already too much self-focus and any more would only threaten the public realm further. And yet, there is an important relationship between the self and our public or professional roles. Self-identity is drawn from many sources. When we narrow our definition of self to include only private pursuits, we give up a part of ourselves. Earlier cultures seem to have recognized the importance of a full and fulfilling public life of theatrical play, civic celebration, political involvement, and conversational enjoyment. Sociologist Ray Oldenburg has argued that the best cultures have always had what he calls "third places" (beyond the family and workplace) where neighbors could congregate and experience a public life. Neighborhood cafés, pubs, beauty parlors, and a host of assorted places qualify for third places if we but use them. An important aspect of self-expression awaits us there.

## Professional Relationships and Goal Competence

How can we improve goal competence at work and elsewhere in the public realm? In the early 21st century, we seem to be charting a course that moves precariously between a work life that must be fulfilling, a pleasure-filled private life, and a subtle but nagging need to reengage ourselves in the public life of our communities. The problem is one of balance. How do we avoid the tendency for work to become all-consuming? How do we make the time for our families and close friends that we so desire? And what energy will be left to invest in the public realm if we are to save our cities, reinvent democracy, and leave our children a healthy planet? Balancing these concerns in our lives requires skillful communication. We must provide a convincing rationale to the boss that time off from work to spend with family or in the community is not only well deserved, but will ultimately refresh us and make us more productive at work. In order to fulfill our responsibilities to community and family, we need to demonstrate the value of the entire family giving up its weekend to help a local recycling effort. These are issues that require goal competence. Without careful consideration of our own and other's goals, we will likely bounce back and forth, attempting much but accomplishing little.

## Professional Relationships and Message Competence

Translating our professional and public goals into effective verbal and nonverbal messages is the final challenge. Knowledge of how interpersonal communication works is valuable in any organization, but that knowledge must be con-

verted to specific skills to do any good. Over the course of your college education, you will want to develop your public speaking, writing, and interviewing skills. These will enable you to present yourself as an organized and skilled communicator both at work and in public roles. You will also have need to call on many of the interpersonal skills that we have described in this text: listening actively, overcoming stereotypes, managing conversations, taking the perspective of others, and occasionally expressing your feelings or showing empathy. One of the most useful skills in the public realm is the ability to hear diverse points of view and find meaningful ways to integrate or sort them out. In the skill building section of this chapter, we show how to develop the art of negotiation and conflict management.

# Skill Building: Creative Conflict Management and Negotiation

Conflicts and differences of opinion are normal parts of all communication contexts, professional or private. On the job or in the home, you can expect to encounter many situations in which your interests conflict with those of others. As a competent communicator you need to know how to use talk to resolve these conflicts of interest; that is, you need to know how to negotiate.

**Negotiation** is a process whereby two or more parties whose interests are initially opposed use communication to reach a joint decision. When the foreign ministers of two superpowers sign a peace treaty, when business executives enter into an international joint venture, or when city officials and union leaders end a strike, negotiation has taken place. Similarly, when students and teachers agree on an extra credit assignment, when parents and children decide on a fair allowance, or when two friends choose an evening's entertainment, they too have taken part in negotiation. In all these cases, people use talk to get what they want from one another. When their communication works, everyone involved benefits and the relationship is strengthened. When it fails, frustration, anger, and exhaustion are likely results. Thus, the ability to negotiate effectively is an important interpersonal skill.

In this section we'll give you some hints on how to improve your negotiating skills. We'll begin by introducing you to five different styles of conflict, discussing the situations in which each is appropriate, and asking you to think about your own style. We'll then look at some ways people can turn conflict situations into opportunities for creative problem solving. Finally, we'll end with some general rules for cooperative negotiation. While we'll only be able to skim the surface of this complex subject, we hope you'll think about your negotiation behavior as you read this section.

## Choosing Your Conflict Style

Without realizing it, you have probably already developed a negotiation style. Most people have. Some people are overwhelmed by conflict and either walk away from it or give in to keep the peace. Some see conflict as a contest and will do anything to win. Some seek to compromise, while others view conflict as an opportunity for creative problem solving. We can define the five basic conflict styles in terms of their ability to meet two kind of goals: personal and relational. Figure 12.1 shows the relationship between these two goals and conflict style. Let's begin with the lower right-hand quadrant. Here we place people whose primary concern is with achieving personal goals, even at the expense of a relationship. For these people conflicts are competitive games; they may even enjoy fights—as long as they win. We call their style the **aggressive style.** David Johnson compares each conflict style to a different animal.[51] He describes those who use the aggressive style as sharks.

Moving clockwise, we come to the lower left-hand corner. Individuals who fit here try to avoid conflict. For them nothing is worth the hassle of a fight. When faced with disagreement, they use the **withdrawing style,** backing away from conflict both physically and psychologically. Johnson calls them turtles.

In the upper left-hand quadrant is the **accommodating style,** in which concern for the relationship is high while the need to achieve personal goals is low. People who fit this quadrant try to smooth over all disagreements. If you are the one who gives in just to keep the peace, you fill the role of accommodator. Johnson would describe you as a teddy bear.

In the middle of Figure 12.1 are those who have a moderate concern for personal and relational goals. These individuals often try to cut a deal by using a **compromising style.** Johnson compares them to foxes.

Finally, in the top right-hand quadrant we have individuals who are committed both to personal and relational goals. They seek solutions through which everyone will benefit. Raymond and Mark Ross describe their **problem-solving style** this way: "It is an enlightened style based on the assumptions that conflicts are natural in the human experience; conflicts are amenable to rational, cooperative problem solving; and a sensitive openness is the necessary first step."[52] Johnson likens people who use this style to owls.

Which style is the best? It all depends. While the problem-solving style is the most idealistic choice, it takes skill and effort and may not be right for all situations. There are times when each style should be used. For example, when a goal is more important than a relationship, an aggressive (or at least assertive) style may be called for. When buying a used car, it is not particularly important to forge a close relationship with the salesperson, but it is important to get a good buy. Here the shark will do better than the teddy bear. In some cases neither maintaining the relationship nor getting your way is very important. This is when it makes sense to withdraw. If a very large person wearing leather and chains wants to

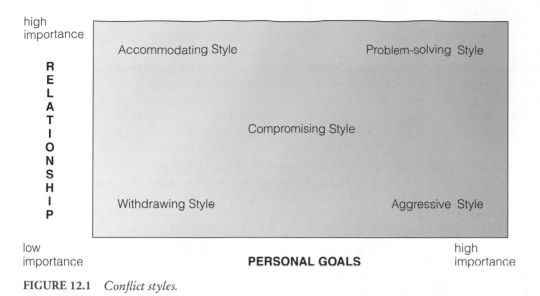

**FIGURE 12.1** *Conflict styles.*

park a motorcycle in the spot you've been eyeing, why not park somewhere else? Unless you have something to prove, avoidance may be the better part of valor.

When the relationship is important, a more accommodating style is called for. If you and a close neighbor are pooling your money to buy a wedding gift for a friend but you disagree on what to buy, you may decide it is better to give in. If you really don't care a lot about the gift but do care about your neighbor, accommodating may be best.

If your emotional involvement and your needs are equal and moderate, then try to compromise. Perhaps you are involved in business negotiations. You want to maintain a reasonably good business relationship, but you also want to do well for yourself. Negotiating the best overall compromise is the strategy called for here.

Finally, when a lot is at stake, it's a good idea to take time to work things out using a problem-solving strategy. For example, serious disagreements with long-time coworkers or romantic partners need this kind of response. The point is that you should develop the ability to enact all of these styles in the proper circumstances.

## Taking a Problem-Solving Approach to Negotiation

Although all the conflict styles we've discussed are appropriate in some circumstances, one stands out as particularly important: the problem-solving or integrative approach. Because this style takes the most interpersonal skill and sensitivity, it warrants further analysis in terms of (1) how it differs from negotiation and (2) what specific strategies are available.

### The Difference Between Compromise and Problem Solving

Initially, it's easy to confuse compromise with problem solving, but the two are not identical. Perhaps an example will help illuminate the differences. A husband and wife disagree about where to go for vacation. He wants to go to the mountains, while she wants to go to the seashore. A compromise solution might be to split their two-week vacation into equal parts: one week in the mountains and one week at the shore. While this is certainly better than nothing, it is not the ideal solution, for, at least half of the time, one party has to give in to the other. A problem-solving solution looks for a novel alternative that results in at least some benefits to both parties. If, after discussing the reasons for their initial preferences, the couple finds out that what the husband wants from a mountain vacation is the opportunity to hunt, fish, and hike and what the wife likes about the shore is the swimming, sunning, and social interaction, then they are in a position to look for a problem-solving solution. They may find an alternative that meets both their needs: a resort in a warm part of the country, one that has a sandy beach and plenty of activities, but one in an area where hunting and fishing are plentiful.[53]

*Problem-Solving Strategies*

While the advice to look for a creative solution that will increase the rewards and decrease the costs to both parties is obviously good advice, it's not always obvious how we are to find such solutions. Students of negotiation have identified several ways to reach integrative solutions. In the first two we will look at, one actor gets the other to agree by reducing the other's costs or increasing the other's rewards. In the second two, both parties change their initial positions.

The first strategy is called **cost-cutting.** Usually, when one party objects to a solution, it is because that solution leads to costs. If a way can be found to minimize or eliminate the costs of the objecting party, then agreement can be reached. Geoff may object to going to Serena's home for the holidays because the drive is long and tiring. Serena can cut his costs by promising to drive, by suggesting that they stop at a nice resort on the way, or by arranging to fly.

Of course, not all the costs of an agreement are that concrete—sometimes they are psychological. Once people have taken a position, they often refuse to give in as a matter of pride. One way of cost-cutting is to help the other person save face. We've already discussed the importance of maintaining one's own face and line. The competent communicator is also willing to help others maintain theirs. Suppose that, without thinking, Dr.

Foster assigns a test the day after the big homecoming dance. His students would like him to change the date. So far as they can see, there are no costs involved in his making such a simple change. Foster, however, sees the matter differently. He agrees that it would be possible to rearrange his lesson plan without too much trouble. Two things, however, are at stake: his principles and his status. Foster objects to changing his course simply to accommodate the social needs of his students. He feels that such a change would signal that dances are more important than classes, and more significantly, he feels that if he gives in, he will lose face. The student negotiators must acknowledge these concerns. They should be careful to show him respect and to let him know that they understand the importance of class work. They should frame their discussion as problem solving rather than confrontation, and they should be careful not to challenge his authority. By stressing his reputation for being flexible as well as fair and firm, by trying to minimize the size of the change they are asking, and by offering to take the test earlier rather than later, they may have a better chance to convince him. How would you cut the professor's costs if you were the students involved? What would you agree to if you were the professor?

A second way of reaching a mutually beneficial agreement is **compensation,** or finding a way to pay back the party who is accommodating. An interesting example of compensation occurred during the 1961 Cuban Missile Crisis. In 1961, the Russians began placing nuclear missiles in Cuba. In return for agreeing to remove them, the Russians secretly convinced the United States to withdraw its missiles from Turkey. Compensation allowed the Russians to feel that their decision did not represent unilateral accommodation but instead involved mutual benefits. Interestingly, the U.S. withdrawal was delayed for four months, to help U.S. leaders avoid domestic criticism and save face.[54]

On a more mundane level, if your mother agrees to lend you her car, you could compensate by offering to pick up the cleaning on your way home or, at the very least, by returning it with a full tank of gas. We generally expect some compensation when we do favors for others. Insensitivity to this simple principle can wreck relationships, making one party feel that he or she is being taken advantage of or taken for granted. Often, a simple "thank you" is all that another party wants by way of compensation, illustrating how important simple verbal responses are in maintaining relationships.

A third method of creative negotiation is called **logrolling.** Here both sides make concessions on issues that are important to the other but relatively unimportant to them. That is, the first party concedes on positions A and B while the second concedes on C and D. Assume, for example, that members of a union are asking for a 20 percent increase in the overtime pay rate (a position that is very important to them) as well as 20 minutes more of rest breaks (a position of secondary importance). Assume also that management strongly opposes the rest breaks but is not as concerned with the overtime issue. In this case the union might be willing to drop its request for breaks if management gives up its position on overtime. As Dean Pruitt tells us, "This will typically be better for both parties than a compromise on the two issues (e.g., a 10 percent increase in overtime rate and 10 more minutes of rest time)."[55]

Let's look at another example of logrolling. Geena and Ellen are looking for an apartment. Geena's primary concern is that the place be close to work; secondarily, she would like to live in a modern high-rise. Ellen, on the other hand, can't stand modern apartments; she wants an older place with a fireplace and a large kitchen. Location is of less concern although she would prefer a house in the country. Perhaps both can get their major needs met if they look for a converted duplex in town. Although Geena doesn't get to live in a high-rise and Ellen doesn't get to live in the country, both may be relatively satisfied.

The final strategy we'll look at is **bridging.** Bridging involves finding a new option that satisfies both parties, without either having to concede. Let's look at a classic example. Two people are working in the library. One feels the library is stuffy and so decides to open the window. The other is made uncomfortable by the draft and insists the window be closed. No compromise (for example, opening the window halfway) seems possible. The librarian who comes to investigate the disturbance thinks for a minute and then opens a window in the next room, bringing in fresh air without the draft.

Another way of bridging is called **expanding the pie.** If a conflict arises over sharing resources, one way to solve the problem is to increase the resource. Assume a couple is quarreling over who will get sole possession of a second bedroom. One party, a composer, wants it as a music room. The other, an architect, wants it as a design area. Sharing the room, a compromise solution, won't do, as there isn't enough space for both to spread out and the activities of one would disturb the other. One solution is to build on an addition to the house, thereby expanding the available space so both can have what they want.

## Rules for Cooperative Problem Solving

Negotiating creatively takes imagination and sensitivity. Here we offer some things to think about the next time you find yourself in a conflict situation.

**1.** *Diagnose your personal and relational goals.* As we have seen, there are times to walk away from a conflict, times to give in, times to take a hard line, and times to compromise. When you encounter a conflict of interest, begin by honestly evaluating your personal and relational goals. If both are high, then a cooperative problem-solving strategy is called for.

**2.** *Make an effort to understand the other's interests and emotions.* Don't forget the human element. The parties involved in negotiation are flesh-and-blood people who are often frustrated, fearful, or angry and who have their own unique thoughts and perceptions. In Chapter 3 we discussed attribution biases. We saw that it is much easier for people to understand their own motivations than those of others. While seeing things from the other's point of view is not easy, it is worth a try. Often the other's demands are not as arbitrary and unreasonable as you might think.

One block to understanding the other is distinguishing *their* intentions from *your* fears. Roger Fisher and William Ury illustrate how easy it is for us to let our own fears and expectations color our interpretations. They recount the following story: "They met in a bar, where he offered her a ride home. He took her down unfamiliar streets. He said it was a short cut. He got her home so fast she caught the 10 o'clock news." Most people find the ending surprising because they make an assumption based on their own fears and prejudices.[56] Our suspicions are often made even worse during negotiation. The cost is an unwillingness to look for creative solutions.

If you can put aside your prejudices and sense the other's position, you may be better able to reach a settlement. If a father understands that a child's opposition to an early bedtime is prompted by a desire for autonomy rather than a desire to stay up late, he may be able to find another way to let the child feel grown up and important. It's also a good idea to ask yourself how your behavior looks to the other. One party's shyness may seem to the other to be coldness or disdain. If the first person realizes this, he or she can violate the other's perceptions by being more outgoing. Finally, understanding a partner's perceptions also allows you to help the partner save face. Remember that people may be trapped into a proposal long after they've ceased to believe it. You need to find a way to help them back out gracefully.

**3.** *Realize that emotions may run high during negotiation and accept them as legitimate.* In public negotiations parties may feel the need to vent anger, either to show a constituency they are not being soft or simply to release tension. While one's first response might be to walk out or shout an angry partner down, a better response is to let the other talk. The same is true of personal disagreements. Once your roommate has expressed anger, he or she may be better able to talk rationally. Fisher and Ury cite a useful rule developed during an industrial negotiation: Members agreed that only one person could get angry at a time. That made it easier for the party being criticized to listen to the other and say, "That's OK. It's his [or her] turn now."[57]

**4.** *Focus on interests, not positions.* Let's return to the example we gave of opening the library window. Each disputant had an initial position: "The window should be opened" versus "The window must be closed." A **position** is the initial solution to the conflict that each proposes. **Interests,** on the other hand, are the underlying needs or concerns of each party. In this example the interests are "to get fresh air" and "to avoid a draft." The disputants couldn't find a solution because they were focusing on positions. The librarian realized what interests were at stake and found a solution that fulfilled both interests.

It is essential to search for the interests behind the position. Assume the parents in a given community are concerned about a dangerous building site.[58] They are afraid that their children will get hurt playing there, so they demand that the construction company fence off the area immediately. The company doesn't understand the reasons behind the demands but rather sees it as unnecessary harassment. The company is likely to respond defensively if the parents' committee begins discussion by saying, "We demand that you put up a fence within the next 48 hours or we'll bring suit." A better way is to start with common ground: "We believe that we have a problem that needs to be solved. We're concerned about safety, as we know you are. It would be a terrible thing for both of us if an accident occurred. What can we do to make sure that one doesn't occur?" In addition, the parents should demonstrate that they recognize the company's interests as well: "We understand that it's in your interests to get your job done at minimum cost while preserving your reputation for safety and responsibility. Are we correct? Do you have any other important interests?" By responding to interests rather than positions, both parties are more likely to be able to solve the problem.

5. *Consider turning to third parties for help in negotiation.* Many conflicts can be solved if the people involved sincerely want to solve them and if they have the necessary sensitivities and interpersonal skills. But not all can. It is no crime to turn to others for help in the face of conflict. The literature on negotiation distinguishes three types of third-party intervention. Pruitt tells us that "in **mediation,** the third party works with the disputants, helping them reach agreement. In **fact-finding,** the third party listens to arguments from both sides and produces a set of nonbinding substantive recommendations. **Arbitration** is like fact-finding except that the recommendations are binding."[59] Conflicts between management and unions often make use of the latter two types of intervention. Mediation is used for a wide range of personal and community disagreements.

When negotiations reach a deadlock, third parties can help. For professional disputes people often turn to a professional mediator. For personal problems people generally turn to a friend. In both cases the individual chosen must have certain qualities: the ability to establish rapport with both parties, good interpersonal and persuasive communication skills, perceived impartiality, assertiveness, a strong power base, and a reputation for trustworthiness.[60] Most importantly, the mediator must be skilled at empathic listening. If you believe you have these skills and want to develop them, you might consider taking a course in group problem solving, conflict management, negotiation, or mediation. Each of these areas will build on your interpersonal skills and make you better able to take problem-solving approaches to personal and professional problems.

# Process to Performance

## Review Terms

The following is a list of major concepts introduced in this chapter. The page where the concept is first mentioned is listed in parentheses.

deference (341)
avoidance rituals (341)
presentational rituals (341)
demeanor (342)
playacting (342)
third places (344)
organizational culture (345)
organizational vocabulary (348)
grapevine (350)
personality traits (350)
leadership (351)
dyadic linkage theory (352)
cohesion (353)
groupthink (353)
relationship marketing (357)
persuasive internal marketing (357)
negotiation (363)
aggressive style (364)
withdrawing style (364)
accommodating style (364)
compromising style (364)
problem-solving style (364)
cost-cutting (366)
compensation (366)
logrolling (367)
bridging (367)
expanding the pie (367)
position (368)
interests (368)
mediation (369)
fact-finding (369)
arbitration (369)

## Suggested Readings

Conrad, Charles, and Marshall Scott Poole. *Strategic Organizational Communication in a Global*

*Economy.* Belmont, Calif.: Wadsworth, 2004. An excellent exploration of communication in organizations, this book is sophisticated yet accessible.

Sennett, Richard. *Respect in a World of Inequality.* New York: W.W. Norton, 2003. Sennett challenges us to overcome what he calls modern society's profound lack of positive ways to express respect and recognition for others, especially when our economic standing and talents differ dramatically.

---

### Topics for Discussion
www.oup.com/us/trenholm

---

### Observation Guide

1. Visit a public square, park, or business area where impersonal transactions are likely to take place. Record examples of avoidance rituals and presentational rituals. Note what happens when one person oversteps the boundaries, such as being too polite or too personal. Also, try to label any other rituals or behaviors that you think make impersonal interactions more or less effective.

2. Observe a wide range of customer-clerk interactions. On the sales floor, record the communication patterns on the sale of big-ticket items such as furniture or automobiles as well as small purchases like shoes, groceries, or health foods. In addition, hang around the customer service desk, where you can overhear people returning merchandise. Take notes following each observation, writing down message patterns. Then rate the results of the transaction as (1) very effective, (2) OK, (3) somewhat problematic, or (4) not effective at all. Summarize what you have observed, noting which patterns of communication are most or least effective.

3. Every college campus is an organization. From your perspective as a student, try to identify as many different informal communication networks as you can. Who are the key members of the grapevine? Who are the most influential decision makers? Who is tapped into the off-

campus network? Which faculty members seem to be most "connected" on your campus? What influence do these networks have on the goings-on at your campus? You can conduct similar observations at work.

### Exercises

1. Your instructor will assign everyone a role in a fictitious manufacturing organization. (Instructors, see directions for "Hi-Fli, Inc." in the *Instructor's Guide* to Farace, Monge, and Russell's *Communicating and Organizing,* available from Addison-Wesley.) For two or three class periods, the class will role-play an actual organization going about its everyday work routines. Students should observe their own communication with supervisors, coworkers, messengers, top management, and so on, and write down observations during assigned "coffee breaks." After the exercise is completed, discuss the communication patterns observed: status differences, upward distortion, leadership styles, and so on.

2. Rent a videocassette or film version of one or more movies that include work settings and scenes as a major part of the story line. Films such as *9 to 5, Network,* and *Games Mother Never Taught You* are good examples. Choose several interesting segments to show in class. Small groups of students may be assigned to analyze different segments. The analysis should reflect research and theory presented in this chapter. For instance, a group could analyze the nature of supervisor-subordinate communication as portrayed in the film clip. Another group might choose to discuss the decision-making style and roles being played in a business meeting, and so on. Each group should organize its analysis for a 15-minute presentation to the class.

3. Each student should think of the best and worst supervisor-subordinate relationship in which he or she has been involved. These relationships may have taken place at work, in a volunteer agency, or in a classroom work group—anywhere a clear leader was established. As a class, compile two lists. The first one should include the charac-

teristics of the most and least effective supervisor known. The second list should include characteristics of the most and least effective relationships observed. Be careful to distinguish characteristics attributed to the supervisor from those attributed to the relationships. Once you have completed the two lists, discuss which is the most instructive. Is it better to think in terms of personal traits or relational attributions? Why?

4. Divide the class into groups of three and assign one person each to play the role of therapist, help seeker, and observer. Then role-play the following informal therapeutic relationships. In each situation the "therapist" should try to enact the three essential traits recommended by Carl Rogers: warmth, genuineness, and accurate empathy. The "observer" should record the verbal or nonverbal messages that communicate (or fail to communicate) the three characteristics.

## Situation 1:

THERAPIST   Bartender

HELP SEEKER   Regular patron at bar, an independent accountant

SITUATION   Patron reveals a problem relating to a potential client in the basket-weaving mailorder business. He wants the account but cannot find a single topic of conversation on which to conduct small talk. He asks the bartender for advice.

## Situation 2:

THERAPIST   Best friend

HELP SEEKER   East Coast young urban professional (yuppie)

SITUATION   Yuppie tells friend about a job offer on the West Coast. She really wants the job but can't seem to convince her boyfriend that there will be opportunities for him. He likes his current job and friends, but she thinks the move will do them good—if he gives it half a chance. She asks her best friend for advice.

## Situation 3:

THERAPIST   Attorney

HELP SEEKER   A recent widow, 45 years of age, one child

SITUATION   The young widow consults her attorney. She is trying to put her life back together but cannot decide whether to sell the house and move into an apartment or keep the house and rent out rooms. She is on the verge of tears as she thinks about the changes ahead of her.

When finished role playing, the observer should report what he or she saw, and all three students should discuss how to improve informal therapeutic interactions. When, for instance, is a problem beyond informal help? How can you tell someone he or she needs to seek professional help?

This painting of a wedding festival provides a window to a culture different than ours, with different norms, expectations, and communication settings.

Araujo Yaponi, *Nuptial Dance*, 1968

## CHAPTER 13

# Cultural and Historical Influences
# Communication Competence
# in Context

Throughout this text we have emphasized the part that context plays in communication competence. In examining family, intimate, and professional communication, we have already seen how important context can be. Here we expand that discussion by looking at more general contextual influences on communication. In this chapter we consider how culture and history affect the forms and functions of interpersonal communication.

We will begin by looking at some of the ways culture affects interpersonal interaction. In the first half of this chapter we will define culture and examine some of the ways cultures differ from one another. We will then look at problems that can occur when people from different cultures confront one another, and we will offer suggestions for improving cross-cultural communication.

In the second half of the chapter we will look at the impact of historical change on interpersonal communication. Our goal will be to demonstrate that interpersonal communication is not only affected by geographic or spatial factors, but by temporal factors as well. Cultures grow and change, and the competent communicator recognizes and adapts to this process.

## Cultural Influences

**Culture** is that set of values and beliefs, norms and customs, rules and codes, that socially define groups of people, binding them to one another and giving them a sense of commonality. Because we are humans, we ask questions about the world and our place in it. And because we are social beings, we turn to others for answers. In a sense culture is the collective answer to the fundamental questions that puzzle all of us: Who are we? What is our place in the world? How are we to live our lives? Although each of us develops our own responses to these questions, we also carry with us the answers our cultures have given us. And these cultural understandings play a large part in determining how we perceive the world, how we think about ourselves and our relationship to others, how we set and achieve goals, how we define the self, and how we exchange messages.

Although there may have been a time when Americans could sit back complacently and ignore everything that was "foreign," that time is gone. In today's shrinking world it is impossible to avoid cultural contact. More and more of us are crossing cultural boundaries each year, and even those of us who stay "safely" at home find our cultural worlds changing. As a result of technological and social changes, the worlds we are born into are likely to be quite different from those we later work and live in. To get along today, we must be able to adapt to cultural change. One way to begin is to become aware of the diversity of culture patterns.

## How Cultures Differ

Sometimes it's easy to see cultural differences. If you've ever traveled to another country, you realize that what *they* do is often not what *you* do at home. People dress, move, and speak differently. They listen to different music, live in different kinds of shelters, and eat different food. If these were the only differences to separate us, cross-cultural communication might not be so difficult. But there are other, more subtle differences that you can't see from the windows of a tour bus, differences in the ways people within cultures view the world and their place in it. These differences make up a culture's **worldview,** its "orientation toward such things as God, [humans], nature, the universe, and the other philosophical issues that are concerned with the concept of being."[1]

To understand what separates us from people from other cultures, we need to understand how others think and why they think that way. We need to notice more than what lies on the surface. We need, for example, to understand that while some people believe they control their own fates, and that they have no one to blame for their failures but themselves, others believe just as strongly that the outcomes of their efforts are predestined by forces greater than themselves. We

need to learn to accept that some people live by the clock and measure their lives by goals achieved, and others see time as fluid and measure their lives by the strength of their relationships. We need to realize why some people stubbornly try to define themselves as unique individuals while others are willing to submerge themselves in groups. And we need to appreciate that while clarity and directness are the hallmarks of good communication for some, indirectness and ambiguity are preferred by others. In this section we try to look below the surface at five dimensions that describe cultural difference: (1) locus of control, (2) activity orientation, (3) attitudes toward time, (4) connections to others, and (5) communication styles.[2]

### Locus of Control: Control vs. Constraint

People differ in the extent to which they believe they can control the world through their own actions. In some cultures it is assumed that people control their own destinies. Members of such cultures feel that there are no limits to what people can do if they are determined and hard working. A belief in one's own ability to control destiny is called internal locus of control, and cultures in which this belief is prevalent are referred to as **control cultures.** "Don't let anything stand in your way" might be the motto of a control culture.

Not all cultures locate control internally; some have an external locus of control. These cultures hold that people have very little control over their lives and believe there is little the individual can do to change his or her fate. In these cultures events are thought to be fixed by chance, luck, or supernatural forces. "One does not make the wind, but is blown by it" is a proverb that illustrates the values of **constraint cultures.**

Control and constraint cultures have different relationships with the environment. Control cultures tend to separate the natural and civilized worlds; for them humans are distinctly different from (and more highly developed than) other living organisms. Nature is something to be mastered, an inexhaustible resource to be exploited for humanity. If there are floods, members of control cultures build dams. If insects threaten crops, they spray their fields with pesticides. Although this view contributes to the material wealth of control cultures, it can also lead to vast environmental damage. Unlike control cultures, constraint cultures are often resistant to change, and are more likely to accept things the way they are. Members of constraint cultures feel it is presumptuous to believe that humans can change nature. K. S. Sitaram and Roy T. Cogdell explain the difference in the following way. If you ask a member of a constraint culture why his yield of corn was so small while other farmers got much more, he would likely say "It is the wish of God." A farmer from a control culture might answer, "I guess I didn't work hard enough."[3]

### Action Orientation: Doing vs. Being

Closely related to locus of control is action orientation. In some cultures, people are very task driven; for them it's important to set and accomplish goals. Members of this kind of culture dismiss activities that are "unproductive." These cultures are called **doing cultures**. Their watchword might be "Just do it." Members of doing cultures worry about wasting time and judge their own worth in terms of their accomplishments and material achievements. They generally feel that people should be judged by how well they do a job rather than by how well they relate to others. For them product is more important than process.

In contrast, other cultures stress personal relationships over task accomplishment. In these cultures, called **being cultures,** personal compatibility is more important than job competence. Members of being cultures are not as driven as members of doing cultures. Time spent hanging out or just relaxing is not wasted time. "People are more important than things" might sum up their worldview. Although members of being cultures tend to live more for the moment than do members of doing cultures, they should not be considered passive. Rather they value relationships more than activities.[4]

Differences on this dimension often surface in the workplace. When faced with a family problem, for example, a worker from a being culture may simply stop coming to work for several weeks until the problem has been resolved, even if this means that the job doesn't get done. In a doing culture, the worker would be expected to come to work and resolve personal problems in his or her spare time. When negotiating contracts or setting up business partnerships, members of doing cultures expect to get to the point quickly; members of being cultures, however, may meet three or four times without even mentioning business; for them, it is important to establish a personal relationship before getting down to business.

### Attitudes Toward Time: M-Time and P-Time

Attitudes toward time also vary culturally, and are connected to other dimensions of difference. Edward Hall describes two kinds of time orientations.[5] In some cultures, people segment and organize time in a linear way. Things are done in sequence, one thing at a time; appointments are taken seriously; and speed is valued over sloth. In these cultures time is divided into uniform segments, and the time we spend in a given activity is regulated not by the nature of the act itself, but by the clock. Members of these monochronic or **M-time cultures** make their activities fit their schedules rather than fitting their schedules to their activities. For them, "time is money."

It may be hard to imagine another way of organizing time, but there are cultures in which time is much less tangible. In what Hall has labeled polychronic or **P-time cultures** preset schedules are seldom followed and several tasks may be undertaken at the same time. People do not queue up or take a number to indicate who is next, and meetings and appointments seldom start on time. For them, "haste makes waste."

Members of M-time cultures can be extremely frustrated when doing business in a P-time country. The M-time businessperson expects an appointment to start on time and to be private. But

## Collectivism and Individualism

## *Antz*

Eric Darnell and Tim Johnson, 1998

Z (Woody Allen) is a lowly worker ant, an insignificant cipher in a colony where no one stands out. Despite overwhelming pressures to conform, Z has big dreams and a quirky individuality that ultimately allows him to win the hand of the beautiful princess (Sharon Stone) and to transform the social structure of the colony. While much of the fun of this computer-animated movie lies in identifying the actors whose voices bring the ants to life (including Sylvester Stallone, Jennifer Lopez, Gene Hackman, and Christopher Walken), there is a message: that individuality trumps conformity and that everyone—even ants—should learn to think for themselves.

When a view of the world pervades a culture, you'll find traces of it everywhere, including animated films. Although Antz is primarily meant to entertain, it reflects our culture's distrust of conformity and authoritarianism and our glorification of independent action. Yet the final message is somewhat ambivalent, for it is a combination of Z's willingness to act as an individual and the ability of the ants to work as a unit that ultimately saves the colony from disaster. Thus Antz seems to suggest that every culture must find the right balance between individualism and collectivism.

in P-time culture, a meeting may start an hour late, and there may be several other people, with other business to transact, being attended to at the same time. In P-time cultures, those in charge conduct business with more than one person at a time, stop and start, switch from one problem to another, take phone calls, and break for coffee without missing a beat. This attitude toward time may leave the M-time individual wondering how anything ever gets done.

Of course, the frustration can work both ways. To a P-time person, M-time scheduling may feel rigid and unnecessary. Why, he or she may ask, should appointment times be set? After all, sometimes an hour appointment is more than enough time to accomplish one's goals, while at other times an hour appointment is way too short. Why not let events unfold as they will? Why not "just take your time"? Similarly M-time insistence on private appointments may feel alienating to P-time people, for it separates the individual from the group.

### Connections to Others: Individualism and Collectivism

To whom should I be loyal? To myself or to others? Do I owe allegiance to my family, clan, or company, or should my first allegiance be to myself? These are questions all cultures must answer. In some cultures, called **individualist cultures,** the basic unit is the individual. Individuals are expected to make their own decisions, to take personal responsibility for their actions, and to look out for their own best interests. Loyalty to self is a higher loyalty than loyalty to others. In **collectivist cultures,** on the other hand, the basic unit is the group.[6] Collectivists believe the individual must be subordinate to the group. In return, the group protects its members. In these cultures anything that makes the individual stand out as different from others in the group is a threat. Publicly praising an individual's achievements or encouraging competition is frowned upon, while conformity and consensus are sought.

Not all individualist or collectivist cultures are the same, although in all individualist cultures, independence and autonomy are valued and in some individualist cultures everyone is equal in status while in others status differences are recognized and accepted. Scholars have used the term **horizontal individualism** to refer to the first case and **vertical individualism** to refer to the second. Similarly, we can speak of **horizontal collectivism,** where the group is primary and everyone within the group is treated as equal, and **vertical collectivism,** where a strict status hierarchy is maintained within the group.[7]

Difficulties can arise when individualists and collectivists work together. After all, countries that believe "the squeaky wheel gets the grease" and encourage individuals to stand up for their own rights may have trouble understanding countries where "the uneven nail gets hammered down." To collectivists, individualists may seem boastful and competitive; to individualists, collectivists may seem hypocritical and conforming. Box 13.1 illustrates some of the difficulties that can arise when individualists and collectivists interact.

### Communication Styles: Low-Context and High-Context Communication

Given all the differences we have looked at so far it should come as no surprise to find that communication styles also differ across cultures. Directness, formality, and expressiveness are a few of the communication variables that differ from country to country.[8] But the style variable that has achieved the most attention is context-dependence.[9] In **low-context cultures,** context does not play a large part because meaning is explicitly stated in words. People in low-context cultures are expected to say what they mean, and mean what they say. Accuracy and clarity are the hallmarks of good communication. The receiver should not have to guess at meaning; meaning should be clearly laid out by the speaker.

In **high-context cultures,** on the other hand, a lot of the meaning is implicit and unstated. Receivers are expected to look to the context (who they are dealing with, what the situation is, what common beliefs people share) to understand the speaker's meaning. In high-context cultures people are expected to read between the lines and to guess one another's meaning *despite* what is actually said. In many high-context cultures being too direct can cause others to lose face and can create disharmony. By making messages subtle, individuals protect one another. Box 4.1, Speaking with Names, has already provided an example of high-context communication used to avoid embarrassment.

Obviously, problems can occur when speakers from high- and low-context cultures interact. High-context receivers may feel low-context communication is too blatant and may, in some cases, look for hidden meanings, assuming that the stated message is not the true message. Low-context receivers may simply be confused by high-context communication and wonder what prevents speakers from saying what's really on their minds.

### American Cultural Patterns

As you read the previous section, you may have tried to figure out how Americans fare on the dimensions we've described. If you haven't, take a minute to look back and see if you can identify mainstream American cultural patterns.

*Americans, in general, have a control, can-do orientation to life.* As a culture, we believe in **effort optimism,** the idea that if people work hard, they can achieve most goals. We do not hesitate to make innovations and we are not particularly frightened of change. Rather than accepting our lot in life, we try to improve it, believing in progress and in the goals of material well-being and physical comfort. In fact, we may look down on members of "underdeveloped" countries who have not achieved a comparable standard of living,

BOX 13.1

## When East Meets West

# Hidden Differences in Corporate Communication Styles

Not so long ago, an American company sent one of its best young managers to Japan to take over the Tokyo office. His first decision concerned a new advertising campaign, which he found completely unacceptable. When the New York office urged him to accept the plan anyway, he felt angry and frustrated. These feelings only deepened over time. Meetings seemed disorganized, and department heads were vague about their plans. His plans to reorganize the office and put his own mark on the company met with passive resistance. Six months later, after his top Japanese manager resigned, the young man was recalled.

What happened? In *Hidden Differences: Doing Business with the Japanese*, Edward T. and Mildred Reed Hall explain that cultural misunderstandings lay at the root of the problem. Sending a young man to head the Tokyo office was the first mistake, as Japanese businessmen respect age and experience. The fact that the young man himself failed to do research on Japanese language, culture, and business practices was another error. Finally, sending an ambitious person with a desire to put his own ideas into practice was the third mistake. The Japanese find a competitive, aggressive attitude uncongenial and distressing. The Halls feel that, "despite popular beliefs to the contrary, the single greatest barrier to business success is the one erected by culture."

One difference between Japan and the United States is that Japan, like many countries in East Asia, Africa, and South America, is a collectivist culture, while the United States is an individualist country. When collectivists and individualists interact without understanding the hidden differences that characterize their corporate styles, misunderstandings result. According to Harry C. Triandis, Richard Brislin, and C. Harry Hui, individualism-collectivism is a major cultural difference that affects work values, personal styles of interaction, and even concepts of morality. They believe that anyone who wants to work effectively in international business should be trained in how to diagnose and adapt to differences along the individualism-collectivism continuum.

What is the difference between collectivist and individualist cultures? Briefly, collectivists have a "we" orientation. Loyalty to the group is more important than individual achievement, and the smallest "unit of survival" is the collective, whether it be extended family, clan, or organization. In contrast, individualist cultures have an "I" orientation. Here the smallest unit of survival is the individual.

The behaviors of collectivists can seem surprising or distasteful to individualists, and collectivists may find individualist attitudes and actions equally inexplicable. What should Americans, as individualists, do when working in a collectivist culture? Triandis and his colleagues offer a number of guidelines, a few of which are listed below.

First, individualists should understand that collectivists let themselves be guided by group norms rather than individual goals. This means that when collectivists change group memberships, their opinions, attitudes, and even their personalities may change. Individualists need to be aware of this factor and not be taken aback.

In addition, collectivists are likely to stress harmony and cooperation more than individualists. Competitive or confrontational situations cause discomfort and embarrassment. If criticism of a coworker becomes necessary, the individualist must be sure the interaction takes place in private and should offer as much positive feedback as possible to allow the other to save face.

Because harmony is so important, individualists should not be put off by unusual shows of modesty from collectivists. It is not uncommon for a collectivist to begin a presentation by saying something like, "Please forgive this unworthy effort." Individualists who give presentations should begin in a more modest way than they are generally used to. Attempts to build credibility by stressing expertness will seem like boasting and will create a negative impression.

Although collectivists are not competitive or boastful, they do recognize and respect status differences. Unlike individualists, they feel more comfortable in vertical than in horizontal relationships. They therefore feel uncomfortable interacting until they know what position in society their partner occupies. Individualists should not hesitate to let collectivists know their age, rank, place of birth, and even income. This information allows collectivists to decide how to proceed. Individualists should also seek out this kind of information and give special respect to collectivists' status and age.

Individual decision making is not as highly valued by collectivists as it is by individualists. Individualists should expect negotiations to take time as collectivists seek out group consensus. Negotiations also take time because collectivists feel the need to establish personal relationships with their individualist partners. In some cases, individualists may feel their privacy is being violated. In an attempt to establish long-term relationships, collectivists may spend a great deal of time visiting their individualist partners, or they may ask personal questions that individualists feel are intrusive. Although establishing a per-

sonal relationship takes time, once the relationship has been defined, collectivists will expect a great deal more loyalty and commitment than an individualist is normally likely to give to a business partner.

Finally, the actual mechanics of doing business may differ dramatically. Collectivists rely less on written contracts than do individualists and may not understand the necessity for signed documents. They may also engage in some acts which are considered illicit in individualist countries. Whereas an individualist might consider paying a government official to expedite paperwork to be a bribe, collectivists may see it as a natural part of doing business. Nepotism and other personal connections are much more acceptable in collectivist cultures than in individualist cultures.

Of course, not all collectivist countries are the same, and individualists doing international business must recognize the particular patterns in the country to which they are assigned. Nevertheless understanding the general nature of collectivism can be an important first step in successful intercultural interaction. If you should find yourself working in a collectivist culture some day, you will have to find a way to maintain your own value system while respecting that of others. This is by no means an easy task, but it is absolutely essential in adapting to the hidden differences you are sure to encounter.

SOURCE Harry C. Triandis, Richard Brislin, and C. Harry Hui, "Cross-Cultural Training Across the Individualism-Collectivism Divide," *International Journal of Intercultural Relations* 12 (1988): 269–89.

**ADDITIONAL READING**

Hall, Edward T., and Mildred T. Hall. *Hidden Differences: Doing Business with the Japanese.* Garden City, N.Y: Anchor Press Doubleday, 1987.

particularly if they hold a constraint orientation. To us, people in these cultures may seem too accepting of things that we feel can be changed. We also place a high value on science and technology as ways of exploiting and mastering nature, and this value is reflected in our communication. Larry Samovar points out, "Americans tend to value objectivity, empirical evidence, rationality, and concreteness in their communication, and they often experience considerable difficulty in understanding persons who do not reflect these values."[10]

*Americans, in general, value doing over being and M-time over P-time.* As a culture we pride ourselves on our achievements, we strive to get ahead, and we feel uncomfortable "wasting" time. These values translate into a concern with direct and rapid channels of communication. Americans expect to be able to communicate instantly and effectively, and may feel bereft if parted from their cell phones or computers, even for an instant. When Americans encounter countries in which the telephones don't work and the mail services is unreliable, their response is likely to be anguish or frustration.

It should be clear that *America, in general, is an individualist country.* In *Habits of the Heart,* Robert Bellah and his colleagues describe the centrality of individualism in the American value system: "We believe in the dignity, indeed the sacredness, of the individual. Anything that would violate our right to think for ourselves, judge for ourselves, make our own decisions, live our lives as we see fit, is not only morally wrong, it is sacrilegious."[11] Because we are so individualistic, we do not hesitate to make ourselves stand out from the crowd and celebrate our unique accomplishments. One example of this can be seen in the way we define and emphasize individual credibility. If you have even taken a public speaking class, you know that the good speaker is expected to emphasize expert qualifications at the beginning of a speech. In certain Native American cultures a more collectivist view is taken. It is considered rude to display one's own credentials; the speaker instead opens by apologizing for his or her lack of knowledge, telling audience members that they alone can judge the worth of the speech. In so doing, they subordinate the individual to the group.

Our concern with individual difference is also evidenced by our belief in open self-disclosure. In the interpersonal realm the majority of Americans believe that healthy relationships are built through self-disclosure and that it is important to share personal details. Although we realize self-disclosure is most appropriate with those close to us, Americans are notorious for opening up to strangers. In many collectivist cultures, the sharing of intimate details in a public context is embarrassing and shameful, and even husbands and wives seldom share their thoughts or feelings with each other.

Given all this, it is not surprising that *America is a direct, low-context culture.* We believe in being direct, in getting to the point, in avoiding lengthy digressions or details (details that in high-context cultures establish context). When Americans disagree they don't hesitate to say so and they expect the listener to accept their directness. "What part of 'no' don't you understand?" is a typically American saying. In many high-context cultures, where maintaining group harmony is essential, it is considered rude to say "no" directly. Disagreement may be indicated by "perhaps" or "that's an interesting idea" or even by a "yes" (said with enough hesitation to let the receiver know that "yes" actually means "no"). High-context cultures appear to give receivers a larger part in the communication process than Americans do. The fact that in our culture speakers have the major responsibility for creating meaning may explain why we are such notoriously bad listeners.

When we cross cultural boundaries, we carry with us, without being aware of it, cultural "baggage" that can affect our ability to interact successfully. Successful cross-cultural communication means being aware of our assumptions as well as accepting the fact that the people with whom we interact may not share our worldviews and may think and communicate in very different ways.

## Ethnic, Regional, and Class Differences

Nationality is not the only influence on our lives. Ethnic, regional, and class identities are other sources of cultural identity. They can also be a major source of communication problems, for although members of different ethnic groups may share common worldviews, they also differ from the larger culture in ways that reflect their own unique experiences. These differences can lead to misperceptions and misunderstandings. As the study outlined in this chapter's Research in Review section illustrates, members of minority cultures within America can often feel invisible. In the remainder of this section, we look at some of the ways the subcultures that Americans belong to shape our lives.

### Shifting Cultural Identities

None of us belongs to a single culture. Rather, we belong to a number of hierarchically embedded cultures and subcultures, each contributing in its own way to our understanding of the world. Some of the groups to which we belong are very large and diffuse, while others are much smaller and more specific. Some are very important sources of influence and identity, while others affect us only slightly. Some complement each other, and some conflict. Yet each contributes to cultural identity.

Our cultural identities shift back and forth. Sometimes we are influenced by national identity, sometimes by regional or class loyalties. In some situations ethnic and gender identifications shape our attitudes and behaviors, while in others, religious identity comes to the fore. If we are successful, we choose, from among the many voices telling us who to be and what to do, that advice that best fits our own sense of self.

### Black and White Communication Patterns

A few years ago it was common to deny that there were any true linguistic differences in black and white language patterns. By now, however, there is substantial agreement that grammatical and stylistic differences exist between the English associated with the dominant ethnic group in American (whites of European ancestry) and the English associated with members of predominantly African-American communities. Although it is true that we all, regardless of our ethnicity, use language to give meaning and coherence to our lives, it is also true that the groups we belong to provide us with different ways of expressing our uniqueness. Standard **American English (AE)** reflects one kind of experience, while what has come to be called **African-American Vernacular English (AAVE)** or **Ebonics** reflects another.[12]

Before we look at the unique characteristics of AAVE in more detail, it's important to recognize that what blacks and whites share in terms of word usage, grammar, and style is much greater than what separates us. It is also important to emphasize the fact that not all African Americans use the vernacular language, just as not all European Americans speak standard AE.

What is AAVE? It is most decidedly not bad grammar, nor is it the speech of "street people" or uneducated ghetto dwellers, although it has been characterized in these ways. Indeed, linguist Geneva Smitherman estimates that AAVE is "spoken at various times by some 90 percent of the Black community—regardless of socioeconomic status—including poets and professors, entertainers and elites, reverends and revolutionaries." (Think Maya Angelou, Henry Louis Gates, Queen Latifah, Clarence Thomas, Jesse Jackson, and H. Rap Brown, all of whom have used African-American language patterns in public discourse, and you begin to see the range and power of AAVE.)[13] For Smitherman, as for many linguists, both black and white, AAVE is a set of communication practices rooted in the black American oral tradition, made up of a combination of African language patterns (Niger-Congo) and Euro-American English. Marcyliena Morgan lists three factors that account for the unique the structure of African-American verbal style: adaptation of African styles of interaction during slavery; face-to-face rules for black/white interaction enforced prior to the end of segregation; and

## When Nobody Knows Who You Really Are

# Perceptions of Minority Invisibility

Many Americans avoid thinking about racial or ethnic differences. They prefer to oversimplify, ignore, or downplay them. In doing so, however, they may be rendering members of minority groups invisible, "their voice . . . unheard, their needs unfulfilled, their self-identities assailed." In "Perceptions of Minority Invisibility Among Asian American Professionals," Wei Sun and William J. Starosta look at how 14 Asian-American professionals perceive and react to invisibility.

The authors identified 14 Asian-American professionals who worked in largely white environments. These individuals were asked to comment on their own experiences in regard to visibility/invisibility, as well as to discuss those of other Asian Americans. They were also asked whether they thought other groups in the United States were mistreated or misunderstood and to offer suggestions for ways to raise minority visibility.

Regarding individual invisibility, all but three of the respondents felt they had, in some ways, been made to feel unequal and invisible. One respondent remarked that half of the time she was ignored, while the other half she was an object of fascination. Others reported being stared at because of their appearance and noted that, ironi-

cally, this extra visibility contributed to their invisibility. Still others admitted to being invisible, but accepted it as a part of life that should just be ignored.

When asked about the overall invisibility of Asian Americans, even the interviewees who denied personal experience agreed that members of their own ethnic group are often neglected and ignored by mainstream culture. To deal with this problem, some Asian Americans strive to achieve economic or professional success, some resist by retreating from mainstream culture, and still others simply accept invisibility as a part of life. All except one of the respondents said that other groups within American were also misunderstood and treated unfairly.

Given these feelings, what solutions did the interviewees propose? First, in analyzing the problem, participants recognized that invisibility is a long-term problem that is hard to fight because it is subtle. Overall, two suggestions were offered for increasing visibility. One was to establish coalitions with other minority members; the other was to work even harder to achieve individual success and to "get over it, get on with your lives and not let people who don't matter affect the way you live in this world."

Many members of American mainstream culture don't give the experiences of their friends and colleagues from minority cultures much thought, rarely considering what it must feel like to be disconfirmed on a daily basis. Most of us ignore the problems of people who are different. This study shows that, in doing so, we can inadvertently create invisibility.

Sun, Wei, and William J. Starosta. "Perceptions of Minority Invisibility Among Asian American Professionals." *The Howard Journal of Communication* 17 (2006): 119–42.

"urbanization and popular culture's role in the co-alescence of a national Black youth identity."[14]

Although there are identifiable differences in grammatical structure between AE and AAVE (with the latter having, in some cases, a more complex grammar than the former), stylistic differences may be of more interest. These include use of what appears to nonusers as exaggerated language, as well as mimicry, use of proverbs and aphoristic phrasing, punning and plays on words, spontaneity and improvisation, indirection, and tonal semantics.[15] Stylistic variables like these make African-American language seem more animated and high-keyed, while European-American language may appear more low-keyed, dispassionate, and impersonal.[16] It is clear that differences in key can lead to misunderstanding. AAVE speakers may seem (to AE speakers) to be too emotional, while AE speakers may appear (to AAVE speakers) to be hiding their true feelings.

This effect is increased by differences in turn-taking. Thomas Kochman tells us that European-American speakers generally wait for a pause or a direct invitation to take their turn at talk, then address all of the points that have been made up to that time. African-American speakers, on the other hand, follow a rule that tells them to come in assertively after a single point has been made, but to restrict comments to this one point. Because of these differences both groups may see each other as "hogging the floor."

Another style difference involves the use of the **call and response pattern.** Jack Daniel and Geneva Smitherman describe this aspect of AAVE. "Briefly defined, this African-derived process is the verbal and nonverbal interaction between speaker and listener in which each of the speaker's statements (or 'calls') is punctuated by expressions ('responses') from the listener."[17] Speakers who are accustomed to this interaction style feel that overt responses are necessary to let the speaker know how he or she is "getting over." When interacting with people who give feedback in more subdued ways, they may assume they are not being understood and may "repeatedly punctuate 'calls' with questions such

as 'Are you listening to me?' 'Did you hear me?' etc."[18] Of course, speakers who are not acquainted with this pattern may not understand what is going on when speakers interject calls or when listeners offer responses like "Tell it," "I hear you," or "Go 'head, run it down," during conversation. These indications of interest and involvement may be heard as intrusive and interruptive by people not familiar with the pattern.

There are additional style differences that have been well documented, including differences in eye contact and listening behavior.[19] Box 13.2 discusses a final example by describing a language game associated with the African-American cultural practice, "playing the dozens."

It is important to reiterate that the differences we have looked at are general, group-based differences—they don't apply to every African American or European American that you know. Still, they should indicate how easy it is for people whose communication styles differ to misunderstand one another. Table 13.1 provides additional examples of ways in which patterns common to one cultural group (the in-group) may be misinterpreted by members of another (the out-group) when people fail to respect and celebrate diversity.

### Regional and Class Differences

Ethnic differences are not the only sources of communication misunderstandings. Social class and regional identity also give rise to communication differences. Carley Dodd, for example, lists some of the differences in interpersonal style one is likely to find between the West and East coasts of America. His list includes perceived abruptness; speed of delivery; amount of verbal buffering (that is, introductory phrases in a sentence); amount of eye contact, touch, space, and verbal pausing; manner of leaving a conversation; amount of warmth and openness; amount of animation; amount of dominance; and amount of contentiousness.[20]

Class also determines communicative activity, as we saw in our discussion of Bernstein's elaborated and restricted codes in Chapter 4. There

BOX 13.2

## If You Can't Stand the Shame, Don't Play the Game:

# Playing The Dozens as a Conflict-Reducing Ritual

Playing the dozens is a language game in which players use ritualized insults about each other's mothers to score off one another. It is part of a rich tradition of verbal gaming that includes related forms such as signifying, snapping, busting, and capping. Although originally associated with young urban black males, this improvisational game is now played by all ages and by both males and females. It is played in front of an appreciative audience that reacts to the cleverness of the insults, showing their appreciation for the player who comes up with the most humorous insult. "Your mother is so skinny she ice-skate on a razor blade," "Your mother's so ugly she went into a haunted house and came out with a job application." "Your mother's so bald headed, every time she gets in the shower she gets brainwashed," and "Your mother's so fat, her blood type is Ragu" are examples of some of the milder sounds. At their best, sounds can be clever and even poetic. Players must be quick-witted and highly verbal.

There have been many explanations for this ritual. Some have seen it as displaced aggression resulting from social and economic pressures, while others have viewed it (when played by adolescent males) as a working through of Oedipal impulses. Most current scholars now view it as a safe way of resolving conflict in daily interaction. Morgan, for example, ties it to the need to present a social face that exemplifies *cool*, "the ability to react with eloquence, skill, wit, patience, and precise timing" (p. 253). Thurmon

Garner believes that players learn important lessons about conflict by playing this game. They learn to confront conflict by talking rather than fighting, to keep cool in tense situations, and to keep their wits about them.

Participants can benefit personally, learning inventiveness, assertiveness, and poise. They achieve a personal sense of power, since successful players are highly regarded in the community. They also learn not to lose their temper and to "hang in" when the going gets tough. Participants learn to remain composed, calmly taking whatever failures fall their way. Finally, because contestants must play off one another, following the flow of the game, they learn to coordinate their thoughts and actions.

The community can also benefit. In this ritual, conflict is dealt with, not by repression, but through dramatization. Hostility can be expressed, but in an indirect and ritualized form, giving the community a nonviolent forum for conflict. In the words of Smitherman, "Today the dozens, with its infusion into other cultures, still serves as a release from the pressures of daily existence, a safe, nonviolent method of venting hostility and suppressed rage within acceptable confines. Surely a healthier alternative than the rat-tat-tat-tat of glocks, domestic abuse, and other kinds of violence ranging throughout *all* communities today" (p. 225).

**SOURCE** Thurmon Garner, "Playing the Dozens: Folklore as Strategies for Living," *Quarterly Journal of Speech* 69 (1983): 47–57.

**ADDITIONAL READINGS**

Morgan, Marcyliena. "More than a Mood or an Attitude: Discourse and Verbal Genres in African-American Culture." Chapter 9 in *African-American English: Structure, History and Use.* Salikoko S. Mufwene et al., eds. New York: Routledge, 1998.

Smitherman, Geneva. "'If I'm Lyin, I'm Flyin': The Game of Insult in Black Language," Chapter 12 in *Talkin That Talk.* New York: Routledge, 2000.

The information included in this table highlights some specific examples of how verbal and nonverbal cues can generate various meanings depending on in-group and out-group perceptions. They are offered here not as generalizations applicable to all ethnic group members in any one group but as information to assist you in recognizing potential sources of miscommunication.

| Specific behavior | Possible in-group perception | Possible out-group perception |
|---|---|---|
| Avoidance of direct eye contact by Latino/as | Used to communicate attentiveness or respect | A sign of inattentiveness; direct eye contact is preferred |
| An African American who aggressively challenges a point with which she or he disagrees | Acceptable means of dialogue; not regarded as verbal abuse, nor a precursor to violence | Arguments are viewed as inappropriate and a sign of potential immediate violence |
| Asian-American use of finger gestures to beckon others | Appropriate if used by adults for children, but highly offensive if used to call adults | Appropriate gesture to use with both children and adults |
| Interruptions used by African Americans | Tolerated in individual/group discussions; attention is given to most assertive voice | Perceived as rude or aggressive; clear rules for turn-taking must be maintained |
| Silence used by Native Americans | A sign of respect, thoughtfulness, and/or uncertainty/ambiguity | Silence indicates boredom, disagreement, or a refusal to participate/respond |
| The use of touch by Latino/as | Perceived as normal and appropriate for interpersonal interactions | Deemed as appropriate for some intimate or friendly interactions; otherwise perceived as a violation of personal space |
| Public displays of intense emotions by African Americans | Personal expressiveness is valued and regarded as appropriate in most settings | Violates U.S. societal expectations for self-controlled public behaviors; inappropriate for most public settings |
| Asian Americans touching or holding hands of same-sex friends | Seen as acceptable behavior that signifies closeness of platonic relationships | Perceived as inappropriate, especially for male friends |
| Latino/as use of lengthy greetings or the exchange of pleasantries prior to business meetings | Regarded as an important element of establishing rapport with colleagues | Seen as a waste of time; getting to the business at hand is valued |

Source: Mark P. Orbe and Tina M. Harris, *Interracial Communication: Theory into Practice* (Belmont, Calif.: Wadsworth, 2001), p. 65.

| TABLE 13.2 | Perceptions of Poverty Culture in the United States |
| --- | --- |

| Concept | Poverty culture's view |
| --- | --- |
| Success | Generally unattainable, limited only to people with a lot of luck |
| Failure | Inevitable, no hope to overcome inherent failure |
| Emotions | Emotions are made to be expressed, publicly or privately |
| Future | Difficult to envision, so live for now |
| Money | To be used before it gets away, not saved for the future |
| Police | Unfriendly, out to get us, and should be avoided |
| Education | Useful for poor people with upward aspirations, an obstacle for individuals with low aspirations |
| Fate | Dominates some people, since various seen and unseen forces control our destiny |

Reprinted from Carley H. Dodd, *Dynamics of Intercultural Communication*, 2nd ed. (Dubuque, Iowa: Brown, 1987), p. 80.

can be great differences between those who have lived in affluence and those who have grown up in poverty. Dodd describes some of the attitudes one is likely to find in poverty-level subcultures. Members of the poverty culture are much more likely to be fatalistic than are the affluent. Many poor people feel that the future is beyond their control, that success is impossible, and failure almost inevitable. Reared in environments in which achievement is difficult, their aspirations are often very limited. This leads to a here and now attitude in which desires are satisfied as rapidly as possible rather than deferred to a future date. Members of poverty cultures are often traditional and conservative, resisting innovations and sticking to tried-and-true ways of doing things. Because of these differences, communication between the rich and poor is often frustrating for both parties. Table 13.2 summarizes some poverty-culture values. The fact that these values differ from those of the middle class means that when middle-class people intervene in poverty neighborhoods, fundamental misunderstandings may occur.

## Communicating Across Culture

Whenever we interact with others who have been taught a different set of understandings about the world, we are engaging in **cross-cultural communication.** As we have seen, this kind of communication is not always easy. Although sensitive and intelligent people can often find communicative common ground, even the most well-meaning people experience problems in communication if cultural differences are large. In this section, we'll look at some of the reasons problems occur and we'll discuss some ways these problems can be avoided.

Cross-cultural communication is difficult because we are unaccustomed to dealing with differences. As we have seen throughout this text, people seek out similar others and avoid those who are different. In conversational openings, for example, we try to find something in common to talk about ("Oh, you're from New Jersey, do you know so-and-so?"). Similarity is such a strong basis for attraction we may actually dislike dissimilar others. As social comparison

## Fear and Prejudice

# Crash

Paul Haggis, 2005

*Crash*, set in Los Angeles, examines the intersecting lives of a group of strangers: a racist cop (Matt Dillon), a spoiled Brentwood housewife (Sandra Bullock), a world-weary homicide detective (Don Cheadle), a successful TV producer and his beautiful wife (Terrence Howard and Thandie Newton), an Iranian merchant (Shaun Toub), a Mexican locksmith (Michael Pena), and a philosophical car thief (Ludicris). Divided by race and class, blinded by fear, unable to see or hear one another, their lives collide in the aftermath of a car jacking. While the characters could easily be one-dimensional caricatures, one of the strengths of the movie is that they continually surprise us. Each character exhibits moments of appalling bigotry, yet each also reveals a vulnerability and humanity that suggest that the cause of their behavior may lie outside of them, that it may be a product of a society where racism makes communication impossible and collision inevitable.

When fear and racism are common, alienation is a natural result. Graham (Don Cheadle) sums up one of the major themes of the film, our inability to make connections. "In any real city, you walk, you know? You brush past people, people bump into you. In L.A., nobody touches you. We're always behind this metal and glass. I think we miss that touch so much, that we crash into each other, just so we can feel something." Racism is a difficult subject, one most people would rather ignore. By addressing it directly *Crash* provides an important opportunity for dialogue.

theory points out, if we find ourselves interacting with someone who is too different, we exert subtle pressures on that person to conform.

One of the reasons we avoid those who are different is that cross-cultural communication usually takes extra effort. Rather than relying on old routines, we have to take the trouble to define new scripts and negotiate new understandings. While this may be a disadvantage in terms of time and energy, it can also be rewarding. Cross-cultural communication forces us to see the world in fresh ways and allows us to make new connections.

## Barriers to Intercultural Understanding

Given the kinds of differences we have described, it is no wonder that communication sometimes fails. In this section, we'll look at three barriers to intercultural understanding. We'll begin with prejudice, then briefly discuss two additional problems: ethnocentrism and assumed similarity.

### Prejudice

Communicating interculturally means communicating with people who are different, and people who are different often make us feel uncomfortable. We can do two things in response to this discomfort: (1) we can think about the parts of the new culture we find strange, try to see why people in the culture act as they do, and relish the opportunity to communicate in new ways; or (2) we can reject, devalue, and avoid contact with anyone from the new culture. As we all know, the latter course is too frequently

*Entering a culture means celebrating its unique values.*

chosen, resulting in prejudice, discrimination, and intergroup conflict.

**Prejudice** is a negative social attitude held by members of one group toward members of another group, an attitude that biases perceptions and often leads to discrimination. To better understand this definition, let's break it down into separate parts, following the analysis given by Tuen van Dijk.[21]

First of all, *prejudices are attitudes.* An **attitude** is a generalized evaluation of a stimulus object. To see how attitudes work in general, let's take a fairly neutral stimulus object, the horse. People respond to horses in various ways. Some people are crazy about them, some people are scared to death of them, and others simply don't care. Suppose as a young child Bob spent his summers on a farm, where he was allowed to feed the horses. His friends were all crazy about riding and talked about the horses they would one day own. Bob also read books about horses, and for a while *Black Beauty* was his favorite book. Over time he took these experiences and messages and used them to construct a general schema of what a horse was like: strong, swift, and beautiful. He stored this schema in memory,

accessing it whenever the topic of horses came up, and using it to color later perceptions. When, on a vacation, he was given a mean-tempered, ill-kempt, sway-backed horse to ride, he measured the poor beast against his original schema, saw that the horse was atypical, and felt sorry that it had been so neglected and mistreated. Compare Bob's experience with Cathy's. Cathy was always told to stay away from horses because they were dangerous and wild. She had no personal experience with the animal, but picked up a fear of horses from her mother. Her schema was negative, and when she saw the pitiful sway-backed nag we just described, she said to herself, "See, I was right. Horses are large, dumb, nasty beasts." The generalized conception, or attitude, each developed acted as a guide to perception and action.

Second, prejudices are a special kind of attitude. *Prejudices are attitudes based on group rather than individual opinions.* Some attitudes are merely matters of personal taste. You, for example, may not like people who are tall. If this attitude is not shared by other members of your culture and not used to limit the freedom of those who are tall, it is not a prejudice, although it is a foolish and biased opinion. Other attitudes are developed through communication with **in-group members** (people who share a common group identity) and used to describe **out-group members** (people who come from a different social group). These attitudes, if they are negative, are prejudices.

In all cases of ethnic prejudice, there is a strong emphasis on group identity, on "them" versus "us." "They" are to be feared or mistrusted primarily because they are not like "us." Ethnic prejudices are, in fact, created and reproduced through intergroup communication. Ironically, many people who are strongly prejudiced have never had personal experiences with the targets of their prejudice. Their negative attitudes come from secondary experience, from the talk or texts that make up their cultures.

Third, *prejudice is, by definition, a negative attitude.* Through prejudice we devalue members of other groups for not being the same as us. In a study of the attitudes of the Dutch toward foreign workers (primarily Surinamese, Moroccans, and Turks), van Dijk found three areas of negative evaluation. Out-group members were devalued for being different, for competing for scarce resources, and for threatening the Dutch way of life. First, van Dijk's subjects complained that the foreign workers were lazy, noisy, clannish, dirty, and sexually promiscuous, characteristics often used to describe out-group members regardless of nationality. Second they accused the foreign workers of taking away their neighborhoods, jobs, and houses, even though, as van Dijk points out, the jobs and houses they took were generally unacceptable to Dutch workers. Again, this complaint is a common one: that out-group members are favored over in-group members, even when by objective measure this perception is untrue. Finally, van Dijk's subjects saw the out-group as threatening to their territory, cultural identity, safety, well-being, and material interests.[22] With such fear, it is no wonder that intergroup conflicts so easily erupt into violence.

Fourth, *prejudices are based on biased cognitive models.* When prejudiced people think about out-group members, they are not trying to represent the world accurately. Rather, their purpose is to draw a line between in-group and out-group members, a line that divides those who are "superior" from those who are "inferior." To do this, prejudiced people often distort reality. Van Dijk explains:

> When in-group members interpret "ethnic encounters," their goal in doing so is not primarily to establish a truthful and reliable representation of "what is really going on." Rather, just as in the interpretation of other encounters, people construct a model that is subjectively plausible . . . is coherent with previous models of ethnic encounters, and is a partial instantiation of general knowledge and attitude schemata.[23]

Several cognitive biases maintain prejudice: negative interpretations, discounting, attribution errors, exaggeration, and polarization. By **negative interpretations** we mean interpreting everything that minority members do as negative. If, for example, we see an out-group member sitting in the yard and soaking up the sun, we may interpret this activity as shiftlessness, while an in-group member doing the same thing may be seen as enjoying a well-deserved rest. If out-group members hang out together, they are clannish; if in-group members do so, they are being sociable. Whenever people see what "they" do as bad and what "we" do as good, they are using negative interpretations.

**Discounting** is a cognitive bias often linked to prejudice. Discounting means dismissing information that doesn't fit preconceived schemata. If, for example, you believe that out-group members are incapable of success and you encounter a very successful individual, you may discount this information by telling yourself that he or she is merely the "exception that proves the rule." Or you may convince yourself that the success was only due to luck or favoritism. In this way your schema never has to be changed, and you can continue to hold your prejudice in the face of contrary evidence.

People also tend to make the **fundamental attribution error** of interpreting another's negative behaviors as due to their disposition rather than due to their situation. This error is particularly strong in prejudiced people. If a prejudiced person finds that an out-group member is unemployed, he or she will believe the reason lies in the out-group member's inherent lack of ability and motivation rather than in an external circumstance like job discrimination. Of course, if the prejudiced person should lose a job, the attribution will be reversed. This time the unemployment will be blamed on external circumstances, for example, that all the jobs are being stolen by out-group members.

Finally, the biases of exaggeration and polarization are often used to support prejudices. Because of fear and anger, individuals may engage in **exaggeration** when they describe the negative character of out-group actions. An out-group member disagreeing with an acquaintance will be perceived as engaging in a violent argument. A mother who scolds her child in public may be seen as abusing the child. Individuals are not the only ones guilty of exaggeration; media reports about out-group members also show this bias. Thus, van Dijk reports that in the Netherlands newspapers frequently use a "flood" metaphor to describe immigration—for example, a "tide" of Tamil refugees "flood" into the country. These word choices are particularly unfortunate in the Netherlands, given its tradition of battling against the sea for survival.[24]

**Polarization** is the tendency to magnify differences between in-groups and out-groups. Polarization is also used to categorize people as more different than they are. Thus, an immigrant who has become a citizen and who, for all intents and purposes, is very similar to in-group members will still be excluded and seen as one of "them."

A final characteristic of prejudices is that *prejudices are often used to support discriminatory behavior;* that is, they legitimate the treating of out-group members as inferior. Prejudices make it acceptable to deny out-group members the same rights and privileges given to in-group members. Thus, prejudices are often used to support the power and dominance of in-group members.

### Communicating Prejudice

These biased perceptions are kept alive through everyday communication, both mediated and interpersonal. The mass media reproduce prejudices in several ways. First, news items are often written in ways that encourage alarm or anger. Often the most sensational and violent aspects of interethnic interactions are stressed, presumably because this practice sells papers and raises ratings. But whereas minority group members often take center stage in violent happenings, their roles are generally "nonspeaking." That is, they are seldom given the opportunity to explain their perception of events. In addition, the number of minority journalists, especially in high positions,

is small. Thus, ethnic events are often described from the majority points of view. Finally, "topics that are relevant for the ordinary daily life of ethnic groups, such as work, housing, health, education, political life, and culture, as well as discrimination in these areas, are hardly discussed in the press, unless they lead to 'problems' for society as a whole or when they are spectacular."[25]

Individuals also spread prejudice through stories, anecdotes, and jokes; through persuasive argument; and through everyday conversations. Because most prejudiced people know that prejudice is considered bad, they try to hide it or to disguise it by using disclaimers ("Some of my best friends are . . . ," "I'm not prejudiced, but . . . ," or "Some of them are perfectly nice, however . . ."). These language forms give the illusion of fairness. Unfortunately, statements such as these are usually followed by negative stereotypes. Because these patterns cloak prejudice and racism, they are generally resented by out-group members.

In a classic 1970 study, Jack Daniel asked black respondents to report statements that white speakers had made to them that indicated insincerity.[26] In analyzing his results, Daniel put the responses into four categories. The first was made up of white attempts to show affinity for black people and included comments like "One of my best friends is a Negro," "You are as good as I am," "My maid is a Negro," and "My son goes to school with a Negro." The second category contained attempts to show an understanding of the black person's experiences through comments like "I am a member of a minority group," "I know exactly how you feel," "I used to live in the Hill District (a black district in Pittsburgh)," and "Once I didn't have what you have." The third category included stereotypic and derogatory comments like "you people," "little colored child," and "show me the latest dance." Finally, the last category consisted of comments that indicated the majority speaker did not understand the problems of minority members: "Negroes should be more grateful," "You have a chip on your shoulder," "If you just wait a little longer . . . ," and "What exactly does the Negro want?"

Do these comments appear prejudiced to you? Have you heard comments like them? If you are a minority group member, you probably have (although the language and content may be updated), and chances are you've found them offensive. If you're a majority group member you may not have realized how inappropriate some of these comments are.

### Ethnocentrism

Another barrier to effective intercultural communication, and one that is closely tied to prejudice, is **ethnocentrism,** the belief that our culture is better than any other. While our way of life may be best for us, that does not mean it is best for others, or that our cultural patterns are widely shared. Samovar and his colleagues ask us to consider the possibility that every culture has something to offer and that our culture may not always be the best.

> The Jew covers his head to pray, the Protestant does not—is one more correct than the other? In Saudi Arabia women cover their faces, in America they cover very little—is one more correct than the other? The Occidental speaks to God, the Oriental has God speak to him—is one more correct than the other? The American Indian values and accepts nature, the average American seeks to alter nature— is one more correct than the other? A listing of these questions is never-ending. We must remember, however, that it is not the questions that are important, but rather the dogmatic way in which we answer them.[27]

Currently, many colleges are trying to combat ethnocentrism by exposing individuals to multicultural studies. Traditional curricula are being revamped to include the contributions of writers and thinkers from a variety of cultural backgrounds. Because allegiance to one's own cultures is so strong, this attempt has been controversial.

### Assumed Similarity

There is a final barrier to cross-cultural understanding that may surprise you. This barrier consists of **assumed similarity;** it occurs whenever we ignore differences and assume that everyone is exactly the same. At first glance, this hardly seems like a problem; it seems instead to support the goals of open-mindedness and equality. The problem comes, however, when we ignore true differences and assume everyone is just the same as us. Many of the cross-cultural misunderstandings we have discussed so far have occurred precisely because the participants did not consider that their partners might be seeing the world differently and acting in accordance with those different perceptions. Competent communicators recognize the powerful effects of culture on every aspect of their lives. When interacting with people from another culture they are sensitive to differences in perspective.

# Communicative Competence and Culture

It should be clear by now that culture is a powerful force that affects every aspect of our lives. In this section we will look at the relationship between culture and interpretive schema, social roles, goal achievement, notions of the self, and message choices. We will see how sensitivity to cultural norms and values can increase our competence as communicators, and how ignoring the effects of culture can lead to unsuccessful and unrewarding interactions.

## Culture and Interpretive Competence

William Brooks gives an excellent example of how cultural sets affect perception. He tells the story of a professor at London University who showed his African students a film about improving health conditions in African villages. After the film he asked the class what they had seen. One student answered, "A chicken!" and the others all agreed. The professor was surprised, for to his knowledge there was no chicken in the movie. He carefully went through the entire film, frame-by-frame, and sure enough he found in the bottom corner of two or three frames, a chicken taking flight. Although the chicken's cameo performance lasted only part of a second, the students saw it quite clearly; what they did not see was the important information (important at least to the professor) on eradicating mosquitoes. Several theories were offered for the students' response: the African students' sharp eye for hunting, the religious significance of the chicken, and even the fact that novice film viewers tend to focus on details within a frame rather than on the whole frame. Regardless of the reason, the students' culture clearly had taught them to see the world differently than the professor's culture had.[28]

The example of the chicken points out that people from different cultures see the content of scenes differently. Someone brought up on a farm in Nebraska and someone from inner-city Chicago, if transported to each other's environments, will not see them in the same way. Each will miss a lot of what the other considers to be important. Yet each will probably notice things that are so commonplace to the other that they've become invisible.

Not only does culture determine what we see, it determines how we see. There is evidence that general patterns of information processing also differ culturally. Carley Dodd tells us that general thought patterns, including the kind of logic we use and the ways we sequence events, may also be the products of culture. Members of some cultures, for example, think in terms of linear, sequential, time-ordered patterns, while members of other cultures think in terms of pictures or configurations.[29]

## Culture and Role Competence

All cultures categorize people by role. A good example of role-related behavior is the way we react to age. In many cultures the elderly are treated with great respect. The Ashanti of Ghana, for example, address all elderly men by a term that translates as "my grandfather," and they regard older people as repositories of wisdom.[30] In China old age is also respected, and the Chinese have difficulty understanding why Americans separate the generations, paying to send our children to day-care centers and our grandparents to old-age homes. In comparison to the Ashanti and the Chinese, we place less value on old age. In our culture the elderly are often seen (even by themselves) as useless and nonproductive.

The values placed on being men or women are also culture-specific, and everyday customs reflect these values. In parts of India women do not eat at the table with men; they are served separately after the men have finished eating.[31] In Vietnam women must eat smaller portions of food than men, regardless of their hunger.[32] And, of course, in some cultures women wear veils and are completely isolated from the world of men. Not only do gender values differ, but so too do our ways of being masculine and feminine. Although many Americans are brought up to believe that men are naturally more aggressive, more logical, and less emotional than women, in some cultures this pattern is reversed. Edward Hall tells us that in Iran, it is the men who read poetry, express their emotions freely, and act on intuition rather than logic; women, on the other hand, are considered to be coldly practical.[33]

## Culture and Goal Competence

Not only does culture specify appropriate role behaviors, it also affects individual goals and aspirations. Carley Dodd discusses the fact that some cultures emphasize task goals, while others emphasize social goals. Members of task cultures believe that self-worth can be measured by how much one has accomplished. Dodd tells us that in such cultures, themes such as "no pain, no gain," "get ahead," and "make it to the top" are "the surface structures of a deeper, underlying cognitive dimension of how people are viewed in comparison with tasks. Americans, for instance,

*Concepts such as goal setting, roles, and even interpersonal space are highly determined by our cultural background.*

arc considered highly task oriented."[34] In a more people-oriented culture, task achievement is less important. People develop a more personal style of conversation. In traditional societies, power and prestige are differentially distributed. The place of women in such societies is likely to differ sharply from that of men.

Cultures also tell us whether we should even try to set goals. Certain cultures, marked by fatalism, believe that individuals can do nothing to control their future. Members of these cultures meet their fate with acceptance, endurance, and passivity, assuming that it is wrong to attempt to change what is God's will. Larry Samovar illustrates the difference between fatalism and a sense of accomplishment. "If you ask a Hindu why he got only ten bags of corn from his land while

nearby farmers got much more he would say it was the wish of God. An American farmer's answer to the same questions would be, 'Hell, I didn't work hard enough.'"[35] Obviously, members of fatalistic cultures communicate differently from those of more active cultures. They may consider our communication efforts to be aggressive, persistent, and even arrogant.

## Culture and Self Competence

As we saw in Box 13.1, cultures also differ in the value they place on the self. Collectivist cultures emphasize what Stella Ting-Toomey calls a "we" identity, valuing shared interests, harmony, and collective judgments. Individualist cultures, on the other hand, place a premium on an "I" identity, valuing personal identity, competition, and individual decision making.[36] North American and European countries (like the United States, Canada, and Great Britain) are individualist, while many South American and Asian countries (like Venezuela, Peru, Taiwan, and Thailand) stress collectivism. The individualist countries value freedom, creativity, and economic incentive, but at the same time may inadvertently encourage materialism, alienation, and ecological arrogance. As for communication style, collectivists try to avoid conflict and, when this is impossible, use indirect styles of conflict resolution, while individualists are more confrontational and direct. Collectivists also try to discourage individual accomplishment. In distributing rewards they are more likely to use an **equality norm** (where each member receives the same reward regardless of input) than an **equity norm** (where distribution is based on individual merit); in individualist countries the opposite is true. Because harmony is so important, collectivist cultures value obedience, emphasize smooth intergroup relations, and stress politeness. Family and interpersonal obligations are also important. As Ting-Toomey says, "To be attracted to a member of a collectivistic culture means to take on additional responsibilities and obligations toward the member's social networks."[37]

## Culture and Message Competence

One of the most obvious signs of cultural difference is language difference. Dodd tells us that there are over 3,000 language communities on earth, many of which have yet to be recorded in writing. One of the best points of access to a culture is its language, for language is the primary tool by which a culture transmits its values and beliefs. Yet learning a new language is difficult, because languages differ in what they make expressible. As we saw in our discussion of the Sapir-Whorf hypothesis in Chapter 4, different language communities organize the world in different ways.

While differences in verbal behavior between cultures are obvious, nonverbal differences are equally important but less obvious. When we cross international borders, we are usually aware of the difficulties of translating our language; we are less aware of the difficulties of translating nonverbal meanings. As we saw in Chapter 3, one area of nonverbal difference is in the meaning and use of space. As Hall tells us:

> *Space is organized differently in each culture. The associations and feelings that are released in a member of one culture almost invariably mean something else in the next. When we say that some foreigners are "pushy," all this means is that their handling of space releases this association in our minds.*[38]

Hall explains that in Latin American countries people feel comfortable talking at much closer distances than North Americans are used to. The distance that makes a Latin American feel comfortable may signal either sexuality or hostility to a northerner. Thus, a North American will move away from a Latin American during conversation. "As a consequence, they think we are distant or cold, withdrawn and unfriendly. We, on the other hand, are constantly accusing them of breathing down our necks, crowding us, and spraying our faces."[39] Americans who work closely with Latin Americans have been known to erect physical barricades of desks and chairs to give themselves room, a tactic that so disturbs Latin Americans that they may even climb over the obstacles in order to find a comfortable speaking distance.

Body language and eye contact also differ from culture to culture. In Indonesia, for example, people talk while sitting on the floor, but it is very important for them not to point the soles of their feet toward their conversational partner, for that would indicate the other was beneath them.[40] And even so seemingly natural a behavior as eye contact can carry many messages. E.C. Condon outlines the meanings that are attached to a widening of the eyes in several cultures. For instance, in the dominant American culture widened eyes signify surprise or wonder. If Chinese widen their eyes, however, they may be expressing anger or resentment. For the French the identical movement means "I don't believe you," while for Hispanics, it may signal a lack of understanding.[41]

The examples in this section have shown that culture affects all aspects of communicative behavior. To be an effective communicator, an individual must be sensitive to cultural norms and values. He or she must also be aware that cultural understandings change over time. In the remainder of this chapter, we look at the temporal dimension of communicative contexts.

# Historical Influences

As our discussion of cultural influences has shown, communication changes as we travel around the globe. What counts as good communication in San Diego may not be effective in San Juan, and what is acceptable in Berlin may be taboo in Beijing. The same kind of changes occur as we move through time. Communication practices that were acceptable to your parents' generation seem old fashioned now, just as today's communication patterns will seem obsolete to the next generation. No culture can afford to remain static; if a culture is to survive, it must evolve. Understanding a culture therefore involves more than understanding what separates it from other cultures. It also involves understanding how that culture develops over time.

In this section we'll examine temporal changes in the interpersonal communication patterns of Americans—changes that we think will surprise you. We'll discover that the ways our ancestors interacted with friends and neighbors, thought about their families, raised their children, communicated their love to one another, and felt about themselves have changed dramatically over the years. And we'll see that these changes in the private sphere are closely related to social and economic changes in the public sphere.

We'll begin by looking at social conditions in America in three historical periods: the colonial period, the early industrial period, and the modern period. There will, of course, be gaps in our survey, and we will limit ourselves to understanding the lives of middle-class citizens. Nevertheless, this brief overview should give you a general sense of the ways in which personal relationships have evolved over time.

## The Colonial Period (1600–1780)

Let's begin with the **colonial period,** a period that extends from about 1600 to about 1780. During this period the early colonists set out to establish themselves in what was to them the New World. Of course, there were regional variations in the ways they went about this task. The Puritans who settled in New England, for example, lived in small, tight-knit villages, closely supervised by religious leaders. Colonists in the Middle colonies were more religiously and economically diverse and experienced greater class disparity. And Southern communities, where much of the population was made up of single males between the ages of 20 and 29, was characterized by a less stable culture involving "conspicuous consumption, profiteering, and hospitality."[42] Despite these differences, however, there were commonalities. The colonial period was characterized by strong social consensus and interdependence, by an acceptance of inequality and rank, and by patriarchal power.

### The Colonial Household

The basic interpersonal unit in colonial times was the household, not the nuclear family. Households were large, consisting of husband and wife, children from their marriage and (because of high death and remarriage rates) from previous marriages as well, indentured servants, apprentices, and unmarried relatives. No special favoritism was shown to blood relatives, all household members lived and worked together, and there was no separation between work and family life. The colonial home was a site of production. There food was grown, cloth was woven, furniture was made, schooling was undertaken, and religious instruction was offered.

For most colonists (except the very few who lived on large Southern plantations) personal space was limited. A large family might share a two- or three-room dwelling and might all sleep together in the same room or even many in the same bed. The modern concept of privacy was simply unknown. Community leaders could interfere in the lives of the colonists whenever they liked, removing a child from, or assigning an unmarried adult to, a household. No household was exempt from community scrutiny. Court records, for example, frequently cited testimony of neighbors who just happened to be peering through a window at the time a crime was committed. In one case a couple testified that they heard snoring in the next room. To satisfy their curiosity they stood on a hogshead of tobacco and peered over the wall. Upon catching a glimpse of a couple in bed together, one of the observers pried loose a board to get a better view.[43] Under such close supervision, it is not surprising that individualism and nonconformity were rare.

### Rank and Patriarchy

Colonial political life was hierarchical, with older males making all important community decisions. In the words of historian Stephanie Coontz, "the glue that bound individuals to households and households to community was patriarchy."[44] Under **patriarchy** older males ruled all aspects of life. So accepted was male authority that household heads who failed to control their wives, servants, or children could be punished. Inequality and male superiority were seen as a natural part of God's plan. In such a society, knowing how to communicate one's own rank and how to show deference to those of higher rank must have been an important communication competence.

### Codes of Conduct

One of the most surprising aspects of colonial life was the relative earthiness of the people. Be-

haviors we would consider rude or crude today were quite common, although advice manuals of the time did their best to encourage a more civilized code of conduct. A popular advice manual of the time offered the following advice:

*Foul not the table cloth.*

*Put not thy hand in the presence of others to any part of thy body not ordinarily discovered.*

*Spit not in the room but in the corner, or rather go out and do it abroad.*[45]

Accounts of foreign travelers confirm the fact that uncouth behaviors occurred frequently. A Frenchman who visited Virginia in the 1780s marveled at the fact that the people he observed blew their noses either with their fingers or with a single silk handkerchief that also doubled as a necktie and a napkin.[46] It was clear that our colonial ancestors did not have a strong sense of cleanliness or of human boundaries. Nor did the majority view personal violence and cruelty as wrong. Brawling was a major and accepted part of male culture. The problem became so bad, in fact, that legislatures in Virginia, North Carolina, and South Carolina made it illegal to "cut out the Tongue or pull out the eyes," or to bite or cut off the nose "[of] the King's Liege people."[47] Only gradually did more "civilized" sets of manners develop.

### Sex, Love, and Marriage

Given such impulsivity, it is not surprising that sex was openly enjoyed and discussed. Sex during colonial times was not a matter for false prudery; it was talked about with great directness, and marriage manuals advised couples to engage "with equal vigor" in the conjugal act.[48] Nevertheless, the proper setting for sex was considered marriage, and sexual practices that did not lead to legitimate procreation were severely punished. Adultery, defined as sex between a man and a married woman, was one such practice, although its prohibition seems to have been as much a matter of protecting (men's) property rights as it was a way of enforcing morality.

Today we believe that love is a necessary prerequisite to marriage. This was not the case in colonial times. Love was a duty, something one learned to feel after marriage. Romantic love, as we know it today, did not develop until the 19th century. Colonial couples based their choice of partners on compatibility rather than on romance and were anxious to pick a mate their parents approved of. According to a popular advice manual of the time: "Children are so much the goods, the possessions of their Parents, that they cannot without a kind of theft, give away themselves without the allowance of those that have the right in them."[49]

### Concepts of Identity

In colonial times, identity was clearly fixed by rank and gender. Men and women were considered to be different from one another by nature. Men were controlled, rational, and moral. Women, on the other hand, having inherited Eve's sinful nature, were passionate and tempestuous. Because of these essential differences, men were to guide and teach their wives; and wives were to submit to such teaching. In the words of John Winthrop, governor of the Massachusetts Bay Colony, writing in 1645, "A true wife accounts her subjection [as] her honor and freedom, and would not think her condition safe and free, but in subjection to her husband's authority."[50] This was not an era in which gender roles were questioned or individuality accepted.

Although colonial conformity pressures may seem stifling to us, they did not seem that way to the colonists. Independent decision making had little value, and families made no attempt to teach children social attitudes that might conflict with community standards. It simply never occurred to parents to foster individuality in their children. And the idea that people should look inside themselves to find what makes them unique and should share that uniqueness with others was not to occur for another hundred years or so. Rather than worrying about an individual self, the colonists worried about being accepted by their communities and their God.

## The Early Industrial Period (1830–1880)

The simple agrarian life of the colonial period did not last long. By the early 19th century, America was experiencing rapid urbanization and industrialization. Young men and women in increasing numbers were leaving the safety of small rural communities and seeking their fortunes in towns and cities. The new conditions they faced led to a great deal of uncertainty.

### Social Change and Anxiety

Historian Karen Haltunnen has identified some of the fears that preoccupied Americans during this period.[51] First, 19th-century Americans feared political instability. Now that political leaders were elected rather than appointed by the crown, there was concern about the influence of corrupt politicians. Fear of mob rule was real and immediate. Second, 19th-century Americans feared economic change. The emergence of industrial capitalism ushered in a new era of competition and greed. People worried about the instability of a money economy. Third, 19th-century Americans feared the new social freedoms that surrounded them. No longer under the watchful eye of their elders, suddenly responsible for their own conduct, young men and women found their new freedoms frightening.

S. W. Nissenbaum sums up the situation in which urban migrants found themselves:

> They were on their own, then, in mind and body . . . what loomed before them was not just a bleak future, but an unknowable future—and a far wider range of options than their parents had ever known, and for which nobody was equipped to prepare them. . . . Neighbors were unfamiliar; the new communities were often demographically skewed; the seasonal cycle of seed-time and harvest no longer serve to regulate the rhythm of their

*lives; even their bodies, which had served to confirm their identity through the physical labor imposed by farm work, were useless and "alien" to the kind of activities demanded of them in colleges or cities.*[52]

Social historians argue that it was in response to insecurity brought on by new social conditions that 19th-century Americans developed new ways of relating to one another and to themselves.

### The 19th-Century Home

In one sense, 19th-century Americans were right to be concerned about the impact of a changing economy on their lives. The emergence of industrial capitalism had far-reaching effects, not the least of which was that work and home became separated. For the first time in American history, men left home to work, leaving women and children behind. This changed the way 19th-century Americans felt about the home. Americans began to think of their lives as occurring in two different spheres, one ruled over by men and the other belonging to women. The public sphere, where men worked and governed, was characterized by competition and greed. The private sphere, the world of the home, was characterized by sentiment and sympathy. No longer a site of production, the home now became a refuge from the harsh realities of capitalist competition, a "haven in a heartless world." Descriptions of the home dating from this period reveal an almost religious fervor.

*We go forth into the world . . . and the heart is sensible to a desolation of feeling; we behold every principle of justice and honor disregarded, and good sacrificed to the advancement of personal interest; and we turn from such scenes with a painful sensation, almost believing that virtue has deserted the abodes of men; again, we look to the* sanctu-ary *of* home; *there . . . disinterested love is ready to sacrifice everything at the altar of affection.*[53]

Not only did the home serve a spiritual function, it also took on a political function. During the Revolution, the patriots had exerted pressure on the British by boycotting foreign products. After the Revolution, the sense that there was a link between patriotism and the home became even stronger. It was in the home that citizens of the new republic were to be educated. The problem of political instability that so worried people of the time could only be solved if young people were educated to be responsible and patriotic. That education took place within the home under the guidance of what came to be called the **republican mother.**

During this period, the physical home was redesigned to reflect changing social conditions, as well as improved standards of living and new notions of propriety. Beds, which in the colonial period, were in open view in the main room of the home, were now placed in separate rooms. Houses became larger and their spaces more specialized. Historian John Kasson says, "by the latter part of the nineteenth century, middle-class houses and apartments were characteristically divided into major zones of society, privacy, and service . . ." Guests were entertained in the parlor and dining room; household members sought privacy in bedrooms and bathrooms; and servants worked in kitchen, pantry, and laundry room.[54]

### Rudeness and Civility

Americans responded to the dramatic changes that were occurring around them by developing new codes of conduct. These codes were closely tied to the new public and private spheres. In public, as we saw in Box. 3.1, behavior was characterized by rigid politeness and self-effacement. Gone was the impulsivity of the colonial times. Now anything that remotely touched on personal feeling or on passionate desire was placed off-limits. The public face of 19th-century America was rigid and prudish in the extreme.

In private, another code of conduct developed. People who guarded against any show of emotion

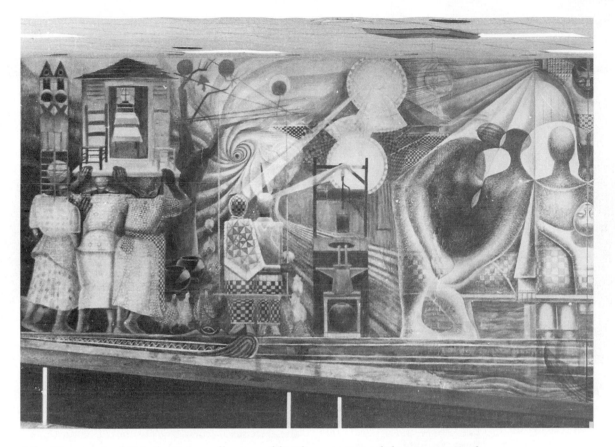

*John Biggers mural,* Family Unity, *talks to us of family structure and the importance of ancestral ties in African-American culture. Notice that the women are shown bearing a house on their shoulders, indicating their central connection to the home. Biggers employs elements of West African iconography to express his unique cultural experience.*

John Biggers, detail of *Family Unity* mural, 1979–1984

in public were free to express their feelings in private, although this emotional expression was expected to be positive and uplifting and was extremely sentimental. One of the reasons communication took this form was that it was considered (as we have already seen in Chapter 8) to be a reflection of the speaker's **character.** Character consisted of a constellation of positive qualities including thrift, hard-work, duty, self-sacrifice, good deeds, integrity, and a spotless reputation, as well as sentimentality, gentility, and kindheartedness.[55] Character was extremely fragile; it could be destroyed by any hint of crudeness. Therefore, it was something to be constantly worried about and improved upon. Within the private sphere almost any occasion could give rise to character-building. Even a normal dinner could be an opportunity for family members to demonstrate "punctuality, order, neatness, temperance, self-denial, kindness, generosity, and hospitality."[56]

### Sex Roles and Personal Identity

As in the colonial period, sex roles were highly differentiated. Men and women were still considered to be different from one another, but the nature of their differences had shifted. Women, who had previously been considered morally inferior to men, now became the moral superiors. No longer could men set the standard for women, for men were now considered to be ruled by base passions. Women were desexualized and described with almost cloying sweetness, as the following passage from a novelist of the time shows:

> But stop. Turn back. We have neglected the
> heart of the house, the mother's room!
> The old temple had no such holy of holies.
> The mother's room! Here came she as a bride.
> Here only God's angels and her own husband
> have heard what words the inmost heart of
> love can coin.[57]

### Love, Desire, and Romance

The direct expression of sexual feeling that characterized colonial communication was muted and transformed in the 19th century. Direct talk about sex became taboo, although the resulting secrecy and censorship may actually have enhanced rather than dampened sexual desire.[58] When couples expressed their passion, they expressed it in terms of an idealized and romantic love rather than in terms of physical desire.

Although love purified and elevated passion, it was not an excuse for premarital intimacy. Sex was to take place only within the bonds of marriage. An advice manual of the day told men to wait until marriage before engaging in physical intimacy: "You can wait, you are a man; be master of yourself."[59] There was no corresponding need to warn women, for their natural purity protected them from temptation.

## The Modern Period (1900–1960)

By the turn of the century, social conditions in America were once again changing. The anxieties of early capitalism had waned, and Americans were embracing the very values they had once feared. Americans had finally adjusted to urban life and industrial development. Many of our current beliefs and attitudes toward interpersonal communication were beginning to emerge.

### Mass Consumption and the American Dream

The early 20th century was a period of unprecedented industrial growth. To Americans of the time, bigger was better. Many towns and cities doubled in size, large corporations began to control the economy, and average citizens began to orient themselves to national news and advertising rather than to local issues.[60] As the economy moved from scarcity to abundance, America became a consumer society. In earlier times, independent families were expected to be self-sufficient, producing all that they needed for themselves. As industries grew, people became dependent "on goods made by unknown hands," on the output of mass production.[61] As Americans wandered through the glamorous new department stores and gazed at piles of brand-name goods, they dreamed of someday displaying these riches in their own homes. For more and more people consumption was a means of reaching happiness. Now every American had an equal right "to desire the same goods and to enter the same world of comfort and luxury."[62]

It was no accident that advertising came into its own at this time. The new mass economy required a high level of consumer demand, the more wasteful and indiscriminate the better. Advertising had to do more than announce the availability of a product, it had to create a demand. In 1919 the associate editor of *Advertising and Selling* made this quite clear: "I want advertising copy to arouse me, to create in me a desire to possess the thing that's advertised, even though I don't need it."[63] Under such pressure, Americans became increasingly materialistic. As Stephanie Coontz points out, "the activity of parents became directed less at ensuring that their children should *be* more than themselves than that they should *have* more than themselves."[64]

*The essential nature of gender roles has changed dramatically over time, in virtually every culture.*

## Home and Family Values

Given this change in attitudes, it is not surprising that the home was no longer seen as a refuge or a temple. It was seen, instead, as a place for further commodification and consumption. The home was a place to display the store-bought goods a family could afford, especially the technological marvels made possible by electricity. The status of a home could be measured by whether it contained an electric range or washing machine; the personality of its owners could be measured by the style and taste of the home's furnishings.

At the same time that the home was becoming filled with consumer goods, it was being emptied of most of its social functions. The moral authority of the home was diminishing, as public schools took over education and government agencies took over the task of providing social welfare. The only social function left was an emotional one. Experts agreed that the primary social purpose of the home was to "foster emotional health in an industrial society."[65] Social maladjustment was no longer blamed on poverty or genetics, but on a failure of the home. Mothers, in particular, were blamed if children did not turn out to be model citizens for it was their responsibility to provide a stable and nurturing psychological setting within the home.

## Personality and Self-Expression

By the early 20th century, the codes of conduct that had characterized the 19th century had almost completely dissolved. Middle-class Americans no longer looked to their "betters" for models of genteel behavior. Instead, in the early part of the century, "imitations of working-class and black culture became the rage: middle-class people listened to ragtime, did the cakewalk, copied the tough dancing pioneered by urban working youth, embraced professional sports, and started going to amusement parks and nickelodeons."[66] The stiffness and formality of the 19th century was replaced by a new freedom, openness, and vitality.

Friendliness was also a key component of the new communication style. Twentieth-century Americans labored to make themselves liked in ways their ancestors had not. One reason lay in the world of work. The modern workplace had become more and more anonymous. To get ahead in the ranks of white-collar workers, it was necessary to get along with others, to make a good impression on the boss, to stand out in a crowd. This took more than character; it took personality.

The careful, self-controlled man or woman of the 19th century was becoming obsolete in the new consumer culture. Success was no longer measured by diligence and self-control but by one's ability to take risks and to make a personal impression. The quality that best allowed one to make such an impression was **personality.** Personality allowed one to be outgoing and expressive; people who had it were fascinating, stunning, attractive, magnetic, glowing, masterful, creative, dominant, and forceful.[67] The individual with personality knew how to draw attention to him- or herself. The individual with personality could win friends and influence people.

### Sex and Self-Discovery

Psychologist Howard Gadlin has identified two major features of interpersonal relationships in the early 20th century: the reemergence of repressed sexuality, and an increased acceptance of personal fulfillment as a goal of relationships.[68] As the modern period advanced, sex became freer and more open. During the 19th century, for a man to glimpse a young woman's ankle was considered shocking and improper. By the 1920s

flappers were wearing skirts that revealed their knees. In fact, between the years 1913 and 1928 the amount of cloth needed to make a woman's dress diminished from a little over 19 to a mere 7 yards.[69] Gradually, people were revealing both their bodies and their minds to one another.

As we saw in Box 11.1, a new form of courtship, the date, developed in the 20th century. As young people escaped the watchful eyes of chaperones, they were free to experiment with new forms of intimacy. Although virginity was still highly prized until late in the century, "necking" and "petting" became more common. In heterosexual couples, it was considered the woman's task to set sexual limits. It was also considered the woman's fault if control broke down and unsanctioned sexual acts occurred. According to the sexual ideology of the time, there were two types of women, "good girls" who successfully fought off their beaus' advances and "bad girls," who somehow gave off subtle cues that they were "cheap" and thus "got what they asked for." A 1945 dating manual addressed to women warned: "Remember that the average man will go as far as you let him go. A man is only as bad as the woman he is with."[70] The fallacies in this system are clear to us today, but they were not at the time. Prior to the 1960s, few seemed to have found the double standard objectionable. Nor were many particularly offended that men were often portrayed as "potential wolves verging on rapists."[71] As in every other period we have looked at, these sexual stereotypes were considered to be "natural."

Marriage was still an important goal for most couples. As in previous eras it provided financial security and legitimized reproduction. But intimate relationships did more than that in the 20th century: they offered self-fulfillment. Couples believed that interpersonal relationships were a path to self-discovery. Increasingly they turned to one another for the satisfaction of all their emotional needs, expecting togetherness to solve all of their problems. When togetherness did not result in new insights into the self, and when partners were unable to provide each other with complete need satisfaction, disappointment was often bitter, with divorce an inevitable result. As current statistics attest, it has become harder and harder over time for couples to stay together, perhaps because expectations are so high.

---

# Communicative Competence and Historical Change

Our discussion of changing social conditions in America shows that, just as culture affects communicative competence, so too does history. In different periods, people process information differently, take on different roles, set different goals, define themselves differently, and construct messages in substantially different ways. Below, we summarize some of the ways historical change affects each aspect of communicative competence.

## History and Interpretive Competence

Having interpretive competence means being sensitive to context; it means understanding, at any given time, what social information to attend to and what to ignore. In order to make appropriate message choices, individuals must be able to read complex social cues. Over time, the nature of these cues changes; factors that are closely tied to effective communication in one era may be completely unimportant in another.

In the colonial period, for example, rank and social standing determined message choices. Americans of the time had to be able to gauge the exact amount of social distance between themselves and those with whom they communicated. In the 20th century, where displays of deference are not as important as they once were, it isn't necessary to pay as much close attention to these details. Similarly, in the 19th century, social occasions were highly formal and etiquette was exact-

ing. Communicators of that time period had to pay careful attention to social cues that we in the 20th century would hardly notice, and they had to follow exactly social scripts. This does not mean that today we no longer need interpretive competence; rather it suggests that we need to be sensitive to other kinds of social information. In some respects, our task today may be harder than that of our ancestors, for rather than looking at outward indications of others' rank or character, we have to look inward, picking up on subtle differences that tell us who others are as individuals. Clearly, interpretive competence is connected to historical change.

## History and Role Competence

Over time roles also change. The clearest example of this kind of change lies in gender roles. As we have seen, concepts of men's and women's essential nature have changed dramatically in the last 400 years. And, of course, they are still evolving today.

In any era, knowing how to fit comfortably into appropriate roles without losing one's identity is an important social skill. In a transitional period when role definitions are changing, this kind of role competence is especially important. Women who were born before World War II, for example, the grandmothers of today's college students, experienced such a role transition. Brought up to believe that their self-worth lay in finding a good husband and in keeping house for him and their children, few considered embarking on a long-term professional career. The woman who chose a career after college ran the risk of being labeled unwomanly or a bad mother or even emasculating. On the other hand, the woman who followed proper role expectations and settled into a domestic role was, by the time she reached middle age, dismissed as "just a housewife." It took exceptional flexibility for a woman of that generation to find her way through the contradictions of being female.

Men today may be in a somewhat similar position. Male roles seem to be in transition. Older, more "macho" images of man as undisputed head of household, principal wage earner, and protector of wife and child are now being questioned. Like women of earlier generations, men today need to use role competence to adapt to new social expectations without losing their identities. Of course, gender roles are not the only roles that change over time. None of our social roles are static; our attitudes toward family roles, age roles, and professional roles also evolve.

## History and Goal Competence

Like interpretive and role competence, goal competence is also affected by historical change. Both the kinds of goals we set for ourselves and the ways we go about achieving them change over time. As we have seen, definitions of personal fulfillment have evolved over the years. Goals such as ambition and competition are good examples. In preindustrial America, where social mobility was severely limited, these goals were not particularly important to the average person. After industrialization, however, they became more common.

Once new goals become popular, individuals must develop the competence to achieve those goals. In the early 20th century, for example, two new ways of impressing others developed: **pluck** and **charm.** Being plucky meant presenting oneself to others as spirited, resolute, and willing to take risks to get what one wanted. People with pluck were not afraid to blow their own horns to advertise their good qualities. People with charm got their way by being physically attractive and cheerful and by exhibiting brash good humour. Today these persuasive qualities are still admired, so it may seem odd to us that in the 19th century they were not highly valued. Indeed, these qualities were deeply distrusted and associated with the tricks of confidence men.[72] In the 19th century had an individual tried to use pluck or charm to achieve a goal, he or she would probably have failed. Today, quite the reverse is true. How we reach our goals changes historically.

## History and Self Competence

If there is one enduring theme in American social history, it is that Americans have become more and more individualistic with the passage of time. Discovering and understanding the self was not of particular concern to our colonial ancestors because they derived their identity through social rank and community membership rather than individual achievement. Individualism became more important in the 19th century, as people began to search for the romantic self, the self that transcended social roles. When personality became a valued attribute in the early 20th century, individuality became even more central to our way of life. Americans turned inward to consider what qualities made them unique and out of the ordinary. Developing a personal style that expressed that self became an essential interpersonal competence.

As the self became increasingly important to Americans, talking about the self became more and more acceptable. In earlier times, discussing one's most private thoughts and feelings was actually considered unacceptable and rude. Today we see it as a basic prerequisite for any healthy relationship. In fact, self-revelation is becoming an important source of entertainment as talk show hosts from Ricki Lake to Oprah have found out. Americans today love talking and hearing about intimate details of their own and others' lives. Knowing when and how to do so is an important social skill in the late 20th century. Self competence, like the other kinds of competence we have reviewed, is historically determined.

## History and Message Competence

As interpretive, role, goal, and self competence change, so too do the message choices we make. Over time, language itself takes on different forms and functions. Throughout this chapter we have included excerpts from 19th-century novels and letters, excerpts that have probably seemed unusually sentimental and florid to you. Most of us simply do not express ourselves in these ways today. The words and sentences we use nowadays are quite different in tone from those used in previous eras.

Nonverbal behaviors have also changed. We dress and move in a much freer and more open way today than ever before. We express emotions differently too. If, today, we were to use the kinds of nonverbal behaviors popular in either the colonial period or the 19th century, we would seem completely incompetent.

Finally our relational messages have undergone change as well. As the kinds of bonds we seek to forge with others have evolved, so too have our ways of sending relational messages. Although emotional bonding would appear to be a spontaneous and natural kind of communication, it, too, like every other form of competence, is deeply affected by context.

# Skill Building: Increasing Sensitivity to Context

In order to communicate effectively, you need to be aware of both historical and cultural contexts. Because it is difficult to predict the future, it is impossible to give specific guidelines for adapting to historical change. At this point all we can say is that the definition of successful communication is constantly changing as new technologies emerge and social conditions change. The more flexible and the more adaptable you can be, the better will be your communication.

It is somewhat easier to discuss cross-cultural skills. So in this section, we'll focus on adapting to cultural differences. We'll begin with some suggestions about how to increase competence in international situations and then offer some suggestions for handling subcultural contact.

## Adapting to International Differences

Many people find it hard to picture themselves in international contexts. Yet statistics show us that more and more people are crossing international borders every year. Here are some guidelines to help you adapt to this kind of communication situation and develop a "third culture" perspective.

1. *Prepare yourself ahead of time. Preparedness is an important aspect of successful adaptation.* While still in this country, read some books, take a course, or try to meet people from your host country. Ask them what you can expect. This knowledge will give you a sense of confidence and will impress host nationals with the effort you've made to understand their culture.

2. *When you travel abroad, expect differences in material culture.* In many countries housing, transportation, sanitation, food, and medical facilities may not meet the standards you are used to. Don't dismiss the importance of these differences, but don't let them overwhelm you either. Know that from time to time the lack of luxury and privacy will be frustrating. Don't take your frustration out on host nationals. Instead of complaining, see how they cope. Above all, practice patience.

3. *Realize that it is naturally stressful to be cut off from familiar customs and landmarks.* When you feel the stress of culture shock, take a break and relax. This may mean periods in which you withdraw a bit until you regain the equilibrium needed to explore your new environment. Give yourself occasional rest periods.

4. *Make friends with host nationals and ask them to introduce you to their culture.* Interpersonal contacts are an important source of information. Host nationals will usually be delighted to show you the ropes, and they can take you places you'd never have the courage to explore on your own. Your trip will be much more rewarding if you have made new friends.

5. *Realize that you will make mistakes.* From time to time you will violate norms of your new culture, and host nationals will undoubtedly violate some of your norms. Laugh off these mistakes and learn from them. If reactions to your behavior suddenly seem strained, ask someone what went wrong and discuss what you should have done instead. Similarly, if a new acquaintance violates one of your customs, explain the

violation in a nonjudgmental and nonthreatening way. Like other forms of communication, cross-cultural misunderstandings are best repaired by metacommunication.

**6.** *Develop an attitude of nonjudgmental curiosity.* While it is natural to see differences as "wrong," it is generally nonproductive. When you encounter a new custom, suspend your judgment and try to find out why the custom exists and how it functions within the culture. Instead of being a critic, be an observer. And remember the old proverb, "To understand all is to forgive all."

## Increasing Subcultural Understanding

Sometimes it seems that the misunderstandings we encounter in our own country are more difficult to correct than those between nations. Members of different subcultures can seem very foreign and very threatening to us. Yet there are some things we can do to increase our ability to understand subcultural communication differences.

**1.** *Open yourself up to new contacts.* As we have seen, prejudiced persons seldom have any direct contact with the targets of their prejudice. Stop for a minute and think about your own circle of friends. How many people do you know who come from a different racial, ethnic, or religious background than yours? If your answer is few or none, you are avoiding potentially rewarding experiences. The first step in increasing subcultural understanding is to make contact.

**2.** *Learn about the history and experiences of different subcultures.* Most people know a lot about the history, problems, and customs of their own or of majority groups and very little about those of other people. This tendency is very limiting. If you are fortunate enough to know people from other subcultures, take the time to ask them about their cultural heritage. If not, read or take courses. Most college campuses offer courses on the history, literature, and art of major subcultures. They also often have workshops on social problems of oppressed groups. Take advantage of these programs while you have the opportunity.

**3.** *Test your stereotypes.* All of us have prejudices of some kind. The person who proudly announces to the world, "I'm not at all prejudiced," probably is. The trick is to be aware of your prejudices. When you feel yourself being judgmental about out-group members, ask yourself why you feel this way and what effect it is having on you. Admit to yourself that you might be wrong, and try to see things more objectively.

**4.** *Develop empathy.* Don't assume that everyone in the world thinks and feels as you do. Observe other people and listen to what they are saying. Try mentally putting yourself in their place. Also be aware that careless comments can be potentially hurtful. Before you say something that might be offensive, ask yourself, "How would I feel if someone said that to me?"

**5.** *Work on becoming more self-confident.* If you feel insecure about yourself, you may use others as scapegoats, taking out your insecurities on them. The better you feel about yourself, the more likely you are to be able to feel good about other people and to be willing to learn from them.

# Process to Performance

## Review Terms

The following is a list of major concepts introduced in this chapter. The page where the concept is first mentioned is listed in parentheses.

culture   (373)
worldview   (374)
control cultures   (374)
constraint cultures   (374)
doing cultures   (375)
being cultures   (375)
M-time cultures   (375)
P-time cultures   (375)
individualist cultures   (376)
collectivist cultures   (376)
horizontal individualism   (377)
vertical individualism   (377)

horizontal collectivism   (377)
vertical collectivism   (377)
low-context cultures   (377)
high-context cultures   (377)
effort optimism   (377)
American English (AE)   (381)
African-American Vernacular English
   (AAVE)   (381)
Ebonics   (381)
call and response pattern   (383)
cross-cultural communication   (386)
prejudice   (388)
attitude   (388)
in-group member   (388)
out-group member   (388)
negative interpretations   (389)
discounting   (389)
fundamental attribution error   (389)
exaggeration   (389)
polarization   (390)
ethnocentrism   (391)
assumed similarity   (391)
equality norm   (394)
equity norm   (394)
colonial period   (395)
patriarchy   (396)
early industrial period   (397)
republican mother   (398)
character   (399)
modern period   (400)
personality   (402)
pluck   (404)
charm   (404)

## Suggested Readings

Samovar, Larry A., Richard E. Porter, and Edwin R. McDaniel. *Communication Between Cultures*, 6th ed. Belmont, Calif: Wadsworth, 2006. This popular text is an excellent introduction to the field of intercultural communication.

Smitherman, Geneva. *Word from the Mother: Language and African Americans*. (New York: Routledge, 2006. Smitherman is a wonderful writer, and in this book she gives an overview of debates about African-American language patterns, arguing convincingly that the speech of African Americans enriches general American English.

**Topics for Discussion**
www.oup.com/us/trenholm

### Observation Guide

1. Interview someone from a different culture. Explore differences in worldview, time and activity orientations, attitudes toward human nature and the individual self, and social organization. Analyze how these differences might affect communication. Ask your informant what difficulties he or she has encountered in your country.

2. If you are a fan of science fiction or utopian literature, take a favorite book and analyze the worldview of the major characters. How does the fictional culture described in the novel differ from your own? How would your communication have to change for you to fit in that world?

### Exercises

1. Often organizations on campus run programs to familiarize students with the problems of minority groups. Invite members of these groups to come to your class and conduct a workshop. If there are no such organizations on your campus, make it a class project to design programs that will increase understanding between majority and minority members.

2. Invite businesspersons or government employees who have worked abroad to attend class and discuss their experiences with you. If your campus has professors who act as consultants in intercultural matters, have them attend too.

3. Work in groups. Assume you have been given the task of putting together a list of guidelines that will help international students understand and adapt to american culture. Outline the issues you would address and what you would say about those issues. Also think about general ways international students could overcome "culture shock."

# References

## Chapter 1

1. Carl Sagan, ed., *Communication with Extraterrestrial Intelligence (CETI)* (Cambridge, Mass.: MIT Press, 1973), p. 344. This book is a transcript of a conference held in 1971 at Byurakan Astrophysical Observatory, Yerevan, USSR. While it is technically difficult, the chapters "Message Contents" and "The Consequences of Contact" are easy to follow and very illuminating.

2. See, for example, Cyril Ponnamperuma and A. G. W. Cameron, *Interstellar Communication: Scientific Perspectives* (Boston: Houghton Mifflin, 1974). For a more popular discussion, see Carl Sagan, *The Cosmic Connection: An Extraterrestrial Perspective* (Garden City, N.Y.: Anchor Press, Doubleday, 1973).

3. Sagan, *Cosmic Connection*, p. 42.

4. For an excellent history of the study of communication, see Nancy Harper, *Human Communication Theory: The History of a Paradigm* (Rochelle Park, N.J.: Hayden, 1979).

5. Frank E. X. Dance and Carl E. Larson, *Speech Communication: Concepts and Behavior* (New York: Holt, Rinehart & Winston, 1972).

6. S. S. Stevens, "A Definition of Communication," *The Journal of the Acoustical Society of America* 22 (1950): 689–90. Quoted in Frank E. X. Dance and Carl E. Larson, *The Functions of Human Communication* (New York: Holt, Rinehart & Winston, 1976), p. 25.

7. Dean Barnlund, *Interpersonal Communication: Survey and Studies* (Boston: Houghton Mifflin, 1968), p. 6. Quoted in Dance and Larson, *Functions*, p. 25.

8. John T. Masterson, Steven A. Beebe, and Norman H. Watson, *Speech Communication: Theory and Practice* (New York: Holt, Rinehart & Winston, 1983), p. 5.

9. Bernard Berelson and Gary A. Steiner, *Human Behavior: An Inventory of Scientific Findings* (New York: Harcourt Brace Jovanovich, 1964), p. 527. Quoted in Dance and Larson, *Functions*, p. 24.

10. Sarah Trenholm, *Human Communication Theory* (Englewood Cliffs, N.J.: Prentice-Hall, 1986), pp.4–5.

11. Aldous Huxley, "Words and Their Meanings," in *The Importance of Language,* ed. Max Black (Englewood Cliffs, N.J.: Prentice-Hall, 1962), pp. 4–5.

12. Joost A. M. Meerloo, "Contributions of Psychiatry to the Study of Human Communication," in *Human Communication Theory: Original Essays,* ed. Frank E. X. Dance (New York: Holt, Rinehart & Winston, 1967), p. 132.

13. Ibid.

14. Clifford Geertz, "Deep Play: Notes on the Balinese Cockfight," in *Myth, Symbol and Culture,* ed. Clifford Geertz (New York: Norton, 1971), p. 7.

15. John C. Condon, "When People Talk with People," in *Messages: A Reader in Human Communication,* 3rd ed., ed. Sanford B. Weinberg (New York: Random House, 1980), p. 58.

16. Erving Goffman, "On Face-Work," in *Interaction Ritual,* ed. Erving Goffman (Garden City, N.Y.: Anchor Books, 1967).

17. Ibid., p. 10.

18. Donald J. Cegala, "Interaction Involvement: A Cognitive Dimension of Communicative Competence," *Communication Education* 30 (1981): 109–21; Brian H. Spitzberg and Michael L. Hecht, "A Component Model of Relational Competence," *Human Communication Research* 10 (1984): 575–99; John M. Weimann, "Explication and Test of a Model of Communicative Competence," *Human Communication Research* 3 (1977): 195–213; David R. Brandt, "On Linking Social Performance with Social Competence: Some Relations Between Communicative Style and Attribution of Interpersonal Attractiveness and Effectiveness," *Human Communication Research* 5 (1979): 233–37.

19. Dell H. Hymes, "On Communicative Competence," in *Sociolinguistics,* ed. J. B. Pride and Janet Holmes (Harmondsworth, England: Penguin, 1972), pp. 269–93; Ruth Ann Clark and Jesse G. Delia, "Topoi and Rhetorical Competence," *The Quarterly Journal of Speech* 65 (1979): 187–206.

20. Stephen W. Littlejohn and David M. Jabush, "Communication Competence: Model and Application," *Journal of Applied Communication Research* 10 (1982): 29–37; Brian H. Spitzberg, "Communication Competence as Knowledge, Skill, and Impression," *Communication Education* 32 (1983): 323–29.

21. Clark and Delia, "Topoi."

22. John A. Bargh and Katelyn Y. A. McKenna, "The Internet and Social Life," *Annual Review of Psychology* 55 (2004): 573–90.

**23.** Robert D. Putnam, "Bowling Alone: The Collapse and Revival of American Community" (New York: Simon & Schuster, 2000); Bargh and McKenna also offer a discussion of Putnam's research on p. 577.

**24.** Tom Standage, *The Victorian Internet: The Remarkable Story of the Telegraph and the Nineteenth Century's On-line Pioneers* (New York: Berkley Books, 1998), pp. 129–42.

**25.** Bargh and McKenna, p. 576.

**26.** Ibid., 576. For the original story, see Reuters, "Miss France Not a Man," April 27, 2001.

**27.** Nancy K. Baym. "Interpersonal Life Online," in *Handbook of New Media: Social Shaping and Social Consequences of ICTs, Updated Student Edition,* ed. Leah A. Lievrouw and Sonia Livingston (Thousand Oaks, Calif.: Sage Publications, 2006), pp. 35–52. For more information about how young people are using new media, see Amanda Lenhart, Mary Madden, and Paul Hitlin, "Teens and Technology: Youth Are Leading the Transition to a Fully Wired and Mobile Nation" (Washington, D.C.: Pew Internet & American Life Project, July 2005), pp. 1–33. Retrieved September 20, 2005, from http://www.pewinternet.org/PPF/ r?162/report_display.asp.

**28.** Sadie Plant, "On the Mobile: The Effects of Mobile Telephones on Social and Individual Life, pp. 1–85; quote p. 64. Retrieved July 5, 2006, from http://www.motorola.com/mot/doc/0/234_MotDoc.pdf. For a discussion of mobile telephone text-messaging, see Crispin Thurlow, "Generation txt? The Sociolinguistics of Young People's Text-Messaging." Retrieved September 20, 2005, from http://www.shu.ac.uk/daol/articles/v1/n1/a3/thurlow2002003-paper.html.

## Chapter 2

**1.** For a discussion of the form of "inner speech," see Lev Semenovich Vygotsky, *Thought and Language,* ed. and trans. Eugenia Hanfmann and Gertrude Vakar (Cambridge, Mass.: MIT Press, 1962). An interesting source for a discussion of the elliptical and condensed quality of intrapersonal communication is Sigmund Freud, *The Interpretation of Dreams,* ed. and trans. James Strachey (New York: Avon Books, 1965).

**2.** William W. Wilmot, *Dyadic Communication,* 2nd ed. (Reading, Mass.: Addison-Wesley, 1979), p. 19.

**3.** For an interesting discussion of organizational culture, see Ernest G. Bormann, "Symbolic Convergence: Organizational Communication and Culture," in *Communication and Organizations: An Interpretive Approach,* ed. Linda L. Putnam and Michael E. Pacanowsky (Beverly Hills, Calif.: Sage, 1983).

**4.** Robert Cathcart and Gary Gumpert, "Mediated Interpersonal Communication: Toward a New Typology," *Quarterly Journal of Speech* 69 (1983): 267–77.

**5.** Sarah Trenholm, *Human Communication Theory* (Englewood Cliffs, N.J.: Prentice-Hall, 1986), pp.17–18.

**6.** Gerald R. Miller, "The Current Status of Theory and Research in Interpersonal Communication," *Human Communication Research* 4 (1978): 164–78.

**7.** Gerald R. Miller and Mark Steinberg, *Between People: A New Analysis of Interpersonal Communication* (Chicago: Science Research Associates, 1975), p. 22.

**8.** See, for example, John Shotter, *Cultural Politics of Everyday Life: Social Constructionism, Rhetoric, and Knowing of the Third Kind* (Toronto: University of Toronto Press, 1993). For an early, classic formulation of the importance of joint interaction, see Paul Watzlawick, Janet Beavin, and Don D. Jackson, *Pragmatics of Human Communication* (New York: Norton, 1967).

**9.** See, for example, Peter A. Andersen, "Cognitive Schemata in Personal Relationships," and James M. Honeycutt, "Memory Structures for the Rise and Fall of Personal Relationships," in *Individuals in Relationships,* ed. Steve Duck (Newbury Park, Calif.: Sage, 1993).

**10.** See, for example, William Wilmot, *Relational Communication* (New York: McGraw-Hill, 1995). See also T. L. Morton and M. A. Douglas, "Growth of Relationship," in *Personal Relationships,* vol. 11, ed. Steve Duck and R. Gilmour (New York: Academic Press, 1981), pp. 3–26; Kenneth Gergen, *Realities and Relationships: Soundings in Social Construction* (Cambridge, Mass.: Harvard University Press, 1994).

**11.** See, for example, Leslie A. Baxter and Barbara M. Montgomery, *Relating: Dialogues and Dialectics* (New York: The Guilford Press, 1996); William K. Rawlins, *Friendship Matters: Communication, Dialectics, and the Life Course* (New York: Aldine de Gruyter, 1992).

**12.** Wilmot, *Relational Communication,* p. 3.

**13.** Wilmot, *Dyadic Communication,* pp. 9 10.

**14.** Shotter, *Cultural Politics,* 1993.

**15.** W. Barnett Pearce, *Interpersonal Communication: Making Social Worlds* (New York: HarperCollins, 1994), p. 76.

**16.** Andersen, "Cognitive Schemata in Personal Relationships," in *Individuals in Relationships,* p. 9.

**17.** Honeycutt, "Memory Structures for the Rise and Fall of Personal Relationships," in *Individuals in Relationships,* pp. 60–86. For a discussion of MOPs, see R. C. Shank, *Dynamic Memory: A Theory of Reminding and Learning in Computers and People* (Cambridge: Cambridge University Press, 1982).

**18.** Honeycutt, "Memory Structures," p. 63.

**19.** Wilmot, *Relational Communication,* p. 19.

**20.** William W. Wilmot and Leslie A. Baxter, "The Relationship Schemata Model: On Linking Relationships and Communication." Paper presented to the Western Speech Communication Association Convention, Spokane, WA, 1989.

**21.** Niall Bolger and Shannon Kelleher, "Daily Life in Relationships," in *Social Context and Relationships,* ed. Steve Duck (Newbury Park, Calif.: Sage, 1993), pp. 100–108.

**22.** Niall Bolger et al., "The Contagion of Stress Across Multiple Roles," *Journal of Marriage and the Family* 51 (1989): 175–183.

**23.** Bolger, "Daily Life," p. 104. See also J. Mirowsky and C. E. Ross, "Social Patterns of Distress," *Annual Review of Sociology* 12 (1986): 23–45.

**24.** Wilmot, *Relational Communication,* p. 4. The quote is from C. Humphreys, *Buddhism* (Harmondsworth, England: Penguin Books, 1951).

**25.** Arthur P. Bochner, "The Functions of Human Communication in Interpersonal Bonding," in *Handbook of Rhetorical and Communication Theory,* ed. Carroll C. Arnold and John Waite Bowers (Boston: Allyn and Bacon, 1984), p. 547.

**26.** William K. Rawlins, "Openness as Problematic in Ongoing Friendships: Two Conversational Dilemmas," *Communication Monographs* 50 (1983): 1–13, and "Negotiating Close Friendship: The Dialectic of Conjunctive Freedoms," *Human Communication Research* 9 (1983): 255–66.

**27.** The tendency of our culture to desire intimacy in all relationships has been discussed by a number of historians and social critics. See, for example, Howard Gadlin, "Private Lives and Public Order: A Critical View of the History of Intimate Relations in the United States," in *Close Relationships: Perspectives on the Meaning of Intimacy,* ed. George Levinger and Harold L. Raush (Amherst: University of Massachusetts Press, 1977), pp. 33–72; Christopher Lasch, *The Culture of Narcissism* (New York: Norton, 1978); Robert N. Bellah and others, *Habits of the Heart: Individualism and Commitment in American Life* (Berkeley and Los Angeles: University of California Press, 1985); Judith Martin, *Common Courtesy* (New York: Atheneum, 1985).

**28.** Judee K. Burgoon, "Privacy and Communication," in *Communication Yearbook* 6, ed. Michael Burgoon (Beverly Hills, Calif.: Sage, 1982), p. 225.

**29.** Ibid., p. 225.

**30.** Steve Duck, "Our Friends, Ourselves," in *Bridges Not Walls: A Book About Interpersonal Communication,* 6th ed., ed. John Stewart (New York: McGraw-Hill, 1995), p. 312. This article is an excerpt from Chapter 1 of Duck's *Understanding Relationships* (New York: The Guilford Press, 1991).

**31.** Our discussion of relational competence is loosely adapted from the work of Linda Harris. In explaining her model, however, we have omitted its theoretical grounding in CMM theory. For a fuller understanding of her model, see Linda Harris, "Communication Competence: An Argument for a Systemic View," unpublished paper, Department of Communication Studies, University of Massachusetts, 1979.

**32.** Julia T. Wood, "Engendered Relations: Interaction, Caring, Power, and Responsibility in Intimacy," in *Social Context and Relationships* (Newbury Park, Calif.: Sage, 1993), pp. 26–54.

**33.** Graham Allan, "Social Structures and Relationships," in *Social Context and Relationships,* ed. Steve Duck (Newbury Park, Calif.: Sage, 1993), p. 7.

## Chapter 3

**1.** Frances Mayes, *Under the Tuscan Sun: At Home in Italy* (New York: Broadway Books, 1996), pp. 63–67.

**2.** Judee Burgoon and Thomas Saine, *The Unspoken Dialogue: An Introduction to Nonverbal Communication* (Boston: Houghton Mifflin, 1978), pp. 6–10.

**3.** Ross Buck, *The Communication of Emotion* (New York: Guilford Press, 1984).

**4.** C. Wedekind and S. Furi, "Body Odor Preferences in Men and Women: Do They Aim for Specific MHC Combinations or Simply Heterozygosity?" *Proceedings of the Royal Society of London, Series B,* 260 (1997): 245–49.

**5.** Desmond Morris, *Manwatching: A Field Guide to Human Behavior* (New York: Abrams, 1977), pp.86–91.

**6.** Paul Ekman and Wallace Friesen, *Unmasking the Face: A Guide to Recognizing Emotions from Facial Expressions* (Englewood Cliffs, N.J.: Prentice-Hall, 1975).

**7.** Albert Mehrabian, *Nonverbal Communication* (Chicago: Aldine-Atherton, 1972), p. 2.

**8.** Daphne E. Bugental, Jacques W. Kaswan, Leonore R. Love, and Michael N. Fox, "Child Versus Adult Perception of Evaluative Messages in Verbal, Vocal, and Visual Channels," *Developmental Psychology* 2 (1970): 367–75.

**9.** Jeffrey G. Shapiro, "Responsivity to Facial and Linguistic Cues," *Journal of Communication* 18 (1968): 11–17. See also Leon Vande Creek and John T. Watkins, "Responses to Incongruent Verbal and Nonverbal Emotional Cues," *Journal of Communication* 22 (1972): 311–16.

**10.** Miles Patterson, *Nonverbal Behavior: A Functional Perspective* (New York: Springer-Verlag, 1983), p. 9.

**11.** Dale Leathers, *Successful Nonverbal Communication: Principles and Applications,* 3rd ed. (Boston: Allyn and Bacon, 1997).

**12.** Laura K. Guerrero and Kory Floyd, *Nonverbal Communication in Close Relationships* (Mahwah, N.J.: Lawrence Earlbaum, 2006), pp. 57–83.

**13.** Marvin Zuckerman and R. E. Driver, "What Sounds Beautiful Is Good: The Vocal Attractiveness Stereotype," *Journal of Nonverbal Behavior* 13 (1998): 67–82.

**14.** Ashley Montagu and Floyd Matson, *The Human Connection* (New York: McGraw-Hill, 1979), p. 17.

**15.** Abraham Maslow and Norbert L. Mintz, "Effects of Esthetic Surroundings I: Initial Effects of Three Esthetic Conditions upon Perceiving 'Energy' and 'Well-Being' in Faces," *Journal of Psychology* 41 (1956): 247–54.

**16.** See, for example, Mark L. Knapp, *Nonverbal Communication in Human Interaction* (New York: Holt, Rinehart & Winston, 1978), pp. 83–113; Lawrence Rosenfeld and Jean Civikly, *With Words Unspoken: The Nonverbal Experience* (New York: Holt, Rinehart & Winston, 1976), pp. 161–85.

**17.** Steven Kaplan, Rachel Kaplan, and John S. Wendt, "Rated Preference and Complexity for Natural and Urban Visual Material," *Perception and Psychophysics* 12 (1972): 334–56.

**18.** Albert Mehrabian and James Russell, *An Approach to Environmental Psychology* (Cambridge, Mass.: MIT Press, 1974).

19. Rosenfeld and Civikly, *With Words Unspoken,* p.147.

20. Stanford Lyman and Marvin Scott, "Territoriality: A Neglected Social Dimension," *Social Problems*15 (1967): 235–49.

21. Edward T. Hall, *The Silent Language* (New York: Doubleday, 1959).

22. Edward T. Hall, *The Hidden Dimension* (Garden City, N.Y.: Doubleday, 1969), pp. 133–34.

23. Edward T. Hall, *Beyond Culture* (Garden City, N.Y.: Anchor Press, 1970).

24. For a summary of this research, see Burgoon and Saine, *The Unspoken Dialogue,* pp. 93–94.

25. Laura K. Guerrero and S. M. Jones, "Differences in Conversational Skills as a Function of Attachment Style: A Follow-up Study," *Communication Quarterly* 53 (2005): 305–21.

26. Paul Ekman and Wallace Friesen, "The Repertoire of Nonverbal Behavior: Categories, Origins, Usage, and Coding," *Semiotica* 1 (1969): 49–98.

27. Morris, *Manwatching,* pp. 50–51.

28. Adam Kendon, "Some Functions of Gaze-Direction in Social Interaction," *Acta Psychologica* 26 (1967): 22–63.

29. Ekman and Friesen, *Unmasking the Face,* p. 40 and p. 52.

30. For a brief review, see D. R. Rutter, *Looking and Seeing: The Role of Visual Communication in Social Interaction* (Chichester, England: Wiley, 1984), pp.49–54.

31. P. C. Ellsworth, "The Meaningful Look," *Semiotica* 24 (1978): 15–20; Miles Patterson, "An Arousal Model of Inter personal Intimacy," *Psychological Review* 83 (1976): 235–45.

32. Irenaus Eibl-Eibesfeldt, "Similarities and Differences Between Cultures in Expressive Movements," in *Nonverbal Communication,* ed. Robert Hinde (Cambridge: Cambridge University Press, 1972), pp. 297–312.

33. Michael Argyle, Mansur Lalljee, and Mark Cook, "The Effects of Visibility on Interaction in a Dyad," *Human Relations* 21 (1968): 3–17.

34. Clara Mayo and Marianne LaFrance, "Gaze Direction in Interracial Dyadic Communication," paper presented at the annual meeting of the Eastern Psychological Association, Washington, D.C., 1973. Cited in Clara Mayo and Nancy Henley, eds., *Gender and Nonverbal Behavior* (New York: Springer-Verlag, 1981).

35. Rutter, *Looking and Seeing.*

36. Ibid.

37. G. B.Ray and Kory Floyd, "Nonverbal Expressions of Liking and Disliking in Initial Interaction: Encoding and Decoding Perspectives," paper presented at the annual conference of the Eastern Communication Association (May 2000), Pittsburgh; Kory Floyd and G. B. Ray, "Human Affection Exchange IV: Vocalic Predictors of Perceived Affection in Initial Interactions," *Western Journal of Communication* 67 (2003): 56–73.

38. Ekman and Friesen, *Unmasking the Face.*

39. For a review of these studies, see Judith Hall, *Nonverbal Sex Differences: Communication Accuracy and Expressive Style* (Baltimore: Johns Hopkins University Press, 1984), pp. 59–84.

40. James G. Martin, "Racial Ethnocentrism and Judgments of Beauty," *Journal of Social Psychology* 63 (1964): 59–63; A. H. Illife, "A Study of Preferences in Feminine Beauty," *British Journal of Psychology* 51 (1960): 267–73.

41. Elaine Walster, Vera Aronson, Darcy Abrahams, and Leon Rottman, "Importance of Physical Attractiveness in Dating Behavior," *Journal of Personality and Social Psychology* 4 (1966): 508–16.

42. James E. Maddux and Ronald W. Rogers, "Effects of Source Expertness, Physical Attractiveness, and Supporting Arguments on Persuasion: A Case of Brains over Beauty," *Journal of Personality and Social Psychology* 39 (1980): 235–44.

43. Morris, *Manwatching,* p. 282.

44. D. Symons, *The Evolution of Human Sexuality* (New York: Oxford University Press, 1979).

45. See Guerrero and Floyd, *Nonverbal Communication in Close Relationships,* pp. 64–65.

46. Ibid, pp. 65–68.

47. See, for example, L. Aiken, "Relationships of Dress to Selected Measures of Personality in Undergraduate Women," *Journal of Social Psychology* 59 (1963): 119–28; Lawrence Rosenfeld and Timothy G. Plax, "Clothing as Communication," *Journal of Communication* 27 (1977): 24–31; Mary B. Harris and Hortensia Baudin, "The Language of Altruism: The Effects of Language, Dress, and Ethnic Group," *Journal of Social Psychology* 91 (1973): 37–41.

48. Thomas F. Hoult, "Experimental Measurement of Clothing as a Factor in Some Social Ratings of Selected American Men," *American Sociological Review* 19 (1954): 324–28.

49. G. L. Trager, "Paralanguage: A First Approximation," *Studies in Linguistics* 13 (1958): 1–12.

50. David W. Addington, "The Relationship of Selected Vocal Characteristics to Personality Perception," *Speech Monographs* 35 (1968): 492–503.

51. James McCroskey, Carl E. Larson, and Mark Knapp, *An Introduction to Interpersonal Communication* (Englewood Cliffs, N.J.: Prentice-Hall, 1971), p. 117.

52. Susan Milmoe, Robert Rosenthal, Howard T. Blane, Morris E. Chafetz, and Irving Wolf, "The Doctor's Voice: Postdictor of Successful Referral of Alcoholic Patients," *Journal of Abnormal Psychology* 72 (1967): 78–84.

53. David M. Buss, "Human Mate Guarding," *Neuroendocrinology Letters* 23 (2002): 23–29.

54. K. L. Egland, M. A. Stelzner, P. A. Andersen, and B. H. Spitzberg, "Perceived Understanding, Nonverbal Communication, and Relational Satisfaction, in *Intrapersonal Communication Processes,* ed. J. Aitken and L. Shedletsky (Annandale, Va.: Speech Communication Association, 1997), pp. 386–95.

55. R. A. Baron, "Olfaction and Human Social Behavior: Effects of Pleasant Scent on Attraction and Social Perception," *Personality and Social Psychology Bulletin* 7 (1981): 611–16;

R. K. Aune, "The Effects of Perfume Use on Perceptions of Attractiveness and Competence, in *The Nonverbal Communication Reader: Classic and Con-temporary Readings,* 2nd ed., ed. L. K. Guerro, J. A. Devito, and M. L. Hecht (Prospect Heights, Ill.: Waveland Press, 1999), pp. 126–32.

56. Ashley Montagu, *Touching: The Human Significance of the Skin* (New York: Columbia University Press, 1971).

57. Brenda Major, "Gender Patterns in Touching Behavior," in *Gender and Nonverbal Behavior,* pp. 15–37.

58. Richard Heslin, "Steps Toward a Taxonomy of Touching," paper presented at the annual meeting of the Midwestern Psychological Association, Chicago, 1974.

59. Major, "Gender Patterns," p. 33.

60. Nancy Henley, "Status and Sex: Some Touching Observations," *Bulletin of the Psychonomic Society* 2 (1973): 91–93.

61. Judee K. Burgoon, "A Communication Model of Personal Space Violations: Explication and an Initial Test," *Human Communication Research* 4 (1978): 129–42; Judee K. Burgoon and B. A. LePoire, "Effects on Communication Expectancies, Actual Communication, and Expectancy Disconfirmation on Evaluations of Communicators and Their Communication Behavior," *Human Communication Research* 20 (1993): 75–107.

62. Judee K. Burgoon and Jerold L. Hale, "Nonverbal Expectancy Violations: Model Elaboration and Applicability to Immediacy Behaviors," *Communication Monographs* 55 (1988): 58–79.

63. W. A. Afifi and Sandra Metts, "Characteristics and Consequences of Expectation Violations in Close Relationships," *Journal of Social and Personal Relationships* 15 (1998): 365–92.

64. Laura K. Guerrero, S. M. Jones, and Judee K. Burgoon, "Responses to Nonverbal Intimacy Change in Romantic Dyads: Effects of Behavioral Valence and Degree of Behavioral Change on Nonverbal and Verbal Reactions," *Communication Monographs* 67 (2000): 325–46.

65. Peter Andersen, "Nonverbal Immediacy in Interpersonal Communication," in A. W. Siegman and S. Feldstein (eds), *Multichannel Integrations of Nonverbal Behavior.* (Hillsdale, N.J.: Erlbaum, 1985), pp. 1–36; Peter Andersen, "A Cognitive Valence Theory of Intimate Communication," paper presented at the annual conference of the International Network on Personal Relationships Conference, Iowa City, IA, 1989; L. Wertin and Peter Andersen, "Cognitive Schemata and Perceptions of Sexual Harassment," paper presented at the annual conference of the Western States Communication Association, Pasadena, Calif., 1996.

66. Wertin and Andersen, "*Cognitive Schemata ...;*" Laura K. Guerrero, "A Test of Cognitive Valence Theory," manuscript in preparation, 2005. Cited in Guerrero and Kory Floyd, *Nonverbal Communication in Close Relationships,* p. 46.

67. James Averill, "A Constructivist View of Emotion," in *Emotion: Theory, Research, and Experience,* Vol. 1, ed. R. Plutchik and H. Kellerman (New York: Academic Press, 1980), pp. 305–39.

68. Richard Buttny, "The Discourse of Affect Display in Social Accountability Practices," paper presented at the International Communication Association annual convention, Chicago, 1991.

69. Example cited in ibid., pp. 20–21, and slightly modified for use here.

70. Ronald Adler, *Confidence in Communication: A Guide to Assertive and Social Skills* (New York: Holt, Rinehart & Winston, 1977), p. 178.

71. Janet Beavin Bavelas, Alex Black, Nicole Chovil, and Jennifer Mullett, *Equivocal Communication* (Newbury Park, Calif.: Sage, 1990).

72. Jane Austen, *Sense and Sensibility,* 2nd ed. (Oxford: Oxford University Press, 1982, 1811).

73. Lawrence M. Brammer, *The Helping Relationship: Process and Skills* (Englewood Cliffs, N.J.: Prentice-Hall, 1973), pp. 90–93.

# Chapter 4

1. Helen Keller, *The Story of My Life* (Garden City, N.Y.: Doubleday, 1905), p. 36.

2. Daniel J. Boorstin, *The Discoverers* (New York; Vintage Books, 1983), Book One: Time.

3. For a nice summary of the differences between verbal and nonverbal codes, see Judee K. Burgoon and Thomas Saine, *The Unspoken Dialogue: An Introduction to Nonverbal Communication* (Boston: Houghton Mifflin, 1978), pp. 18–20.

4. For an attempt at a structuralist breakdown of nonverbal behavior, see Ray L. Birdwhistell, *Introduction to Kinesics* (Louisville: University of Kentucky Press, 1952), and *Kinesics and Context* (Philadelphia: University of Pennsylvania Press, 1970); for a critique of this attempt, see Allen T. Ditmann, "Review of Kinesics in Context," *Psychiatry* 34 (1971): 334–42.

5. Umberto Eco, *A Theory of Semiotics* (Bloomington: University of Indiana Press, 1976), p. 7.

6. Our list is a composite made up of functions suggested by the following authors: Joost A. M. Meerloo, "Contributions of Psychiatry to the Study of Communication," in *Human Communication Theory: Original Essays,* ed. Frank E. X. Dance (New York: Holt, Rinehart & Winston, 1967), pp. 130–59; Roman Jakobson, "Closing Statement: Linguistics and Poetics," in *Style in Language,* ed. Thomas Sebeok (Cambridge, Mass.: MIT Press, 1960), pp.350–77; and Dell Hymes, "The Ethnography of Speaking," in *Readings in the Sociology of Language,* ed. Joshua Fishman (The Hague: Mouton, 1968), pp.99–138.

7. Sigmund Freud, *Introductory Lectures on Psychoanalysis,* trans. and ed. James Strachey (New York: Norton, 1966), pp. 25–79.

8. For a full discussion of the relationship between language and uncertainty, see Charles R. Berger and James J. Bradac, *Language and Social Knowledge: Uncertainty Reduction in Interpersonal Relations* (London: Edward Arnold, 1982).

**9.** Michael Stubbs, *Discourse Analysis: The Sociolinguistic Analysis of Natural Language* (Chicago: University of Chicago Press, 1983), pp. 48–49.

**10.** If you are not familiar with language structure, you may find Frederick Williams, *Language and Speech: Introductory Perspectives* (Englewood Cliffs, N.J.: Prentice-Hall, 1972), a useful introduction to the subject.

**11.** *Webster's Third New International Dictionary* (Springfield, Mass.: Merriam-Webster, 1981).

**12.** Dan I. Slobin, *Psycholinguistics* (Glenview, Ill.: Scott Foresman, 1971), p. 96.

**13.** John R. Searle, *Speech Acts: An Essay in the Philosophy of Language* (Cambridge: Cambridge University Press, 1969).

**14.** CMM theory is one of the most popular of recent communication theories; there are many articles on the subject. We suggest you try W. Barnett Pearce, Vernon E. Cronen, and Forrest Conklin, "On What to Look at When Analyzing Communication: A Hierarchical Model of Actors' Meanings," *Communication* 4 (1979): 195–220, and Vernon E. Cronen and W. Barnett Pearce, "Logical Force in Interpersonal Communication: A New Concept of the 'Necessity' in Social Behaviors," *Communication* 6 (1981): 5–67. For an overview and bibliography, see Vernon E. Cronen, W. Barnett Pearce, and Linda M. Harris, "The Coordinated Management of Meaning: A Theory of Communication," in *Human Communication Theory: Comparative Essays,* ed. Frank E. X. Dance (New York: Harper & Row, 1982), pp. 61–89.

**15.** Edward Sapir, *Selected Writings of Edward Sapir in Language, Culture and Personality* (Berkeley and Los Angeles: University of California Press, 1958), and Benjamin Lee Whorf, *Language, Thought and Reality* (Cambridge, Mass.: MIT Press, 1966).

**16.** Sapir, *Selected Writings,* p. 162.

**17.** Henry Allan Gleason, Jr., *An Introduction to Descriptive Linguistics,* rev. ed. (New York: Holt, Rinehart & Winston, 1961), p. 4.

**18.** Slobin, *Psycholinguistics,* p. 125.

**19.** Whorf, *Language, Thought and Reality,* p. 240.

**20.** Ibid., p. 243.

**21.** Julia T. Wood, *Gendered Lives: Communication, Gender, and Culture* (Belmont, Calif.: Wadsworth, 1994), p. 130; Julia T. Wood, "Defining and Studying Sexual Harassment as Situated Experience," in Gary Kreps, ed., *Communication and Sexual Harassment in the Workplace* (Cresskill, N.J.: Hampton Press, 1993).

**22.** Basil Bernstein, ed., *Class, Codes and Control,* Vol. 2 (London: Routledge and Kegan Paul, 1973).

**23.** The sample dialogue is taken from Raymond S. Ross and Mark G. Ross, *Relating and Interacting* (Englewood Cliffs, N.J.: Prentice-Hall, 1982), p. 93.

**24.** Two useful reviews of the early studies can be found in Chapters 2 and 3 of Barbara Westbrook Eakins and R. Gene Eakins, *Sex Differences in Human Communication* (Boston: Houghton Mifflin, 1978), and in Chapter 6 in Judy Cornelia Pearson, *Gender and Communication* (Dubuque, Iowa: Brown, 1985).

**25.** Laurie Arliss also provides a review, *Gender Communication* (Englewood Cliffs, N.J.: Prentice-Hall, 1991).

**26.** See, for example, Deborah Tannen, *You Just Don't Understand: Women and Men in Conversation* (New York: Ballantine, 1990), and Daniel N. Maltz and Ruth A. Borker, "A Cultural Approach to Male-Female Miscommunication," in *Language and Social Identity,* ed. John J. Gumperz (Cambridge: Cambridge University Press, 1982).

**27.** Candace West and Don Zimmerman, "Small Insults: A Study of Interruptions in Cross-Sex Conversations Between Unacquainted Persons," in *Language, Gender and Society,* ed. Barrie Thorne, Cheris Kramarae, and Nancy Henley (Rowley, Mass.: Newbery House, 1983), pp. 102–17; West and Zimmerman, "Doing Gender," *Gender and Society* 1, no. 2 (1987): 125–51.

**28.** The original impetus for much of the work on these and the following variables began with Robin Lakoff, *Language and Woman's Place* (New York: Harper and Row, 1975).

**29.** The findings on tag endings are somewhat mixed. A large number of studies report that women use more tag endings than do men. These include Janet Holmes, "Women's Language: A Functional Approach," *General Linguistics* 24, no. 3 (1984): 149–78; Janet Holmes, "Sex Differences and Mis-communication: Some Data from New Zealand," in *Cross-cultural Encounters. Communication and Miscommunication,* ed. J. B. Pride (Melbourne: River Seine Publications, 1985), pp. 24–43; Anthony Mulac and Torborg L. Lundell, "Linguistic Contributions to the Gender-linked Language Effect," *Journal of Language and Social Psychology* 5, no. 2 (1986): 81–101; Bent Preisler, *Linguistic Sex Roles in Conversation* (Berlin: Mouton de Gruyter, 1986); Linda Carli, "Gender, Language, and Influence," *Journal of Personality and Social Psychology* 59 (1990): 941–51. Other studies, however, have found no effect or the opposite. Deborah Cameron, F. McAlinden, and K. O'Leary, "Lakoff in Context: The Social and Linguistic Function of Tag Questions," in *Women in Their Speech Communities: New Perspectives on Language and Sex,* ed. J. Coates and D. Cameron (New York: Longman, 1988), pp. 74–93; Betty Lou Dubois and Isabel Crouch, "The Question of Tag Questions in Women's Speech: They Don't Really Use More of Them, Do They?" *Language in Society* 4 (1975): 289–94; Judy Lapadat and Maureen Seesahai, "Male Versus Female Codes in Informal Contexts," *Sociolinguistic Newsletter* 8 (1977): 7–8; M. Baumann, "Two Features of 'Women's Speech?" in *Proceedings of the Conference on the Sociology of the Languages of American Women,* ed. B. L. Dubois and I. Crouch (San Antonio, Tex.: Trinity University Press, 1976, pp. 33–40.

**30.** Elizabeth Aries, *Men and Women in Interaction: Reconsidering the Differences* (New York: Oxford University Press, 1996), p. 179; Mulac and Lundell, "Linguistic Contributions"; Carli, "Gender, Language, and Influence."

**31.** Patricia Bradley, "The Folk-Linguistics of Women's Speech: An Empirical Examination," *Communication Monographs* 48 (1981): 73–90.

**32.** Deborah Tannen, *You Just Don't Understand: Women and Men in Conversation* (New York: Balantine Books, 1991).

**33.** Aries, *Men and Women in Interaction*, p. 28. See also Fred L. Strodtbeck and R. D. Mann, "Sex Role Differentiation in Jury Deliberations," *Sociometry* 19 (1956): 3–11. For a critique of the original study, see Lynn R. Anderson and P. Nick Blanchard, "Sex Differences in Task and Social-emotional Behavior," *Basic and Applied Social Psychology* 3, no. 2 (1981): 109–39.

**34.** Robert K. Leik, "Instrumentality and Emotionality in Family Interaction," *Sociometry* 26 (1963): 131–45; Jerold Heiss, "Degree of Intimacy and Male-Female Interaction," *Sociometry* 25 (1962): 197–08.

**35.** Aries, *Men and Women in Interaction*, p. 16.

**36.** Ibid., p. viii.

**37.** Cathryn Johnson, "Gender, Legitimate Authority and Leader-Subordinate Conversations," *American Sociological Review* 59 (1994): 122–35.

**38.** Deborah Tannen, *Gender and Discourse* (New York: Oxford University Press, 1994), p. 60.

**39.** Holmes, "Women's Language"; Cameron, "Lakoff in Context."

**40.** Carol Gilligan, *In a Different Voice* (Cambridge, Mass.: Harvard University Press, 1982).

**41.** Littlejohn, *Theories of Human Communication*, p. 241; see also Dale Spender, *Man Made Language* (London: Routledge & Kegan Paul, 1980), pp.76–105.

**42.** Eakins and Eakins, *Sex Differences in Communication*, p. 121.

**43.** Ibid., p. 120.

**44.** Ibid., p. 141.

**45.** Robin Lakoff, "Language and Women's Place," *Language in Society* 2 (1973): 45–80.

**46.** See Alan Garner, *Conversationally Speaking: Testing New Ways to Increase Your Personal and Social Effectiveness* (New York: McGraw Hill, 1981); and Sharon A. Ratliffe and David D. Hudson, *Skill-Building for Interpersonal Competence* (New York: Holt, Rinehart & Winston, 1988).

**47.** Mark L. Knapp and others, "The Rhetoric of Goodbye: Verbal and Nonverbal Correlates of Human Leave-Taking," *Speech Monographs* 40 (August 1973): 182–98.

**48.** S. I. Hayakawa, *Language in Thought and Action*, 3rd ed. (New York: Harcourt, Brace, Jovanovich, 1972).

## Chapter 5

**1.** Paul Watzlawick, Janet Beavin Bavelas, and Don D. Jackson, *Pragmatics of Human Communication* (New York: Norton, 1967), p. 52.

**2.** Ibid., p. 51. See also Jurgen Ruesch and Gregory Bateson, *Communication: The Social Matrix of Psychiatry* (New York: Norton, 1951), pp. 179–81.

**3.** Watzlawick et al., *Pragmatics,* p. 52.

**4.** Stephen W. King and Kenneth K. Sereno, "Conversational Appropriateness as a Conversational Imperative," *Quarterly Journal of Speech* 70 (1984): 264–73.

**5.** Julia T. Wood, "Communication and Relational Culture: Bases for the Study of Human Relationships," *Communication Quarterly* 30 (1982): 75–83. See also Mary Anne Fitzpatrick and Patricia B. Best, "Dyadic Adjustment in Relational Types: Consensus, Cohesion, Affectional Expression and Satisfaction in Enduring Relationships," *Communication Monographs* 46 (1979): 167–78; and Gerald M. Phillips and Nancy J. Metzger, *Intimate Communication* (Boston: Allyn and Bacon, 1976).

**6.** Robert C. Carson, *Interaction Concepts of Personality* (Chicago: Aldine, 1969); see in particular Chapter 6, "Contractual Arrangements in Interpersonal Relations."

**7.** Ibid., p. 184.

**8.** See, for example, Gregory Bateson, "Culture Contact and Schismogenesis," *Man* 35 (1935): 178– 83; William C. Schutz, *The Interpersonal Underworld* (Palo Alto, Calif.: Science and Behavior Books, 1966); Timothy Leary, *Interpersonal Diagnosis of Personality* (New York: Ronald Press, 1957). For a summary of early relational work, see Malcolm R. Parks, "Relational Communication: Theory and Research," *Human Communication Research* 3 (1977): 372–81.

**9.** Judee K. Burgoon and Jerold L. Hale, "The Fundamental Topoi of Relational Communication," *Communication Monographs* 51 (1984): 193–214.

**10.** Frank E. Millar and L. Edna Rogers, "A Relational Approach to Interpersonal Communication," in *Explorations in Interpersonal Communication,* ed. Gerald R. Miller (Beverly Hills, Calif.: Sage, 1976).

**11.** B. Aubrey Fisher, *Small Group Decision Making,* 2nd ed. (New York: McGraw-Hill, 1980), p. 327.

**12.** Burgoon and Hale, "The Fundamental Topoi," p. 198.

**13.** Ibid.

**14.** For a general overview of some classic research on similarity and attraction, see Ellen Berscheid and Elaine Walster, *Interpersonal Attraction* (Reading, Mass.: Addison-Wesley, 1969). For a discussion of similarity as a device in developing relationships, see Steve Duck, "Interpersonal Communication in Developing Acquaintance," in *Explorations in Interpersonal Communication.* For experimental evidence of the effects of attitude similarity on attraction, see the work of Michael Sunnafrank; for example, "Attitude Similarity and Interpersonal Attraction in Communication Processes: In Pursuit of an Ephemeral Influence," *Communication Monographs* 50 (1983): 273–84.

**15.** Evelyn Sieburg, "Dysfunctional Communication and Interpersonal Responsiveness in Small Groups," unpublished dissertation, University of Denver, 1969. For a good summary of Sieburg's theory, see Frank E. X. Dance and Carl E. Larson, *Speech Communication: Concepts and Behavior* (New York: Holt, Rinehart & Winston, 1972), pp. 140–43.

**16.** Watzlawick et al., *Pragmatics.* See Chapter 6 for a discussion of the "logic" of paradox.

**17.** Gregory Bateson, Don D. Jackson, Jay Haley, and John H. Weakland, "Toward a Theory of Schizophrenia," *Behavioral Science* 1 (1956): 251–64; Jay Haley, *Strategies of Psychotherapy* (New York: Grune & Stratton, 1963).

**18.** Lynda Rummel, Sarah Trenholm, Charles Goetzinger, and Charles Petrie, "Disconfirming (Double Bind) Effects of Incongruent Multichannel Messages," in *Interpersonal Communication: A Rhetorical Perspective*, ed. Ben Morse and Lyn Phelps (Minneapolis: Burgess, 1980).

**19.** The Palo Alto group includes Gregory Bateson, John H. Weakland, Paul Watzlawick, Janet Beavin Bavelas, Don D. Jackson, and Jay Haley. To understand this approach, see the section on the pragmatic perspective in B. Aubrey Fisher, *Perspectives on Human Communication* (New York: Macmillan, 1978).

**20.** For an overview and model of interact sequences, see B. Aubrey Fisher and Leonard C. Hawes, "An Interact System Model: Generating a Grounded Theory of Small Groups," *Quarterly Journal of Speech* 57 (1971): 444–53.

**21.** See Watzlawick et al., *Pragmatics,* pp. 54–59 for the original example.

**22.** William W. Wilmot, *Dyadic Communication* (Reading, Mass.: Addison-Wesley, 1979).

**23.** Ibid., p. 127.

**24.** Vernon E. Cronen, W. Barnett Pearce, and Lonna M. Snavely, "A Theory of Rule-Structure and Types of Episodes and a Study of Perceived Enmeshment in Undesired Repetitive Patterns ('URPs')," in *Communication Yearbook* 3, ed. Dan Nimmo (New Brunswick, N.J.: Transaction Books, 1979).

**25.** Wilmot, *Dyadic Communication,* p. 128.

**26.** Gerald R. Miller and Mark Steinberg, *Between People: A New Analysis of Interpersonal Communication* (Chicago: Science Research Associates, 1975), pp. 167–73.

**27.** Ross Buck, "Recent Approaches to the Study of Nonverbal Receiving Ability," in *Nonverbal Communication: The Social Interaction Sphere*, ed. John Wiemann and Randall Harrison (Beverly Hills, Calif.: Sage, 1983), pp. 209–42.

**28.** Ross Buck, "Emotional Communication in Personal Relationships: A Developmental-Interactionist View," in *Close Relationships*, ed. Clyde Hendrick (Newbury Park, Calif.: Sage, 1989), p. 159.

## Chapter 6

**1.** Ellen J. Langer, *The Power of Mindful Learning* (Reading, Mass.: Addison-Wesley, 1997).

**2.** Becca Levy and Ellen J. Langer, "Memory Advantage for Deaf and Chinese Elders: Aging Free from Negative Premature Cognitive Commitments," *Journal of Personality and Social Psychology* 66 (1994): 989–97.

**3.** Ellen J. Langer, *Mindfulness* (Reading, Mass.: Addison-Wesley, 1989).

**4.** Langer, *The Power of Mindful Learning*, p. 4.

**5.** Joseph LeDoux, *Synaptic Self: How Our Brains Become Who We Are* (New York: Penguin Books, 2002), p. 174.

**6.** Antonio Damasio, *The Feeling of What Happens: Body and Emotion in the Making of Consciousness* (San Diego: Harvest Books, 1999), pp. 35–81.

**7.** Elizabeth Phelps, K. J. O'Connor, W. A. Cunningham, E. S. Funayama, J. C. Gatenby, J. C. Gore, and M. R. Banaji, "Performance on Indirect Measures of Race Evaluation Predicts Amygdale Activation," *Journal of Cognitive Neuroscience* 12 (2000): 729–38.

**8.** Elizabeth Phelps and Laura Thomas, "Race, Behavior, and the Brain: The Role of Neuroimaging in Understanding Complex Social Behaviors," *Political Psychology* 24 (2003): 747–58.

**9.** Joseph LeDoux, *The Emotional Brain: The Mysterious Underpinnings of Emotional Life* (New York: Simon & Schuster, 1996), p. 206.

**10.** G. Bower, "How Might Emotions Affect Learning?" in *Handbook of Emotion and Memory: Research and Theory*, ed. S. A. Christianson (Hillsdale, N.J.: Lawrence Erlbaum, 1992).

**11.** Gordon B. Moskowitz, *Social Cognition: Understanding Self and Others* (New York: Guilford Press, 2005), p. 85.

**12.** Gordon B. Moskowitz, "Preconscious Effects of Temporary Goals on Attention," *Journal of Experimental Social Psychology* 38 (2002): 397–404. See also P. M. Gollwitzer, "The Volitional Benefits of Planning," in *The Psychology of Action: Linking Cognition and Motivation to Action* P. M. Gollwitzer and J. A. Bargh, ed. (New York: Guilford Press, 1996), pp. 287–312; G. B. Moskowitz, A. R. Salomon, and C. M. Taylor, "Implicit Control of Stereotype Activation Through the Preconscious Operation of Egalitarian Goals," *Social Cognition* 18 (2000): 151–77.

**13.** T. L. Chartrand and J. A. Bargh, "Automatic Activation of Impression Formation Goals: Nonconscious Goal Priming Reproduces Effects of Explicit Task Instructions," *Journal of Personality and Social Psychology* 71 (1996): 464–78.

**14.** Gordon Allport, *The Nature of Prejudice* (Cambridge, Mass.: Addison-Wesley, 1954).

**15.** See R. Hastie, "Schematic Principles in Human Memory," in *Social Cognition: The Ontario Symposium 1*, ed. E. T. Higgins, C. P. Herman and M. P. Zanna (Hillsdale, N.J.: Lawrence Erlbaum, 1981). See also S. E. Taylor and J. Crocker, "Schematic Basis of Information Processing," in *Social Cognition: The Ontario Symposium 1.*

**16.** Moskowitz, *Social Cognition*, p. 154.

**17.** F. I. M. Craik, "Human Memory," *Annual Review of Psychology* 30 (1979): 63–102.

**18.** Moskowitz, *Social Cognition*, pp. 163–64.

**19.** D. L. Medin, "Concepts and Conceptual Structure," *American Psychologist* 44 (1989): 1469–81.

**20.** Nancy Cantor and J. F. Kihlstrom, *Personality and Social Intelligence* (Englewood Cliffs, N.J.: Prentice-Hall, 1987).

21. Moskowitz, *Social Cognition*, p. 164.

22. George Kelly, *The Psychology of Personal Constructs* (New York: Norton, 1955).

23. C. McCauley, C. L. Stitt, and M. Segal, "Stereotyping: From Prejudice to Prediction," *Psychological Bulletin* 87 (1980): 195–208.

24. Mara Mather, Marcia K. Johnson, and Doreen M. DeLeonardis, "Stereotype Reliance in Source Monitoring: Age Differences and Neuropsychological Test Correlates," *Cognitive Neuropsychology* 16 (1999): 437–58.

25. Jeffrey W. Sherman and Gayle R. Bessenoff, "Stereotypes as Source Monitoring Cues: On the Interaction Between Episodic and Semantic Memory," *Psychological Science* 10 (1999): 100–10.

26. T. Holtgraves, T. K. Srull, and D. Socall, "Conversational Memory: The Effects of Speaker Status on Memory for the Assertiveness of Conversational Remarks," *Journal of Personality and Social Psychology* 56 (1989): 149–60.

27. Quote taken from the Stanford Prison Experiment Slide show on Philip Zimbardo's website, www.prisonexp.org, retrieved June 27, 2006. See also P. G. Zimbardo, "Pathology of Imprisonment," *Society* 6 (1972): 4,6,8.

28. Mark W. Baldwin, John P. R. Keelan, Beverly Fehr, Vicki Enns, and Evelyn Koh-Rangarajoo, "Social Cognitive Conceptualization of Attachment Working Models: Availability and Accessibility Effects," *Journal of Personality and Social Psychology* (in press, 2006).

29. N. L. Collins and S. J. Read, "Adult Attachment, Working Models, and Relationship Quality in Dating Couples," *Journal of Personality and Social Psychology* 58 (1990): 644–63.

30. Antonio Damasio, *The Feeling of What Happens: Body and Emotion in the Making of Consciousness* (San Diego: Harvest Book, 1999).

31. Moskowitz, *Social Cognition*, pp. 158–59.

32. Hazel Markus, " Self- Schemata and Processing Information About the Self," *Journal of Personality and Social Psychology* 35 (1977): 63–78.

33. Robert Abelson, "Script Processing in Attitude Formation and Decision–Making," in *Cognition and Social Behavior*, ed. J. S. Carroll and J. N. Payne (Hillsdale, N.J.: Lawrence Erlbaum, 1976).

34. Robert Abelson, "Psychological Status of the Script Concept," *American Psychologist* 36 (1981): 715–29.

35. Joseph Forgas, "Affective and Emotional Influences on Episode Representations," in *Social Cognition: Perspectives on Everyday Understanding*, ed. Joseph Forgas (London: Academic Press, 1981), pp. 165–80.

36. F. I. M. Craik, "Human Memory," *Annual Review of Psychology* 30 (1979): 63–102.

37. William James, *The Principles of Psychology*, 2 vols. (New York: Dover Books, 1890/1950).

38. E. Pronin, D. Y. Lin, and L. Ross, "The Bias Blind Spot: Perceptions of Bias in Self Versus Others," *Personality and Social Psychology Bulletin* 28 (2002): 369–81.

39. R. P. Vallone, L. Ross, and M. R. Lepper, "The Hostile Media Phenomenon: Biased Perception and Perceptions of Media Bias in Coverage of the Beirut Massacre," *Journal of Personality and Social Psychology* 49 (1985): 577–85.

40. Marilynn Brewer, "A Dual Process Model of Impression Formation," in *Advances in Social Cognition*, Vol. 1, ed. T. K. Srull and R. S. Wyer (Hillsdale, N.J.: Erlbaum), pp. 1–36; S. Chaiken and Y. Trope, eds., *Dual-Process Theories in Social Psychology* (New York: Guilford Press, 1999).

41. L. Z. McArthur, "What Grabs You? The Role of Attention in Impression Formation and Causal Attribution," in *Social Cognition: The Ontario Symposium*, Vol. 1, ed. E. T. Higgins, C. P. Herman, and M. P. Zanna (Hillsdale, N.J.: Erlbaum, 1981), pp. 201–46.

42. Brewer, "A Dual Process Model."

43. Ibid, p. 22.

44. Daniel T. Gilbert and P. S. Malone, "The Correspondence Bias," *Psychological Bulletin* 117 (1995): 21–38.

45. Stanley Deetz and Sheryl Stevenson, *Managing Interpersonal Communication* (New York: Harper & Row, 1986), p. 58.

46. Michael Brenner, "Actors' Powers," in *The Analysis of Action: Recent Theoretical and Empirical Advances*, ed. M. von Cranach and Rom Harre (Cambridge: Cambridge University Press, 1982), pp. 213–30.

47. Daniel T. Gilbert, B. W. Pelham, and D. S. Krull, "On Cognitive Business: When Person Perceivers Meet Persons Perceived," *Journal of Personality and Social Psychology* 54 (1988): 733–40.

48. Steven Duck, "Interpersonal Communication in Developing Acquaintances," in *Explorations in Interpersonal Communication*, ed. Gerald R. Miller (Beverly Hills, Calif.: Sage, 1976), pp. 127–47.

49. Seymour Rosenberg and Andrea Sedlak, "Structural Representations of Implicit Personality Theory," in *Advances in Experimental Social Psychology* 6, ed. Leonard Berkowitz (New York: Academic Press, 1972).

50. Harold H. Kelley, "The Warm–Cold Variable in First Impressions of Persons," *Journal of Personality* 18 (1950): 431–39.

51. P. E. Tetlock, "Accountability and Complexity of Thought," *Journal of Personality and Social Psychology* 45 (1983): 74–83; S. L. Neuberg and S. T. Fiske, "Motivational Influences on Impression Formation: Outcome Dependency, Accuracy-Driven Attention, and Individuating Processes," *Journal of Personality and Social Psychology* 53 (1987): 431–44.

52. Mark L. Snyder, "The Self-Monitoring of Expressive Behavior," *Journal of Personality and Social Psychology* 30 (1974): 526–37.

53. Mark L. Snyder, "Self-Monitoring Processes," in *Advances in Experimental Social Psychology*, ed. Leonard Berkowitz (New York: Academic Press, 1979), pp. 86–131.

54. Mark W. Baldwin and J. G. Holmes, "Salient Private Audiences and Awareness of the Self, *Journal of Personality and Social Psychology* 53 (1987): 1087–98.

**55.** Mark W. Baldwin, "Relational Schemas as a Source of If- Then Self- Inference Procedures," *Review of General Psychology* 1 (1997): 326–35.

**56.** L. M. Levine, L. M. Bogart, and B. Zdaniuk, "The Impact of Anticipated Group Membership on Cognition," in *Handbook of Motivation and Cognition*, Vol. 3, ed. R. M. Sorrentino and E. T. Higgins (New York: Guilford, 1996), pp. 531–69.

**57.** Baldwin, "Relational Schemas."

**58.** Sally Planalp, "Relational Schemata: A Test of Alternative Forms of Relational Knowledge as Guides to Communication," *Human Communication Research* 12 (1985): 3–29.

**59.** Robert Carson, *Interaction Concepts of Personality* (Chicago: Aldine, 1969).

**60.** B. Park, "Trait Attributes as On-line Organizers in Person Impressions," in *On-line Cognition in Person Perception*, ed. J. N. Bassili (Hillsdale, N.J.: Erlbaum), pp. 39–60.

**61.** Gordon Moskowitz and J. S. Uleman, "The Facilitation and Inhibition of Spontaneous Trait Inferences at Encoding," poster presented at the 95th annual convention of the American Psychological Association, New York (cited in Moskowitz, *Social Cognition*, p. 294).

**62.** Matthew D. Lieberman, Johanna M. Jarcho, and Junko Obayashi, "Attributional Inferences Across Cultures: Similar Automatic Attributions and Different Controlled Corrections," *Personality and Social Psychology Bulletin* 31 (2005): 889–901.

**63.** Sam Gosling, Sei Jin Ko, Thomas Mannarelli, and M. E. Morris, "A Room with a Cue: Personality Judgments Based on Offices and Bedrooms," *Journal of Personality and Social Psychology* 82 (2002): 379–98.

**64.** D. T. Gilbert, B. W. Pelham, and D. S. Krull, "On Cognitive Business: When Person Perceivers Meet Person Perceived." *Journal of Personality and Social Psychology* 75 (1988): 733–40.

**65.** J. Jaspers and M. Hewstone, "Cross-Cultural Interaction, Social Attribution, and Intergroup Relations," in *Cultures in Contact*, ed. S. Bochner (Elmsford, N.Y.: Pergamon Press, 1982), B. Park and M. Rothbart, "Perceptions of Outgroup Homogeneity and Levels of Social Categorization: Memory for the Subordinate Attributes of In-Group and Out-Group Members," *Journal of Personality and Social Psychology* 42 (1982): 1051–68.

**66.** L. Ross, T. M. Amabile, and J. L. Steinmetz, "Social Roles, Social Control, and Biases in Social Perception and Attribution Processes," *Journal of Personality and Social Psychology* 35 (1977): 484–94.

**67.** Taken from the home page of the International Listening Association website, www.listen.org, retrieved December 29, 2005.

**68.** Judi Brownell, *Listening: Attitudes, Principles, and Skills*, 3rd ed. (Boston: Allyn & Bacon, 2006), pp. 9–10.

**69.** See, for example, Andrew D. Wolvin and Carolyn Gwynn Coakley, *Listening* (Dubuque, Iowa: Brown, 1996); and Florence I. Wolff and Nadine C. Marsnick, *Perceptive Listening* (Fort Worth, Tex.: Harcourt, Brace, Jovanovich, 1993).

**70.** For a definition and discussion of the construct of intelligence, see the report of the APA Task Force: Ulric Neisser et al., "Intelligence: Known and Unknown," *American Psychologist* 51, no. 2 (1996): 77–101.

**71.** Howard Gardner, *Frames of Mind: The Theory of Multiple Intelligences* (New York: Basic Books, 1983). See also Robert J. Sternberg, *Beyond IQ: A Triarchic Theory of Human Intelligence.* (New York: Cambridge University Press, 1985).

**72.** For the original definition, see John D. Mayer and Peter Salovey, "What Is Emotional Intelligence?" in *Emotional Development and Emotional Intelligence: Educational Implications*, ed. Peter Salovey and David Sluyter (New York: Basic Books, 1997), pp. 3–31. For a more recent review of the theory and relevant research, see John D. Mayer, Peter Salovey, and David R. Caruso, "Emotional Intelligence: Theory, Findings, and Implications." *Psychological Inquiry* 15 no. 3 (2004): 197–215, 197.

**73.** Daisy Grewal and Peter Salovey, "Feeling Smart: The Science of Emotional Intelligence," *American Scientist* 93 (2005): 330–39, 399.

**74.** Ibid., p. 338.

**75.** Mayer, Salovey, and Caruso, "Emotional Intelligence," p. 209.

**76.** For an evaluation of EI research to date, see Gerald Matthews, Richard D. Roberts, and Moshe Zeidner, "Seven Myths About Emotional Intelligence," *Psychological Inquiry* 15 no. 3 (2004): 179–96.

**77.** See Voncile Smith, "Listening," in *A Handbook of Communication Skills*, ed. Owen Hargie (New York: New York University Press, 1986), pp. 250–51.

## Chapter 7

**1.** Peter L. Berger, *Invitation to Sociology: A Humanistic Perspective* (Garden City, N.Y.: Anchor Books, 1963), p. 66.

**2.** Ibid., p. 78.

**3.** Ruth Benedict, *Patterns of Culture* (New York: Penguin Books, 1946), p. 2.

**4.** Theodore M. Newcomb, Ralph H. Turner, and Philip E. Converse, *Social Psychology: The Study of Human Interaction* (New York: Holt, Rinehart & Winston, 1965), p. 326.

**5.** George J. McCall and J. L. Simmons, *Identities and Interactions* (New York: Free Press, 1966), p. 67.

**6.** Charles Horton Cooley, "The Social Self: On the Meanings of I," in *The Self in Social Interactions, Vol. I: Classic and Contemporary Perspectives*, ed. Chad Gordon and Kenneth J. Gergen (New York: Wiley, 1968), pp. 87–91.

**7.** Leon Festinger, "A Theory of Social Comparison Processes," *Human Relations* 2 (1954): 117–40.

**8.** Daryl J. Bem, "Self-Perception Theory," in *Advances in Experimental Social Psychology* 6, ed. Leonard Berkowitz (New York: Academic Press, 1972).

9. McCall and Simmons, *Identities and Interactions,* p. 67.

10. Erving Goffman, "On Face-Work," in *Interaction Ritual* (Garden City, N.Y.: Anchor Books, 1967).

11. Ibid., p. 226.

12. Erving Goffman, *The Presentation of Self in Everyday Life* (Garden City, N.Y.: Doubleday, 1959), p. 24.

13. Sarah Trenholm, *Human Communication Theory* (Englewood Cliffs, N.J.: Prentice-Hall, 1986), p. 105.

14. Erving Goffman, "Role Distance," in *Encounters: Two Studies in the Sociology of Interaction* (New York: Bobbs-Merrill, 1961), p. 108.

15. Goffman, *Presentation of Self,* pp. 212–28.

16. Morris Rosenberg, "Psychological Selectivity in Self-Esteem Formation," in *Attitude, Ego Involvement, and Change,* ed. Carolyn W. Sherif and Muzafer Sherif (New York: Wiley, 1967), pp. 26–50. Quoted in William Wilmot, *Dyadic Communication* (Reading, Mass.: Addison-Wesley, 1979).

17. W. Barnett Pearce, "The Coordinated Management of Meaning: A Rules-Based Theory of Interpersonal Communication," in *Explorations in Interpersonal Communication,* ed. Gerald R. Miller (Beverly Hills, Calif.: Sage, 1976), pp. 17–35.

18. William F. Lewis, "Telling America's Story: Narrative Form and the Reagan Presidency," *Quarterly Journal of Speech* 73 (1987): 282.

19. Vivian Paley, *Bad Guys Don't Have Birthdays* (Chicago: University of Chicago Press, 1991).

20. Jerome Bruner, "Life as Narrative," *Social Research* 54 (Spring 1987): 15.

21. Lewis, "Telling America's Story," p. 282.

22. Ellen J. Langer, "Minding Matters: The Consequences of Mindlessness-Mindfulness," *Advances in Experimental Social Psychology* (1989): 137–73.

23. Milton Rokeach, *The Open and Closed Mind* (New York: Basic Books, 1960), p. 57.

24. Langer, "Minding Matters," p. 140.

25. Ibid., p. 167.

## Chapter 8

1. John McCrone, *The Ape That Spoke: Language and the Evolution of the Human Mind* (New York: Morrow, 1991).

2. *The New Shorter Oxford English Dictionary,* Vol. 1. (Oxford: Clarendon Press, 1993), p. 483.

3. Philip Rieff, *The Triumph of the Therapeutic: Uses of Faith after Freud.* New York: Harper & Row, 1966, p. 2, quoted in Warren I. Susman, *Culture as History: The Transformation of American Society in the Twentieth Century* (New York: Pantheon Books, 1984), pp. 271–285; Charles Taylor, *Sources of the Self: The Making of the Modern Identity* (Cambridge: Harvard University Press, 1989).

4. Susman, *Culture as History,* p. 273.

5. Ibid., p. 273.

6. Ibid., p. 277.

7. Henry Laurent, *Personality: How To Build It* (New York: Funk & Wagnalls, 1915), p. iv, quoted in ibid, p. 277.

8. See, for example, John Kihlstrom and Nancy Cantor, "Mental Representations of the Self," in *Advances in Experimental Social Psychology* 17, ed. Leonard Berkowitz (Orlando, Fla.: Academic Press, 1984), pp. 1–47.

9. Don P. McAdams, *The Stories We Live By: Personal Myths and the Making of the Self* (New York: Guilford Press, 1993), p. 11.

10. Hazel Markus, "Self-Schemata and Processing Information About the Self," *Journal of Personality and Social Psychology* 35 (1977): 63–78.

11. Hazel Markus, M. Crane, S. Bernstein, and M.Siladi, "Self-Schemas and Gender," *Journal of Personality and Social Psychology* 42 (1982): 38–50.

12. Eric Berne, *Games People Play* (New York: Grove Press, 1964).

13. W. Barnett Pearce and Vernon E. Cronen, *Communication, Action and Meaning* (New York: Praeger, 1980), p. 136.

14. Steven Berglas and Edward E. Jones, "Drug Choice as an Externalization Strategy in Response to Noncontingent Success," *Journal of Personality and Social Psychology* 36 (1978): 405–17. See also E. E. Jones and S. Berglas, "Control of Attributions About the Self Through Self-Handicapping Strategies: The Appeal of Alcohol and the Role of Underachievement," *Personality and Social Psychology Bulletin* 4 (1978): 200–206.

15. Daryl J. Bem, "Self-Perception Theory," in *Advances in Experimental Social Psychology* 6, ed. Leonard Berkowitz (New York: Academic Press, 1972).

16. Charles Horton Cooley, "Looking-Glass Self," in *Symbolic Interaction: A Reader in Social Psychology,* 3rd ed., ed. Jerome G. Manis and Bernard N. Meltzer (Boston: Allyn and Bacon, 1978), p. 169.

17. A. G. Greenwald, "The Totalitarian Ego: Fabrication and Revision of Personal History," *American Psychologist* 35 (1980): 603–18.

18. Linda Lederman, "Internal Muzak: An Examination of Intrapersonal Relationships," in *Interaction and Identity: Information and Behavior,* vol. 5, ed. Hartmut Mokros (New Brunswick, N.J.: Transaction Publishers, 1996): 197–214.

19. Ibid.

20. D. C. McClelland, R. Koestner, and J. Weinberger. "How Do Self-Attributed and Implicit Motives Differ?" *Psychological Review* 96 (1989): 690–702.

21. Robert Norton, *Communicator Style: Theory, Applications, and Measures* (Beverly Hills, Calif.: Sage, 1983), p. 58.

22. Donald Darnell and Wayne Brockriede, *Persons Communicating* (Englewood Cliffs, N.J.: Prentice-Hall, 1976), p. 176.

23. Ibid., p. 178.

24. Roderick Hart and Don Burks, "Rhetorical Sensitivity and Social Interaction," *Speech Monographs* 39 (1972): 75–91.

25. Roderick Hart, Robert Carlson, and William Eadie, "Attitudes Toward Communication and the Assessment of Rhetorical Sensitivity," *Communication Monographs* 47 (1980): 1–22.

26. James C. McCroskey, "Oral Communication Apprehension: A Summary of Recent Theory and Research," *Human Communication Research* 4 (1977): 78–96.

27. Ibid.

28. Michael J. Beatty and Ralph R. Behnke, "An Assimilation Theory Perspective of Communication Apprehension," *Human Communication Research* 6 (1980): 319–25.

29. J. Bowlby, *Attachment and Loss: Separation, Anxiety, and Anger* (New York: Basic Books, 1973); C. Hazan and P. R. Shaver, "Love and Work: An Attachment-Theoretical Perspective," *Journal of Personality and Social Psychology* 52 (1990): 511–24; Eric P. Simon and Leslie Baxter, "Attachment Style Differences in Relationship Maintenance Strategies," *Western Journal of Communication* 57 (1990): 416–30.

30. See J. Feeney and P. Noller, "Attachment Style as a Predictor of Adult Romantic Relationships," *Journal of Personality and Social Psychology* 58 (1990): 281–91; J. Feeney and P. Noller, "Attachment Style and Verbal Descriptions of Romantic Partners," *Journal of Social and Personal Relationships* 8 (1990): 187–215; Hazan and Shaver, "Love and Work"; N. Collins and S. Read, "Adult Attachment, Working Models, and Relationship Quality in Dating Couples," *Journal of Personality and Social Psychology* 58 (1990): 644–63; M. Levy and K. Davis, "Lovestyles and Attachment Styles Compared: Their Relations to Each Other and to Various Relationship Characteristics," *Journal of Social and Personal Relationships* 5 (1988): 439–71; J. Simpson, "Influence of Attachment Styles on Romantic Relationships," *Journal of Personality and Social Psychology* 59 (1990): 971–80.

31. K. Bartholomew and L. Horowitz, "Attachment Styles Among Young Adults: A Test of a Four Category Model," *Journal of Personality and Social Psychology* 61 (1991): 226–44; R. Kobak and C. Hazen, "Attachment in Marriage: Effects of Security and Accuracy of Working Models," *Journal of Personality and Social Psychology* 60 (1991): 861–69; R. Kobak and A. Sceery, "The Transition to College: Working Models of Attachment, Affect Regulation, and Perceptions of Self and Others," *Child Development* 88 (1988): 135–46; M. Mikulincer and O. Nachshon, "Attachment Styles and Patterns of Self-Disclosure," *Journal of Personality and Social Psychology* 61 (1991): 321–31; M. Senchak and K. Leonard, "Attachment Styles and Marital Adjustment Among Newlywed Couples," *Journal of Social and Personal Relationships* 9 (1992): 51–64; J. Simpson, W. Rholes, and J. Nelligan, "Support Seeking and Support Giving Within Couples in an Anxiety-Provoking Situation: The Role of Attachment Styles," *Journal of Personality and Social Psychology* 62 (1992): 434–46.

32. D. P. McAdams, "Human Motives and Personal Relationships," in *Communication, Intimacy, and Close Relationships*, ed. V. Derlega (New York: Academic Press, 1984) p. 45.

33. D. P. McAdams, S. Healy, and S. Krause, "Social Motives and Patterns of Friendship," *Journal of Personality and Social Psychology* 47 (1984): 828–38; D.P.McAdams, R. J. Jackson, and C. A. Kirshnit, "Looking, Laughing and Smiling in Dyads as a Function of Intimacy Motivation and Reciprocity," *Journal of Personality* 52 (1984): 261–73.

34. Judy-Anne Craig, Richard Koestner, and David Zuroff, "Implicit and Self-Attributed Intimacy Motivation," *Journal of Social and Personal Relationships* 11 (1994): 491–508.

35. Mark Knapp and Gerald Miller, eds., *Handbook of Interpersonal Communication* (Beverly Hills, Calif.: Sage, 1985), p 72.

36. Barbara Montgomery, "Behavioral Characteristics Predicting Self and Peer Perceptions of Open Communication," *Communication Quarterly* 32 (1984): 233–40.

37. Robert E. Owens, Jr., *Queer Kids: The Challenges and Promise for Lesbian, Gay, and Bisexual Youth* (New York: The Haworth Press, 1998), p. 39.

38. Ritch C. Savin-Williams and Kenneth M. Cohen, *The Lives of Lesbians, Gays, and Bisexuals* (New York: Harcourt Brace, 1996), p. 114.

39. Ibid., p. 128.

40. Mary V. Borhek, *Coming Out to Parents: A Two-Way Survival Guide for Lesbians and Gay Men and Their Parents* (Cleveland, Ohio: The Pilgrim Press, 1993), p. 53.

41. Betty Berzon, *Permanent Partners: Building Gay and Lesbian Relationships that Last* (New York: Plume Books/Penguin, 1990), pp. 298, 300.

42. Borhek, *Coming Out to Parents*, pp. 46–54, has some excellent advice for dealing with parental reactions.

43. Owens, *Queer Kids*, p. 45; Savin-Williams, *The Lives of Lesbian, Gay, and Bisexual Youth*, p. 129. See also S. K. Telljohann and J. H. Price, "A Qualitative Examination of Adolescent Homosexuals' Life Experiences: Ramifications for Secondary School Personnel," *Journal of Homosexuality* 26 (1993): 41–56; G. Herdt and A. M. Boxer, *Children of Horizons: How Gay and Lesbian Teens Are Leading a New Way Out of the Closet* (Boston: Beacon Press, 1993).

44. This guideline and the others in this section are suggested by Owens, *Queer Kids*, p. 197, Table 9.2.

45. At the time of this writing, the address for P-FLAG was PO Box 27605, Washington, D.C. 20038. A national organization, it can easily be found on the Internet as well.

46. Owens, *Queer Kids*, p. 98.

## Chapter 9

1. For a full account of the case consult any of the online news services; the CNN account can be found at http://www.cnn.com/2005/LAW/03/14/atlanta.hostage/ (Retrieved July 10, 2006).

2. Robert E. Sanders and Kristine L. Fitch, "The Actual Practice of Compliance Seeking," *Communication Theory* 11, no. 3 (2001): 263–89, p. 263.

3. One of the earliest studies of interpersonal strategies was that of Gerald Marwell and David R. Schmitt, "Dimensions of Compliance–Gaining Behaviors: An Empirical Analysis," *Sociometry* 30 (1967): 357–58. See also Michael E. Roloff, "Validity Assessments of Compliance Gaining Exemplars," *Communication Theory* 4 (1994): 69–81.

**4.** Kristine L. Fitch, "Cultural Persuadables," *Communication Theory* 13, no. 1 (2003): 100–23.

**5.** Ruth Ann Clark and Jesse G. Delia, "Topoi and Rhetorical Competence," *The Quarterly Journal of Speech* 65 (1979): 187–206.

**6.** For a recent discussion of the importance of face, see Kathy Domenici and Stephen W. Littlejohn, *Facework: Bridging Theory and Practice* (Thousand Oaks, Calif.: Sage, 2006). See also William R. Cupach and Sandra Metts, *Facework* (Thousand Oaks, Calif.: Sage, 1994); and Penelope Brown and Stephen C. Levinson, *Politeness: Some Universals in Language Usage* (New York: Cambridge University Press, 1987). For a discussion of recent studies in speech communication, see Danette Ifert Johnson, Michael E. Roloff, and Melissa Riffee, "Responses to Refusals of Requests: Face Threat and Persistence, Persuasion and Forgiving Statement," *Communication Quarterly* 52, no. 4 (2004): 347–56.

**7.** Daena J. Goldsmith, "Content–Based Resources for Giving Face Sensitive Advice in Troubles Talk Episodes," *Research on Language and Social Interaction* 32, no. 4 (1999): 303–36.

**8.** The original source is I. P. Pavlov, *Conditioned Reflexes* (London: Oxford University Press, 1927).

**9.** Robert B. Cialdini, *Influence: Science and Practice*, 4th ed. (Boston: Allyn & Bacon, 2001), p. 168. See also George J. S. Razran, "Conditional Response Changes in Rating and Appraising Sociopolitical Slogans," *Psychological Bulletin* 37 (1940): 481.

**10.** Recently a spate of books on cults have been published. See, for example, Janja Lalich, *Bounded Choice: True Believers and Charismatic Cults* (Berkeley: University of California Press, 2004); Lorne L. Dawson, *Comprehending Cults: The Sociology of New Religious Movements*, 2nd ed. (New York: Oxford, 2006); and James R. Lewis, *Cults: A Reference Handbook* (Santa Barbara, Calif.: ABC–CLIO, 2005). For a description of cult recruitment techniques, see Eileen Barker, *The Making of a Moonie: Choice or Brainwashing?* (London: Basil Blackwell, 1984).

**11.** See, for example, B. F. Skinner, *Science and Human Behavior* (New York: Macmillan, 1953).

**12.** Albert Bandura, *Social Learning Theory* (Englewood Cliffs, N.J.: Prentice-Hall, 1977).

**13.** Mary John Smith, *Persuasion and Human Action: A Review and Critique of Social Influence Theories* (Belmont, Calif.: Wadsworth, 1982), p. 202.

**14.** George Caspar Homans, *Social Behavior: Its Elementary Forms* (New York: Harcourt Brace Jovanovich, 1959); John W. Thibaut and Harold H. Kelley, *The Social Psychology of Groups* (New York: Wiley, 1959).

**15.** Good discussions of relational currencies are provided in Kenneth L. Villard and Leland J. Whipple, *Beginnings in Relational Communication* (New York; Wiley, 1976), and Kathleen M. Galvin and Bernard J. Brommel, *Family Communication: Cohesion and Change* (Glenview, Ill.: Scott, Foresman, 1982).

**16.** Cialdini, *Influence*, p. 54.

**17.** For the original formulation of balance theory, see Fritz Heider, *The Psychology of Interpersonal Relations* (New York: Wiley, 1958); for a statement of congruity, see Percy H. Tannenbaum, "The Congruity Principle Revisited: Studies in the Reduction, Induction, and Generalization of Persuasion," in *Advances in Experimental Social Psychology 3*, ed. Leonard Berkowitz (New York: Academic Press, 1967).

**18.** For the original formulation of dissonance theory, see Leon Festinger, *A Theory of Cognitive Dissonance* (Stanford, Calif.: Stanford University Press, 1957).

**19.** Robert H. Gass and John S. Seiter, *Persuasion, Social Influence, and Compliance Gaining* (Boston: Allyn & Bacon, 2003), p. 60.

**20.** Cialdini, *Influence*, p. 62.

**21.** Ibid., p. 76.

**22.** D. J. Howard, "The Influence of Verbal Responses to Common Greetings on Compliance Behavior: The Foot-in-the Mouth Effect," *Journal of Applied Social Psychology* 20 (1990): 1185–96.

**23.** Milton Rokeach, *Beliefs, Attitudes, and Values* (San Francisco: Jossey-Bass, 1968), *The Nature of Human Values* (New York: Free Press, 1973), and "Value Theory and Communication Research: Review and Commentary," in *Communication Yearbook 3*, ed. Dan Nimmo (New Brunswick, N.J.: Transaction Books, 1979).

**24.** Walter J. Carl and Steve Duck, "How to Do Things with Relationships...and How Relationships Do Things with Us," in *Communication Yearbook* 28, ed. Pamela J. Kalbfleisch (Mahwah, NJ: Lawrence Erlbaum, 2004), pp. 1–34.

**25.** Ibid., p. 3.

**26.** Ibid., p. 5

**27.** Daniel Katz, "The Functional Approach to the Study of Attitudes," *Public Opinion Quarterly* 24 (1960): 163–204.

**28.** Aristotle, *Rhetoric,* trans. W. Rhys Roberts, and Poetics, trans. Ingram Bywater (New York: Modern Library, 1954), pp. 24–25. For more modern formulations of the notion of credibility, see Carl I. Hovland and W. A. Weiss, "The Influence of Source Credibility on Communicative Effectiveness," *Public Opinion Quarterly* 15 (1951): 635–50, and David K. Berlo, James B. Lemert, and Robert J. Mertz, "Dimensions for Evaluating the Acceptability of Message Sources," *Public Opinion Quarterly* 33 (1969): 563–76. For critiques of the credibility construct, see Gary Cronkhite and Jo Liska, "A Critique of Factor Analytic Approaches to the Study of Credibility," *Communication Monographs* 43 (June 1976): 91–107, and Gerald R. Miller and Michael Burgoon, "Persuasion Research: Review and Commentary," *Communication Yearbook* 2, ed. Brent D. Ruben (New Brunswick, N.J.: Transaction Books, 1978), pp.29–47.

**29.** John R. French and Bertram Raven, "The Bases of Social Power," in *Studies in Social Power* (Ann Arbor: University of Michigan Press, 1959).

**30.** Edward E. Jones and Thane S. Pittman, "Toward a General Theory of Strategic Self-Presentation," in *Psychological*

*Perspectives on the Self,* ed. Harry Suls (Hillsdale, N.J.: Lawrence Erlbaum, 1980).

**31.** Karen Tracy and others, "The Discourse of Requests: Assessment of a Compliance-Gaining Approach," *Human Communication Research* 10 (1984): 513–38.

**32.** Gerald R. Miller and others, "Compliance-Gaining Message Strategies: A Typology and Some Findings Concerning Effects of Situational Differences," *Communication Monographs* 44 (1977): 37–51; Michael E. Roloff and Edwin F. Barnicott, "The Situational Use of Pro- and Anti-Social Compliance-Gaining Strategies by High and Low Machiavellians," in *Communication Yearbook* 2, ed. Brent D. Ruben (New Brunswick, N.J.: Transaction Books, 1978), pp. 193–205.

**33.** Gerald Marwell and David R. Schmitt, "Dimensions of Compliance-Gaining Behavior: An Empirical Analysis," *Sociometry* 30 (1967): 350–64.

**34.** Laura K. Guerrero, Peter A. Andersen, and Walid A. Afifi, *Close Encounters: Communicating in Relationships* (Mountain View, Calif.: Mayfield, 2001).

**35.** See Yukie Aida and Toni Falbo, "Relationships Between Marital Satisfaction, Resources, and Power Strategies," *Sex Roles* 24 (1991): 43–56.

**36.** For an interesting study on face and directness, see Larry A. Erbert and Kory Floyd, "Affectionate Expressions as Face–Threatening Acts: Receiver Assessments," *Communication Studies* 55, no. 2 (2004): 254–70.

**37.** Guerrero et al. *Close Encounters,* p. 299.

**38.** Ibid., p. 293. See also L. M. Sagrestano, "Power Strategies in Interpersonal Relationships," *Psychology of Women Quarterly* 16 (1992): 481–95.

**39.** Guerrero et al. *Close Encounters,* p. 296.

**40.** Robert E. Sanders and Kristine L. Fitch, "The Actual Practice of Compliance Seeking," *Communication Theory* 11, no. 3 (2001): 263–89.

**41.** Ibid., p. 281.

**42.** Ibid., p. 271.

**43.** Ibid., pp. 286–87.

**44.** Harold H. Dawley, Jr., and W. W. Wenrich, *Achieving Assertive Behavior* (Monterey, Calif.: Brooks/Cole, 1976), p. 15.

**45.** Ibid., p. 97.

## Chapter 10

**1.** John Cheever, "Goodbye, My Brother," in *The Stories of John Cheever* (New York: Knopf, 1978), p. 3. Reprinted with permission.

**2.** See, for example, Salvador Minuchin, *Families and Family Therapy* (Cambridge, Mass.: Harvard University Press, 1974), pp. 50–51.

**3.** Virginia Satir, *Peoplemaking* (Palo Alto, Calif.: Science and Behavior Books, 1972).

**4.** Kathleen M. Galvin and Bernard J. Brommel, *Family Communication: Cohesion and Change* (Glenview, Ill.: Scott, Foresman, 1982), p. 4.

**5.** Ronald E. Cromwell and David Olson, eds., *Power in Families* (New York: Halstead Press, 1975), p. 5.

**6.** Basil Bernstein, *Class, Codes, and Control* (London: Routledge and Kegan Paul, 1971).

**7.** Ralph Turner, *Family Interaction* (New York: Wiley, 1970), pp. 97–116.

**8.** Minuchin, *Families,* p. 53.

**9.** David Kantor and William Lehr, *Inside the Family* (San Francisco: Jossey-Bass, 1976).

**10.** Minuchin, *Families,* pp. 54–56.

**11.** Christopher Lasch, *Haven in a Heartless World* (New York: Basic Books, 1977).

**12.** David Olson and Hamilton McCubbin, *Families: What Makes Them Work* (Beverly Hills, Calif.: Sage, 1983), pp. 30–34.

**13.** D. R. Entwistle and S. G. Doering, *The First Birth* (Baltimore: Johns Hopkins University Press, 1980); B. C. Miller and D. L. Sollie, "Normal Stress During the Transition to Parenthood," *Family Relations* 29 (1980): 459–65.

**14.** J. H. Meyerowitz and H. Feldman, "Transition to Parenthood," *Psychiatric Research Reports* 20 (1966): 459–65.

**15.** Hilary Lips and Anne Morrison, "Changes in the Sense of Family Among Couples Having Their First Child," *Journal of Social and Personal Relationships* 3 (1986): 393–400.

**16.** S. A. Anderson, C. S. Russell, and W. R. Schumm, "Perceived Marital Quality and Family Life Cycle Categories: A Further Analysis," *Journal of Marriage and the Family* 45 (1983): 127–39; B. C. Rollins and K. L. Cannon, "Marital Satisfaction over the Family Life Cycle: A Re-evaluation," *Journal of Marriage and the Family* 36 (1974): 271–82.

**17.** S. A. Anderson, "Changes in Parental Adjustment and Communication During the Leaving-Home Transition," *Journal of Social and Personal Relationships* 7 (1990): 47–68.

**18.** Ibid.

**19.** Anne-Marie Ambert, "Relationship Between Ex-Spouses: Individual and Dyadic Perspectives," *Journal of Social and Personal Relationships* 5 (1988): 327–46.

**20.** F. F. Furstenberg, "The New Extended Family: The Experience of Parents and Children After Remarriage," in *Remarriage and Step-parenting,* ed. K.Pasley and M. Ihinger-Tallman (New York: Guilford Press, 1987), p. 342.

**21.** Ambert, "Relationship Between Ex-Spouses."

**22.** Galvin and Brommel, *Family Communication,* p.234.

**23.** Steven Mintz and Susan Kellogg, *Domestic Revolutions: A Social History of American Family Life* (New York: The Free Press, 1988).

**24.** Jane Howard, *Families* (New York: Simon and Schuster, 1978). Cited in Galvin and Brommel, *Family Communication,* pp. 299–300.

**25.** See John M. Gottman, *Marital Interaction: Experimental Investigations* (New York: Academic Press, 1979).

**26.** Mary Anne Fitzpatrick, "A Typological Approach to Marital Interaction: Recent Theory and Research," in *Advances in Experimental Social Psychology* 18, ed. Leonard Berkowitz (New York: Academic Press, 1984), pp. 1–47. See also Mary Anne Fitzpatrick and Diane M. Badzinski, "All in the Family: Interpersonal Communication in Kin Relationships," in *Handbook of Interpersonal Communication,* ed. Mark Knapp and Gerald R. Miller (Beverly Hills, Calif.: Sage, 1985), pp. 687–736.

27. Fitzpatrick and Badzinski, "All in the Family," p.700.

28. B. Rollins and R. Galligan, "The Developing Child and Marital Satisfaction of Parents," in *Child Influences on Marital and Family Interaction: A Lifespan Perspective,* ed. Richard Lerner and Graham Spanier (New York: Academic Press, 1978), pp. 71–106.

29. Alice Rossi, "Transition to Parenthood," *Journal of Marriage and the Family* 30 (1968): 26–39.

30. Linda K. Acitelli, "When Spouses Talk to Each Other About Their Relationship," *Journal of Social and Personal Relationships* 5 (1988): 185–200.

31. Michael Ross and Diane Holmberg, "Are Wives' Memories for Events in Relationships More Vivid Than Their Husbands' Memories?" *Journal of Social and Personal Relationships* 9 (1992): 585–604.

32. Paul H. Zietlow and Alan L. Sillars, "Life-stage Differences in Communication During Marital Conflicts," *Journal of Social and Personal Relationships* 5 (1988): 223–46.

33. Ibid.

34. See, for example, B. Rollins and D. Thomas, "Parental Support, Power, and Control Techniques in the Socialization of Children," in *Contemporary Theories About the Family,* Vol. 1, ed. Wesley R. Burr and others (New York: Free Press, 1979), pp. 317–64. See also S. Steinmetz, "Disciplinary Techniques and Their Relationship to Aggressiveness, Dependency, and Conscience," in *Contemporary Theories About the Family,* Vol. 2, pp. 405–38.

35. Desmond Morris, *Intimate Behavior* (New York: Bantam Books, 1971), pp. 252–54.

36. Gene Brody and David Shaffer, "Contributions of Parents and Peers to Children's Moral Socialization," *Developmental Review* 2 (1992): 31–75.

37. R. R. Sears, E. E. Maccoby, and H. Levin, *Patterns of Childrearing* (Evanston, Ill.: Row, Peterson, 1957).

38. Brody and Shaffer, 1982, p. 39.

39. M. L. Hoffman, "Identification and Conscience Development," *Child Development* 4 (1971): 400–406.

40. E. M. Hetherington, M. Cox, and R. Cox, "The Aftermath of Divorce," in *Mother-Child, Father-Child Relations,* ed. J. H. Stevens and M. M. Mathews (Washington, D.C.: NAEYC, 1978); T. S. Parish, "The Relationship Between Factors Associated with Father Loss and Individuals' Level of Moral Judgement," *Adolescence* 15 (1980): 535–41.

41. James Applegate, Brant Burleson, Julie Burke, Jesse Delia, and Susan Kline, "Reflection-Enhancing Parental Communication," in *Parental Belief Systems: The Psychological Consequences for Children,* ed. Irving Sigel (Hillsdale, N.J.: Lawrence Erlbaum, 1985), pp. 107–42.

42. Roger Jon Desmond, Jerome L. Singer, Dorothy G. Singer, Rachel Calam, and Karen Colimore, "Family Mediation Patterns and Television Viewing: Young Children's Use and Grasp of the Medium," *Human Communication Research* 11 (1985): 461–80.

43. Ibid.

44. William Rawlins and Melissa Holl, "Adolescents' Interaction with Parents and Friends: Dialectics of Temporal Perspective and Evaluation," *Journal of Social and Personal Relationships* 5 (1988): 27–46.

45. Anderson, "Changes in Parental Adjustment."

46. Mark Fine and Lawrence Kurdek, "Parenting Cognitions in Stepfamilies: Differences Between Parents and Stepparents and Relations to Parenting Satisfaction," *Journal of Social and Personal Relationships* 11 (1994): 95–112.

47. For a brief review of this research, see Fitzpatrick and Badzinski, "All in The Family," pp. 713–17.

48. A. Goetting, "The Developmental Tasks of Siblingship over the Life Cycle," *Journal of Marriage and the Family* 48 (1986): 703–14.

49. Victor Cicirelli and Jon Nussbaum, "Relationships with Siblings in Later Life," in *Life-Span Communication: Normative Processes,* ed. J. Nussbaum (Hillsdale, N.J.: Lawrence Erlbaum, 1989), pp.283–99.

50. D. T. Gold, "Sibling Relationships in Retrospect: A Study of Reminiscence in Old Age," doctoral dissertation, Northwestern University, Evanston, Illinois, 1986. (Cited in Cicirelli and Nussbaum, "Relationships with Siblings.")

51. Michael Nichols, *The Power of the Family: Mastering the Hidden Dance of Family Relationships* (New York: Fireside Books, 1988).

52. James Patterson and Peter Kim, *The Day America Told the Truth* (New York: Prentice Hall, 1991).

53. Virginia Satir, *Peoplemaking* (Palo Alto, Calif.: Science and Behavior Books, 1972).

54. J. Bowlby, *The Making and Breaking of Affectional Bonds* (London: Tavistock, 1979); J. A. Simpson, "The Influence of Attachment Styles on Romantic Relationships," *Journal of Personality and Social Psychology* 59 (1990): 971–80.

55. Brant R. Burleson, "Age, Social-Cognitive Development, and the Use of Comforting Strategies," *Communication Monographs* 51 (1984): 140–53.

56. D. R. Lehman, J. H. Ellard, and C. B. Wortman, "Social Support for the Bereaved: Recipients' and Providers' Perspectives on What Is Helpful," *Journal of Consulting and Clinical Psychology* 54 (1986): 438–46.

57. James L. Applegate, "Adaptive Communication in Educational Contexts: A Study of Teachers' Communicative Strategies," *Communication Education* 29 (1980): 158–70.

58. Brant R. Burleson and Wendy Samter, "Consistencies in Theoretical and Naive Evaluations of Comforting Messages," *Communication Monographs* 52 (1985): 103–23.

## Chapter 11

1. The authors would like to thank Vernon Cronen for providing this example. We have paraphrased the account; any inaccuracies are our own.

2. Howard Gadlin, "Private Lives and Public Order: A Critical View of the History of Intimate Relations in the

United States," in *Close Relationships: Perspectives on the Meaning of Intimacy,* ed. George Levinger and Harold Raush (Amherst, Mass.: University of Massachusetts Press, 1977), pp. 33–72.

**3.** Richard Sennett, *The Fall of Public Man: On the Social Psychology of Capitalism* (New York: Vintage Books, 1976), p. 102.

**4.** Timothy Stephen, "Communication in the Shifting Context of Intimacy: Marriage, Meaning, and Modernity," *Communication Theory* 4 (1994): 191–218.

**5.** Ellen Berscheid, Mark Snyder, Allen Omoto, "Issues in Studying Close Relationships: Conceptualizing and Measuring Closeness," in *Close Relationships,* ed. Clyde Hendrick (Newbury Park, Calif.: Sage, 1989), pp. 63–91.

**6.** Ibid.

**7.** See William K. Rawlins, "Friendship as a Communicative Achievement: A Theory and an Interpretive Analysis of Verbal Reports," Ph.D. dissertation, Temple University, 1981. See also Kaspar D. Naegele, "Friendship and Acquaintances: An Exploration of Some Social Distinctions," *Harvard Educational Review* 28 (1958): 232–52.

**8.** Virginia Kidd, "Happily Ever After and Other Relationship Styles: Advice on Interpersonal Relations in Popular Magazines, 1951–1973," *Quarterly Journal of Speech* 61 (1975): 31–39.

**9.** Diane Prusank, Robert Duran, and Dena DeLillo, "Interpersonal Relationships in Women's Magazines: Dating and Relating in the 1970s and 1980s," *Journal of Social and Personal Relationships* 10 (1993): 307–320.

**10.** For models of relationship development that portray participants as making rational choices and being highly aware of the process, see Irwin Altman and Dallas Taylor, *Social Penetration: The Development of Interpersonal Relationships* (New York: Holt, Rinehart & Winston, 1973); Charles Berger and Richard Calabrese, "Some Explorations in Initial Interaction and Beyond: Toward a Developmental Theory of Interpersonal Communication," *Human Communication Research* 1 (1975): 99–112. For arguments that people are less conscious of these processes, see Charles Berger, "Self-Consciousness and the Adequacy of Theory and Research into Relationship Development," *Western Journal of Speech Communication* 44 (1980): 93–96; Jesse Delia, "Some Tentative Thoughts Concerning the Study of Interpersonal Relationships and Their Development," *Western Journal of Speech Communication* 44 (1980): 97–103.

**11.** Harriet Braiker and Harold Kelley, "Conflicts in the Development of Close Relationships," in *Social Exchange in Developing Relationships,* ed. Robert Burgess and Ted Huston (New York: Academic Press, 1979), pp. 136–68.

**12.** Mark L. Knapp, *Interpersonal Communication and Human Relationships* (Boston: Allyn and Bacon, 1984), p. 192.

**13.** Warren Shibles and Charles Zastrow, "Romantic Love vs. Rational Love," in *The Personal Problem Solver* (Englewood Cliffs, N.J.: Prentice-Hall, 1977), p. 21.

**14.** See Stanley Schacter and Jerome Singer, "Cognitive, Social, and Physiological Determinants of Emotional State," *Psychological Review* 69 (1962): 379–99; Miles Patterson, "An Arousal Model of Interpersonal Intimacy," *Psychological Review* 83 (1976): 235–45.

**15.** Gregory L. White, Sanford Fishbein, and Jeffrey Rutstein, "Passionate Love and the Misattribution of Arousal," *Journal of Personality and Social Psychology* 41 (1981): 56–62.

**16.** Richard Sennett, *The Fall of Public Man* (New York: Random House, 1978).

**17.** Steven Duck, "Interpersonal Communication in Developing Acquaintance," in *Explorations in Interpersonal Communication,* ed. Gerald R. Miller (Beverly Hills, Calif.: Sage, 1973), pp. 127–48.

**18.** Elaine Walster, Vera Aronson, Darcy Abrahams, and Leon Rottman, "Importance of Physical Attractiveness in Dating Behavior," *Journal of Personality and Social Psychology* 4 (1966): 508–16.

**19.** For a summary of this research, see William Griffitt, "Attitude Similarity and Attraction," in *Foundations of Interpersonal Attraction,* ed. Ted L. Huston (New York: Academic Press, 1974), pp. 285–308.

**20.** Brant Burleson and Wayne Denton, "A New Look at Similarity and Attraction in Marriage: Similarities in Social-Cognitive and Communication Skills as Predictors of Attraction and Satisfaction," *Communication Monographs* 59 (1992): 268–287.

**21.** Brant Burleson, Wendy Samter, and A. E. Lucchetti, "Similarity in Communication Values as a Predictor of Friendship Choices: Studies of Friends and Best Friends," *Southern Communication Journal* 57 (1992): 260–276; Brant Burleson, Adrianne Kunkel, and Jennifer Birch. "Thoughts about Talk in Romantic Relationships: Similarity Makes for Attraction (and Happiness, Too)," *Communication Quarterly* 42 (1994): 259–273.

**22.** Charles Backman and Paul Secord, "The Effect of Perceived Liking on Interpersonal Attraction," *Human Relations* 12 (1959): 379–81. See also Fritz Heider, *The Psychology of Interpersonal Relations* (New York: Wiley, 1958).

**23.** Benjamin J. Broome, "The Attraction Paradigm Revisited: Responses to Dissimilar Others," *Human Communication Research* 10 (1983): 137–52.

**24.** See David R. Mettee and Elliot Aronson, "Affective Reactions to Appraisal from Others," in Huston, *Foundations of Interpersonal Attraction,* pp. 235–83.

**25.** William C. Schutz, *FIRO: A Three-Dimensional Theory of Interpersonal Behavior* (New York: Holt, Rinehart & Winston, 1958).

**26.** Kenneth Villard and Leland Whipple, *Beginnings in Relational Communication* (New York: Wiley, 1976); U. G. Foa, "Interpersonal and Economic Resources," *Science* 171 (1971): 345–51.

**27.** John Berg and Richard Archer, "The Disclosure-Liking Relationship: Effects of Self-Perception, Order of Disclosure, and Topical Similarity," *Human Communication Research* 10 (1983): 269–82.

**28.** Rawlins, "Friendship as a Communicative Achievement."

**29.** Margaret E. Gruhn, "German-American Language Patterns as Indicators of Cultural Communication Boundaries: A Cross-Cultural Analysis," paper presented at the Speech Communication convention, Denver, Colorado, November 1985.

**30.** Michael Monsour, Sam Betty, and Nancy Kurzweil, "Levels of Perspectives and the Perception of Intimacy in Cross-Sex Friendships: A Balance Theory Explanation of Shared Perceptual Reality," *Journal of Social and Personal Relationships* 10 (1993): 529–50.

**31.** Paul H. Wright, "Self-Referent Motivation and the Intrinsic Quality of Friendship," *Journal of Social and Personal Relationships* 1 (1984): 115–30.

**32.** Robert B. Hays, "The Day-to-Day Functioning of Close Versus Casual Friendships," *Journal of Social and Personal Relationships* 6 (1989): 21–38.

**33.** Suzanna Rose and Felicisima Serafica, "Keeping and Ending Casual, Close and Best Friendships," *Journal of Social and Personal Relationships* 3 (1986): 275–88.

**34.** Ibid., p. 280.

**35.** Knapp, *Interpersonal Communication,* pp. 29–58.

**36.** Paul Mongeau, Jerold Hale, Kristen Johnson, and Jacqueline Hillis, "Who's Wooing Whom? An Investigation of Female Initiated Dating," in *Interpersonal Communication: Evolving Interpersonal Relationships,* ed. Pamela Kalbfleisch (Hillsdale, N.J.: Lawrence Erlbaum, 1993) pp. 51–68.

**37.** Liana Koeppel, Yvette Montagne-Miller, Dan O'Hair, and Michael Cody, "Friendly? Flirting? Wrong?" in *Interpersonal Communication: Evolving Interpersonal Relationships,* ed. Pamela Kalbfleisch (Hillsdale, N.J.: Lawrence Erlbaum, 1993), pp. 13–32.

**38.** Robert A. Bell and John A. Daly, "The Affinity-Seeking Function of Communication," *Communication Monographs* 51 (1984): 91–115.

**39.** Leslie A. Baxter and William Wilmot, "'Secret Tests': Social Strategies for Acquiring Information About the State of the Relationship," *Human Communication Research* 11 (1984): 171–202.

**40.** James H. Tolhuizen, "Communication Strategies for Intensifying Dating Relationships: Identification, Use and Structure," *Journal of Social and Personal Relationships* 6 (1989): 413–34.

**41.** Malcolm R. Parks and Mara B. Adelman, "Communication Networks and the Development of Romantic Relationships: An Expansion of Uncertainty Reduction Theory," *Human Communication Research* 10 (1983): 55–80.

**42.** Leslie A. Baxter, "Symbols of Relationship Identity in Relationship Cultures," *Journal of Social and Personal Relationships* 4 (1987): 261–80.

**43.** Robert Fulghum, *It Was on Fire When I Lay Down on It* (New York: Random House, 1989.

**44.** William Rawlins, "Openness as Problematic in Ongoing Friendship: Two Conversational Dilemmas," *Communication Monographs* 50 (1983): 1–13; Leslie A. Baxter, "Dialectical Contradictions in Developing Relationships," *Journal of Social and Personal Relationships* 7 (1990): 69–88.

**45.** Baxter, "Dialectical Contradictions."

**46.** Betty Berzon, *Permanent Partners: Building Gay and Lesbian Relationships that Last* (New York: Plume, 1990), p. 83.

**47.** Ibid., p. 86.

**48.** Jeanne Marecek, Stephen E. Finn, and Monda Cardell, "Gender Roles in the Relationships of Lesbians and Gay Men," *Journal of Homosexuality* 8, no. 2 (1982): 45–50.

**49.** Berzon, p. 87.

**50.** Alan L. Sillars and Michael D. Scott, "Interpersonal Perception Between Intimates: An Integrative Review," *Human Communication Research* 10 (1983): 153–76.

**51.** Ibid.

**52.** Laura K. Guerrero, Peter A. Andersen, and Walid A. Afifi, *Close Encounters: Communicating in Relationships* (Mountain View, Calif.: Mayfield, 2001), p. 227.

**53.** For a discussion of maintenance in different kinds of relationships see Daniel J. Canary et al., "An Inductive Analysis of Relational Maintenance Strategies: Comparisons Among Lovers, Relatives, Friends, and Others," *Communication Research Reports* 10 (1993): 5–14. See also Laura Stafford and Daniel J. Canary, "Maintenance Strategies and Romantic Relationship Type, Gender and Relational Characteristics," *Journal of Social and Personal Relationships* 8 (1991): 217–42.

**54.** Steven Duck, *Relating to Others* (Chicago: The Dorsey Press, 1988), pp. 102–21.

**55.** Sally Planalp and James Honeycutt, "Events That Increase Uncertainty in Personal Relationships," *Human Communication Research* 11 (1985): 593–604.

**56.** John Gottman with Nan Silver, *Why Marriages Succeed or Fail: And How You Can Make Yours Last* (New York: Simon & Schuster, 1994).

**57.** Ibid., pp. 32–67.

**58.** Ibid., pp. 59–61.

**59.** Ibid., pp. 71–72.

**60.** Ibid., pp. 79–80.

**61.** Ibid., p. 95.

**62.** John W. Lannamann, "Interpersonal Communication Research as Ideological Practice," *Communication Theory* 1 (1991): 179–203; Sarah Trenholm and Arthur Jensen, "The Ideology of Intimacy: Public Selves/Private Selves," paper presented at the Eastern Communication Association's annual conference, Atlantic City, May 1986.

**63.** Elizabeth House, "Sex Role Orientation and Marital Satisfaction in Dual- and One-Provider Couples," *Sex Roles* 14 (1986): 245–59; Linda Nyquist, Karla Slivken, Janet Spence, and Robert Helmreich, "Household Responsibilities in Middle-Class Couples: The Contributions of Demographic and Personality Variables," *Sex Roles* 12 (1985): 15–34.

**64.** Morton Deutsch, "Conflicts: Productive and Destructive," in *Conflict Resolution Through Communication,* ed. Fred E. Jandt (New York: Harper & Row, 1973), pp. 155–97.

**65.** Joyce Hocker Frost and William W. Wilmot, *Interpersonal Conflict* (Dubuque, Iowa: Brown, 1978), pp. 17–19.

66. Raymond S. Ross and Mark G. Ross, *Relating and Interacting* (Englewood Cliffs, N.J.: Prentice-Hall, 1982), p. 124.

67. George R. Bach and Peter Wyden, *The Intimate Enemy: How to Fight Fair in Love and Marriage* (New York: Avon Books, 1970).

68. David W. Johnson, *Reaching Out: Interpersonal Effectiveness and Self-Actualization,* 3rd ed. (Englewood Cliffs, N.J.: Prentice-Hall, 1986), pp. 81–83.

69. Frost and Wilmot, *Interpersonal Conflict,* pp.136–38. See also Roger Fisher, "Fractionating Conflict," in *Conflict Resolution: Contributions of the Behavioral Sciences,* ed. Clagett G. Smith (Notre Dame, Ind.: University of Notre Dame Press, 1971).

70. Frost and Wilmot, *Interpersonal Conflict,* p. 138.

## Chapter 12

1. Leon Battista Alberti, *Ten Books on Architecture,* ed. and trans. J. Leoni (New York: Transatlantic Arts, 1966), p. 175.

2. Lawrence Rosenfeld, "Central Park and the Celebration of Civic Virtue," in *American Rhetoric: Context and Criticism,* ed. Thomas W. Benson (Carbondale: Southern Illinois University Press, 1989), pp. 221–66.

3. Warren Leland, "Turning Reality Round Together: Guides to Conversation in Eighteenth-Century England," *Eighteenth Century Life* 8 (1983): 65–87.

4. Henry Fielding, "An Essay on Conversation," in *Miscellanies,* Volume One, ed. Henry Knight Miller (Middletown, Conn.: Wesleyan University Press, 1972), p. 120.

5. Gerald Miller and Mark Steinberg, *Between People: A New Analysis of Interpersonal Communication* (Chicago: Science Research Associates, 1975).

6. Richard Sennett, *The Fall of Public Man* (New York: Random House, 1974).

7. Rom Harre, *Social Being: A Theory for Social Psychology* (Totowa, N.J.: Littlefield, Adams, 1979), pp. 22–26.

8. For example, see Sennett, *The Fall of Public Man.* See also Christopher Lasch, *The Culture of Narcissism: American Life in an Age of Diminishing Expectations* (New York: Norton, 1979).

9. Erving Goffman, *Interaction Ritual: Essays on Face-to-Face Behavior* (Garden City, N.Y.: Anchor Books, 1967), pp. 47–95.

10. Ibid., p. 76.

11. Ibid., p. 79.

12. Sennett, *The Fall of Public Man.*

13. James Kunstler, *Home From Nowhere: Remaking Our Everyday World for the 21st Century* (New York: Simon and Schuster, 1996), p. 39.

14. Ibid., p. 39.

15. Ray Oldenburg, *The Great Good Place: Cafes, Coffee Shops, Community Centers, Beauty Parlors, General Stores, Bars, Hangouts and How They Get You Through the Day* (New York: Paragon House, 1989).

16. James Taylor, *Rethinking the Theory of Organizational Communication: How to Read an Organization* (Norwood, N.J.: Ablex, 1993), p. 96.

17. Charles Conrad, *Strategic Organizational Communication: An Integrated Perspective* (Fort Worth: Holt, Rinehart and Winston, 1990), p. 6.

18. Karl Weick, *The Social Psychology of Organizing,* (Reading, Mass.: Addison-Wesley, 1979).

19. Daniel C. Feldman, "The Multiple Socialization of Organization Members," *Academy of Management Review* 6 (1981): 309–18.

20. Fredric M. Jablin, "Task/Work Relationships: A Lifespan Perspective," in *Handbook of Interpersonal Communication,* ed. Mark Knapp and Gerald R. Miller (Beverly Hills, Calif.: Sage, 1985), p. 633.

21. Gareth Morgan, *Images of Organization,* 2nd ed. (Newbury Park, Calif.: Sage, 1997).

22. W. Barnett Pearce, *Using CMM: The Coordinated Management of Meaning.* Manuscript available at www .pearceassociates.com, August 1999.

23. Julie Foehrenbach and Karen Rosenberg, "How Are We Doing?" *Journal of Communication Management* 12 (1982): 3–11.

24. Keith Davis, *Human Behavior at Work* (New York: McGraw-Hill, 1972), p. 280.

25. William Davis and J. Regis O'Connor, "Serial Transmission of Information: A Study of the Grapevine," *Journal of Applied Communication Research* 5 (1977): 61–72; Evan E. Rudolph, "Informal Human Communication Systems in a Large Organization," *Journal of Applied Communication Research* 1 (1973): 7–23; Eugene Walton, "How Effective Is the Grapevine?" *Personnel Journal* 38 (1961): 45–49.

26. For a review of trait research, see R. D. Mann, "A Review of the Relationship Between Personality and Performance in Small Groups," *Psychological Bulletin* 56 (1959): 241–70. For a more current review of personality influences, see Mark Snyder and William Ickes, "Personality and Social Behavior," in *The Handbook of Social Psychology,* Vol. 2, 3rd ed., ed. Gardner Lindzey and Elliot Aronson (New York: Random House, 1985), pp. 883–947.

27. Max DePree, *Leadership Jazz* (New York: Doubleday, 1992), pp. 220–25.

28. Charles O'Reilly and David Caldwell, "Informational Influence as a Determinant of Task Characteristics and Job Satisfaction," *Journal of Applied Psychology* 64 (1979): 157–65.

29. Irving Janis, *Victims of Groupthink: A Psychological Study of Foreign Policy Decisions and Fiascos* (Boston: Houghton Mifflin, 1972).

30. Daniel Katz and Robert L. Kahn, *The Social Psychology of Organizations* (New York: Wiley, 1966), pp. 239–45.

31. Gerald A. Goldhaber, *Organizational Communication* (Dubuque, Iowa: Brown, 1983), p. 226.

32. Fredric M. Jablin, "Superior-Subordinate Communication: The State of the Art," *Psychological Bulletin* 86 (1979): 1208.

33. Charles Redding, *Communication Within the Organization: An Interpretative Review of Theory and Research* (New York: Industrial Communication Council, 1972), p. 443.

34. Fredric M. Jablin, "An Exploratory Study of Subordinates' Perceptions of Supervisory Politics," *Communication Quarterly* 29 (1981): 269–75.

35. Don Peppers and Martha Rogers, *The One to One Future: Building Relationships One Customer at a Time* (New York: Currency/Doubleday, 1997).

36. Ibid., p. 22.

37. Kathleen Reardon and Ben Enis, "Establishing a Companywide Customer Orientation Through Persuasive Internal Marketing," *Management Communication Quarterly* 3 (1990) 376–87.

38. J. H. Fritz, "Men's and Women's Organizational Peer Relationships: A Comparison," *Journal of Business Communication* 34 (1997): 27–46.

39. P. M. Sias and D. J. Cahill, "From Coworkers to Friends: The Development of Peer Friendships in the Workplace," *Western Journal of Communication* 62 (1998): 273–99.

40. Ibid.

41. Ibid.

42. James Dillard, "Close Relationships at Work: Perceptions of the Motives and Performance of Relational Participants." *Journal of Social and Personal Relationships* 4 (1987): 179–93.

43. Ibid.

44. Patrice Buzzanell, "Managing Workplace Romance," paper presented at the annual convention of the Speech Communication Association, Chicago, November, 1990.

45. G. R. Spruell, "Daytime Drama: Love in the Office," *Training and Development Journal* 39 (1985): 21–23; Dennis Mumby and Linda Putnam. "Bounded Rationality as an Organizational Construct: A Feminist Critique," paper presented at the annual conference of the Academy of Management, San Francisco, 1990.

46. Linda Harris, "Communication Competence: An Argument for a Systemic View," unpublished paper, University of Massachusetts, 1979.

47. Arlie Hochschild, *The Time Bind: When Work Becomes Home and Home Becomes Work* (New York: Owl Books/ Henry Holt, 2001).

48. Charles Berger, "Perceptions of Information Sequencing in Relationship Development," *Human Communication Research* 3 (1976): 29–46.

49. Frances Moore Lappé and Paul Martin DuBois, *The Quickening of America: Rebuilding Our Nation, Remaking Our Lives* (San Francisco: Jossey-Bass, 1994), pp. 137–163.

50. Price Pritchett, *Culture Shift: The Employee Handbook for Changing Corporate Culture* (Dallas: Pritchett & Associates, 1993).

51. For a discussion of relational and personal goals in a management context, see Robert R. Blake and Jane S. Mouton, *The Managerial Grid* (Houston: Gulf, 1964), and Jay Hall, *Conflict Management Survey* (Woodlands, Tex.: Teleometrics International,1969). See also Raymond S. Ross and Mark G. Ross, Relating and Interacting (Englewood Cliffs, N.J.: Prentice-Hall, 1982), and David W. Johnson, *Reaching Out: Interpersonal Effectiveness and Self-Actualization,* 3rd ed. (Englewood Cliffs, N.J.: Prentice-Hall, 1986), pp. 207–10.

52. Ross and Ross, *Relating and Interacting,* p. 145.

53. Our discussion of negotiation strategies is based on two basic sources: Dean G. Pruitt, *Negotiation Behavior* (New York: Academic Press, 1981), and Roger Fisher and William Ury, *Getting to YES: Negotiating Agreement Without Giving In* (Boston: Houghton Mifflin, 1986).

54. Pruitt, *Negotiation Behavior,* pp. 149, 152.

55. Ibid., p. 153.

56. Fisher and Ury, *Getting to YES,* p. 24.

57. Ibid., p. 32.

58. See ibid., pp. 51–56, for a development of this example.

59. Pruitt, *Negotiation Behavior,* p. 201.

60. Ibid., pp. 215–17.

## Chapter 13

1. Larry A. Samovar, Richard E. Porter, and Nemi C. Jain, *Understanding Intercultural Communication* (Belmont, Calif.: Wadsworth, 1981), p. 46.

2. The material that follows is taken from a number of sources, including Terence Brake, Danielle M. Walker, and Thomas Walker, *Doing Business Internationally: The Guide to Cross-Cultural Success* (Burr Ridge, Ill.: Irwin Prof. Pub., 1995); William B. Gudykunst and Young Yun Kim, *Communicating with Strangers: An Approach to Intercultural Communication,* 3rd ed. (New York: McGraw-Hill, 1997); and Larry A. Samovar, Richard E. Porter, and Lisa A. Stefani, *Communication Between Cultures,* 3rd ed. (Belmont, Calif.: Wadsworth, 1998), pp. 152–72.

3. K. S. Sitaram and Roy T. Cogdell, *Foundations of Intercultural Communication* (Columbus, Ohio: Merrill, 1976, p. 51; cited in Samovar, Porter, and Jain, *Understanding Intercultural Communication,* p. 94.

4. The distinction between being and doing is well articulated by Brake et al. in *Doing Business Internationally;* although based on the work of Edward T. Hall, Florence Kluckhohn, and Fred Strodbeck, it appears to be similar to Geert Hofstede's distinction between masculine and feminine cultures. See Geert Hofstede, *Cultures and Organizations: Software of the Mind* (London: McGraw Hill, 1991).

5. Edward T. Hall, *The Dance of Life: The Other Dimension of Time* (New York: Doubleday and Company, 1983).

6. Harry C. Triandis is the researcher most associated with the individualist/collectivist distinction. See, for example, H. C. Triandis, "Cross Cultural Studies of Individualism and Collectivism" in *Nebraska Symposium on Motivation,* 1989. (Lincoln: University of Nebraska Press, 1990), J. J. Berman ed., pp. 41–133.

7. For a discussion of horizontal and vertical aspects of these two factors, see T. M. Singelis et al., "Horizontal and Vertical Dimensions of Individualism and Collectivism: A Theoretical and Measurement Refinement," *Cross Cultural Research* 29 (1995): 240–75.

8. See Brake, *Doing Business Internationally,* pp. 54–59.

9. Edward T. Hall, *Beyond Culture* (Garden City, N.Y.: Anchor/Doubleday, 1976).

10. Samovar, Porter, and Jain, *Understanding Intercultural Communication*, p. 68.

11. R. Bellah et al. *Habits of the Heart: Individualism and Commitment in American Life* (New York: Harper and Row, 1985), p. 142.

12. AE and AAVE seem to be the terms most often used by linguists to describe these two languages. However, there are many others, and the decision of what term to use carries some political shadings. BE or Black English is sometimes used to refer to AAVE, and Geneva Smitherman has referred to standard American English as LWC, the language of wider communication.

13. Geneva Smitherman, *Talkin that Talk: Language, Culture and Education in African America* (New York: Routledge, 2000), p. 364.

14. Marcyliena Morgan, "More than a Mood or an Attitude: Discourse and Verbal Genres in African-American Culture," in *African-American English: Structure, History and Use.* Salikoko S. Mufwene et al., eds., (New York: Routledge, 1998), pp. 251–281; p. 254.

15. Smitherman, *Talkin that Talk*, p. 217.

16. Thomas Kochman, *Black and White Styles in Conflict* (Chicago: University of Chicago Press, 1981), p. 18.

17. Jack L. Daniel and Geneva Smitherman, "How I Got Over: Communication Dynamics in the Black Community," *Quarterly Journal of Speech* 62 (February 1976): 26–39, 27.

18. Ibid., p. 38.

19. Molefi Kete Asante and Alice Davis, "Encounters in the Interracial Workplace," in *Handbook of International and Intercultural Communication* (Beverly Hills, Calif.: Sage, 1979), p. 387.

20. Carley H. Dodd, *Dynamics of Intercultural Communication*, 2nd. ed. (Dubuque, Iowa: Brown, 1987), p. 71.

21. Tuen A. van Dijk, *Communicating Racism: Ethnic Prejudice in Thought and Talk* (Newbury Park, Calif.: Sage, 1987).

22. Ibid., p. 220.

23. Ibid., pp. 235–36.

24. Ibid., p. 372.

25. Ibid., pp. 44–45.

26. Jack L. Daniel, "The Facilitation of White-Black Communication," *The Journal of Communication* 20 June 1970): 134–41.

27. Samovar and others, *Understanding Intercultural Communication*, p. 195.

28. William D. Brooks, *Speech Communication* (Dubuque, Iowa: Brown, 1974), p. 24. The original source for this anecdote is John Wilson, "Film Literacy in Africa," *Canadian Communications* 7 (4) (Summer 1961): 7–14.

29. Dodd, *Dynamics of Intercultural Communication*, p. 49.

30. Ibid., p. 44.

31. Samovar and others, *Understanding Intercultural Communication*, p. 119.

32. Dodd, *Dynamics of Intercultural Communication*, p. 45.

33. Edward T. Hall, *The Silent Language* (Garden City, N.Y.: Doubleday, 1959), p. 67.

34. Dodd, *Dynamics of Intercultural Communication*, p. 92.

35. Samovar and others, *Understanding Intercultural Communication*, p. 94. The quote is from K. S.

36. Stella Ting-Toomey, "Identity and Interpersonal Bonding," in *Handbook of International and Intercultural Communication*, p. 352.

37. Ibid., p. 364.

38. Hall, *The Silent Language*, p. 191.

39. Ibid., p. 209.

40. Dodd, *Dynamics of Intercultural Communication*, p. 174.

41. E. C. Condon, "Cross-Cultural Interferences Affecting Teacher-Pupil Communication in American Schools," *International and Intercultural Communication Annual* 3 (1976): 108–20.

42. Stephanie Coontz, *The Social Origins of Private Life: A History of American Families 1600–1900* (London: Verso, 1988), pp. 74–78.

43. John D'Emilio and Estelle B. Freedman, *Intimate Matters: A History of Sexuality in America* (New York: Harper & Row, 1988), p. 29.

44. Coontz, *Social Origins*, p. 79.

45. Eleazar Moody, *The School of Good Manners* (Portland, Me.: Thomas B. Wait, 1786), pp. 7, 8, 10; quoted in John F. Kasson, *Rudeness and Civility: Manners in Nineteenth-Century Urban America* (New York: Hill & Wang, 1990), p. 13.

46. Kasson, *Rudeness and Civility*, p. 14.

47. Ibid., pp. 15–16.

48. Coontz, *Social Origins*, p. 89.

49. D'Emilio and Freedman, *Intimate Matters*, p. 21.

50. Coontz, *Social Origins*, p. 96.

51. Karen Haltunnen, *Confidence Men and Painted Women: A Study of Middle-Class Culture in America, 1830–1870* (New Haven: Yale University Press, 1982).

52. S. W. Nissenbaum, "From Pleasure to Intimacy: The Glorification of Sexual Love in Early Victorian America, 1830–1860," mss. University of Mass., Amherst, 1966, p. 27; quoted in Howard Gadlin, "Private Lives and Public Order," in *Close Relationships: Perspectives on the Meaning of Intimacy*, ed. George Levinger and Harold L. Raush (Amherst: University of Massachusetts Press, 1977), p. 43.

53. Kirk Jeffrey, "The Family as Utopian Retreat from the City," *Soundings* 55 (1972), p. 28; quoted in Stephanie Coontz, *The Way We Never Were: American Families and the Nostalgia Trap* (New York: Basic Books, 1992), p. 54.

54. Kasson, *Rudeness and Civility*, p. 170.

55. Warren I. Susman, *Culture as History: The Transformation of American Society in the Twentieth Century* (New York: Pantheon Books, 1984), pp. 273–74.

56. Glenna Matthews, *"Just a Housewife:" The Rise and Fall of Domesticity in America* (New York: Oxford University Press, 1987), p. 25.

57. Ibid., p. 20.

58. Karen Lystra, *Searching the Heart* (New York: Oxford University Press, 1989), p. 88.

59. Ibid., p. 116.

60. Coontz, *Social Origins*, p. 335.

61. William Leach, *Land of Desire: Merchants, Power, and the Rise of a New American Culture* (New York: Vintage, 1993), p. 7; quote taken from Wesley Clair Mitchell, *Business Cycles* (Berkeley: University of California Press, 1913), p. 12.

62. Leach, *Land of Desire*, p. 6.

63. Matthews, *"Just a Housewife,"* p. 180.

64. Coontz, *Social Origins*, p. 351.

65. Matthews, *"Just a Housewife,"* p. 182.

66. Coontz, *Social Origins*, p. 337.

67. Susman, *Culture as History*, p. 277.

68. Gadlin, "Private Lives and Public Order," p. 57.

69. Ibid., p. 62.

70. Beth Bailey, *From Front Porch to Back Seat: Courtship in Twentieth-Century America* (Baltimore: Johns Hopkins, 1989), p. 90.

71. Ibid., p. 93.

72. Haltunnen, *Confidence Men and Painted Women*.

# Author Index

# Subject Index

# Illustration Credits

*Photo research by Linda Sykes Picture Research, Inc., Hilton Head, S.C.*

*Page ii and cover,* Liz Wright, *Sushi and Beer,* Brooklyn, 1993. © 2006 Liz Wright/Private Collection/Bridgeman Art Library

*Pages 2, 9, 19,* Margaret Loxton, *Celebration,* late 20th century. Private Collection/Bridgeman Art Library/ © 2006 Margaret Loxton.

*Page 8,* Pablo Picasso, *Girl Before a Mirror,* 1932. Oil on canvas, 64″ × 51¼″. Collection, The Museum of Modern Art, New York, Gift of Mrs. Simon Guggenheim. © 2008 Estate of Pablo Picasso, Artist's Rights Society (ARS), New York/SPADEM, Paris

*Page 13,* Francks Deceus, *Old Love,* 1995. Private Collection/Bridgeman Art Library

*Pages 24, 38, 45,* Edward Hopper, *Nighthawks,* 1942. Art Institute of Chicago. Friends of American Art Collection, 1942.51

*Page 34* figure 2.2, Michael Newman/Photo Edit

*Page 35,* Michael Escoffery, *Circle of Love,* 1996. Private Collection/Michael Escoffery/Art Resource, NY, © 2008 Artist Rights Society (ARS), NY

*Page 41,* Michael Mortimer Robinson, *Away Thoughts,* 1995. SuperStock

*Pages 50, 74,* Archibald Motley, Jr., *Black Belt,* 1934. Hampton University Museum, Hampton, Virginia

*Page 52,* Tony Freeman/Photo Edit

*Page 57,* Michael Newman/Photo Edit

*Page 69,* figure 3.2, Paul Ekman and Wallace F. Friesen, *Pictures of Facial Affect* (Palo Alto, Calif.: Consulting Psychologists Press, 1976)

*Page 80,* Gerald Nailor (Toh Yah), *Untitled,* 1937. Museum of Indian Arts and Culture, Museum of New Mexico, Santa Fe, NM. Photo Blair Cox 51404/13

*Pages 86, 96,* Lily Furedi, *Subway,* 1934. Smithsonian Art Museum, Washington DC/Art Resource, NY

*Page 89,* figure 4.2, Helen Keller, *The Story of My Life.* New York: Doubleday, 1954

*Page 94,* Tomb relief of the *King's Scribe Amenhotep and His Wife Renut,* c. 1275 B.C. Painted limestone, w. 123.1cm. Egypt, Deir Durunka, Dynasty XIX, 1307–1196. © The Cleveland Museum of Art, 1995, Leonard C. Hanna Jr. Fund, 63.100

*Page 105,* Bas Jan Ader, *I'm Too Sad to Tell You,* 1970. Museum Boijmans Van Beuningen, Rotterdam

*Pages 116, 131,* Emiliano di Cavalcanti, *Five Girls from Guaratingueta,* 1930. Archivo Iconografico, S. A./Corbis

*Page 123,* Grant Wood, *Daughters of the Revolution,* 1932. © Estate of Grant Wood/Licensed by VAGA. New York/Cincinnati Art Museum, The Edwin and Virginia Irwin Memorial (1959.46)

*Page 124,* Gary Conner/Photo Edit

*Page 134,* Dale Kennington, *Cocktail Party II,* 20th century. © Dale Kennington/SuperStock

*Page 138,* *London Street Scene,* 1926. Eileen Tweedy/The Art Archive

*Pages 142, 151, 153,* Franklin McMahon, *Irish Pub,* late 20th century. Franklin McMahon/Corbis

*Page 163,* Michael Newman/Photo Edit

*Page 167,* Claudio Bravo, *Ole Sobre Lienzo,* 1979. © Claudio Bravo, courtesy, Marlborough Gallery, New York

*Page 170,* Jeff Greenberg, Photo Edit

*Pages 178,187,* Marcel Duchamp, *Sonata,* 1911. Philadelphia Museum of Art/Corbis/© 2006 Artist Rights Society (ARS), NY

*Page 182*, Barbara Kruger, *You are Not Yourself.* Christie's Images/Corbis

*Page 190*, Bob Daemmrich/Photo Edit

*Page 198, 209*, Edvard Munch (1863–1944), *Self Portrait with a Wine Bottle*, 1906. Munch Museum, Oslo, Norway/Scala/Art Resource, NY/© 2008 (ARS), NY

*Page 203*, Elaine De Kooning (1920–1989) *Self Portrait*, 1946. Oil on masonite. National Portrait Gallery, Smithsonian Institution/Art Resource, NY

*Page 207*, Myrleen Ferguson Cate/Photo Edit

*Page 217*, Alexej von Jawlensky, *Head Kopf*, 1920. Watercolor. SuperStock/© 2008 Alexej von Jawlensky/Artist Rights Society (ARS), NY

*Pages 226, 240*, Edward Mortelmans, *Reflections*, 20th century. © Edward Mortelmans/Private Collection/The Bridgeman Art Library

*Page 236*, Randy Faris/Corbis

*Page 244*, Michael Newman/Photo Edit

*Page 252*, Robert Delaunay, *Runners*, 1924–1925. Archivo Iconografico, S. A./Corbis

*Pages 258, 260, 274*, Honore D. Sharrer, *Tribute to the American Working People*, panel from five-part painting (family in interior), 1951. © Honore Sharrer/Smithsonian Art Museum, Washington, D.C./Art Resource, NY

*Page 277*, Gerrit Greve, *Celebrating the Birth of Jake*, last quarter of the 20th century. Gerrit Greve/Corbis

*Pages 278, 279*, *A Harlot's Progress* by William Hogarth, Scene I, Sean Shesgreen, ed., Engravings by Hogarth: 101 Prints. New York: Dover, 1973

*Page 286*, David Young-Wolff/Photo Edit

*Pages 294, 306*, John Carroll (1892–1952), *Two Figures*, 1929. Oil on Canvas. The Newark Museum, Gift of Mr. and Mrs. Lesley G. Sheafer, 1954 INV.:54.209/Art Resource, NY

*Page 296*, Edouard Manet, *Chez Le Pere Lathuille*, 1879. Musee des Beaux-Arts, Tournai, Belgium/SuperStock

*Page 308*, David Kelly Crow/Photo Edit

*Pages 315, 328*, Spencer Grant/Photo Edit

*Pages 336, 349*, Steve Chenn/Corbis

*Page 340*, William Gropper (1897–1977), *The Senate*, 1935. Oil on canvas. Digital Image © The Museum of Modern Art, New York/Gift of A. Conger Goodyear (108.1936)/Licensed by SCALA/Art Resource, NY

*Page 356*, George Tooker, *Government Bureau*, 1956. Metropolitan Museum of Art, George A. Hearn Fund, 1956

*Pages 372, 388*, Araujo Yaponi, *Nuptial Dance*, 1968. SuperStock

*Page 393*, © Lawrence Migdale/www.migdale.com

*Page 399*, John Biggers, detail of *Family Unity* mural, 1979–1984. Sterling Student Life Center, Texas Southern university, Houston. Photo by Earlie Hudnall, Jr.

*Page 401*, David H. Wells/Corbis